The Ashley Reader:
Redeeming Reason

The Ashley Reader:
Redeeming Reason

Benedict Ashley, OP

Sapientia Press
of Ave Maria University

Requests for permission to make copies of any part of the work should be
directed to:

Sapientia Press
of Ave Maria University
1025 Commons Circle
Naples, FL 34119
888-343-8607

Cover Design: Eloise Anagnost

Printed in the United States of America.

Library of Congress Control Number: 2006922392

ISBN-10: 1-932589-26-0

ISBN-13: 978-1-932589-26-9

Table of Contents

Foreword

IT IS A PARTICULAR PLEASURE FOR ME TO PROVIDE THIS foreword, since Father Benedict Ashley is so linked with Chicago. He did his undergraduate work at the University of Chicago, a deeply formative experience in which he passed through Marxism to the Catholic Church; he later contributed to the intellectual life of the Church in the archdiocese during the years he spent at Aquinas Institute of Theology, where he became president.

This volume, which offers the distillation of a life devoted to philosophical and theological research in the Catholic Church, comes like a sign of spring in the intellectual landscape. Father Benedict, fully aware of its historical development and its limitations, sets out to demonstrate that the thought of St. Thomas Aquinas has given "perfect and scientific expression" to a common fund of doctrine and that it has an irreplaceable role in expounding the "great truths to which reason, especially when it is healed by the grace of faith, can attain and which can form a solid foundation for all scholarship and education." He defends Thomism as "clear, unambiguous, scientific, based on human experience and perennially able to withstand the assault of other systems of thought." In doing so, he challenges Catholic theologians to return to what is theirs and awakens hope for intellectual life beyond the hopelessness of postmodernism.

Father Ashley's own life and experience are an assurance of the value and role of the theologian in the community of believers. His theological understanding is a response to his supernatural sense of faith, rooted in the magisterial teaching of the Church. This is a style of discourse I met when, as a seminarian, I first heard him lecture at the Catholic University of America almost forty years ago.

In this book Fr. Ashley begins by exposing the philosophical bases of his moral arguments for the divine answers to human questions about good and evil and the meaning of human life which are in accord with human reason. He goes on to discuss issues of systematic theology and ecclesiology because "doctrine comes before morals; the gospel is the grace of God before it is the demand of God." (A. Nichols, *The Shape of Catholic Theology*, 319). This conversation is verified in the integrated theology offered by Aquinas.

He looks at issues of moral theology in the light of an appreciative but critical evaluation of Pope John Paul II's theology of the body, indicating where the Holy Father's thought still needs to be developed in order to respond to current bioethical problems. He assesses the inadequate and sometimes misleading attempts of some Thomists to come to grips with modernity and the changing scientific attitudes and the pressures on human behavior to which it gives rise. This affords him the opportunity of proposing foundations for a revised moral theology. Father Ashley's moral theory speaks to human beings in the actual situations of life; he works his theory out with great conviction in writing about bioethics.

This collection of essays is a gift to the Church; it cannot be overlooked by any serious moral theologian or bioethicist reflecting on issues of human life, its propagation and protection.

—Francis Cardinal George, OMI
Archbishop of Chicago

Philosophical Issues

CHAPTER 1

"The Church Has No Philosophy of Its Own"

A Shocking Pronouncement

THE CATHOLIC CHURCH TEACHES THAT IN OUR FALLEN state the human intellect, without the assistance of divine grace, is prone to err. Nevertheless, it has always resisted the tendency of Protestant theology to regard human reason as so weakened by original sin that faith must stand in isolation from reason. Thus it was no surprise that John Paul II, the most philosophically educated of any recent popes, strongly defends the harmony of reason in his great encyclical *Faith and Reason*.[1] Yet the terms in which he has done so are quite startling and markedly different from those found in many statements of previous popes, especially of Leo XIII who in 1879 in another great encyclical, *On the Restoration of Christian Philosophy*,[2] made the theology and philosophy of St. Thomas Aquinas the basis of all Catholic education. John Paul II, however, says quite flatly:

> The Church has no philosophy of her own nor does she canonize any one particular philosophy in preference to others. [Note] The underlying reason for this reluctance is that, even when it engages theology, philosophy must remain faithful to its own principles and methods. Otherwise there would be no guarantee that it would remain oriented to truth and that it was moving towards truth by way of a process governed by reason. A philosophy that did not proceed in the light of reason according to its own principles and methods would serve little purpose. At the deepest level, the autonomy which philosophy enjoys is rooted in the fact that reason is by its nature oriented to truth and is equipped moreover with the means necessary to arrive at truth. A philosophy conscious of this as

---

[1] *Fides et Ratio.*
[2] *Aeterni Patris.*

its "constitutive status" cannot but respect the demands and the data of revealed truth.[3]

John Paul II has support for his statement in the fact that while the drafts of the Preliminary Commission on the Second Vatican Council had proposed a 20-page defense of the authority of Aquinas, this was hotly debated and rejected by the Council. As a result the *Declaration on Christian Education*[4] has only one reference to St. Thomas. After urging universities to preserve the proper autonomy of each discipline and to give "careful attention to the current problems of these changing times" in such a way as to maintain the harmony of reason and faith, this *Decree* says "[t]his method follows the tradition of the doctors of the Church and especially of St. Thomas." Moreover, in the Council's *Decree on the Priestly Training*[5] the section on the studies required of priests, which was later to be followed closely in the revised *Code of Canon Law* #251–2, does not retain the former Canon 1366 that "canonized" Thomism in both philosophical and theological education, but mentions it only in relation to theology.

> #251. Philosophical subjects should be taught in such a way as to lead the students gradually to a solid and consistent knowledge of man, the world and God. The student should rely on that philosophical patrimony which is forever valid, but should also take account of modern philosophical studies, especially those which have greater influence in their own country, as well as recent progress in the sciences. Thus, by correctly understanding the modern mind students will be prepared to enter in dialogue with their contemporaries.[6]

The mention of Aquinas in Vatican II's *Decree on Priestly Training*,[7] (also followed by the Revised Code #252) merely says that priestly candidates "should learn to examine more deeply, with the help of speculation and with St. Thomas as teacher, all aspects of these mysteries [of the Faith], and to per-

---

3 *Fides et Ratio,* v, #49.
4 *Gravissimum Educationus,* October, 18, 1965, n. 10, in Austin Flannery, OP, *Vatican Council II: The Conciliar and Post Concilar Documents* (Vatican Collection), vol. 1, new rev. edition, 725–37.
5 *Optatum Totius,* Oct. 28, 1965, nos. 13–18.
6 Canon 1366: "Philosophiae rationalis ac theologiae studia et alumnorum in his disciplinis institutionem professores omnino pertractent ad Angelici Doctoris rationem, doctrinam, et principia, eaque sancta teneant." (Professors should treat studies in rational philosophy and theology and the preparation of graduates in these disciplines wholly according to the reasoning, doctrine, and principles of the Angelic Doctor and hold them sacred.)
7 *Optatam Totius,* n. 16.

ceive their interconnection." This seems a much weaker approbation than that of St. Pius X who said in his Motu Proprio *Doctoris Angelici* (1914):

> Since we have said that Aquinas' philosophy was "carefully to be followed and we did not say "solely," some thought to comply with or at least not to oppose our will by taking the philosophy of any of the scholastic doctors indiscriminately, even when such a philosophy was in repugnance to the principles of St. Thomas. But these greatly deceived themselves. It is quite evident that when we set up St. Thomas as the leader of the scholastic philosophy, we have wished to be understood especially of his principles, upon which such a philosophy is established, because, as we must reject that old opinion which held as irrelevant for the faith what anyone thinks about creatures, if he thinks rightly about God—since an error on the nature of creatures originates false knowledge about God—so we must keep reverently and inviolately St. Thomas' principles on philosophy from which flows such a doctrine on creatures as is in harmony with faith. . . . For if the Catholic truth be deprived of his valuable help, in vain would anyone seek help from that philosophy whose principles are common with, or not opposed to Materialism, Monism, Pantheism, Socialism, or Modernism. Consequently we have already instructed all teachers of philosophy and theology that to deviate a single step from St. Thomas, especially in metaphysical questions, would not be without great detriment. Now furthermore we say that those who have perversely interpreted or absolutely denied the principles and chief propositions of St. Thomas' philosophy, those not only do not follow St. Thomas, but wander widely from him.[8]

Furthermore Pius X backed this up by approving the famous (some thought them infamous) *Twenty-Four Theses*[9] that, according to the Dominican scholars of the day codified Aquinas' thought, especially in contrast to that of Suarez's alleged reconciliation of the Thomistic metaphysics based on the *analogia entis* with Scotist metaphysics based on the *univocatio entis*. Are we then to agree with conservatives who see this as another example of what they consider the weak and compromising spirit that has infected church authorities as a result of Vatican II? It is evident that the great majority of the bishops (only 58 did not favor the final version of the

---

[8] *Doctoris Angelici,* June 24, 1914, *AAS* 6 (1914), 336–41, trans. Jacques Maritain; *St. Thomas Aquinas,* trans. by J. F. Scanlon, 189–214.

[9] Most readily accessible in Latin and English, trans. Hugh McDonald, "Decree of Approval of Some Theses Contained in the Doctrine of St. Thomas Aquinas and Proposed to the Teachers of Philosophy" www.vaxxine.com/hyoomik/aquinas/theses.eht. The standard commentary on these is Edouard Hugon, OP, *Les Vingt-Quatre Thèses: Principes de Philosophie,* 9th ed.

Decree on Priestly Training) wanted to avoid any appearance of a narrow adherence to Thomism or Neo-Scholasticism in Catholic education, lay and clerical, and John Paul II has followed this expression of the views of the episcopacy.

The Autonomy of the Human Disciplines

The popes did not wait for Vatican II to qualify their commendation of the thought of Aquinas. While it is true that St. Pius X found it necessary in his difficult struggle against the Modernist heresy to enforce his authority in doctrinal questions in a very strict manner ("to deviate a single step from St. Thomas, especially in metaphysical questions, would not be without great detriment"), the initiatives of Leo XIII that Pius was reaffirming were expressed only with some important qualifications. Thus Leo wrote in *On the Restoration of Christian Philosophy*:

> We exhort you, Venerable Brethren, in all earnestness to restore the golden wisdom of St. Thomas, and to spread it far and wide for the defense and beauty of the Catholic faith, for the good of society, and for the advantage of all the sciences. The wisdom of St. Thomas, we say; for if anything is taken up with too great subtlety by the scholastic doctors, or too carelessly stated—if there be anything that ill agrees with the discoveries of a later age, or is, in a word, improbable in whatever way, it does not enter Our mind to propose that for imitation to our age.[10]

At the time of *On the Restoration of Christian Philosophy* and as late as Maurice M. de Wulf's widely used *History of Philosophy*, first published in 1900, it was supposed that the scholastics were in fundamental agreement. Later research, however, especially the work of Étienne Gilson, made clear how fundamental were some of their disagreements in philosophy, in spite of the fact that the scholastics were generally orthodox in faith. No doubt, it was this realization on the part of Pius XII that led him both to reaffirm the contemporary value of Thomism in very strong terms in his 1950 encyclical *Concerning Some False Opinions Threatening to Undermine the Foundations of Catholic Doctrine*,[11] and in 1953 to qualify this affirmation in an allocution to the professors of the Jesuit Gregorian University in which he said:

> For every professor it is legitimate, within the limits laid down (which are not to be overreached), to adhere to any school which possesses the right of domicile in the Church, provided that he completely distinguish the truths which must be held by all from those things which are

[10] *Aeterni Patris,* n. 31.
[11] *Humani Generis.*

the distinctive and characteristic element of that school, and note these distinctions in his teaching, as becomes a well-balanced professor.[12]

In fact a review of the previous papal documents from Leo XIII to Pius XI will make clear that this qualification made by Pius XII was by no means something wholly new. Generally the popes in approving the doctrine of St. Thomas Aquinas and prescribing it for Catholic schools have been very careful to leave room for a legitimate liberty in scholarly research and discussion. They have made special provisions for the Franciscans and for the Society of Jesus in order to permit, and indeed to encourage them in the study of and explanation of their own traditions that form a precious part of the heritage of the Church, although in both cases they have also emphasized the primary authority of the doctrine of St. Thomas.

Therefore, it remains to determine what Pius XII in the passage quoted above meant by "the limits laid down" and "the truths which must be held by all." Certainly he had made very clear in *Concerning Some False Opinions Threatening to Undermine the Foundations of Catholic Doctrine* that these limits do *not* make room for the introduction of systems of philosophy that are alien to the method and basic principles of the traditional scholastic philosophy. In the allocation to the professors of the Gregorian he first praised the scholastic method for its precision and clarity and then says: "The various systems of doctrine permitted by the Church should entirely agree with whatever has been tested by ancient and Christian philosophy from the first days of the Church." He then more exactly specifies these "truths which must be held by all":

> As an example of the truths We have just mentioned, take those which pertain to the nature of our knowledge, the proper meaning of truth, the metaphysical being; and transcendental principles founded on truth, the teachings on God as infinite and person, the Creator of all things, or the nature of man, the immortality of the soul, the dignity of the human person, the duties which the natural moral law reveals to man and imposes on him by his very nature.[13]

From this passage some have drawn the conclusion that Pius XII intended to put all thinkers on an equal footing provided that they all support the basic truths just ennumerated. This reading, however, would reduce the approval of St. Thomas to little more than saying that he, like many others, was an orthodox Christian philosopher. The pope, however, also said in this address:

---

[12] *Animus noster gaudio, AAS* 45 (1953), 682–90, translated in *Irish Ecclesiasical Record* (August 1965): 121–30.

[13] Ibid.

No other Doctor has accomplished this (concordance with the tradition of Christian philosophy) so clearly, or so perfectly, whether one considers the harmony of the individual parts or their union and wondrous coherence with the truths of faith, nor has any other Doctor formed such a solid and unified system, as St. Thomas Aquinas.

Yet to this he added a qualification, similar to that made by Leo XIII:

> To these things which demand unhesitating assent, however, should not be added others which, because they concern what is true in the factual order, are still matters of controversy among the great commentators and outstanding disciples of St. Thomas, nor those points about which there is dispute whether they form part of the teaching of the Angelic Doctor, or how they should be interpreted. We here pass over in silence as outmoded teachings that are based on the defective and meager knowledge of the ancients concerning physics, chemistry, biology and like natural science.

Thus for Pius XII as for Leo XIII and Pius X the approbation given by the Church to the doctrine of St. Thomas Aquinas is bestowed not merely because there is nothing in his doctrine that is unorthodox, nor merely because with other scholastic doctors he defends certain basic philosophical truths that furnish the natural preparation for the Catholic faith, but because he defends them in a manner that makes his teaching the most secure basis for Catholic education and scholarship. Note also that Pius XII used without qualifications the term "*all* Catholic schools," not interpreting this Canon 1366 of the *Code of Canon Law* as it then existed as applying only to seminaries, as some interpreted that canon. John XXIII in his time reaffirmed this strong commendation of Aquinas in an address to the Fifth International Thomistic Congress:

> Since St. Thomas' teaching above others, is consonant with the truths revealed by God and the pronouncements of the Holy Fathers and with the principles of right reason, Holy Church has adopted it as her own and has called its author Doctor Communis, that is, the Universal Doctor.[14]

Thus the papal documents just quoted and cited also in the documentation of *Faith and Reason* and many others give a carefully nuanced meaning, but a very strong one, to the papal support of Thomism. They approve Thomism principally because St. Thomas gave a sound exposition of certain great truths to which reason, especially when it is healed by the grace of faith,

---

[14] *Singulari sane animi*, Sept. 16, 1960, translated in *The Pope Speaks* 6 (1959–60): 325–28.

can attain, and which can form a solid foundation for all scholarship and education. Pius XII said in *Concerning Some False Opinions Threatening to Undermine the Foundations of Catholic Doctrine*:

> It is well known how highly the Church regards human reason, for it falls to reason to demonstrate with certainty the existence of God, personal and one; to prove beyond doubt from divine signs the very foundations of the Christian faith; to express properly the law which the Creator has imprinted in the hearts of men; and finally to attain to some notion, indeed a very fruitful notion, of divine mysteries.[15]

Thus, to be quite explicit, this encyclical and other papal documents enumerate these principles as follows:

1. The distinction and harmony of reason and faith.

2. The nature of human knowledge and the truth to which it has access.

3. The basic metaphysical principles.

4. The existence of God, and his attributes as an infinite, personal, free Creator.

5. The nature and dignity of the human person and the immortality of the soul.

6. The existence and basic principles of the natural moral law.

The Church is not intruding into the secular realm by insisting that the defense of these truths should be basic to scholarship and education. The light of faith itself instructs her that these truths of reason can be attained by human reason, and should be attained for the full maturity of faith. Yet reading this list some have concluded that, since such truths are to be found in one form or another in all great scholastic writers, the work of St. Thomas is approved only as regards those points which he holds in common with other doctors. This interpretation, however, cannot be squared with the unique approbation given to it by the consistent papal tradition. What then is unique about the way in which St. Thomas presents these truths that has gained him a seal of approval from the Church that she has not given to others? The answer is obvious from the words of the popes. It is the special merit of the thought of St. Thomas that he has given a defense of these truths that is clear, unambiguous, scientific, based on human experience, and perennially able to withstand the assaults of other systems of thought.

---

[15] *Humani Generis,* n. 29.

Does this mean that St. Thomas is a "mere apologist" as some would phrase it? As Leo XIII made clear in *On the Restoration of Christian Philosophy*, the Christian view of philosophy finds in Aquinas's thought three great values:

1. It satisfies the natural human need for truth.

2. It provides a sound apologetics preparing the way for Christian faith.

3. It is a helpful instrument of sacred theology in the explanation of the strictly supernatural mysteries of that faith.

The fact that for Aquinas the truth of revelation is infinitely superior to that of reason does not minimize the very great value of sound human reason. St. Thomas's philosophy is of great apologetic value precisely because it is strictly scientific in method, free of rhetoric and polemic. As a result his thought remains more contemporaneous than that of many contemporary philosophers whose view of the world is narrowed by their anguished preoccupation with especially urgent problems. Progress in philosophy depends not only on a sense of urgency, but also on clear vision and abiding purpose. As Pius XII wrote in *Concerning Some False Opinions Threatening to Undermine the Foundations of Catholic Doctrine*:

> As we well know from the experience of centuries, the method of Aquinas is singularly preeminent both for teaching students and for bringing truth to light; his doctrine is in harmony with divine revelation, and is most effective both for safeguarding the foundation of the faith, and for reaping, safely and usefully the fruits of sound progress.[16]

Thus I personally hope that the future period of Catholic philosophy in the United States will see more attention given to the expansion and development of the common fund of doctrine given such perfect and scientific expression by St. Thomas, and that all scholars of every tradition and opinion will work to enlarge this fund by bringing to it both the criticisms and the special contributions of the past and of the present. This enlargement cannot be accomplished, however, by an eclecticism that would weaken the solid foundations on which the doctrine of St. Thomas is built. The methods, principles, and major doctrine of St. Thomas must remain the norm by which, in the words of Pius XI, "the diverse systems of philosophers are to be examined and judged." Finally we must strive to make our *philosophia perennis* so well formulated by St. Thomas truly live for our times. As Pius XII said in note 30 of the encyclical just quoted:

---

[16] Ibid., n. 31.

Then in these fundamental questions, we may clothe our philosophy in a more convenient and richer dress, make it more vigorous with a more effective terminology, divest it of certain scholastic aids found less useful, prudently enrich it with the fruits of the progress of the human mind. But never may we overthrow it, or contaminate it with false principles, or regard it as a great, but obsolete relic. For truth and its philosophic expression cannot change from day to day, least of all where there is question of self-evident principles of the human mind or of those propositions which are supported by the wisdom of the ages and by divine revelation, whatever new truth the sincere human mind is able to find certainly cannot be opposed to truth already acquired, since God, the highest Truth, has created and guides the human intellect, not that it may daily oppose new truths to rightly established ones, but rather that, having eliminated errors which may have crept in, it may build truth upon truth in the same order and structure that exist in reality, the source of truth.

CHAPTER 2

Transition to Historical Mindedness

BERNARD LONERGAN'S ANALYSIS OF THE TWENTIETH century as a transition from what he called "the classical world-view to historical mindedness"[1] is often thought to be the explanation of the decline of Thomism in America. Is not the Thomistic tradition of philosophy and theology redolent of the "classicist" mentality? And is not such a mentality utterly unable to deal with the dynamic, subject-centered, existentialist, personalist, and pluralist mindset of our times, which Vatican II called Catholics to address positively?

If Thomism is to have a future, therefore, it must shed its classicist mentality and assume historical-mindedness without losing its integrity and uniqueness. Since what is described as classicist in the thought of the past is best typified by Platonism and its *essentialism*, and since Maritain, Gilson, and others in the first half of this century seem to have firmly established the *existential* character of Thomism,[2] such a renewal seems possible.

Historical-mindedness in philosophy is the recognition that truth exists only in the minds of persons.[3] Hence, when these persons are human, it exists only in historical events of knowing, each of which is conditioned by the experiences of the past, the pragmatic situation of the present, and anticipations of

---

[1] Bernard J. F. Lonergan, SJ, "The Transition from a Classicist World-View to Historical Mindedness" in *A Second Collection.*

[2] For a history and analysis of this achievement see Gerald A. McCool, SJ, *Catholic Theology in the Nineteenth Century,* 241–67, and *From Unity to Pluralism,* 114–99. See also Helen James John, *The Thomist Spectrum,* and Georges Van Riet, *Thomistic Epistemology,* and Romanus Cessario, OP, *A Short History of Thomism.*

[3] "Such is the objectivity of truth. But do not be fascinated by it. Intentionally it is independent of the subject, but ontologically it resides only in the subject: *veritas formaliter est in solo judicio.*" Lonergan, "The Subject" in *A Second Collection,* 3.

the future. Consequently, truth in its existentiality is perspectival, that is, it is an envisioning of reality from a particular point-of-view determined by the knower's historical situation. Thus, inevitably, human truth is one-sided. The achievement of truth is a social activity in which a plurality of points-of-view must be brought into a reasonable conversation. For such a conversation to proceed, no one point-of-view can claim a priori a superior validity, unless a super-human participant intervenes.

Why, then, do we Thomists have so much difficulty entering into the intellectual dialogue in this concrete time in history, a time when historical-mindedness and acquiescence to the pluralism of truth are so in style? I suggest that it has been our "metaphysicism," our tendency to reduce philosophy to metaphysics, a tendency foreign to Aquinas himself, and of fairly recent origin, which has stultified us and caused the post-Vatican II decline of Thomistic influence in Catholic life.

In Greek and medieval thought,[4] and in Aquinas's own texts,[5] the term "philosophy" was taken broadly to include the entire range of human disciplines (other than the *sacra doctrina* of Christian theology) from logic to metaphysics. The last was indeed, philosophy *par excellence*, but it did not absorb, indeed it presupposed, the other kinds of philosophy. So true was this, that in the medieval schools, metaphysics was ordinarily not an item in the curriculum, since it seemed to overlap with sacred theology, which for Christians had replaced metaphysics or natural philosophy as queen of the sciences.[6]

We need to recall that it was not until Christian Wolff, a follower of Leibnitz working in a Cartesian perspective, that the division within physics between a philosophy of nature and an empirical science of nature was introduced.[7] Only then did the field of philosophy begin to be set against the field of the sciences, natural and humane. Furthermore, Wolff reduced all branches

---

4 See John Passmore, "Philosophy" in *Encyclopedia of Philosophy*, vol. 6, 216–30.

5 Robert Busa, SJ, ed., *Index Thomisticus,* vol. 17, n. 62201. See also James A. Weisheipl, "Classification of the Science in Medieval Thought."

6 James A. Weisheipl, "Curriculum of the Faculty of Arts at Oxford in the Early Fourteenth Century," finds no statutory mention of a requirement to study metaphysics before 1407. Nancy G. Siraisi, *Arts and Sciences at Padua*, 109–42, shows that the study of Aristotle's Metaphysics at that university was linked with the study of his *Physics* and given only secondary importance.

7 This metaphysicism has a long history. Suarez, whose Scotistic tendencies are well-known, in *Disputationes Metaphysicae, Opera Omnia* Dist. I, Sect. IV, 13, 29, attributes the reduction of the other sciences to material parts of metaphysics to Giles of Rome (*I Metaphysics*, q. 22 and the beginning of *Posterior Analytics*) but advocates the traditional order of learning. In fact, however, Scotus's metaphysics absorbs much of philosophy, and this Wolff carried out in full, *Discursus Praeliminaris de Philosophia in Genere*, 3 nn. 56, 86–87. See also Richard Blackwell, "The Structure of Wolffian Philosophy," and Jose Ferrata Mora, "Suarez and Modern Philosophy."

of philosophy to applications of metaphysics. When Thomism was revived by Leo XIII in its Neo-Scholastic form, many Thomists, notably Cardinal Mercier and the Thomistic Institute of the University of Louvain, which dominated the first period of this revival, accepted and refined this notion.[8]

In the second phase of the Thomistic revival, under the leadership on the one hand of Joseph Maréchal and on the other of Jacques Maritain and Étienne Gilson, closer attention to the text of Aquinas and its historical setting gradually eliminated this Wolffian notion. Maréchal and his followers, however, accepting the Cartesian "turn to the subject" and the Kantian transcendentalism, also accepted a dichotomy between philosophy as transcendental, and the sciences as categorial or empirical, and thus continued to identify philosophy with metaphysics (or the critique of metaphysics). While they admitted the possibility and desirability of a "correlation" between the two realms of knowledge, they viewed them as completely autonomous.[9]

Gilson, while quite unsympathetic to Transcendental Thomism, shared with it the identification of philosophy with metaphysics, and has even been accused of identifying metaphysics with Christian theology. Certainly he justified his position on this issue by insisting that Aquinas was a theologian. Hence for Gilson, although St. Thomas recognized a formal distinction between philosophy and theology, existentially his philosophy subsists only within the structure of his theology, and is definitively formulated only in the *Summa theologiae*.[10] Consequently, for Gilson, the other human disciplines simply are not philosophy at all, although philosophy, by which he seems to

---

[8] The evolution of views at the Institute Superieur de Philosophie of the University of Louvain on the philosophy of nature can be traced in widely used textbooks: Desiré-Joseph Cardinal Mercier, in *Cours de Philosophie* (vol. 1, 26–30), attacked Wolff's views as *un divorce desastreux* (p. 26, n. 1), but followed him in distinguishing the "sciences of observation" from the philosophical disciplines of cosmology, psychology, and natural theology, which were their *complement*. Fernand Renoirte, in *Cosmology*, returned to the Wolffian conception of cosmology as "metaphysical."

[9] See McCool, *From Unity to Pluralism*, 87–113. Robert J. Henle, SJ, "Transcendental Thomism," argues that Transcendental Thomism is really not Thomism, but he notes (pp. 92–93) that Maréchal did not intend this transcendental approach to replace but only to complement that of Aquinas.

[10] McCool, *From Unity to Pluralism*, 161–200, and John F. Wippel, "Thomas Aquinas and the Problem of Christian Philosophy," in his *Metaphysical Themes in Thomas Aquinas*, 1–33, see nn. 71, 76, of that work for other authors on this issue. Wippel (pp. 26–29), while disagreeing with Gilson, seems to me too cautious when he requires corroboration in Aquinas's other philosophical works to accept safely any position in the Aristotelian commentaries as Aquinas's own. I prefer the view of James A. Weisheipl, *Friar Thomas d'Aquino*, 281–85. Medieval authors so respected the *auctoritates* that in their commentaries either they interpret them benignly to fit their own conviction as to the truth or, if they doubt the truth of the text, they carefully distance

mean metaphysics—has the right to criticize them when they illicitly make metaphysical claims.[11]

Maritain never accepted this reduction of philosophy to metaphysics, as his *Degrees of Knowledge* and his *Natural Philosophy* clearly show.[12] He recognized the existence of a variety of disciplines, including a philosophy of nature, ethics, politics, and esthetics, which can properly be called "philosophy" by analogy to metaphysics as *prima inter pares*. These are not, as Wolff thought, mere applications of metaphysics, since each discipline has its own self-evident first principles not reducible to those of metaphysics. Maritain not only defended Aquinas's position on this, he exemplified it in essays that contributed positively and originally to many of these diverse philosophies in their own proper terms.[13]

Nevertheless, Maritain was not able to free himself completely from the prevailing notion that the modern sciences, whether natural or humane, are postmedieval "new" sciences quite unlike their medieval counterparts in principles and methods. Instead he accepted the autonomy of these new sciences and tried to explicate exactly what their proper objects and proper principles were in contradistinction to those of the correlative types of philosophy. Thus for him, just as for Wolff, there is a formal distinction between the philosophy of nature and the empirical sciences of nature. The philosophy of nature was *dianoetic*, having first principles of a philosophical type, while modern science is *perinoetic*, and is to be subdivided into *empiriometric* or *empirio-schematic* depending on whether it uses or does not use mathematical models.[14] Unfortunately, this interesting but dubious proposal of Maritain, based largely on a passé view of the history of science, has over-

---

themselves from it (as St. Albert the Great frequently does in his Aristotelian commentaries), but they seldom simply report the meaning of the text, as modern commentators often do. It seems to me anachronistic to attribute this modern "objectivity" to Aquinas. See also John M. Quinn, OSA, *The Thomism of Etienne Gilson*, 94–124, and Leo Elders, "S. Thomas D'Aquin et Aristote."

[11] In *The Philosophy of St. Thomas Aquinas* (translation of the 3rd edition of *Le Thomisme*, chapter 9, 186–203), Gilson simply follows the *Summa theologiae* in order, method, and content in presenting Aquinas's views of sub-angelic reality. It should be noted, however, that Gilson used his interpretation of Thomism in writing brilliantly on literary, esthetic, and even scientific topics in *Painting and Reality*, and *From Aristotle to Darwin and Back*.

[12] Jacques Maritain, "The Philosophy of Nature" in his *Science and Wisdom* and *Distinguish to Unite or the Degrees of Knowledge*, 21–70, 136–201; and *The Philosophy of Nature*, with the review by William H. Kane, OP, in *The Thomist*.

[13] The range of Maritain's thought is manifest in the essays on his work in *Jacques Maritain: The Man and His Metaphysics*, edited by John F. X. Knasas.

[14] See James A. Weisheipl, "Commentary on Maritain's 'Epistemology of Modern Science' by Jean-Louis Allard."

shadowed his defense of the plurality of philosophies.[15] As a result, Gilson's radically reductionist view has been much more influential.[16]

Thomist philosophy in the period immediately before Vatican II was thus presented chiefly as a metaphysics. This alone guaranteed its decline in the United States where analytical philosophy looking back to the empiricism of Hume and native pragmatism have produced a culture in which metaphysics is dismissed as "nonsense" or at least "irrelevant."[17] But even where the Cartesian–Kantian tradition of continental Europe has been dominant, transcendentalized Thomism has been caught up in the steady march toward the "forgetfulness of being," as Heidegger named it, ending in the present lamentations over "the death of philosophy."[18]

In both empiricist and Kantian traditions, philosophy has been identified with metaphysics, and metaphysics with an analysis of the conditions of knowledge, while the *content* of knowledge has been surrendered to the non-philosophical sciences. Certainly Thomism has important things to say about the subjective aspect of knowledge, but for Aquinas this is so sharply subordinated to the objective content of knowledge that a Thomism that has been restricted in this way to metaphysics or to "cognitive theory"[19] can have little to say in any contemporary conversation about the topics that dominate our historical perspective.

The way out of this dead-end, I would suggest, is a *ressourcement,* a return to Aquinas's own point-of-view. Historical mindedness not only calls our attention to our own historical situation and concerns, but also frees us from clinging to our own restricted point-of view, so that there can be a "fusion of horizons."[20] Today we are imprisoned in a set of fixed convictions that philosophy and science are two utterly diverse enterprises; that philosophy is metaphysics, that if certitude in knowledge is possible at all it is only by a transcendental critique, and that modern science is so successful it

---

[15] Maritain's view of the history of science depended largely on the great work of Pierre Duhem (1861–1916), *Le système du monde: histoire des doctrines cosmologiques de Platon à Copernic,* who considered empirical science merely a "saving of the appearances" and exaggerated the role of Nominalism in its development. For a different approach, see my *Theologies of the Body,* 253–344, and William A. Wallace, OP, *From a Realist Point of View.*

[16] See J. F. X. Knasas, "Immateriality and Metaphysics," *Angelicum* 65 (1988): 46–76, for recent literature.

[17] For what the noted historian of philosophy Frederick Copleston, SJ, calls the "recurrent waves of metaphysics and anti-metaphysics" (p. 130), see "The Nature of Metaphysics" in his *On the History of Philosophy and Other Essays.*

[18] On the current "death of philosophy," see the essays in Hugh J. Silverman, ed., *Philosophy and Non-Philosophy Since Merleau-Ponty.*

[19] Developed by Bernard Lonergan in *Insight.* For his account of his own relation to Maréchal, see his essay, "Insight Revisited," in *A Second Collection.*

[20] Hans-Georg Gadamer, *Truth and Method,* 269–74, 337–38, 358.

could only be hindered in its progress by a radical philosophical critique of its basic principles.

Aquinas shared none of these restrictive presuppositions. For him the proper object of human intelligence is material things as they are known through the senses.[21] In studying such things, we must first establish their existence by sensible observation, primarily by the sense of touch.[22] Our intellectual concepts have scientific relevance only through reduction to such existential facts and the principles of our scientific knowledge are judgments verified in such existential facts, never simply in nominal concepts.[23]

Although our sense knowledge shows us a world of great variety in a constant process of change, our intelligence can analyze this world only by a step-by-step process of insight by which we separate the randomly variable aspects of reality from the more stable and uniform aspects, the natural from the chance or artificial—going always from more general and vague insights toward more and more specific and precise ones, yet never losing sight of the fact that the beings we are considering are changing beings, *ens mobile,* knowable by us only through their changes.[24] So much for the classicist mind obsessed with fixed essences! For Aquinas the goal of science is not the intuition of essences but the establishing of causal relations that explain the coming into existence and perishing of sensible realities.[25]

---

[21] Aquinas compares the human intellect to that of God and angels and then says, *Est autem alius intellectus, scilicet humanus, qui nec est suum intelligere[as is God's], nec sui intelligere est objectum primum ipsa eius essentia [as is an angel's, or the separated human soul], sed aliquid extrinsecum, scilicet natura materiali rei. S.Th.* I, q. 87, a. 3 c.; cf. *III Sent.,* dist. 23, q. 1, a. 2, ad 3; *SCG* II, 75; *De Veritate* q. 10, a. 9; *In de Anima,* II, 6.

[22] See Charles De Koninck, "Sedeo, ergo sum." There is also a Laval dissertation by Thomas Feeley on the subject for which I do not have the exact citation at hand.

[23] The "order of questions" discussed in the *Posterior Analytics* (cf. Aquinas, *In Posterior Analytics,* II, lect. 1) requires that the question *An sit?* be answered affirmatively before the question *Quid sit?* can be raised. Only then will a definition be a "real" rather than a "nominal" one, and only real definitions can be used in scientific demonstrations. Hence (contrary to common misconceptions) Thomistic philosophy is never an essentialist deduction from mere concepts, but is always existential, and presupposes critical acts of judgment concerning the existence of the things defined.

[24] For Aristotle and Aquinas sense knowledge always requires a change in the sense organ by the action of the sensible object, hence the object is immediately known precisely as it enters into the process of change through its active qualities *(sensibilia propria).* Other spatio-temporal aspects *(sensibilia communia)* of the object are known only mediately through these qualities. Hence, the human intellect, because its own proper object is changeable being, knows the physical world not as something static but precisely in its dynamism (cf. *In De Anima,* II, lect. 13, 386–94).

[25] The goal of science is to answer the question *proper quid,* i.e., the causes of the fact studied *(In Post. Analyt.* I, lect. 4, 30–43 *bis).* This answer is to be found in the essential definition of some subject, but this definition must be a real, i.e., existential, definition. Thus scientific method always moves from establishing the existence of a subject and of

One problem that convinced Maritain and his disciples to hold that modern science does not arrive at a knowledge of the essences of natural thing *(dianoesis)* but can only "save the phenomena" *(perionoesis)* was that they thought Aristotle's and Aquinas's hold on the *philosophia* (or *scientia*) *naturalis* was only able to define the human species as "rational animal" and merely generically distinguish animals from plants and from inanimate minerals. Hence any further exploration could only be phenomenal. Thus Joseph Owens, a noted expert on Aristotle, has written:

> Aquinas emphasized repeatedly, in various contexts and at every period of his writings, the impenetrable nature of corporeal essences. Although insisting upon the generic explanation of bodies in natural philosophy by substantial principles, matter and form, he maintained without qualification that this intellectual penetration did not reach a thing's specific differentiae. For human knowledge the specific characteristics of things were not open to explanation through substantial form. Rather, what was known of them specifically had to be gathered always in piece meal fashion through observation of qualities and activities. [26]

Thomists of this opinion cited numerous texts of Aristotle and Aquinas, such as the following:

> Because the essential differences of things are often unknown and unnamed, it is sometimes necessary to use accidental differences to designate substantial differences, as the Philosopher says. [27]

One has only to examine these texts, however, to see that Aristotle and Aquinas are saying that our knowledge and definition of the essences of natural things are not directly and immediately evident, yet from the proper accidents of things we *can* come to some genuine though imperfect understanding of these essences. This is because the properties of bodies are the effects of their

---

its properties and finishes by finding an essential, causal relationship among them. All existential definitions must be reduced to sense knowledge, and ultimately to the sense of touch.

[26] Joseph Owens, "St. Thomas and Modern Science," *Transactions of the Royal Society of Canada* 1 (June 1963): 289.

[27] *De Potentia,* I. q. 9, a. 2 ad 5. Joseph Owens, 289, n. 4, cites an incomplete and not entirely accurate list of such texts in Roland-Goselin's edition and commentary on the *De Ente et Essentia*, 40, n. 2, in which Owens also refers to Joseph Le Rohellec, CSSp., "Utrum juxta S. Thomae doctrinae essentiae rerum sensibilium statim in simplici apprehensione percipiantur," *Xena Thomistics,* vol. 1, 285–303 that essay, however, understands these texts in much the same way as I have explained them above, and so does R. B. Gehring, "The Knowledge of Material Essences according to S. Thomas Aquinas," who does not draw from these texts Owen's unwarranted opinion.

substantial essences and hence can be known by arguments from effect to cause. This knowledge is indeed "through observation of qualities and activities," but that is also the way we know human nature to be rational animality. Thus to say that corporeal natures are "impenetrable" to human reason is grossly exaggerated and surrenders to a merely phenomenalist account of natural science that cuts Thomism off from modern scientific advance. Aquinas, in commenting on Aristotle, says explicitly in one of the very texts to which Owens refers,

> Since the essential principles of things are not known to us, therefore, it is necessary that we use accidental differences in designating essential ones. Thus "two-footed" [in the definition of man] is not essential. Yet through accidental differences we come to the knowledge of essential ones. [28]

It is true, however, that the more specific our exploration of the sensible world the more difficult it becomes to separate the essential from the non-essential and to discover causal relationships. Only by the use of careful observation and experimental isolation of phenomena, and by dialectical reasoning based on hypothetical models, especially mathematical models, can we make progress.[29]

Fortunately, there are no limits to this progress. As we build up a scientific understanding of the natural world around us, the need for other sciences and their possibility becomes evident. First of all, the difficulties we meet, and the divergences of opinion that arise among our fellow explorers of nature, lead us to see the need for rigorous modes of thinking and the exact use of language. Thus we discover the logical disciplines as necessary to progress in learning.[30] These disciplines, although instrumental to natural

---

[28] "Sed quia principia essentialia rerum sunt nobis ignota, ideo oportet quod utamur differentiis accidentalibus in designatione essentialium: bipes enim non est essentiale, sed ponitur in designatione essentialis. Et per eas, scilicet per differentias accidentales, devenimus in cognitionem essentialium." *In De Anima,* I, lect. 1, n. 14.

[29] Dialectical reasoning is employed by Aristotle and Aquinas to arrive at a discrimination of the essential features of a state of affairs from the accidental features. The "controlled experimentation," which is characteristic of modern science and of which Aristotle and Aquinas knew only a few rudimentary examples, would have been accepted by them as a technology (art) in the service of dialectical thinking. If dialectic succeeds, it makes possible an act of intellectus (insight) expressed in a real definition. Such a definition is then a principle of scientific (as distinguished from dialectical) argument. An example of this process is provided by Aristotle's search for a definition of "soul" at the beginning of the *De Anima* (cf. Charles De Koninck, "Introduction a l'etude de l'ame," *Laval Theologique et Philosophique* 3 (1947): 9–65, and Emile Simard, "Le hypothese," *Laval Theologique et Philosophique* 3 (1947): 89–120.

[30] *In De Trin.* (Decker), q. 5, a. 1, ad 2. That logic originated in the difficulties met in studying nature is clear from Aristotle's dialectical procedure in *Physics* I, and *De Anima* I.

science, have principles distinct from those of natural science because they are concerned not with existing, sensible realities and their relations, but with mental and linguistic constructs and their relations. The condition of such logical sciences, however, is that we have no mental relations except between concepts derived from the physical world, and no language whose ultimate reference is not to that same world.[31]

Mathematization of Thought

The need and possibility of mathematics also emerges from natural science when it demonstrates that all sensible things are quantitative (that is, they can be measured and counted). Thus we discover that human intelligence, because it is served also by the interior sense we call imagination, has the ability to idealize quantities by a mentally constructive process that results in abstract figures and numbers that differ from physical figures and numbers in that they are absolutely uniform and unchanging. Hence they are not subject to efficient or final causality, and have only imaginary existence.[32]

Because of its fixity, simplicity, and precision of relations, mathematics makes possible an application of logic much more elaborate than that in natural science and permits the perfecting of logic as a discipline. Moreover, mathematical models, although they apply only approximately to the existing physical world, are very helpful in forming hypotheses about that world and testing them dialectically. They can even produce certitude that some hypothetical physical situations are impossible.[33] Thus for Aquinas the theory of

---

31 The object of logic is the purely mental relations formed between "objective concepts" by intellectual acts. Such concepts are ultimately derived from the material changeable things that are the proper object of natural science. The logician does not know these relations as psychological objects (that pertains to natural science, of which psychology is only a subdivision), but precisely as mental relations (e.g., the relation of predication) that cannot exist in the real world, but only in the process of our thinking about it. Such relations, however, imitate real relations found in nature, as exemplified in Venn diagram circles standing for relations of logical classes. Thus the validity of logical rules presupposes our knowledge of the material world; it is not a priori. For example, the principle of contradiction as a logical rule is grounded in the principle of contradiction as an existential ("ontological") assertion about the sensible world that we experience. Only subsequently can metaphysical reflection on this sensibly grounded principle show it to have absolute (metaphysical) necessity as applying not merely to *ens mobile* but to *ens commune*.

32 *In De Trin.,* q. 5, a. 3. The most thorough treatment of Aquinas's views on mathematics that I am acquainted with is by Bernard Mullahy, CSC, "Thomism and Mathematical Physics"; cf. also Charles De Koninck, *The Hollow Universe.*

33 On the "subalternation" of natural science to mathematics see *In De Trin.,* q. 5, a. 3, ad 6 and 7 and the article by Mullahy above.

the "liberal arts" provides instruments for the successful development of natural science.[34]

Natural science in its own proper development arrives at two important conclusions, which make clear that the realm of material things, which it studies and which supplies the conditions of the other sciences I have mentioned, is not identical with all that is. These are the famous demonstrations that although all existing material things require a cause of their existence other than themselves, the First Cause of them all—though of course it too must exist in order to cause them to exist—is not material. Hence the sense of the term "being" must be analogically extended to signify not just *ens mobile* but *ens commune*, that is, being common to material and immaterial existents.[35]

The second demonstration is that there exists substantially united with the material human body an immaterial subsistent form that is not the First Cause, namely, the human soul. This second proof presupposes the first, since the former establishes (a) the existence of a First Cause and, therefore, (b) that not all being is material; while the latter establishes another instance of such immaterial being, namely the human soul, which depends on the First Cause for its own existence.[36]

The existence of immaterial being raises the question of whether a science of being in this new inclusive sense is possible, but it also indicates the great difficulties the formation of such a science would entail, since the immaterial realm is not within the proper object of our intelligence, in that it is metaphysical. If it were, then "being as such" (usually said to be the proper object of metaphysics), it would be *ens mobile* and natural science would be "first philosophy" not only *quoad nos* but *in se*.[37]

Because of these difficulties about developing metaphysics as a science, there has to be sufficient reason for its pursuit. That reason is provided when we consider that the fact of the immateriality of our intelligence means that we differ from all other things of the material world in that our activities are not wholly determined by nature, but at least in part are a matter of *free*

---

[34] The chief texts of Aquinas on this subject are listed in Pierre H. Conway, OP and B. M. Ashley, OP, *The Liberal Arts in St. Thomas Aquinas,* 62–64. See also Pierre H. Conway, OP, *Principles of Education.* Armand Maurer's introduction to his translation, *The Division and Method of the Sciences,* has many useful bibliographical notes on this topic.

[35] The summary presentation by Aquinas of the fundamental proof from motion in *Summa theologiae* I, q. 2, a. 3 must be read with the much fuller development in *Summa contra Gentiles* I, 13–16. For an accurate exposition of the argument and discussion of why it has not been rendered obsolete by modern physics, see Vincent E. Smith, *The General Science of Nature.* For discussion of common misunderstandings of Aquinas's argument, see Thomas C. O'Brien, *Metaphysics and the Existence of God.*

[36] *Summa theologiae* I, q. 75, a. 1–2, aa. 5–6; q. 89. See Anton Pegis, *The Problem of the Soul in the Thirteenth Century.*

[37] *In Meta.* (Marietti), III, 6, 398; VI, 1, 1170; 11, 7, 2267.

choice.[38] Hence, we have a need for the ethical disciplines by which our intelligence guides free human actions and for the technologies by which it invents and produces artifacts.[39]

The ethical disciplines develop the theme of the *summum bonum* both for the individual and for the society in which alone the human individual can achieve actual freedom. Aquinas comes to the conclusion that the *summum bonum* proper to human beings is the achievement of wisdom and above all such knowledge of the First Cause as is possible for us by human efforts.[40]

Since such knowledge, however difficult, is the goal of human existence, the need and possibility of a metaphysics as the first philosophy is established. The proof of the existence of the First Cause by the science of nature is the necessary condition of such a science, but nevertheless metaphysics is autonomous, based, as is every science, on an intuition of its own formal subject, an intuition, however, which presupposes certain conditions.[41]

The thesis that the necessary condition of metaphysics is the proof provided by natural science that immaterial being exists provoked a heated controversy in the 1950s that still continues. In 1979 the various opinions were collected and carefully analyzed in a Catholic University of America thesis by John V. Wagner.[42] After showing the fallacies of the attempts to deny that

---

[38] *Summa theologiae* I, q. 83; *De Veritate*, q. 24, a. 1–2; *De Malo*, q. 6.

[39] *In Ethic.*, I, lect 1, 1–6 (Marietti).

[40] Ibid., VI, lect. 5, 1180–83; X, lect. 11, 2098–2210.

[41] This is analogous to the Thomistic doctrine that the senses are the material condition of intellection, and that rational credibility is the material condition of faith. In each case the more perfect kind of knowledge is formally independent, because it has its own proper principles that are known by some intuitive type of knowledge *(intellectus)*, but this intuition presupposes a material condition without which it is impossible. On the nature of intuition *(intellectus)* in Aquinas, see Julien Peghaire, CSSp., *Intellectus et ratio selon S. Thomas d'Aquin.*

[42] John V. Wagner, *A Study of What Can and Cannot be Determined about* Separatio *as it is Discussed in the Works of St. Thomas Aquinas.* Wagner's main reason for doubting that Aquinas accepts Aristotle's position without qualification is "An approach [such as Aquinas'] that describes metaphysics as beginning with the discovery of primary beings and then includes the rest of being in its field of study because it is caused by them is not the same as an approach [such as Aristotle's] that discovers an immaterial being and on the basis of that discovery widens the notion of being" (p. 353, n. 56). This opposition disappears if we note that for Aristotle and Aquinas the proof of the First Mover in the Physics goes all the way to God as the primary being, whose existence is easier to prove than that of lesser immaterial beings. "Et sic terminat philosophus considerationem communem de rebus naturalibus in Primo Principio totius naturae, qui est super omnia Deus benedictus in saeculo saeculorum. Amen." (8, lect. 23, 2550 Marietti). Although for Aquinas, God (as Wagner shows correctly) is not the subject of metaphysics, but its principle, his existence known by natural science, establishes the reality of *ens commune* (common to material and immaterial beings) as its subject.

Aquinas held the position in question, Wagner concluded, nevertheless, that the texts that expound this position do not absolutely exclude other ways of accessing the subject of metaphysics. The strongest alternative is to be found in Aquinas's arguments that it is not impossible for forms that are not the forms of matter to exist. Lawrence Dewan, OP, has recently supported this proposal, but admits that it only establishes the *possibility* that being can be immaterial.[43]

If this is the case, is it not paradoxical to suppose that so "existential" a philosopher as Aquinas would anticipate Leibnitz by constructing his metaphysics on mere possibility? In my judgment, these texts, which are evidently the last resort of those who want to cut Thomistic metaphysics loose from any necessary relation to natural science, do not even establish the positive possibility of immaterial being, but are intended by Aquinas simply to refute arguments that claim to prove its impossibility.

It was the great accomplishment of Gilson, to which L. B. Geiger and Cornelio Fabro also greatly contributed,[44] to bring out in a way that had become obscure even in the major commentators on Aquinas how the Common Doctor was able to explicate in his metaphysics the philosophical truth that Christian faith confirms: that God is the *Ipsum Esse Subsistens*, who by the utterly free act of creation calls all other existents into a participation in *esse*.[45] Thus that by which realities are real is being in the (analogical) sense of the act of existing, known by us in an intellectual judgment.[46]

To say that the act of existing is the ultimately reality of all things, however, is meaningful only if we also add that this act of existing in creatures is

---

There is no circularity in using this physical proof as the condition of metaphysics, and then in metaphysics showing that this same proof has not only physical but metaphysical certitude and necessity. The essentially reflective, critical character of metaphysics requires it to inquire into the facts established by the special sciences in order to determine their type of necessity or contingency.

[43] See "St. Thomas Aquinas against Metaphysical Materialism" in *Studi Tomistici, Problema Metafisici.*

[44] See Étienne Gilson, *Being and Some Philosophers;* L. B. Geiger, OP, *La Participation dans la philosophie de S. Thomas d'Aquin;* Cornelio Fabro, *La nozione metafisica di partecipazione.* On the last see Mario Pangallo, *L'essere come atto nel Tomismo essenziale di Cornelio Fabro.*

[45] It must be noted, however, that Aquinas himself believed that this Christian insight was already achieved by Aristotle, since he says quite plainly, after expounding the Stagirite's views, that "From this is manifest the error of the opinions of those who teach that Aristotle thought that God is not the cause of the substance of the heavens, but only its motion." "Ex hoc autem manifest falsitas opiniones illorum, qui posuerunt Aristotelem sensisse quod Deus non sit causa substantiae caeli, sed solum motus est," *In Meta.,* VI, 1, 1164 on Aristotle, Meta. VI, 1026a 11–18. "Substance" here certainly includes *esse,* since substance as such can be caused only by giving it existence.

[46] Gilson, *Being and Some Philosophers;* Fabro, *La nozione metafisica di partecipazione.*

limited and specified by essence, while in God it is identical with essence.[47] "Being" taken as the metaphysician takes it to cover all that exists as material and non-material is an empty term until it is filled with an array of analogical and univocal concepts developed in the special sciences. To say that God is Pure Act means just as much or just as little as we have learned of him through the actualities of this world.[48]

Thus for Aquinas metaphysics is a reflective science, or better still, a contemplative wisdom[49] and if it has no content supplied by the special sciences to reflect on and contemplate, it remains merely verbal and thus otiose. Hence, if studied in isolation from the special sciences, it either suffers reduction to the natural sciences or is forced to claim transcendental intuitions unavailable to public discourse.

Nor is it necessary to accept the view, Platonic in its origin but reinforced today by the rapid progress of the special disciplines and the prevalence of the hypothetico-deductive method, that these disciplines can never achieve anything more than probability. In fact these disciplines have proper principles that have a genuine certitude, although of different types. Hence, they continue to accumulate a set of solid, demonstrated conclusions, although these are few in relation to the large body of shifting hypothetical conclusions that constitute the bulk of current opinion in the field.[50] Therefore, the material dependence of metaphysics on these disciplines does not imperil the certitude of metaphysics itself.

Thus the future of Thomism depends on whether our increasing sense of history will enable us to look once more with sympathy and without apologies on the way Aquinas viewed the variety of sciences, and on the manner in which he saw their unification by a transphysical wisdom. I believe we will then find that he can, through us, enter into the modern philosophical dialogue as a living and magisterial voice.

---

[47] See discussion in Wippel, *Metaphysical Themes in Thomas Aquinas,* 107–61, 191–214, and literature there referred to.

[48] No doubt this is why Aquinas makes so much use of the now obsolete Aristotelian sciences in his writings that today prove a source of embarrassment to modern commentators and teachers.

[49] *In Meta.* I, l, n. 34.

[50] See William A. Wallace, "Demonstration in the Science of Nature," in *From a Realist Point of View.*

CHAPTER 3

Why First Philosophy Is Last[*]

Part I: The Contemporary Domination of Scientism

IN HIS ENCYCLICAL *FIDES ET RATIO*, JOHN PAUL II explains the importance of sound human reasoning for understanding divine revelation. He especially notes the difficulty of doing this today when human knowledge has advanced but also has greatly fragmented. A chief cause for this fragmentation he says is scientism, a distortion of natural science that he defines as follows:

> This is the philosophical notion that refuses to admit the validity of forms of knowledge other than those of the positive sciences; and it relegates religious, theological, ethical and aesthetic knowledge to the realm of mere fantasy. In the past, the same idea emerged in positivism and neo-positivism, which considered metaphysical statements to be meaningless. . . . The undeniable triumphs of scientific research and contemporary technology have helped to propagate a scientistic outlook, which now seems boundless, given its inroads into different cultures and the radical changes it has brought.[1]

John Paul II points out that this can lead to a crass *pragmatism* or to postmodern nihilism. Yet in distinction from scientism, the Pope commends the achievements of modern science and says,

---

[*] This essay, in its present form previously unpublished, was first drafted and delivered at a summer conference held by the Jacques Maritain Center, Notre Dame University. It summarizes the chief conclusion of my book *The Way Toward Wisdom* soon to be published.

[1] *Fides et Ratio,* n. 88.

Finally, I cannot fail to address a word to *scientists*, whose research offers an ever greater knowledge of the universe as a whole and of the incredibly rich array of its component parts, animate and inanimate, with their complex atomic and molecular structures. So far has science come, especially in this century, that its achievements never cease to amaze us. In expressing my admiration and in offering encouragement to these brave pioneers of scientific research, to whom humanity owes so much of its current development, I would urge them to continue their efforts without ever abandoning the *sapiential* horizon within which scientific and technological achievements are wedded to the philosophical and ethical values which are the distinctive and indelible mark of the human person. Scientists are well aware that "the search for truth, even when it concerns a finite reality of the world or of man, is never-ending, but always points beyond to something higher than the immediate object of study, to the questions which give access to Mystery."[2]

Thus what John Paul II writes about "philosophy" chiefly concerns the discipline of metaphysics. Yet he does not tell us exactly what the relation between "science" and "metaphysics" ought to be. Nor does he tell us how we are to convince philosophers today that metaphysics is a valid form of truth and not merely, as some analytic philosophers declare, a mere "language game" without empirical foundation.

The Damage Done to Our Culture by Scientism

Few scientists would admit they are guilty of the "scientism" that John Paul II deplores. They sincerely believe that they are honestly pursuing the scientific method that has proved so enormously successful in modern times. Yet the Pope is certainly right in claiming that scientism as he describes it has many negative effects on our culture, which is largely the product of science and scientific technology. Can this denial by scientists of the harm caused by scientism be because scientists today tend to limit objective truth to the "value free" study and explanation of observed data?

A second disastrous result of scientism is that instead of eliminating "theology" and even "religion," because some agnostic scientists see them as obscurantist and oppressive, scientism has produced a substitute for religion that is even more obscurantist and oppressive, namely, secular humanism.[3] It is

---

[2] Ibid., n. 106.

[3] For a clear statement of what secular humanists believe, see "Spirituality Without Faith," at www.naturalism.org/spiritual.htm. For my argument that secular humanism is in the sociological sense a "religion," since its function is to provide the worldview and value system necessary for every person and human community, see my books *Theologies of the Body: Humanist and Christian* and *Choosing a Worldview and Value System.*

obscurantist because it popularizes current scientific speculations as if they were true "discoveries" and it is oppressive because it effectively fosters a world-view in which human rights have no other basis than the arbitrary preferences of powerful elites. Without a belief in a Creator who governs the universe to promote the happiness of his creatures, to which he guides them by the purposes he has built into nature, there can be no effective, rational defense of morality. Yet physics 101 teaches that "teleology," and therefore any notion of purpose or value in nature, must be systematically excluded from true science.

A third baneful effect of scientism is that it empties the universe of human meaning. The famous physicist Steven Weinberg when asked what his deep investigations of the universe meant to him replied, "The more I study the universe the more *pointless* the universe seems."[4] The immense, expanding universe seems utterly indifferent to our human existence. We may hope that there is other intelligent life out there, but even if there is, we are all doomed. Our brief lives seem a mere accident of an evolution that has no predictable outcome in a universe of which we are a meaningless product of chance. For a value-free scientism, if our lives are to have any value at all, we must, without any objective basis in science, create it for ourselves.

Some theologians in their efforts to dialogue with Eastern religions have succumbed to the speculations of the physicist Fritjof Capra in his well-known *The Tao of Physics*[5] to conclude that the "organic" view of the universe presented by current physics argues for pantheism, contrary to the fundamental article of Judaeo-Christian faith in a God who absolutely transcends the universe he has freely created for its own good. This pantheism was supported by Einstein who said "I believe in Spinoza's God, who reveals himself in the harmony of all being, not in a God who concerns himself with the fate and actions of men."[6] Other theologians are so fascinated by the paleontologist Teilhard de Chardin's views on evolution as moving toward the noösphere and the Omega point[7] that they tend to override the Church's teaching that God directly creates the human soul.

---

[4] See the interview with Weinberg in Alan Lightman and Roberta Brawer, *Origins: The Lives and Worlds of Modern Cosmologists,* 451–66: the majority of the other scientists interviewed in this book are less blunt but seem to have similar views.

[5] Fritjof Capra, *Tao of Physics: An Exploration of the Parallels between Modern Physics and Eastern Mysticism.*

[6] Spinoza held that matter and mind are simply two aspects of one Absolute or "God." See Arnold Sommerfeld, "To Einstein's 70th Birthday," in Paul Arthur Schlipp, *Albert Einstein Philosopher-Scientist,* 99–105, esp. 103. See also 659ff. Ilse Rosenthal-Schneider, "Presuppositions and Anticipations of Einstein's Physics," ibid., 129–46, shows 144ff. that Einstein believed, while granting it could not be proved, that this is the only possible universe and hence God was not free to create any other. This was the meaning of his famous dictum, "God does not play dice."

[7] Pierre Teilhard de Chardin, *The Phenomenon of Man.*

First, environmentalists point out that the technologies fostered by value-free science have devastated the very order of nature that science studies and have led to the spread of previously unknown "weapons of mass destruction." Even when technology is not misused it is engendering modes of human living that are so complex and unnatural to human persons, especially to the institution of the human family, that new diseases and psychological maladies have arisen and even the human genome has become imperiled. The controversy over human cloning is only one example of this endangerment of our species. Another example is that some predict the eventual replacement of human persons with intelligent machines!

The fourth tragic effect of scientism (and for Catholics the worst of all) is that it has led some Catholic theologians laudably concerned to "meet the modern mind" to distort not just natural theology but the revealed faith. Let me mention a few examples of such errors.[8] I pass over the evolutionist–creationist controversy because the Catholic Church does not teach a fundamentalist reading of Genesis, but there are many other less publicized scientistic distortions of Catholic teaching.

Again, the search for extraterrestrial intelligence promoted by the astronomer Carl Sagan has led some theologians to so qualify their discussions of the doctrine of Incarnation as the unique source of redemption that the Vatican was forced to reassert this central Christian truth with a directness that has seemed to some offensive to ecumenism.

The mind-body controversy also has made some theologians hesitate to claim that the human intelligence is other than the operation of the brain. The famous *Dutch Catechism* was required by the Vatican to remedy its deliberate omission of any mention of angels for whom there seems no room in a scientistic universe, although there is ample room for an infinity of possible purely material worlds.[9] Christologies "from below" that overshadow the "from above" divinity of Christ seem to fit better into this sort of universe.[10]

Some of these deplorable effects of scientism on theology result from rather crude misunderstandings of science. Thus a number of distinguished theologians were led by their mistaken notion that science had eliminated the traditional distinction between "substance" and "accidents" to attempt new and very dubious theories of "transignification" to replace the orthodox formula of "transubstantiation" in the Eucharist.[11] Some theologians have

---

8 While it might make my argument stronger to name names, for the sake of fairness I will not do so in this section because some of these theologians seem not to be aware that they are basing their revisions of traditional doctrines on scientism rather than on sound science.

9 See my essay "The Existence of Created Free Spirits" in this collection.

10 See my essay "Christology from Above" in this collection.

11 For an example from a widely used theological reference book, "The 'tota substantia', that is, the material substance composed of matter and form with its inherent accidents,

even attempted to revive Aquinas's and even Duns Scotus's views, orthodox in principle but outmoded as to embryological facts, on the "delayed hominization" of the human embryo and fetus in order to permit certain medical practices that are in fact abortions.

Of course, as regards most of these doctrines all but a few Catholic theologians submit to the Church's teachings and I do not question their sincerity in doing so. Yet they have been so frightened by the difficulties of harmonizing orthodoxy with the results of science in its scientistic interpretation that they give minimalist interpretations to these doctrines. Or they are content to make their submission to orthodoxy in footnotes to readings of biblical texts that minimize the value of these texts in supporting this orthodoxy. While these theological waverings are usually more directly affected by the historical-critical method in Scripture study than by the theologians' knowledge of science, of which they disclaim expertise, it is obviously scientism that has fostered the "demythologizing" of the Bible.

This kind of scientism is not at all what the founders of modern science thought that they were working so hard to develop. Galileo, Descartes, Boyle, Harvey, Newton,[12] even Einstein who accepted the pantheism of the "God intoxicated" Spinoza, supposed that science would reveal "the glory of God." They hoped it would enhance the meaning of the universe and the dignity of the human person as capable of scientific thought. I don't mean to complain that much of current science is still very speculative; that is inevitable as science advances. The problem that must concern all of us is that today science has increasingly become a set of mathematical hypotheses that are more and more impossible to interpret in a consistent physical way and hence seems empty of human meaning.[13]

What remedy does John Paul II propose? He writes, "To be consonant with the word of God, philosophy needs first of all to recover its *sapiential dimension* as a search for the ultimate and overarching meaning of life." What is needed, the Pope says, is

> A philosophy of *genuinely metaphysical* range, capable, that is, of transcending empirical data in order to attain something absolute, ultimate and foundational in its search for truth. This requirement is implicit in sapiential and analytical knowledge alike; and in particular it is a

---

is not in accord with the world-picture presented by physics and philosophy at the present time." Karl Rahner, *Encyclopedia of Theology: The Concise Sacramentum Mundi,* 1753.

12 See Eugene M. Klaaren, *Religious Origins of Modern Science: Belief in Creation in Seventeenth-Century Thought,* especially the many quotations from Robert Boyle.

13 See Anthony Rizzi, *The Science Before Science,* especially 1–6.

requirement for knowing the moral good, which has its ultimate foundation in the Supreme Good, God himself.[14]

Where is such wisdom to be found? John Paul II holds up St. Thomas Aquinas as a model for Christian thinkers; yet says, "the Church has no philosophy of its own. (n. 43)[15]" While there are some current philosophers who still speak of "metaphysics," their conception of this discipline is often very far from that of Aquinas, and the majority of contemporary thinkers seem to deny its validity. It is necessary, therefore, to raise the question that in Aquinas's time it was seldom discussed because the authority of Aristotle's *Metaphysics*—although it received very different interpretations—was taken for granted.

Part II: The Validity of "Metaphysics"

The Discovery of "Metaphysics"

It was Aristotle who first proposed that there must be an intellectual discipline that can unite other more specialized disciplines without destroying their autonomy. Plato had held that there is really only one wisdom to which all others are reducible, as Pythagoras and Parmenides had in different ways also supposed. After Aristotle, the Stoics and Epicureans tended to reduce all knowledge to ethics. In our universities today we have fragmented knowledge into dozens of "fields" and "departments," which though they jealously defend their own turf actually are divided into two great camps. As C. P. Snow in his famous book *The Two Cultures* showed, these are the "hard sciences" and the "soft humanities."[16]

While the Greeks gave the name "philosophy" to all critical disciplines, today philosophy and theology are relegated to the "soft humanities." These humanities are deemed "soft" in the sense that their pronouncements are considered to be more a matter of taste and opinion than of truth. Thus the apparent autonomy of modern disciplines has been reduced to the hard sciences and these to mathematical physics. Hence, it would seem that Aristotle's hope of "dividing in order to unite," as Jacques Maritain put it,[17] in order to maintain a genuine plurality of intellectual disciplines has been abandoned. Therefore, I would like again to raise the question that Aristotle first asked, "Is there a way to overcome the fragmentation of knowledge without reducing different modes of thought to a single dominating discipline?"

[14] *Fides et Ratio,* n. 83.
[15] Ibid., n. 43.
[16] C. P. Snow, *The Two Cultures: A Second Look* (Cambridge: Cambridge University Press, 1964).
[17] This is the original French title of his work *The Degrees of Knowledge,* translated under the supervision of Gerald B. Phelan, 1959, reprinted as vol. 7 of *Collected Works of Jacques Maritain* (Notre Dame: IN: University of Notre Dame Press, 1995).

Aristotle called the discipline he sought for this purpose "First Philosophy" and sometimes, for reasons I will touch on later, "Theology." After his death some disciple or editor gave it, for reasons that are not certain, the name "metaphysics," that is "post-physics."[18] By "first" Aristotle did not necessarily mean *epistemologically* or even *pedagogically* prior to the more specialized disciplines. Some insist that we must establish an epistemology before we can begin any science, since we need to have truth criteria by which to judge its first principles. Therefore, because they assume that epistemology is part of metaphysics, they hold that metaphysics precedes all other sciences. But "epistemology" is a modern term reflecting the Cartesian "turn to the subject." For Aristotle and Aquinas every autonomous science justifies the truth of its own principles and proper methodology. Only First Philosophy considers "truth" as a transcendental property of every kind of reality, of Being as such. But Being as such is analogical and hence it is a *confused* concept. Hence the meaning of the judgment "Being is" must also be confused. There is no way to begin to clarify its confusion except by distinguishing the various meanings of "Being" by referring to what we have learned about them in the special sciences.

For Aristotle what this "First"—in the sense of Ultimate—"Philosophy" might be was so difficult to determine that all but one of the fourteen books of his *Metaphysics*, at least as I read that work, are devoted to examining that question. Only Book XII is clearly devoted to actually expounding First Philosophy itself. The other thirteen books argue that this First Philosophy can be neither a reduction of all disciplines to a single science, as Plato had thought, nor can it be any of the special disciplines whose autonomy Aristotle recognized and wished to defend.

He concludes that First Philosophy presupposes natural science, as do the other special sciences that depend on it for its data.[19] It cannot, therefore, pretend to correct the *certain* conclusions achieved by these special sciences. Yet it can assist them in several ways important ways. First, it can sometimes decide whether all or some of the first principles of these special sciences are

---

[18] I recommend the translation by Hippocrates G. Apostle, *Aristotle's Metaphysics,* Peripatetic Press, for its fidelity to the Greek, its commentaries and helpful glossary. On the issue of the unity of Aristotle's thought and of his metaphysics in particular, see Charlotte Witt, "The Evolution of Developmental Interpretations of Aristotle," in William Wians, ed., *Aristotle's Philosophical Development: Problems and Prospects,* 67–82.

[19] I argue this at length in chapters IV and V of my *The Way Toward Wisdom*; cf. also Ralph McInerny of the University of Notre Dame, who writes, "The only conclusion which I offer is that the order of learning which makes metaphysics consequent upon the philosophy of nature, not only for its terminology, which can be extended and purified, but even for the suggestions of its formal subject as not restricted to material conditions, follows on the very nature of our mind . . . ," "The Prime Mover and the Order of Learning," *Being and Predication: Thomistic Interpretations,* 49–58.

merely conditionally true or have absolute necessity. For example, it shows that the Principle of Non-Contradiction used in natural science applies to all Being and hence with absolute necessity. Second, it can compare the findings of one discipline with another and show their similarities and differences. Third, it can often solve apparent contradictions in the special disciplines that arise from semantic confusions. Fourth, it can relate all beings to their First Cause and by the analogy of effect to cause arrive at some understanding, although an imperfect one, of the nature or essence of that First Cause. In this sense First Philosophy is, as Aristotle says,[20] also a theology, although one founded not on revelation but on human experience and reason; God is not included in its proper subject but is the goal of its explorations of being.

The Division of the Sciences

What autonomous disciplines did Aristotle recognize?[21] In the tradition of Parmenides, Plato reduced human knowledge of reality to innate ideas and hence did not clearly distinguish the mental from the real. Aristotle, to the contrary, separated the field of logic taken in a broad sense as including poetics, rhetoric, dialectics, and demonstrative logic from the real sciences, because it deals only with the mental relations we use in thinking and speaking about reality. Hence, Aristotle does not even call logic an *episteme* or "science." Yet he showed that logic is a rigorous, critical discipline whose rules can be demonstrated by reducing them all to the Principle of Contradiction. Thus the knowledge of logic is valuable because it helps us to be consistent in our thinking. But whence comes the Principle of Non-Contradiction? Surprisingly, this principle on which all logic is based and which guarantees its autonomy is derived from its employment in natural science. This is because it is natural science, as the epistemologically first discipline dealing with reality, must be the one that renders evident the Principle of Non-Contradiction on which all human reasoning depends.

Natural science grounds the Principle of Non-Contradiction by resolving the debate between Parmenides and Heraclitus, in which Plato sided with Parmenides, as to whether truth can be derived from sense knowledge. Aristotle concedes to Heraclitus that the world we know is in flux, but shows that our changing world also has a certain order and stability that makes it intelligible. Everything is changeable but this very fact means that when any being is actual it exists as a definite kind of thing and not as something else, nor as nothing.

---

[20] *Meta.* VI, c. 1, 1026a 18 and XI c. 7, 1064b 2.

[21] On this see St. Thomas Aquinas, *The Division and Methods of the Sciences,* Questions V and VI of the *Commentary on Boethius'* De Trinitate.

Other than natural science and the art of logic grounded in natural science, are there other autonomous disciplines that deal with reality? Plato, in the tradition of Pythagoras, maintained that mathematics has a certainty not possible in natural science. Hence for him mathematical knowledge was at least a bridge to the Idea of the One and Good to which all knowledge could be reduced. Aristotle in the *Metaphysics* devotes more space to refuting this Platonic view than to any other topic. He does this by showing that the two mathematical disciplines he recognizes, namely geometry and arithmetic, although paradigms of logical thinking, are not logic, nor are they part of natural science.[22]

The distinction between mathematics and natural science, however, was not easy to make, because for both Pythagoras and Plato, it was mathematics that enables us to understand the order of the universe. This view has persisted throughout western history and triumphed when Galileo, well trained as an Aristotelian, was seduced by his genius for mathematics into adopting Pythagoreanism. Today it reigns supreme in modern science because of its evident success and the technological control it has given us. Furthermore, since modern mathematics has been reduced more and more to logic, this seems to say again that Aristotle's project has failed. He had argued that since the object of mathematics is quantity abstracted from the physical quantities studied by natural science, its abstract character guarantees its autonomy, yet presupposes that natural science has first established the existence and definition of physical quantity. Fortunately, Kurt Gödel, by his famous Theorem or Theorems, has now shown mathematically that arithmetic cannot be known to be either consistent or complete without reference to real quantity.[23]

While the theoretical disciplines of natural science, geometry, and arithmetic are studied simply for the sake of knowing, and logic is studied only to assist in this knowing, there are also purely practical disciplines. These practical disciplines are studied either to produce something, the technologies, or to guide human living, the ethical sciences. It is obvious that the technologies presuppose natural science because we must know natural materials and use natural forces to make anything real.

As for the ethical sciences, Aristotle distinguished individual and domestic ethics, politics, and military leadership, but argued that politics is architectonic with regard to the others.[24] Ethics deals with the satisfaction of human needs that are necessary to human nature, while the technologies

---

[22] For Aristotle's views on mathematics, see Sir Thomas L. Heath, *Mathematics in Aristotle,* and Hippocrates Apostle, *Aristotle's Philosophy of Mathematics* (Chicago: University of Chicago Press, 1952).

[23] Ernest Nagel and James R. Newman, *Gödel's Proof,* new ed., Harry J. Gensler, *Gödel's Theorem Simplified,* and Egon Boerger, Erich Grädel, and Yuri Gurevich, *The Classical Decision Problem.*

[24] *Nichomachean Ethics* VI. c, 8, 1141b 23 sq.; *Politics,* 1, c.1, 1252a sq.; *Aquinas, Summa theologiae* II–II, q. 50.

deal proximately with freely chosen goals that are not absolutely necessary for our happiness.

Thus it would seem that Aristotle should have concluded that the discipline that unifies human knowledge, yet at the same time respects its diversity by a division of that knowledge into the special theoretical and practical sciences, is natural science, since all these other special sciences are grounded in natural science because it is epistemologically first among human intellectual disciplines. This would be consonant with modern thought that, though it claims to value the autonomy of the different forms of human thought, in fact tends to reduce their objective truth to empirical natural science.

Why then is natural science not First Philosophy, since it is epistemologically prior to all other human sciences? Aristotle was born in a family whose sons were traditionally physicians and he had a genius for the exploration of nature. When asked why he demeaned himself by studying the entrails of worms, he answered that even there he found the wonderful art of the Maker of all things.[25] Might he not then have thought of natural science as not only First, that is chief among sciences, but also as theology, a study of the divine?[26]

Why the First Must be Last

It was precisely Aristotle's profound exploration of natural science, both in its foundations and its ultimate reaches that showed him that natural science, though it is epistemologically first, couldn't be the ultimate, unifying science. Werner Jaeger in his famous but inconclusive effort to date Aristotle's works thought that the Stagirite had moved away from Plato's belief in a spiritual reduction of all knowledge to the empiricism of natural science.[27] But it was precisely Aristotle's empirical epistemology that led him both to reject Plato's reduction of the autonomous special disciples and at the same time to agree with Plato that the order of material reality depends on a superior order of spiritual reality. This became evident to him at three progressive levels of natural science.

First, and most important in Book VIII of the work called the *Physics*, in which Aristotle lays the foundations of natural science, he discovered that changeable, material beings exist ultimately only as the effects of non-material causes, of which one must be the ultimate cause of all existing change-

---

[25] *De Partibus Animalium* I, c. 5, 644b 21 sq.

[26] According to Abraham P. Bos, *Cosmic and Metacosmic Theology in Aristotle's Lost Dialogues* (New York: Brill, 1989), Aristotle probably dealt with religious topics in his lost dialogues rather than in the extant corpus because the dialogue was considered the literary form appropriate to more transcendent speculations.

[27] On the history of such theories, see the essays in *Aristotle's Philosophical Development: Problems and Prospects*, William Wians, ed. (Lanham, MD: Rowman & Littlefield, 1996).

ables, the Unchangeable Cause of all changeables, both in their existences and their essences. Let me stress that for him this is a conclusion of natural science, not, as we are sometimes told, of a "*philosophy* of nature." For Aristotle and for western thought, natural science was never placed in opposition to "philosophy" until the eighteenth century when Christian Wolff, the disciple of Descartes and Leibniz, identified "philosophy" with "metaphysics," which he defined as the "science of possible being." Consequently Wolff placed "cosmology" as that part of "philosophy" that studies the features common to all possible worlds in opposition to non-philosophical "science of physics," which studies the actual world empirically.[28] In fact, as I have just stated, even for the Platonic tradition physics was only the shadow of philosophy because material nature imitated the spiritual ideas through the mediation of mathematics, while for the Aristotelian it was the most evidently valid philosophy precisely because it was empirical.

Second, Aristotle in Book III of *De Anima* found that at the summit of natural science the human intelligence is discovered to transcend the material order. Because we have spiritual souls we are able to know something of the spiritual causes of the material order by analogy from what we know of their effects in the material order.

Third, Aristotle realized that the system of changeable bodies that make up our material universe requires the existence not only of a First Immaterial Cause, but in addition to spiritual human intelligences dependent on material bodies, the existence also of a number of purely spiritual intelligences subordinate to the First Cause.[29] This must be the case, he concluded, because the unity of the universe, like the unity of the sciences, is one of coordination of a number of autonomous but merely physical agents that must be actuated by separate spiritual agents.[30] For these three reasons First Philosophy is not epistemologically first but last. Furthermore, it alone can also properly be called theology and as such is developed in Book XII of his so-called *Metaphysics*.

This First Philosophy, therefore, would not be needed and indeed could not be valid unless natural science first established at least the existence of the First Cause and its transcendence of matter. Once grounded by the certain demonstration that "being" is not merely material, it is possible for First Philosophy to look back over all the more special sciences, compare and contrast them, distinguish the contingent from the necessary, the probable from

---

[28] See Giorgio Tonelli, "Wolff, Christian," *The Encyclopedia of Philosophy*, edited by Paul Edwards, vol. 8, 340–44, and Blackwell, "The Structure of Wolffian Philosophy," 203–18.

[29] Some commentators think that Aristotle thought these spiritual intelligences were the souls of the celestial spheres, but Aquinas shows this would be inconsistent with Aristotle's other views; see Aquinas, *Summa contra Gentiles* I, 13, n. 112.

[30] *Metaphysics* XII, c. 8, 1073a 13 sq.

the certain in the exploration of these special sciences, and finally coordinate them into a unified worldview.

Imperfect as our understanding of the totality of reality may be, since it is only analogical, nevertheless Aristotle in his *Ethics*[31] and *Politics* concluded that the rational contemplation of divine things is the goal of human existence, true though imperfect happiness. Hence the study of First Philosophy, however meager its results, is worth the effort. It is true human wisdom, far more desirable than the illusory mystical wisdom that Plato's system claimed.

Bernard Lonergan's characterization of the thought of the twentieth century as a "transition from the classical worldview to historical mindedness"[32] is often thought to be the explanation of the decline of Thomism in America in the last half of that century. Is not the Thomistic tradition redolent of the "classicist" mentality? And is not such a mentality utterly unable to deal with the dynamic, subject-centered, existentialist, personalist, and pluralist mindset of our times that Vatican II called Catholics to address more positively? If Thomism is to have a future, therefore, it must shed this classicist mentality and assume historical-mindedness without losing its integrity and uniqueness. Already in 1937 the great French medievalist M.-D. Chenu, and other like-minded Thomists had argued this.[33]

Since what is described as classicist in the thought of the past is best typified by Platonism and its essentialism, and since Maritain, Gilson, and others in the first half of the last century seem to have firmly established the *existential* character of Thomism, such a renewal seems possible.

As Bernard Lonergan said, historical-mindedness in philosophy is the recognition that truth exists only in the minds of persons.[34] Since, however, truth is not mere consistency in thought as Kant held, but the conformity of the mind to reality, we all have a responsibility to seek agreement of minds based on such conformity to reality and not on any other grounds. To be both historically-minded and yet fulfill this responsibility requires, therefore, that no matter how different our perspectives we seek jointly to transcend our historical limitations. Metaphysics therefore must recognize the historical limits

---

[31] *Nicomachean Ethics* X, cc. 6–8; *Pol.* VII, cc. 1≠3.

[32] See my essay "Transition to Historical Mindedness" in this collection.

[33] *Une École de théologie: le Saulchoir,* G. Alberigo, et al. This book was put on the Index, probably under the influence of Thomists of the Garrigou-Lagrange persuasion because it seemed to incline toward the "modernism" that was then a great problem for the Church. See the article "Due maestri in una scuola di teologia: Cordovani Chenu," *Vita sociale* 40 (1983): 166–76 on www.utenti.lycos.it/emilioweb/minor/p_fe8311.htm. Yves Congar, OP, so influential in Vatican II and later made Cardinal, was closely associated with Chenu in this transition to historical Thomism.

[34] As Lonergan rightly says in "The Subject" (*A Second Collection,* 3), "Such is the objectivity of truth. But do not be fascinated by it. Intentionally it is independent of the subject, but ontologically it resides only in the subject: *veritas formaliter est in solo judicio.*"

of any expression of the truth about reality, but should not be afraid to remain faithful to truths once it has found them to have been well attested evidentially by any of the sciences according to their proper criteria.

Part III: Thomistic "Metaphysics"

Eight Readings of Thomism and Their Reconciliation

So much for Aristotle, as I read him: Now I want to move on to consider how St. Thomas Aquinas read him. I believe that Aquinas accepted and defended Aristotle's views on First Philosophy, but pursued them well beyond what Aristotle had been able to accomplish. My reading is based on the totality of Aquinas's works, but is especially concerned to separate St. Thomas's position as a philosopher from his position as a Christian theologian, and thus to avoid those readings, which depend too much on the *Summa theologiae* in which Aquinas uses philosophical positions more thoroughly established in his other, properly philosophical works.[35]

In doing this I at once run into the difficulty that currently there are many apparently inconsistent readings of Aquinas relative to his Aristotelian sources. I can identify eight such readings that are current and influential: (1) Essentialist, (2) Platonizing, (3) Transcendental, (4) Existential, (5) Phenomenological, (6) Analytic, (7) Semiotic, and (8) Aristotelian Thomisms

The first phase of the Thomist Revival was centered on the efforts, principally by members of the Dominican Order, to present an authentic Thomism instead of the Suarezian Thomism of the seventeenth century, which tried to synthesize Thomas with Scotus. By the 1930s the fundamental differences between these two giants of metaphysics were generally recognized. The effort to recover an authentic reading of Aquinas was a chief occupation of the French Dominicans and is exemplified by the work of Reginald Garrigou-Lagrange (1877–1964), characterized by his critics as *Essentialist or Conceptualist Thomism.*[36] This school holds that the subject of metaphysics is conceived in the third degree of abstraction according to the analysis of the Dominican Thomist Cardinal Cajetan, OP (1468–1534). According to Cajetan, natural science is in the first degree of abstraction, mathematics in the second, and metaphysics and logic in the third. Thus

---

[35] In my opinion it was such an excessive dependence on the *Summa theologiae* as a source for Aquinas's philosophical views that led Gilson to a basically faulty interpretation of Aquinas's metaphysics.

[36] On Garrigou-Lagrange, see Richard Peddichord, OP, *The Sacred Monster of Thomism* (South Bend, IN: St. Augustine's Press, 2004). Garrigou-Lagrange's metaphysics is well represented by his *Reality: A Synthesis of Thomistic Thought*, now available on www.ewtn.com/library/theology/reality.htm. See Richard Peddichord, *The Sacred Monster of Thomism: An Introduction to the Life and Legacy of Reginald Garrigou-Lagrange, OP.*

Essentialists generally assume without further discussion that this degree of abstraction is realistically valid. This reading of Aquinas was formulated in the famous "XXIV Theses" approved by Pius X as expressing the "solid doctrine of St. Thomas" as it had been canonized by Leo XIII.[37]

Secondly, Arthur Little, Cornelio Fabro, and Fr. W. Norris Clarke, SJ, have provided us with *Platonizing* readings of Aquinas.[38] These authors point out that Aquinas assimilates to his Aristotelian position a vast amount of the Platonic tradition as he knew it chiefly through Neo-Platonism. This influence is to be found mainly in Aquinas's doctrine of *participation*, a central theme for Plato, which Aristotle seldom develops. This raises no special difficulty for the reading I prefer if it is granted that Aquinas is always very careful to use these Platonic sources in a manner consistent with his Aristotelian epistemology, as well as with the doctrine that the First Cause produces the universe not by emanation but by efficient causality.

Although the doctrine of *creatio ex nihilo* is not explicit in Aristotle's works, Aquinas considers it a necessary consequence of his argument for an immaterial First Cause.[39] As for participation, this is formal causality, which is entirely consistent with what I have said of Aristotle, even if, in his anti-Platonic polemic, he is disinclined to emphasize it. Since First Philosophy treats of the transcendental properties of Being as such, that is of the different kinds of being in their analogical unity, it deals with that transcendental property that is truth, the conformity of mind to reality, a type of formal causality and participation.

The third reading of Thomism is that of the Transcendental Thomists, initiated by Joseph Maréchal (1878–1944)[40] and notably represented by Karl Rahner, SJ (1938–99) and in a somewhat different way by Bernard Lonergan, SJ (1904–84).[41] In an effort to read Aquinas in a way more acceptable to modern philosophy dominated by Kant and enlivened by the "philosophy of

---

37 These theses can be found with history and commentary in Pedro Lumbreras, OP, *The XXIV Fundamental Theses of Official Catholic Philosophy.*

38 Arthur Little, SJ, *The Platonic Heritage of Thomism,* Cornelio Fabro, *La nozione metafisica di partécipazione secondo S. Tommaso d'Aquino,* 3rd ed. rev. and augmented, and *Participation et causalité selon S. Thomas d'Aquin;* W. Norris Clarke, SJ, *The Philosophical Approach to God: A Neo-Thomist Perspective* who, however, in his more recent *The One and the Many* adopts the Transcendental reading of Aquinas.

39 On this question see Mark F. Johnson, "Did St. Thomas Attribute a Doctrine of Creation to Aristotle?," *The New Scholasticism* 63 (1989): 129–55, who with great textual detail answers this question affirmatively. See also his "Aquinas' Changing Evaluation of Plato on Creation," *American Catholic Philosophical Quarterly* 66 (1992): 81–88.

40 Maréchal, *Le points de depart de la metaphysique: Lecons le Developpement historique et théorique du problème de la Connaissance.* 3rd ed. Essential passages are available in *A Maréchal Reader,* edited and translated by Joseph Donceel.

41 David Tracy, *The Achievement of Bernard Lonergan* (New York: Herder and Herder, 1970).

immanence" of Maurice Blondel (1861–1949) and of evolutionary "process," influenced by biological evolutionary theory and represented by Henri Bergson (1859–1941), these thinkers found what they believed to be an a priori element in Aquinas's presentation of Aristotle's epistemology. They found this in the dynamism of the human intelligence that cannot be satisfied until it rests in the Absolute. Consequently this horizon of Absolute Being conditions all of human knowledge and constitutes in its depths as metaphysical.

In this way the "turn to the subject" of Descartes that initiated modern thought seems to be discovered within Thomism. The very helpful histories of modern Thomism by Father Gerald McCool interpret that history as the triumph of this transcendental reading of Aquinas.[42] Proponents of other schools of Thomism have done so thorough a job in attacking this position that I will not attempt to do so here. Rather I want to acknowledge the contribution that the members of this school have made to a genuine modernization of Thomism.

The great achievement of modern thought has been to bring to attention the subjective aspects of human knowledge, which Aristotle and Aquinas certainly recognized, but that are less developed in their thought because they were so anxious to get its objective elements right. While they placed problems in a dialectical context of opinion, they seldom touched on the way history and culture color our view of the world, or on the way that individual and social tendencies enter its construction. The Transcendental Thomists have opened up such questions and I am convinced that if Thomism is to survive in our times it must also deal with these issues.

The fourth reading of Aquinas, the Existential, which has been most influential in the United States, was chiefly the work of Jacques Maritain (1882–1973)[43] and Étienne Gilson (1884–1978).[44] They were both ardent defenders of St. Thomas's originality and fully conscious of the problem raised by the contrast between its medieval and modern historical contexts. They vigorously opposed Transcendental Thomism because of its Cartesian, Kantian, idealist tendencies, but also attacked essentialist, Neo-Scholastic Thomism. This reading has many proponents. Fr. Joseph Owens, an expert of Aristotle gave it a special twist.[45] It is most fully presented with textual arguments by Fr. John F. Wippel in his recent *The Metaphysical Thought of St. Thomas Aquinas*.[46]

What distinguishes this school is its insistence, with variations, on resting the validity of metaphysics on the "judgment of *esse* or existential act," *independent* of any other discipline, especially of natural science. The problem

---

[42] *From Unity to Pluralism* and *The Neo Thomists.*

[43] See Joseph W. Evans, ed., *Jacques Maritain: The Man and His Achievements;* and Ralph McInerny, *Art and Prudence: Studies in the Thought of Jacques Maritain.*

[44] No good recent study of Gilson seems available but see A. C. Pegis, *A Gilson Reader.*

[45] See Owens's *An Elementary Christian Metaphysics.*

[46] John F. Wippel, *The Metaphysical Thought of Thomas Aquinas.*

this raises, of course, is that they also grant that for Aquinas *esse* and *essentia,* the existence and the essence, of anything except God in whom these are identical, are related as act to potency and hence are correlative. But does this not mean that just as we cannot say anything meaningful about matter except in relation to form, so we cannot say anything meaningful about existence except in relation to some essence? That is why Aquinas insisted that the term Being is analogical, and hence that First Philosophy does not have as its subject one kind of being but many kinds of being that it carefully distinguishes. Hence to talk about *esse* without at the same time distinguishing its various kinds that are only analogically one is empty talk and has opened Thomists to the accusation of mouthing impressive nonsense.

Since it is the business of the special sciences to study these various kinds of being, it follows that First Philosophy when it talks about Being as Being must do so as a reflection over the similarities and differences of the beings whose existences and essences are properly studied by the special sciences. Thus it is "First" by being epistemologically last. To deny that it presupposes the special sciences is to empty it of content, or to go down the road that Scotus, working in the Platonic tradition, took when he made the subject of metaphysics univocal Being and thus epistemologically prior to all others forms of knowledge.[47]

Yet I would not for a moment deny the great contribution Gilson made to Thomism by placing Aquinas in historical perspective, or what Maritain did by his emphasis on the importance of the division of the sciences and their autonomy. Maritain also advanced our understanding of the intuitive and connatural aspects of knowledge. Joseph Owens and John Wippel have also contributed to a better understanding of these sources. Owens in particular granted that the way to immaterial being has to be through material being, although, mistakenly in my opinion, he circularly assigned this task to First Philosophy instead of seeing that, until it has been achieved, the First Philosophy is natural science.

The fifth reading, *Phenomenological Thomism,* has gained prominence especially through its use by Karol Wojtyla (Pope John Paul II, 1920–2005) and the Thomists of the Polish University of Lublin.[48] Wojtyla was a pupil of Garrigou-Lagrange and remained faithful to an unquestionably authentic Thomism, but attempted to meet modern concerns by the adopting the phenomenological method of Husserl, while retaining the critical realism of Aquinas against Husserl's constitutive idealism. This approach to metaphysics focuses on Personalism (as Maritain had also done), that is, on the human person as manifest-

---

[47] For Scotus's view see Cyril L. Schircel, *The University of the Concept of Being in the Philosophy of Duns Scotus,* and Peter King, "Scotus on Metaphysics" in Thomas Williams, ed., *The Cambridge Companion to Duns Scotus,* 69–99.

[48] The best exposition in English of his philosophy is Rocco Buttiglione, *Karol Wojtyla: The Thought of the Man Who Became Pope John Paul II,* foreword by Michael Novak.

ing the harmony of the material and the spiritual in the analogy of Being. Its special concern is to emphasize the dignity of the human person and its moral responsibilities in the face of modern materialism and moral relativism.

Analytic Thomism, the sixth reading, exemplified in Great Britain by Gertrude Elizabeth Anscombe, Peter Geach, Anthony Kenny, Fr. Brian Davies, OP, John Haldane, and in the United States by my colleague at St. Louis University, Eleonore Stump, is also concerned to be authentically Thomist by applying the methods of analytical philosophy to the clarification and defense of the logical meaningfulness of metaphysical terms and the logical consistency of its arguments.[49] In common with other analysts, however, these Thomists usually avoid epistemological questions as self-defeating, and thus so far have often been content to show that those who call metaphysics "nonsense" are talking nonsense. Who can deny that one of the great strengths of both Aristotle and Aquinas is their attention to clear definitions, distinctions, and "good reasons" for their views? I recently complained to Professor Stump that analytic Thomists seem more concerned with language than First Philosophy. She insisted that it is precisely metaphysics in the sense of ontology, the reality to which language refers, that is currently the emphasis of analysts. But concern for reality is the purpose of every science except logic and I am not sure that the analysts have yet awakened to the question of what First Philosophy is.

The seventh school, *Semiotic Thomism,* is only in formation under the leadership of John Deely, who in its development was assisted by my good friend, recently deceased, Ralph Austin Powell.[50] This approach holds that it is possible to save metaphysics from the dead-end debate between Idealism and Realism that characterizes all of modern philosophy only through semiotics. This discipline was initiated by St. Augustine, but was first critically developed by a Thomist contemporary of Descartes, Jean Poinsot, OP (John of St. Thomas, 1589–1644), and later by the American Charles Saunders Pierce (1839–1914).[51] According to this view we must return to an initial concept of thought that transcends the real and the ideal (mental), that is, Being and Non-Being, and hence through this distinction overcome Cartesian solipsism. The initial concept of Being is a sign that confusedly contains both mind-independent signs and mind-dependent signs and thus transcends

---

[49] For an introduction see John Haldane, "Thomism and the Future of Catholic Philosophy," Blackfriars Aquinas Lecture 1998.

[50] *Tractatus de Signis* (1632): *The Semiotic of John Poinsot,* with the assistance of Ralph A. Powell, OP, bilingual edition with commentary. For a bibliography of Deely's extensive publications see his *Four Ages of Understanding: The First Postmodern Survey of Philosophy from Ancient Times to the Turn of the Twenty-first Century.* See also his recent *What Distinguishes Human Understanding?*

[51] See Richard J. Bernstein, ed., *Perspectives on Peirce: Critical Essays;* Jacqueline Brunning and Paul Foster, eds., *The Rule of Reason: The Philosophy of Charles Sanders Peirce,* and James J. Liska, *A General Introduction to the Semeiotic of Charles Sanders Peirce.*

their opposition. Hence it includes both the inseparable though distinguishable real and subjective mental aspects of human knowledge. Modern thought has the merit of fully recognizing the subjective or mental aspects of knowledge that premodern thought too much neglected, but has been unable to reconcile these with the knowledge of real, existent being that premodern thought had dealt with more adequately.

Finally, and eighth, is what I candidly call *Aristotelian Thomism*. Among its advocates were the Charles De Koninck of Laval University, James A. Weisheipl (c. 1923–84) of the Medieval Institute, Toronto, both deceased and, Ralph McInerny of Notre Dame. William A. Wallace, formerly of the Catholic University of America and now the University of Maryland, and myself, are still working to present it as the only form of Thomism able to assimilate the contributions of the other schools and defend and implement a valid metaphysics in twentieth-century science-dominated culture.[52]

Conclusion

For this position, which I have sketchily expounded in part in Part II of this essay, the validity of metaphysics depends on two conditions:

1. There can be no valid metaphysics formally distinct from natural science unless its subject, Being as Being *(esse)* as it analogically includes both material and immaterial being, has first been validated in a manner proper to the foundations integral to natural science by a demonstration of the existence of immaterial being as the cause of material beings.

2. Modern natural science can achieve such a demonstration, but only if its own foundations are rendered unequivocally consistent with sense observation by an analysis such as is exemplified by Aristotle's *Physics* in Aquinas's interpretation of that work.

In my own opinion, the reason that Aquinas so successfully used philosophy in his primary work as a theologian was that he alone among patristic and medieval theologians fully appreciated the full significance of the epistemolog-

---

[52] See James A. Weisheipl, OP, ed. and introduction, *The Dignity of Science: Studies in The Philosophy of Science Presented to William Humbert Kane, OP*, xvii–xxxiii, and my articles, "The River Forest School of Natural Philosophy" in Long, *Philosophy and the God of Abraham*, 1–16; "Thomism and the Transition from the Classical World-View to Historical-Mindedness," in *The Future of Thomism*, edited by Deal W. Hudson and Dennis W. Moran, 109–22; "The Loss of Theological Unity: Pluralism, Thomism, and Catholic Morality," in Mary Jo Weaver and R. Scott Appleby, *Being Right: Conservative Catholics in America*, 63–87; and "The End of Philosophy and the End of Physics: A Dead End" in Roman T. Ciapalo, ed., *Postmodernism and Christian Philosophy*, 12–22.

ical stance of Aristotle. Although he certainly advanced Aristotle's thought, he never, I believe, deviated from Aristotle's epistemological commitment to the grounding of all purely human knowledge in our experience of a material changing world known through the senses. This position, therefore, seeks a *positive* dialogue with natural science looking toward the integration of *philosophia naturalis* with the foundations of modern science and the establishment of a valid metaphysics formally distinct from natural science yet open to the possibility of Christian revelation or some other divine revelation. As a Catholic I am convinced that it is only in this way that we can adequately meet the challenge of Pope John Paul II in *Fides et Ratio* to help our times bring faith and reason into a positively working and productive relationship.

CHAPTER 4

The Existence of
Created Pure Spirits[*]

Current Neglect of Angelology

ST. THOMAS AQUINAS IS TRADITIONALLY KNOWN AS the *Doctor Angelicus* because of his extensive and beautiful treatise on the angels in the *Summa theologiae* (I, qq. 50–64) and their role in the divine governance of the universe (qq. 106–14). Francisco Suarez, SJ, and Jean Poinsot, OP (John of St. Thomas), also wrote extensively on this subject from a theological perspective. Most Thomists today consider the arguments discussed by these authors for the existence of pure spirits to be *ex convenientia*, that is, that they conclude only to the "fittingness" or probability of angelic existence, so that certain knowledge of that existence is possible only through revelation.

After Vatican II it even began to be questioned whether the treatment of the angels in the Bible was to be taken literally, rather than mythologically or symbolically. Thus the famous *Dutch Catechism* omitted any mention of the angels.[1] This led the Magisterium to reaffirm that their existence pertains to Christian faith, as is also asserted in the *Catechism of the Catholic Church*.[2]

---

[*] This unpublished essay was the Edith Stein Lecture for 2004 sponsored by the Philosophy Department of Franciscan University, Steubenville, Ohio, that I was invited to give through the kindness of Professor Patrick Lee.

[1] "Declaration of the Commission of Cardinals on the 'New Catechism'" *(Die Nieuwe Katechismus)*, which, in "II Doctrinal Part," says, "It is necessary that the Catechism teach that God, besides this sensible world in which we live, has created a realm of pure spirits whom we call Angels" (Cf. Conc. Vat. 1, Const, *Dei Filus*; Conc. Vat. II, *Lumen Gentium,* n. 49, 50). Furthermore, it should state explicitly that individual human souls since they are spiritual (Cf. Conc. Vat. II, Const. *Gaudium et Spes,* n. 14) are created immediately by God (Cf. v.g., *Encyclical Humani Generis.* See *Acta Apostolicae Sedis: Commentarium officiale*).

[2] *Catechism of the Catholic Church,* nn. 327–30, 350.

Nevertheless, after Vatican II some theologians tried to explain away the many biblical references to angels and devils as the mythology of ancient times used in the Bible in a merely metaphorical sense to refer to God's providence or to human sin.

These theological doubts were in part due to the fact that modern science seems to explain the cosmos without supposing any such beings and that the widespread belief in them in pre-scientific times can (supposedly) be accounted for by depth psychology. Another reason, however, was the concern of some theologians, notably Karl Rahner, to build a theology on anthropology led them to minimize the traditional role of the angels.[3] Of course it would be a serious mistake to encourage the already widespread occultism, which, as Christian faith has declined in the face of secularism, has stimulated interest in "psychics," theosophism, UFOs, satanism, gnosticism, and all manner of superstitions. The very term "spirituality" has been debased to mean a hunger for consoling feelings rather than a hunger for truth. This caution, however, should not prevent us from asking about the truth of the matter. If we observe effects in our empirical world that can only be caused by spirits their existence must be honestly admitted.

Aquinas's Principle Ways of Proving the Existence of Pure Spirits

Aquinas himself was not content to leave belief in the existence of pure spirits merely to biblical faith. He attempted to show that the existence of angels, like the existence of God, is also accessible to reason by means of three principal arguments, all based on what he calls the "perfection of creation."

First, since the concept of *substance* is not, as such, corporeal and since immaterial substances are more actual than bodies and hence superior to them, both bodies and spirits must exist within the universe for creation to be perfect.

Second, since it is evident that in case of humans spirits united to bodies do exist, pure spirits independent of bodies and thus more like the Creator must exist within the universe for creation to be perfect.

Third, since the perfection of the universe consists principally in intelli-

---

[3] Thus Kenelm Foster in Appendix I of vol. 9 of the bilingual edition of the *Summa theologiae* (New York: McGraw-Hill/Blackfriars 1968), 304, lists four "chief shortcomings . . . of Patristic and medieval angelology" emphasized by Rahner in "Angel," which appeared in *Sacramentum Mundi*, in which, while supporting church teaching, Rahner makes observations similar to those of Foster and says: "From the kerygmatic point of view there is no necessity at the present time to place truths concerning the angels particularly in the foreground of preaching and instruction" (p. 34). This de-emphasis has gone so far that I have heard preachers who on a feast of the angels manage to say nothing about them!

gent beings, but human intelligence, dependent as it is on a body to know, is the least possible kind of intelligence, pure spirits independent of bodies and thus more like the all-knowing Creator must exist within the universe for creation to be perfect.

From these arguments it follows that pure spirits, as intelligences more like the Creator than material things or the human species of such inferior intelligence, must exist in greater numbers than all bodily species. Also the first and third arguments can be reduced to the second, since the first goes no further than to establish the existence of *at least* the human, embodied intelligence, while the third only accentuates the specifying intellectual activity of spiritual substances. Thus we can combine them in a single argument as follows.

> The perfection of creation requires that the universe contain not only the material beings we observe with our senses, but also spiritual beings endowed with intelligence. These must consist not only in the human species, which though endowed with spiritual souls require a body to exercise their intelligence, but also pure spirits that more perfectly resemble the Creator, who is Thought Thinking Itself.

Such an argument obviously presupposes that our universe was created as "perfect." Yet Aquinas certainly did not ascribe to the notion, later urged by Leibnitz and derided by Voltaire in *Candide,* that ours is "the best of all possible worlds." St. Thomas recognized that an omnipotent God could make any universe that he had freely created still better if he wished. Thus the perfection of the universe that he assumes in this argumentation is not absolute, but is *relative to the purpose for which God created it.* The Creator chose this purpose among all the infinite possibilities that his omnipotence includes. Thus the perfection of the universe is a *teleological* perfection; it perfectly achieves the purpose the Creator had in mind. Consequently, the certitude of the argument is necessarily one of "fittingness" *(ex convenientia),* yet such a "fit" will not be merely probable, but certain, if we can be certain just what purpose the Creator intended.

When one finds a previously unknown artificial object it is often possible to be certain from its design that it was made for some definite use. Who can reasonably doubt that a pair of scissors was made to cut? No one doubts either that the marks on ancient tablets found on the island of Crete called Minoan A, even though we cannot yet decipher them, were intended for much the same purposes as those on other tablets found there called Minoan B that we can decipher. Thus what Aquinas is arguing is that the universe exhibits a perfection or order with a purpose that can be known with certitude.

Reason can be certain that the Creator is all wise and all good, as well as almighty, and hence that he made our universe not for his own benefit, but in order to enable his creatures to share his eternal happiness. This purpose could not have been achieved unless the universe included intelligent—and therefore spiritual—creatures endowed with freedom. Yet the universe also needs to include material substances, as from our perspective it obviously does, because created spirits need the whole range of possible objects from the material to the spiritual to come to an appreciation of the wisdom and power of God. In the beatific vision this will be given them by grace, but in the natural order they need to contemplate God in the mirror of his creation. Aquinas argues that pure spirits do this through co-created innate ideas, but we humans must observe the material creation with our bodily senses and by this means come to some intellectual knowledge of spiritual reality by analogical reasoning from material effects to their spiritual causes. The very fact, however, that embodied spirits can thus transcend their material limitations further manifests God's wisdom and power, even to pure spirits far superior to us.

Yet for all created spirits, embodied and pure, the universe in its hierarchic range from lowly matter to lofty spirituality is marked by *mystery* that exceeds creaturely understanding and inspires both human and pure spirits to explore and contemplate God's universe as it unfolds, like a vast drama, in its providential history. This mystery manifests a Creator who is infinitely and inexhaustibly wise and good. The human urge to study our material universe through natural science and to imitate the Creator in further controlling and perfecting subhuman creatures flows from the fascination of this mystery.

Finite intelligences, both those of humans and of pure spirits, know not through a perfectly unified vision, but through at least more than one idea even in the highest spirits; in the human case many ideas are required. Hence our knowledge is assisted by the *contrast* of opposite ideas. Therefore, the existence of the *physical* evils natural to the material order, because of chance through conflict of one good natural force with another, and even of *moral* evils that are possible because of creaturely finite intelligence and free will, actually assists intelligent creatures in their efforts to understand the Creator and his providence. We are like spectators at a great drama that, in moving to a perfect resolution, has to pass through moments of suspense and fear.

Today some scientists find our universe "pointless," just one of an infinite number of possible worlds that we happen to be in. This is because they are interested only in obscure details of our world and tend to overlook its obvious intelligibilities without which their scientific enterprise could not even get started. This alleged pointlessness simply manifests the cosmic mystery that is at once full of order and beauty, yet unfathomable. Aquinas's understanding of this mystery was so profound that for him this argument for the existence of pure spirits based on the perfection of the universe was not merely probable but rigorously demonstrative. Obviously it is so only if its premises are sound, and to test these thoroughly requires an examination of St. Thomas's total philosophy that cannot be engaged in here. What is possible here is only to understand the outline of this argument from the perfection of creation.

Therefore, I want to pursue a fourth argument that Aquinas usually mentions and then passes over. It can be found, along with Aquinas's commentary in Aristotle's *Metaphysics* XII and in the *Summa contra Gentiles* II, c. 19. The reason St. Thomas gives for seeking other arguments is that this fourth argument depends on Aristotle's unhappy choice of the hypothesis that the material universe is eternal. Since this flawed Aristotelian argument for the existence of pure spirits is found in the *Metaphysics*, Thomists have often taken it for granted that if a valid rational proof of angelic existence is to be had it must be "metaphysical" in character, as the first three arguments already discussed certainly are because they presuppose a consideration of the whole range of being. Yet for Aquinas, as I have already stated, it is natural science that provides the existential proofs for the existence of God and of the human soul that metaphysics presupposes in its own treatment of spiritual reality. Hence we should not neglect the possibility that the existence of pure spirits may also be demonstrated in natural science prior to its metaphysical treatment. Long ago the distinguished exegete of Aquinas, Charles De Koninck, dean of Laval University, pointed out to me that such a proof can be made. De Koninck did not publish his reading of Aristotle's argument, but I will try to develop and update it here.

Aristotle's Argument for the Existence of Contingent Created Spirits

In Aristotle's hypothetical model the universe is eternal, without beginning or end. Yet it is dependent, at least for the activity of the substances that compose it, on a First Cause, exterior to the universe and absolutely necessary, that is, free of all kinds of change. That the universe exists as a relatively stable system—a portion of which is, at least, constituted of sensible, changing, interacting material substances—is certain from the evidence of our senses. Moreover, from the fact that these substances are changing, at least by local motion, it can be demonstrated that the First Cause of these motions exists and that the First Cause is immaterial and totally independent in its existence from the universe.[4]

To explain the eternity of the world Aristotle hypothesized a geocentric universe in which the earth and its atmosphere up to the sphere of the moon is

---

[4] *Physics*, VIII, cc. 4–6, 244b, 7–260a, 18, according to Jean-Pierre Torrell, "The Person and His Work," in *Saint Thomas Aquinas*, vol. 1, 342, this work was commented on by Aquinas at Paris in 1268–69.

composed of matter that is subject to both motion and alteration, but that the heavenly spheres are composed of an essentially different kind of matter that is inalterable and subject only to local motion that is perfectly circular and perpetual. The motion of these spheres is therefore natural to them and "emanates" from them not by efficiency causality but as a necessary property. This leaves open the question of how the motion of these heavenly bodies is subordinate to the First Cause, yet undoubtedly it is, since otherwise the perpetual existence of the universe is inexplicable. On the other hand the sublunar matter is alterable and hence imperfectly actualized by its forms. Thus the regular (law-like) behavior of material substances is only "for the most part" *(in pluribus).*

Aristotle identified the physical prime mover of the heavens with the outermost heaven of the fixed stars that naturally rotates forever every 24 hours. Yet the planets, whose motion is somehow subordinated to this outer sphere, are known by astronomical observation to have a degree of independence in their movements that are in cycles other than our 24-hour one. Consequently, their subordination to the sphere of the fixed stars is one of coordination necessary for the stability of the cosmic system, but not one of perfect unification.[5]

Since the motion of stellar and planetary spheres is natural and does not require an efficient cause, but emanates from each as a property,[6] this leaves open the question of how the motion of the heavenly bodies is subordinate to the First Cause. Yet, it must be, since otherwise the perpetual existence of the universe is inexplicable. On the other hand the sublunar matter is alterable and, hence, imperfectly actualized by form. Thus the regular (law-like) behavior of material substances is only "for the most part" *(in pluribus),*[7] since the activities of these terrestrial-type bodies can interfere with each other and produce true chance events that are not possible in the heavens.[8]

---

[5] This model is developed in the whole of Aristotle's *De Caelo et Mundo* with an unfinished commentary (through beginning of Bk III) by Aquinas at Naples about 1273 (Torrell), and presumed in *Metaphysics* XII, c. 8 1073a–1074b 14, commented by Aquinas in Paris after the middle of 1271 (Torrell).

[6] For the complexities of this question, see Eric A. Reitan, "Aquinas and Weisheipl: Aristotle's Physics and the Existence of God," and David B. Twetten, "Why Motion Requires a Cause: The Foundation for a Prime Mover in Aristotle and Aquinas," both in *Philosophy and the God of Abraham: Essays in Memory of James A. Weisheipl, OP*, with their references to the article of Weisheipl that corrected many common misunderstandings of Aquinas on this point.

[7] Aristotle argues for the reality of chance in the sub-lunar region in *Physics* II, c. 4–6, 195b 31–198a 12 commented on by Aquinas *In Phys.* II, lects. 7–10.

[8] The famous physicist and mathematician Pierre La Place (1749–1827) boasted that if he knew the position and momentum of every particle of matter in the universe at a given time he could predict the entire future. This determinism has so influenced modern scientists that they still regard it as amazing that modern quantum mechanics has

Therefore in the sublunar, terrestrial portion of the universe there are different lines of causality each ending in a body that is a mover that is prime, that is, unmoved in respect to that causal series. Aristotle identified these with the four elements of earth, water, air, and fire, each having a natural motion; that is, a motion to a natural place in the universe, which motion, like that of the spheres, is natural to them and simply emanates from them as a property. Since, however, these elements are alterable and therefore can be converted into other substances, the fact that they have these innate powers of motion requires explanation that is provided by the fact that they are generated by the action of the heavenly spheres.

As we study the various terrestrial substances we discover that besides the four elements and their inanimate combinations, there are living plants and animals that are highly complex substances made out of these elements. These organisms are naturally self-moving, and in the case of animals, capable of sense knowledge. Human animals are also capable of intellectual, abstract knowledge, dependent on the senses for information, yet transcending them so as to attain to essential knowledge and self-consciousness, as well as freedom of choice. Humans therefore have immaterial souls, whose origin Aristotle does not discuss, but that are prime movers with respect to the physical world, since they enable us to transcend both determinism and chance in our freedom, and enable us to gain technological control over material things,. inanimate and animate.[9]

Since the existence of human souls shows that spiritual beings other than the First Cause are possible, we have an analogy to explain the actions of the heavenly spheres, which must receive their power to move eternally from spiritual principles; but since these spheres do not have an organic structure, these souls cannot be embodied in the spheres, but must be unembodied intelligences that move the spheres. Thus the universe to be a complete system as it is observed to be must contain both material substances of many sorts, including human beings whose souls are spiritual, and also at least as many pure spirits as there are heavenly spheres with independent motion, all of them subordinate to the First Cause whose existence is totally other than that of the universe.

---

turned out to be fundamentally and irreducibly indeterministic. Thus the law-like determinism of nature turns out to be intrinsically probabilistic and the order of the universe seems to emerge out of a chaos of chance events. Indeed "chaos theory" shows that very slight differences in a physical situation can, in the course of time, produce vast differences in outcome, so the future is predictable, if at all, only in a very broad way. What is, in fact predicted is the eventuality that the universe will run down, although from time to time in small regions there is counter-rise in negentropy or order, but these regions inevitably dissipate.

[9] *De Anima* III c. 4–8, 427a 16–432a 13.

Aquinas's Revision of Aristotle's Argument

Aquinas accepted Aristotle's principles but criticized his conclusions and developed them further. The only additional empirical information he had in doing this was supplied by the Ptolemaic astronomy that remained geocentric, but added eccentrics in order to give a better account of the observed planetary motions. This was inconsistent with Aristotle's model but did not raise fundamental questions.[10] The first important criticism Aquinas made was to show that the hypothesis of an eternal world cannot be demonstrated, as neither can its contrary. He defends Aristotle's preference for an eternal world as a hypothesis that is more economical than its contrary.[11]

It was not until Galileo's telescopic sighting of sunspots that the notion of inalterable celestial matter was eliminated, but this still leaves open the possibility of world-cycles, and so on. Such notions, however, as endless cycles of change, other possible worlds, the infinity of space or time are scientifically futile since *ex hypothesi* these situations are inaccessible to our knowledge: They would either be part of our finite universe or they would not have to be part of it and, therefore, would have no causal effects on our world from which we could infer their existence.[12]

Aquinas, however, accepted Aristotle's First Way of proving the existence of a First Immaterial Cause through motion and developed the other Four Ways that presuppose it. Yet he showed that this First Cause is not only the cause of motion in the universe but of *the contingent existence* of these agents (the real distinction in them of essence and existence), that is, the First Cause is truly, even in the hypothesis of an eternal world, the Creator of the universe *ex nihilo.*[13] Thus the problem is solved of how the primary natural movers have their natural efficiency by emanation as properties of their nature, since they receive these from their natural generators and ultimately from their creation *ex nihilo* by God in whom alone essence and existence are identical.

Consistency of Aquinas's Argument with Modern Science

Once we have accepted from modern science that there is only one kind of matter in the universe and that it is subject to alteration as well as motion, then the question of whether the universe began at a certain time in the past becomes open and the modern cosmological theory of the evolution of the

---

10 On the differences between Aristotelian and Ptolemaic geocentrism, see Thomas S. Kuhn, *The Copernican Revolution,* 78–99
11 See Leo Elders, *The Philosophy of Nature of St. Thomas Aquinas,* 129–31.
12 See Joseph Silk, *The Big Bang,* 390–91.
13 The articles in R. James Long, ed., *Philosophy and God of Abraham* referred to in a previous note provide extensive discussion of the issues involved in the origin of the human species.

university from a "singularity" (the Big Bang) replaces Aristotle's steady-state universe. According to modern theory the immense heat in the original plasma of the original singularity caused it to expand and very quickly differentiate into its present four fundamental natural forces (gravity, electromagnetism, and the weak and strong nuclear forces internal to atoms). Quantum theory also removes rigid determinism in the universe and leaves space for true chance. Thus the future of the universe becomes unpredictable in any detailed way, although the Second Law of Thermodynamics and its continuing spatial expansion seem to make inevitable a final state of the material world in which matter is so spread out and entropy so maximized that no change will take place except in the form of random quantum "fluctuations."[14] The history of the universe that began with a Big Bang will end in a Big Crunch, that will obliterate every differentiation of matter produced in this cycle, or, more probably, in either a Big Freeze or a Big Rip that will end cosmic history.

Therefore, nothing in modern physics disproves—indeed it all seems to support—Aquinas's view that a universe that contains alterable matter and therefore true chance must also contain more than one relatively independent line of causality going back to certain physical prime movers endowed with natural powers given them by the agents that bring them into existence, ultimately the First Cause. Furthermore, since the spirituality of the embodied human soul can be demonstrated as Aristotle does, and the question of its individuation by the human body is cleared up affirmatively by Aquinas, it can be demonstrated that each of these lines of causality in the material universe, whatever their physical prime movers, must also be moved by intelligences, as Aristotle supposed the planets were moved.

Thus we have proved the existence of either extraterrestrial embodied intelligences or disembodied ones. Yet, since extraterrestrial embodied intelligences could not explain the basic natural forces in the universe from which they themselves would have evolved, we must conclude *that natural science demonstrates that the universe contains at least as many pure spirits as there are fundamental forces in the universe.*

If there are objections to the idea that these different lines of physical causality could all be caused by the First Cause, it can be answered by saying that, of course, they are *ultimately* caused by the First Cause, but if there were not intermediate, created, pure spirits as prime movers interior to the universe, the universe would not be a complete and relatively stable system. An ontologistic model of reality that ascribes all causality to the First Cause and gives no genuine autonomy to secondary causes is contradictory to the true existence of a universe and would reduce our phenomenal world to a mere dream of the Absolute of Advaita Hinduism or The Void of Buddhism

---

[14] See Joseph Silk, *The Big Bang,* for an account of modern cosmology.

or the ineffable One of Neo-Platonism. Such worldviews have historically provided no stimulus for a realistic natural science such as has developed in western culture, but is now threatened by postmodern skepticism.

Thus an adequate defense of a realistic natural science against this skepticism requires that it be open to the existence both of God as First Cause and to pure spirits as part of the universe. This conclusion is also supported by the fact of evolution that modern science has established. Such deterministic concepts of cosmic evolution as the Greek notion of the "primeval egg," St. Augustine's *rationes seminales*,[15] Bergson's and Teilhard de Chardin, *élan vital*, Whitehead's "creativity,"[16] Stuart Kaufmann's "Self-Organization,"[17] and other *autopoetic* theories fail to explain how something can give itself what it does not already have.[18]

Complex substances contain extensive information, but inanimate matter as we know it in the elements and their constitutive particles contains a comparatively very small amount of information. A living embryo develops from a single cell to a mature animal because it has an intrinsic genetic code that contains the complex information necessary to guide the differentiation and inter-relation of its parts. Nothing we know about the matter of which our universe is composed indicates that such information is naturally intrinsic to it. Not only is the universe a true system, but in at least one of its regions there exist human bodies prepared for the reception of spiritual souls from the Creator who alone can produce spiritual entities *ex nihilo*. These body-dependent spiritual souls have free will and independent action. Hence

---

[15] On St. Augustine's view of evolution, see Ernest C. Messenger, *Evolution and Theology: The Problem of Man's Origin*.

[16] Henri Bergson's 1907 *Creative Evolution* influenced both Alfred North Whitehead, *Process and Reality: An Essay in Cosmology*, and Pierre Teilhard de Chardin, *The Phenomenon of Man*.

[17] See Stuart A. Kauffman, *The Origins of Order: Self-Organization and Selection in Evolution* and *At Home in the Universe: The Search for the Laws of Self-Organization and Complexity*. On the scientific difficulties of this now popular notion, see Deal L. Overman, *A Case Against Accident and Self-Organization*.

[18] For this reason I must disagree with the views of my good friend Cletus Wessels in his interesting books *The Holy Web: Church and the New Universe Story* and *Jesus in the New Universe Story* that see modern science as presenting an "emerging" universe. Spiritual substances cannot "emerge" from matter but must be created by God. Modern science presents not an emerging natural order but a "running-down" universe in which more complex bodies and systems of bodies emerge only temporarily as mere episodes in this general decay. Because current science does not recognize the action of spiritual entities and hence can find no adequate cause for the emergence of complex substances from simpler substances, it is forced ultimately to ascribe the natural order to chance and declare that it just happens that the world we live in all the infinity of possible worlds is the way it is.

it is not possible to assign an adequate cause for evolution except that some intelligence or intelligences have all the information necessary for such complex constructions.

The First Cause, of course, has such information, but we human beings did not produce evolution, although by studying the natural processes of evolution we may someday be able to produce life and guide its evolution. Since we did not guide evolution and neither did any extraterrestrial embodied intelligences, since they too evolved[19] the cause of biological evolution in our universe cannot be reduced to the interaction of material causes that are inevitably subject to many chance interferences with each other. Therefore, the guidance of cosmic and biological evolution can only be ascribed to that part of the universe that is a community of pure spirits. These spirits cannot create natural forces, as only God can do, but they can guide their operation, as a human chemist guides natural forces in producing higher chemical compounds from simpler compounds or elements.

Pure spirits must share information with each other and freely choose to unite in a community, or reject that community and become evil and destructive. The continued existence and evolution of the universe is evidence that the good spirits, by help of the First Cause who must be perfectly good, outmaster the evil ones, although the presence of intelligent beings, human and pure spirits, is the only way to account for the moral evil in the universe and even for what appears to be an excess of physical evil. This fact of community is the ultimate explanation of how the unity of the universe is intrinsic and natural to it and not simply imposed by the First Cause.

This conclusion is not contrary to Darwinism since natural selection depends causally on environmental changes that in turn depend causally on cosmic evolution that in its turn depends on the fundamental natural forces. It is questionable, however, whether Darwinism is an adequate theory of the physical aspects of evolution since it does not well explain how a history of so many chance events has resulted in the human body adapted to a human soul, although natural selection certainly has played an important part in this history.[20] We must, therefore, conclude that modern science far from disproving the Aristotelian-Thomistic argument for the existence of pure spirits seems to support it. Yet this proof of the existence of created pure spirits, just

---

[19] The "Extra-terrestrial Intelligences," concerning which there is much speculation today but no actual evidence, are assumed to be embodied, although in Arthur C. Clark's novel (which was made into the famous Stanley Kubrick film *2001: A Space Odyssey*) the origin of man from ape was produced by extraterrestrials who had themselves so far evolved that they no longer had any body but empty space!

[20] See John N. Deely and Raymond J. Nogar, OP, eds., *The Problem of Evolution: A Study of the Philosophical Repercussions of Evolutionary Science,* which is still not out of date; R. Jeffrey Grace, "The Transcendental Method of Bernard Lonergan," at www.lonergan.on.ca/reprints/grace-method.htm.

as it did not depend on Aristotle's particular model of a steady-state eternal universe, does not depend on any of the particular modern theories of scientific cosmological and biological evolution, but on more basic principles and observed facts fundamental to the whole of natural science.

Rational Proof of the Existence of Pure Created Spirits

I conclude this discussion with a formal presentation of this demonstration:

Major Premise		
Prime movers, intrinsic to the universe, of independent lines of physical causality	*are*	necessary to the universe as a as a complete, unified system.
Minor Premise		
Pure, unembodied spirits	*are*	the prime movers, intrinsic to the universe, of independent lines of physical causality.
Conclusion		
Pure, unembodied spirits	*are*	necessary to the universe as a complete, unified system.

The Major Premise presupposes that there are in fact independent lines of physical causality in the universe, but this can be shown from the fact that the matter of this universe is subject to alteration and, therefore, is imperfectly actualized. Hence the independence of one line of causality is evidenced by the observance of chance events disturbing the regularity of natural laws. Given the demonstration that every line of causality must have a prime mover, the proposition must be true since to be a complete, unified system the universe must contain the prime movers of all activity within it.

The Minor Premise is proved by showing that the prime physical mover in any line of physical causality is such by its natural properties that emanate from its specific nature. Hence it must receive this nature from the First Cause, either by direct creation, or by being generated directly by some agent intrinsic to the universe; but since it is prime in the physical order this generator must be a spiritual being.

The Middle Term is simply a case of the proof of the necessity of a prime mover for any line of causality, which must ultimately be, even for physical causality, a spiritual mover, either an agent that is part of the universe, or the First Cause that transcends it. While it can be objected that the universe might be, as Aristotle thought, eternal and in that case the prime physical movers, like his celestial spheres, were never generated, Aquinas answers this objection by pointing out that since in such a model the physical movers act for an infinite time, this cannot be attributed simply to their natural powers, since no physical substance could produce an infinite act.

Finally we may ask whether this argument means that there are only four or so angels corresponding to what science today supposes are the fundamental natural forces? Not necessarily, since these few forces may very well be generic, admitting of any number of more specific, relatively independent forces involved in cosmic evolution than present theories have accounted for.

On the other hand, it could be objected that an evolutionary and entropic universe, such as proposed by modern science, is not an intrinsically complete, unified system. To this it can be replied that although such a universe lasts as an active system only for a finite time, nevertheless, at present it exhibits a fundamental stability that has enabled it to keep operation in a unified way for billions of years. This is long enough for it to serve its purpose as a mirror in which pure spirits naturally contemplate the Creator and as a necessary material home for embodied human spirits who are thus able to join the pure spirits in this contemplation.

CHAPTER 5

Truth and Technology*

Technology and Presence

ACCORDING TO MARTIN HEIDEGGER, "TECHNOLOGY is a mode of revealing. Technology comes to presence in the realm where revealing and unconcealment take place, where aletheia, truth, happens."[1] Thus for Heidegger the essence of technology is not practical instrumentality but a way of openness to the disclosure of Being. Paradoxically he also claims that technology so dominates our world as to conceal Being so completely

---

* Published as "Truth and Technology," *American Catholic Philosophical Association Proceedings: The Importance of Truth*, 68 (1993): 27–40.

[1] My account of Heidegger's views on this topic is based principally on his essay "Die Frage nach der Technik," in *Die Technik und die Kehre*, translated with an excellent introduction by William Lovitt in *The Question Concerning Technology and Other Essays*. My references will be to this translation. This quote is found on 1 and is the conclusion of the following argument: "The current conception of technology, according to which it is a means and a human activity, can therefore be called the instrumental and anthropological definition of technology" (5). But this entirely "correct instrumental definition of technology still does not show us technology's essence" (6). Heidegger then shows that "instrumentality" implies "means and ends" and this implies "causality" (i.e., Aristotle's Four Causes). He then argues that since causality is "being responsible for" and "being indebted to," its essence is "bringing-forth (6–12). This leads him to conclude that since "Truth is a revealing of Being" and "to bring-forth" is "to reveal," therefore, "Technology is no mere means. Technology is a way of revealing. If we give heed to this, then another whole realm for the essence of technology will open itself up to us. It is the realm of revealing, i.e., of truth" (12). I have particularly profited from Egbert Schuurman, *Technology and the Future: A Philosophical Challenge,* and Michael E. Zimmerman, *Heidegger's Confrontation with Modernity: Technology, Politics, Art,* for the historical context of Heidegger's thought; and John Loscerbo, *Being and Technology: A Study in the Philosophy of Martin Heidegger,* and the essays in John Sallis, ed., *Heidegger and the Path of Thinking* for detailed analysis.

that western civilization is collapsing.[2] Yet, he prophetically proclaims that its collapse will open us up once more to a new disclosure of Being, a new epoch of civilization.[3]

"Being" is traditionally studied by metaphysics, but Heidegger believed traditional metaphysics was really about "beings" not "Being." For him, Being is the reflective experiencing of the flow of historical events not just by the individual but also in the culture of an age. Being is "remembered" by a phenomenological reflection describing the how (not the causal why) of events.[4]

For the controversy on Heidegger and National Socialism that is closely related to his views on technology, see the survey of recent literature in Thomas Sheehan, "Heidegger and the Nazis," and "A Normal Nazi," a review of Richard Wolin, *The Heidegger Controversy: A Critical Reader,* and Ernst Nolte, "Heidegger and Nazism: An Exchange."

[2] "The essence of technology, as a destining revealing, is the danger. The transformed meaning of the word 'Enframing' *[Gestell]* will perhaps become somewhat more familiar to us now if we think Enframing in the sense of destining and danger. The threat to man does not come in the first instance from the potentially lethal machines and apparatus of technology. The actual threat has already affected man in his essence. The rule of Enframing threatens man with the possibility that it could be denied to him to enter into a more original revealing and hence to experience the call of a more primal truth." *The Question Concerning Technology,* 28. *Gestell* is that state of affairs in our technological society where Being is reduced to a standing reserve *(Bestand),* that is, matter and energy to be used in the expression of the will to power, the very opposite of Nature in its primordial sense of that which gives birth from within itself. See Loscerbo's discussion, *Being and Technology,* 136–41.

[3] "Enframing cannot exhaust itself solely in blocking all lighting up of every revealing, all appearances of truth. Rather, precisely the essence of technology must harbor in itself the growth of the saving power." *The Question Concerning Technology,* 28. "Technology, whose essence is Being itself, will never allow itself to be overcome by men. That would mean, after all, that man was master of Being. . . . On the contrary, the coming to presence of technology will be surmounted in a way that restores it into its yet concealed truth. This restoring surmounting is similar to what happens when, in the human real, one gets over grief or pain. But this surmounting of a destining of Being-here and now, the surmounting of Enframing-each time comes to pass out of the arrival of another destining, a destining that does not allow itself either to be logically and historiographically predicted or to be metaphysically construed as a sequence belonging to the process of history." "The Turning," 38–39, translated in Lovitt, *The Question Concerning Technology,* 86–49.

[4] "Being may perhaps best be said to be the ongoing manner in which, in the lastingness of time, everything encounters man and comes to appearance through the openness that man provides." Lovitt, *The Question Concerning Technology,* xv. For a fuller discussion of what "Being" meant for Heidegger, see John N. Deely, *The Tradition via Heidegger: An Essay on the Meaning of Being in the Philosophy of Martin Heidegger,* and Ralph A. Powell, OP, "The Late Heidegger's Omission of the Ontic-Ontological Structure of Dasein," in Sallis, *Heidegger and the Path of Thinking,* 116–87.

In the occasional revelatory event *(Ereignis)*, Being becomes immediately present to us, somewhat as in great poetry.[5]

To "forget Being" is to lose contact with such events by preoccupation with concerns about controlling the world, and first of all with controlling one's way of seeing the world, rather than remaining open to it. Technology (from Greek *techne*, "art," "craft," "skill" in the broadest sense) is such a concern that has given rise to philosophy (traditional metaphysics) and to science. In the first or Greek period, truth was experienced as the immediate self-presencing of *physis*, nature in the inclusive sense of the flow of concrete, temporal experience, that is, of history. In the second or Christian period, truth became certitude guaranteed by a highest, timeless being, God. In the third, modern, post-Cartesian period, this certitude became guaranteed by the interior self-control of the knowing subject.[6]

Environmentalism

Today environmentalism shows the relevance of Heidegger's question about technology, but has he set us on the right path to answer it? Are not his notions of "Being" and truth too much bound up with modernity to be relevant to our postmodernity? For him, still thinking in Kantian perspectives, Being remains phenomenal, temporal, historical. Although he struggled valiantly against Cartesian subjectivism, he had no way of distinguishing within the "world" of a given epoch between its mind-dependent and its mind-independent components, and was forced to submit to cultural relativism. He could do no more than proclaim the end of modernity and await the coming of a new revealment of Being in a new age.

Since Heidegger presents his view in historical terms, I want to propose an alternative account of the origins of our technological crisis.[7] Heidegger attributed its source to Plato and Aristotle because they began the transformation of truth *(aletheia)* as openness into that of *techne* or control. Plato and Aristotle did indeed begin the progress of natural science that has continued until today. Plato saw in mathematics the ideal of a strictly theoretical, analytic, critical discipline. Aristotle showed that such a discipline is possible even in the study of our changing, empirical world. Unlike Plato, he was convinced that theories

---

[5] On the sense in which philosophy and art merge for Heidegger, see C. D. Keys, "Truth as Art: An Interpretation of Heidegger's *Sein Und Zeit* and *Der Ursprung des Kunstwerkes*" in Sallis, *Heidegger and the Path of Thinking*, 65–84.

[6] See Loscerbo, *Being and Technology*, 1–96, and Lovitt, *The Question Concerning Technology*, xxiv–xxvi, for discussion of these stages.

[7] For a somewhat different scenario of the history of science from a Christian point of view, see S. L. Jaki, *The Road of Science and the Ways to God*, the Gifford Lectures 1975, and Paul Haffner, *Creation and Scientific Creativity: A Study in the Thought of S. L. Jaki*, 20–32.

about nature could do more than "save the appearances," they could be a true science.[8] Thus in the Greek period, the logic, the mathematics, and the empiricism of modern science were already in place.

Yet sustained advance in science was held back by four factors: (1) a slave economy with its contempt for servile works until Christianity gradually removed this contempt for work; (2) the decline of educational institutions, until the rise of the medieval universities; (3) the lack of economic motivation, until the rise of capitalism in the Renaissance; (4) the lack of the concept of controlled experimentation aided by a technology of observation. This last factor was overcome when Galileo began to use the telescope and the inclined plane. Consequently in the sixteenth century, science, still motivated by Christian aims, began to flourish.

No doubt if the development of science had remained under Christian auspices this progress would have been shaped by the conviction that inspirits its origin, that the ultimate purpose of all knowledge is to enable humanity to know and glorify God in creation and that its use of technology must be moderated by the principle that human dominion is a stewardship of God's gifts.[9] But the religious wars of the sixteenth and seventeenth centuries had disillusioned the intelligentsia with revealed religion. In the Enlightenment and continuing through "modernity" to our own times, the dominant worldview has increasingly become one in which not God but man is in control of the world. Hence the Enlightenment coopted science, and gave to it a reductionist interpretation.

This scientism, however, insisted that objective truth is "fact-free." Consequently it provoked within the Enlightenment a polarization between scientism and romanticism, the latter claiming to supply the needed value system, by a subjective creation of values. The distinguished physicist Freeman Dyson writes,

> As soon as we mention the words "value" and "purpose," we run into one of the most firmly entrenched taboos of twentieth-century science. Hear the voice of Jacques Monod, high priest of scientific rationality, in his book *Chance and Necessity.* "Any mingling of knowledge with values is unlawful, forbidden."[10]

It is this polarization, still with us, which accounts for the two extreme attitudes toward technology today: on the one hand are the proponents of scientism who understand technology as the reduction of nature to raw material

---

8 For a more detail discussion see my *Theologies of the Body: Humanist and Christian,* 101–203.

9 On this see the essay "Dominion or Stewardship" in this collection.

10 Freeman Dyson, in *Infinite in All Directions,* 100.

and the reconstruction of the world according to human whim;[11] on the other hand are the romantic environmentalists who deplore the ravages of technology and propose a return to nature.[12] In this respect at least Heidegger clearly is a thinker in the romantic tradition.[13]

Is there a way to reconcile these extreme notions of technological truth? Obviously it will have to reinterpret modern science so that it escapes the reductionism of scientism and finds a relation between nature and human values. As a first step in this task I will now briefly attempt what Heidegger would call a "retrieval" of a theory of technological truth in the Greek tradition of Aristotle and the medieval tradition of Aquinas.

The Greek and Medieval Conception of Technological Truth

Since for Heidegger, still working in a perspective fixed by Descartes and Kant, "Being" is temporal, the question of whether there is an immaterial, and therefore, supratemporal Being is not raised. He speaks of the fourfold aspects of a world: earth, sky, mortals, and gods, but these "gods" of a given historical epoch will pass away with the times.[14] Hence we must ask, "Is it possible to be open to a revealment of a supra-temporal Being concealed from us by modern technology?"

For Aristotle that question occupies most of the work we call the *Metaphysics*: "Is there a First Philosophy?"[15] Heidegger thought that in fact Aristotle's First Philosophy did not deal with the essence of technology, since it was itself a *techne* concerned only with beings, an art of controlling thought rather than opening it up to Being as such. On the contrary, Aristotle in fact held that First Philosophy must be a theoretical discipline, because human action presupposes an understanding of the world and of ourselves that is prior to our actions in changing them.[16]

Plato, influenced by Pythagoras, inclined to the view that First Philosophy is mathematics because of its clarity and certitude. The successful

---

[11] Schuurman, *Technology and the Future,* 77–312. Schuurman is a member of the Dutch Reformed Church and writes from a Christian perspective.

[12] See Schuurman, *Technology and the Future,* 51–176, for a discussion of several of these thinkers, and Zimmerman, *Heidegger's Confrontation,* 46–65 on Ernst Jünger. In 77–93 Zimmerman demonstrates in detail Ernst Jünger's influence on Heidegger, and Schuurman (pp. 100–102) argues that Ernst's brother Georg Friedrich Jünger was also an important influence.

[13] See Schuurman, *Technology and the Future,* 80–124.

[14] This aspect of Heidegger's thought is treated in detail by V. Vycinas, *Earth and Gods.*

[15] It is not until Book XII (Lambda) of the *Metaphysics* that Aristotle finally gets to treating Being in its full scope as including both immaterial and material Being. The last two books, XIII and XIV, are devoted to showing that mathematical being is not Being in this wide sense.

[16] *Metaphysics* VI, c.1, 1025bff

mathematicization of natural science since Galileo and Descartes seems to support that view. Aristotle, however, rejected mathematics as a candidate, because it deals with timeless abstractions, while the world of our experience is, as Heidegger affirms, a temporal world of change and process. Therefore, Aristotle was inclined to consider natural science the First Philosophy until he discovered, in the course of developing a natural science, that a world of change cannot be self-explanatory but must have non-material first causes.[17] Since the cosmos is pluralistic in its processes there must be many such first causes, of which human intelligence is an instance. Yet the unity of the universe requires the coordination of these relatively first causes by the existence of an absolute First Cause.[18] Aquinas further made explicit, what is ambiguous in Aristotle, that each human person is endowed with its own intelligence and free will, so that each is a relative first cause.[19]

Hence First Philosophy cannot be technology, or any other practical discipline, or the theoretical sciences of mathematics or of nature, but must be a theology that deals with non-temporal, spiritual realities, of which God, the Thought Thinking Itself is the first principle.[20] Yet, since Aristotle rejects knowledge not founded in the senses, and such a theology has no empirical data of its own, building, as it does, on the effects of non-sensible causes, it can only reflect on the results of the other sciences and coordinate them in an inter-disciplinary manner in analogical terms, such as Being and Truth.

The "metaphysics" Heidegger accuses of being essentially a technology, a way of control, not openness to Being, and whose death he announces, is not Aristotle's or Aquinas's theological First Philosophy, but a Cartesian discipline independent of the special sciences and rooted in the subject's self-consciousness. Unhappily, it is this conception of metaphysics in a variety of crude and very subtle forms that still passes for Thomism.[21]

Metaphysics and Truth

How would a First Philosophy of the Aristotelian type deal with "truth"? Truth is a transcendental term in the sense that it applies analogically to all

---

17 *Physics* VIII, c. 5–10, 256a 4ff.; *De Anima* III, c. 4–5, 429a–430a 8. See the commentaries of St. Thomas Aquinas, *In libros Physicorum* VIII, lect. 11–23 and *In libros De Anima* III, lect. 7–10.

18 *Metaphysics* XII (Lambda) c. 6–10, 1071b 3ff. See Aquinas, *In XII libros Metaphysicorum* XII, lect. 5–12

19 Aquinas, *De unitate intellectus contra Averroistas* and *Summa contra Gentiles* II c. 73; *Summa theologiae* I, q. 79. a. 5.

20 *Metaphysics* VI, c. 1; Aquinas, *In libros XII Metaphysicorum* VI, lect. 1.

21 See my essays "Transition to Historical Mindedness" in this collection and "The River Forest School of Natural Philosophy," in Long, *Philosophy and the God of Abraham,* 1–16, in which I defend an Aristotelian interpretation of Aquinas.

the univocal terms found in the special sciences. All are somehow "true" but in very different ways. Truth is a property of a proposition by which what it asserts is verified in its referent. Thus it is an *adequatio rei et intellectus*, not in the Cartesian sense rightly attacked by Heidegger, that the thinking subject forms a mental representation of the object within itself to substitute for the object which remains extra-mental, but in the Aristotelian sense that the thinking subject is identified with the object.[22] The late Heidegger came close to Aristotle's view when he spoke of Being revealing itself to man and thus inducing man to open himself, to become a "clearing" in which Being might manifest itself. Unfortunately, Heidegger, still too influenced by Kant for whom causality is only a mental category, avoids speaking of knowledge in terms of causality.[23]

Although propositional truth (logical truth) is the proper sense of "truth," it implies that the entity to which a true proposition refers in expressing this adequation of mind and reality can analogically also be called "true" (ontological truth). Technology is first of all a kind of knowledge, and this knowledge is propositionally true or false. While for theoretical truth the *adequatio* is *adequatio intellectus ad rem*, for practical truth, of which technology is a species, it is *adequatio rei ad intellectum*, the production of something measured by the mind.[24]

It is this fact that led Heidegger to think of technology as "control," the mind controlling Being, and since Being utterly transcends human control, dissolving Being into beings which can be controlled. This seems right, when we think of practical action as having no standard external to the "creative" human mind. For Aristotle and Aquinas, however, human freedom, although real, is limited. It has to do with the means to goals, while ultimate

---

[22] "Actual knowledge is identical with its object." *De Anima* III, c.5, 430a 20; c.7, 431a. "The soul is in a way all existing things; for existing things are either sensible or thinkable, and knowledge is in a way what is knowable, and sensation is in a way what is sensible; in what way we must inquire." C. 8, 20–24. c. 7, 431a.8 20–24. On this last text, see Aquinas, *In libros De Anima* II, lect. 13.

[23] Heidegger seems to favor an organicist conception according to which nature *(physis)* develops from within. "Not only handcraft manufacture, not only artistic and poetical bringing into appearance and concrete imagery, is *poesis*. *Physis* also, the arising of something from out of itself, is a bringing-forth, *poesis*. *Physis* is indeed *poesis* in the highest sense. For what presences by means of *physis* has the bursting open belonging to bringing-forth, e.g., the bursting of a blossom into bloom, in itself *(en heautoi)*. In contrast, what is brought forth by the artisan or the artist, e.g., the silver chalice, has the bursting open belonging to bringing-forth not in itself, but in another *(en alloi)*, in the craftsman or artist." In *The Question of Technology*, 10ff., Heidegger seems to have forgotten Aristotle's efforts to show that while nature is an intrinsic principle of change, nothing moves itself.

[24] Aquinas, *Summa theologiae* I, q. 14, aa. 5–6.

goals that provide a measure or standard for means are fixed in nature.[25] Thus technology as practical truth must ultimately have its standard not in the human mind or will but in nature. The propositional truth about technology, therefore, will be conformity to some principles that refer to these fixed goals.

To speak of a "goal" for a free human being, however, is not to refer merely to knowledge. Something known as achievable becomes a goal only when persons commit themselves by an act of will to achieve it.[26] The psychology of human beings is such that we cannot will simply by thinking abstractly. Our imagination and sensuous appetites that are bodily faculties also come into play.[27] Thus practical knowledge to be fully practical involves the whole human person, and will not be practically true unless the person is virtuous, that is, unless in body and soul they are disposed to act "according to nature."

Thus true practical action is first of all prudent (moral, ethical) action that conforms to the standard of human action, the goals set by our human nature.[28] The discipline of ethics is one that investigates and arrives at true conclusions (propositions) about what is to be done or not done in order to achieve these goals and to render the human agent fully human, "a good or virtuous person."[29] Strangely, Heidegger largely avoided ethical questions in his later works, but in his earlier phase the notion of existential "authenticity" is the equivalent of "virtue."

Technology, however, deals, not with *doing*, the concern of ethics, but with *making*. Yet obviously *making* is a form of *doing*, so that technology is intrinsically subordinated to ethics. One can know how to do something without yet deciding actually to do it.[30] Thus prudence is absolutely practical, but art (technology) is only conditionally practical. Thus a technological act can be false or "bad" in two ways: (1) it can fail to produce what the maker intends; and (2) the maker can intend to produce what is not according to moral standards.

While persons are free to use or not to use moral truth to guide their actions, if they follow it they can only act rightly, and they primarily perfect themselves, although they may also perfect others and other things. Persons are also free to use or not use technological truth, but they can abuse it, either to produce something that is morally wrong or technically bad. The moral goals of human life are fixed, but there are many ways of achieving

---

25 Aristotle, *Nicomachean Ethics* III, c. 8, 1112b 13–1113a 14; Aquinas, *In Ethic.*, III, lect. 8–9.

26 Aquinas, *Summa theologiae* I–II, q. 10, a. 1.

27 Ibid., I, q. 9, aa. 2–3

28 Ibid., II–II, q. 47, aa. 4–7.

29 Aquinas, *In Ethic* I, lect. 1

30 Aristotle, *Nicomachean Ethics* IV, c. 4, 1140aff.

these goals. Consequently, technology either seeks to satisfy our necessary or our free needs. Modern technology is characterized by an enormous expansion of these free needs. Obviously arts that serve acquired needs should be subordinated to those that meet necessary needs.

The ancients also distinguished between liberal and servile arts. A servile art is an art in the strictest sense, since it produces a work that exists extramentally, while a liberal art produces a purely mental work. What today we call the fine arts are liberal because they primarily serve communication between persons, although by the medium of external works of art that they produce.[31]

Nevertheless, no matter whether a technology be necessary or free, servile or liberal or fine, it is not a *creatio ex nihilo*, but *mimesis*, an imitation of nature, not in the sense of a mere copy, but in two respects: (1) its material is pre-existent natural material, and (2) the form which is given to that matter is derived by analogy from natural forms. Hence arise the axioms "Art imitates nature" and "Art perfects nature." In short, according to an Aristotelian First Philosophy, the truth of a technology as a discipline consists in its capacity to guide us in producing instruments of virtuous human living by imitating and perfecting nature. Of course technologies undergo immense historical developments, but the fixed and permanent point on which all these developments, helpful and hurtful, turn is the goal of human life intrinsic to human nature, enduring as long as we remain one human community.

Ethics and Prudence

If this is indeed the truth of technology we need to inquire further about the question concerning which Heidegger said little, but which is familiar enough in the other branch of practical knowledge, the field of ethics and prudence. It is this: "What is the relation between facts and values, the "is" and the "ought"?[32] In other words, just how is practical truth grounded in the truth of nature, which it imitates and perfects? In the field of ethics this has given rise to endless debate. Its origin, as I hoped I have already made clear, is in the modern separation of fact and value that polarized the Enlightenment into scientism and romanticism.

The high degree of mathematization in modern science has been necessary and useful, but it has caused many to forget that it is only instrumental. Natural science uses mathematics, but it uses it only to understand nature and nature is Being that exists only in becoming, in change, in process, and cannot be understood except in terms of that dynamism. This means to understand nature not only in its actuality but also in its potentiality, its

---

[31] See my article "Significance of Non-Objective Art," *Proceedings of the American Catholic Philosophical Association* (1965): 156–65.

[32] See also my article "Integral Human Fulfillment" in this collection.

form and its matter. It also means to understand it in terms of the plurality of natural units and their interaction, that is, of, in terms of one thing acting on others and being acted upon by them—efficient causality. But efficient causality is correlative to final causality or teleology.[33]

Mathematical objects, since they have no dynamism, have no final cause, or purpose.[34] They can be described completely in terms of formal and material causality, and their material aspect is reduced to the blank homogeneity of empty ideal space and of time conceived as an already present fourth dimension. This has led scientists to suppose that they can successfully describe the world without any reference to teleology, which they mistakenly suppose is purposed as an occult, non-observable force. Actually, however, every mathematical theory becomes implicitly teleological the moment it is given a physical interpretation. A mathematical model that did not contain terms that could be physically interpreted as forces (energy, efficient causes) would never be mistaken for a physical theory. Such forces either regularly produce an effect (are law-like) or their results are random. Hence, although allowance must be made for events that happen either by chance or human freedom, yet the concept of nature and of a science of nature demand that at least some events are empirically law-like, deterministic.

Furthermore, some of these regular processes must be not merely destructive, but constructive, that is, they produce stable, unified entities engaged in regular activities—atoms, molecules, organisms, astronomical and ecological systems. If all processes were purely entropic, a constant breaking down of all forms of stable order in the world, the world would not last long. Although in the end our world may meet entropic doom, yet in the epoch in which we live stable entities come into existence and perdure for a significant time. Aristotelian final causality refers to this empirical fact that natural processes often produce natural objects.

Today, the environmental movement is based on the fact that the environment is complexly organized in a way that makes life possible. Physicists who acknowledge the "Anthropic Principle," at least in its weak form, recognize that the evolution of life and of human beings could never have taken place if our solar system and our universe had a structure much different than it actually has.[35] The universe is not an infinite mass of matter and

---

[33] See my articles in *The New Catholic Encyclopedia*, "Final Causality" (5:162–66) and "Teleology" (13: 979–81); also "Research into the Intrinsic Final Causes of Physical Things," published under the title "Problem: The Relation of Physical Activity to Essence and End," 185–97.

[34] Aquinas, *In libros XII Metaphysicorum* II, lect. 4.

[35] See J. D. Barrow and F. J. Tipler, *The Anthropic Cosmological Principle*. The weak form of the principle states that the universe as we observe it must be consistent with the fact that we exist as its observers. The strong form is that for the universe to exist it must have the properties that will allow intelligent life to develop in it at some stage

energy endlessly turning out every possible combination of its elements in random sequence.[36] It is a finite dynamic whole so structured that it has produced human persons who can scientifically understand its structure and its history.

In present day science three situations, which I have space only to mention, provide the opening for a reinterpretation of science to acknowledge the teleological character of nature. First, present cosmology holds that the universe originated in a Big Bang. If this was preceded by a Big Crunch, such epochs other than our own are in principle unknowable.[37] Second, the mind-body problem cannot be solved by the computer analogy because human intelligence can always make a better computer.[38] Third, modern science tends more and more to explain the universe not by natural laws, but by its evolution, its history, and thus by unexplainable initial conditions.[39] To try to eliminate these conditions by a mathematical model is once more to reduce natural science to mathematics and belie its dynamism.

Human persons are part of nature, and the goals that they must satisfy are fixed by nature, but as regards the means to these goals they are free. Hence their analogical intelligence that gives them the capability both of imitating and perfecting nature makes possible the advance of technology, provided that technology is controlled by moral virtue. Prudence or ethics is the practical science that enables us to judge what is virtuous to do in various situations and it leaves plenty of room for individual freedom of choice.

---

of its history. Barrow and Tipler also propose a Final Anthropic Principle that says that once intelligent life has developed it will never die out. For criticism, see Willem E. Drees, *Beyond the Big Bang: Quantum Cosmologies and God,* 78–88.

[36] Dyson, *Infinite in All Directions,* 103: Although he still argues for a universe infinite in time and space in which intelligent life will survive forever, admits he is "mixing science with science fiction."

[37] On this see Stephen W. Hawking, *A Brief History of Time,* 150–53. Even in the contracting phase conditions would not be suitable for the existence of intelligent human beings, and the Crunch would wipe out all traces of any previous cycle.

[38] I have argued this in detail in "Theology and the Mind-Body Problem," in *Mind and Brain*, edited by Robert Brungs, SJ. See also Essay 4 in this volume.

[39] The Nobel Laureate in Physics Stephen Weinberg is reported in Lightman and Brawer, *Origins,* 465, as saying: "The question always comes up, 'What was there before the big bang?' And I spend so many minutes waffling about that, saying, 'Well maybe there was no time. . . .' But I share their perplexity. I find it more comfortable to think about infinite time as well as infinite space, no boundary in time any more than a boundary in space, and with everything being explained by physics without any arbitrary historical elements entering it." The interviewer then asks, "No initial conditions?" and Weinberg answers, "Yes." No initial conditions at all. That would be appealing, especially if we could show that for a certain set of laws of physics, any set of initial conditions would always evolve into the steady state, so that you wouldn't even have to ask, "Well, why are we in the steady state?".

Thus the extremes of scientism and romantic environmentalism can be reconciled, if our First Philosophy leads us to correct the current interpretation of science by restoring final causality. This will give us an understanding of human nature that is teleological and this will furnish us with a guide to the proper use and care of the environment. But what are the purposes of human life intrinsic to human nature that a good technology is supposed to serve? Thomas Aquinas showed there are at least four.[40] First of all we have a need for bodily health and security. Second we need the family, without which the species cannot be preserved or brought to maturity. Third we need the larger human community, all of these bound together by true friendship in love. Fourth we need knowledge practical and theoretical, and this knowledge ought to extend not merely to things, but above all, to the knowledge of persons, supremely the knowledge of God. It must also include the knowledge of a variety of species of things, since every species is a unique revelation of the Creator, as well as telling us something about ourselves, by way of contrast or similarity. Hence comes our human need to preserve the variety of species in our environment.

Because we are bodily beings, all the activities leading to these ethical ends require appropriate technology. Even the worship of God requires churches, sacred objects, musical instruments, books, and the like. Yet in these technologies a simplicity of life is necessary both because of the limitation of resources and because of the ever present danger that the means will become ends and greed will lead to the injustice of depriving some so that others may indulge themselves at their expense.

Of these four values, a society centered in contemplation is the highest good since it is in the loving knowledge of persons and of God, that is, in the social good and the good of truth, that human happiness finally consists.[41] Thus it is that the essence of good technology is to supply the means necessary to know Being, the Being which is history, as Heidegger said, but more than that—what Heidegger did not say—the Being that is the blessed society of persons centered in God in a universe preserved and perfected by technology so as to serve the Creator.

At the end of "The Question Concerning Technology" Heidegger says enigmatically,

> All that is merely technological never arrives at the essence of technology. It cannot even once recognize its outer precincts. Therefore, as we seek to give utterance to insight into that which is, we do not describe the situation of our time. It is the constellation of Being that is uttering

[40] Aquinas, *Summa theologiae* I–II, q. 94, a. 2
[41] This is the conclusion of Aristotle's *Politics* VII, c. 3, 1325b, 14–32. If only Heidegger had asked himself whether the Third Reich was such a state!

itself to us. But we do not yet hear, we whose hearing and seeing are perishing through radio and film under the rule of technology. The constellation of Being is the denial of world, in the form of injurious neglect of the thing. Denial is not nothing; it is the highest mystery of Being within the rule of Enframing. Whether the god lives or remains dead is not decided by the religiosity of men and even less by the theological aspirations of philosophy and natural science. Whether or not God is God comes disclosingly to pass from out of and within the constellation of Being. So long as we do not, through thinking, experience what is, we can never belong to what will be.[42]

Heidegger is surely right in saying we can never get free of our modern technological imprisonment until the light of Being, that is, of objective Reality, breaks through the walls of our artificiality and subjectivism. It is true also that God makes himself known to us through the events of history. It may even be true that the crisis of western civilization at the end of the twentieth century is destined to awaken us to the God that has been concealed so long.

Must we, however, await the advent of God in history, or has he already come and is being rejected by a culture that falsifies technology by making it an idol? The truth of technology is the truth of humble service, service to the real physical needs of all members of our society and, even more important, to their spiritual needs, to help reveal and communicate to all a true and ever-deepening understanding of the world, our true human selves, and our Creator. Heidegger scorned the "religiosity of men" and "the theological aspirations of philosophy and natural science," and preferred to issue Delphic oracles about a new epoch of Being. Is it not more fruitful to ask ourselves what is false in our scientific thinking and misguided in our design and use of scientific technology and strive to correct it?

---

[42] Heidegger, *The Question Concerning Technology*, 49.

CHAPTER 6

Contemporary Understandings of Personhood*

Classicist and Historicist Worldviews

EVERY CONTEMPORARY WORLDVIEW HAS ITS OWN understanding of the human person—Christian, Judaic, or Islamic; Hindu, Buddhist, or Confucian; Marxist or Humanist—each subdivided into a spectrum from fundamentalist to liberal. A superficial scan of this vast array of images of the human person would be unprofitable. The differences in understanding the human person between Catholic theologians today, although considerable, seem to me less significant than their common conviction that the "classicist worldview" of the person needs to be revised in accordance with modern "historical-mindedness."[1] Therefore, I will concentrate on this area of current agreement.

The leading systematic theologians of the Vatican II period—Karl Rahner, Edward Schillebeeckx, Hans Urs Von Balthasar, Yves Congar, Hans Küng—were all marked by their "historical-mindedness,"[2] and most younger

---

* Published as "Contemporary Understandings of Personhood," *The Twenty-Fifth Anniversary of Vatican II: A Look Back and A Look Forward,* Proceedings of the Ninth Bishops' Workshop, Dallas, Texas, Russell E. Smith, ed., 35–48.

[1] Lonergan, "The Transition from a Classicist World-View to Historical Mindedness," 1–9.

[2] For the anthropologies of these theologians, see the following: Karl Rahner, SJ, *Hearers of the Word,* with discussion by Louis Roberts, *The Achievement of Karl Rahner*; for Bernard J. F. Lonergan, SJ, see David Tracy, *The Achievement of Bernard Lonergan.* See also Robert J. Schreiter, CPPS, and Mary Catherine Hilkert, OP, eds., *The Praxis of Christian Experience: An Introduction to the Theology of Edward Schillebeeckx.* For Hans Urs von Balthasar, see *A Theological Anthropology,* republished as *Man in History* (1982); with discussion by Louis Roberts, *The Theological Aesthetics of Hans Urs von Balthasar*; for Hans Küng, see his *On Being a Christian,* 249–73; with discussion by Catherine Mowry LaCugna, *The Theological Methodology of Hans Küng.* Yves Congar's

theologians have followed in their paths, though they sometimes lack the grounding in the classicist worldview possessed by most of these masters. Since none have better described the difference between these two views of the human person than Bernard Lonergan, I will quote him in full from his well-known essay, "The Transition from a Classicist World-View to Historical-Mindedness."

> One can apprehend man abstractly through a definition that applied *omni et soli* and through properties verifiable in every man. In this fashion one knows man as such; and man as such, precisely because he is an abstraction, also is unchanging. It follows in the first place, that on this view one is never going to arrive at any exigence for changing forms, structures, methods, for all change occurs In the concrete, and on this view the concrete is always omitted. It follows . . . , that this exclusion of changing forms, structures, methods, is not theological; it is grounded simply upon a certain conception of scientific or philosophic method; that conception is no longer the only conception or the commonly received conception; and I think our Scripture scholars would agree that its abstractness, and the omissions due to abstraction, have no foundation in the revealed word of God.
>
> On the other hand, one can apprehend mankind as a concrete aggregate developing over time, where the locus of development, and so to speak, the synthetic bond is the emergence, expansion, differentiation, dialectic of meaning and of meaningful performance. On this view intentionality, meaning, is a constitutive component of human living; moreover, this component is not fixed, static, immutable, but shifting, developing, going astray, capable of redemption; on this view there is in the historicity, which results from human nature, an exigence for changing forms, structures, methods; and it is on this level and through this medium of changing meaning that the Church's witness is given to it.[3]

If we look at the human person with this historical-mindedness characteristic of contemporary theology, what are the chief emphases? It seems to me that there are five on which most theologians would agree. I will also indicate in a sentence or two what a classicist theologian might have to say about each. Why assume that what Lonergan calls the "transition" from one worldview to another has ended the dialogue between them?

Subjectivity of the Human Person

The historicist worldview seems to have originated in the so-called "Copernican revolution" in philosophy initiated by Descartes and brought to its climax

---

point of view can be gathered from his little work still untranslated, *Esprit de l'homme, Esprit de Dieu.*

[3] Ryan and Tyrrell, eds., *A Second Collection,* 5ff.

by Immanuel Kant, often spoken of as "the turn to the subject," in response to the value-free objectivity claimed by natural science in its remarkable progress after Galileo. In a mechanistic Newtonian world human persons refused to be machines or mere objects, and became aware of their existence as subjects, feeling, thinking their own thoughts, making their own choices.

This *subjectivity* of the human person is not the same as "subjectivism." Rather it is a term for our humanity in its difference from all other beings in our visible world. Among the objects that make up the world, only we persons are "subjects," that is, self-conscious and free. Consequently we cannot be defined as being this or that as objects are, since we are responsible for making ourselves whatever we become by our own choices. Therefore, to speak of human "nature" is to risk reducing the person to an object, of losing precisely what makes us persons.

Hence, many contemporary theologians prefer to make use not of the classical philosophies of being that began by an analysis of the objects of knowledge but of the post-Kantian "critical philosophies," which begin with an analysis of the subjective conditions of knowledge and the phenomena of experience. The question of objectivity and real existence is dealt with only subsequently.

Thus, for example, in the theology of Karl Rahner, the human subject is analyzed in depth by a method of "transcendental deduction" a priori to concrete experience and then "correlated" with that experience.[4] In the method of Lonergan, on the other hand, one begins with concrete experience, but fixes attention not on the content of that experience but on the process of inquiry by which the subject can fully appropriate that experience as its own;[5] while in Schillebeeckx's later thought subject and object are "inextricably intertwined" yet the phenomenological viewpoint remains dominant.[6] What would a classicist say to all this? Certainly what makes us more than animal is our intelligence and through intelligence we are self-conscious, but do we first of all and with fundamental certitude know ourselves as subjects? Or are we first aware of the objective world, and secondly and reflexively that we are knowers of that world? Yet no doubt modern culture emphasizes this reflexive awareness.

I believe this is why so many people in our culture find the Church's pro-life arguments against abortion cast in the terms of classical theology

---

[4] Cf. Anne Carr, *The Theological Method of Karl Rahner.*

[5] A concise summary of Lonergan's conception of method is found in the first chapter of his *Method in Theology*, 3–26. For his conception of subjectivity, see his essay "The Subject" in A Second Collection, 69–86.

[6] Edward Schillebeeckx, *Christ: The Experience of Jesus as Lord,* chapter 2, 731–43, explains his idea of "experience" as the "inextricable intertwining" of the subjective and objective in the encounter with reality. Religious experiences are ones that point to something that transcends experience.

unpersuasive. They grant that persons have rights, but persons are subjects; and therefore pregnant women are possessed of subjective feelings and interests and have rights. But the fetus is only potentially a subject since it is yet not self-conscious and lacks feelings and interests. Is it so obvious then that it is a person? Consequently Catholic theologians who are pro-life today have to labor strenuously to show that even the pre-embryo is a person by beginning with understanding of the person, rather than denying as Kant did that we can know the "noumenal" (objectively real) self.

Historicity of the Human Person

The second feature of this contemporary understanding is the *historicity* of the human person. The classicist worldview included human history, but it did not appreciate the historical consciousness of the human person. Human persons are fundamentally marked by historicity, because their existence as they actually experience it cannot be separated from its historical context. Sartre said, "Man has no nature, but a history."[7] It would be truer to say that our nature is our liability to be shaped by and our capacity to shape history.

We are in Heidegger's term "thrown into" a world we did not make.[8] We are defined by our relations to the objects and persons of our world, yet we are responsible by our free decisions for creating ourselves and for remaking the world into which the next generation will be born. We are, therefore, not simply persons, but persons of our time, inescapably modern or postmodern.

This does not mean that we are confined to the limits of the present. It is the very essence of our historicity that we remember the past and anxiously anticipate the future. Yet past and future are known to us and have significance only in terms of the present. Consequently, this recognition of human historicity does not imply an acceptance of "historicism," the notion that we can stand outside our present and view the march of history with a neutral eye. No, our historicity requires us to use the past to build the future, not to try impossibly to relive it. We must, therefore, cease trying to define ourselves as persons by some timeless abstraction called "human nature."

This theological emphasis on historicity became very evident in Vatican II where for the first time an ecumenical council was primarily concerned not with orthodoxy, which was hardly in question, but relevance and communication. Therefore, today Catholic theology and biblical scholarship is above all marked by a historical consciousness just as scholastic theology was marked by a metaphysical consciousness. Hence, also we have witnessed an anguished traditionalist reaction against the Council. For traditionalists the

---

[7] Thomas C. Anderson, however, shows in his *The Foundation and Structure of Sartrean Ethics*, 57–60, that even for Sartre ethics is teleological and recognizes certain universal human needs that must be met.

[8] Martin Heidegger, *Being and Time*, I, 5, 174.

very function of theology is to help the Church transcend the variations of history, which may be inevitable, but which traditionalists see as erosive of orthodoxy. The historically minded, on the contrary, see the Council as accepting a view of the human person according to which orthodoxy can be maintained only at the price of rethinking the faith in every generation and through every cultural change.

Relationality of the Human Person

For the historically-minded, a third characteristic of the human person is its relationality.[9] Objects may be conceived in isolation, but human persons exist only in relation to persons within that world of objects. We must constantly deal with these persons and it is in these relational efforts that each of us discovers who we are as persons. Our self-consciousness cannot be a Cartesian *ego*, although it was Descartes who first made "the turn to the subject." *Cogito,* I think always of myself in relation to a world that manifests itself to me as I am in relation to other subjects with whom I communicate. Since this network of relations is a society with a particular historical culture, it seems difficult to avoid a certain cultural relativism in our view of Christian life, How can we separate a "natural law" from the culture in which that law is actually lived? While today we would be horrified at the burning of heretics at the stake, in the social context of the Middle Ages the greatest and most saintly theologians not only did not deplore but applauded this horrid deed!

The linkage of subjectivity and relationality explains why "modern man" (and woman) is at once intensely *individualistic* yet intensely *socializing*.[10] As subjects, human persons must be free of all external coercion to take possession of their own lives, but these lives can have meaning only in involvement in the reconstruction of social reality. We see this exemplified often in the modern intelligentsia who demand total freedom of personal expression, yet are constantly propagandizing for the restructuring of all traditional institutions according to their own ideals. Note that modernist "conservatives" are just as caught up in this paradox as are modernist "liberals." The modernist conservative is a libertarian as regards private life, but a social activist in his or her determination to apply the "magic of the market" to rendering society economically efficient in the manner of Social Darwinism.

---

[9] See Remy C. Kwant, *The Phenomenology of Social Existence,* for a discussion of human relationality.

[10] This paradox is well illustrated by Wade Clark Roof and William McKinney in their study, *American Mainline Religion,* which hypothesizes that the main reason for the high rate of Church affiliation in the United States compared with most European countries, along with an extreme pluralism of belief, is the need Americans feel for some kind of community support in a culture that is extremely individualistic. They quote Thomas Jefferson's famous remark, "I am my own sect."

This relationality of the human person, while often resulting in pressures to conform, also puts a premium on the personal in the sense of the idiosyncratic. We make ourselves interesting and important by becoming obviously unique. We have to have something to offer that others lack in the free market of living. Hence we are no longer so much interested in what is common to all human beings, but rather in the variety of persons. We feed on confessional autobiographies and personal "profiles" that reveal the most intimate details of personal lives in order to achieve recognition in the confusion of human names and faces.

Consequently, the notion of universal moral norms, whether of a natural or a divine law, seems irrelevant to the actual lives of persons, each one unique and lived in unique circumstances. Moral good or evil is not to be found in the conformity to some general rule usually inapplicable, but in the effort or neglect to construct a life rich in human values. In this perspective it is easier to see why the "mainstream" moral theologians of today, having opted for the "paradigm shift" to modernity, find a moral methodology of proportionate reason so much more realistic and personalist than the classical moral method.[11]

Language and the Human Person

Since social relations are maintained by communication and communication is through language, and language expresses meanings, a fourth emphasis of the historically minded is on the human person as the *creator of meaning through language.* As subjects we think and choose, but this is possible only through symbols of some sort, through a language, which is not natural, instinctive, or universal to humankind, but a human invention, differing from culture to culture and from age to age, that is, through our historicity. Not only do we, in our relationality and for the sake of our relations, create languages, but through languages we also create meaning. In even a deeper way as Heidegger and Ricoeur have emphasized, language once created creates us, because we are born into a culture whose symbols largely determine how the world appears to us.

From this arises the great concern today for *hermeneutics* and *semiotics,* that is, for problems of translation and interpretation of symbolic expressions whether verbal or non-verbal.[12] To think about the human person as

---

[11] For a survey of the controversy (favorable, however, to proportionalism), see Bernard Hoose, *Proportionalism: The American Debate and Its European Roots* (Washington, DC: Georgetown University Press, 1987). For a criticism of this moral system, see my essay "Integral Human Fulfillment" in this collection.

[12] For an introduction to the current state of these disciplines, see Richard E. Palmer, *Hermeneutics: Interpretation Theory in Schleiermacher, Dilthey, Heidegger, and Gadamer,* and John Deely, *Introducing Semiotic: Its History and Doctrine; Basic Semiotics;* and *Four Ages of Understanding.*

religious necessarily requires that we understand the symbols that speak to faith, that reveal God to us, whether in the liturgy, the Scriptures, or the preached Word and the teaching of the church and its tradition. But as history changes and the network of social relations change and individuals in their subjectivity receive the Word in terms of their own varied and changing experience, the old symbols lose their meaning or take on false meanings, unless they are somehow renewed. This is why the very nature of the human person makes it necessary for contemporary theology to rethink and re-express classical theology, and why it becomes so frustrated if it lacks the freedom for this task.

The postmodernists have pushed this theme of human linguistic rivalry to the extreme of "deconstructionism" which amounts to a denial that communications between human persons can ever succeed, because nobody says what they really mean. Even if we tried to be wholly honest, we run up against the barrier that the other will be interested only in what he agrees with, namely, what he already thinks.[13] This pessimism need not be accepted as final, but it is a striking way of recalling the biblical account of the Tower of Babel and pointing out that only the Pentecostal miracle of tongues can hope to overcome this consequence of our sinful condition. Pluralism is a fact, but it should not make us give up our ecumenical efforts at communication.

Liberation of the Human Person

The fifth mark of the modern understanding of the person is the emphasis on the *need of persons to liberate themselves.*[14] Persons exist always in a power struggle to be free of control by others or to gain control over others. "Truth" is a function of ideologies used as weapons in this struggle. We are not just subjects as self-conscious; we are either "subjects" of domination by others, or we are subjectors. The freedom of the self-conscious subject is an illusion, if we suppose that we are free to live our own lives without a struggle to attain that freedom against the oppression of the powers that be.

Modern theology has more and more carried on a self-criticism of the elitist tendencies of modernity, with the result that one of the features of postmodernity is the emphasis on political theology, on liberation theology, and feminist theology. The hermeneutic of today is a "hermeneutic of suspicion" and deconstruction that seeks to uncover in all the documents of the past and the institutions of the present the hidden agenda of the struggle for power. This demands the abandonment of classical ideas of scholarly objectivity and

---

[13] For a discussion of these recent developments see David Ray Griffith, William A. Beardslee, and Joe Holland, *Varieties of Postmodern Theology,* especially Griffith, 32–40.

[14] Ibid., 81–94 and 129–48.

neutrality, and requires conversion and commitment. But this "conversion" is not merely the conversion in faith and morals of traditionalism, nor even the "conversion" of understanding urged by Bernard Lonergan, but an option for one side or the other in the power struggle. Vatican II's "preferential option for the poor" is understood in this sense, and the "poor" or "oppressed" become the side with which one has identified, while one's opponents are by definition the "oppressors." Theology thus is no longer merely a study but a "praxis" that formulates the concerns of the oppressed and motivates their efforts to break their bondage. This bondage is not just personal sin but rather "sinful social structures."

An Historical-Minded Evaluation

I have tried to describe the chief points of emphasis that are being developed by contemporary theology in its efforts to revise the classical view of human nature. That these features of the human person are of great significance often neglected in pre-Vatican II theology ought to be taken into account by all theologians today, and especially by the Church in teaching and preaching, who can deny?

A serious question is raised, however; by statements like the following by Bernard Lonergan:

> The old foundations of theology will no longer do. In saying this I do not mean that they are no longer true, for they are true now as they ever were, I mean they are no longer appropriate. One type of foundations suits a theology that aims at being deductive, static, abstract, universal, equally applicable to all places and to all times. A quite different foundation is needed when theology turns from the deductivism to an empirical approach, from the static to the dynamic, from the abstract to the concrete, from the universal to the historical totality of particulars, from invariable rules to intelligent adjustment and adaptation.[15]

In taking this stand for a new foundation for theology, Lonergan was not unaware of the risks of this approach and he warned that "our disengagement from classicism and our involvement in modernity must be open eyed, critical, coherent, surefooted."[16] Certainly theologians like Lonergan, Rahner, and Schillebeeckx made great efforts to show that they were not disloyal to the

---

[15] Lonergan, "Theology in its New Context" in *A Second Collection*, 63ff.

[16] Lonergan's whole emphasis is on the "self-appropriation" of our knowledge. For him "objectivity" is achieved by a disciplined awareness of our subjective processes in knowing. But is it not rather that we test the validity of our knowing processes by their success in letting objects "speak for themselves"? On the contrary, Heidegger (although he never wholly freed his thought from phenomenological idealism) in his second phase came to stress the contemplative passivity of human knowledge and to

work of Aquinas, but were engaged in an effort at what Heidegger called "retrieval," an effort to maintain a dialogue with the classical past in which new questions were being raised that St. Thomas in his historical context had never thought of asking. Yet Lonergan was certainly correct when he said that contemporary theologians generally conceive modern theology as a paradigm shift from what they perceive as classical theology, especially that of Aquinas. As Lonergan put it, this does not mean they deny the truth of Aquinas's theology of the human person, but they have simply lost interest in it. The result of this shift of attention is that, unlike Lonergan, Rahner, and Schillebeeckx, they no longer feel any special obligation to relate their understanding of the human person to the classical view (often caricatured) except by way of contrast.

Yet is it possible to treat of human historicity, subjectivity, relationality, and the like without grounding these characteristics in a metaphysical and a theologically dogmatic understanding of human nature as it transcends cultural relativity? And was not this precisely the foundation firmly laid by classical theology? The great theologians of Vatican II, for all their talk of new foundations, in fact worked very hard to show that the "turn to the subject," which in one way or another they took, ultimately led back to an affirmation of this metaphysical and dogmatic tradition and confirmed it. The question, therefore, is whether in fact their adoption of this "turn to the subject," for all the stimulus to fresh thinking about the human person it has produced, really opens a path to the future, or is it now proving a dead end?[17]

Perhaps the mistake of much of the theology of the Vatican II period has been not to be historical-minded enough about the wisdom of making this turn to the subject. Common to the period of theology just preceding Vatican II was the feeling that official Thomism, for all its merits, had become a serious obstacle to dialogue with "the modern mind." Rahner sought to surmount this barrier by transcendentalizing Thomism and historicizing it with help from Heidegger. Lonergan took another path of finding in Thomism a way to metaphysics through cognitional theory. Schillebeeckx sought a way out through a theory of religious experience. What was common to all was the turn to the subject and an effort to find something of Kant's a priori foundation for knowledge even in Aquinas. What was lacking, I believe, was a critical exploration of the historical situation in which European thought turned to the subject.

When we look at the research that has been done on this question in the last thirty years, different possibilities of explanation open up. The modern

---

attribute the "forgetting of Being" to the tendency of western man to manipulate reality rather than let it reveal itself.

17 See Fergus Kerr, *Theology After Wittgenstein*, 7–16, and also on Hans Küng, 15–16; and David Braine, *The Reality of Time and the Existence of God*, 232–36 and 250ff. for rather severe criticisms of Rahner from the viewpoint of analytic philosophy.

mind is polarized between the objectivity of modern science and the subjectivity of modern philosophy and theology. Was this split, which we are now struggling to overcome, historically inevitable? Was it made necessary by a dialectic intrinsic to the nature of human self-understanding? That seems to be the hidden assumption of our theologians that leads them to conclude that the Church must accept this situation and make the best of it. Or was this polarization due rather to strictly historical factors that, although we must recognize and deal with them, do not of themselves tell us what attitude to take toward this crisis?

I believe the second explanation is the better, and I suggest the historical hypothesis that the turn to the subject was due to a previous questionable turn taken by the natural sciences in the seventeenth and eighteenth centuries when the teleological approach to nature was abandoned for mechanism. Because the remarkable subsequent development of science and scientific technology was, mistakenly, attributed to this turn, it became and still is a dogma of science that our world and consequently human nature are without intrinsic purpose. Consequently the objective scientific picture of the world is value-free, and silent both about the world's Creator and the relation of humanity to its Creator.

If we were to ask further why science took this disastrous turn to mechanism, I suggest a second historical hypothesis, that this interpretation of natural science in an antiteleological way served the ideological interests of the intellectual elites of the Enlightenment whose concern was to promote a secular humanism as a substitute for Christianity. Furthermore, the Enlightenment was the result, and we can very well say the divine punishment, on the Church for its negligences that led to the Reformation schisms and the subsequent religious wars. The European intelligentsia, disillusioned with a fratricidal and fanatic Christianity, turned to a religion of humanity whose hope was in the power of a science and technology unrestricted by any divine purposes for nature and for art.

If these historical hypotheses can be substantiated, and I have given evidence for them elsewhere,[18] then what is needed in theology today is not an effort to understand ourselves by starting with questions posed in the perspectives of Secular Humanism, for that is what the turn to the subject really was, but from the perspectives of our own Christian tradition, whose formulation as the classical worldview, although certainly not final, was essentially sound.[19] Of course, this does not exempt us from showing how on this solid

---

[18] This is the thesis of my *Theologies of the Body: Humanist and Christian.*

[19] For efforts at a Thomistic anthropology from a modern point of view, see John Paul II's *The Acting Person*, translated by Andrezej Potocki; also John H. Walgrave, OP, *Person and Society: A Christian View*; and Mieczyslaw A. Krapiec, *I–Man: An Outline to Philosophical Anthropology*, the title of which needs to be rendered "inclusive."

foundation, all the truth to be found in modern science and in modern philosophy with its emphasis on historicity, subjectivity, and so on, can be consistently integrated. Vatican II, I believe, called us to that task. We must be grateful to the theologians who contributed to this decision by the Council, but Vatican II did not—I repeat—did not declare that these theologians had demonstrated the right way to accomplish that task. Rather the Council affirmed the solid foundations already laid in the metaphysical and dogmatic achievements of its classic tradition as the grounds for future progress.[20]

---

[20] On this continued recommendation of Aquinas as a preferential exemplar for Catholic theology, see the letter of Paul VI, *Lumen Ecclesiae, The Pope Speaks,* 19 (4:1975): 287–307, in which he especially praises St. Thomas's "cognitive and ontological realism," and the addresses of John Paul II, "Perennial Philosophy of St. Thomas for the Youth of Our Times (November 17, 1979), *Osservatore Romano* (English edition) (December 17, 1979): 6–8, and "Method and Doctrine of St. Thomas in Dialogue with Modern Culture" (September 13, 1980), *Osservatore Romano* (October 20, 1980): 9–11. In the first of these addresses (n. 9) John Paul II states his own understanding of the human person, "We are indebted to St. Thomas for a precise and ever valid definition of that which constitutes man's essential greatness: 'he has charge of himself' " (*ipse est sibi providens, Summa contra Gentiles* III, c. 81). Man is master of himself, he can make provision for himself and form projects toward fulfilling his destiny. This fact, however, taken by itself, does not settle the question of man's greatness, nor does it guarantee that he will be able, by himself, to reach the full perfection of his personality. The only decisive factor here is that man should let himself be guided in his actions by the truth, and truth is not made by man; he can only discover it in the nature that is given to him along with existence. It is God who, as creator, calls reality into being, and, as revealer, shows it forth ever more fully in Jesus Christ and in his Church. The Second Vatican Council, when it speaks of this self-providence of man 'in so far as it involves knowing what is true' *(sub ratione veri)* as a 'kingly ministry' *(munus regale)*, goes to the heart of this intuition. This is the teaching that I set out to call to mind and bring up to date in the Encyclical *Redemptor Hominis*, by drawing attention to man as 'the primary and fundamental way for the Church.' " (n. 14) See also my essay "The Church Has No Philosophy of Its Own" in this collection.

Systematic Theology Issues

CHAPTER 7

"The Truth Will Set You Free"*

Reflections on the Instruction on the Ecclesial Vocation of the Theologian *of the Congregation for the Doctrine of the Faith, May 24, 1990.*

Two Ways to Serve the Truth

THIS INSTRUCTION ON THE *ECCLESIAL VOCATION OF the Theologian* (EVT) begins by proclaiming, "The truth which sets us free is a gift of Jesus Christ (cf. Jn 8.32)." The Christian community lives by faith in God's Word. Within this community bishops and theologians both serve that Word, but differently. Must these two ways to serve the truth compete with rather than complete each other?

EVT says the theologian's role "is to pursue in a particular way an ever deeper understanding of the Word of God found in the inspired Scriptures and handed on by the living Tradition of the Church."[1] Today, however, we

---

* I was asked to submit this article in its original form by the then chairman of the National Conference of Catholic Bishops Committee on Doctrine to *Origins*, whose editor, however, felt it was too inopportune to publish. I do not here give any attention to the heated debate over Canon 812 that prescribes that Catholic theologians obtain a *mandatum* from their bishop or religious superior to teach and the application of the Apostolic Constitutions *Ex Corde Ecclesiae* and *Sapientia Christiana* to Catholic schools. In my opinion parents of undergraduate college students and students themselves should be regularly informed by the local bishop as to which faculty members of colleges and universities in their diocese have the *mandatum*, since they have a right to know from whom their children can obtain orthodox instruction.

[1] *Ex Corde Ecclesiae,* n. 6; in n. 29 the role of the theologian is defined as follows: "Bishops should encourage the creative work of theologians. They serve the Church through research done in a way that respects theological method. They seek to understand better, further develop and more effectively communicate the meaning of Christian Revelation as transmitted in Scripture and Tradition and in the Church's Magisterium. They also investigate the ways in which theology can shed light on specific questions raised by contemporary culture. At the same time, since theology seeks an understanding of revealed truth whose authentic interpretation is entrusted to the

more commonly define a theologian as an expert in a certain scholarly discipline pursuing an academic career of research, teaching, and publication. It was not always so.[2] Theology became an academic discipline only with the rise of the medieval universities. Previously theologizing occurred chiefly in the catechizing, preaching, or polemics of bishops or in the spiritual writings of contemplatives. Soon the reign of scholastic theology was disrupted by the wars of theological schools in defense of the traditions of religious orders. Then it was challenged by the antischolastic Renaissance academies, and split by the Reformation. Finally, the secularized universities excluded or marginalized theological faculties. After Trent, Catholic theologizing was largely confined to seminary manuals narrowly focused on preparing priests.

In modern times, some European state universities instituted theological faculties, but in the United States Catholic schools paralleled the secular universities, and for a time gave a certain pride of place to departments of theology. Today they are pressured to copy secular universities by substituting departments of "religious studies" neutral to religious commitment.

The Acceptance of Authority

Authority cannot be effective unless its subjects accept it. Acceptance must be threefold. First Catholics ought to listen to the guidance by authority and the reasons it gives for its judgments and if these reasons are objectively valid submit to their objective truth. Second, Catholics must also intelligently accept the guidance of authority even when authority cannot give convincing reasons. Third, Catholics must refuse acceptance of authoritative teachings only when authority exceeds its legitimate limits, or contradicts itself or the evident truth. The notion that we ought to decide everything for ourselves and reject whatever we do not understand pervades our individualistic culture, but is absurd, since in fact we must often trust the guidance of others more qualified than we are. Since to be a Christian requires us to accept God's guidance, whether we understand it or not, and to be a Catholic Christian we must believe that God has chosen to guide us through the successors of the apostles, it is totally contradictory to refuse to accept that guidance, within its proper limits and when one is not certain that it is mistaken.

Today the great majority of Catholics do not reject the guidance of church authority altogether, but they limit it very narrowly, often to infallible

Bishops of the Church, it is intrinsic to the principles and methods of their research and teaching in their academic discipline that theologians respect the authority of the Bishops, and assent to Catholic doctrine according to the degree of authority with which it is taught. Because of their interrelated roles, dialogue between Bishops and theologians is essential; this is especially true today, when the results of research are so quickly and so widely communicated through the media."

2 See Yves M.-J. Congar, *A History of Theology*, for a periodization of the development of theology as a systematic discipline

pronouncements and then they are not at all sure how to recognize an infallible pronouncement. Our democratic individualism, the frightening experience of the disasters of totalitarianism, and the clamor of the media, make us skeptical of authority as an imposition of power. Yet actually today's Church compared to other human institutions of the past and present is neither totalitarian nor power hungry. The Church of Vatican II and recent popes teaches human solidarity, respect for conscience, and the primacy of charity. While it can be criticized for excessive centralization, much has been done since the Council to implement the principles of subsidiarity and collegial consultation. Moreover, it is not easy to see how a global church faced by so many divisive and hostile forces can carry on its mission without a fair degree of centralization and a clear and unified voice. I believe that the real source of the internal crisis is the fact that many Catholics are confused as to what the Church actually teaches and the degrees and limits of its authority. The notorious case of Charles Curran who claimed freedom of opinion on all teachings that were not clearly infallible, and then questioned whether any of the Church's moral teachings had ever been infallibly declared, typifies this confusion. It is also illustrated by the frequent attacks on the *Catechism of the Catholic Church* that was the fruit of the most complete consultation of all the bishops of the Church that has ever taken place in history.

What is essential for overcoming this crisis is a clear understanding of the role of the Holy Spirit in the church and the development of doctrine. The revelation of God has been given once and for all in Jesus Christ. It is all infallibly true. Nothing can be added to it or taken away nor can any of its truths be changed. Yet our understanding of it as a Church can be deepened in the course of history by the enlightenment of the Holy Spirit. To this development of doctrine all members of the Church can contribute since all are members of Christ's Body, are animated by his Holy Spirit, and share in his threefold ministry of governing, teaching, and sanctifying, although in different and complementary ways. Yet as regards the final discernment and judgment of what is true insight as distinguished from the foolishness of worldly opinion, Christ has established the college of bishops under the headship of the successor of St. Peter "to bind and to loose," that is, to pass judgment. This judgment can be final and therefore infallible or it may have various degrees approaching finality and therefore requiring various types of acceptance. Ordinarily the discernment of these degrees of authority does not raise any problem for the informed Catholic, but when such a problem arises it is the responsibility of each of us to find out the intention of authority and give the appropriate kind of acceptance. I am afraid that the present confusion is largely due to theologians who have been eager to purpose new interpretations of tradition without doing so in a manner that assists the faith and lives of ordinary Catholics.

This understanding of the development of doctrine certainly implies that the bishops and the pope should be open not only to the views of theologians but also to the experiences of all members of the Church, especially those whose lives testify to the strength of their faith and love. If authority does not do so it is deaf to the voice of the Holy Spirit and fails to implement his guidance in the problems of our day. What I know of John Paul II, the bishops that I know, and the Roman curia, convinces me that the authority in the Church today does in fact strive hard to listen. To be effective church authority must judge between many discordant voices. But, like any good judge, a bishop must hear all sides impartially and then have the courage to winnow the wheat from the chaff having concern only for the truth.

My solution to this problem of reconciliation in the Church may be thought simplistic and overly optimistic, but it is a growing conviction. We need to work together at two things. The first is the effective communication of the actual teaching of Vatican II embodied in the *Catechism of the Catholic Church*. Most Catholics, I believe, remain quite uninformed or misinformed on what Vatican II taught. Many others have heard its teachings presented in such a manner that they either suppose it diluted Catholic tradition or they think its importance was chiefly in opening the door to new proposals for reform. Such biases have to be overcome by an objective listening to what was actually said. It is foolish for any party in the Church to suppose that there can be any other grounds for Church unity in faith and mission than the guidance of the Holy Spirit given to our times by Vatican II. This must be the common ground of any dialogue.

Granted this fundamental teaching as our point of departure dialogue is certainly necessary and to this the Common Ground Initiative[3] is devoted. Other attempts at a dialogue of mutual understanding and reconciliation are going on in the Church, but this is far from enough. We cannot resign ourselves to the negativistic calumnies in which *The National Catholic Reporter* and *The Wanderer* waste their energies in the illusion that they are promoting or defending the Gospel. Dialogue that fails to take Vatican II seriously, whether by supposing that it was a hopeless attempt to address an apostate world or that its real importance was an opening to novelty, cannot be fruitful. Nor can a dialogue that is simply a delaying tactic, an excuse to refuse to listen to the authoritative judgment of authority, achieve anything.

We must all begin with the truth of revelation understood according to the historic point of the development of doctrine reached in our century by Vatican II. Granting that in this teaching there are levels of finality we must sincerely attempt to discriminate those levels and give to them the appropriate kind of assent. In light of this teaching we must then ask what are the most pressing problems of the Church and seek to find ways in which we can

---

3 The website of the Common Ground Initiative is www.nplc.org/commonground.htm.

agree to cooperate in their solution. Where we cannot find common ground we should all be willing to give preeminence in action to those matters on which we can find general agreement, leaving the other matters to study, prayer, and continued patient dialogue. As for those having the heavy responsibility of authority, I would suggest that they should try to do two things. First, they should put their main energies into communicating to all the faithful the teachings of Vatican II and the *Catechism* in ways accommodated to different groups in the Church. Second they should promote dialogue of the type described among the various conflicting parties, calling on them in the name of the Church itself to listen to each other and seek reconciliation.

CHAPTER 8

Catholicism as a
Sign System[*]

Three Religious Languages

"SEMIOTICS," WRITES JOHN DEELY, "IS NOT SO MUCH a method as a point of view." He defines this as follows:

> The semiotic point of view is the perspective that results from the sustained attempt to live reflectively with and follow out the consequences of one simple realization: the whole of our experience, from its most primitive origins in sensation to its most refined achievements of understanding, is a network or web of sign relations.[1]

Thus from the semiotic perspective the various religious faiths can each be studied as "a network or web of sign relations." Protestants often claim Roman Catholics emphasize Tradition and the sacraments, while the Reformers stressed the Bible and preaching.[2] Thus Catholicism appears to be more a system of non-verbal signs than of words. On the other hand, the Orthodox churches generally treat Tradition as fixed by the first seven ecumenical councils rather than by the process of the "historical development of doctrine" as do Catholics.[3] Both Protestants and Orthodox think Catholics emphasize institutional authority and legality to the neglect of spirituality,[4] and Protestants also accuse Catholics of preferring law to Gospel.[5]

---

[*] *The American Journal of Semiotics,* 13.
[1] Deely, *Basic Semiotics,* 13.
[2] Louis C. Bouyer, *The Word, Church, and Sacrament in Protestantism and Catholicism.*
[3] John Meyendorff, *Living Tradition,* 13–26, 45–62; Jaroslav Pelikan, *Imago Dei: The Byzantine Apologia for Icons,* 41–66.
[4] Meyendorff, *Living Tradition,* 76–79.
[5] Joseph A. Burgess and Brother Jeffrey Gros, FSC, eds., "Lutheran-Roman Catholic Dialogues: Justification by Faith," in *Building Unity: Ecumenical Documents, IV, Ecumenical Dialogues with Roman Catholic Participation in the United States,* 217–90.

Thus the three great expressions of Christianity can be understood as three ways of interpreting and using the language of the Christian faith, that is, as three different sign-systems.[6] Ecumenical dialogue largely depends, therefore, on skillful translation of these languages.[7] Here I will only try to sketch the sign-system of Catholicism to prepare for such mutual interpretation.

I will use the term "sign" as the genus and "symbol," not in opposition to sign, but as a species of sign characterized by polysemy. I also distinguish between "natural," "conventional," and "historical" signs.[8] Natural signs are based on a similarity or analogy between sign and signified, while conventional signs are arbitrary. The sign-system of Christianity is made up chiefly of historical signs. These are natural insofar as they refer to historical persons or events that have a universal significance, but they are also conventional insofar as they have been selected and modified by custom and tradition. For example, the historical Abraham is the model of monotheistic faith for Judaism, Christianity, and Islam, but by custom in the traditions of these three religious communities Abraham plays somewhat different symbolic roles.

I also assume that there are *archetypes*, namely natural symbols having cross-cultural significance. I am not committed, however, to Jung's theory of a collective unconscious;[9] nor to the alternative theory of cultural diffusionism.[10] It seems more economical to explain archetypes as derived from common human experiences of the body and basic human relationships. These universal signs, however, are modified historically by particular environments, societies, and cultures.

Bible and Tradition

Catholicism as a symbol system is first of all a *tradition* rooted in Israel's history and colored by the Hellenistic and European cultures where it first developed. With Vatican II it has entered a new global, multicultural, and ecumenical phase. For our times this tradition was summed up in the decrees of Vatican II that confirmed its normative expression to be the Catholic Bible interpreted by the college of bishops under the pope and its chief devotional expression to be a vernacular liturgy with its seven sacraments centered in the Eucharist.[11]

---

6 Clifford Geertz, "Religion as a Cultural System," in Michael Banton, ed., *Anthropological Approaches to the Study of Religion*, 1–46.

7 Joseph Cardinal Ratzinger, *Principles of Catholic Theology: Building Stones for a Fundamental Theology*, 367–93.

8 Deely, *Introducing Semiotic*, 17, 53–62.

9 Carl Jung, *Archetypes and the Collective Unconscious: The Collected Works of C. G. Jung*, Vol. 9, Pt. 1, and Jung, et al., *Man and His Symbols*.

10 G. S. Kirk, *Myth: Its Meaning and Function in Ancient and Other Cultures*, 273–80.

11 Ratzinger, *Principles of Catholic Theology*, 367–93.

Vatican II in speaking of the relation of the Bible and Tradition indicated that the Bible is an inspired and normative expression of Tradition but did not declare it to be an exhaustive expression, since the Bible grew out of Tradition and must be interpreted in its terms.[12] Moreover, this Tradition is not simply the transmission of an explicit and static message, but of a symbol-system whose implicit meaning is inexhaustible and therefore open to organic development, as well as to occasional obscuration. Thus it is true that Catholicism differs from Orthodoxy in that Catholicism explicitly accepts the historical development of its biblical and doctrinal sign-system.[13]

Although Protestants have tended to regard such Catholic "developments" as corruptions of the original Gospel, modern Protestant biblical scholars recognize that the Bible is the product of a long developing tradition[14] and thus must be interpreted in the context of a living tradition. Yet the Catholic Church resists the "modernism" of Liberal Protestantism that interprets biblical symbols "existentially" without reference to their historic truth.

Law and Gospel

The Orthodox and Protestant complaint that Roman Catholicism is too legalistic also has a semiotic basis, since it involves a contrast between "the literal" and "the symbolic." Law is an effort to designate values in precise, literal, behavioral terms: "You shall not commit adultery" (Ex 20:14). Symbols embody values in polysemic, metaphorical, or analogical form: "The kingdom of heaven is like a treasure hidden in a field" (Mt 13:44). The scribes and Pharisees cited the Law; Jesus taught in parables.

Yet the Old Testament is not just a law book, nor the New Testament just a collection of parables. Although the Torah or Law (better "Instruction") is the core of the Old Testament, this Law is a practical expression of the Covenant (Testament) between God and his People, a transcendent personal relationship symbolized as a marriage (and a stormy one). Moreover, in the biblical canon the Torah is interpreted not merely through the Talmudic legal hermeneutic of later Judaism, but by its narrative context and through the rhetoric and poetry of the Writings and the Prophets. "You shall not commit adultery" becomes the story of David and Bathsheba and an encomium of faithful love in the *Song of Songs*.

Protestant exegetes have often criticized Catholic commentators for employing the patristic and medieval theory of the "four-fold senses of Scripture" as a hermeneutical strategy for elevating the "spiritual" over the "literal" sense of the Bible to make room for spurious "developments." But Catholic

---

[12] *Dei Verbum, Dogmatic Constitution on Divine Revelation,* Vatican II (November 18, 1965): 7–10; 750–65.

[13] Ratzinger, *Principles of Catholic Theology,* 85–152.

[14] F. F. Bruce, *Tradition Old and New,* 163–74.

exegetes have always held that the three spiritual senses must be firmly grounded in the literal sense.[15] As one Reformer, John Calvin, acknowledged,[16] the Gospel message of the New Testament cannot simply erase the "letter of the Law," but can only infuse it with a deeper meaning. For semiotics the "letter of the Law," although it is to be interpreted literally and not symbolically, is nevertheless still a sign, a pragmatic sign of what is commanded or forbidden. Furthermore, all written laws must be understood *historically* (cf. the debate over "strict" and "constructive" interpretations of our federal Constitution). The laws of the Pentateuch are the result of a long development and even after they were finally codified the interpretive and casuistic process continued. Thus the Gospel is one among many Jewish interpretations of the Law, not that of a scribe or rabbi, but of the messianic prophet, Jesus of Nazareth. The *Sermon on the Mount* fuses Law and Gospel, legal exegesis and parabolic symbolization.

Hence, whatever one may be justified in saying about the ecclesiastical politics of the Roman Catholic Church, from a semiotic perspective, its literal "legalism" cannot simply be opposed to the symbolic spirituality of the Gospel. Instead this legalism should be understood as an effort (no doubt reinforced by the immensely pragmatic character of classical Roman culture) to interpret the symbols of faith in concrete, practical, institutional, and hence historically conditioned terms. Canon law is not the Gospel, but it attempts to realize the Gospel in the changing circumstances of history. Thus while Catholicism's sign-system certainly has strong legal elements, this is consistent both with the semiotic range of the Old or New Testament and with an equally strong emphasis on the symbolic and sacramental.

The Catholic Symbol System

The Old Testament as the source of the absolute monotheism inherited by Christians and Muslims, had to meet a baffling semiotic problem: How to name the ineffable One God.[17] Iconoclasm, the destruction of all idols, could not be the whole solution.[18] God himself had to provide the right God-language and did so by telling Moses to call him the "I Am" (Yahweh), which Jews still hesitate to pronounce.[19] Furthermore, since the canonical

---

15 St. Thomas Aquinas, c. 1266, *Summa theologiae* I, q. 1, a. 9–10, and Henri de Lubac, SJ, *The Sources of Revelation,* 42–71.

16 John Calvin, *Institutes of the Christian Religion,* 2.7, 12–17, 360–66.

17 See Frederick M. Jelly, OP, "The Relationship Between Symbolic and Literal Language in Naming God," in Robert P. Scharlemann, ed., *Naming God,* 52–64.

18 Aidan Nichols, OP, *The Art of God Incarnate: Theology and Symbol from Genesis to the Twentieth Century,* 13–29; Pelikan, *Imago.*

19 See Tryggve N. D. Mettinger, *In Search of God: The Meaning and Message of the Everlasting Names,* for extensive discussion of this issue.

scriptures are believed to be the very Word of God speaking through a human author and using human language, they set the mode and the limits of proper God-language. Although no idol of God was permitted lest the sign be mistaken for the Signified, the Jews used the sacred Tent (Tabernacle) in the desert and later the Temple in Jerusalem, its altar, and the Ark within the Holy of Holies, to signify God's presence. Such signs—to use a Heideggerian oxymoron[20]—reveal by concealing, and conceal by revealing.

Many such revealing-concealing symbols of God are used in the Bible, but also there is always concern to indicate God's unity by some central symbol. Thus Deuteronomy insists there be but one Temple, that in Jerusalem. But what is the unifying, central symbol in the Old Testament—the Chosen People, the Covenant, the Law, the Temple, or the Messiah?[21] For historic Judaism the Temple and the Messiah are less central than the Law, and today for many Jews not the Law but the Land is their chief symbol of identification.

Perhaps it is best to see these as a network of mutually connotative and determinative signs.[22] The Chosen People made a Covenant with God to keep the Law. The Messiah will restore the Temple and perfect observance of the Law, and the Law is the Wisdom of God by which heaven and earth were created, are preserved, and in the light of which they are to be understood and used. Since the Law expresses the Creator's wise and loving purposes, the creation of the community of Israel by the Covenant and the Law is not an isolated incident but the interpretative key to the meaning of history. This history is not to be read as a cycle, as in many religions, but as a drama having a beginning, middle, and end: the story of a creation always threatening to return to chaos under the evil onslaught of fallen angels and sinning humanity, yet moving surely by the power of the Creator toward redemption and transformation.[23]

God's instrument in this redemptive task is the People of God, chosen in Abraham, wedded by God in the Covenant at Sinai, established in the Davidic Kingdom, restored after the Exile in Babylon, and, purified by its suffering as God's Servant. It patiently awaits the advent of the Messiah under whose anointed kingship God's reign will be established so that all nations will stream to the Jerusalem Temple to worship the One God in peace and justice (Is 66:7–24).

---

[20] Martin Heidegger, "On the Essence of Truth" in *Martin Heidegger: Basic Writings*, 130–35.

[21] John Hayes and Frederick Prussner, *Old Testament Theology: Its History and Development,* 257–60.

[22] Karl Hermann Schelkle, *Theology of the New Testament,* vol. 1, ix–xi.

[23] Northrop Frye, *The Great Code: The Bible and Literature,* 106–38.

Signs and texts require an interpreter in order to have actual significance.[24] In the Catholic symbol-system this interpreter or "Teacher of Righteousness," the Messiah as paradigmatically the Suffering Servant, is identified
with the historic Jesus of Nazareth, the New Adam by whom at last the
Covenantal Law is reinterpreted, brought to perfection, and perfectly exemplified.[25] Jesus is acknowledged as the incarnate, cosmically creative Wisdom
(Word) of God and his "body" (that is, his human nature, body and soul) is
the living Temple of God in which the Chosen People, expanded to embrace
all believing humanity, is incorporated as the visible, social reality of the
Church.[26] This Messianic community is animated by the Holy Spirit whose
descent is the result of Jesus' sacrificial death on the Cross that defeats Satan,
sin, and death (the ancient Serpent of chaos). This proleptic triumph of the
Cross over evil inaugurates the final, indefinitely prolonged, phase of history
by sending the Holy Spirit to animate the Church and cause the organic
development and transformation of humanity and the cosmos.

Signs require not only an interpreter, but also *hearers* to whom what is
signified is interpreted and by whom it is received and given concrete realization. Without this community signs are a dead language. In a historic, ongoing community they take on life and begin to undergo development. The
Torah as interpreted by Jesus found its listening community not in the Chosen People as a whole, but in a "remnant" of Jews and then in proliferating
groups of non-Jewish believers, identified with Jesus as his "mystical body."
To emphasize the genuine humanity of Jesus against the Gnostics and other
Docetists, increasing attention was given to his Virgin Mother, who as a
"corporate personality" linking the Old to the New Testament both gave
Jesus his humanity and served as the first of his disciples.[27]

In Mary all the sanctifying work of God in the Old Testament came to
completion, preserving her from all effects of the sins and failures of human
history, thus preparing her to be the New Eve, the faithful bride of God and
virgin mother of the Messiah. Hence, by joining the risen Jesus in her bodily assumption into heaven, she became the sign of the ultimate bridal union
of the Church with him in the consummation of history. Hence for
Catholics Mary is the symbol of the Chosen People, the Church, and the
redeemed Creation.[28] She is not God, but beloved of God and faithful to
God. Thus Mary as symbol of Creation and God as Creator are two infi-

24 Umberto Eco, "The Role of The Reader," in *The Role of the Reader: Exploration in the Semiotics of Texts*, 3–43.
25 E. P. Sanders, *Jesus and Judaism*, 267–69.
26 Nichols, *The Art of God Incarnate*, 30–48.
27 André Feuillet, *Jesus and His Mother*, 189–242.
28 George A. Maloney, SJ, *Mary: The Womb of God—A Vivid and Powerful Study of the Greatest Woman Who Ever Lived*, 10–11.

nitely separated extremes, which find their union and center in Jesus, Son of God and Son of Mary, "true God and true Man."

In the time during which the Church is developing and expanding to convey its message to the whole human race in all its diversity, the struggle against the forces of Satan and human sin goes on and the visible Church must constantly renew its life and strength in the Spirit. For this Jesus remains accessible in the Church through the teaching authority of the Church and the sacraments. This teaching authority is found in the Spirit-anointed pastors of the Church who interpret the Bible and discern authentic Tradition, while the sacraments (the liturgy) transmit the power of Jesus' Spirit to the members of the Church by re-presenting Jesus' earthly work.

The sacraments make the hidden Christ tangible, since they are material instruments of his bodily humanity.[29] This work of interpreting the sacred Tradition is not only that of private prayer and Bible study, but also a corporate task of the whole Church. The legal authority and unity of this interpretation is guaranteed by the pastors (shepherds) of the Church centering in the Bishop of Rome, successor of St. Peter whom Jesus appointed as chief of the apostles.[30] The validity and unity of the sacraments are to be found in the Eucharist, the symbol which includes all the other symbols, the Covenant, the Temple sacrifices, the death of Christ, the nuptial unity of the Church with Christ, and so on.[31] The other sacraments, beginning, through baptism, with rebirth to the life of grace and incorporation in the Church, are preparatory rites for the Eucharist, the sacramental wedding feast of Christ and the Church.

These symbols are both archetypal (natural) and historical. Their natural character derives from their use of fundamental experiences of human life: birth, death, struggle, sexual union, the believing community, food, drink, touching, light and darkness, the parallelism of human community to the order of the cosmos.. They occur in most of the world religions, and even the secular substitutes for religion such as Enlightenment Humanism and Marxism have been forced to use them in their ideologies and public ceremonies. They are modified historically, however, by their identification with actual persons and events in Jewish history and the ongoing history of the Catholic Church.[32]

How does this complex symbol-system help to answer the Old Testament problem of how to name God? From the foregoing it is evident that the historical, developmental character of revelation in Scripture and Tradition in

---

[29] Thomas Aquinas, c.1265, *Summa theologiae* III, q. 62, a. 1 and 5.
[30] *Lumen Gentium, Dogmatic Constitution on the Church,* Vatican II (21 November 1964).
[31] *Sacram liturgiam, Constitution on the Sacred Liturgy* (4 December 1963): nn. 47–48.
[32] Michael G. Lawler, *Symbolism and Sacrament,* 10–21.

the ongoing life of the Church is summed up in the Trinitarian doctrine of God, whereas the Old Testament portrays God as Creator and governor of history, the New Testament reveals God as "the Word of God made flesh" in Jesus of Nazareth, and predicts the work of the Spirit-animated in which Jesus remains sacramentally present until the end of history when God will be "all in all" (1 Cor 15:28).

This Trinitarian symbol (formulated in the Nicene Creed, the "symbol" of faith) must not, however, be interpreted in the manner of the heresy of "modalism." "Father, Son, and Holy Spirit" are not three names of the One God; they are the proper names of the Three Persons who are One God. Christianity is inherently communitarian, since its God is not as an isolated individual, but a community of mutually related but distinct persons.[33] The New Testament maintains the absolute monotheism of the Old, but develops it through the apostolic experience of Jesus as the incarnate Son, and the Holy Spirit as the animator of the Church in its universal mission. The communication of the divine existence and life from the Father to the Son (the "Word" and "Image" of the Father) and through the Son to the Holy Spirit (the "Breath" and "Voice" of God) is so absolute, so total, that these three Persons (manifest in human history each in his own way) are only one God.

The ineffable mystery of the One God is thus best expressed as an act in which the Three Persons are the signs in which the "message" of Divinity is communicated from Father to Son and through the Son to the Holy Spirit; since to be a "person" is to be able to know and to love in freedom, that is, to signify by revealing to other persons what one truly is. God the Father reveals himself to and in the Word and through the Word to the Holy Spirit in whom Father and Word are united in love.[34]

While the Orthodox defend the Trinitarian conception of God formulated in the Nicene Creed, they reject the doctrine, which Catholics and Protestants accept, of the *Filioque*, that is, that the Holy Spirit proceeds from the Father *and the Son*; both because it was added to the Creed after the first Seven Councils which alone the Orthodox recognize, and because the Orthodox understand it as a denial that the Father is the sole principle (the *monarchia*) of both Son and Holy Spirit. They believe it has led the Roman Church to neglect the Spirit's role in the liturgy and resulted in the legalism and overcentralized papal authority.[35]

---

[33] William Hill, OP, *The Three-Personed God,* 111–48, 225–37, and Mary Ann Fatula, OP, *The Triune God of Christian Faith,* 76–81, 100–17.

[34] See my articles "An Integrated View of the Human Person," in *Technological Powers and the Person,* 313–33, and "Contemporary Understandings of Personhood," in chapter six of this volume.

[35] Yves Congar OP, *I Believe in the Holy Spirit,* vol. 3.

Catholics, however, believe the *Filioque* is a legitimate doctrinal development based on the principle that the order of the historical manifestation of the Three Persons (the "economic Trinity") is a revelatory sign of the inner, eternal order by which the Divine Being is communicated (the "ontological Trinity").[36] In this ontological order the Father is indeed the sole source of the Divine Being, which he communicates totally to the Son and through the Son to the Holy Spirit who as Love Itself consummates the unity of Father and Son as one God.

Semiotic Shifts

This Catholic sign-system, precisely because it is historical and developmental, is constantly confronted by new experiences that may threaten a "paradigm-shift" in the system, such as the Gnostic crisis of the second century, the Arian crisis of the fourth, the Reformation crisis of the sixteenth, or the Enlightenment crisis of the eighteenth.

The Vatican II crisis is best characterized not as the confrontation of the Church by "modernity" (that was the crisis of the Enlightenment; we are now in "postmodernity"), but as the confrontation of the Church with global multiculturalism and the problems of individual rights and "special interests" that it raises. To exemplify the semiotic complexity of such problems, I will discuss one that happens to be acute not only for Catholics but for Anglicans: the validity of priestly ordination of women.

Many Catholic theologians see no serious "theological" problem about women's ordination except as a power struggle between a male hierarchy fearful of its authority and women (i.e., the active majority of church membership) who claim full recognition as persons and equal opportunity to participate in policy and ministry.[37]

That the "power" in question, however, is not economic power or brute force, but the power of symbols or sacraments is evident from the great concern feminists also have for "horizontal and vertical inclusive language" in liturgy and preaching. Priesthood is a sacrament, and the sacraments, we have seen, are a kind of language. Hence proponents of women's ordination also argue that gender is irrelevant to the symbolism of priesthood, since as St. Paul says, "in Christ there is neither Jew nor Greek, male or female" (Gal 3:26–29), so that all Christian language and the sacraments in particular should be gender-neutral or at least androgynous.[38]

Can this feminist claim be squared with the assumption I made earlier that the ultimate roots of symbolism, particularly the symbol-system of the

---

[36] Hill, *The Three-Personed God.*

[37] For such views, see the selections in Leonard Swidler and Arlene Swidler, eds., *Women Priests: A Catholic Commentary on the Vatican Declaration.*

[38] Ann E. Carr, *Transforming Grace,* 19–60.

Christian Bible and Tradition, are to be found in the human body and its basic biological, sexual, and familial relationships?

We seen that it is God who teaches us how to name God because divine names reveal who God is and how to call on God.[39] Names for God have to be analogous, that is, taken from a comparison to something we can name in our ordinary experience, yet implying that God is more unlike than like the analogues we use to name God.[40] The likeness on which such names are based is either *superficial* as when the Bible calls God "The Rock" (metaphor) or *essential* as when it calls God, "Truth Itself" (proper analogy). Theology strives to reduce the metaphors of the Bible and the liturgy to proper analogies so as to avoid anthropomorphism. Because we are created in God's image, the best analogies of both types are taken from the human person, our lives and relations.

The human relation most analogous to our creaturely relation to God is that of *child* to *parent*, since children depend on their parents for existence, as we do on God. A parent is a person, a knowing and loving being; hence God also is personal. To call God simply "Parent," however, is too impersonal. A parent is either mother or father. Thus to speak to God as Person and Parent, we must choose either masculine or feminine names (to use *both* depersonalizes God as a neuter thing). Hence our choice must be determined by whether our relation to our Creator is more like our relation to our mother or our father.

A child's relation to its mother is that of *identity*, because the child comes from the mother's body, is nursed at her breasts, and kept close in infancy. On the contrary, the child's relation to its father is that of *otherness* (but still relatedness), because the father, while present, is not so close as the mother. In pantheistic religions, which name God as the Whole and the creature a part of God, God is often Mother; but theistic religions (Judaism, Christianity, Islam) have always called God "Father," because he is the "Wholly Other," who brings creation into existence by a free act, not as part of himself. Since this doctrine of a transcendent Creator is the fundamental article of Christian faith, Christians must, as Jesus taught them, call God "Father," showing that God is utterly Other, yet the Other that loves and cares for his children, male and female, created "in his image and likeness" (Gn 1:26,27)

Jesus called God "Father," not simply as an adopted son like other human beings, but as the Divine Son, Second Person of the Trinity.[41] Why did this Second Person become incarnate to save all humanity, men and women, as a man rather than as a woman? Three related reasons can be given.

---

[39] Mettinger, *In Search of God.*
[40] Thomas C. O'Brien, "Names Proper to the Divine Persons," in St. Thomas Aquinas, *Summa theologiae,* Appendix, 239–51.
[41] Thomas Hopko, ed., *Women and the Priesthood.*

First, because the Second Person is in all ways equal to the Father his perfect image (Col 1:15). Hence, if the Father is named by a masculine name, so it is more revelatory for the Second Person to be called "Son" than "Daughter."

Second because in the family the father is generally said to be the "head" and "representative" of the family, not because he is more human than his wife, but because the unity of the family requires that one parent be head, and the male by his greater physical size, strength, and aggressiveness, and (since he does not bear the burdens of pregnancy and nursing) by his easier access to the world beyond the family, more commonly fills this role. Consequently, in the Bible, Adam represents all humanity (Gn 2:15–17), and Jesus is called the New Adam (Rm 5: 12–21).

Third, because the Incarnation is for our redemption from sin, and is an emptying (*kenosis,* Phil 2:7) or humbling of God who becomes our Servant in order to teach us to overcome Adam's original sin of pride. Thus Jesus by his celibacy and non-violence overcomes that masculine pride that is the root of the oppression of women and the powerless. To manifest this lesson of humility, it was necessary that Jesus be a male who willingly accepted the role of Suffering Servant. If the Incarnation had been female it would not have taught this lesson of the liberation of women from male violence and sexual abuse.

What then of the Holy Spirit?[42] The Hebrew *ruah* is feminine in form but sometimes neuter in meaning, while the Greek *pneuma* is neuter. Nevertheless in the New Testament the Third Person of the Trinity, the Holy Spirit is referred to as masculine to indicate his absolute identity in being with the Father and Son who, as we have seen, had to be named as masculine. In the Old Testament the name of "Wisdom" is used to indicate the manifestation of God in the Creation, in God's providence over Creation, and in the Mosaic Law. This Wisdom or cosmic and moral order is personified metaphorically as feminine, yet pantheism is avoided by portraying the link between God and creation (or the Chosen People as the summit of creation) not as a relation of identity but of covenantal partnership. Wisdom is God's Bride.

The relation between man and wife in which all questions of superior and inferior are overcome in the equality of mutual love is thus the best analogy for the relation between God and his People.

In the New Testament "Wisdom" is also sometimes identified with Christ as the supreme manifestation of God (1 Cor 1:24; Col 2:3), but more properly with the Holy Spirit sent by Christ to be the Soul of the Church, the Universal People of God. Thus Wisdom *(Sophia)* is most clearly manifest to us in the Blessed Virgin Mary, whom the Spirit overshadowed, and who is the New Eve,

---

[42] H. M. Manteau-Bonamy, OP, *The Immaculate Conception and the Holy Spirit: The Marian Teaching of Father Kolbe,* and Donald L. Gelpi, SJ, *The Divine Mother: A Trinitarian Theology of the Holy Spirit,* 215–38.

Eve, the New Paradise, "the mother of all the living" (Gn 3:20), Creation redeemed from sin. Thus feminine names are not used of God in the Bible or Tradition, but of the Bride of Christ: the Cosmos, the Church, the Virgin Mother, who is not God, but who is his divinized Creation.

Since the mystery of salvation in the Bible and Tradition is symbolically presented as liberation from every form of injustice and oppression, it is paradoxical indeed when this symbol-system is interpreted as a warrant for oppressing women, or exalting male pride and domination, since its whole purpose is to declare that God "has thrown down the rulers from their thrones, but lifted up the lowly" (Lk 1:52). Thus the question of women's ordination can only be answered in terms of a consistent interpretation of the Christian symbol-system. To oppose the pagan fertility cults with their priestesses, the Old Testament priesthood was exclusively male, and it was hereditary. The chief function of the priest was to offer the animal sacrifices of the Temple. The New Testament knows only one priest, Jesus Christ, who has offered himself on the Cross once and for all. He is also king (Messiah) and prophet (Teacher), offices usually divided in the Old Testament.[43]

All Christians by the anointing of baptism and confirmation manifest the power and presence of this One Priest to the world not simply as individuals but as members of the Mystical Body of Christ, the Church. This is not possible, however, unless Christ is effectively present in our world as its Head and Bridegroom, no longer visibly but *sacramentally* in a special sign, and this special sign is the priestly college of bishops and presbyters headed by the successor of St. Peter.

As we have seen, Jesus had to be male to reveal his Sonship with the Father, and to offer that priestly act of self-sacrifice in which the male pride of domination is humiliated to the role of Suffering Servant. Therefore male gender is an essential element of those chosen by the Church for this sacramental signifying of Christ.[44] Yet, the exclusion of women does not in any way diminish the perfect equality of all members of the Church, female and male, since the distribution of different charisms in the Church is for the good of the whole Church and every member in it, not for the aggrandizement of those on whom these special gifts are bestowed.

Is there then no role in the Church proper to women and from which men are excluded? The Christian mystery, as we have seen, is symbolized by a Covenant between God and the New Creation completed in Christ, true God and true Man. The priest is chosen in the Church as the icon of Christ, but in Church tradition the consecrated virgin is chosen as the icon of the

---

[43] Jean Galot, SJ, *Theology of the Priesthood*, 65–66, 166–68.

[44] Sacred Congregation for the Doctrine of the Faith, *Declaration on the Question of Admission of Women to Ministerial Priesthood*, October 14, 1975. www.ewtn.com/library/CURIA/CDFINSIG.htm.

Church.[45] Feminists may not want to be consecrated virgins, but, judging by the decline of vocations in our secularized society, neither do many males today want to be celibate priests.

Feminists may also object that priesthood is a position of superiority and power, while the consecrated virgin seems consigned to the passivity of the contemplative life. But in Catholic tradition the contemplative life is superior to the active life to which ministry pertains.[46] Throughout the history of the Church the Virgin Mary has been honored above ordained priests, even above popes. As for active ministry, consecrated virgins can share in all its forms, except the priesthood, as male religious can share in the contemplative life. The gender-exclusive aspect of roles in the Church is found only in the symbolism of the priest as the male Christ humbled to be a servant of all, the virgin as the female Church exalted to be the one bride of God.

This example shows, I believe, how hopeless it is to make sense of the Bible and Tradition in a Catholic perspective unless we widen our analysis to include the whole semiotic range. Most of the debate today about women's ordination and inclusive language is couched in the legal vocabulary of "rights," "equality," "discrimination," "power," and "competency." As I have indicated, such literal, legal terms are by no means foreign to the Bible or Catholic Tradition, and must enter into any reasonable debate about women's ordination. But they must be coordinated with metaphorical symbolic terms without which God-language becomes impossible.[47]

Obviously the status of women in society today is undergoing historic changes that confront the Church with problems not hitherto squarely faced. Therefore, the Catholic principle of the historical development of its doctrines, canon law, and sign-system must be called upon to help the Church deal with the questions these changes raise about gender-justice in Church structures and life. To acknowledge the historicity of Christian truth and practice, however, means also to turn to the Bible and Tradition to discover the roots from which any historical development must draw its vitality. If these roots are cut the tree will wither and die, not grow and bear fruit.

A major representative of the Catholic tradition, St. Augustine, a bishop, a Doctor of the Church, the father of semiotics,[48] teaches us that without skill in the liberal arts, that is, in semiotics, the Bible cannot be rightly interpreted. St. Catherine of Siena and St. Teresa of Avila, consecrated virgins,

[45] Louis Bouyer, *Woman in the Church*, 96–106.

[46] Pius XII, *Sacra Virginitas*, 244, n. 32. www.vatican.va/holy_father/pius_xii/encyclicals/documents/hf_p-xii_enc_25031954_sacra-virginitas_en.html.

[47] Aidan Nichols, OP, *Holy Order: Apostolic Priesthood from the New Testament to the Second Vatican Council*, 144–55.

[48] Deely, *Introducing Semiotic*, 17–18.

108 ■ | II. SYSTEMATIC THEOLOGY ISSUES

mystics, and also Doctors of the Church, teach us that without meditation on the great symbols of the Bible and Tradition their inner life and power cannot be deeply experienced.[49] Whether this "web and network of sign relations" signifies *reality*, and how that invisible reality is knowable by tangible signs to faith is another topic open (but on another occasion) to semiotic analysis.

---

[49] Paul VI, Homilies of September 27, 1970 and October 24, 1970, *The Pope Speaks*, 15:196–202; 218–22.

CHAPTER 9

Christology From Above:
Jesus' Human Knowledge According to the Fourth Gospel[*]

The Problem

IN THE VATICAN II PERIOD MANY THEOLOGIANS HAVE emphasized a "Christology from below," that is, they have begun with Jesus' humanity and asked how it manifests his divinity, rather than beginning with his divinity and asking how this became incarnate. They have done so for two defensible reasons: (1) to avoid the Platonic dualism and the monophysitism that it often engendered in popular piety, and (2) because they believed this might make the doctrine of the Incarnation more intelligible to persons in our materialistic, scientistic culture.

Yet for St. Thomas Aquinas's view of the nature of Christian theology as a science of God revealing to our faith what he is in his most intimate being, this procedure seems misleading. Theology begins, as Aquinas does in his *Summa theologiae*, with a study of the doctrine of the Triune God in his self-revelation and then proceeds to explain why such a God has freely chosen to send his Divine Son in person to be humanly incarnate so that we might know and love God more intimately. The First and Second Parts of the *Summa theologiae* of St. Thomas Aquinas prepare for his exploration of the mystery of the Person and work of Jesus Christ our Savior. His treatment of the Church, the Sacraments, and the goal of history are all considered as the completion of Jesus' own work during his earthly and risen life.

Of course, Aquinas had to reconcile this properly theological order with his Aristotelian philosophical epistemology according to which the nature of anything is revealed through what it does. Hence it is through the work of

---

[*] This paper was read at a conference titled "Reading John with St. Thomas Aquinas," sponsored by Ave Maria College and held at Deaborn, Michigan, October 5–6, 2001 and also in *Reading John with St. Thomas Aquinas: Theological Exegesis and Speculative Theology*, ed. by Michael Dauphinais and Matthew Levering, 241–53.

Christ that we best recognize who he is. St. Thomas, therefore, fits a Christology from below in which he gives great attention to the humanity of Jesus into a Christology from above that begins with his Divine Personhood, not the other way around as some of our theologians today are attempting to do. For the Common Doctor to begin Christology from below would be good *apologetics* for the Faith to an unbelieving world, but it is not proper to theology as a science since that must begin from the viewpoint of the Faith.

In his exploration in the Third Part of his *Summa theologiae* of the Person and work of Jesus, St. Thomas Aquinas drew heavily on his previous study of the Fourth Gospel. In the *Prologue* of his commentary on this Gospel (n. 1), he cites the words of St. Augustine that "While the other Gospel writers inform us in their Gospels about the active life of Jesus, John in his Gospel informs us also as to his contemplative life." Note that "also," since St. Thomas tells us that the task of a member of the Dominican Order, as he was, must be to imitate the Lord by "giving to others what one has first contemplated."[1]

According to revelation, Jesus as a Person is the Son of God, the Second Person of the Trinity, entirely equal with the Father and that Person through whom the Holy Spirit proceeds from the Father, who is the source of both Son and Spirit. Yet in obedience to the Father and in the power of the Holy Spirit he has chosen to become human like us in all but sin, in order not only to redeem us from our sins but also to raise us up with him to eternal life in the community of the Trinity. This truth raises for us the difficult theological problem much discussed today as to the nature of Jesus' human contemplation of the Father in the Holy Spirit during his earthly life. Did he in his humanity enjoy the beatific vision of his Father even in this life, or only in his divine nature?

Gerald O'Collins, SJ, and Daniel Kendall, SJ, have reviewed this question in their article, "The Faith of Jesus."[2] They are concerned to refute the

---

1 *The Commentary on St. John (Super Evangelium S. Ioannis Lectura)*, edited by P. Raphaelis Cai, OP, of which, regrettably only Part I, chapters 1–7, have been translated into English by James A. Weisheipl, OP. and Fabian R. Larcher, OP.): the prologue and first five chapters are by Aquinas and the rest a *reportatio* by Reginald of Piperno, corrected by Aquinas, was probably written 1270–72 during St. Thomas's second period of teaching at Paris. The Third Part of the *Summa theologiae* was written at Naples, about 1272, until left uncompleted in 1273; see James A. Weisheipl, OP, *Friar Thomas D'Aquino: His Life, Thought and Works,* 246–47, 361–62, 372, and Torrell, "The Person and His Work," *Saint Thomas Aquinas,* vol. 1, 198–201, 261–66, 333, 339ff. Probably, however, at least the first 20 or perhaps 35 questions of the Third Part were already completed when he went to Naples, and this is the part we are chiefly concerned with here. Yet it remains probable that the *Commentary* is the earlier work.

2 "A life of teaching and preaching, by which we give others the fruits of our contemplation, is more perfect than the life that stops at contemplation. For this life is built on an abundance of contemplation, and such was the life Christ chose." *Summa theologiae* III,

thesis boldly defended by St. Thomas that Jesus, since even in his earthly life he had the beatific vision of the Trinity, unlike Christians, did not have the virtue of faith! Collins and Kendall carefully discuss the three documents of the Holy See that are sometimes quoted as adopting Aquinas's view, held also by other medieval theologians. They conclude, however, that, as the International Theological Commission has also seemed to recognize, these documents do not constitute a definitive magisterial pronouncement on the subject, which thus remains open for theological debate.

In reviewing the various theological opinions on the question the authors list six principal difficulties for the assumption that Jesus had the beatific vision in this life:

1. How could he have truly suffered if he was already beatified?

2. How could he have had free will?

3. How could he have been tempted and gained merit through trials?

4. How could he have experienced the human process of learning?

5. The Gospels (e.g., Mk 5:30–32; 13:32) seem to indicate that his human knowledge was limited.

6. The hypostatic union in Christ of a divine and human nature does not necessarily imply that Jesus possessed the beatific vision in his human nature.

Magisterial Teaching

On this question, in 1907 the Holy See declared in *Lamentabili* that:

> A critic cannot assert that Christ's knowledge was unlimited unless by advancing the hypothesis, which is historically inconceivable and morally repugnant, that Christ as man had God's knowledge and yet was unwilling to communicate so much knowledge to his disciples and posterity. (*DS* 3434)[3]

40, 1, ad 2. See Mary Ann Fatula, OP, "*Contemplata Aliis Tradere*: Spirituality and Thomas Aquinas, The Preacher," *Spirituality Today* 43 (1; Spring 1991): 19–43, and Giles Hibbert, OP, "*Contemplata aliis tradere*: The Vocation of the Dominican Order." www.english.op.org/vocations/contemplata.html.

[3] Gerald O'Collins, SJ, and Daniel Kendall, SJ, have reviewed this question in their article, "The Faith of Jesus," *Theological Studies* 53 (September 3, 1992): 403–23.

The Holy Office in 1919 also declared that it could not be "taught safely" that

> It is not certain that the soul of Christ during his life among men had the knowledge that the blessed, that is, those who have achieved their goal *(comprehensores)*, have. *(DS* 3645)[4]

Pius XII in *Mystici Corporis,* 1943, affirms:

> Christ in his human intellect possessed the beatific vision and knew all future members of the Church from conception.[5]

On this last statement and the previous ones, however, O'Collins and Kendall comment:

> Yet it needs to be pointed out that the encyclical was concerned with the mystery of the church and not as such with doctrines about Christ. In short, contemporary Catholics should continue to give these documents a respectful hearing. But we fail to see any clear obligation to endorse the view that Christ during his earthly existence enjoyed the beatific vision. Neither his unique personal dignity as Son of God nor his unique function for revelation and redemption necessarily and clearly requires such extraordinary knowledge.[6]

They then add that,

> The International Theological Commission in its Christological documents, "Select Questions of Christology" (1979), "Theology, Christology and Anthropology," 1981, and "The Consciousness of Christ Concerning Himself and His Mission" 1985, do not assert beatific vision but only "the consciousness that Jesus had of his mission implied an awareness of his 'preexistence.'"[7]

These difficulties were certainly known to Aquinas, although as regards the fifth concerning the exegesis of the Gospels, he was not acquainted with modern exegetical methods. Yet he firmly maintains in the *Summa theologiae* III, q. 9, a. 2 that Jesus, even as he journeyed to God in this life in his human nature possessed the beatific vision in its fullness.[8] In q. 7, a. 3, he

---

4 *Enchiridon symbolorum, definitionum et declarationum de rebus fidei et morum,* edited by Henry Denzinger and Adolph Schönmetzer, n. 3434.
5 Ibid., n. 3645.
6 *Mystici Corporis Christ,* n. 75.
7 O'Collins and Kendall, "The Faith of Jesus," 410.
8 *Catechism of the Catholic Church,* nn. 417–74.

concludes therefore Jesus did not have the virtue of faith since he possessed what is superior to faith, namely vision.

It is easy to see why such a thesis is unacceptable to many theologians today when the trend is to work out a "Christology from below" that emphasizes the truth of Jesus' humanity. This is believed to be necessary both to avoid Gnostic and Monophysite heresy, but also to make Jesus more credible and lovable to our secular humanist culture. These are good intentions, but of course, as in all matters of Christology they involve the risk of minimizing the *mystery* of the Incarnation. My purpose in this essay is not to answer all these difficulties nor to evaluate O'Collins and Kendall's very nuanced proposal for a solution, but to consider how Aquinas's *Commentary on the Gospel According to St. John* enabled Aquinas to present his final views in the *Summa theologiae.*

St. Thomas's Comments

In his commentary on the *Prologue* Aquinas explains that when in verse 4b (n. 101) it is said of the Divine Word—"And that Life was the light of men"—that this can be understood in two ways:

> First it is called the light of man as an object visible only to men, because only intelligent creatures can see it, since only they are capable of the divine vision. . . . Second it can be called the light in which all men participate. For we are only able to see the Word and that light through that participation that is in our nature in the superior part of our soul, namely the light of the intellect.

And later (n. 104) he adds that this is true not only as regards our creation but also regards our restoration from sin:

> And the light was the light of all men, not simply of the Jews, because the Son of God in becoming flesh came into the world that he might illuminate all men with grace and truth.

As to the words "Full of grace and truth" (Jn 1:14 b) said of the Word made flesh, Aquinas comments (n. 188) that,

> Anyone is given grace as he is united to God. Therefore that one is full of grace who is most perfectly united to God. But others are joined to God through the sharing of a natural likeness (Gn 1:16: "Let us make man in our image and likeness"), others through faith (Eph 3:17: "May Christ dwell in your hearts through faith"), and others through charity since he who "remains in charity remains in God," as is said in

1 Jn, 4:16. But these ways are not perfect since neither through natural participation is anyone perfectly united to God, nor is God seen through faith as he is, nor loved through charity as he is loveable; since He is infinitely good and therefore infinitely lovable, and this infinite lovableness no creaturely love can match, and therefore [in these ways] no perfect union is possible. In Christ, however, in whom human nature is united to divinity in the unity of person is to be found a complete and perfect union to God, since that union was such that all acts both of the divine and human nature were acts of that one person. He was, therefore, full of grace in that he did not receive from God some special gift of grace, but was God himself. (Phil 2:9: "The Father, gave the Son that name that is above every name" and Rm 1:4: "He who was predestined the Son of God in power.") He was also full of truth, since the human nature in Christ attained to the divine truth itself so that a man was the divine truth itself. For in other men are many particular shared truths by which the First Truth shines in their minds in many representations, but Christ is the Truth itself. Hence it is said on Col 2:3 that "in him are hidden all the treasures of wisdom."

Thus for Aquinas Christ in his human nature possesses Truth in the fullest way possible. On another verse, "For God does not give the Spirit according to measure" (Jn 2: 34), he similarly comments (n. 543),

This is said of Christ both as God and as man. . . . God the Father gives the Spirit without measure since he gives Christ both the strength and power of breathing forth the Holy Spirit whom, since the Holy Spirit is infinite, the Father gives without limit; and indeed gives the Holy Spirit to the Son just as he, the Father himself possesses the Spirit so that the Spirit proceeds "also from the Son." And the father gives the Holy Spirit to the Son through the Son's eternal generation. Similarly also Christ, as he is man has the spirit without measure, for to other humans the Holy Spirit is given according to measure since his grace is given to them within limits. But Christ as man does not receive grace according to measure and therefore he does not receive the Holy Spirit according to measure.

Jesus has this grace in three ways: (1) as the grace of the union of his human nature to his divinity, (2) as his habitual grace as an individual man, and (3) as his grace as the Head of the Church. His grace of union is infinite, but his habitual grace as an individual man and his grace of the Head of the Church have certain limits. Nevertheless, it can still be said that Christ received theses graces "without measure" in three senses: (1) as regards the total capacity of his human nature; (2) as regards the infinity of the gift received; and (3) as he is the cause through whom others receive grace. As to the last of these three senses, St. Thomas comments (n. 544):

> It is evident from all that has been said, that the grace of Christ that is called "the grace of headship" according to which Christ is the head of the Church is infinite as to its influence. For from the fact that he himself possesses the gifts of the Spirit "without measure," he has the power of pouring them out without measure. In other words, the grace of Christ is sufficient not only for some men but for all men, according to 1 Jn 2:2, "He is the propitiation for our sins and not for our sins only but for the those of whole world" and even of many worlds, if such exist.

Thus Aquinas derived two fundamental principles from this Gospel that he used to answer the two important questions with which we are here concerned. These are: (1) Jesus by reason of the union of his human nature to his divine person had the fullness of grace and truth in the unlimited degree possible to a created nature, and (2) that this was necessary for his mission of redemption as head of the Church of those predestined to be redeemed.

St. Thomas's View in the *Summa theologiae*

In *Summa theologiae* III q. 9, a. 2, the question is asked, "Whether Christ had any science other than that of a blessed one or *comprehensor*?" The *Sed Contra* cites the words of the Fourth Gospel 8, 55, "For I know Him and I keep his word." Aquinas in his commentary (n. 1286) says that this applies both to Christ's speculative intellectual knowledge and to his affective consent to the Father's will. He then says in his reply to the question,

> That which is in potency is reduced to act through that which is in act; for others are heated only through that which is hot. Human beings, however, are in potency to that beatific knowledge that is the vision of God as they are ordered to it as to their end: for it is only rational creatures that are capable *(capax)* of that beatific vision inasmuch as they are images of God. Humans are brought back to this ultimate end through the humanity of Christ, according to Hebrews 2:10, "For it was fitting that He [God the Father], for whom and by whom all things exist, in bringing many sons to glory, should make the pioneer of their salvation [Christ] perfect through suffering." And it was also fitting that the beatific knowledge that consists in the vision of God should belong to Christ in the most excellent manner, since a cause should always be more powerful than its effect.[9]

---

[9] See also "A man is called a pilgrim *(viator)* from tending to beatitude and a beholder *(comprehensor)* from having already obtained beatitude. . . . Now man's perfect beatitude

To the objection (ad 3) that such knowledge is beyond human nature, Aquinas replies,

> The beatific vision or knowledge is in a certain way beyond the nature of the rational soul insofar as that soul cannot attain to it by its own power; but in another way . . . it is in accord with that nature insofar as according to its nature it is made in the image of God and hence capable of that vision. Yet [God's] uncreated knowledge is in every way above the nature of the human soul.

Aquinas then in *Summa theologiae* III, q. 7 asks about the individual habitual grace of Christ in his human person and declares that he had all the virtues and gifts, including hope and love, but not faith (a. 3 c).

> It is written (Heb 11:1): "Faith is the evidence of things unseen." But there was nothing that was not visible to Christ, according to what Peter said to Him (Jn 21:17): "Thou knowest all things." Therefore there was no faith in Christ. . . . As was said above (II–II, 1, 4), the object of faith is of something divine that is unseen. Now a virtuous habit, as every other habit, takes its species from its object. Hence, if we deny that the something divine was unseen, we exclude the very essence of faith. Nevertheless, Christ, as will be made clear (q. 34, a. 4) from the first moment of His conception saw God's Essence fully, Hence he could not have had faith.

In replying to the obvious objections to this answer he concedes that faith is a more noble virtue than the moral virtues, yet unlike them it implies a deficiency that Christ could not have had. Nor did Christ lack the merit of faith since he obeyed God in all matters as do the blessed in heaven who also no longer need the virtue of faith, since it is replaced by the beatific vision.

Answer to Current Approaches

Before attempting to deal with O'Collins and Kendall's special objections, it seems useful to say something about the classical Protestant approach to Christology and some of the concerns expressed currently by other Catholic

---

consists in that of both soul and body-in the soul as regards what is proper to it inasmuch as the mind sees and enjoys God-in the body inasmuch as the body will be resurrected. . . . Now before his passion Christ's mind saw God perfectly and thus he had beatitude as far as regards what is proper to the soul, but beatitude was lacking as regards all else, since his soul could suffer and his body was both liable to suffering and to death. Hence he was at once beholder inasmuch as he had the beatitude proper to the soul and at the same a pilgrim inasmuch as was still tending to beatitude as regards what was lacking for his beatitude." *Summa theologiae* III, q. 15, a. 10 c.

theologians. Classical Protestant Christology inherited a confusion already found in medieval theologians and in subsequent Catholic catechesis clear down to the present by the idea of the "vicarious atonement" taken in the sense that God's justice demanded that the human race be condemned and punished for its sins, but that in his mercy he chose to satisfy this justice by punishing his Son Jesus in our place. This fostered the idea of God as "a vengeful God" who needs to soothe his feelings of revenge by "taking it out" on somebody. The Scriptures do indeed use this metaphor of "vindication," as they also use the metaphor of "redemption" (i.e., buying back a slave from the Devil master) and other metaphors. Theology should not take these too literally, but instead seek a consistent interpretation.

For Aquinas the essential purpose of the Incarnation is for God to reveal himself to us perfectly as the God of Love, so that we may be able to respond to his love with all our heart and soul. As Plato said in *The Republic* (II, 511), the righteous man's righteousness can be revealed and made evident to all only if he dies as a criminal rather than desert the truth of his ethical teaching. Jesus exposed himself to death by his enemies rather than desert the truth of his preaching about his Father that "God is love."

What then of the "vicarious atonement"? Punishment is not revenge, that is, its purpose is not to assuage (or, as we say today, "bring closure") to the feelings of a victim of injustice, but should (a) be to deter others from committing the injustice; (b) aid in the rehabilitation of the criminal; and (c) "maintain the order of justice" in our culture, since to ignore injustice tempts people to forget that it is evil. This third effect of punishment, according to Aquinas, (*Summa theologiae* II–II, q. 108 c.) is fundamental, since if the order of justice is obscured there can be no deterrence or rehabilitation. Therefore, God had to punish sin, not to get his vengeance, but so that in the eyes of men, his justice might not be obscured. Yet God in his mercy took this punishment on himself in his Son, who is one with him, in order to keep the message clear that he is the God of Love. Thus the disorder of sin in the world is corrected and the punishment due is "satisfied" by a perfect act of divine-human love that manifests what God is really like.

Thus the purpose of the incarnation is God's self-revelation as Truth and Love, and this was most clearly manifested by God the Son's allowing himself to be killed by the wicked as a scapegoat for their own sins. God did not want his Son to die, nor did he cause his death, but he wanted him to manifest the divine love and mercy in the clearest most convincing way possible, that is, by showing that love even unto to death and the forgiveness of his enemies. Thus we are saved by the Holy Spirit that God sent as the reward of his Son's obedience, by his merits on the Cross, and throughout his life. This Thomistic understanding of soteriology is important in order to fully appreciate Aquinas's insistence that Jesus even in this life had the beatific vision because the goal of the incarnation is not simply to "cover over" human sins, as Protestant theology tended to say, but to deify us by enabling us to enter into the community of the Trinity's wisdom and love.

As for theologians today, the principal concern seems to be that they think that (a) the Chalcedonian formula lacks sufficient grounding in Scripture understood by the historical-critical method; (b) it is not sufficiently "from below," that is, intelligible in terms of our human experience, since the concept of a *hypostasis* derived from Greek metaphysics is unintelligible to modern man; and (c) it seems to deprive Jesus of human personhood.

Such worries, however, neglect the essential point that in the Old Testament God promised that someday he would become "personally" present to His people. In Jesus, therefore, in his complete humanity as head of God's people, God is present in person through that Divine Person who is his Son. Any Christology that falls short of this personal presence of God in true humanity fails and this is the case if Jesus is simply a human person, or even if he is both a human person and a Divine Person. Thus Küng's theology of Jesus as "the final prophet"[10] will not do, because the prophet speaks in God's name but is not the personal presence of God.

The metaphysical problem of how a Divine Person can be truly human has to be solved in any philosophical theology, but it should be remembered that the Divine Person of the Second Person of the Trinity is only *analogically* (although eminently) a "person," so that there need be no logical contradiction between Jesus being a human person and simultaneously but in another sense a Divine Person. However, since the term "person" as used by Chalcedon simply means what is signified by "I", that is, the ultimate unifying supposit of nature and its attributes, it is better to speak of Jesus as only one Person, the Divine Person. Yet this Person "includes" all that is to be found in a human person, so that Jesus lacks nothing of what it is to be human (except sin). As for the scriptural problems, the historical-critical method suffices for apologetic purposes, but it cannot provide a properly theological resolution of the question.

Thus, the Chalcedonian formula remains theologically best: Jesus is fully and truly a member of our human community, yet in him the Second Person of the Eternal Trinity has become unequivocally present to us as God's Self-Revelation. Aquinas, who fully accepts the Chalcedonian formula, therefore, finds no difficulty in attributing the beatific vision to the human nature of a Divine Person as the prototype and ultimate cause of the beatific vision to which all human persons are called in grace.

What then are we to think of the specific objections of O'Collins and Kendall to this view so confidently argued by the Angelic Doctor? It is noteworthy that they do not explicitly raise the difficulty that has so troubled

---

[10] Hans Küng, *On Being a Christian.*

those who want to emphasize a "low" Christology so as to emphasis Jesus' humanity, namely, "Doesn't this make the earthly Jesus less human?" The answer to that, of course, is that if we attain the beatific vision in heaven we will be no less human than we are; we will be perfectly human. "Grace perfects nature" and restores us to the perfect humanity that God intended for us in the creation. It is true that Aquinas does not claim that Adam and Eve had the beatific vision, since they too had to be prepared for it by a meritorious life of faith. Nor does Aquinas ever suggest that Our Lady, the new Eve had that vision in this life. Nevertheless, it cannot be argued that its possession would diminish rather than complete Jesus' perfect humanity.

O'Collins and Kendall avoid stating any such direct argument, but implicitly raise it in the first three and seemingly strongest of their objections. If Jesus was already possessed of the beatific vision, how could he have merited our salvation by freely obeying his Father, an obedience that involved many trials and suffering, "even death on the Cross"? The answer to this is found in Aquinas's teaching that it is not the simple fact of trials and suffering that gain anyone merit before God but the obedience with which they are accepted.[11] Jesus' obedience was perfect and therefore every action he performed had infinite merit. The reason that God required that he undergo such great trials and suffering was not that any one of his simple acts of love was insufficient to save the whole world, but it was rather to manifest to us the perfection of his obedience, since this would not have been sufficiently evident to us in his more ordinarily human acts. Furthermore in *Summa theologiae*, q. 34, a. 4, ad 1, Aquinas points out that Christ did not need to merit the glory of his human soul, only the glorification of his human body. Thus, since we are the "Body of Christ," we need his merit on our behalf.[12]

Moreover, from a psychological perspective Aquinas argues in III q. 34 that although in this life human intellectual activity is dependent on the senses, this is not absolutely necessary since the separated soul will have knowledge in somewhat the same manner as the angels or pure spirits. Hence at the very moment of conception Christ could have human knowledge and thus could have human freedom.[13]

---

[11] *Summa theologiae* III, q. 46, a. 3, Aquinas argues that although Christ's death on the Cross was for many reasons appropriate to his mission (a. 2), it was not absolutely necessary for our salvation, since God could have saved us in other ways.

[12] In *Summa theologiae* III, q. 19, a. 3, Aquinas shows Christ merited for himself and also for his outward glory, while in a. 4 he shows that as Head of the Church he merited for all. In III q. 48 he shows he merited (a. 1) as Head of Church, (a. 2) as to atonement, (a. 3) as a worthy sacrifice, (a. 4) as our redeemer, and (a. 5) as a Divine Person, but also through his human nature as his instrument.

[13] In *Summa theologiae* III, q. 18. a. 4, Aquinas argues for Christ's free will, and shows in a. 5 that this will though free was always conformed in obedience to God's will in such a way that there was no contrariety between it and Christ's human passions,

Hence Jesus, even while he enjoyed the beatific vision in this life, retained his free will by which he carried out his mission in perfect obedience to his Father. Our freedom is given to us in our human nature to enable us to be happy and thus we are not free with respect to happiness itself. Yet in this life we can sin because the nature of our happiness remains somewhat obscure. Hence we can choose goods that are more evidently desirable than true happiness although in conscience we know that they are only deceptive. In the beatific vision, however, we will experience a happiness that is so perfect that we will no longer be free to sin. Yet we will in no way lose our freedom, since we will still be able to choose for enjoyment among created goods whatever is not inconsistent with our love of God and neighbor. In this life also we do not lose our freedom by basing every decision on the love of God and neighbor, but remain free as to the virtuous ways in which this love can be expressed. Thus Jesus by reason of the beatific vision could not sin, but this did make him less free, but more free in his willing obedience to the plan of God. Indeed perfect obedience to a superior is not robotic, but should be an application of our gifts of intelligence and ingenuity to realize the superior's command in the best way possible in the circumstances. A good workman follows the blueprint in building a house but not just mechanically. He shows his own craftsmanship.

A further consideration concerning Christ's consciousness is that human consciousness has many levels of awareness. I am only dimly conscious of the room in which I am writing but fully conscious of the page before me. The great writers on the mystical life tell us that in the unitive state the presence of God is evident to the mystic even when she or he is engaged in very ordinary practical matters, and perhaps even in sleep! In this state of union God is still known only in the darkness of faith. Yet faith has become like the sky at dawn and the beatific vision of God, like the sun at that time, is just below the horizon.

Thus from such facts of mystical experience it is evident that there is no contradiction in supposing that Jesus had ordinary human knowledge by which he engaged in the daily routine of life, even though in the profound depths of his consciousness he was fully aware of himself as a Divine Person, the Son of God: "No one knows the Son except the Father, and no one knows the Father except the Son, and any one to whom the Son wishes to reveal him" (Mt 11:27: Lk 10:22).[14] Thus Karl Rahner, who dealt profoundly with this

---

     even as regards his natural human fear of death (a. 6). See also q. 20, a. 1, in which Aquinas holds that Christ was perfectly subject to his Father in human nature although equal to him in his Divinity.

[14] Note that this text belongs to Q, supposed by many scholars to be our most authentic source for Jesus' teaching. In *Summa theologiae* II, q. 46, a. 7, Aquinas argues that Christ had beatitude in the highest part of his soul even on the Cross and when he cried out, "My God, my God, why have you forsaken me!" (Mt 27:46).

question in view of his own transcendental philosophy of the human subject, argued that the Hypostatic Union required that Jesus be immediately aware that he was the Son of God.[15] The reason Rahner gave for this was that it belongs to human nature and human intelligence to have an indirect self-consciousness of the knowing subject in every direct act of knowledge. Since the human Jesus was a Divine Person, he therefore, must have had— precisely in order to be human—an immediate awareness of his own Person. For Rahner, however, this was not a direct, objective awareness, as would be the beatific vision, but a background awareness, or "horizon" of consciousness that we possess as subjects.

In this way Rahner sought to reconcile this background awareness that he claims Jesus had of his own Divine Person with Jesus' human life of learning, willing, and acting in an entirely human manner. Rahner based this solution on his Transcendental Thomistic philosophy that seized on Aquinas's teaching that we have an indirect self-consciousness as the horizon of all of our direct consciousness of the material world and our own body. This direct awareness of the world and our bodily selves is the proper object of human intelligence that acquires all it knows only through the senses. Most Thomists, however, do not accept this interpretation of Aquinas since it colors his thought with the philosophy of Kant who claimed for us an a priori element in human knowledge independent of the senses.

For Aquinas our indirect self-consciousness is in no wise a priori since it arises in us only through and in our direct consciousness of the material world. Only reflexively do we know ourselves directly and clearly. For Aquinas, therefore, Christ's self-awareness of his divinity would have been possible only through the objective beatific vision of God. Yet there is no contradiction in claiming that at the same time he had ordinary human thought processes. Nevertheless, Aquinas's claim that Jesus knew himself as God in the beatific vision attributes to him a more perfect way of knowing his Divine Person than the merely indirect, horizon-like mode that Rahner suggests. A child, just as an adult, has an indirect self-consciousness but very little direct self-understanding. Human maturity, on the other hand, consists in achieving a direct objective understanding of one's self. In Aquinas's theory Jesus had that mature knowledge from the moment of his conception and hypostatic union with the Divine Son; yet this did not prevent him from also acquiring knowledge in the ordinary human way in the course of a maturing lifetime.[16]

15 Karl Rahner, SJ, "Dogmatic Reflections on the Knowledge and Self-Consciousness of Christ," *Theological Investigations*, vol. 5, 193–218.

16 Aquinas's claim that Jesus had not only the beatific vision but mature human knowledge at the moment of his conception does indeed seem extravagant. One must take into account his Aristotelian embryology that today concerns the abortion question; cf. the essay "When Does a Human Person Begin to Exist?" in this collection. St. Thomas thought that God creates the human spiritual soul with its intelligence only

O'Collins and Kendall raise two other related difficulties for Aquinas's teaching. The Gospels seem to indicate that Jesus in his earthly life experienced the human process of learning and in certain passages such as Mark 5:30–32, 13:32 seem to indicate that his human knowledge was limited. Thus we read in Mark, "And Jesus, perceiving in himself that power had gone forth from him, immediately turned about in the crowd, and said, 'Who touched my garments?' . . . And he looked around to see who had done it" (5:30, 32), and also that Jesus said of the Last Judgment, "But of that day or that hour no one knows, not even the angels in heaven, nor the Son, but only the Father" (13:32). There are similar passages in all four Gospels.

Aquinas, of course, was well aware that these passages had been troubling to the Church Fathers. He did not claim that the human intelligence of Christ was comprehensively omniscient as he was in his divinity, since the human soul, while by grace it is open to the vision of God as he truly is finds his infinite truth inexhaustible.[17] Yet Jesus in the beatific vision that he possessed in this life knew all about creatures that there is to know.[18] In addition to this, according to Aquinas, Jesus acquired knowledge in the human manner by the intellectual analysis of the information received through his bodily senses.[19] We humans learn in two ways: by finding out the truth for ourselves or by being taught. Aquinas says that the former way is superior and therefore, "It was more fitting for Christ to have his acquired knowledge

---

when its bodily instrument is sufficiently formed some weeks after conception. This instrument is the central organ or prime mover of the body that is the organ of sensation; for Aristotle and Aquinas, the heart, for us the brain. Hence the child from the first moment it exists can have the sense of touch that is the minimal requirement of intellection. Since, however, Jesus' conception was miraculous, St. Thomas supposed that for Jesus this happened with Mary's consent to Gabriel's message. With modern embryology we must conclude that human conception and creation of the soul naturally occurs at fertilization of the ovum when the human genome is complete since from then on the maturation of the human person is self-development. The brain does not yet exist. However, what is primordial to the brain, namely the information in the nucleus of the zygote that will build the brain, exists in the genome. Hence, contrary to Aquinas, it seems impossible to attribute to the zygote body any actual capability of sensation. This, however, does not negate Aquinas's principal argument, namely, that Jesus' human intelligence could have had "infused" knowledge, like the separated soul or an angel, since that is not derived form the senses. Hence, Jesus in the womb of Mary, even before his body had developed a brain, could have been miraculously conscious of his Father, his own Divine Person as Son, and of his mission from his Father and thus have freely committed himself to that mission for our sake. Since John the Baptist at a later stage in the womb was already a prophet (Lk 1:41), why would we deny this was more perfectly true of Jesus? To assert this in no way minimizes the humanity of either John or Jesus.

[17] *Summa theologiae* II, q. 10, a. 3.

[18] Ibid., III, q. 9, a. 1.

[19] Ibid., III, q. 9, a. 4.

by his own efforts than from teaching."[20] This does not seem absolutely to exclude that Jesus learned from others, but simply to say that he was first and foremost a teacher not a pupil.

The Fourth Gospel is more insistent than the Synoptic Gospels on Jesus' "clairvoyance." Thus on John 6:15, "Then Jesus, because he knew they were going to come and seize him by force to make him king, withdrew again up the mountainside alone," Aquinas comments:

> In Christ was a threefold knowledge. First, he had sense knowledge and in this respect was like the Prophets in that certain sensible images could be formed in Christ's imagination by which future or hidden things could be represented which was appropriate to his state in this life. Second was an intellectual knowledge and in this he was unlike the Prophets but was above the angels because he was in more excellent possession [of the beatific vision] than any creature. Third was the divine cognition and in respect to this he was the inspirer of the Prophets and the angels, since all cognition is a participation in the Divine Word.[21]

Thus for Aquinas the first of the foregoing texts in Mark and others like them refer to Jesus' behavior that was appropriate to his human nature in ordinary situations, in this case, to ask the people about him to point out the woman who had touched him when he was not looking, just as any prophet might do even if he at the same time was clairvoyant. As Jesus did not work miracles except for special reasons, so he would not have used his clairvoyance openly except for some special reason. As for the second statement that even the Son does not know the time of the judgment, the Fathers of the Church recognized that this is a rhetorical way of emphasizing that Jesus' mission from the Father did not permit him to make this particular revelation and cannot be taken literally.

The final objection of our authors is their assertion that the hypostatic union in Christ of a divine and human nature does not necessarily imply that Jesus possessed the beatific vision in his human nature. On this fundamental problem a distinction, based on Aquinas's statements already quoted, is necessary. If we consider only the ontology of this unfathomable mystery we find no absolute reason to say that it would have been impossible for the Divine Word to have assumed human nature without bestowing the beatific vision on its intellectual power. Yet if we take into consideration, as Aquinas does, the purpose of the Incarnation, then Aquinas's argument for his thesis has great force. The Word became incarnate in order to make it possible

---

[20] Ibid., II, q. 9, a. 4 ad 1.
[21] *Super Ioannis,* c. vi, lect. 2, n. 870.

again for all humanity to attain the beatific vision. Since the cause must contain what it effects, a fountain must be filled with water, and it is the Word in his human nature that is the source of the gift of the beatific vision that we hope to enjoy and which he himself enjoys in a supreme way.

It could still be objected that while this argument holds for the Risen Christ ascended to the Father in eternity it need not have been so during his earthly life, since our salvation comes after his resurrection. I believe that is really what O'Collins and Kendall have in mind. But this would not satisfy Aquinas. For him Christ's salvific mission and meriting of our salvation begins as soon as he assumes human nature. It is not the Risen Christ that merits our salvation but the earthly Christ as present among us. Every moment of his life is the fulfillment of his saving mission and this is possible only because he already has attained in his human nature the goal that he has been sent to bring us to at last.

At the very end of the Fourth Gospel (21:25) we read: "There are many other things that Jesus did. If every one of them were written down, I suppose the whole world would not have room for the books that would be written." St. Thomas comments on this text:

> To write down one by one the signs and works of Jesus Christ is to summarize the power of each and all these words and doings; but the words and works of Christ are also those of God. And if anyone might wish to explain each of them, he would be utterly unable; for the whole world could not do this, because all the words we humans have cannot say as much as the One Word of God. Thus from the beginning of the Church all writing was about Christ but it was never enough; furthermore if the world should endure for a hundred thousand years books can be written about Christ but not enough to perfectly sum up what he has done and said. As it is said at the end of Ecclesiasticus 12, "There is no end to writing books," and Psalm 40:5 says, "I have uttered these things and spoken them, but they are too numerous to recount!"[22]

Thus with Aquinas we must humbly kneel in contemplation and adoration before the mystery of the Word made flesh.

---

[22] Ibid., concluding words of commentary, c. xii, lect. 6, n. 2660.

CHAPTER 10

The Priesthood of Christ, of the Baptized, and of the Ordained*

Priest or Presbyter

CANDIDATES FOR ORDINATION TO THE PRIESTHOOD need to know in what the Christian priesthood—for all the many forms it has taken and may take historically—essentially consists. All the baptized also need to know both what is the essential character of their own general priesthood and its relation to the ordained priesthood. Sound theological methodology seems to demand that we look for this answer first of all in Scripture in the context of Sacred Tradition. Moreover, we need to consider how contemporary experience as a part of that living tradition is renewing that understanding in its application to the present situation of the Church.

The very term "priest" is, as we shall see in some detail later, not very clear to many. In a recent study of comparative religion, Dale Cannon identifies six functions common to almost all known religions that he calls the "ways" of dealing with "ultimate reality": (1) "sacred rite"; (2) "right action"; (3) "devotion"; (4) "shamanic mediation" (5) "mystical quest; and, (6) "reasoned inquiry." He defines "priest" or "priestess" as "a master of sacred ritual, a keeper of the rites, who is duly authorized to perform them." A "sacred rite" is an action that symbolizes some "ultimate reality" and connects those who perform it and those for whom they perform it with this "ultimate reality."[1]

At least one of the reasons that Vatican II[2] preferred the term "presbyter" to "priest" was that it also assigned to the presbyterate a participation in the

---

* This was published in Donald J. Goergen and Ann Garrido, eds., *The Theology of Priesthood* (Collegeville, MN: The Liturgical Press, 2001), 139–64.

[1] Dale Cannon, *Six Ways of Being Religious: A Framework for Comparative Studies of Religion.*

[2] For Vatican II's extensive teaching on the priesthood, see the documents *Lumen Gentium*, No. 21, 1964; *Christus Dominus*, October 28, 1965; *Presbyterorum Ordinis*,

threefold offices *(munera)* of Christ as prophet, king, and priest.[3] In this way it avoided the confusion of saying that a "priest" who had the threefold offices of prophet, king, *and priest* thus using "priest" in two senses, first as the name of a threefold office, and second as the name of only one of these offices. Yet in some later magisterial documents there has been a reversion to the term "priest" in the first sense. Two factors have favored this reversion. First, the term "priest" is much more familiar than the term "presbyter," and in the United States the latter tends to be confused with the "Presbyterian" denomination. Second, for traditional theology the priestly office is given preeminence over the other two offices. It is precisely this evaluation that is today in question, since some argue that it is the shepherd (king) of the community who presides at the Eucharist and hence the pastoral (kingly) role has preeminence. While others argue that since, as St. Paul says, "faith comes through hearing"(Rm 10:17) and Christian community and worship flow from faith, preaching (prophecy) is preeminent. Others hold that the three offices are co-equal. Others even question whether this is really the best way to describe Christian ministry. To avoid taking a position at the outset, I will use the term "presbyter" for the ordained minister who by ordination is empowered to lead the community in the celebration of the Eucharist and also to be preacher. I will until its proper place in my argument make no claim that one or other of the three offices is to be ranked above the others. I also will not here distinguish between the "bishop" and the "presbyter" According to Vatican II consecration to the episcopacy is a true and distinct sacrament that confers the

---

December 7, 1965; *Optatam Totius,* October 28, 1965; *Apostolicam Actuositatem,* November 18, 1965. This conciliar teaching has also been synthesized and precisely formulated in the *Catechism of the Catholic Church* I, Article 9, nn. 748–975 on the Church and II, chapter 3, Article 6, nn. 1536–40, and on the Sacrament of Holy Orders. Theological analyses taking into account Vatican II teaching are David Power, OMI, *Ministers of Christ and His Church: The Theology of Priesthood*; Albert Vanhoye, SJ, *Old Testament Priests and New Priests According to the New Testament*; and Jean Galot, *Theology of the Priesthood.*

[3] See Peter J. Drilling, " 'The Priest, Prophet and King Trilogy' Elements of Its Meaning in *Lumen Gentium* and for Today," *Église et Theologie* 19 (1988): 179–206, who warns that these are not "divided functions of ministry" but inseparable aspects of "service." I would add that this concept had roots in Jewish Christianity as is evident from the following passage in the Jewish Christian *Clementine Recognitions and Homilies,* Basic Source (B), dated by Harnack c. 220 B.C. See Edgar Hennecke and Wilhelm Schneemelcher, *New Testament Apocrypha,* 128–43. "Now also if someone else was anointed with that oil, in the same way having received power from it he became either a king, a prophet or a high priest. If this temporal grace composed by humans was this powerful, then understand how great that ointment is that was taken by God from the tree of life, for the one that was made by humans confers such exceptional dignities among humans. For what in the present age is more glorious than a prophet, more celebrated than a high priest, more sublime than a king?" (1.46.3–5).

"fullness of the priesthood." Evidently the term "priesthood" here refers to the entire threefold ministry to which both presbyter and bishop are ordained, but the bishop has a greater sacramental power since he can confer Holy Orders. No doubt his preaching and pastoral functions also have a fullness not given to the presbyter, but that issue will not be discussed here.

My concern in this paper is to give a precise theological answer based on Sacred Scripture and Sacred Tradition to the question of the candidate for presbyteral ordination, as well as to the laity, as to the essential nature of this office. I can think of three ways to answer this question from the New Testament. The first is by a historical reconstruction of the development of church order in the first century. After the time of Ignatius of Antioch in the first half of the second century and of Irenaeus in the second half the threefold system of the Sacrament of Holy Orders, bishop, priest, and deacon and the primacy of the Bishop of Rome is historically stable. The difficulty with this way, however, is that the New Testament evidence is very sparse and difficult to interpret because the terminology is ambiguous and the data very indirect. This route has been thoroughly researched with little or no new data for over one hundred years. Scholars now largely agree that in this period church structure was evolving and varied from place to place and in particular that monepiscopy was not yet established. They seem especially sure that in Rome there were many heads of house churches, who were in effect bishops, none of whom was the Bishop of Rome. The trouble with this consensus, however, as has been well pointed out by David Albert Jones, OP, in his answer to Eamon Duffy's *Saints and Sinners: A History of the Popes* when he says:

> Yet though sensitive historians like Chadwick can see the dangers of idealising the apostolic order of ministry, they are consistently unaware how deeply this mindset has informed the interpretation of the evidence. The whole notion of the evolution, revolution, or supposed radical development in ministry in the first century is in fact a supposition *imported* by the observer. It is a classic case of theory distorting observation. There is a pervasive underlying mindset that idealises early ministry as free, loose, inspired and lay, and sees the emergence of clerical forms as a fall from primitive innocence.[4]

This bias is evident in such terms as "the Jesus Movement" and is favored by concerns to maximize flexibility to accommodate ecumenical dialogue and to open the way to changes in church structure that might permit more room for lay ministry or even women's ordination. Since theology ought not to fall into either the extreme of anachronism or that of evolutionary bias, I believe that this way of historical reconstruction is not satisfactory.

---

[4] "Was There a Bishop of Rome in the First Century?" *New Blackfriars* 60 (March 1999): 128–43.

This does not mean that historical research is irrelevant. It provides a historical context in which to read the Scriptures even if it cannot give us a definitive answer to our question.[5] A second route to an answer to our question is to study the texts of the New Testament, beginning with the Words of Institution of the Eucharist documented by St. Paul (1 Cor. 11:23–26) as early as A.D. 56–57[6] and supported by the Synoptic Gospels. To this key text one can then add other materials in which Jesus seems to portray himself as the Suffering Servant whose death will redeem the world and St. Paul's references to his own sufferings and that of other Christians as sacrificial, since such texts make use of metaphors derived from the Jewish sacrificial worship.[7] I believe that this way is valid, but it runs into problems because of the current controversies about "metaphor" and "analogy."[8] Hence I prefer here to treat it as secondary and supportive of my thesis but not its foundation.

The third way of answering the question from Scripture is to begin with the only text in Scripture in which the problem is directly addressed in terms of the relation of the "priesthood" of the New Testament in relation to that of the Old Testament. This is the Epistle to the Hebrews (Heb 3:3) that explicitly uses the term *hiereus* (*sacerdos,* priest) to translate the Hebrew *kohen.* To this datum can then be added the only other texts of the New Testament where

---

[5] My own hesitancy to accept the consensus criticized by Jones is reinforced by reflection on the history of the beginnings of the Dominican and Franciscan Orders. I am suspicious of the assumption that the traditional structure of religious institutions must have had a protracted period of evolution. The Franciscan Order did have such a period, and a very stormy one, because the Seraphic Saint had no interest in organization; but the Order of Preachers received essentially the same structure it has today at its first two General Chapters in 1220 and 1221 under the presidency of St. Dominic, whose gifts as a political organizer were remarkable. One can, of course, think that Our Lord was like St. Francis, but since I think Jesus was also like St. Dominic, I think we cannot assume that the evolution of the basic structure of the Christian community took long to crystallize.

[6] Raymond E. Brown, *Introduction to the New Testament,* 510–15.

[7] In the conference out of which this article was written, I several times objected to the use of the term "cultic" as having pejorative connotations today. As is well known, Protestant writers often compare the "prophetic" to the "cultic" in depreciation of the latter. Moreover, the term "cult" today is associated with religious aberrations. I believe in the interests of objectivity it is better to avoid the term.

[8] For some of the problems about metaphor and symbol see Louis-Marie Chauvet, *Symbol and Sacrament: A Sacramental Reinterpretation of Christian Experience.* The concern of such authors to avoid the "idolatry of onto-theology" due to their reliance on Martin Heidegger seems to me based on a misunderstanding of Aquinas's analysis of analogy and causality and that it results in an excessively apophatic theology. Of course God is infinitely other than our conceptions of his Mystery, but He has taken the trouble to reveal himself to us in human nature and human language and it is theology's business to try to understand that message not simply to play a game of hide-and-seek of "revealing and concealing" in the pretentious manner of Heidegger.

this term is also used, 1 Peter 2:9–10, which is quoting Exodus 19:6 which is also referred to in Revelation 1:6 and 20:6.[9]

Was Jesus a Priest *(Hiereus, Sacerdos)*?

The Gospels make quite clear that the early church considered Jesus a prophet. They all portray John the Baptist as a genuine prophet and then argue that Jesus was far greater than John. They also portray his ministry as one of preaching the coming of the Kingdom of God that was witnessed by miracles just as had been the ministry of Elijah, type of all the Old Testament prophets. The early Church was also concerned to show that Jesus was a king, the Messiah (Greek *Christos*, the Anointed One) as was evident in the Infancy Narratives that trace his descent from David. He was to fulfill the Old Testament prophecies by being invested by a ceremony of anointment with the same divine authority conferred on David as King and on his successors. To avoid a political understanding of his mission, however, Jesus did not make this claim for himself publicly or permit the Twelve to do so. Yet privately he accepted Peter's profession of faith in him as the Christ (Mk 8:27–30, Mt 16:13–20; Lk 9:18–21). According to the Synoptics, Jesus, even when asked by Pilate at his trial whether he was "the King of the Jews," only replied, "You say so" (Mk 15:2; Mt 27:11; Lk 23:3) and remained silent. Yet according to the Johannine tradition (Jn 18:8–40) Jesus further explained this by saying "My kingdom is not of this world."[10]

There was question, however, whether Jesus was also a priest. Certainly Jesus was not a "priest" as Jews understood the term. He was not even an ordained rabbi.[11] In the eyes of his contemporaries Jesus was just a layman. His legal father, Joseph, was a member of the tribe of Judah, not of Levi

---

[9] *The Exegetical Dictionary of the New Testament,* article *hiereus*, vol. 2, 174ff., the noun is used 31 times, of which 14 are in Heb; Mk, 2; Mt, 3; Lk, 5; Acts, 3; Jn, 1; and Rev 3 times, but refer only to Old Testament or pagan priests except in 1 Pt and Rev as cited in my text. *Hierateia* (priestly office) occurs only in Lk 1:9, where it refers to Jewish presthood; *hierateuma* (priesthood) only in 1 Pt 2, 5, 9. These terms are derived from *hieros* (holy) for which, however, the more common term is *hagios*. Holz Goldstein in the article on *hierateuma*, 173, makes the point that, "the four terms *hierateuma, hagios, thusia* and *pneumatikos* interpret one another." He also notes that "the author of 1 Pt in 2:4–5 introduces this quote with the phrase 'let yourselves be built into a spiritual house to be a holy priesthood *(herateuma)* to offer spiritual sacrifices acceptable to God through Jesus Christ.' Thus the inspired writers understand that the defining function of the New Testament priesthood is to 'offer spiritual sacrifices.' "

[10] Raymond E. Brown, SS, *The Death of the Messiah: from Gethsemane to the Grave: a Commentary on the Passion Narrative in the Four Gospels*, deals in detail with the different traditions of the passion narrative.

[11] The date at which rabbis began to be "ordained," not as priests, of course, but as authentic students of the Torah, is uncertain, but it was probably after the fall of the Temple.

from which the hereditary Jewish priesthood had to come (Mt 1:1–18; Lk 2:4–5, 3:1–38).

Was this a problem for early Christians? And if so, why? There is some evidence in the Dead Sea Scrolls that at least Jews of Jesus' time expected both a "Messiah of David" and a "Messiah of Aaron," and perhaps thought of these titles as joined in one person. However that may be, what really raised the question was the destruction of the Temple in A.D. 70 which the Gospels claim was predicted by Jesus himself. That destruction meant the end of Old Testament sacrificial worship. How then could the Christians, most of whom were still Jews, carry on worship? It is true that the Jews had worshipped in the Exile before the rebuilding of the Temple, continued to do so in the Diaspora before its fall, and that worship has continued among Jews without the Temple. But this had and has always a provisional character until the Messiah comes. For the Jewish Christians, since they believed Jesus was the Messiah, this could not be an adequate answer. It was necessary, therefore, that someone give this answer and it was given by the anonymous author of Hebrews. The urgency of this question may not be evident to us today because we are used to a separation of church and state. In the ancient world, however, the idea that a nation could exist without its gods, and therefore, without a priesthood to carry on their worship was unthinkable.

Was Jesus a priest? For the church of New Testament times and today for all those who accept the inspiration of the Bible, the Epistle to the Hebrews settles that question without ambiguity. Even from a literary point of view Hebrews is one of the most impressive books of the New Testament, although we are not sure who was its author.[12] Because of the style of the epistle many of the Church Fathers doubted that St. Paul was its author and so do most exegetes today. Nevertheless, it is an inspired, canonical work and may have been written before the Fall of the Jerusalem in A.D. 70 since it seems to assume that the Temple services were still continuing (Heb 10:1–3, etc.). Some exegetes explain these passages as mere references to the Old Testament

---

[12] Possible authors are Apollos (Acts 18:24–28; 1 Cor 3:6, etc.) or Clement of Rome (Phil 4:3; Origen) or even Barnabas. On this whole question, see the recent work of Roland Minnerath, *De Jerusalem a Rome: Pierre et l'Unite de l'Eglise Apostolique,* 495–501. Hebrews, as its contents and traditional title indicate, was probably sent to a predominantly Jewish-Christian community, and probably to one in Rome. It must be before I Clement, which is commonly dated A.D. 95 but by some recent authors as early as A.D. 70. See Minnerath, 558–67, and T. J. Herron, *The Most Probable Date of the First Epistle of Clement to the Corinthians.* Marie E. Isaacs, *Sacred Space: An Approach to the Theology of the Epistle to the Hebreux,* JSNT. Supplement Series 73, places Hebrews near A.D. 70. Paul Ellingworth, *The Epistle to the Hebrews: A Commentary on the Greek Text,* 31–33, holds it written to Rome before A.D. 70 and cites many authors of the same opinion. Raymond E. Brown and John Meier, *Antioch and Rome: Cradles of Catholic Christianity,* 139–49, are less certain but do not put it beyond the second Christian generation.

prescriptions for these services. Yet surely if the author wrote after the destruction of the Temple, he would have mentioned the abolition of the temple sacrifices as a striking proof of his thesis that the services of the Old Law were only temporary, a mere shadow of the things to come.[13]

It is obvious enough why this epistle, in spite of the obscurity of its author, was thought by the early Church to be important enough to be included in the canon. On the basis of many Old Testament references it eloquently argues that (1) Jesus Christ is the Son of God superior to all creation; (2) yet he is also truly human, in all but sin like one of us; and (3) and therefore, as the Christ, he is our Mediator.[14] He is the only true priest who is able with us and for us to offer himself to God as a worthy sacrifice and thus bring us the gift of salvation from God, his Father. Thus, although St. Paul and the Gospels never speak explicitly of Jesus as a priest, Hebrews firmly insists that he is not only a priest but also the only true priest. Moreover, though the Synoptics and Paul do not speak of Jesus as a "priest," they relate his solemn words and actions at the Last Supper. What could be more clearly a priestly act than his sharing of the bread and wine as he said to the Twelve, "This is my body that is for you. . . . This cup is the new covenant in my blood. Do this, as often as you drink it, in remembrance of me," thus symbolizing the coming sacrifice of the Cross (1 Cor 11:23–34; cf. 10:16–17; Mk 14:22–26; Mt 26:26–29; Lk 22:14–23)? Certainly these many references make clear that the early Church understood the Last Supper as a cultic, sacrificial, priestly act on Jesus' part to be continued as a central practice in the Christian community.

Central to the whole argument of Hebrews is its claim that this sacrificial death of Jesus was one true sacrifice that can take away sin.[15] Hence, Jesus is the one and only true High Priest of whom the Aaronic priests of the Old Testament were merely prophetic types. Thus the author of Hebrews surely would have granted that the Last Supper that prefigures Jesus' sacrificial death was itself also a prophetic, priestly action. For some exegetes who favor the Protestant emphasis on preaching the Word as against Catholic emphasis on the priestly

---

[13] This argument is supported by both Isaacs and Ellingworth.

[14] In my analysis of Hebrews I have used Albert Vanhoye, SJ, *La Structure littéraire de l'"Épître aux Hébreux,"* and Louis Dussaut, *Synopse Structurelle de l'Épître aux Hebreux: Approche d'Analyse Structurelle.*

[15] St. Thomas Aquinas, *Summa theologiae* II–II, q. 85, a. 1, explains why the duty to offer *sacrifice* to God pertains to the natural law. On this universality see D. M. Knope's article in *The Perennial Dictionary of World Religions*, edited by Keith Crim et al., 637–40. The current tendency to avoid the notion of the Eucharist as "sacrifice" and to emphasize the notion of "meal," neglects the fact that a sacrifice is not just "giving up something" but a *gift* by which the giver and God are united. Hence the sacred banquet in which the sacrificial gift is shared by both parties is a symbol of their union. See 1 Corinthians 10:18–21 in which St. Paul clearly compares the Eucharistic banquet to both the Temple sacrifices and pagan sacrifices.

administration of the sacraments, the term "cultic" has negative connotations. These scholars also exaggerate the contrast between the prophetic and the priestly traditions of the Old Testament. It is true that the prophets often denounce those who obey the cultic prescriptions of the Law while neglecting its moral commandments. "Obedience is better than sacrifice" (1 Sm 15:22). "Cult," however, simply means "worship" and nowhere in the Bible do "worship" or "priest" as such have negative connotations. Quite the contrary "priesthood" and "worship" (whatever may be said of particular priests and their fidelity to their calling), when they are in the service of the One God, are for the Bible always positive terms (Gn 14:18). That is why Hebrews (3:3) is so concerned to show that Jesus was not only a priest, but also the High Priest, the Supreme Priest. Thus, any attempt to address the question of Christian priesthood theologically ought to begin with the truth of revelation that so profoundly establishes it. Strictly speaking there can be only one priest, Jesus Christ, as true Man and True God, the sole Mediator between God and humanity who has offered one sufficient sacrifice, the sacrifice of himself on the Cross.[16]

The Priesthood of the Baptized

Protestant Christians sometimes ask, "If, as Hebrews so clearly teaches, Jesus is the only priest and his offering on the Cross was a wholly sufficient sacrifice for sins (Heb 10:11–18), how can priests be ordained to daily offer the Eucharist as a sacrifice? Is not the Christian minister ordained to be a preacher of the gospel not a cultic priest?" They also point out that the leaders of the New Testament communities are called not "priests" but "elders" (presbyters).[17] Yet at the same time Protestants cannot pass over important biblical texts outside Hebrews. In the First Epistle of St. Peter we read,

> You are a chosen race, a royal priesthood, a holy nation, a people of his
> [God's] own, so that you may announce the praises' of him who called

---

[16] Joseph A. Fitzmeyer, SJ, *New Jerome Biblical Commentary*, 1395ff., shows that Jesus clearly underwent death in voluntary obedience to his mission from the Father, that is, he "offered" himself for the salvation of the people. Thus he, not his killers, was the priest of that sacrifice. Fitzmeyer thinks that though Paul emphasizes the salvific effect of Jesus' death and resurrection, he did understood Jesus' death as a sacrifice, remembered in the Eucharist, in which Christians share by baptism, and in which his own mission as apostle was a participation. Moreover, it is clear that in this teaching Paul was transmitting the *kerygma* handed down to him. Note also that theologically the canonization of Hebrews makes its interpretation of the tradition a part of the *depositum fidei*.

[17] A Protestant author who has recently studied this question thoroughly, R. Alastair Campbell, *The Elders: Seniority Within Earliest Christianity*, concludes that in the Early Church milieu "elder" was simply a title of dignity in general. Thus it was appropriate for those holding an office of leadership in the early church before a more specifically theological term had been established.

you out of darkness into his wonderful light. Once you were "no people" but now you are "God's people."[18]

This text, which quotes Exodus 19:6 with reference to the Chosen People, is also supported by the prophecy made to the Jews that in the Messianic age, "You yourselves shall be named priests of the Lord, ministers of our God you shall be called" (Is 61:6). The meaning of these texts is that God has chosen and consecrated Israel as his own people in a Covenant by which they are bound to worship him only. This thought is carried further by two other texts of Trito-Isaiah:

And the foreigners who join themselves to the Lord,
    ministering to him,
Loving the name of the Lord
    and becoming his servants
All who keep the sabbath free from profanation
    and hold to my covenant,
Them, I will bring to my holy mountain
    and make joyful in my house of prayer.
Their holocausts and sacrifices
    will be acceptable on my altar,
For my house shall be called a house of prayer
    for all peoples. (Is 56:6–7)

I come to gather nations of every language;
    they shall come and see my glory . . .
Some of these I will take as priests and Levites,
    says the Lord." (Is 66:18–21)

Thus the Jewish people are called to be the mediator by which the True God will become known to all nations; and the Gentiles too will come to worship God in the Jerusalem Temple and from even these pagans some will be chosen to be priests. Hence these prophecies in their Christian fulfillment are not primarily made to individuals, but to the Church as a corporate body and hence to its members who by baptism have become parts of that corporate whole. "We," says St. Paul, "are one body in Christ, and individually parts of

---

[18] William J. Dalton, SJ, *New Jerome Biblical Commentary,* 903ff., holds that 1 Peter is Petrine (perhaps St. Peter through a secretary) and says, "[T]here is good reason for dating 1 Pt just before Peter's death, which took place probably in A.D. 65," and he holds that this epistle is of Roman origin. Unless a later date for Hebrews is proved, the two works were probably written in the same period and have much in common with the Pauline literature. On the relation of 1 Peter to 2 Peter, which is probably the last book in the New Testament canon and pseudonymous, see Jerome H. Neyrey, SJ, *New Jerome Biblical Commentary,* 1017ff.

one another" (Rm 12:5). The Christian Community, the Church, is a "chosen race" or "nation," who are "God's people," his very "own" consecrated by Christ as "holy," and as a "royal" "kingdom." The Church is "priestly" because it is called to "announce his [God's] praises" in a worthy way, that is, through Christ as God has himself willed.

The Book of Revelation confirms this teaching of First Peter when it speaks of Christ, "who has made us into a kingdom, priests for his God and Father, to him be glory and power forever. Amen" (Rv 2:6). You made them a kingdom and priests for our God, and they will reign on earth" (Rv 5:9). "The second death has no power over these; they will be priests of God and Christ, and they will reign with him for the thousand years" (Rv 20:6). This is the universal priesthood of all the baptized, recognized by the Second Vatican Council. It is symbolically effected in the chrismatic anointing of the Sacrament of Confirmation that follows baptism.

In Vatican II's *Dogmatic Constitution on the Church* we read:

[The] faithful are by baptism made one body with Christ and are established among the People of God. They are in their own way made sharers in the priestly, prophetic, and kingly functions of Christ. They carry out their own part in the mission of the whole Christian people with respect to the Church and the world. (n. 31)[19]

We can conclude that the term "priest" (Greek *hierous*, Latin *sacerdos*) can and must be applied to all Christians, not indeed univocally but by analogy to the perfect priesthood of Christ. All other priesthood than Christ's can only be some form of participation in Christ's from which it must derive its whole meaning and power. When Jesus said, "Call no one on earth your father, you have one Father in heaven" (Mt 23:9), he was not denying that we have fathers and mothers whom we are commanded by God the Father to honor (Mt 15:4). Rather he was teaching that human fatherhood is only a share in that of the Supreme Father and Creator, the one perfect father.

Similarly, though Christ is the one priest, all those baptized as members of Christ's body, and who through him worship the Father in the Holy Spirit, truly share in his priesthood. I might, therefore, have said to the young priest, "You may be right that Jesus was a layman, but certainly you were wrong to say that he was not a priest. Christ is the only Priest and we baptized Christians are priests only in and for him as we are the Church. The Church is Christ's holy body nourished on his Eucharistic Body and Blood offered for the world once and for all time on the Cross.[20]

---

[19] *Lumen Gentium*, n. 10, 2.

[20] *Apostolicam Actuositatem*, n. 2, "The characteristic of the lay state being a life led in the midst of the world and of secular affairs, layperson are called by God to make their apostolate, through the vigor of their Christian spirit, a leaven in the world."

The Ordained Priest

The teaching of Hebrews that Christ is the only priest implies a certain ecclesiology.[21] As Moses was the mediator of the imperfect former Covenant, so Christ is the mediator of the perfect new and final Covenant. Since the first Covenant was not made merely with individuals but with the Chosen People, Israel, so the new Covenant is made with the new Israel, the Christian community, the Church. Since for Hebrews the Church owes its very existence as a priestly people to its Head, Jesus Christ the High Priest, it is a *hierachical* organization.[22] The term "hierarchy,"[23] although it was used by Vatican II in *Lumen Gentium* without apology, today is anathema to some for whom it

---

[21] See Jean Delorme, General Ed., Paul Bony et al., *Les ministère et les ministeres selon le Nouveau Testament: dossier exegétique et réflexion théologique.* Chapter VI on Hebrews is by Charles Perrot, 118–37. The first Part is on the New Testament, book by book. The second part is theological reflections.

[22] St. Paul greets the "bishops and deacons" at Philippi (Phil 1:1). In the Pastoral Epistles, dated (Brown) in the late first century we read of "bishops" and "deacons" and "widows." In 1 Clement (c. 70–95) no mention is made of a bishop at Rome, but the letter concerns rebellion against "presbyters" at Corinth. By the time of St. Ignatius of Antioch (d. 107–17) there is a monarchical bishop in Jerusalem and the churches of Asia Minor, along with a presbyterate and deacons. In the *Didache* (c. A.D. 100) we read of "bishops," "deacons," and itinerant "prophets." By the time of St. Irenaeus (fl. 177), who knew St. Polycarp who knew St. John and St. Ignatius, the threefold hierarchy and the Bishop of Rome are well established. Our data, however, is haphazard and scanty. Hence various reconstructions of the data are possible, but the essential points are: (1) The Church was never just a "Jesus Movement" but an organized community of communities; (2) Though the whole community participated in selecting leaders, *apostolic authority* was required for valid Church office. E. Schillebeeckx tried to question this in *Ministry* and *The Church with a Human Face*, but has been well answered by Pierre Grelot, *Église et ministères: pour un dialogue critique avec Edward Schillebeeckx.* Albert Vanhoye, SJ, and Henri Crouzel, SJ, "The Ministry in the Church: Reflections on a Recent Publication," *The Clergy Review* 5 (68; May 1983): 156–74; and Walter Kasper, "Ministry in the Church: Taking Issue with Edward Schillebeeckx," *Communio* (Summer 1983): 185–95. The Sacred Congregation for the Doctrine of the Faith had a formal dialogue with Schillebeeckx on his position and asked him to correct it. This he attempted in the second of the books above, but the Congregation declared his answer did not meet their objections. (*Lettera Sacerdotium ministeriale, Circa il ministro dell'eucaristia,* 1983. *Notificazoine della Congregazione per la Dottrina della Fede,* 15 September 1986. In *L'Osservatore Romano,* 24 September 1986.) On modes of choice of leaders, see Alexandre Faivre, *Naissance d'une hiérarchie: Les premières étapes du cursus clérical* and Jean Gaudemet, "The Choice of Bishops: A Tortuous History," in *Concilium* 1996, 3; and *From Life to Law,* edited by James Provost and Knut Walf, 59–65.

[23] On the introduction of the term "hierarchy" into theology by the Pseudo-Dionysius and the difference between his ecclesiology and that of Aquinas, see my essay, "Cosmic Community in Plotinus, Aquinas, and Whitehead," *Cultura y Vida* (XX Semana Tomista, 1995), Appendix A, 33. This essay is included in the present collection in revised form with the title "Hierarchy in Ecclesiology."

seems to mean "an oppressive power." In fact it is derived from the Greek *hieros*, sacred, and *arche*, a principle of order, and hence simply means "sacred order." The Church is no mere mob or loose "Jesus Movement," but an organic, well-structured, dynamically acting community whose organization is determined by its spiritual mission. This is well brought out by two biblical metaphors. The First Epistle of St. Peter (1 Pt 2:4–8) compares Christians to "living stones" to "be built into a spiritual house to be a holy priesthood to offer spiritual sacrifices acceptable to God through Jesus Christ." Of this edifice Christ is himself also a "living stone," but he is the "corner stone. The second metaphor elaborated by St. Paul in the twelfth chapter of First Corinthians compares the Church to a living body with its differentiated organs among which Christ is the head. Since Paul used this metaphor to restore order in the Corinthian church he evidently had in mind not just Christ invisibly present, but the community leaders who represented Christ in that church.

These metaphors, therefore, make clear that the Church is hierarchical, that is, has a sacred order in which Christ as High Priest is the *hierarch*, the principle of that organic order. Since the Church is Christ's body by which he remains visibly present and active in mission in the world, its leaders must also sacramentally signify that priestly presence *within* the Church. To say, as do some Protestant theologians, that Christ's presence is sufficiently manifested in the preaching of his Word minimizes the Incarnation. Christ is indeed present through the preacher, but also through the sacraments, and above all through the communal offering of the Eucharist. All three offices of Christ, pastoring, preaching, sanctifying are inseparably related in Christ as Head of the Church and therefore also in his sacramental representative within the community.[24] Precisely because the ordained priest represents Christ his role cannot be that of oppressive domination but like Christ's is that of a servant. Did Jesus not say of himself, "The Son of Man did not come to be served but to serve and to give his life as a ransom for many" (Mt 20:28)?

Hebrews itself does not, like the Gospels and St. Paul, speak of Jesus as "head of the body, the Church" nor as "servant." Yet it conveys the same truth by emphasizing Christ's priestly role as a mediator. Unless Christ was both "head of his body, the Church" (Eph 5:23) and also its Servant, he could not mediate between God and the People. As supreme head of his people, the

---

24 As a Dominican I call attention to the way this is put for members of the Order of Preachers in our *Fundamental Constitution*, V: "Since by priestly *[sacerdotalem]* ordination, we are co-workers with the episcopacy, we have as our special charge the prophetical function by which-with due regard for the changing conditions of men, times, and places-the Gospel of Jesus Christ is announced by word and deed throughout the world, so that divine faith is aroused or more profoundly penetrates the whole of the Christian life and builds up the body of Christ-which work is completed in the sacraments of faith.

Church, he is their representative before God.[25] Yet as Son of God he is also God's representative to the people. Probably one of the earliest Christian creedal formulas, a version of the Jewish creed, the *Shema*, was,

> For there is one God.
> There is also one mediator between God
>   and the human race,
> Christ Jesus, himself human,
> Who gave himself
>   as a ransom for all (1 Tm 2:5–6).

Yet Jesus' servanthood did not contradict his leadership role as priest. At the Last Supper after washing the feet of the Twelve, he said,

> You call me "teacher" and "master," *and rightly so,* for indeed I am. If I, therefore, the master and teacher, have washed your feet, you ought to wash one another's feet. I have given you a model to follow, so that as I have done for you, you should also do. (Jn 13:13–15, italics added)

Certainly Jesus did not hesitate to teach with an authority far more confident than that of the scribes and Pharisees with their legalistic quibbling (Mt 7:29). Yet he did not claim this authority to teach and to judge (Jn 6:27) as his own right but based it on the mission he had from his Father, a mission not of condemnation but of salvation (Jn 3:26–21). Hence he chose for himself the title of "shepherd" ("I am the good shepherd," Jn 10:14), an ancient Jewish title for kings and other leaders (Ez 34). The task of a shepherd was to protect his flock and above all to keep them moving together in spite of their exasperating tendency to scatter and stray into danger. For the Christian community to remain a community and carry out its mission as the Church, there must be "one flock, and one shepherd" (Jn 10:16).

Since Jesus was always conscious that his earthly life would end on the Cross, it was imperative that he provide for the continuation of this leadership after he had departed. Although he would always be invisibly present to his Church in faith ("I am with you always, until the end of the age" (Mt 28:20), nevertheless, this headship of the Church must somehow continue visibly. This is why Jesus so carefully chose and prepared the Twelve to whom he explained the full meaning of his teaching. "The knowledge of the mystery of the kingdom of heaven has been given to you, but to them [the crowds] it has

---

[25] For a thorough recent treatment of the various opinions on this issue, see Melvin Michalski, "The Relationship between the Universal Priesthood of the Baptized and the Ministerial Priesthood of the Ordained in Vatican II and in Subsequent Theology: Understanding 'essentia et non gradu tantum,'" *Lumen Gentium*, n. 10.

not been granted" (Mt 13:10–11). He gave to the Twelve his own titles of "shepherd" (pastor) as when he said to Peter, "Feed my sheep" (Jn 21:17), "judge" ("Whatever you bind on earth will be bound in heaven, and whatever you loose on earth will be loosed in heaven" Mt 16:19; cf., Mt 19:28) and "teacher" ("He who hears you, hear me," Lk 10:16). "All power in heaven and on earth has been given me, go, therefore, and make disciples of all nations, baptizing them in the name of the Father, of the Son, and of the Holy Spirit, teaching them to observe all that I have commanded you" (Mt 28:18–19).

It could be asked why in such texts no mention of the word "priest" is made.[26] But in the text just quoted it is clear that the Twelve are to baptize. As already mentioned, at the Last Supper they were commanded to continue the celebration of the Eucharist. They were also authorized to forgive sins ("Receive the Holy Spirit. Whose sins you forgive are forgiven them, and whose sins you retain are retained" Jn 20:22). Thus it is clear that in preparing and leaving leaders in his Church, Jesus intended that they should share in his headship of the Church not only as shepherds and teachers but also as ministers of the sacraments, that is, as priests. That the term "priest" is not used of them is explained by the need of the infant Church to avoid any suggestion that its leaders claimed merely to be Old Testament priests. As Hebrews argues, the Christian priesthood is the reality of which the Aaronic priesthood was only a metaphor.

It has also been objected that in the texts I have cited and similar ones, it is not always clear whether Jesus is conferring powers exclusively on the Twelve and their successors or on *all* his disciples then and now. Vatican II answered this, as I have already shown, by teaching that while the whole Church is priestly in that it shares in Jesus' mission and his threefold ministry of shepherd, teacher, and priest, it cannot do so without visible leadership. These leaders are not outside and over the Church, but are members of a living body as its head is also part of the body. They too receive their life from that body. Indeed, they live and act in the service of the unity and mis-

---

26 Jean Colson, *Ministre de Jésus-Christ ou le Sacerdoce de l'Evangile,* says the New Testament avoids the term "priest" for presbyters to avoid confusion with Old Testament priesthood, but the extra-biblical writers of the first two centuries can be understood to admit a kind of priesthood instrumental to that of the one priest Jesus Christ (p. 346 conclusion). See André Lemaire, *Les ministères dans l'église and Les Ministères aux origines de l'Église, naissance de la triple hiérarchie: évêques, presbytres, diacres,* 93–97, on why Vatican II preferred the N.T. "presbyter." Also see Vanhoye, *Old Testament Priests New Priests,* who remarks: "At the present time the opposite tendency seems to have become dominant, one that tends to reject the priestly expression of the Christian reality. Would this not be just another form of regression-where one has not taken the trouble to assimilate the new conception of priesthood, such as it is worked out in the New Testament, and continues, in discussing the question, to take for granted the Old Testament ideas of priestly worship, as if no other possibility existed?" (378).

sion of that body only by the power of the Holy Spirit that animates the Church, head and members.[27]

Hence those who are authorized by Christ to teach and govern are also authorized to lead the community in worship, especially by presiding at the Eucharist, the Church's supreme act of worship. Only by this ordering of ecclesial leadership to presidency in worship can the essentially spiritual purpose of their leadership be manifest. In this way it fits the model set by Jesus at the Last Supper.[28] The Fathers of the Church very reasonably saw a reference in Hebrews to the Eucharist in the text, "It is good to have our hearts strengthened by grace and not by foods, which do not benefit those who live by them. We have an altar from which those who serve the tabernacle have no right to eat,"(Heb 13:10).[29] It is common today, however, for biblical scholars to see

---

[27] In my *Justice in the Church: Gender and Participation,* The McGivney Lectures 1992, Appendix 1, 169–88, I discuss recent opinions that, influenced by democratic egalitarianism, exaggerate the *in persona Ecclesiae* aspect of priesthood at the expense of its *in persona Christi* aspect. In this matter, as in Christology, neither Christ's divinity nor his humanity can be neglected. The Sacrament of Holy Orders is a divine action elevating the priest's humanity by a charism and thus authorizing his representation of the community; it is not merely a blessing on the inaugurating in office of a representative of the human community.

[28] Power says, *Ministers of Christ and His Church,* 189: "We seem to be moving into an era when there be no question of defining a presbyter only in terms of his power to celebrate the eucharist, and when there will be a more vivid expression of the collegial nature of the ordained priesthood through a wider diversification of function, allowing for greater specialization, made possible by a greater sense of collaboration and communion among pastors." Yet it would be wrong to think the medievals defined priesthood *only* in terms of the power to celebrate the Eucharist. St. Thomas, *Summa theologiae* III Suppl., q. 37, a. 2, only says that the orders are distinguished by their *relation* to the Eucharist as the supreme act of worship. Vatican II, *Lumen Gentium,* n. 28, describes the three ministries, without explicitly ranking them, but *Presbyterium Ordinis,* n. 2, says: "The ministry of priests is directed toward this work [offering the Eucharist] and is consummated by it. For their ministry, which takes its start from the gospel message, derives its power and force from the sacrifice of Christ." The Council, *Sacrosanctum Concilium,* paraphrases this: "Nevertheless, the liturgy is the summit toward which the activity of the Church is directed: at the same time it is the fountain from which all her power flows." This classical position has been recently disputed. See Jean Galot's brief survey, *Theology of the Priesthood,* 129–37; Yves Congar, H. Bouëssé, and J. Lécuyer support the classical view but C. Dillenschneider, L. Bouyer, K. Rahner, D. Olivier, and S. Dianich give priority to preaching. W. Kasper, and W. D. Dodd opt for "leadership" (governance). These critics of the classical view, however, seem to be insisting that preaching and pastoring are necessary conditions for authentic community worship and not really denying that worship is the community's supreme act.

[29] The disputed passage is "Do not be carried away by all kinds of strange teaching. It is good to have our hearts strengthened by grace and not by foods, which do not benefit those who live by them. We have an altar from which those who serve the tabernacle have no right to eat." (Heb 13:9–10). The Church Fathers understand

no more in these words than an allusion to the heavenly altar, that is, the once and for all, eternal sacrifice of Christ. This reading requires one to suppose that the text rather strainedly uses "eating" to mean an act of faith in the Cross. Yet it seems more natural to understand it as a comparison between the Old Testament sacred meal shared by those who offer a sacrifice in the temple and the Eucharist as a sacred meal that commemorates and makes present the sacrifice of the Cross. Even if this is not to be taken as a reference to the Eucharist, we need not be surprised that the author of Hebrews preferred to rest his arguments on Old Testament texts at a time that the New Testament was not yet written. His understanding of the shedding of Christ's blood as the inauguration of the New Covenant (Heb 9:18) seems to reflect the Eucharistic words of institution in the tradition reported still earlier by St. Paul, "This cup is the new covenant in my blood" (1 Cor 11:25). A final question that has been raised is why in the New Testament we find no talk of "ordination" for the priestly leaders of the early Church. The meaning of the Sacrament of Holy Orders, whether for bishops, priests, or deacons,[30] is that these leaders in the Church do not act on their own but precisely as members of Christ's Body. They do not act in their own right nor only *in persona ecclesiae*, that is, as representatives of the Christian community. They also and primarily act *in persona Christi* since their special role is to make Christ visible within the community as its head just as the other sacraments are the signs that make the forgiving, healing, and feeding acts of the invisible Christ symbolically visible. Therefore while the community can testify to the suitability of the candidate for priesthood and, receive and acclaim him as legitimately their representative once he is ordained, they cannot make the final decision as to his ordination, nor can they confer the sacrament of Holy Orders on him. Only the bishops who have the fullness of the sacrament have the authority from Christ through

---

this to be a warning against the Judaizers who insisted on the Old Testament dietary laws. Thus it says that such material food is of no spiritual profit, since Christians have the spiritual food of the Christian altar, namely the Eucharist. Protestants often reject this reading and say that the "altar" is a metaphor for the Cross. The Protestant exegete Ellingworth, *The Epistle to the Hebrews*, 708–12, notes, however, that it can mean both the Cross and the Eucharist, since the Eucharist commemorates the Cross. I would add that in the context of a final exhortation a veiled reference to the Christian Eucharist as a sacred meal replacing those of the Jews seems entirely appropriate.

30 Jean Colson, *La Fonction diaconale aux origines de l'Église* on *diakonos* in the New Testament, 8–81, inclines to the view (p. 40), now become common, that the Seven in Acts 6 were presbyter-bishops for the Greek-speaking Jews since they also exercised other ministries than "serving at table." But if "serving at tables" means celebrating the Eucharist, how did this hinder the apostles from preaching? On the contrary, the complaints of the widows must have been about ordinary food for the poor. The traditional view, still accepted in the rite of diaconal ordination, is that deacons first of all carry out the charitable work of the Church (serving at tables) to the poor, but can share with priests preaching, baptism, and witnessing marriages.

their predecessors the Apostles to confer this sacrament. This conferring of the same apostolic authority that Jesus conferred on the Twelve must be by some public act that makes it clear to the flock who their shepherds are. Otherwise the flock will be scattered by "savage wolves" (Acts 20:29).

While it has been argued by some that an isolated Christian church that for a long time lacked a bishop might on its own authority choose one of its members as a priest, there would be no way to know that such a leader has this apostolic authority until it would be recognized by the whole Church as such by regular ordination. Some theologians have speculated that an isolated Christian church lacking a bishop for a long time might be able by right of its own participation as a Christian community in Christ's priesthood to appoint its own priests.[31] Nevertheless, if they were to attempt this in good faith, there would still be no way for them or the whole Church to know that such a leader has priesthood by apostolic authority until he would be ordained by a legitimate bishop by a certainly valid sacramental act. Although the ministry of this supposed priest might be even more pastorally fruitful than that of some ordained priests, this would not make him a sacramental sign nor validate the sacraments he might attempt to perform.

By valid ordination a priest sacramentally symbolizes Christ not merely in a hidden manner but visibly as Christ is the head of the historic Church in its unity throughout time and space. Of course Christ can confer graces of ministry outside the sacraments as he instituted them. Nevertheless, as the Council of Trent, Session XXI, c. 2 declared,[32] not even the college of bishops or its head, the Bishop of Rome, can substantially change or replace the sacraments, but only the manner of their liturgical performance. The essential permanence of the sacraments incarnationally manifests the historic unity and continuity of the Church.

From very early in the Church's history this sacramental sign of "ordination" has been conferred by the "laying on of hands"[33] by those recognized to

---

[31] Among the very different reconstructions of the development of Church polity based on the scanty data available, see Daniel Donovan, *What Are They Saying about the Ministerial Priesthood?* For a survey, see Kenan B. Osborne, OFM, *Priesthood: A History of the Ordained Ministry in the Roman Catholic Church,* and Patrick J. Dunn, *Priesthood.* R. Alastair Campbell, *The Elders,* argues that, besides the traveling apostles, the local house churches were first headed by "elders," who were often the well-to-do owners of houses large enough for Church meetings. Next, in large cities the leaders of several such house churches formed a presbyterate under a leader (the overseer or proto-bishop). Finally this leader became the monarchical bishop of a city with several presbyters of second rank under him. But how long did this development take? Surely not very long.

[32] *Enchiridion symbolorum, definitionum et declaratioinum de rebus fidei et morum,* ed. Henry Denzinger and Adolph Schönmetzer, n. 931. See also *Catechism of the Catholic Church,* n. 1125.

[33] It is quibbling to say, as do some authors, that "ordination" was a later development, since it is more probable that from the first some sort of ceremony gave public evidence

be successors of the original Apostles (the bishops) with appropriate prayers expressing the rank and meaning of the office being conferred. This laying on of hands is a very natural sign, redolent of Jesus' own practice of conferring grace by reaching out and touching the one in need (Mt 8:15, etc.). In Acts (13:3) we read how the church of Antioch sent Paul and Barnabas on the first mission to the Gentiles. After fasting and prayer, "they laid hands on them and sent them off," thus acknowledging the need of God's grace for such an impossible task. While this laying on of hands was practiced in both the Eastern and Western Church the claim that it is the essential act of ordination was not always recognized by theologians nor formally and finally declared until Pius XII did so in 1947.[34] What is clear is that from the beginning it was always considered necessary that for Church leaders to have priestly as well as pastoral and teaching authority they must receive it by some form of public ordination performed by other leaders who could rightly claim apostolic authority.

There are many other problems connected with the theology of priesthood. Why must the Christian priest be male to symbolize Jesus, and why was Jesus Son and not Daughter of God? Is there a role of equivalent dignity for women in the Church? Why is it fitting that the priest and the bishop in the Latin Church be celibate, but in the Orthodox Church only the bishop? I have discussed these difficult questions elsewhere.[35] Any adequate answers to them must also rest on the understanding of both the general and ordained priesthood as participation in that of Christ the High Priest.

Thus my answer to the question of my friend, the young priest, can be summarized as follows. (1) The bible explicitly teaches in Hebrews that Jesus indeed was a priest, the One Priest foreshadowed by the Old Testament priesthood. (2) The Church as the Body of Christ shares in his priestly or sanctify-

---

of the conferring of apostolic authority. In many places in the New Testament "laying on of hands" is mentioned as an action of blessing, healing, bestowing the Holy Spirit, etc. (Acts 8:17, 18, 19; 19:6; 14:23; 2 Tm 4:1–8. Heb 6:2) and is used to send Paul and Barnabas on an apostolic mission (Acts 13:3) and to install the Seven in office (Acts 6:6, 1 Tm 4:14; 2 Tm 1:6, 5:22) as a sign of transmitting divine power.

34 Apostolic Constitution, *Sacramentum Ordinis*, 1947, *DS*, n. 3858; see *Catechism of the Catholic Church,* n. 1573.

35 See my *Justice in the Church: Gender and Participation*, 67–117. Regrettably many attacks on *Inter Insigniores*, October 15, 1996, of the Congregation for the Doctrine of the Faith, and John Paul's Apostolic Letter *Ordinatio Sacerdotalis*, May 22, 1994, and on mandatory priestly celibacy facilely assume that these are based on cultural sexism and obsolete views on sexuality. These attacks show little knowledge of recent historical-theological studies such Christian Cochini, SJ, *Apostolic Origins of Priestly Celibacy,* and R. Cholij, *Clerical Celibacy in East and West,* and Stefan Heid, *Celibacy in the Early Church: The Beginnings of a Discipline of Obligatory Continence for Clerics in East and West,* that show the great antiquity of priestly celibacy in the Church both East and West and that this had roots in New Testament teaching that was not sexist. See also Manfred Hauke, *Women in the Priesthood?* on the theological reasons for exclusively male ordination.

ing office, as well as in his kingly or shepherding office, and in his teaching office, in its mission of evangelizing the world and offering worship—especially Eucharistic worship—to God. (3) The Church cannot, however, act as a unified and indefectible body whose faith is unfailing without a leadership empowered by ordination with apostolic authority from Christ to act as his representatives and instruments in the service of the Church and its mission. (4) The priesthood of the ordained is inseparable from that of all the baptized, and vice versa, so both are inseparable from the one priesthood of Christ, which is their source and their whole rationale.

Addendum: Laicization of Spirituality: Christian Perspectives[36]

In Buddhism, at least in the Theravada version, those alone who have in this life taken a vow to "enter the Path" leading directly to Nirvana can hope to enter Nirvana at death. Others committed to Buddhism can expect only to arrive at this final stage of freedom from the Wheel of Karma in some future reincarnation.[37] On the contrary the Christian Gospel promises that those who have taken the vows of baptism can hope to achieve the goal of their spiritual journey in a single lifetime. It is true that in Catholicism this entry into the vision of God may take place not immediately at death but only after a period of purification (Purgatory), but those who die in the Lord are certain to pass through this purification to God before the Resurrection and Last Judgment. It follows also that those who die having rejected God's mercy have no further hope but, like the fallen angels, have of their own free will forever excluded themselves from God.[38]

When in the third century A.D. the great scholar Origen speculated whether the notion of reincarnation might be assimilated to Christian doctrine, the Church immediately and definitively rejected this view as incompatible with the doctrine of Resurrection.[39] In certain Gnostic, Manichaean, and Albigensian heresies it was maintained that only a group of "the perfect" could achieve holiness, while others of the sect can only rely on the prayers of the perfect for salvation. The Catholic Church also rejected this view, although it survives in popular belief.

---

[36] I have added this section from my brief article in the *Encyclopedia of Monasticism*, in order to make clearer that the goal of priests and laity is the same.

[37] For a discussion of this topic, see a statement by current followers of Theravada Buddhist and Buddhist Corner, Schools of Buddhism, www.onmarkproductions.com/html/schools-three-vehicles.shtml.

[38] *Catechism of the Catholic Church,* nn. 988–1065.

[39] See *Origen on First Principles,* for references on souls in this text. On "Origenism," see www.newadvent.org/cathen/11306b.htm, and its condemnation and on the II Council of Constantinople, XI 553, see www.iclnet.org/pub/resources/text/history/council.2constan.txt.

In authentic Christianity, however, there cannot be two essentially different types of spirituality. All the baptized are called to holiness and all who remain true to their baptism at death or in Purgatory will achieve total holiness, though of different degrees according to a person's degree of love of God at death. This Catholic doctrine is based on the command of Jesus in the Sermon on the Mount "Be perfect as your heavenly Father is perfect," since he would not have given such a command without also offering the grace for all his disciples to fulfill it. Yet in the seventeenth century to correct an exaggerated interest in mysticism then current, Alonso Rodriguez, SJ, (d. 1616) proposed the distinction of an "ordinary way" of spirituality based on "active contemplation" and an "extraordinary way" to which only a few are called based on "infused contemplation."[40] Though for long widely accepted, this distinction is now largely abandoned after being effectively refuted by Juan Arintero, OP, and Reginald Garrigou-Lagrange, OP, who argued that "infused contemplation" is simply Christian faith operating at its fullness under the influence of the Gifts of the Holy Spirit. Since these Gifts are given to all Christians, all the baptized receive a general call to infused contemplation, though not all actually progress in this life to the point of receiving a proximate call to open themselves to this gift.[41]

Further discussion of this subject has, however, led to certain qualifications. For example, Garrigou-Lagrange noted that, as is evident in the biographies of some saints, those living the active life may sometimes achieve a higher degree of charity than those in the contemplative life and hence be at a higher degree of holiness.[42] Yet their actual enjoyment of infused contemplation may be delayed by the circumstances of their charitable activities. Hence they may not arrive at the fullness of infused contemplation until late in life when they are more free for prayer. Moreover in some souls this form of contemplation may take more hidden forms than in others. Consequently, spiritual directors should not conclude that those whose prayer remains merely active are spiritually retarded through some habit of sin.

Furthermore, one should not without qualification accept the common view that distinguishes the Christian life of observance of the Commandments and the more perfect life of the Counsels. This was a questionable interpretation of the Gospel narrative (Mk 10:17—31, Mt. 19:16–30; Lk 18:18–30) in which Jesus tells the young man who has observed the commandments that he

---

[40] Alphonsus Rodriguez, *Practice of Perfection and Christian Virtues.*

[41] Reginald Garrigou-Lagrange, OP, *Christian Perfection and Contemplation, according to St. Thomas Aquinas and St. John of the Cross.*

[42] For the history of this, see Jordan Aumann, OP, *Christian Spirituality in the Catholic Tradition,* chapter 10, last section on "Systematic Spiritual Theology," and bibliography. Also, Juan González Arintero, OP, *The Mystical Evolution in the Development and Vitality of the Church.*

ought also to "go and sell what you possess, give to the poor, and come follow me." In this view the "counsels" are taken to be celibacy, poverty, and obedience that are vowed in the consecrated life of religious. These, however, are only means to the better observance of the Commandments and are not appropriate for Christians in every vocation or circumstance. Rather, all Christians are alike called to keep the Commandments and to grow in the faith, hope, and charity that specify Christian holiness. Yet they may take different means to this growth, of which the counsels are preeminent, but remain a matter of free choice according to a person's personal vocation.

It would be entirely wrong, therefore, simply to suppose that the consecrated life of the monk and nun or the other forms of religious life are invested with a higher form of spirituality than the life of marriage or single life in the world. For all Christians spirituality means principally growth in the theological virtues of faith, hope, and love of God and neighbor and in the moral virtues that support them. Even the highest mystical prayer, we are told by St. John of the Cross, the great spiritual Doctor of the Church, are nothing but intense acts of faith, hope, and love.[43] Other extraordinary phenomena, visions, revelations, the stigmata, the working of miracles, and the like, do not of themselves constitute holiness, but are given by God either to encourage Christians to greater trust in God or to manifest the beauty and meaning of the Christian life to others. The deifying union *(theosis)* effected by these theological virtues is identical in earthly as in heavenly life, except that the union of faith is dark, while the union of vision is face to face in the light of God. Whether on earth or in heaven it is an immediate person-to-person union between the creature and its Creator.

Thus the fundamental elements of spirituality must be the same for all Christians whether clerical, vowed, or lay. Yet the life in the world that is proper to the laity as such has its specific problems that require appropriate modes of this fundamental spirituality. Unfortunately today many Catholics are unacquainted with the Catholic spiritual tradition and seek to satisfy their hunger for a deeper spirituality by turning to eastern religions with their emphasis on meditation techniques. Some Christians even turn to New Age spirituality, theosophy, or occultism, which are highly questionable and may even be demonic.

The Second Vatican Council both in its *Dogmatic Constitution on the Church* (*Lumen Gentium,* 1964), Chapter V, and more specifically in its *Decree on the Apostolate of Lay People* (*Apostolicam actuositatem,* 1965) explained the basis for such an authentic lay spirituality. After consultation with the entire episcopate, this was further formulated in the *Catechism of the Catholic Church* issued by Pope John Paul II in 1994. These documents emphasize that the

---

[43] "The Ascent of Mount Carmel," II, 28, 8; www.ccel.org/j/john_cross/ascent/book2.html.

basis of a sound spirituality for those whose vocation is to a life in the world is first of all a deep respect and understanding of the graces of their baptism.

The laity also need a profound appreciation of the graces of the Sacrament of Confirmation, and of Christian community in the Eucharist, and for most laypersons the Sacrament of Matrimony, as well as of the Sacraments of Reconciliation and Anointing of the Sick for their purification from sin. To be received fruitfully these sacraments must be acts of Christian faith in response to the proclamation of the Gospel. Hence they constitute both the celebration of the gifts of grace and their source for further growth in holiness. The laity, whose lives are not shaped by monastic rules but by the shifting requirements of domesticity and work that often leave little room even for prayer, are often tempted to use the sacraments only irregularly and prepare for them carelessly. They must therefore develop a practical pattern of regular reception of the sacraments and communal worship. They must be vividly aware of the doctrine of the communion of the saints and the reality of the Church as the Body of Christ, in which all the members are concerned for each other. A merely private, individualistic piety cannot be authentically Christian.

A second feature of lay spirituality must be learning to pray not only vocally but meditatively at times and in a manner compatible with their necessary occupations in the world. While there are many techniques of prayer (and here much can be learned from non-Christian spiritualities), it is essential to understand that the goal of prayer is not some "experience" or "altered state of consciousness." It is the deifying union with God in the only way possible in this life, that is, in acts of faith, hope, and love.

Prayer must first of all be a petition to God for an increase of his better gifts he has already given by which we are able to come before him. Then prayer is thanksgiving for these gifts and praise of God not only for the divine generosity but for the community of the Triune God itself in infinite power, truth, and love. Laypersons who take time in their busy lives for meditation thus come to know God as source of all the good that they do each day in any activity however humble or mundane. In this way their daily work, which John Paul II has said in his encyclical *On Work* (*Laborem exercens,* 1981) is the duty of all, sanctifies the laity. This requires, of course, that this work be also a practice of the Christian moral virtues of moderation, courage, justice, and prudence and be motivated by the theological virtues of faith, hope, and charity.

Traditionally the work of Christ is threefold, prophecy (teaching, preaching), governance (pastoral ministry), and priesthood (prayer, worship, intercession). Vatican II teaches that the laity share in this "general priesthood" and its threefold function, since they are "a chosen race, a royal priesthood, a holy nation, a people of His own" (1 Pt 2:9). The clergy are chosen from this people and ordained by the Church acting in the name of Christ in the power of the Holy Spirit to serve the people so as to assist them in their own witness to the Gospel. Thus an essential part of lay spirituality is to witness to the Gospel to the world in which they live and work. This evangelization and transformation of the world as a leaven within it is the special apostolate of the laity, whether done on its own initiative or in collaboration with the clergy. Thus the roles of clergy and laity are essentially different but mutually supportive.

The spirituality of the laity does not, however, render the tradition of monastic spirituality useless. In the Church the clergy and religious are at the service of the whole People of God in the building up of the Body of Christ (Eph 2:19–22). St. Thomas Aquinas says that for contemplatives the rule should be *contemplare, et contemplata aliis tradere,* "To contemplate in order to share with others what one has contemplated." Thus throughout the ages, monasteries have been and should continue to be centers of spiritual inspiration and renewal. Yet the laity ought to support monastic life and share with monks and nuns not only the problems but also the insights of the Holy Spirit in their own lives. For all Christians Christ remains the model to be imitated and the source of grace by which to be transformed into his image. Yet perhaps the recent development, chiefly under the influence of liberation theology, of "basic communities" may in the future serve some of the animating functions exercised in the past by monasteries, but will still need centers of contemplative life. The Taizé community in France has demonstrated in recent years that monasteries can also serve ecumenism. In so enormous a community as the Catholic Church centers of more intense communal and contemplative life serve to raise the level of participation in the laity as a whole.

CHAPTER 11

Moral Theology and Mariology*

The Imitation of Mary

THE GREEK TERM *ANTHROPOS*, AS THE LATIN TERM *homo*, though both are masculine, grammatically signify both female and male human persons. Not long ago the English *man* could also be so understood, but no longer since those who claim to be feminists have forced usage to take an exclusively masculine sense. What a Christian can hardly deny is that good theology must be based on an *anthro*pology and that on a Christology. On the *imitatio Christi* all seem to agree.[1] Any explanation of dogmatic and ethical revelation not intelligible in terms of our experience of human beings who have actually lived good lives as God's children would be a mere system of ideals. Yet what human being has a rightful claim to goodness except Christ? Hence, the "imitation" of Christ cannot be taken literally but only analogically. The saints are good because they live *in Christo*, as St. Paul keeps saying (Rm 9:1, 12:5; 16:7; 1 Cor, 4:17; 15:18, 15:22, and so on). They are members of Christ's Body, instruments of his holy grace. Yet in them are expressed aspects of human goodness that could not find full expression in Jesus' humanity, limited by time and space, and in his human individuality. St. Paul could rightly speak of his own sufferings as "filling up the sufferings of Christ" (Col 1:24) that could not be experienced in Jesus' own flesh and lifetime.

So it is only in the Mystical Body of Christ throughout history that the fullness of what it is to be human *in Christo* will finally be made explicit. One limitation of Jesus was and is that he is only a male, and therefore, no matter

---

* Published in *Anthropotes* 7 (2; December 1991): 137–53.

[1] For a discussion of the different current views on the specificity of Christian ethics, see David Hollenbach, SJ, "Fundamental Theology and the Christian Moral Life," in Leo J. O'Donovan and E. Howland Sanks, eds., *Faith Witness: Foundations of Theology for Today's Church,* 167–84.

how "androgynous" we may imagine him, could not have exhibited the gifts proper to the female half of the human race. If he could not have even exhibited all the gifts of human males, since he chose to be a carpenter and not a warrior, a politician, an artist, or a scientist, he certainly could not take on the role of mother, or nun, or any of the other countless roles to which women today bring a special feminine contribution. It is to holy women that we must look to see these feminine aspects of total humanity if we are to develop a moral theology in its full amplitude.

Of course one might object that morality is morality, virtue is virtue, whether found in man or woman. The virtues, however, are skills in dealing with life problems, and while both sexes have many life problems in common, they also have to meet different problems arising from sexual differences and the different experiences that result from them. Even the feminist literature, when it attempts to describe the de facto psychological differences, gives much the same picture as I have given.[2]

Feminists, however, generally maintain that this de facto difference is not rooted in nature but is a reformable product of a patriarchal culture.[3] Yet, no man has to meet the problems of motherhood or of sexism in the way a woman must, just as no woman struggles with the Oedipus complex. Consequently there are important distinctions in the virtues and moral life of men and women that moral theology, generally androcentric in view, while never denying, has largely neglected.

Feminine and Masculine Virtue

What in general could be the difference between the male and female types of virtue? Nancy Chodorow has argued that the psychological differences of the sexes are cultural in origin, yet she presents a theory of how the basic relations of the boy or girl to its mother and father (which certainly have a natural biological and transcultural basis!) result in a different pattern of psychosocial development.[4] The most basic way to discover and formulate this difference is to begin with the fact that femaleness is ordered to motherhood, maleness to fatherhood. To be a human mother or father is not merely a biological but also an educational and spiritual task, since begetting a child entails the moral responsibility to help that child develop into a mature adult, and for the Christian parent to help that child attain union with God.

---

[2] See Mary Roth Walsh, *The Psychology of Women: Ongoing Debates.*

[3] For this see Nancy Chodorow, "Feminism and Difference: Gender, Relation, and Difference in Psychoanalytic Perspective," and the critique by Alice S. Rossi, in Mary Roth Walsh, *The Psychology of Women,* 246–73.

[4] Chodorow, "Feminism and Difference," 259ff. For Freud's very different theory of the development of sexual identity, see Christopher Lasch, *Haven in a Heartless World: The Family Beseiged.*

Hence we can speak both of biological and spiritual parenthood. Males, no matter what tasks they undertake in life, whether as artisans, artists, statesmen, teachers, priests, or soldiers, precisely as male ought to bring to these tasks some of the qualities of spiritual fatherhood; and women as women likewise bring to all non-domestic works they engage in today some of the qualities of spiritual motherhood.

What morally characterizes good and bad mothering and fathering? These roles cannot be adequately grasped in any simple formula, but if we try to list the tasks a successful mother must perform at both the physical and the spiritual level, we must include the following: A women must accept and cooperate with the sexual advances of her partner, live with serenity and patience the nine months of pregnancy, undergo the hard work of delivery, nurse and fondle the child, watch over and tend it in infancy, encourage and support its growing independent activity, be ever available to comfort and reassure it in its misadventures. She must maintain the domestic environment and keep her husband contentedly near at home, share with him their common experiences by which they grow as human persons, encourage and console the husband in his own difficulties. She must also instruct the children by word and example in the basic tasks of living and basic moral attitudes, transmit religion as a daily way of life, advance herself intellectually and in prayer and spiritual union with God. She must unselfishly permit the children to grow up and leave the home, extend what she has learned as mother to her own gifts and competencies and thus enter into the service of the larger community in the work-a-day world, bringing to these tasks the spiritual motherhood she has learned. In all these efforts she must remain always available to her children and friends for counsel and comfort and to her husband as a companion in later life and old age.

As we look awe-struck over this list we can understand why it is usually said that what is specifically feminine is the ability to "nurture," that is, to enable other persons to grow by providing for them the environment, physical and psychological and spiritual, which they need to grow. To speak of this as "passivity" or "receptivity" or "matter" or "potency" is not wrong if these terms are not understood merely negatively, but rather as connoting the wonderful capacity of a woman to allow another person to act in that person's own right, supporting, encouraging, and stimulating that growth and action without trying to impose what is alien to it. The complaint of some feminists that this capacity implies a lack of self-identity is mistaken; rather it implies a healthy autonomy unthreatened by confronting others. No wonder that in many cultures the feminine is symbolized by "water" which gives life, yet remains a liquid, transparent, cleansing ambience in which other things may move and grow freely. When this capacity for mothering fails or is perverted we find a mother who is negligent, hard, lacking in empathy, critical, or (even more frequently) possessive, smothering, destructive. Such mothers leave their children starved for love or imprisoned and unable ever to adequately mature.

Fathering, on the other hand,[5] requires a man to seek a mate; fight off rival males; win over the woman by his attention and love; actively embrace, penetrate, and impregnate his wife, yet do so tenderly and with vulnerable self-surrender on his own part. He must provide her and the children with food and protection during her pregnancy and their infancy; give his family a sense of security by his constant presence and reliability. He must provide shelter; share with his wife his experiences of the extra-domestic world so that she can grow with him intellectually and spiritually; convince her of his enduring fidelity when he must be absent. He must share increasingly in the guidance and education of the children, giving to them an objective realism of thought and discipline they need to meet the outer world; yet act as priest of the family by representing to them the presence of God as an objective fact. Finally he must help his wife to widen her relations with the wider society; and be evermore her companion in sickness and old age as they prepare for heaven.

In trying to characterize this fathering task we note that while the woman nurtures, the man tends to "construct," that is, to impose an order on things, whether it is the simple physical fact of initiating pregnancy, providing the home as shelter and protection, or the more spiritual tasks of disciplining the children physically and mentally, or undertaking the work of the wider social order. Whereas the woman "allows" the child to grow, the father "causes" the child to grow.

When fathering fails or is perverted, the wife and child are neglected, left in insecurity, or treated as objects without dignity, or (and this is perhaps more common) they are dominated and used for the father's egoistic purposes. The masculine principle when perverted tends usually toward *violence*, to destruction rather than construction, as the perverted feminine principle to "possessiveness," to smothering rather than nurturing.

Woe to the child whose mother smothers and whose father tyrannizes! What I have described are, of course, merely types, and if taken too literally and mechanically become stereotypes; but they indicate the kind of gifts and contributions possible to men and women precisely as such to the moral fabric of the world.

Jesus as God is the Son of the Father, and as man he was a male. According to the Fourth Gospel when Jesus washed the apostles' feet to show them they must not act as domineering masters but as servants, he said, "You call me teacher and master, and rightly, for so I am (Jn 13:14)." Thus the Gospels always show Jesus acting with authority, as a leader, in a thoroughly masculine manner, and demanding the loyalty and obedience of his disciples.

---

[5] See John W. Miller, *Biblical Faith and Fathering.*

He was their "Lord." Yet he was also their "servant" and demanded that his apostles also be "servants" in the sense that as leaders having authority and dominion, they were to use that power not for their own aggrandizement, but purely for the good of those they served. Therefore, while we must turn to the *imitatio Christi* to find the fundamental norm of all Christian virtue for women as for men, as well also for the norm of distinctly masculine virtue, we still need an *imitatio Mariae* to establish the norm of distinctly feminine virtue. The complementary harmony between these two aspects of human virtue reflects Adam's need for Eve, and the need of Jesus, the New Adam, for Mary, the New Eve.[6]

Historical Data for Mariology

Yet it can well be asked whether such a mariological aspect of moral theology can be responsibly developed, considering how little historical data there is out of which to construct a picture of Mary's life and personality. The earliest stratum of New Testament witness, the authentic epistles of St. Paul, say nothing about her, and only in the Third and Fourth Gospels are we given any information on her and that is not at all detailed. Furthermore, modern historical-critical exegesis tends to reduce even this meager data to a tissue of "theological constructs" built on only three or four historically trustworthy facts: Mary was a woman of Nazareth, mother of Jesus, wife of Joseph the carpenter, who was probably present at the crucifixion and at the events of Pentecost.

Most exegetes also admit that the tradition of the virgin conception of Jesus goes back to a period prior to the Gospels of Matthew and Luke that they seem to witness independently of each other.[7] The theologian can answer

---

[6] See *La Nouvelle Eve, Bulletin de la Societe Francaise d' Etudes Mariales,* 1954–57, four numbers.

[7] For the current views of Catholic exegetes on the historicity of the Marian biblical data see Raymond E. Brown, SS, *The Birth of the Messiah,* supplemented by his "Gospel Infancy Research from 1976–86," *Catholic Biblical Quarterly* 48 (3 & 4, 1986): 468–83, 660–80, with up-to-date bibliography; and Joseph A. Fitzmyer, SJ, *The Gospel According to Luke I–IX.* These two exegetes hold the virginal conception of Jesus to be historically probable and a doctrine of faith, but they judge Matthew and Luke's narratives to be in the main theological constructs modeled on Old Testament stories and contend that their theological content was retrojected from the Paschal faith. On the contrary, André Feuillet, *Jesus and His Mother,* and Rene Laurentin, *The Truth of Christmas: Beyond the Myths,* with a preface by Joseph Cardinal Ratzinger, hold that both accounts (and especially Luke's) are based on a Jerusalem tradition that must in part go back to Mary herself. If we grant that "Luke" was a disciple of Paul who with him visited Jerusalem (Brown admits this as possible) at a time when he must have at least met acquaintances of Mary, this seems entirely credible.

this difficulty to a degree by recalling that theological certitude does not rest directly on historical evidence, but on the witness of the Tradition and especially on the normative expression of that Tradition in the canonical Scriptures. The doctrine of biblical inspiration guarantees to us that what the canonical writers assert to be relevant to our salvation and also historically real did in fact happen.[8] Thus, although there is no possibility of establishing the virginal conception of Jesus by historical evidence, we can be theologically certain of it as a historical fact on the inspired word of the evangelists.[9]

The same evaluation applies also to some of the other Mariological information given by these writers, although we must be careful to discriminate what they intend to assert as historical truth and what they supplied as dramatization or interpretation. For example, according to some exegetes the *Magnificat* that Luke places in Mary's mouth cannot be certainly attributed to her composition, but can perhaps be taken simply as Luke's dramatization in the manner of classical historians, expressing what Mary might appropriately have said.[10]

Yet even granted that we can garner a certain number of facts about Mary with theological certitude, the number is small; and what are we to say of her immaculate conception, her perpetual virginity, her assumption, or the interior sentiments throughout the ministry of her Son, which traditional piety attributes to her and which seem guaranteed only by the official dogmatization of the Church on the basis of a tradition for which historical evidence is lacking for many years after the events? Can it be that this expansion of Mariological data is the work of a kind of myth-making by popular piety and of theological justification through a sort of transcendental deduction? Beginning from the historical fact that Mary of Nazareth was the mother of Jesus, whom we Christians believe to be God Incarnate, the Church seems to have drawn many conclusions about her on the principle that God gives to those he has chosen for a special role in his plan of salvation the qualities and graces they need to fulfill that role.

[8] Vatican II, *Dei Verbum*, n. 3.

[9] See Feuillet, *Jesus and His Mother*, 130–88; Laurentin, *The Truth of Christmas*, 432–65; the survey of recent discussion by James T. O'Connor, "Mary, Mother of God and Contemporary Challenges," *Marian Studies* 29 (1978): 26–43; and Raymond E. Brown, "Gospel Infancy Research."

[10] Brown, *The Birth of the Messiah*, 346–65, thinks it probably was composed in a Jewish Christian "*anawim* circle" and borrowed by Luke for his narrative, Fitzmyer, *The Gospel According to Luke I–IX*, 59, says "Since there is no evidence that the Magnificat ever existed in a Semitic (Hebrew or Aramaic) form, there is no reason to think of Mary as the one who composed it. It has not been preserved by a family tradition." Laurentin, *The Truth of Christmas*, 379–83, defends its Marian authenticity.

Are not those exegetes who hold that Luke's narrative is primarily a theological construct based solely on the resurrection faith in Jesus' divine Sonship in effect attributing to the evangelist this same kind of deductive reasoning?[11] To this principle, however, it can be objected, that such reasoning seems to ignore the "contingency" of history. Is it not true that, although the successor of St. Peter plays a very important role in God's plan for our salvation and is undoubtedly endowed by God with many graces of office, there have been some very negligent and even wicked popes? How, then can we argue that Mary, as historical personage, "necessarily fulfilled all that was appropriate to the mother of the Savior"?

There seems here to be a gap between historical contingency and a type of reasoning based on metaphysical necessity. The reply to this very serious objection is, I believe, that given the plan of God for our salvation revealed to us in the Scriptures, we can apply the principle of appropriateness to the degree that a certain event is absolutely necessary to that plan. Thus, the dogmatic infallibility of the pope is necessary to God's plan of salvation, and we can conclude that it is historically impossible that any pope has erred in making a solemn definition. Only if it could be established with certitude that some successor of St. Peter has so erred would we in honesty have to renounce the Catholic faith. But the moral rectitude or competence of this or that occupant of the Holy See is not essential to God's plan of salvation, so there is no difficulty in admitting the sins and failures of certain popes. Similarly, our certitude that Mary was not only the mother of Jesus, but also the entirely worthy mother of the Incarnate Word, arises from the fact that Mary's role in God's plan of salvation was absolutely necessary to the fulfillment of that plan.

Thus the insight of Catholic piety that Mary must have been wholly without sin, and therefore immaculately conceived and assumed body and soul at her passing, and that her heart was always conformed to the heart of her Son depends not on historically tracing the tradition of the Church to its source, nor to explicit statements in the Scripture, but to a profound appreciation by the faithful of the plan of God revealed in the Gospel, which the Magisterium, guided by the Holy Spirit, is able to confidently confirm. Thus it has been possible to develop within the Church a methodologically sound Mariology of considerable amplitude, quite sufficient for a consistent and credible theology. Such a theology is authentically feminist precisely because it shows us in Mary, the New Eve, the Mother of God the Son, the unique

---

[11] For a discussion on the methodological shift in Mariology from an excessively deductive to a more historical and analytic approach, see Cyril Vollert, SJ, *A Theology of Mary*, 19–41, and on the development of Marian dogma, 223–50.

gifts God has given to women, complementary to the other unique gifts God the Father has given to men, so that man and woman might be "one flesh" in the Holy Spirit.

Mary's Virginity

Why was the Mother of Our Lord a virgin? In the age of the sexual revolution feminists find the ancient emphasis on the value of virginity an unjust imposition on female as compared to male freedom. Yes, a true virgin is one who waits to give her love entirely to only one husband. In the Old Testament again and again the Chosen People are called "the Virgin Daughter Israel" or "the Virgin Daughter Zion" because they were betrothed to God in the covenant, to be always faithful to Him as he was always faithful to them. Tragically, however, Israel was not true to its covenant. It fell into idolatry and took other gods for her lovers. As the prophets wept over the unfaithfulness of the Chosen People it seemed to them that all was lost. But the Word of God came to them with the reassurance that there was a remnant that remained faithful to God. Thus in the Gospel of Luke we read about Zachariah and Elizabeth, about Anna who in her widowhood prayed night and day in the Temple, and of Simeon who awaited the coming of the Lord. These, and other faithful Jews like them, were God's remnant, still true to their virgin love of God.

When we read the Old Testament, therefore, we see that through its many stories of war and disaster, of idolatry and decadence, the fact that the Holy Spirit of God continued to prepare his people for the great moment when the Son of God would finally appear in their midst. He permitted all the tragedies and failures only as an education and a purification of the remnant that remained faithful. These long centuries of gradual sanctification were finally to come to their completion in a daughter of Israel in whom no stain of sin, not even of the sin of Adam and of Eve, remained; who was in the fullest sense the virgin bride to whom God had betrothed himself in the covenant. Thus the virginity of Mary, her perfect answer of faith to God, the fruitfulness of her divine motherhood are all one single mystery of the union of humankind with God in an eternal covenant. And we can add that her Assumption into heaven with her risen son is also joined to that same mystery, since it was God's fitting response to her perfect fidelity to him.

Sometimes we Catholics are asked why we make so much of Mary, when there is only a little about her in the Bible, a little in the Gospels of Matthew and Luke, and the story of Cana and Jesus' putting her in the care of John at the Cross. But in fact that whole Old Testament is about Mary, since it is the story of the preparation of the Jews for the coming of the Messiah, and in her that preparation was complete. What then does all this mean for us? We are not Jews and we do not belong to Old Testament times. The answer, of course, is that because Mary is the mother of Our Lord, she is also our Mother, the Mother of the Church. Jesus is the head of the Church, and the Church, says St. Paul, is truly his body. All of us who are baptized and who receive the Eucharist are truly the very body of which Christ is the head. As Mary is the mother of the head, so she is mother of the body. That is why Pope Paul VI after Vatican II gave her the title of "Mother of the Church" in the liturgy. While Jesus is both God and man, Mary is only human, but she has given to Jesus his humanity, and she gives us in our humanity the right to call Jesus our Brother.

The Immaculate Conception

Therefore, in being joined to Christ our only Savior as his brothers and sisters through our common mother who is Mary and the Church she symbolizes, we live one life in the Holy Spirit of love with, through, and in them. The Immaculate Conception of Mary cannot be understood simply as a personal event related to her alone. No, it is the completion of God's work in restoring all of creation from its fallen state, summed up in the holy remnant of the Chosen People. She is the summation of the Chosen People, who through the grace of God was ready to speak the word of faith on their behalf. As in a marriage the virgin bride says to her groom, "I do" and thus makes covenant with him, so in Mary the believing Jews said the words, "Behold the handmaid of the Lord. Be it done to me according to your Word." She could not have spoken those words with entire truthfulness if in her had remained even a trace of sin or its effects. Her faith had to be as perfect in its humanity as God's Word in its divinity so that the covenant might be entirely firm on both sides.

Mary's immaculate conception, therefore, is not just hers. We share in it. Although we were born in original sin, our baptism is a rebirth in grace in the Church, and therefore in sinless Mary, and we began to share in her freedom from sin given her by God that she might be the perfect covenant partner of the sinless Jesus. The more we live in the Church, receive its sacraments, strive to live its life of love of God and neighbor, the more we are clothed in her total holiness, and in heaven we will share with her that fullness of grace which God bestowed on her at the very moment he created her soul, so that we might also come in time to that same perfect holiness. In the Book of Revelation we read of the New Jerusalem, descending like a bride from heaven, in which Christ the King will reign. That New Jerusalem, the heavenly Zion is Mary, it is the Church, it is the saints who have been born in her.

The Mariological Theme in the Whole Bible[12]

In the light of such a Mariology and the rehabilitation of patristic typological exegesis[13] it also becomes evident that the Scriptures have much more to tell us about Mary than the few passages in Luke and John. The Eve–Mary typology is as old as Irenaeus and the series of barren women who miraculously bear a child to be the savior of his people which runs from Sarah (Gn 17:15–22), through the mother of Samson (Jdg 13), Hannah, mother of Samuel (1 Sm 1–2:11), to Elizabeth, mother of John the Baptist (Lk 1:5–5), and finally Mary (Lk 1:26–56), forms the background of Luke's narrative.[14] Along with these women are such heroines who saved their people as Esther and Judith, and women prophetesses such as Deborah (Jdg 4–5) and Huldah (2 Kg 22:14–20). In this way the whole of salvation history as narrated in the historical books of the Bible is patterned in relation to the Virgin Mother of the Messiah.

In the prophetic books beginning with Hosea, the great metaphor of the Chosen People as the Bride of Yahweh is developed (Hos 1:2–3:5; Is 1:21, 50:1, 54:6–7, 62:4–5; Jr 2:2, 3:1, 3:6–12; Ez 16 and 23) and culminates in Mary as the personification of her people, the Virgin Daughter of Zion.[15] Finally, in the Wisdom literature of the Bible, the wisdom of the Creator as it is reflected in creation and in the Law (Ps 19; Bar 3:9–4:4) is also personified as a feminine figure, which Catholic liturgy has rightly identified with Mary, who is type of the Church itself.[16]

Thus, the whole of the Old Testament is capable not only of Christological but a Mariological interpretation and this is confirmed in the New Testa-

---

12 The most authoritative affirmation of this theological achievement is to be found in the fact that so much of it has been taken up in the teachings of the Magisterium, notably in Vatican II, *Lumen Gentium,* 21 November 1964, chapter 8, nn. 52–69; Paul VI's Apostolic Exhortation *Marialis Cultus* (February 2, 1974): 113–68, www.papalencyclicals.net/Paul06/p6marial.htm, and especially John Paul II's Encyclical *Redemptoris Mater,* 1987, 361–433, www.vatican.va/holy_father/john_paul_ii/encyclicals/documents/hf_jp-ii_enc_25031987_redemptoris-mater_en.html, English edition, *Mary: God's Yes to Man,* with an introduction by Joseph Cardinal Ratzinger and commentary by Hans Urs von Balthasar.

13 See Henri de Lubac, *The Sources of Revelation,* with an interesting exchange of letters with Hugues Vincent of the Ecole Biblique of Jerusalem on the views of M.-J. Lagrange on this question. For a critique of de Lubac, which, however, approves typological exegesis, see G. W. H. Lampe and K. J. Woolcombe, *Essays on Typology, Studies in Biblical Theology,* vol. 22.

14 Feuillet, *Jesus and His Mother,* 104; Laurentin, *The Truth of Christmas,* 399–431.

15 See Feuillet, *Jesus and His Mother,* 11–16; Laurentin, *The Truth of Christmas,* 52–53. For critique, see Raymond E. Brown, *The Birth of the Messiah,* 320–28.

16 See Charles De Koninck, *Ego Sapientia . . . La sagesse qui est Marie,* and Louis Bouyer, "The Scriptural Themes of Mariology: The Divine Wisdom" in his *The Seat of Wisdom,* 20–28.

ment by the infancy narrative of the Lucan Gospel and by the symbolic way in which the Johannine Gospel treats Mary as "the Woman."[17] In "Revelation" all these symbols are collected in the sign of the Woman Clothed with the Sun who is the New Jersualem, Bride of the Lamb.[18] Even Paul's silence about Mary yields to the fact that Luke, who was Paul's companion,[19] says so much of her, and indeed makes her virginal conception of the Savior a metaphor that seems an equivalent for Paul's doctrine of "salvation by faith.[20]

The Formation of Christian Character

Therefore, without in any way neglecting the results of modern historical-critical scholarship, we can proceed on solid theological grounds to construct a rich Mariology that can serve for a study of the *imitatio Mariae* to complete a full theology with a feminist contribution of moral insight. Christian moral theology does not merely concern how to make particular difficult moral decisions, as it is sometimes presented today, but with mapping out what the Bible calls "the way of life" in contrast to the "way of death" (Dt 30:15). To this way of life it applies the great metaphor of the Exodus. Life is a journey, a dynamic struggle to attain a goal. Hence it is also a process of building a kingdom, the Community of God in which he will eternally reign as in his temple. And it is finally a process of creating the persons who will be citizens of that kingdom, of forming their characters in the strength necessary to travel to the end of that way and in the holiness needed to live in that kingdom in everlasting peace (Eph 2:19–22, 4:15–16; Heb 12:1–2).

As we act so we become, and as we are so we act. Hence theology in its moral dimension is a narrative of the victorious life of a Christian through whose carrying of the Cross unto death comes the transformation of the risen life. That narrative of passage, however, to be intelligible must be understood

---

[17] Feuillet, *Jesus and His Mother*, 118–29.

[18] Rev. 29:9

[19] Ibid., pp 17–33. Also see Feuillet's "La Femme vêtue de soleil (Ap 12) et la glorificatoiin de l'Epouse du Cantique des Cantiques (6, 10)," *Nova et Vetera* 59 (1984): 36–67; 103–28.

[20] Against the widely received opinion of P. Vielhauer, available in English in L. E. Keck and J. L. Martyn, eds., *Studies in Luke-Acts: Essays Presented in Honor of Paul Schubert,* based principally on the fact that Luke-Acts does not stress Paul's views on grace as much as Protestant theology likes to do, that the author of these two works could not have been a companion of Paul, see Fitzmyer, *The Gospel According to Luke I–IX,* 51, "Most of the arguments brought forth in modern times to substantiate the distance of Luke from Paul do not militate against the traditional identification of the author of the Third Gospel and Acts with Luke, the Syrian from Antioch, who had been a sometime collaborator of the Apostle Paul." On the historical reliability of Luke, see also W. G. Kümmel, "Luc en accusation dans la theologie contemporaine" in F. Neirynck, ed., *L'Évangile de Luc: The Gospel of Luke,* 3–19.

in terms of the kind of person who is being created through the process. The three great gifts by which a person becomes truly a disciple of Christ, truly a Christian, are, as St. Paul reiterates, faith, hope, and love (1 Cor 13:13 and also 1 Th 1:3, 5:8; 13:7; Rm 5:1–5; 12:6–12; Gal 5:5–6; Eph 1:15–18; 4:2–5; Col 1:4–5; 1 Tm 6:11; Tit 2:2; Heb 6:10–12; 10:22–24; 1 Pt 1:3–9, 21–22).[21]

To these "theological" virtues (so named because their direct object is God himself) can be related what the Greeks called the great moral virtues, named in the Book of Wisdom (8:7): *prudence, justice, fortitude,* and *temperance*. Prudence is much the same as what the Bible usually calls "wisdom" and this wisdom is the practical aspect of faith, the light by which one walks the way and which grows brighter through the experiences of the way. Justice is the biblical "righteousness" and is linked to Christian love, since genuine love first of all respects the dignity and rights of others and the order given the world by its Creator. Temperance (or moderation) detaches us from the pursuit of the pleasures of the world, and fortitude (or courage) makes us steadfastly enduring in the troubles and persecutions of the world.

The necessity of these two latter virtues, so manifest in Christian chastity and martyrdom, explains why asceticism, the bearing of one's Cross, is so essential to traveling the Way, and they are therefore intimately connected with Christian hope that makes us confident that the Promised Land is worth the effort and can really be attained by the power of God. Thus the complete Christian is one who has been forged in the fire of suffering through faith, hope, and love.

Mary's Faith and Prudence as the New Eve

Let us now trace the story of how God formed Mary as the feminine counterpart of the New Adam. Luke presents Mary for the first time at the moment of the annunciation and the commencement of her virgin motherhood. Where Eve, mother of all the living (Gn 3:20 or 25, "Eve" itself resembles the Hebrew for "living"), yielded to the temptation of Satan to seek autonomy from God, Mary to be the mother of all who live by grace, consented to total cooperation in God's plan for the salvation of the world from sin.[22]

This free consent that involved her whole being and her whole life vocation was not merely a private act. In the faith of the Old Testament she knew that she spoke for her whole people, God's chosen people, and through them for all humanity. What she consented to, moreover, was to be the mother of

---

[21] See Laurentin, *The Truth of Christmas,* 38–43, 222–46.
[22] *The New Jerusalem Bible,* 1907, footnote e, suggests that this trilogy of virtues probably antedates Paul.

the Messiah, and hence the mother of all Israel, and through them of all humanity, the New Eve, mother of all the living through grace.[23] Her faith, therefore, was not just the imperfect faith we have as Christians, but a "consummate" faith, that total faith that alone was adequate to receive the supreme gift of the Incarnation of God's Son.

Such a consummate and total faith would hardly have been possible to a man. Motherhood requires of a woman that she place complete faith in the husband who causes her to become pregnant and in whom she must trust for care during her pregnancy and nursing period. To be able to trust in this way requires a special way of thinking, of which few men are capable. Today feminist scholars are explaining just how women think differently than men, and indeed in some ways better than men.[24] In what does this feminine mode of thought consist? From such empirical studies as are available, the common saying that women are more "intuitive" than men is probably correct.[25] Human intelligence, as St. Thomas Aquinas pointed out,[26] has two phases. The first phase is *intellectus (ratio superior)* "insight," or "intuition," by which we grasp certain seminal truths directly from our sense experience with a certainty based immediately on that experience. The second phase is *ratio (ratio inferior)*, "reason," by which we explicate and develop these seminal truths by a logical calculus. Persons differ as to the effectiveness with which they use these two phases of their intelligence.

It is not strange, however, that women on average rely more on insight, men on reason. While this can be attributed to the support given by our culture to these different modes of thought, yet they are perhaps more deeply and genetically rooted in the fact that women in order to succeed in their biological role as mothers have needed a more penetrating intuition than do men in order to deal effectively with the personal relations so needed in the family.

Logic is not of much use in understanding other human beings because of their great complexity and interiority. Personal understanding comes rather through empathy, the power to place oneself in another person's shoes, to

23 St. Justin Martyr, *Dialogue with Trypho,* 100, PG 6,710; St. Irenaeus of Lyons, *Adversus Haereses,* 3:22, PG 7, 958–9; Tertullian, *De Carne Christi,* 17, PL 2, 782. See also Feuillet, *Jesus and His Mother,* 6–10.

24 See Abbe Pintard, "Mater viventium" in *La Nouvelle Eve,* 1957, 61–86.

25 See Carol Gilligan, *In a Different Voice: Psychological Theory and Women's Development*; also her "In a Different Voice: Women's Conceptions of Self and of Morality," with the review by Ann Colby and William Damon, in Mary Roth Walsh, *The Psychology of Women: Ongoing Debates,* 274–322 with bibliographies. From a popular view, but based on extensive clinical experience in marriage counseling see John Gray, *Men Are from Mars, Women Are from Venus: A Practical Guide for Improving Communication and Getting What You Want in Your Relationships.*

26 See Mary F. Belensky et al., *Women's Ways of Knowing: The Development of Self, Voice, and Mind.*

notice the small clues that reveal the other's inner attitudes and feelings. In her long evolutionary development the human female has become adapted to this sensitivity in a way males have not. Such empathetic sensitivity has little place in logical thinking that depends on universalizing and objectivizing our experience in an abstract manner, but it gives a great advantage to intuitive thinking that rests on immediate experience and subjective cues.

Mary's great act of faith was made at the Annunciation, but we can understand her readiness only if we consider how she was prepared for that act from the very beginning of her existence as a person. The doctrine of the Immaculate Conception states that "by a singular privilege and grace of almighty God in view of the merits of Christ Jesus, Savior of humanity, Mary was from the first moment of her conception preserved immune from all taint of original sin" (*DS* 2804). This was not an isolated event, but the culmination of the entire history of the world in which, after the fall into sin of Adam and Eve, God had been preparing a worthy human mother for his Divine Son who he was to send as savior of fallen humanity.

Thus the whole development of moral insight that the Old Testament recounts: from Adam to Noah, from Noah to Abraham, from Abraham to Moses, with the Old Law and then through the many stages of its writing and rewriting and through the teachings of the prophets and the sages, gradually prepared the Jewish people to receive the Messiah. Although this people, like all peoples, in many ways fell short of its calling, it produced a Remnant ever more faithful, ever more conformed by grace to God's will. In Mary this grace was complete, so that she is the true Israel, the masterpiece of all God's preparatory work, in whom nothing of the ruin produced by the sin of the ages remained.

This was necessary that she might, in the name of all Israel, and through Israel of all humanity, speak the word of perfect faith, the only condition for the reception of the Incarnate Son of God, the Anointed. If her faith had not been perfect, her "May it be done to me according to your word" (Lk 1:38), could not have been proportionate to the gift of God. Indeed, if there had been left in her even the least trace of the work of sin her faith would not have been perfect.

Moreover, Mary's perpetual virginity is intimately linked with her need for perfect faith. Luke, in true Pauline manner, wanted to show that the Incarnation was entirely an act of grace. The Messiah did not come to the Jews because of any merits on their part, nor simply because they are "children of Abraham," but purely because of the faith of the patriarchs and of the Remnant. Hence Jesus has no earthly father, but is simply and absolutely the Son of God the Father, and his mother must be a virgin mother, one utterly dedicated to God alone in faith. Mary's virginity is thus in a real sense her faith, but her faith understood as a total dedication of soul and body to God alone, as Israel can have no other God than God. It has often been remarked that women find it easier than men to enter into contemplative life and hence to attain mystical union with God, as we see in Catherine of Siena and Teresa of Avila.

Thus women's faith is more open, receptive, transparent. They do not feel, as men to tend to do, that they must impose their formulations and systems on God's revealing word, but simply allow that Word to be heard in their innermost being, to be impregnated by it. Luke shows this contemplative gift of women when he repeats that "Mary pondered all these things in her heart" (Lk 2:19, 51), constantly seeking the meaning of the mystery of Jesus as he grew up in her home, even when she did not understand him perfectly. Like Mary, the sister of Martha (Lk 10:38–42), Mary the mother of Jesus, was ready simply to listen to him.

Thus Mary's faith is a supremely "fertile" faith, a faith that makes it possible for God to work through her to transform the world, and bring about a new creation. No wonder then, that the liturgy applies the name of "Wisdom" to her, that wonderful "prudence" by which we respond to the message of faith by living the faith. This prudence of Mary is manifested by Luke, in the way she carefully tries to understand the meaning of the angel's message before answering it (Lk 1:29, 34), and by John, in the way Mary gets Jesus to assist the young married couple at Cana who have run out of wine, in spite of the fact that his "time has not yet come" (Jn 2:1–11).

Why then do Aristotle and Aquinas seem to deny "prudence" to women?[27] Perhaps what they intended was that kind of prudence that ordinarily makes a man head of the household or a military or political ruler, and which depends both on a wider experience of the world and a more objective attitude than is typical of most women's experience and ways of thinking. Aquinas certainly believes that women have personal prudence, since without it no other virtues are possible. Thus the prudence of women has more the character of "tact" and "sensitivity" in dealing with persons, than of decision in dealing with things and affairs, more typical perhaps of men. When masculine prudence becomes vicious, it becomes a carnal prudence of fraud, treachery, and lust for power, as vicious feminine prudence becomes manipulation, seduction, and deception.

Mary's Hope, Moderation and Courage

From Mary's perfect faith sprang her wonderful hope. Mary could not have been ready for the Incarnation if she had not embodied in herself the great messianic hope of Israel for the fulfillment by the power of God of all the promises he had made to his Chosen People through the prophets. The

---

[27] *Summa theologiae* I, q. 79, a.9; *2 Sent.*, d. 24, q. 2, a. 2; *De Veritate,* q. 15, a. 2.

Magnificat (Lk 1:46–55) expresses this confidence that in spite of all appearances, God will raise the lowly from the dung-hill and cast down the tyrants. This hope grew in Mary through the prophecy of Simeon and the words of the aged Anna, through the strange visit of the Magi, and the unfathomable words of the boy Jesus, "I must be about my Father's work?" (Lk 2:49).

Like a mother she must have retained confidence through the long years when Jesus seemed to pursue nothing more than a carpenter's trade that someday he would "amount to something." Who can doubt that during all this time, as so many mothers have done, she shared with him his growing dreams of mission, since at the wedding of Cana she actually prompted him to perform his first great miracle (Jn 2:1–12)? When he began to succeed in his public ministry and the crowds began to gather around him, her hope must have swelled, yet at the same time it must have been beset by the anxieties that prompted her to come with his other relatives to see how he was doing and to warn him of the dangers he faced (Mk 3:31–34; Mt 12:46–50; Lk 8:19–21). The other relatives even wondered if he was "losing his head" with all this popularity. She knew him too well to think that, yet she needed to see him again. He did not permit her to come in, lest his hearers lose confidence in his complete dedication to them. Thus Mary's hope, like that of many mothers, had to be tempered by disappointment. She had to wait in a hope based on her complete faith.

Christian hope for the coming Kingdom always produces the tension between this life and the next, and demands therefore the asceticism that moderates our desires for present satisfaction and strengthens our courage to persevere and endure in the journey. Mary did not need the purification from sin that this asceticism is necessary to effect, but she shared with her son that suffering for others by which love comes to its ultimate intensity. For Christians the grace of virginity typifies the perfection of moderation (temperance), as well as the humility that keeps virginity a state of openness to God rather than a kind of narcissism, and martyrdom typifies the perfection of fortitude. Mary's virginity was joined to perfect humility, a willingness to be the least and the most powerless of God's creatures, which in fact exalted her to her sublime mission as Mother of God. Her courage in martyrdom was joined to perfect patience at the foot of the Cross, when her own heart was pierced through in compassion for her Son.

What is especially feminine about such humility and compassion is that they arise from a good mother's ability to totally identify with her children without possessiveness or demanding of them to be other than their true selves. The purity of love and the profound strength that this requires is quite beyond measure. It should not be confused with its caricature found in the self-pitying woman who loudly declares herself a martyr to her children or the depersonalized woman who "sacrifices" her own dignity as a human being to be a slave to her children. A doormat cannot be a mother. The true mother brings her children to birth and maturity in their own independent existence. She gives them life out of her own strong and abundant life.

When Jesus sees Mary at the foot of the Cross and before he entrusts her to John's care, he first says, "Woman, behold your son" (Jn 19:26). She is not annihilated by grief, but stands ready to take up a new mission, a new motherhood. Thus Mary is not only a humble handmaid, she is also "the Woman" with a capital letter, "great-souled," "magnanimous," ready for great tasks, and for the "magnificence" which Aquinas associates with courage,[28] because like the widow who put her mite into the temple treasury, she "from her poverty, has contributed [to God] all she had, her whole livelihood" (Mk 12:44).

Mary's Love and Righteousness

Mary's faith and hope were the foundation of her charity, her love in which was summed up the whole of the Old and New Covenant, and with it that perfect righteousness or justice which consists in fulfilling the holy will of God to its greatest and least demand. The piety of the Old Testament and of Judaism today is the unremitting study of the will of God expressed in the Torah and the carrying out of its requirements to the letter.

The Pharisees were imbued with this zeal, but they knew that the prophets had taught that faithfulness to the letter of the law was not enough. Jesus rebuked them not for this literalism as such, since he too held that the Law must be observed to "the least letter" (Mt 5:18), but because they were to be "perfect as the heavenly Father is perfect" (Mt 5:48), with that perfection which is more than the letter. The observance of the Law must be done in the right spirit, since only in that spirit can the weighty things of the Law be distinguished from the lesser things, and all observed in proper measure. That spirit is the Great Commandment of Love that sums up all the rest (Mt 22:38–40). The love to which this Commandment refers is not *eros* but *agape*, not love for what one needs for oneself, but love that seeks to share with another what one already possesses for one's own self.[29]

Eros is not evil; it is necessary that we love what we need; we even love God with *eros*. But *agape* is a participation in God's love for us, a love that arises not because God needs us for his happiness, but because he wants to share his perfect happiness with us, who do need it. It was at Mary's breast and in Mary's home that Jesus in his humanness was formed in *agape*, in the love of generosity, which does justice and more than justice to all the needy. He was formed both in the letter and the spirit of the law. Men have a tendency to be

---

[28] Aquinas, *In VIII Libros Politicorum Aristotelis,* I, lect. 10.
[29] *Summa theologiae* II–II, q. 134, a.4.

concerned with the letter, women with the spirit because for them what matters first of all is the personal relationship to God and to God's children. This personal relationship of love is that inner empathy that gives life to the external letter.

Another way to put this is to remember the teaching of Aquinas that true love has two aspects: (a) it is *beneficence*, a seeking of what is good for the beloved; but (b) it is also desire for *union*.[30] It seems to me that the masculine side of *agape* is beneficence, because male virtue tends to do things for people; but the feminine side is union, because female virtue tends to identify with the one loved, it is empathetic, not merely constructive. Mary's love, therefore, produces in the Christian community that sense of inner unity, of unanimity, of "peace" in the deepest sense of the word. It is this interiority that makes the Law something that gives life, rather than imposing external restraints. It sets us free while maintaining perfect harmony.

What this means in moral theology is that the divorce that has come about between morality and spirituality can be overcome only if we understand that moral laws have to be vivified by the inner spirit of love and union, of community. Christian morality is a morality of community, of mutual respect and mutual help and mutual understanding. Competition and controversy and pluralism are stimulating and necessary for the Church but only within that atmosphere of love that is the special gift of women. That need of the vivifying and unifying power of love is shown us by Luke when in a single sentence he tells us that when the apostles were awaiting the coming of the Holy Spirit at Pentecost, Mary and the women were present praying with them (Acts 2:14). This is the last historical word we hear about her in the Bible, although in the *Book of Revelation* she appears again in allegory as the Woman clothed in the sun (Rv 12:1–18) and as the Bride of the Lamb (Rv 21:1–4, 22:17). We must remember that the early Church was soon divided by the struggle over the question whether Gentile converts had to observe the Law. No doubt it was Mary's prayers that held the Church of those days together in the Spirit.

With justice or righteousness Aquinas links many other virtues which cannot adequately pay a debt, or do not owe a strict debt.[31] Of these the first, the greatest, is *religion*, a willingness to give God his due through reverence and worship, and along with it *piety* to our parents and country, and *obedience* to all legitimate superiors in society. In every Catholic family, I believe, it is commonly the mother who is most mindful of religious obligations, of getting everyone to Mass on Sunday, of keeping fasts and feasts. Certainly Luke shows us the Holy Family fulfilling its duties in the Temple (Lk 2:22–50). It must have been Mary who taught Jesus' his prayers. It is she

---

[30] See Ceslaus Spicq, OP, *Agape in the New Testament.*
[31] *Summa theologiae* II–II, q. 27 a. 2 c; cf. I–II, q. 28, a. 1; II–II q. 23, a. 1.

who says to him when he was found in the Temple, "Your father and I sought you in sorrow" (Lk 2:48). Everything we hear about Jesus shows that he had grown up in a home of regular worship, of reverence for parents ("He was subject to them," Lk 2:51) of a spirit of sincere obedience. It is precisely a woman's sensitivity for human relationships that makes the peaceful good order of a family and a community possible.

Also related to justice are the virtues of *mildness* in correction, *gratitude* for every gift, and *truthfulness*. That Mary restrains the just punishments of God by invoking his infinite mercy is a fundamental feature of her traditional image. Her gratitude to God appears in the first lines of her *Magnificat* (Lk 1:46–49). She is the Mother of Truth itself. Truth is sacred because all society rests on trustworthiness, but truth can be harsh and brutal; it can kill as well as quicken. A truthful woman, however, because she thinks first of the person to whom she speaks, can make truth a healing and a nourishing message.

Jesus' preaching sometimes is a "hard saying" (Jn 6:60), yet what most characterizes it is that it is "Good News" (Mk 1:15) and in that Good News we hear Mary's tenderness, manifest in the tact she shows at the wedding feast of Cana, when Jesus resists her suggestion of a miracle and she says to the waiters very simply, "Do what he tells you" (Jn 2:5).[32] With justice are also associated *liberality* or mercy, *affability*, and *equity* or fair dealing. Who is more merciful, friendlier, more concerned that everyone has a share than a good mother, than Mary? Thus Mary exemplifies justice, righteousness in its entire range of dutifulness, in every letter even the least letter of the moral Law. She gave to the righteousness of her Son that wonderful feminine quality we sum up in the word "mercy." "Take my yoke upon you and learn from me, for I am meek and humble of heart" (Mt 11:29).

It is said that Pope John Paul II consulted 23 Mariologists about whether at beginning of the Third Millennium he should honor Our Lady by declaring *ex cathedra* that she is Co-Redemptrix of all humanity. They unanimously advised against it lest it raise further barriers for ecumenical dialogue. On the other hand John Paul II has received petitions with over a million signatures from the faithful all over the world begging for such an infallible definition. Seeing that the theologians who today choose Mariology as their field are usually toward the conservative end of the theological spectrum, this raises a rather paradoxical situation. Usually liberal Catholics appeal to the *sensus fidelium* against the conservative theologians. In this matter the situation is reversed. On the other hand liberal theologians claimed to be outraged by the recent document *Dominus Jesus* of the Congregation for the Doctrine of the Faith that said:

---

[32] *Summa theologiae* II–II, q. 80.

5. As a remedy for this relativistic mentality, which is becoming ever more common, it is necessary above all to reassert the definitive and complete character of the revelation of Jesus Christ. In fact, it must be *firmly believed* that, in the mystery of Jesus Christ, the Incarnate Son of God, who is "the way, the truth, and the life" (Jn 14:6), the full revelation of divine truth is given: "No one knows the Son except the Father, and no one knows the Father except the Son and anyone to whom the Son wishes to reveal him" (Mt 11:27); "No one has ever seen God; God the only Son, who is in the bosom of the Father, has revealed him" (Jn 1:18); "For in Christ the whole fullness of divinity dwells in bodily form" (Col 2:9–10). [33]

Certainly the title "Co-Redemptrix" can be understood in a way entirely consistent with the Gospel truth that, as St. Peter preached, "There is no salvation through anyone else, nor is there any other name [except that of Jesus] under heaven given of the human race by which we are to be saved" (Acts 4:12), since according to the doctrine of her Immaculate Conception Mary herself is saved through her Son. Yet I agree with these other theologians that the Orthodox Churches might resent another papal definition that did not come from an Ecumenical Council in which they participated, while Protestants might see this as another example of confusing the human Mary with her divine Son.

When the Reformation drew the attention of Protestant Christians away from Mary, moral teaching tended to become pessimistic and when her spirituality no longer infuses our Catholic moral theology it becomes once again the legalism of the Pharisees. The culmination of moral theology, therefore, is not in the casuistic discussions that occupy moralists so much today, especially in the field of bioethics, nor in the reformist theories of liberation, but in the study of the way the Gifts of the Holy Spirit facilitate the full flowering of faith, hope, and charity. Not that this means that therefore moral theology is not concerned with social justice. Christian love is so intimately connected with justice that Our Lord says we will be finally judged on whether we have loved him in the poor and the oppressed (Mt 25:31–45). This justice cannot transform the social order unless it really does flow from an inner spirituality. The letter of justice will kill in politics just as it does in private life. We cannot transform society, or liberate anyone except in the spirit of love.

In her *Magnificat* Mary speaks plainly of how God will put down the rich oppressors and raise the poor, hungry, and oppressed, thus foreshadowing the theme of the Beatitudes, "Blessed are you who are poor, for the kingdom of God is yours" (Lk 6:20).[34] This is at the heart of the spirituality of

[33] Feuillet, *Jesus and His Mother*, 8–10, 120–24, 137–38, 257–58.
[34] See John Paul II, *Redemptoris Mater*, n. 37; Laurentin, *The Truth of Christmas*, 156–57, 167–68, 379–93.

the New Testament, nowhere more explicit than in the Lucan Gospel, namely the expectation of the imminence of the Reign of God, a feast from which no one will be excluded unless he excludes himself (Lk 14:15–24). Its principle is what is now called "the preferential option for the poor," which means that the Christian Community under the headship of the Good Shepherd first of all seeks out those in the world who are the outcast, the neglected, the homeless of every other community. It does so because the Kingdom of God, just because it is God's, is directed to righting every injustice in a spirit of love that goes beyond justice. Mary, because she had experienced poverty, as we see when she and Joseph offer two pigeons to redeem the infant Jesus at the Temple, the sacrifice of the poor (Lk 2:22–24; Lv 12:8), and because she represents the Jewish people, a people whose history is one of exile and persecution, stands with the poor.

Historically it has been the humble people of the Church who recognized her as the Immaculate when the greatest theologians hesitated and who find in her motherliness a confidence that even their confused image of Jesus does not always inspire in them.

CHAPTER 12

Hierarchy in Ecclesiology*

Cosmic Community

PROBLEMS OF WORLD COMMUNITY AND WORLD ECOLOGY are central ethical and spiritual issues today, and they raise the question of "natural law" in new contexts. We are part of nature, but as persons in community we give meaning and unity to the universe; we make it truly a whole. Therefore, any discussion of natural law today requires an examination of the world order as community.

Some thinkers deny the value of the search for world order. Existentialists say that the world is absurd. The best we can do is put a little order into our own brief lives. Analytic philosophers humbly prefer to clarify small areas of discourse, without tackling the cosmos. Yet these disclaimers cannot conceal the cosmic assumptions of both schools of thought. The classical problem of the "whole and the part" cannot be evaded. This is the question of the "universe" and of the "cosmic order," because the notion of "order" (or "system" or "structure") implies a diversity of entities (distinct in number and usually in kind) that are unified by relations.[1] To classify world orders we must speak in terms of "many," "one," "part," "whole," and "relation." We must also consider how these static structures exist in "process" or "change" or "evolution."

---

* Published as "Cosmic Community in Plotinus, Aquinas, and Whitehead," *Cultura y Vida* (XX Semana Tomista, 1995), (Buenos Aires: Sociedad Tomista Argentina, 1995), Appendix A, 1–27.

[1] "A system can be defined as a complex of interacting elements. Interaction means that elements, p, stand in relations, R, so that the behavior of an element p in R is different from its behavior in another relation, R'." Ludwig von Bertalanffy, *General System Theory: Foundations, Development, Applications,* 55 f.; cf. also 83–86. For a recent discussion of this notion, see Errol E. Harris, *Cosmos and Anthropos: A Philosophical Interpretation of the Anthropic Cosmological Principles,* chapter 2, "Wholes," 17–30.

In this essay my purpose is to compare examples of an ancient, a medieval, and a modern world system, chosen for both their historical importance and their typical character. All three models can still be useful in our search for better worldviews today, at least because they raise questions about the assumptions we uncritically or unconsciously make. In each worldview the notion of "natural law" has a different meaning, and each implies a different ethic, especially because each involves a different concept of "community."

Plotinus

The world order of Plotinus (A.D. 270) was built on the principle of perfect *hierarchy*.[2] Not only does all reality flow from the One and return to it, but at every level of "the Great Chain of Being," the whole of the inferior order is also contained in the superior in a more perfectly simple, unified condition. The One contains the Cosmic Intelligence (*Nous* or Mind in which exist the Platonic Ideas). The Cosmic Intelligence in turn contains the World-Soul, in which again are contained in perfect linear order all particular souls and the forms of all inanimate things. Matter alone is not contained in the higher entities, because Matter is only a limit of Being. Matter is Non-Being and the principle of evil.

In descent from the superior to the inferior, the lower differs from the higher only in an ever-decreasing unity and increasing plurality or dispersion. The timeless simplicity of the One becomes "spread out" more and more in time and space, less and less intensely concentrated. Each inferior being is prevented from complete dispersion by its "return" toward the One. Each returns toward the One by imitating it and (in the case of rational beings) by contemplating it (mediately or immediately), thus achieving a certain simplification and unification after the likeness of the absolute One.

As each interior being becomes more unified by its tendency to return to the One, it also imitates it by producing a new inferior. Then this inferior by imitating or contemplating its superior is inflamed with love, becomes impregnated by its energy, and begets an offspring. Thus the famous Neo-Platonic axiom, "The Good is diffusive of itself" means that the One produces the Cosmic Intelligence because it has an absolute tendency to express itself. In turn each member of the cosmic hierarchy is compelled by its need to imitate its superior to continue this cascading process until the uttermost

---

[2] The single surviving work of Plotinus, edited by his pupil Porphyry, is called the *Enneads*. For recent interpretation, see A. H. Armstrong, *The Architecture of the Intelligible Universe in the Philosophy of Plotinus*; Philip Merlan, *Monopsychism, Mysticism, Metaconsciousness: Problems of the Soul in Neo-Aristotelian and Neo-Platonic Tradition*; and J. M. Rist, *Plotinus: The Road to Reality*.

limit of Matter or Non-Being is reached, where light fades into the darkness of the void.

This whole process is absolutely necessary and exhaustive of all possibilities of Being, so that our cosmos (in the phrase of Leibnitz) is the "best of all possible worlds." In one sense the Plotinian universe is dynamic since each entity that it contains is not so much an independent substance as it is a phase of the total process of overflow and return to the One; yet it is also static in the sense that this process *taken as a whole* is everlasting, without novelty. Time, like space, is only an aspect of the dispersion of the One in the Many and manifests itself more and more as we descend the hierarchy.

The most characteristic feature of this hierarchical order of the cosmos is that the inferiors *add nothing* to the superior member of the linear series, except a manifestation or expression of the plenitude and "goodness" of the superior. This forces Plotinus into a curious paradox: He teaches that the production of the universe outside the One is a "fall," a descent into evil, although he also asserts that this results from the very goodness of the One. He attempts to resolve this paradox by insisting on the counterprocess of return by which the fallen world strives upward to imitate the goodness of the One. This redemption of the fallen world is achieved, it would seem, in the mystical ecstatic union of intelligent souls with the One, a redemption as inevitable as the fall, coeternally existent with it. In a strange way the world of Plotinus fits Luther's dialectic formula *simul justus et peccator*, since the world is ever-falling, yet ever-redeemed.

Aquinas

St. Thomas Aquinas (1225–74) made extensive use of the Neo-Platonic system, although he knew the work of Plotinus only indirectly through the Pseudo-Dionysius (5th century A.D.) and others. Yet as a Christian and an Aristotelian he could not accept the basic conception of hierarchic order on which the Neo-Platonic worldview was built.

Of course, in the cosmos of Aquinas there is a kind of hierarchy. At the summit is the Triune God who contains in his own infinite plenitude and in perfect unity the Divine Ideas of all the unlimited, numberless diversity of possible things. Because the Thomistic God is infinite, however, it is impossible for him (because contradictory) to create the "best of all possible worlds."[3] He could always better any particular world he might create, and no possible world could ever completely express his total goodness, nor

---

[3] *Summa theologiae* I, q. 25, a. 6 and *De Pot.* q. 3, a. 16 ad 17. Malebranche and Leibnitz revived the idea that this is "the best of all possible worlds," so savagely satirized by Voltaire in *Candide*.

exhaust the possibilities of his creativity. Plotinus' world is the perfect expression of the absolute, but finite, One,[4] while Aquinas's world is one of the numberless possible likenesses of an infinite God.

Consequently Aquinas holds that God does not produce the universe as a necessary expression of himself, but creates it by a *free choice*, selected from countless possibilities for a wise, but not compelling purpose. Aquinas accepts the Plotinian maxim "the Good is diffusive of itself" not in the order of an *efficient causality*, but of *final* causality, that is, not as applying to the creative *exitus* from God, but to the *reditus* or return to God.[5] God need not have made this world, but once having made it, he cannot help but love his creatures and seek their good, which is to be achieved by their drawing closer to him, and sharing more fully in his power and life. Thus the created world adds nothing to God, but is freely called into being by him to share in what he alone fully possesses,

In the hierarchy of Plotinus the One and each succeeding member *totally* includes the perfection of all succeeding members. In that of Aquinas, however, this is true only of the first in the hierarchy, God himself. The subsequent members include their inferiors only *generically*, but not specifically or individually. For example, humanity contains the general powers of animals, plants, and minerals, but does not contain their specific abilities. Humans cannot swim like fishes, fly like birds, grow out of the earth like the grass, or burn like fire. Even Lucifer, the noblest of creatures, created as the supreme seraph, does not contain in his whole splendor the unique powers of the lowliest worm. Lucifer cannot create any new thing, even acting as an instrument of God.[6] God alone is the Creator because he alone contains the ultimate and specifying powers of every created thing (in a supereminent way). A higher species of creature cannot of itself produce a lower species. Among living, corporeal things the parents produce offspring of their own

---

[4] Many commentators on Plotinus argue that his One is infinite because it "exceeds Being and the Nous" in which there certainly are only a finite number of ideas (*Enneads* VI, 6.18, 7.17, 14–16, etc.; see Armstrong, *The Architecture of the Intelligible Universe*, 34ff., and Rist, *Plotinus*, 22–37 and 250–51, n. 14, with references). It seems to me, however, that the One does not exceed the Nous by a greater *plenitude* of Being, since the One necessarily emanates all that it contains down to the limits of Matter, which is Non-Being, but that the One is "infinite" only in the sense that it is intrinsically and absolutely undivided.

[5] "When it is said that the good is diffusive by its very nature, this effusion is not to be understood as if it meant the operation of an efficient cause, but as meaning a relation to the final cause." *De Veritate* q. 21, a. 1 ad 4; cf. also *Summa theologiae* I, q. 5, a. 4, ad 2.

[6] Ibid., I, q. 45, a. 5 and *Summa contra Gentiles* II, cc. 21; and III, c. 67.

kind, but even then they are not the sufficient cause of the uniqueness of the individual within the species.[7]

This Thomistic view has the startling consequence that in some respects material things more perfectly manifest God than do purely spiritual beings. Thus matter is not, as for Plotinus, the principle of evil, but is a special and unique manifestation of God in that its infinite potentiality to be actualized by an infinite variety of forms corresponds in a manner to the infinite formative power of God, although obviously these two infinities are only analogically comparable.

Therefore, the world order of Aquinas is not primarily a hierarchy or linear cascade from the One to Non-Being, but rather it is a *community of complementary entities with God* as the *coincidentia oppositorum* or *concors discordantium* at the center.[8] Around this center a spiral unfolds in which a hierarchical order as regards generic perfections is combined with a radial order as regards specific perfections.

The complementary perfections of creatures result in a mutual dependence. We human persons need other material creatures for our bodily sustenance. We and the angels need material creatures also as a cosmic mirror in which we see reflected the various perfections of God which we lack in ourselves. In the other direction, inferior beings need the superior to guide them to their own full development, and material beings achieve the psychic level of existence not in themselves, but through being known by rational beings, human and angelic.

For Aquinas, God absolutely transcends the world in his independent existence, undiluted by time, space, or contingency. Yet God is immanent in the world by his creative power and his intimate knowledge and love of each creature in its unique individuality and development. He is "closer to each of His creatures than each of them is to itself."[9] Hence creation is in no sense a

---

[7] Aquinas held that only God can create the species of things as such. Angels and other intermediaries cannot even be instruments of creation (*Summa theologiae* I, q. 45, a. 5). Furthermore, the angels, although they know themselves by their own forms, cannot know lesser things except through innate co-natural forms created in them by God (I, q. 55, a. 1). Human persons can only know inferiors through species abstracted from things (I, q. 85, a. 1). Finally, neither angels nor human persons can produce things inferior to themselves directly, but only by using natural forces (I, q. 90, a. 3 c.). The reason for all this is that only God virtually contains all things, including matter (I, q. 44, a. 2 and 105, a. 1), while each creature is limited by its own specific essence. Hence higher creatures, for Aquinas, contrary to Plotinus, contain their inferiors only generically, not specifically.

[8] These are terms used in Renaissance philosophy, not by Aquinas, but the notions are clearly present in *Summa theologiae* I, q. 47, a. 1 and q. 15, a. 2.

[9] "Therefore as long as anything has existence, so long is it necessary that God should be present to it according to its own mode of existence. Now existence is that which is most interior to anything, and most profoundly interior in all things, since it is the

"fall," but an act by which God as a pure gift grants being to possibilities which he has selected so they can come to share in his power and life. Aquinas agrees with Plotinus that God is both center and circumference of the cosmos. For Aquinas, however, in contrast to Plotinus, the "fall" is not the creation of human persons or angels but is the free choice of some humans and angels to sin.

Because God freely creates and governs his world, and because created persons share God's freedom, the world of Aquinas, unlike that of Plotinus, has a *history*, with a beginning, middle, and end. God, however, cannot be frustrated in his love for his world by the sin of creatures, since in his creative wisdom he also has the power and ingenuity to "bring good out of evil," so as to produce a final result more perfect because of the free choices, good and evil, of his rational creatures. This comes about through the "history of salvation" climaxing in the Incarnation, but the detailed outcome is determined by the actual free choices of rational creatures who accept or reject this supreme self-giving of God.

The communitarian order of the universe as the complementary unity of creatures, especially of created free persons, is for Aquinas an epiphany of the very inner being of God who is not Plotinus' One, but the Trinity. In God himself the eternal procession of the coequal Son and Holy Spirit by generation and spiration from the Father is the ultimate reconciliation of the One and the Many in the mystery of a wholly perfect *community*.[10] This Trinitarian Community surpasses that of creatures, because it is a total communication that results in the perfect equality of the Persons in a single, necessary existence: one life of infinite power, wisdom, and love.

This Triune god, however, has not chosen to live in self-sufficiency, but has created the universe so as to draw angels and humans into this inner divine life by the power of *grace*. Thus all persons are called to share in the inner divine life whose perfect unity is no obstacle to a genuine distinction of unique persons. This community of spiritual life does not obliterate individuality, but fulfills each person in relation to all the others.

---

form of whatever is contained in a thing. . . . Hence it is necessary that God be present in all things and present *intimately*." *Summa theologiae* I, q. 8, a. 1 c.; cf. also a. 2 and q. 22, a. 3 and q. 111, a. 2, where it is shown that an angel cannot move the human will, but God can do so by nature and by grace without any coercion. This is the basis of the famous Thomistic doctrine of the reconciliation of predestination and free will: God can move the free will without destroying its freedom, because he is even more interior to our free will than we are ourselves. It is the presence of the free God to our will that makes it and us free!

10 *Summa theologiae* I, q. 42.

Whitehead

In his "philosophy of organism," Alfred North Whitehead (1861–1947) developed a cosmic model that is strikingly modern in the way it takes account of the following themes unknown to Plotinus or Aquinas: (1) the theory of relativity developed by mathematical physics; (2) the theories of emergent evolution developed by physics, biology, cultural anthropology, and history; (3) the emphasis on pluralism, creativity, and novelty so prominent in modern cultures as a result of our experience of scientific and technological progress; and (4) our modern emphasis on the ethical value of democracy, personal freedom, and equality.[11]

A kind of hierarchical order still remains in Whitehead's universe, since the "actual entities" or "actual occasions" of which it is composed range from very simple entities in which the psychic or subjective aspect is very faint all the way to God who is an everlasting Mind in which exist as "eternal objects" an infinity of possibilities, as well as a full awareness of all the actualities of the past and present. Between these two extremes is an immense array of more or less complex entities.

The ultimate principle of unity in this universe, however, is not simply God but rather *Creativity* that manifests itself supremely in God, but also in every other actual entity. This Creativity is the continual tendency to form new unities out of existing or possibly existing pluralities. Each actual entity, by reason of this Creativity, "be-ings" itself into existence by a unifying process called "concrescence." This is a teleological process, guided by a "subjective aim" that is unique for each actual occasion. It is in some measure a psychic, mindlike process that is consummated in an experiential, subjective "satisfaction." This is achieved at the moment when an actual entity (a "drop of experience") comes into full actuality as a unique event or "occasion." Yet at the very moment of consummation every actual entity, except God, immediately perishes, while achieving "objective immortality" by its inclusion in some new concrescence and also in the mind of God.

Because each actual entity is a synthesis of elements derived from former entities, it mirrors the entire universe as that universe has causally influenced it from the past. In this way the relativistic theory of time and space developed by Einstein enters into Whitehead's cosmos. In the universes of Plotinus and Aquinas causal relations are *simultaneous* and direct communication between substances is possible, but in Whitehead's universe an actual entity

---

[11] Whitehead's chief work is *Process and Reality: An Essay in Cosmology*, original edition from 1929, corrected and edited by David Ray Griffin and Donald W. Sherburne. For useful expositions of his philosophy, see especially Dorothy M. Emmett, *Whitehead's Philosophy of Organism*, 2nd ed.; William A. Christian, *An Interpretation of Whitehead's Metaphysics*; Victor Lowe, *Understanding Whitehead*; Donald W. Sherburne, *A Key to Whitehead's Process and Reality*; and John W. Lango, *Whitehead's Ontology*.

achieves its individuality and distinction from all other entities only at the moment that it attains it own "now." At that moment it fully and actually exists in isolation, and it is related to other entities only through its past as they are contained in it. This is Whitehead's solution of the problem of the One and the Many, since each actual occasion contains all the elements of the universe in itself at that instance in which it completely becomes itself. On the other hand his universe is irreducibly pluralistic, since each entity perishes to make room for new ones in an infinite, endless succession.

What initiates the concrescence of an actual entity? What gives it its novel, unifying, "subjective aim" or germinal idea? Whitehead proposes that God, as the supreme actual entity and embodiment of Creativity, contains within himself an infinity of *possibilities* or "eternal objects." Each new actual entity begins to concresce by "conceptually apprehending" some such as yet unrealized possibility in God, along with other elements which it "physically apprehends" from previously existing entities in its past that have causally influenced it. Thus each actual entity has a psychic or "conceptual pole" by which it apprehends a novel aim by contact with God, and a "physical pole" by which it is related to the other entities of the universe. Once this process of concrescence begins, however, each entity has genuine *freedom* in synthesizing itself, determining the exact manner in which it achieves actual satisfaction.

God, like any other actual entity, is also bipolar. As God contains the infinity of possibilities or eternal objects, Whitehead speaks of God's "antecedent nature;" but as God enters into the ongoing process of the world in achievement of God's own actual experience or satisfaction, Whitehead speaks of God's "consequent nature." This latter consists in God's unification of the divine experience of the plurality of all actual entities that have to be in the universe and this is God's vision of the world as unified order at any given moment of endless time. This vision is not a mere objective observation, but rather an esthetic, creative harmonization that God forms as the divine life experience, just as does every other actual entity in its own concrescence.

God, however, differs from other actual entities because: (1) God initiates the process of creative advance that returns full circle to God; and (2) God does not perish, as all other entities perish, but has a continuous life of everlasting experience, including all past and present events, and moves ever into a future that grows always richer and more unified without ever attaining completion. Thus the infinity of God and universe is that of endless time with a direction but no goal.[12] New events occur constantly, but their novelty is only the actualization of possibilities or "Eternal objects" that pre-exist in God's antecedent nature. This "creative advance" is the working-out in

---

[12] Whitehead, *Process and Reality,* chapter 2, sect. v–vi, 408–12.

the universe and in God's conscious experience of what was already in what we may call "God's unconscious."[13]

Whitehead stresses the inter-relatedness of all actual entities while maintaining a strong pluralism. He conceives this connectedness in terms of Einstein's space-time relativity. Each entity exists in its own here-now. Its universe consists in all those entities in its vicinity and its past that have causally affected it, although as far as it is concerned they have now perished. Yet each entity is also a concrescence of all these influences. Just as God sums up the whole universe in his consequent nature, so each actual entity, in a less explicit, conscious, and comprehensive way, sums up *its* entire universe.[14]

Thus in the moment at which an actual entity comes fully into existence, it is alone with its history.[15] In this same moment it immediately begins to perish, so that time and space are quantized into moments. In its perishing each actual entity "superjects" itself into "objective immortality" by causally influencing new entities that are beginning to concresce. The relation of all actual entities to each other is similar to their relation to God and of God to them. Each actual entity as it perishes also achieves objective immortality in the consequent nature of God, as a part of his advancing vision. In his turn, God enters into the experience of each actual entity, because it is only by "conceptually prehending" some eternal object in God's antecedent nature that each actual entity initiates its own self-creative concrescence.

---

[13] "Thus, when we make a distinction of reason, and consider God in the abstraction of a primordial actuality, we must ascribe to him neither fullness of feeling, nor consciousness." Ibid., sect. ii, 405. "The consequent nature of God is conscious; and it is the realization of the actual world in the unity of his nature, and through the transformation of his wisdom. The primordial nature is conceptual, the consequent nature is the weaving of God's physical feelings upon his primordial concepts. . . . One side of God's nature is constituted by his conceptual experiences. . . . This side of his nature is free, complete, primordial, eternal, actually deficient, and unconscious." Ibid., sect iii, 407. It should be noted that this has some affinity to Plotinus's view that the One is non-conscious or super-conscious; see Rist, Plotinus, 38–52 and Merlan, *Monopsychism, Mysticism, Metaconsciousness,* 4–84, but is by no means identical with it.

[14] This notion again has affinities with the Plotinian notion of the presence of all things in each thing (Enneads VI, 5), but it is not identical with it. This feature of Plotinus's universe comes closest to Aquinas's idea of a community of persons, since in the World Soul and the Cosmic Intelligence the lesser souls exist *in* each other. Aquinas would agree, I believe, with Plotinus's analysis of the nature of "spirit;" yet note that Aquinas holds that one angel cannot know the mind of another without the free consent of the other (*Summa theologiae* I, q. 107).

[15] *Process and Reality* II, chapter 2, 76ff; cf. Christian, *An Interpretation of Whitehead's Metaphysics,* chapter 6, 155ff.

A curious feature of Whitehead's cosmos, considering modern personalism, is that only God is a person or continuous self.[16] Only God maintains a continuous unified existence. For Whitehead the human person is just a "stream of consciousness" made up of a vast number of actual occasions. The created person is a sequence of "drops of experience," or interwoven strands of such sequences. Some of these form the relatively unconscious body, while others, having a more vivid and intense consciousness, form the mind. Except for God there are no enduring selves, and we at death achieve only an objective, not a personal immortality. This position contrasts with that of Plotinus who holds that the human self is an eternal soul that cyclically undergoes reincarnation, and that of Aquinas who teaches that the human person is the unity of a soul and a body, which after death will be resurrected to remain eternally, perhaps to share in the community of the Divine Trinity.

Whitehead explains evil as an inevitable feature of the universe, because in order to exist each actual entity, God excepted, must also negate the existence of other possible entities. The realization of possibilities must always be selective.[17] Every entity must perish to make room for others. This tragic aspect of the universe is compensated by the fact that in perishing each entity survives by its inclusion in new entities and in the imperishable mind of God.

Whitehead's God is often praised as "compassionate," "suffering with the world's suffering," but this is true only in a very peculiar sense. God does not actually undergo any evil or suffering himself, since his synthesis of the experiences of the world is always harmonious and blessed.[18] God is com-

---

[16] "On Whitehead's theory God is an actuality that exists through time without loss of immediacy. His unity is not of a persistent pattern of definiteness with a continuity *between* individual immediacies. It is a continuing unity *within* an individual immediacy. In this one respect Whitehead's conception of God fits our common-sense notion of person existence better than actual occasions and nexus do." Christian, *An Interpretation of Whitehead's Metaphysics,* 411; see his whole discussion of the question, 409–12.

[17] *Process and Reality,* III, chapter 1, sect. iv.

[18] "God prehends actual occasions, but he does not share their immediacy. Actual occasions enter into God's experience, but they do so as objects of his physical prehensions. God's prehension of an actual occasion is the objectification of that actual occasion for God. And an objective entity has perished and lost its subjective immediacy." Christian, *An Interpretation of Whitehead's Metaphysics,* 405. Thus God *remembers* the world, but He does not know it immediately in its presence to Him. "Similarly God prehends and values all the feelings of actual occasions, including their feelings of pain, deprivation, and degradation, and including those decisions which constitute moral evil. It seems that in doing so he accepts and consents to these feelings. He does not reject them but aims at harmonizing them in the unity of his experience." Ibid., 401. See *Process and Reality,* V, chapter 2, sect. vi–vii, 411ff. This does not mean that God is merely a spectator at the world -drama. He initiates all creativity in the world, but does not have omnipotent control over it.

passionate only in the sense that God preserves all that the world achieves by suffering in his own ever-advancing, enriching experience. This history of the cosmos is his history, but in him it is freed of all its confusion and conflict and becomes pure, harmonious vision.

Conclusion

In comparing these three worldviews, either ontologically or ethically, we immediately note that, from a contemporary point of view, Whitehead's cosmology has one immense advantage: It explicitly emphasizes the evolutionary, historical character of the world and humanity. For Plotinus history is a cycle by which the most inferior beings attempt to imitate the eternal stability of the higher world. For Aquinas the universe indeed has a history, the history of salvation, but the subhuman universe of itself has only a steady-state dynamism in which there is no significant advance. In one respect, however, history is more meaningful for Aquinas than for Whitehead, since for Aquinas history has a goal, while for Whitehead it never reaches completion.

It is not true to say, as some do, that in Whitehead the concept of "substance" is replaced by "process." This is in fact truer of Plotinus than Whitehead, since for Plotinus the plurality of entities is simply the radiation of the Divine Goodness and its contemplative return to that Goodness. Whitehead intended to restore the concept of substance by giving it a dynamic, relational character. In this he and Aquinas are quite close together. Actually Aquinas is even more insistent on the relational character of the universe, since for Whitehead things can communicate only through their past, while for Aquinas the goal of each entity is to communicate with others in the immediate present, and ultimately in the eternal present.

This is why Aquinas insists on the dignity of the human person and personal survival in a way Whitehead does not. Plotinus is also less personalistic than Aquinas, since the One is not a community and all souls tend to be assumed into the One. Nevertheless, there is for Plotinus a kind of community of souls in the Cosmic Intelligence and the World-Soul. Nevertheless, it is only Aquinas who insists that the ultimate evil in the universe is not physical but moral, the result of human freedom.

Both Whitehead and Aquinas believe in a personal God who creates freely, although for Whitehead this freedom of creation is qualified by God's need for the world to enrich his own life. But the God of Aquinas is a community of Persons. Creation is a pure gift from which God seeks no gain. Whitehead's God is the *only* Person who requires a world in order to be able to raise to the level of experience and consciousness the possibilities that lie dormant in his antecedent nature. Aquinas and Whitehead both see God as compassionate, yet eternally blissful, but Aquinas believes that the Second

Person of the Godhead has entered bodily into our suffering world and *personally* shared its suffering.

Finally, we may say that for Whitehead there is in God a kind of unconscious in which the eternal objects lie in disjunction or lack of order, so that God is polarized into a static and a dynamic tension; for Plotinus and Aquinas God is purely dynamic, Pure Actuality. For Plotinus and Whitehead, however, God lacks absolute freedom with relation to the world, while for Aquinas God is Freedom Itself; God, by creating, draws created persons into participation in this freedom.

These various similarities and contrasts indicate the need for a new model of the world that could incorporate something of the hierarchical order found in Plotinus and carried on in both Aquinas and Whitehead, plus the communitarian, personalistic aspects of Aquinas and, finally, the evolutionary, historical dimension introduced by Whitehead.

From an ethical point of view the most striking point is the great contribution made by Aquinas in his conception of the world order as a *community*. He understands this community as a plurality of beings that has a certain hierarchical inequality, yet in which every being makes a unique and irreplaceable contribution to the whole. Furthermore, this community, insofar as it is made of *persons*, is an advancing communication of life and experience in which inequality is overcome by mutual sharing, culminating in the graceful invitation of all created persons to enter the Triune Community in which there is perfect coequality of power, awareness, and love.

For Aquinas natural law is our human participation in the eternal law of God's Wisdom, our deepest natural need as human beings is to share in a community of truth and love, and the first commandment of the natural law is for us to seek this communion. Furthermore, it should be noted that historically Christian ecclesiology has been deeply influenced by the Plotinian model of hierarchy transmitted through the work called *The Ecclesiastical Hierarchy* of the Pseudo-Dionysius.[19] With such a model the communitarian notion of the Church as an organism of *complementary* members and offices found in St. Paul (1 Cor 12) has been obscured by a *linear* model of pope-bishop-pastor-laity in which all wisdom and power is contained in the chief and passes down jurisdictionally through various delegates to the passive members of the Church. In such a model the laity have nothing to con-

---

[19] Ronald F. Hathaway, *Hierarchy and the Definition of Order in the Letters of the Pseudo-Dionysius* has shown with regard to the term "hierarchy" in its theological usages that "Pseudo-Dionysius is the virtual author of the term with the lexical meaning which it has possessed ever since" (p. xxi). Hathaway suggests (not very convincingly) that this mysterious author may well have been a Neo-Platonist philosopher (perhaps even a pagan) who, as a result of Christian attempts to suppress pagan Neo-Platonism, resorted to an elaborate Christian disguise under the pseudonym of the disciple of St. Paul to escape censorship.

tribute but obedience. Aquinas's view of cosmic order, however, logically leads to a complementary community, although I do not claim that in this respect Aquinas freed himself entirely from Neo-Platonic influences sufficiently to develop an ecclesiology of a pure Pauline type.

Moral Theology Issues

CHAPTER 13

John Paul II, Theologian of the Body of the Acting Person*

To my knowledge the term "THEOLOGY OF THE body" first appears in those writings of Pope John Paul II (Karol Wojtyla) that so far have been translated into English in the *Wednesday Catechesis*, "By the Communion of Persons Man Becomes the Image of God" of November 14, 1979:

> We find ourselves, therefore, almost at the very core of the anthropological reality, the name of which is "body," the human body. However, as can easily be seen, this core is not only anthropological, but also essentially theological. Right from the beginning, the *theology of the body* is bound up with the creation of man in the image of God. It becomes, in a way, also the theology of sex, or rather the theology of masculinity and femininity, which has its starting point here in Genesis.[1] [i.e., Gn 2:23, italics added]

---

* A previously unpublished paper delivered at the annual meeting of the Catholic Theological Society of America, 1998.

[1] I rely here on the anthology of Karol Wojtyla's writings edited by Alfred Bloch and George T. Czuczka, *Toward a Philosophy of Praxis: An Anthology* (New York: Crossroad, 1981), since these editors were acquainted with Wojtyla's Polish works. They introduce a selection from the Wednesday Catecheses by saying, "We have entitled this series of shared reflections. . . . 'The Theology of the Body.' Our justification is the frequent use of this phrase by John Paul II (p. 57), as if this was the first occurrence of the phrase in his writings." My own *Theologies of the Body: Humanist and Christian* was a reply to Marx's notion that "Someday man will create himself." I began writing that book while teaching in the Texas Medical Center, Houston, in 1970. The title was probably suggested to me by reading John Paul II's *The Original Unity of Man and Woman*. My book, however, refers only to the pope's *Redemptor*

John Paul II was elected pope October 16, 1978. He delivered these talks on the theology of the body in the second to the seventh years of his pontificate (Sept 5, 1979 to Nov. 28, 1984).[2] In this essay I will first summarize the main theses he develops pertaining to this theology of the body. Second, I will analyze the philosophical underpinnings of these theses. Third, I will examine what seems to me to be their theological methodology.

A Theology of the Body

The first chapter of Genesis presents the human person in its *objective* truth. God creates humanity in his own image. Hence we exceed the rest of material creation by virtue of our spiritual nature in its intelligence and freedom. Hence God has also entrusted us with the stewardship of the visible creation. Yet we are also part of that material world as is manifested by the sexual differentiation of our bodies to serve their co-creative transmission of life through reproduction. The second creation narrative in the second chapter of Genesis on the other hand takes more account of human *subjectivity*. This Yahwist narrative does not so much describe human nature as it recounts the experience of humanity's self-discovery not just as an incident of the remote past but as ever present in our lives. Thus these first two chapters of Genesis are complementary accounts, but in these *Catecheses* the Pope prefers to elaborate the latter more subjective, experiential narrative.

The first element of pristine human experience is that of solitude, of otherness in an impersonal world. "It is not good for man to be alone" (Gn 2:18). I experience myself as alone among all the other visible, material, nonpersonal creatures with whom I have so much in common, yet from whom as a person I find myself oddly different even as I name them in their own specificity. I experience myself as a body among bodies, yet differing from them all in my consciousness of being an autodetermining self. Yet as a material being I lack that transparent self-consciousness of a pure spirit such as is God.

The Pope has elaborated this point in his major philosophical work, *The Acting Person,* by analyzing the levels of human self-consciousness. At the center of consciousness is the awareness of our own specifically human acts of self-determination. Yet we are also aware of what is happening *in* us but not by our self-determination, for example, feelings of hunger or of weariness. Below this

---

Hominis, March 4, 1979, Unfortunately, it was only after my work was published that I began to appreciate how much it could have profited from a less superficial acquaintance with John Paul II's thought on the subject as I acknowledge in the new Introduction to my 2nd edition, xviiiff.

2 These *Catecheses* with additional materials are now conveniently available in John Paul II, *The Theology of the Body: Human Love in the Divine Plan,* with a foreword by John S. Grabowski.

conscious-self the human person also is aware that there must be a level of the unconscious that is truly a part of the person that somehow conditions our more conscious acts. Lastly, within this unconscious part of ourselves we also experience a subconscious level that under certain circumstances can rise to consciousness.

After the experience of loneliness comes the experience of confronting not just other things but other human beings precisely as persons like myself. Thus I become aware that my existence is inevitably *relational*. To be a person is to be open to other persons. To show this Genesis 2 relates the most vivid of all interpersonal relationships—that of sexual attraction. With joy Adam cries out "Eve" as it dawns on him that she is "flesh of my flesh, and bone of my bone" (2:23), yet different and complementary to himself. She is not just a desirable object, like the apple "good for food and pleasing to the eyes"(3:6), but a person like himself, with whom he is no longer alone, and to whom he declares his joyful recognition. Adam's own name had the generic meaning of "human" (1:7) or "earthy," because like other animals (2:19) we are formed of matter (2:7). He has given the other animals their diverse names (2:19), but then, when he names his new partner "Woman" *(ishsha)* because "out of her man *(ish)* this one has been taken" (2: 23), he acknowledges that she, like himself and unlike other visible creatures, is a person. Later he is to name her "Eve" as "mother of all the living" (3:20; cf. 4:12), thus acknowledging also that he himself is father of all humanity

This sexual mutuality and complementarity is not, of course, the only basic human experience of relationality. After the origin of humanity, our first experiences have to do with our relationship to our parents, then to siblings, then to peers. But the sexual relationship involves the total person in a special way, as the Yahwist in Genesis (2:24) recognizes by the comment Jesus himself quotes (Mk 10:7), "That is why a man leaves his father and mother and clings to his wife. And the two of them become one body." A theology of the body, therefore, understands the human being as by nature relational in its very essence. It also shows that our consciousness of sexuality is the most vivid realization of the relationality of ourselves in our total personhood. In this experience our bodiliness and our spiritual openness to the other are completely revealed. Thus the paradox of the finitude of our nature with its bodily lack of total transparency, in paradoxical contrast to its spiritual self-consciousness and openness—that is, our solitude and our relationality—are highlighted and in a manner reconciled in the sexual union.

As created in God's image to be stewards of creation, human persons are to share his dominion over other creatures in accordance with his commands and not their own ambitions. They are to "guard and cultivate" the fruitful garden of earth (1:28b, 2:15) and to use its fruits within the limits God has set for them (2:16–17). We have here John Paul II's concern for the ecological question that he was to develop more fully in later writings, for example, in *The Gospel of Life* (1995), n. 42.

We share not only in God's governance of the subhuman world, but also by reason of the command "Be fruitful and multiply and fill the earth" (Gn 1:28a) we cooperate in God's creative action. The union of man and woman expands and perpetuates the human community of persons created in God's divine image and their own. Before he became pope, Wojtyla developed this theme in another major work, *Love and Responsibility*.[3] This work is especially remarkable for its thorough and mainly positive discussion of the relation between erotic desire and love as personal relationality. The relational openness of human personhood manifested in the mutual love of husband and wife requires that their acts, including the act of sexual union, always aim at the common good of both partners. This co-creative and co-operative nature of human acts, therefore, must be retained in the marital act by at least not contradicting its procreative teleology. Thus John Paul II vigorously defends the truth propounded by Paul VI in *Humanae Vitae* of the principle of the inseparability of the unitive and procreative meaning of the marital act not only as a truth of reason but also of faith.

> Precisely against the background of this fuller context [the biblical anthropology he has explained] it becomes evident that the above mentioned moral norm belongs not only to the natural moral order, but also to the *moral order revealed by God*. Also from this point of view, it could not be different, but solely what is handed down by Tradition and the Magisterium and, in our days, the encyclical *Humanae Vitae* as a modern document of this Magisterium.[4] [italics in the original]

Therefore deliberately to render a fertile act of marital intercourse infertile is to treat the partner in that act not as a person but as a mere object of

---

3 John Paul II, *Love and Responsibility* rev. ed., translated by H. T. Willetts. The first edition was published in Polish in 1960.

4 John Paul II writes (after stating that in *Humanae Vitae* Paul VI "stresses that this norm belongs to natural law"), "The Church teaches this norm, although it is not formally (that is, literally) expressed in Sacred Scripture. It does this in the conviction that the interpretation of the precepts of natural law belongs to the competence of the Magisterium. However, we can say more. Even if the moral law, formulated in this way in *Humanae Vitae* is not found literally in Sacred Scripture, nonetheless, from the fact that it is contained in tradition and, as Pope Paul VI writes, has been 'very often expounded by the Magisterium' (*Humanae Vitae*, n. 12) to the faithful, it follows that this norm is in accordance with the sum total of revealed doctrine contained in biblical sources" (cf. *Humanae Vitae*, n. 4), John Paul II, *The Theology of the Body*, 389. This manner of arguing from what is today called "canon criticism," i.e., "the sum total of revealed doctrine contained in biblical sources" and the *analogia fidei* seems typical of John Paul II.

erotic pleasure. This is not simply because contraception artificially alters the act in its biological structure but because it depersonalizes it. Hence a contraceptive act cannot rightly be called an act of love since there can be no truly human love in a depersonalizing act. Even when such a depersonalizing act is used for a good ulterior purpose—for example, to spare an ailing partner the risk of a pregnancy—it remains in itself depersonalizing. As the pope was later to say in the encyclical *The Splendor of Truth*, Catholic moral tradition has always rejected and must continue to reject the illusion that an ulterior good intention can justify the immediate intention to use intrinsically immoral means to achieve that end. A means is intrinsically immoral or moral not just by reason of the proportion of the pre-moral positive and negative values that it may seem to embody but by its conformity or disconformity to the teleology with which the person is endowed as God's image in nature and in grace.[5]

Thus the marital act is an expression of the total person in a supreme act of loving relationship and hence a paradigm of *all* loving relationships. For this reason we can speak of the "nuptial meaning of the body," that is that the human body by reason of its sexuality manifests the spiritual openness of the person to other persons. Most wonderful of all, this relationality manifests what the Old Testament could only suggest, namely that the image of God in which we are created is that of the Trinity of Persons, the divine *Communio*. One can note here the possible influence of Karl Barth on John Paul II since it was the great Protestant theologian who argued that the image of God is found not just in the human nature of the individual but most clearly in the relation between man and woman.[6] Yet, in contrast to the Protestant tradition, the pope emphasizes the sacramentality of marriage. While marriage is a temporal reality of high value, its ultimate meaning is to be a sign, a sacrament of the union of Christ and the Church in eternity.

What then of the celibacy practiced and commended by Jesus and Paul? Beginning in his *Catechesis* of March 10, 1982, John Paul II discoursed at great length on celibacy and virginity "for the sake of the kingdom."[7] Since the essence of human love is found neither in erotic satisfaction nor in fertility but

---

[5] *Veritatis Splendor*, September 6, 1993, n. 72.

[6] For discussion of this, see G. A. Jonsson, *The Image of God: Genesis 1:26–28 in a Century of Old Testament Research*. After reviewing current opinions, Jonsson concludes that of all the many interpretations only two have survived: the Barthian view that the *imago Dei* is the I-Thou relation found in what he calls "the *analogia relationalis*" of man and woman to the Trinity and the other view that it consists in man's resemblance to God by co-dominion over creation (Egyptian kingship origin). The second by far predominates among current exegetes but Claus Westerman, *Genesis I–II: A Commentary*, supports Barth's view.

[7] John Paul II, *The Theology of the Body*, 262–303.

in the relationality of self-giving, it transcends the human temporal condition. The Pope's thesis is expressed as follows:

> [Jesus'] observation, "When they rise from the dead they neither marry nor are given in marriage" (Mk 12:25) indicates that there is a condition of life without marriage. In that condition, man, male and female, finds at the same time the fullness of personal donation and of the intersubjective communion of persons, thanks to the glorification of his entire psychosomatic being in the eternal union with God. . . . [T]he call to continence for the kingdom of heaven finds an echo in the human soul, in the conditions of this temporal life, that is, in the conditions in which persons usually "marry and are given in marriage" (Lk 20:34). . . . [It] is not difficult to perceive there a particular sensitiveness of the human spirit. Already in the conditions of the present temporal life this seems to anticipate what man will share in, in the future resurrection.[8]

Thus the pope discourses at some length on the meaning of Jesus' words, "They [the resurrected] are equal to angels and are sons of god, being sons of the resurrection" (Lk 20:36). To this he joins St. Paul's declaration that the resurrected body will be "not a natural body but a "spiritual body" (1 Cor 15:44) and concludes:

> The glorification of the body, as the eschatological fruit of its divinizing spiritualization, will reveal the definitive value of what was to be from the beginning a distinctive sign of the created person in the visible world, as well as a means of mutual communication between persons and a genuine expression of truth and love, for which the *communio personarum* is constituted. Thus in the resurrection not only will the body be freed of all the blight of sin but it will also arrive at that eternal glory for which God at the beginning created it in grace.[9]

In speaking of these lofty spiritual realities John Paul II does not, however, shut his eyes to our actual historical condition after the Fall. Perhaps the most striking phenomenological description in the *Catecheses* is the pope's reflections on the meaning of the simple declaration of Genesis that when they were created, "The man and his wife were both naked, yet they felt no shame" (2:25). But when they had sinned, "Then the eyes of both of them were opened, and they realized that they were naked" (3:7).

When God came to them and found them hiding among the trees, he asked ironically, "Who told you were naked?" (3:11). The experience of

---

[8] Ibid., 262.
[9] Ibid., 248.

shame reveals the human condition, our sense of alienation from our true selves, from other human persons and from God. Yet at the same time that it obscures our true selves it also reveals our responsibility for ourselves and for others and hence our personhood as sickness reveals the glory of health. It leads us also to acknowledge that God has not abandoned us, since he promises to Eve and all her and Adam's children that the serpent will not have final victory.

> I will put enmity between you [the serpent] and the woman,
>   And between your offspring and hers,
> He will strike at your head,
>   while you strike at his heal (Gn 3:15).

Philosophy in John Paul II's Theology of the Body

John Paul II's "theology of the body" cannot be fully appreciated except in the context of his two previous major works that are available in English, *The Acting Person* and *Love and Responsibility*, which are not principally theological but principally philosophical.[10] It is well-known that John Paul II's thought combines in rather a surprising and problematic way two quite different philosophical methodologies, that of St. Thomas Aquinas and that of modern phenomenology. The two approaches are characterized by some as "a philosophy of being" that is metaphysical and a "philosophy of consciousness" that is phenomenological. They seem obviously opposed in that the former tends to an objective realism and the latter to a subjective idealism.

Kenneth L. Schmitz in his 1991 McGivney Lectures, *At the Center of the Human Drama: The Philosophical Anthropology of Karol Wojtyla/Pope John Paul II,*[11] confronts this paradox. He resolves it by arguing that, while John Paul II has always been and remains a convinced Thomist and a firm realist, he early recognized that classical Thomism in its concern for objectivity gave little attention to human subjectivity. This subjective aspect of knowledge has been the characteristic concern of modern philosophy since Descartes. John Paul II has well-understood that Catholic thought ought to profit from the contributions of this post-Cartesian philosophy. To do so in a critical manner Catholic thinkers must give adequate attention to human subjectivity, without abandoning the achievements of Thomism in supplying the Church with an objective, realistic metaphysics. Moreover, they must recognize more clearly that "human nature" is not "nature" in the same sense that creatures that lack self-consciousness are said to have natures. It pertains to

---

[10] John Paul II, *The Acting Person,* translated by Andrezej Potocki, *Anlecta Husserliana,* vol. 10. The controversy over this translation, which was approved by John Paul II himself, is not significant for this paper.

[11] See also Buttiglione, *Karol Wojtyla,* chapter 5, 117–76.

human nature to transcend the limits of nature in the latter sense by reason of the intelligence and freedom of personhood, that is, a subjectivity that cannot be reduced to pure objectivity.

It is necessary to ask, however, what "phenomenology" and what "Thomism" did Karol Wojtyla, as a philosopher, attempt to synthesize? As regards phenomenology the answer is not difficult, since he himself makes clear that Max Scheler on whom he wrote his dissertation was a principal source.[12] Yet like many other phenomenologists, he explicitly rejected the turn to idealism taken by Edmund Husserl, the chief father of that mode of philosophizing. Phenomenology, for Wojtyla, as originally for Husserl, aims at a "return to the thing," that is a description of immediate human experience without either presuppositions or reductionism. While as an Aristotelian, Aquinas sought always to explain the data of sense experience by demonstration in terms of the four causes, phenomenology seeks to present so accurate a description of the philosopher's own experience that it will intuitively resonate with that of other open-minded observers. Yet it goes beyond the simple reportage of experience to engage in a careful analysis of that experience so as to reveal its essential features and their interrelations. Hence it remains at the intuitive rather than the rational, argumentative level of cognition.

This much is clear, but since many varieties of Thomism were developed in the twentieth century,[13] it is not so clear as to what school Wojtyla belongs. According to Rocco Buttiglione,[14] Wojtyla's 1948 "Angelicum" doctorate dissertation on St. John of the Cross reflected the traditional, so-called "essentialist" Thomism of Reginald Garrigou-Lagrange. Yet it profited most from that noted Thomist's special interest in mystical experience on which he wrote extensively. Upon returning to Poland to do pastoral work, Wojtyla also had the occasion to study the Young Catholic Worker Movement in France and Belgium. There he encountered the "existential" Thomism of Étienne Gilson and especially Jacques Maritain. In the latter's work he also must have noted the interest in mystical experience, connaturality, and "creative imagination."[15]

In Poland itself the "transcendental Thomism" favored by Mieszyslaw Krapiec was especially prominent at the University of Lublin where Wojtyla was soon sent by his archbishop to get a doctorate in philosophy with a

---

12 For the history of Husserl's students, see Hebert Spiegelberg, *The Phenomenological Movement: A Historical Introduction,* 3rd rev. ed., 1–5.

13 For a fuller discussion see the essay "Why First Philosophy Is Last" in this collection.

14 Buttiglione, *Karol Wojtyla,* 34–35, 47–48.

15 Ibid. Maritain made an important contribution to Thomism by his analysis of these aspects of the human cognition; see the discussion of the concept of "creativity" in my *Theologies of the Body,* 312–19 with bibliographical references.

Habilitationschrift on Max Scheler in 1953.[16] He was made an auxiliary bishop in 1958, then archbishop and cardinal, but continued to teach in the Catholic Faculty of the University of Lublin until elected pope. As cardinal he had taken an important role in Vatican II and after it wrote *The Implementation of the Vatican Council.*[17]

The aforesaid types of Thomism put their confidence in a metaphysics that is completely independent of modern science. Essentialist Thomists based metaphysics in the concept of *ens commune.* Transcendental Thomists begin with an a priori consciousness of the self as a being that questions being (Maréchal, Rahner).[18] Existential Thomists rest their case either on an abstractive intuition of *esse* (Maritain) or an existential judgment of esse (Gilson, etc.). As an alternative to these types of Thomism that are metaphysics of being, some theologians today prefer a "metaphysics of becoming," that is, process philosophy (Whitehead, Hartshorne).[19] These various efforts to establish a metaphysics that can serve theology are the result, I believe, of influences stemming from the attempts of Descartes and later Leibnitz and Kant to isolate the certitudes provided by metaphysics from the encroachment of post-Galilean science. This mathematicized science promised nothing but shifting theories of little use to theology.

These efforts to isolate metaphysics from natural science ignored the fact that Aquinas grounded his metaphysics in a natural science that demonstrates the existence of immaterial first causes that are necessary to explain the empirical activities of the universe in general and of the human body in particular. If this existence of immaterial beings as the cause of material beings could not be proved by natural science, natural science itself would be "first philosophy" and a metaphysics would be neither possible or necessary. Post-Galilean science ceased to provide such demonstrations because for the most part it contented itself with mathematical models and failed to grapple with

---

[16] On the influence of Scheler, see the extensive discussion of Buttiglione, 54–82. Wojtyla's dissertation has been translated into Italian, but not English.

[17] Written in 1972 this is available in English translation by P. S. Falla, *Sources of Renewal: The Implementation of the Vatican Council by Cardinal Karol Wojtyla (Pope John Paul II).*

[18] See Otto Muck, SJ, *The Transcendental Method* (New York: Herder and Herder, 1968), for a detailed analysis of Maréchal's work, as well as his influence on Karl Rahner, André Marc, Bernard J. F. Lonergan, and Emerich Coreth.

[19] In my opinion Whitehead's fascinating "hypothetical metaphysics" of process, and even more what Hartshorne and other disciples have made of it, falls short of being a "Radical Process Interpretation of Science," such as I have tried to develop on an Aristotelian basis in my *Theologies of the Body,* 251–412. Whitehead understands change and process simply as an endless series of combinations and recombinations of unchanging "eternal objects" in the "antecedent nature" of God; see my essay in this collection, "Hierarchy in Ecclesiology." For Aristotle material things are subject to genuine novelty.

properly physical explanations of the world, not simply as quantitatively measurable, but as in process. These mathematical models are wholly inadequate to deal with changing reality in its efficiency and teleology, to establish the existence of immaterial reality, or provide the grounds for its metaphysical exploration. Therefore they can be of little service to either a theology of creation or of the human body since creation as a whole and the bodily human person in particular can only be understood dynamically and teleologically.

It is most regrettable that the phenomenological philosophy of Karol Wojtyla, like the Kantian transcendentalism of Karl Rahner and Bernard Lonergan, or the process theology of David Tracy, or the return to Augustinianism and Neo-Platonist metaphysics by Von Balthasar, Ratzinger, and de Lubac, or the Marxist dialectic of liberation theology still operate uncritically with this post-Cartesian understanding of the relation of metaphysics and natural science.

John Paul II has strongly encouraged the efforts of the Pontifical Academy of Science, acknowledged the fact of evolution, and apologized to Galileo, but his conception of metaphysics also appears to be independent of natural science. He does not seem to be aware of the reading of Aquinas that I have just defended, probably because it is current only in Canada and America. Nevertheless, his realistic phenomenology at least has the advantage on the one hand of avoiding unsustainable metaphysical claims and on the other of avoiding the anti-metaphysical reductionism of post-Cartesian science. Its great disadvantage is that its intuitionism opens it up to charges of the deconstructionists that philosophy is mere literature rather than a demonstrative science founded in public, empirical evidence. Unfortunately, in my opinion, all these distinguished Catholic thinkers have failed to face the question of how modern science can be understood so that it is not merely neutral to Christian faith, but can give it positive support. Do not the Scriptures say, "The heavens declare the glory of God" (Ps 19:2), and of the human person, "You formed my inmost being; you knit me in my mother's womb. I praise you, so wonderfully you made me, wonderful are your works!" (Ps 139:13–14). Today a theology of creation that includes a theology of the human body cannot expound these words of the Bible on the basis of empty metaphysical concepts such as "being," "truth," "goodness," "beauty," "love," unless it gives concrete empirical content to them, assimilating what the natural sciences can provide.

What, then, did Karol Wojtyla believe that phenomenology could do for a Thomistic metaphysics understood as independent of natural science? He seems not to have been tempted to follow Husserl into idealism but, like Ingarden and many other disciples of Husserl, believed that it supports a realistic metaphysics.[20] Without attempting here a thorough description of

---

[20] See Spiegelberg, *The Phenomenological Movement* on Ingarden (by Guido King), 223–34.

the many varieties of phenomenology, I would venture that it is the modern equivalent of Aristotle's statement that "Knowledge begins in wonder." To adopt the "phenomenological attitude" rather than what Husserl—very mis-leadingly in my opinion—called the "natural attitude" retained by the empirical sciences is to meditate directly on human experience without pre-suppositions, that is, insofar as possible. To do so is to pass over the distinc-tion between the objective and subjective, the real and the ideal, and thus to insure that subjective and ideal factors in human experience will not be neg-lected. Whether a philosopher who begins with this attitude of open won-derment need end in idealism, as Husserl did, or as John Paul II and others are convinced, in the realism of objective truth within subjective intuition, remains to be seen.

Wojtyla in his chief philosophical work, *The Acting Person,* argues that phenomenology shows that the total person is most fully manifested in human acts, that is, deliberate acts under conscious control and invested with morality, good or bad. Such acts also include in themselves reference to other conscious or unconscious acts that are not as such specifically human but which nevertheless pertain to the whole human person. They also man-ifest not only the person's inner life and relations to the outer world, but also his or her relations to other persons, not as objects but precisely as persons having an inner life of their own. Such an intuitive experience of the person in its totality and not just partially in solipsistic subjectivity necessarily also implies a metaphysical concept of the person as an independently existing substance of a rational nature. Thus Wojtyla was able to claim that in the human act phenomenologically analyzed the metaphysical anthropology of Aquinas is justified and enhanced.

For my own part as a Thomist I, too, am convinced that human acts are the most complete manifestation of the human person, since as the scholas-tics said, "A thing is as it acts." Yet I am not at all satisfied with the phenom-enological method as used by any of its proponents with whose writings I am acquainted, including Wojtyla's. The reliance of phenomenology on a description of experience so accurate that its truth will be intuitively recog-nized by anyone from his or her own experience seems to me inadequate as a philosophical or scientific procedure. You may vividly describe your racist fantasies and I may empathize with them without either of us recognizing their illusory character. It seems to me that such a method at best does not get beyond the truth of plausible fiction.

Frankly I do not find reading Max Scheler's *Formalism in Ethics and Non-Formal Ethics of Value* or Wojtyla's *Acting Person* as helpful as Shake-speare's plays in arriving at an intuition of the essence of the human person. Their language is altogether too abstract and circular to achieve that goal of effective intuition. What I do think is that by this method they have very effectively exposed the reductionism of so much of post-Cartesian philosophy. They have also effectively underlined the failure of neo-scholastic interpreters of Aquinas to build on his anthropology and ethics so as to assimilate to it the rich data of modern psychology and sociology. This, however, is chiefly the result of the too restrictively metaphysical interpretations of Aquinas's thought that have prevailed since the Thomistic revival of Leo XIII and about which I have just complained.

A more positive way to understand such attempts to revitalize Thomism by the use of phenomenology is to note their very justified emphasis on the intuitive as well as the more commonly emphasized rational elements in Aquinas's epistemology. Aquinas argues that while the human intellect is a single faculty it is both *intellectus* and *ratio*.[21] While the angels are pure intelligences, that is, they know by immediate intuition or insight, the human intelligence has such weak and vague insights that it must perfect them by discursive reasoning.

Thus all human knowledge must begin with a few general principles derived immediately from sense experience, such as "The whole is greater than its parts." Then by combining these with additional insights also gained from experience it can reason syllogistically to new conclusions that specify the generic content of the first principles. For Aquinas "deduction" is not a process of "pulling a rabbit out of a hat" of a few "self-evident" axioms, but the illumination of specific experiences by the light of more general truths also drawn from experience but better known to us precisely because of their generality. For example, what I have learned by noting that all experienced wholes are greater than their parts can explain why the parts of the human body that I experience as such depend causally on the total body and can only be understood in relation to that whole. Thus deduction reveals relations between experiences but it cannot substitute for inductive experience. For Aquinas, therefore, human thought is a circular process moving from insights through reasoning to better insights. Yet the reasoning is only as good as the insights derived by the intelligence from sense experience and can advance only by such fresh insights based on further experience.

For Aquinas, as for Wojtyla, intuitive insights are assisted not only by sense cognition but also indirectly by the affective influence of the sense appetites and the will, today often covered by the term "feelings." As the example already mentioned of Garrigou-Lagrange and Maritain shows, modern Thomists independently of phenomenology had already begun to explore the intuitive and affective aspects of Aquinas's epistemology and thus to correct the over-rationalistic presentations of Neo-Scholasticism and the reductionism of current natural science.

---

21 *Summa theologiae* I, q. 54, a. 5 and q. 79, aa. 9–10.

The Hermeneutic of the John Paul II's Theology of the Body

While John Paul II's synthesis of a philosophy of being and a philosophy of consciousness is quite evident in his presentation of a theology of the body in the *Catecheses*, it remains in the background. In the foreground are the texts of the creation narratives in Genesis and the New Testament texts that refer to these foundational narratives. Indeed, it seems to me that the voluminous writings of John Paul II as pope, must be interpreted in a very different light than that provided by his chosen philosophical methodologies. This difference cannot be accounted for merely by the restraints placed on his utterances by his pontifical office. As I have noted, the Wednesday *Catecheses* where the term "theology of the body" first appeared were delivered early in his pontificate (1979–1984) and must have been the fruit of long previous meditation. Moreover, their style and content are too highly personal to be the result of the drafts provided by curial officials. This same style is also notable at least in many features of his later encyclicals.

In all these writings, while the Pope never contradicts essential Thomist positions, and sometimes uses phenomenological description to support them, his manner is more that of a homiletic meditation on the Sacred Scriptures than that either of metaphysics or phenomenological analysis. For example, his discussion of the experience of "shame" might be referred either to Aquinas's quite sophisticated analysis of *verecundia*,[22] or to a phenomenological description of states of moral consciousness, but its focus is on the details of the biblical narrative. Thus these *Catecheses* in style most resemble the manner of a *lectio divina* or a patristic homily. They are reflections on biblical texts quite different than either exegesis in the modern historical-critical and literary modes or from Aquinas's theologically systematic biblical analyses. Yet neither do they examine the "spiritual senses" of Scripture in the manner of Van Balthasar or de Lubac. Instead the *Catecheses* seek to unfold the inner significance of Scripture for an understanding of the total person as manifested in its moral acts. Thus, like the Pope's philosophical synthesis, these mediations are both a "theology of being" and a "theology of consciousness." They are a "theology of being" because they consistently view the human person as an objectively existing, created image of God; but they are also a "theology of consciousness." As God is Being Itself, totally transparent to itself as Truth and Love in divine personhood, so the human person comes fully into being, wholly realizes its created nature, by knowing and loving God, neighbor and its own self *in itself*.

Yet just because I find John Paul II's insight on the nuptial meaning of the body so profound, I ask myself whether and how the tension that so many commentators point out between his Thomism and his phenomenology can

---

22 Ibid., I–II, q. 41, a. 4; see also I, q. 95, a. 3; I–II, q. 24, a. 4, q. 39, a. 1, q. 42, a. 3, ad 4, q. 44, a. 1, ad 3; II–II, q. 116, a. 2, ad 3, q. 151, a. 4; *Suppl.* q. 87, a. 2, ad 3, ad 4.

be adequately overcome. Is it possible to incorporate his phenomenological insights into a more systematic ontological theology? To explore this possibility I first turn to the Aristotelian logic of discourse in order to identify the type to which Wojtyla's phenomenological writing is best referred. Aristotle distinguished four finds of discourse: *poetic* or narrative, *rhetorical* or persuasive, *dialectical* or exploratory, and *scientific* or demonstrative. Thomas Aquinas recognized all four, but his conception of theology implied that for him the first three could only be preliminary to the fourth. Hence for him theology is in a special way a science.

Nevertheless, as Francisco Muniz, OP, once pointed out in criticism of the rationalistic tendencies of the Garrigou-Lagrange school of Thomism,[23] though Aquinas stoutly maintains that theology is *scientia*, he even more emphasizes that it is *sapientia*, a return to first principles. Actually theology does little syllogistic demonstrating; it consists chiefly in the explication of the meaning of the articles of faith. One might at first classify the discourse of John Paul II's Wednesday *Catecheses* as rhetorical or persuasive discourse, since they are in effect sermons intended to persuade his hearers to a deeper faith and love, both married love and celibate love. This is certainly the case, but since, as I have said, like much patristic writing they have the character of a shared meditation, the practical argumentation aimed at motivating an audience characteristic of persuasion is minimized. What is elaborated is primarily a recalling of the Genesis narrative with an exposition of its layers of meaning, much as a literary critic might do with a short story. At the moment "narrative theology" is much in vogue, and I would suggest that John Paul II is practicing it. He uses what is essentially a poetic mode of discourse, just as the Bible itself does in its narrative portions. These narratives, of course, have a "lesson" and are thus properly rhetorical, but it is a rhetoric that largely avoids moralizing and consigns the practical lesson to the auditor's own reflections generated by a story vivid in imagery. Jesus himself chose this mode of preaching in his parables.

Perhaps, following the lead of Muniz, it is best to understand John Paul II's use of phenomenology as dialectical discourse. For Aristotle the discovery of principles is the task proper to dialectics. As argument, dialectics can only yield probable conclusions; but as it clears the way for intellectual insight into the data of experience it provides the conditions of intuitive certitude. Thus John Paul II likes to preface his theological pronouncements by a phenomenological exploration of the Scriptures understood as a search in religious experience for self-understanding. For example, he introduces the encyclical *The Splendor of Truth* with a meditation on the Gospel incident of the Rich Young Man and *The Gospel of Truth* with a meditation on the

---

23 Franciscus Muniz, OP, *De Diversis Muneribus S. Theologiae secundum Doctrinam D. Thomae,* translated by John P. Reid, as The Work of Theology.

Nativity. In this way by meditation on a story, our experiential self-understanding becomes, as Rahner and many other theologians today insist, the opening to a deeper understanding of the revealed Word of God.

Thus the phenomenological method applied to reading the creation accounts has enabled John Paul II to provide a scriptural basis for the Church's teaching on human nature and in particular its sexual character, which exceeds the natural law arguments often used by rooting them in universal human experience. Though the biblical writers lived in a patriarchal culture, if we read them as John Paul II does, they show themselves acutely sensitive to the mystery of the lived relationship of man and woman in its concrete experience. Such experience is more real than any of its particular cultural expressions whether those in which the biblical writers lived or those in which we live. Hence, like the great poets and novelists, the inspired author of Genesis pondered on the mysteries of the equal dignity of man and woman, the complementarity of their gifts, and the tensions, frustrations, and fulfillments of their relationship.

While "patriarchalism" may limit one's understanding of this mystery of the man–woman relationship, so does the current political agenda. To transcend this mystery, as the biblical writer strives to do, it is necessary to turn from political concerns and cultural attitudes to ask, "Why did God make us male and female?" "What did God intend the relation between man and woman should be?" To attempt to answer these questions merely on the basis of the experience of either women or men is to use a tainted source, since both women and men are sinners blinded in part to their true identity. Of course it is impossible to answer these questions without reference to male and female experience since "What is received is received according to the manner of the recipient," but this must be an experience cleansed by the grace of God who speaks to us through his inspired Word.

Thus a Christian doctrine of human relationships, of which the man–woman relation is paradigmatic, must turn to the Word of God and listen carefully, not project our own sin-distorted notions on God. It is precisely here that a "hermeneutic of suspicion" is required. We must be suspicious that current readings of the Scriptures tend to rationalize our modern rejection of those sayings that seem to offend current sensibilities on the grounds that they are culturally conditioned, when in fact it is our rejection of the Word of God that is culturally conditioned. A less anachronistic exegesis of the Genesis texts and of the New Testament texts based on them shows that the final inspired author of that book was facing a problem that is still ours. Far from blindly accepting the patriarchalism of the culture in which he wrote or his own androcentricity, his inspiration made him conscious of these injustices. Hence he wrote to correct them by asserting the original equality and complementarity of the sexes. Certainly Jesus thought so, since he referred to these texts to confirm his own teaching on that equality and complementarity (Mk 10:1–12).

Therefore I believe that John Paul II has provided theologians with a profound phenomenological dialectic by which the true meaning of human sexual experience can be correlated with the revealed Word of God. It remains for us to use this dialectic to establish secure principles on which a systematic theology of the human person can be constructed. Such a systematic theology, however, as John Paul II has rightly seen, cannot securely rest on a phenomenology without a metaphysical grounding. I would argue further that a secure ground for metaphysics itself requires that it too be grounded in a critically revised natural science. Only then will a theology of the body, the human person, or of the total creation meet the needs of the third millenium.

CHAPTER 14

Can We Make a Fundamental Option?*

A. Rahner and the Revision of Moral Theology
Rahner's Fundamental Option of Transcendentalism

IN PRACTICAL THINKING, TECHNICAL OR ETHICAL, THE END OR goal is the first principle that determines whether a proposed means is right or wrong. The term "fundamental option" or "fundamental choice" is now generally used to replace the classical "ultimate end"[1] implying, it seems, a paradigm shift in moral theology due largely to the post-Vatican II hegemony of the thought of Karl Rahner. Rahner wrote a number of essays on moral theology[2] of which the most programmatic was "On the Question of

---

* This essay was read with the title, "Fundamental Option And/Or Commitment to an Ultimate End" at a symposium of the Karl Rahner Society at the national convention of the Catholic Theological Society of America, June 1996, *Philosophy and Theology* 10 (1; January 199):113–41.

[1] On this current usage, see Felix M. Poddimattam, OFM Cap., *Fundamental Option and Mortal Sin.*

[2] I omit consideration of Rahner's works more concerned with spirituality and here consider only Rahner's essays translated into English in *Theological Investigations*, translated and with an introduction by Cornelius Ernst, OP, 23 vols. In vol. 1, "Guilt and Remission: The Borderland between Theology and Psychotherapy," 265–82; vol. 2, "On the Question of a Formal Existential Ethics," 217–34; "The Dignity and Freedom of Man," 235–64; vol. 3, "Some Thoughts on 'A Good Intention,'" 105–28; vol. 4 "Nature and Grace," 165–88; vol. 5, "The 'Commandment of Love' in Relation to the Other Commandments," 439–59; vol. 6, "Theology of Freedom," 178–96; vol. 7, "On Truthfulness," 229–59; "Parresia (Boldness)," 260–67; "The Works of Mercy and Their Reward," 268–74; "Proving Oneself in Time of Sickness," 275–84; "On Christian Dying," 285–93; vol. 8, "On the Evangelical Counsels," 133–67; "Anonymous Christians," 390–98; vol. 9, "The Experiment with Man," 205–24, "The Problem of Genetic Manipulation, " 225–52; vol. 10, "On the Theology of Hope," 242–59; vol. 11, "On

a Formal Existential Ethics." Certain post-Vatican II tendencies in moral theology, recently rejected in the encyclical *Veritatis Splendor*,[3] claim his thought as their inspiration, though it is not at all evident he would have endorsed them.

The revision of moral theology urged by Vatican II, it is generally admitted, ought to replace the voluntaristic, legalistic systems of late medieval theology, predominant until the revival of Thomism at the end of the nineteenth century, with an earlier teleological, means-end system.[4] This revision, still in process today, has run into three great roadblocks: (1) disagreements about how to interpret the text of Aquinas; (2) disagreements about how to relate his thought to modernity; and (3) doubts about whether a return to biblical and patristic sources may not be preferable to a revival of scholasticism. Karl Rahner attempted to overcome these obstacles by making a "fundamental option" in philosophy.[5] To interpret Aquinas he chose the Transcendental Thomism of Joseph Maréchal who sought to dialogue with modern philosophy in its "turn to the subject" with Descartes and Kant, in preference to the Existential Thomism of Jacques Maritain and Étienne Gilson. These Thomists opposed Maréchal's reconciliation of Thomism with modern thought as tainted with the idealism rejected by the Church.[6]

I believe both the Transcendental Thomists and the Existential Thomists misread Aquinas and thereby missed the only real grounds on which a fruitful dialogue with modernity can take place, namely, the rethinking of the

---

the Encyclical *Humanae Vitae*," 263–87; vol. 18, "On Bad Arguments in Moral Theology," 74–85, "Faith as Courage," 211–25, "Christian Dying," 226–58; "Law and Righteousness in the Catholic Understanding," 275–87.

3 John Paul II, *The Splendor of Truth, Encyclical Regarding Certain Fundamental Questions of the Church's Moral Teaching,* August 6, 1993.

4 Ibid., nn. 71–75, has followed current usage in speaking of "teleological ethical theories" and "teleologism" as seemingly identical with proportionalism, a use that originated with Henry Sidgwick, *The Method of Ethics,* original 1874, 7th ed. This terminology identifies "teleology" with the denial of absolute moral norms, and "deontology" with their affirmation. In accordance with etymology I prefer to use "teleological" to mean an ethics based on the relation of means to end, and "deontological" to mean a voluntaristic ethics. In both systems it is possible to affirm or deny absolute moral norms.

5 See Joseph Fuchs, SJ, *Human Values and Christian Morality*; Hugo Rahner, *The Spirituality of St. Ignatius Loyola: An Account of Its Historical Development*; and, George Vass, *Understanding Karl Rahner,* vol. 1: *A Theologian in Search of a Philosophy,* vol. 2: *The Mystery of Man and the Foundations of a Theological System,* are helpful in understanding the spiritual context of Rahner's thought.

6 See my essay *Transition to Historical-Mindedness* in this collection. Also Henle, "Transcendental Thomism: A Critical Assessment," 173–98; and Thomas F. O'Meara, OP, *Church and Culture: German Catholic Theology, 1860–1914.* Georges Van Riet, *Thomistic Epistemology,* 2 vols., reviews the situation systematically.

natural sciences whose remarkable advances, beginning in the seventeenth century, gave birth to modernity and still help it to survive the corrosive doubts of postmodernity.[7]

To defend supersensible reality and even a morality based on a spiritual anthropology, Descartes and Kant and later the Neo-Scholastics were forced, they thought, to find a way to raise metaphysical thought to high ground out of reach of the floodwaters of changing scientific theories. They tried to make philosophy, that is, metaphysics and ethics, wholly independent of natural science and epistemologically prior to it. To achieve this goal the Existential Thomists claimed to ground metaphysics in an intuition of Being (Maritain) or in an existential judgment of *esse* (Gilson). Rahner preferred the approach of the Transcendental Thomists who sought this metaphysical high ground in the self-consciousness of the human subject, as the a priori condition of the possibility of human experience.

Rahner did indeed accept Aquinas's doctrine that the proper object of human intelligence is the essence of material things known only by a "conversion to the phantasm," that is, dependence on sense knowledge.[8] He also insisted against Cartesianism that initially we know ourself knowing *in actu exercitu* only not *in actu signato*. Thus, the knowledge of oneself as a spiritual subject[9] is initially an unthematic, indirect awareness that can be objectified only in reflection and even then never completely. Rahner's revision of Kant so as to insist on the inseparable relation of spirit to world was undoubtedly influenced by his teacher Martin Heidegger. Roberts says,

> It is particularly in Heideggerian themes that we find the strongest influence on Rahner—in themes of Being and Time, dread and fear, death and repetition, time and historicity. True, the influence of the later Heidegger, so strong at present in Protestant theology, is not profound in the case of Rahner. Yet the themes do remain constant. . . . And just as Heidegger himself understood Kant's Critique of Pure Reason to be an answer to the question, "What is man?", so Rahner has taken this as his fundamental issue. Man must *know himself in himself* as opposed to the world in order to be an existent."[10] [italics added]

---

[7] See my essay "The Loss of Theological Unity: Pluralism, Thomism, and Catholic Morality," in Weaver and Appleby, *Being Right: Conservative Catholics in America,* 63–87.

[8] Karl Rahner, *Spirit in the World,* translated by William Dych, SJ, and introduction by Francis Fiorenza, 237–386. See John F. X. Knasas, "*Esse* as the Target of Judgment in Rahner and Aquinas," *Proceedings of the American Catholic Philosophical Association* 59 (1985): 114–31.

[9] Karl Rahner, *Hearers of the Word,* 43, 53–70.

[10] Roberts, *The Achievement of Karl Rahner,* 15–18.

206 ■ | III. MORAL THEOLOGY ISSUES

Yet this self-knowledge is to be pursued, Rahner supposed, not by a detailed study of the world itself, but rather by asking what we must be if we are to experience the world. He writes,

> Why, for Thomas, the totality of the objects able to be reached in metaphysics must already be given simultaneously and implicitly with the light of the intellect which is apprehended simultaneously, is evident from earlier considerations; the first principles are grounded in the light of the intellect, in which principles common to being is elaborated. But a metaphysical object is able to be apprehended by man at all only in the knowledge of common being. Hence, metaphysics is only the reflexive elaboration of all human knowledge's own ground, which as such is already and always posited simultaneously in this knowledge from the outset.[11]

This search for an anthropology through questioning the condition of the subject as it makes possible the subject's life in the world is Rahner's version of the "transcendental method" in philosophy and theology.[12]

Formal Existential Ethics

To apply this transcendental method to moral theology, Rahner found guidance not in Maréchal but in Max Scheler and in Martin Heidegger, two phenomenologists themselves influenced by Edmund Husserl. As Scheler had attempted to overcome the formalism of Kantian ethics by giving it concrete content,[13] so Rahner proposed a "formal existential ethics"[14] that would begin by an analysis of the possible conditions of moral experience and then correlate this formal structure with the concrete matter of daily life in the historical world. For Rahner, this correlation cannot be reduced to any other general principles than those already provided by his transcendental anthropology. Nor can it be achieved by a casuistry of a deductive type. Instead he found a solution to this problem, that is, the possibility of realizing transcendental values in a categorical, concrete world, in St. Ignatius Loyola's "discernment of spirits" central to Rahner's own Jesuit tradition and personal spirituality.[15]

---

[11] Karl Rahner, *Spirit in the World,* 390.

[12] Ibid., 406–8.

[13] On this see Alfons Deeken, *Process and Permanence in Ethics: Max Scheler's Moral Philosophy.*

[14] Karl Rahner, "On the Question of a Formal Existential Ethics," *Theological Investigations,* vol. 2, 217–34.

[15] See Piet Penning de Vries, *Discernment of Spirits According to the Life and Teachings of St. Ignatius Loyola,* and Hugo Rahner, *The Spirituality of St. Ignatius Loyola.*

Fundamental Freedom and the Supernatural Existential

In Rahner's transcendental analysis of the human subject and the conditions it affords for possible experience he first shows that the subject has a dynamism to become transparent to itself through infinite questioning within the horizon of the Absolute Mystery. Then he uncovers a second dimension of human ontology, the power of self-determination or fundamental freedom.[16] Rahner argues that if human beings have free choice as regards particular beings, as evidently we do, then this presupposes a transcendental or fundamental freedom as regards the totality of Being, like Heidegger's *differenz* between "beings" and "Being."

Such a fundamental freedom means a capacity to seek or reject the totality of Being. The human subject who accepts the totality remains open to the continual fulfillment of its dynamism to seek the Absolute, while the subject who rejects this totality becomes imprisoned, unable to transcend itself, in a state of self-contradiction like the damned in hell. By the term "existential" Rahner designates a permanent intrinsic dimension of human subjectivity but not its essence.[17]

Thus the subject's dynamism to know itself and the totality of Being and its fundamental freedom are "existentials" of an anthropology. This question was sharpened for him by the de Lubac controversy concerning the possibility of a natural ultimate end for the human person.[18] Rahner avoided the paradoxes of de Lubac's position (denounced in Pius XII's encyclical *Humani Generis*, 1950)[19] by agreeing with de Lubac's Thomist opponents that the human essence as such, apart from grace, cannot demand the beatific vision. On the other hand, he conceded to de Lubac that the hypothesis of the possibility of a "state of pure nature" inevitably suggests an "extrinsicist" notion of grace. Rahner's own solution was to say that the graced state of the person is a "supernatural existential," that is, an

---

[16] See Karl Rahner, "The Dignity and Freedom of Man," *Theological Investigations,* vol. 2, and the comments of Felix M. Poddimattam, OFM Cap., *Fundamental Option and Mortal Sin,* 25–33; Max Scheler, *Formalism in Ethics and Non-Formal Ethics of Value; A New Attempt toward the Foundation of an Ethical Personalism,* translated by M. S. Frings and R. L. Funk, 29–30; and George Vass, *Understanding Karl Rahner,* vol. 1, 70–75.

[17] Ibid., vol. 2, 65–66.

[18] George Vass, *Understanding Karl Rahner,* vol. 2; Henri de Lubac, SJ, *Surnaturel: Études historiques* and *The Mystery of the Supernatural,* translated by Rosemary Sheed; cf. Raul Berzoa Martinez, *La Teologia del Sobrenatural en los Escritos de Henri de Lubac: Estudio Historico-Teologico, 1931–1980.*

[19] "Concerning some False Opinions Threatening to Undermine the Foundations of Catholic Doctrine," August 12, 1950; www.saint-mike.org/Library/Papal_Library/PiusXII/Encyclicals/Humani_Generis.html.

intrinsic dimension of the graced person's mode of being,[20] not belonging, however, to the human essence (as Scotus claimed and de Lubac was accused of claiming) but to its existential condition.[21]

It is not necessary here to discuss the value of Rahner's solution of this difficulty. What is relevant is that in this way Rahner has provided a transcendental explanation of the elevation of human freedom by grace so that the dynamism of the human person in our actual, existential world is directed not only to an Absolute revealed by our unceasing questioning of Being, but to a "Mystery" in the strict sense of the term, which is utterly beyond the capacity of creatures to attain by their own powers, but which must be received as a gift. Since it is revealed to faith that God wills to grant this gift to all human beings, this supernatural existential is such not only for those in the state of grace, but for all members of the human race, even if they are Christian only "anonymously."[22]

Conceptualization and the Fundamental Option

Rahner, as a phenomenologist, was very sensitive to what to many seemed a serious defect of Thomistic moral theology, namely, its appearance of cold, hard rationalism having little to do with the actual conditions of agonizing human decisions. Are human beings angels with a clear vision of the hierarchy of values leading up the "ultimate end" in light of which they calculate every decision? This seems as unreal as Adam Smith's notion of "economic man"! Is this perhaps the reason that Thomists have always had difficulty in explaining how we can sin even venially without abandoning our commitment to God?

For Rahner, the fundamental option at the level of fundamental freedom is deeper than the level of ratiocination and verbalization and it has various degrees of intensity. Hence it can be said to be "preconceptual." The "reasons" for our deepest commitments such as falling in love or choosing a vocation in life cannot easily be put into words, if at all. Moreover, it does not happen in a moment, nor is it changed in a moment like a decision to buy one brand of detergent rather than another in a supermarket. Thus Rahner's notion of a hidden, transcendental, intuitive level of fundamental option seems far truer to experience than Aquinas's rational, coolly calculative model.

---

[20] Vass, *Understanding Karl Rahner,* vol. 2, 64–84.

[21] See Juan Alfaro, SJ, *Lo Natural y lo Sobrenatural: Historico desde Santo Tomas hasta Cayetano* (1274–1534).

[22] Karl Rahner, *Theological Investigations,* "Anonymous Christians," vol. 8, 390–98; "Anonymous Christians and the Missionary Task of the Church," vol. 12, 161–81; "Observations on the Problem of the Anonymous Christian," vol. 12, 280–94.

B. Some Theories Supposedly Derived From Rahner's Ethics

Venial, Serious, and Mortal Sin

Veritatis Splendor, as I read it, does not condemn theories of fundamental option as such, neither Rahner's nor other versions, just as it does not condemn all teleological theories of ethics. The Magisterium is not concerned with philosophical theories as such. What is censured in *Veritatis Splendor* are certain practical conclusions that some have drawn from the attempts, legitimate in themselves, to revise legalistic and casuistic manual morality by reorganizing ethics either on the principle of teleology or of the fundamental option. These conclusions relate to two main topics: the distinction of mortal from venial sin (nn. 69–70), and the possibility of exceptions to universal moral norms (nn. 71–83).

As regards the distinction of mortal from venial sin, many moralists seem to favor the shift to "fundamental option" in hopes it will resolve certain problems that have long troubled confessors and pastoral counselors, especially in the area of sexual ethics:

1. How is it possible that so many Christians of good will, struggling with "sins of weakness," achieve a state of grace by a sincere confession only to fall back immediately into mortal sin and then just as quickly regain it by a new confession?

2. How is it possible that so many sincere Catholics live in mortal sin because they cannot convince themselves that the universal negative moral norms taught by the Magisterium are absolute when in certain situations making an exception seems more truly responsible?

3. Does our experience really distinguish so sharply between mortal and venial sin?

Therefore, some moralists, using Rahner's transcendental method, have argued that since the notion of fundamental option leaves room for a whole range of categorical acts that are too superficial to change that option, it makes it possible to insert between the traditional "mortal" and "venial" a third type of sins, "non-mortal but serious." To this new third class of sins they assign a good many of the "sins of weakness" and claim that persons who commit "serious" but not "mortal' sins can still remain in the state of grace, that is, retain their fundamental option for God. Furthermore, they argue that the fundamental option is not a single act, but a gradual, largely subconscious process. For it to be mortal, some even claim it has to be a direct act of hatred of God.

Thus, they conclude, mortal sins must be rare, and the obligation to confess most sins seldom binding. Consequently, it would seem that the recidivist in sins of weakness may very well remain in the state of grace in spite of recurring lapses into serious sins, that the many, perhaps majority of Catholics who appear to be in a state of mortal sin by violating the Church's teachings on sexual morality are still in grace, and finally that catechetics should cease to emphasize the categories of "mortal" and "venial" in teaching about sin and confession. The practical effects of these opinions are now evident when we see the entire congregation on Sunday go to communion, although few ever seem to show up in the confessional.

Proportionalism

A second conclusion that some want to draw from the theory of fundamental option is a proportionalist theory of ethical decision according to which all concrete moral norms are only prima facie universal and obligatory because they are always open to exceptions in special circumstances. This inference is based on the fact that Rahner in his essay "On the Question of a 'Formal Existential Ethics,'" is highly critical of the notion of a purely deductive and casuistic ethics.

Yet, as I have already noted, Rahner's concern in his famous essay is quite other than that of either probabilism or proportionalism. He does not deny that there are universally valid and absolute moral norms, nor that the casuistic application of these norms is legitimate and necessary. Thus he says,

> The morally obligatory cannot and must not contradict these norms— this is clear. There can be nothing which actually ought to be done or is allowed in a concrete or individual situation, which could lie outside these universal norms, and to that extent everything which morally ought to be done in the concrete is also the realization of the universal norms. But is it not more than that? Is what is morally done only the realization of universal norms—is what ought morally to be done in the concrete case merely, as it were, the intersection of the law and the given situation? And conversely: if in a certain situation the universal laws leave room for a free choice, i.e., if according to the universal norms several things are still 'allowed' and ethically possible in a determined situation, can we then do what we want, just because *ex supposito* we do not in such a case offend?[23]

What he seeks to show is that a moral theology that stops short with universal norms and casuistic applications is not sufficient to guide unique persons in their unique vocations and circumstances of life. Hence he develops the Ignatian theme of the "discernment of spirits" by which the Christian is rendered sensitive and docile to the guidance of the Holy Spirit. Yet

[23] Ibid., "On the Question of a Formal Existential Ethics," vol. 2, 222–23.

how do we know what the Holy Spirit is saying? How do we discern the divine voice from the promptings of the devil and one's own sinful impulses and rationalizations? Loyola showed that the Christian must develop sensitivity to the guidance of the Spirit by an affective co-naturality. On the level that Rahner conceives as "transcendental" this gradually developed and graced co-naturality makes the soul ever more sensitive to the absolute values of the Gospel.

Consequently when mature Christians form their consciences about decisions at the categorical level they are freed from purely legalistic thinking and enabled to understand what God wants of them in each concrete moral situation in view of their own unique personal vocations. Rahner, encouraged perhaps by the rainbow of Vatican II, seems to have believed that we are entering a period in the Church when the Magisterium will no longer have to promulgate moral norms on every new issue, but will seek to help Christians develop this kind of spiritual discernment that will make it possible for them to meet the extremely varied and constantly changing circumstances of daily life.

Yet in his response to *Humanae Vitae*,[24] Rahner also provided a penetrating analysis of the subjective conditions of moral decision in modern culture that shows us that we need not conclude that dissent from the Church's teaching, as for example the widespread practice of contraception, necessarily means that Catholics are acting in bad conscience.

C. A Thomistic Critique

Transcendental Methodology

Can Thomism, as the classical mode of Catholic theology, better enter into dialogue with modernity by some other route than the transcendental or the existential hermeneutics that try to bypass modern science? Teilhard de Chardin courageously tried—if not very successfully—to open such a path. I would suggest we take Aquinas at his word when he claims that unless natural science has first established that it is not possible to give an ultimate explanation of the visible cosmos nor of the thinking human being who is learning more and more about the cosmos, by causes of the material order, there is no need for or possibility of a "meta-physics" in the service of theology other than physics itself.

This approach, of course, requires a rethinking of modern science to free it from the mechanism and idealism in which Descartes packaged it.[25] Certainly

---

[24] Ibid., "On the Encyclical *Humanae Vitae*," vol. 11, 263–87.
[25] See my "The River Forest School of Natural Philosophy," *Philosophy and the God of Abraham, Essays in Memory of James A. Weisheipl*, edited by R. James Long, 1–16.

the project both of the Transcendental and the Existential Thomists to follow Descartes and Kant in isolating metaphysics from physics as a superior and more reliable kind of knowledge is profoundly contrary to the mind of St. Thomas.

Nevertheless, Rahner and Aquinas come to many of the same conclusions by opposite routes: Rahner by reflection on the human subject as knowing and free, Aquinas by reflection on our detailed, concrete knowledge of the material world in its natural processes. Aquinas's method, however, makes it possible for natural science to contribute positively to metaphysics, while the method chosen by Rahner in hopes of fruitful dialogue with modernity reduces the physical world to a foil for reflection on the knowing subject out of reach of the results of the natural sciences.

I am not claiming, of course—that would be absurd—that Rahner ignored the world in a Neo-Platonic manner, but to deal with concrete reality he had to turn to revelation. As Francis Fiorenza in his excellent introduction to the English translation of *Spirit in the World* has written:

> At this point a basic difference between Rahner and other students of Maréchal becomes evident. Whereas most of Maréchal's followers have carried on their dialogue within the discipline of philosophy, Rahner has seen that a philosophical and existential theology is the only adequate horizon for a dialogue with modern philosophies and their emphasis on the dimension of history. Whereas Lonergan rejects phenomenology and existentialism as merely descriptive and as purified empiricism, Rahner stresses in *Hearers of the Word* (and all his theological writings) the ontological and theological relevance of the problems of historicity and "facticity."[26]

Relying on revelation and his theory of the "supernatural existential" of graced humanity, Rahner in many historical studies and more systematically in his *Foundations of Christian Faith: An Introduction to the Idea of Christianity*, pursued a method of correlating his anthropology developed by transcendental deduction with the concrete data of history.[27] Yet, although he often dealt with topics that involve the relation of science and theology,[28] at the end of his career in a moving passage he said,

---

26 Karl Rahner, *Spirit in the World*, xliiv–xlv.

27 Karl Rahner, *Hearers of the Word*, 111–66.

28 For example, Karl Rahner's essays in *Theological Investigations*, "Theological Reflections on Monogenism," vol. 1, 229–96; "Guilt and Remission: The Borderland between Theology and Psychotherapy," vol. 1, 265–82; "Science as a Confession," vol. 3, 385–400; "Christology with an Evolutionary View of the World," vol. 5, 439–59; "Anonymous Christians," vol. 8, 390–98; "The Experiment with Man," vol. 9, 205–24; "The Problem of Genetic Manipulation," vol. 9, 9, 225–52; "Observations

Certainly, the theologian has ultimately only one thing to say. But this one word would have to be filled with the mysterious essence of all reality. And yet each time I open some work of whatever modern science, I fall as theologian into no slight panic. The greater part of what stands written there I do not know, and usually I am not even in the position to understand more exactly what it is that I could be reading about. And so I feel as a theologian that I am somehow repudiated. The colorless abstraction and emptiness of my theological concepts frightens me. I say that the world has been created by God. But what is the world—about that I know virtually nothing, and as a result the concept of creation also remains unusually empty. I say as a theologian that Jesus is as man also Lord of the whole creation. And then I read that the cosmos stretches for billions of light years, and then I ask myself, terrified, what the statement that I have just said really means. Paul still knew in which sphere of the cosmos he wanted to locate the angels; I do not.[29]

One may, of course, question whether this confessed limitation really makes any great difference in a system of thought that is as comprehensive as Rahner's. But since his aim was to dialogue with a modernity grounded in our present scientific view of the cosmos this limitation raises big questions. Moreover, how can there be a historical-critical approach to theology, which Rahner certainly attempted, without placing human history in a scientific context?

Rahner did occasionally attempt this, as in his important essays on polygenism and evolutionary theory, but not systematically.[30] Thus the advantage of St. Thomas's empirical and analogical approach to metaphysics is that it begins with the problems raised by experience of the world and only gradually and critically works toward the knowledge of the self and God. Hence no gap arises between the empty formalism of the transcendental level of thought and the concrete, categorical world of science and history.

Transcendentality, Intuition, Co-naturality

Yet even if we grant that Thomistic methodology permits us to integrate the findings of the natural and historical sciences into moral theology, is it not true that St. Thomas's analysis of decisionmaking is hopelessly rationalistic?

---

on the Problem of the Anonymous Christian," vol. 12, 280–94; "Theology as Engaged in an Interdisciplinary Dialogue with the Sciences," vol. 13, 80–93; "On the Relationship Between Theology and the Contemporary Sciences," vol. 13, 94–104; "On the Relation between Natural Science and Theology," vol. 19, 3–15.

29　Karl Rahner,"The Experiences of a Catholic Theologian," *Communio* 11 (4; 1984): 412.

30　See Rahner, *Theological Investigations*, "Theological Reflections on Monogenism," vol. 1, 229–96, and "Christology with an Evolutionary View of the World," vol. 5, 439–59.

To answer that question we must refer to a feature of Thomistic psychology that is often neglected. At the beginning of this essay I noted that the fundamental option or the commitment to an ultimate end are for Rahner and Aquinas, respectively, the first principle of ethics. How, for Aquinas, is this first principle known?

Aquinas distinguishes between the *ratio superior* and *ratio inferior* or, in other terms, *intellectus* and *ratio*, intuition and reason.[31] Furthermore, as Jacques Maritain brilliantly showed,[32] Thomists recognize the "co-naturality" of human intuition, a co-naturality enhanced by empathy or love of the object known. The formation of clear and distinct concepts and explicit ratiocination at the level of *ratio*, presupposes intuitional and performative concepts at the level of *intellectus* that can be called "preconceptual" (not very accurately since for Aquinas all intellectual cognition is through some type of concept).

Our knowledge of first principles, whether speculative or practical, is by *intellectus*, theoretical or practical, while the applications of these principles to concrete situations is by *ratio*, theoretical or practical. Moreover, only in the process of using first principle in reasoning do they come to more exact and clear expression. Thus our commitment to our ultimate end is at the level of intuition or the *ratio superior* rather than of the calculative reason.

We can, therefore, credit Rahner with drawing attention to this important question, but whether he answers it better than Aquinas is debatable. One should not confuse the self-knowledge in *actu exercitu*, which Rahner considers as an a priori element in all human knowledge, with preconceptual intuitions *in actu signato* that are "objectifying," although still vague. For example, as Jacques Maritain showed in his *Creative Intuition in Art and Poetry* artists have "preconceptual, formative ideas" of the works they are creating, but this idea becomes fully actual only in the work itself. These ideas are of the work, not of the artist's awareness of himself working.

What then is the essential difference, if any, between Rahner's "fundamental option" and Aquinas's "commitment to an ultimate end"? For both, one's commitment of the total self to the supreme value of which one is aware is the first principle of the moral life and is made at the deepest level of the psyche. For both this commitment admits of degrees of intensity, but it is an either/or choice between openness to the supreme good or an enclosure in self. For both, this commitment is made or changed in some concrete act, but it exceeds the significance of that single act since it becomes the principle of all subsequent life, until it is again changed. Thus the two accounts have much in common,

I believe the difference between them is to be found in a different way of structuring ethics. Aquinas's model is often said to be "deductive," but that

---

31 *Summa theologiae* I, q. 79, a. 9; I–II, q. 57, a. 2 and 4.
32 *Distinguish to Unite,* 260–63.

term is ambiguous. Thomistic ethics is deductive only in the sense that it reduces its conclusions to certain fundamental principles of which commitment to an ultimate end is the first. But it is not "deductive" if that term is understood to mean, as it so often is, that these conclusions are drawn out of the principles without independent reference to moral experience. Quite the contrary, the conclusions in ethics are judgments on which means are effective in achieving the end (the first principle) and which are not, and this requires an independent experiential examination of the means before measuring them by the end, as well as subsequent verification of the conclusions in experience. Aquinas's ethics are thoroughly teleological but also thoroughly experiential (empirical) since only by actually observing the results of human behavior can we discover their effectiveness.

Moreover, Thomistic ethics also determine their first principle, the ultimate end of a good human life, not by postulation but by developing an anthropology through a protracted analysis of human behavior (always open to further refinement) based on the observations of natural science. Thus Aristotle, whom Aquinas follows, arrives at a definition of the ultimate end of individual life in ethics and of communal life in politics only at the conclusion of his *Nicomachean Ethics* and of his *Politics*. It is true that Aquinas in his *Summa theologiae* begins from the end and then treats the means of Christian life, but this is because he is writing theology in which the end is known by revelation. Yet even in the *Summa* the first five questions of the Prima Secundae on the ultimate end are only an initial abstract sketch that becomes ever more concrete as the work proceeds.

The ethics of Rahner, on the other hand, also uses an explicitly "deductive" method, though this deduction is transcendental, that is, it proceeds not from an anthropology based on a scientific study of human behavior, but on the subject's reflection on the conditions of any possible behavior that can be called truly human. Hence, the ethics so derived cannot be well characterized as "teleological." In this methodology moral conclusions are derived not so much by making judgments about the relations of means to an end, as in terms of the realization of ideal values in historical circumstances by "creative" decisions somewhat like those made by artists. The fundamental option, therefore, plays a role not as end measuring means, but as a basic stance either of openness to unforeseen ways of better realizing these values, or of a closure on some finite and self-defeating realization of these values.

This is not to say, however, that Aquinas's teleological model makes no room for growth in moral understanding. In his epistemology our knowledge of the end is just as much based on human experience as is our knowledge of the means. As we grow in understanding of the means by comparing means to the end, so we at the same time grow in understanding of the end by using it in evaluating the means. Thus for both Aquinas and Rahner moral life is open to the mystery of the Goal, which in this life always lies beyond every attempt to realize it.

Fundamental Freedom and Grace

For Rahner, however, as we have seen, this openness to the Mystery is the result of grace accessible to all humanity as the supernatural existential of every human subject. Is not this a manifest superiority of his theological anthropology to that of St. Thomas? Certainly Aquinas, a medieval living in a relatively uniform society, gave little attention to the problem of the salvation of the non-believer of goodwill, a problem typical of the pluralistic modern world, but his analysis of the human act did raise for him the question of the child's first truly human, free act, occurring perhaps about the age of seven.

According to Aquinas free choice is possible only among means in relation to a predetermined end.[33] Ultimately this choice must be in relation to the predetermined end of human nature that in the abstract is "happiness," and in the concrete whatever good appears to our practical moral intelligence to be supreme in the scale of human values. For a Thomistic analysis, therefore, even a child in its first human act makes a judgment of conscience that its first choice ought either to be to commit itself to the greatest good known to it as the concrete realization of its happiness, or to some lesser good, which it perceives to be a true means to this supreme good. If a child makes the latter choice, it also implicitly commits itself to the supreme good, since to will the means to an end is implicitly to will the end. Rahner, in his beautiful essay "Ideas for a Theology of Childhood,"[34] dwells on the child's "openness" but does not discuss the question of children's sins.[35] Of course, since the child is performing a free act, it may act against its judgment of conscience and commit itself explicitly to a concrete object as its supreme good, which it knows has only the appearance of supremacy but which affords more immediate tangible satisfactions. Or it may implicitly choose this illusory happiness by choosing something that is a means to it, but an obstacle to true happiness.

Thus for Thomists there is no philosophical problem in holding that the fundamental option for God or against him is made by every human being, even the merest child, or at any time or anywhere, if that human being is capable of performing a genuinely human, free act of choice. There is, however, a theological problem, since in our existential, fallen state we come into the world with an inherent tendency, aggravated by the sinful condition of

---

33 For an exhaustive study of this theme in Aquinas work, see S. M. Ramirez, OP, *De hominis beatitudine tractus theologicus ad primam secundae Summa Theologicae,* 5 vols.

34 Karl Rahner, *Theological Investigations,* vol. 8, 33–50.

35 Poddimattam, *Fundamental Option,* 112–18.

the world, to act against the judgment of conscience and thus commit ourselves to illusory, false gods, to idolatry. Redemption from this fallen state is
possible in one way only, through the grace of Christ. The child baptized in
infancy has been redeemed through the sacrament, although it still has to
struggle with some effects of our fallen state and with the sinful structures of
that world.

What then of unbaptized children? Thomists have developed two possible answers. First, unbaptized children who die before the age of reason may
attain a state of purely natural happiness (Limbo); or second, as that major
Thomist commentator Thomas del Vio, Cardinal Cajetan, proposed, the
grace of Christ can be mediated to them not by actual baptism, but by the
faith and prayers of their parents and the Church.[36] As for non-Christians
who attain the use of reason, the grace of Christ can be mediated to them in
other ways, above all, as some early Church Fathers taught, by Christ as
Logos acting providentially in history and by the prayers of the Church in
his Name.

Certainly, as Vatican II declared,[37] the founders of the great world religions taught great moral truths (although not with the infallibility of Jewish
prophets and the apostles). Since all truth is from Christ's Holy Spirit, this
teaching may have mediated the grace of Christ to their followers. Therefore, since what is required for salvation is only an obedience to conscience,
however imperfect one's understanding of God and the moral law, the acces-
sibility of salvation to all is real. Yet, since obedience to conscience is beset
by many perils, all humankind still greatly needs the full light of the Gospel
and its sacraments and thus Thomistic soteriology retains an urgent motif
for evangelization and ecumenism.

Rahner's notions of fundamental freedom, fundamental option, and the
supernatural existential lead to much the same result. Fundamental freedom
is the condition of a fundamental option, that is, of the commitment of
one's whole person and one's whole life. The fundamental option is not an
act in itself, but a quality of some categorical acts that, at least implicitly,
involve fundamental freedom. Hence, a child, at whatever age, who per-
forms acts that do not yet involve its fundamental freedom, has not yet
made a fundamental option and is not yet capable either of sin or merit. Yet
when a person does finally perform an act of this profound quality, that act
must either be a choice for God or for self, and thus be a virtuous act or a
mortal sin. Moreover, since both Rahner and Aquinas hold that God has in

---

[36] For further discussion, see my *Theologies of the Body: Humanist and Christian*, 2nd
ed. with new introduction, 600–602.

[37] *Nostra Aetate,* "Declaration on the Relationship of the Church to Non-Christian Religions," October 28, 1965, www.vatican.va/archive/hist_councils/ii_vatican_council/
documents/vat-ii_decl_19651028_nostra-aetate_en.html.

fact invited all human beings to salvation, if that first act is implicitly for God then it is a graced act.

Mortal and Venial Sin

Thus, whether we follow Rahner or Aquinas, mortal sin is a closure of self to God, which, although it involves the total person and penetrates to the depths of the psyche, must take the form of some concrete act in the world of which the sinner is conscious and obliged to confess. In a consistently teleological,[38] means-ends ethic, such as that of Aquinas, morality is not determined by the will of the legislator, but by the objective relation of a certain act considered as a means to the true goal or goals of human life. A sinful act, therefore, is mortal if it raises an impassable roadblock to attaining the goal of union with God, either by rejecting God by an act directly against the theological virtues of faith, hope, and love—in which sins perhaps are rare—or, since loving God and neighbor are inseparable, by an act which seriously harms our neighbor or ourselves—which may not be so rare!

For the ethicist, therefore, the question is how to judge whether a particular kind of act that is harmful to our neighbor is of such a nature to do someone, including the agent, serious harm. Only if it does serious harm is the sin mortal. Venial sin, for Aquinas, is only analogically sin, since it does not break off the relation to God or the life of grace. Such a "superficial" sin is possible only because human reason under the pressure of our disordered appetites is often inconsistent in its judgments. Nevertheless, in the commission of a venial sin, the commitment to the true ultimate end still motivates the act by restraining the doer from going so far as to do serious harm. There is, therefore, no logical possibility of a middle ground between mortal and venial sin.

Yet venial sins can prepare the way for mortal sin and this is why, in the Thomist theory, mortal sin, although it is not itself a process, but a definite act, is the climax of a process, like the critical point at which water boils after being gradually heated. Similarly conversion from sin is ordinarily the culmination of a gradual process of return to God. Yet we cannot class such sins of weakness as drug abuse or genital sexual activity out of marriage as objectively "serious but venial," because they in fact do serious harm to another or ourself.

What is "serious" harm, of course, is sometimes debatable. Is professional boxing moral? There are good arguments that, since the boxer aims at a knockout, which risks serious harm to the victim, professional boxing is a mortal sin and that even attendance at a boxing match is a mortal sin because it promotes a seriously harmful practice, like attendance at the gladiatorial games, which the early Church absolutely forbade. On the other

---

[38] *Veritatis Splendor,* nn. 71–75.

hand, fifty years ago few Christians would have doubted that homosexual genital acts are mortal sins, while many doubt that today.

Questions about what is in fact seriously harmful to human dignity are a legitimate field of research and debate for moralists. It is also their responsibility to suggest changes in the Church's teaching on certain issues where the advance of science and experience show that what was formerly considered seriously harmful is really not so, or what was formerly considered not seriously harmful is so. In the practical order, however, the Magisterium of the Church, the only divinely instituted guide for the Christian conscience, must often decide in controversies, for a time or even definitively, what is seriously harmful to moral and spiritual life and what is not. It does so not by mere legislative fiat, but by discernment in the light of the Gospel of what helps and hurts human progress toward God.

What then is the pastoral solution to the question about the person who seems to fall in and out of grace within days or even hours? Does not the distinction of "transcendental" and "categorical" help us solve this puzzle? A Rahnerian moralist can say that recurring sinful acts at the categorical level, although they do serious harm, involve a relatively superficial aspect of the person, but not the person in its totality, and hence do not change the person's fundamental option, that is, they are venial not mortal sins.

In classical moral theology this same phenomenon was explained by the distinction between objective and subjective morality. A sin may be objectively mortal because it does serious harm yet not be mortally culpable if there are subjective factors, such as ignorance, lack of deliberation, compulsive emotions, and so on, that prevent such harmful acts from being truly or at least fully human acts. Persons struggling with an addiction who have truly determined to overcome it for the sake of God, their family, and themselves have committed themselves to God. If during the course of their treatment they sometimes lapse into objectively seriously harmful acts, yet keep up the treatment, it is probable that these lapses do not reflect a change in commitment but are the result of moments of weakness when the addictive compulsion blinds them to full realization of what they are doing or how to control it. Hence these lapses, though objectively serious because they reinforce the addiction and imperil recovery, may not be subjectively mortal sins. Thus the Rahnerian explanation is in terms of the transcendental and categorical aspects of a human act, the Thomistic in terms of its subjective and objective aspects.

Hence the answer of fundamental option to this pastoral question seems to me to have made little advance over that of classical moral theology, except perhaps to make us still more sensitive to subjective factors in moral behavior. Indeed, this growing sensitivity is a major factor in the revision of moral theology, but it is due not so much to fundamental option theory as to our increased awareness of the limitations of human freedom by psychological and social determination.

Proportionalism Again

Many moralists who have believed themselves to be in the "mainstream" of post-Vatican II theology by adopting the "principle of proportionate reason" as the basic determinate of moral decision are now saying that the rejection by *Veritatis Splendor* of what it names "proportionalism" on the grounds that it denies absolute moral norms is largely the result of misunderstanding.[39]

They point out that proportionalists do not deny that norms such as "Never hate God or neighbor" are absolute, but only claim that such norms are "formal" and hence transcendental not categorical norms. Nor do they even deny that categorical norms are absolute when expressed in terms that imply moral guilt, that is, they do not deny that "murder" is always sinful, as the encyclical seems to charge, but only that what is abstractly defined as "murder" in actual situations is always really murder. Nor, finally, do they deny that some acts, such as torturing innocent children, involve such weighty negative values that it is not imaginable they could be justified by any situation. The real issue, not acknowledged by *Veritatis Splendor*, they claim, is how to define a moral act so as to determine whether it is good or evil.

These protestations of being misunderstood seem to me not very candid. What *Veritatis Splendor* insists on is not that "murder" is always wrong, but that "direct killing of the innocent is always wrong." Nor can its censure be escaped by attempting to redefine "murder" in difficult cases in such a way as to admit of exceptions to traditional norms, for example, by claiming that killing a fetus is not "abortion" if it is gravely deformed.[40] Of course, the problem of exact definition of the moral object in moral theology is often a problem open to debate and refinement, but this does not mean that the contention of proportionalists that the moral object of an act is always indeterminate until qualified by the circumstances and the circumstantial intention of the agent can be sustained.

Aquinas's essential point, confirmed by *Veritatis Splendor*, is that circumstances and intention may make an intrinsically good act evil, but they cannot make an intrinsically evil act good. The significance of this distinction between the essential morality of an act and its accidental modification by circumstances is quite evident in a Thomistic methodology in that we first come to understand the interior acts of the soul through external behavior rather than by reflective insight. No doubt it is not so evident in a Rahnerian

---

[39] See Joseph A. Selling and Jan Jans, eds., *The Splendor of Accuracy: An Examination of the Assertions Made by* Veritatis Splendor.

[40] See the essay "When does a Human Person Begin to Exist" in this collection.

methodology that turns inward to the subject and puts its emphasis on the discernment of spirits.

Such an emphasis on introspection in moral decision, however, has its risks. St. Ignatius himself was well aware of the dangers of such discernment and insisted that it had to be used within the limits set by the Church, legitimate human superiors, and one's confessor or spiritual director.[41] He never countenanced the possibility of "dissent" from the moral teaching of the Church. John Paul II in *Veritatis Splendor* has felt a similar need to insist on the universally obligatory force of certain traditional moral norms. Yet the pope in his encyclical (nn. 6–27) meditates on the dialogue between the Rich Young Man and Jesus in order to make clear that the call of Jesus, "Come follow me!," as St. Ignatius taught, goes far beyond the commandments of the Law.

Similarly some moralists, many of whom favor proportionalism, contend that the Magisteriums's condemnation of some acts, such as contraception, is "physicalist" because it regards the nature of the physical act as an essential element in rendering it objectively and intrinsically evil. This charge may seem more persuasive to Rahnerians who accent the subjective attitude rather than the physical behavior than it does to Thomists who always work from the physical to the spiritual. Rahner himself, however, was concerned not to fall into dualism and wrote eloquently of the body as a symbol expressive of the soul.[42]

Yet, it must be admitted if one demands as a criterion for certain and permanent categorical moral norms that they be grounded by a transcendental deduction from the metaphysical nature of man, as Rahner seems to say in his essay "On Bad Arguments in Moral Theology,"[43] rather than on our empirical experience of human behavior, it becomes difficult to see how such a criterion can ever be met. It is this in Rahner's transcendental methodology that has opened the way to proportionalism.

Prudence and the Gifts of the Holy Spirit

The intention of Rahner's "formal existential ethics" was not, however, to attack absolute concrete moral norms, as I have already indicated, but to show that universal moral norms cannot provide us with the final guidance required in our moral life since they merely mark out the area within which

---

[41] St. Ignatius Loyola, SJ, "Rules for Thinking, Judging, and Feeling with the Church to Have the Genuine Attitude which We Ought to Maintain in the Church Militant," included in his *The Spiritual Exercises*, nn. 353–570 in *Ignatius Loyola: The Spiritual Exercises and Selected Works*, edited by George E. Ganss, SJ, et al., preface by J. W. Padberg, SJ, 211–14; and "Letter on Obedience," ibid., 341–45.

[42] See *Theological Investigations*, "The Dignity and Freedom of Man," vol. 4, 245–52.

[43] Ibid., vol. 18, 74–85.

legitimate choices still have to be made. The final guidance, he says, must be by a "discernment of spirits." What does this issue look like from a Thomistic perspective?

Aquinas distinguishes between three levels in moral decision. First is the level of *moral science*, ethics and moral theology, which attempts to determine universal norms based on an analysis of the kinds of human means that are helpful and harmful to the attainment of the true goal of human life.[44] Ethical science presupposes a view of human anthropology that determines what are the basic needs of the human being and their interrelations. This is also the level of "virtue theory" so much discussed again today.[45] Without a stable and good moral character, consistently good moral behavior is not possible. This character, since it is anterior to concrete moral decisions in unique situations, must be conformed to universal norms.

The second level of moral decision is that of *prudence*. Prudence is a virtue, the foundation of a morally sound character, which enables us to apply general moral norms to special situations.[46] It is not, however, simply casuistry in the classical conception of that term, namely, the correct application of general norms to problematic moral decisions. Prudence differs from casuistry because casuistry places the moral judgment on the level of an impartial judge who is not concerned with what is decided. Prudence, however, is primarily directed toward helping the very person who must make a decision carry it out well and live with it responsibly. It requires an examination not only of the law and the situation but also of the goodwill and capacity to act of the decisionmaker. Or in the case of the governing prudence of heads of families or communities, it requires care for the common good in which they themselves need to participate. Therefore, prudence is not only an intellectual virtue, like casuistic skill, but a moral virtue, the consummation of a good character.

Moreover, for Aquinas, since prudence does not merely consider "cases" abstractly described, but here-and-now singulars involving the decisionmaker and the act of decision itself, it cannot function without the cooperation of sense cognition and sense appetites that condition it. Hence prudent decisions call into play the internal sense that Aquinas calls the *vis aestimativa* or "particular reason," which is not a spiritual but a corporeal faculty, as are the sense appetites. Thus the prudent person needs a sound sense life to live well in this world of the body.

---

44 William A. Wallace, OP, *The Role of Demonstration in Moral Theology: A Study of Methodology in St. Thomas Aquinas.*

45 Romanus Cessario, OP, *The Moral Virtues and Theological Ethics,* 22.

46 See Daniel Mark Nelson, *The Priority of Prudence: Virtue and Natural Law in Thomas Aquinas and the Implications for Modern Ethics,* and William A. Wallace, OP, "The Existential Ethics of Karl Rahner: A Thomistic Appraisal," *The Thomist* 27 (1963): 493–515.

For Thomas there is still a third level of moral perception, that of grace, which consists first of all in the purification and elevation of the human faculties and virtues in view of intimate union with God. It is noteworthy that many proportionalists also reject or minimize the "specificity of Christian ethics," and thus tend to carry on their moral analyses with little reference to the strictly theological aspects of moral theology, reducing it almost totally to philosophical ethics.[47]

For these moralists the Bible and theology in general remain strictly at the transcendental level of presenting certain absolute values to be categorically realized in quite different ways in changing situations. But for Aquinas the values revealed in Scripture penetrate all aspects of the human person, soul and body, and their historical realization in Jesus and the New Testament Church is a concrete norm of what Christian life must be no matter how enculturated—they are not a mere ideal.

Furthermore, this third level of graced morality, which terminates in the theological virtues that directly unite the Christian to God, is not completed just by these "infused" virtues. Aquinas, like St. Ignatius Loyola, is keenly aware that Christians cannot attain their goal by their own prudence without direct guidance by the Holy Spirit through his special gifts.[48] Thus a moral theology inspired by Aquinas, as by St. Ignatius, ought to culminate in spiritual theology, including a theory of the discernment of spirits and supernatural co-naturality.

Conclusion

With *Veritatis Splendor* I am convinced that a revision of moral theology in a proportionalist mode leaves us stuck in the casuistic tradition that we are struggling to escape. Looking for "loop holes in the law" by the pragmatic proportionalist balancing of positive and negative values is no way out of the voluntaristic legalism of the moral manuals tradition from which Rahner also sought to provide an escape by the Ignatian process of discernment.

I believe Rahner has also made a significant contribution to this revision by rethinking theology from the perspective of modern philosophy and its "turn to the subject." Although, I believe, in the long run this cannot provide us with that common ground with modernity that I believe is to be found only by directly entering into dialogue with modern science, it has called our attention to the too much neglected problems of human subjectivity and

---

47 For this contention see authors in Charles E. Curran and Richard A. McCormick, SJ, eds., *Readings in Moral Theology*, No. 2. *The Distinctiveness of Christian Ethics*.

48 On the role of the Seven Gifts in Christian life, see Thomas Aquinas, *The Gifts of the Spirit: Selected Spiritual Writings*, which I edited and Matthew Rzceczkowski, OP. translated, and my *Spiritual Direction in the Dominican Tradition*.

historicity. Remaining true to classical principles, we can now approach the pastoral problem of "gradualism" with a greater Christian compassion and hope.

Finally, I think we ought not to confound Rahner's own intentions with some well-intentioned but untenable interpretations of his theory of fundamental option that have given rise to tendencies incompatible with the Gospel tradition and a truly teleological ethic. These tendencies are more likely to trap us into a return to voluntarism, legalism, and minimalizing casuistry than they are to free us to hear the voice of the Holy Spirit as Rahner hoped to do.

CHAPTER 15

Integral Human Fulfillment
According to Germain Grisez*

I. Moral Theology Under Philosophical Scrutiny

A DEBT OF GRATITUDE IS DUE GERMAIN GRISEZ AND his co-workers John Finnis, Joseph Boyle, and William E. May for bringing to moral theology the philosophical *akribeia*, which recently has been in short supply.[1] Significantly all four are laymen, two (Finnis and Boyle) are philosophers; the other two are theologians who began their teaching as philosophers. In the first few pages of Germain Grisez's remarkable *The Way of the Lord Jesus*[2]

---

* This was published under the title "What is the End of the Human Person: The Vision of God and Integral Human Fulfillment," in *Moral Truth and Moral Tradition: Essays in Honour of Peter Geach and Elizabeth Anscombe*, edited by Luke Gormally (Dublin: Four Courts Press, 1994), 68–96. The IVth section has been added with material from a paper "The Scriptural Basis of Grisez' Revison of Moral Theology" I gave at a conference conference held at Princeton, *Natural Law and Moral Inquiry: Ethics, Metaphysics, and Politics in the Work of Germain Grisez,* edited by Robert P. George (Washington, DC: Georgetown University Press, 1998), 36–49.

[1] The bibliography of this group of writers is extensive. The following are especially important: John Finnis, *Natural Law and Natural Rights*; Germain Grisez (with the help of Joseph M. Boyle, Jr., Basil Cole, OP, John M. Finnis, John A. Geinzer, Jeannette Grisez, Robert G. Kennedy, Patrick Lee, William E. May, and Russell Shaw), *The Way of the Lord Jesus,* vol. 1 of *Christian Moral Principles*, 809–10. See my review discussion, "Christian Moral Principles," in *The Thomist* 48 (1984): 450–60; John Finnis, "Human Good(s) and Practical Reasoning," *Proceedings of the American Catholic Philosophical Association, Practical Reasoning,* vol. 40, ed.Daniel O. Dahlstrom, 23–36; Grisez, Boyle, and Finnis, "Practical Principles, Moral Truth, and Ultimate Ends," *American Journal of Jurisprudence* 32 (1987): 99–151; a select bibliography explains certain changes or clarifications in the theory to meet objections and misreadings Grisez and Russell Shaw, *Fulfillment in Christ*; John Finnis, *Moral Absolutes*; and William E. May, *An Introduction to Moral Theology.*

[2] Grisez et al., *Christian Moral Principles,* 13–22.

he joins the consensus of most current moral theologians, whether "conservative" or "progressive," that the moral theology of the pre-Vatican manuals was
excessively legalistic and in need of serious revision. Thus he commends a leading progressive, Josef Fuchs, SJ, and an influential conservative, Carlo Caf-
farra, for their acknowledgments of this need in the light of the Council.[3]
Thus a revision is the aim of both wings working today in moral theology.

Yet Grisez sharply criticizes the methodology of the revision proposed
by the self-designated "main-stream revisionists." Insofar as the requirement
to assent to Catholic teaching is denied, the minimum set by the new moral
theology is much lower than that set by classical moral theology. But the
new remains as legalistic as the old. It provides no account in Christian
terms of why one should seek human fulfillment in this life, what the specifically Christian way of life is, and how living as a Christian in this life is
intrinsically related to fulfillment in everlasting life.[4]

In this "new moral theology" Grisez opposes not only its dissent from
sacred tradition as embodied in the documents of the living Magisterium of
the Church, but also its untenable interpretation of the Vatican II statements that, "The study of sacred Scripture . . . ought to be the soul of all
theology," and that "Special attention needs to be given to the development
of moral theology. Its scientific exposition should be more thoroughly nourished by scriptural teaching."[5] The prevailing revisionist view seems to be
that since, as even St. Thomas Aquinas admitted, the moral precepts of
Christian life are for the most part materially identical with the natural law
and differ principally only in their supernatural motivation. Therefore, in
view of the modern historical-critical approach to the Bible, the classical
"argument from Scripture" is largely irrelevant to current moral theology,
whose arguments must be based principally on purely rational, philosophical, psychological, or social data.

Grisez, on the other hand holds that there is a specifically Christian
ethics.[6] No doubt this is one reason his work is so strikingly titled *The Way
of the Lord Jesus.* As a Thomist, I heartily agree, since in saying that revealed
moral law and natural moral law are materially identical, Aquinas surely did
not intend to contradict his fundamental principle that matter and form are
proportionate to each other. Hence the formal difference of natural and
revealed ethics also implies the respective modification of their otherwise
materially identical contents. For example, as Aquinas explicitly points out,[7]
although the infused virtue of abstinence has the same material object as the

---

[3] Ibid., 36–37, n. 20.

[4] Ibid., 15.

[5] *Optatam Totius,* "Decree on Priestly Training," October 28, 1965, n. 16.

[6] Grisez et al., *Christian Moral Principles,* 606–8, 661–80.

[7] *Summa theologiae* I–II, q. 63, a. 4 c.

natural virtue, namely, moderation as regards food, the formal difference resulting from the differing supernatural and natural ends to be achieved establishes a different mean for each: In one case the amount of food that best serves earthly health, in the other the amount that best prepares for eternal life in heaven. Thus for actual moral judgment—and that is what moral theology is all about—the Christian can arrive at decisions of conscience quite other than those dictated by reason, although not contradictory to it.

Grisez, therefore, not only has no patience with those who attempt to revise moral theology by dissenting from the Magisterium, but also for those who seek to cut it free from its concrete biblical foundations. Hence, like the rest of us moral theologians who agree with him, he finds himself in an interdisciplinary dilemma. What moral theologian today can claim competence in the highly complex and controverted field of biblical scholarship? On the other hand, has the training and orientation of biblical scholars made them competent to construct a systematic ethics or to apply it to current ethical problems?

Nevertheless, in spite of these strong points, the revision of moral theology proposed by Grisez and his school, often labeled as conservative because of its vigorous defense of Catholic doctrine, is in fact quite radical. Thus Grisez writes,

> St. Thomas Aquinas synthesized Aristotle's concern about the end of man with St. Augustine's articulation of our hunger for the destiny for which God created us. He concluded that human persons naturally desire the beatific vision and described heaven primarily in terms of intellectual knowledge of what God is. It seems to me that the conclusion and description contributed to many of the difficulties I am trying to surmount in this work. My contention is that the human heart is not naturally oriented toward adoption as a child of God and the heavenly inheritance which goes with this status. It is naturally oriented toward human fulfillment, which is found in human goods in which one naturally can participate more and more. No single complete good is naturally available to human persons as their determinate, ultimate end. Of course, in choosing, one seeks a good loved for itself. In this sense, one always acts for an ultimate end—that is, an end not pursued as a means to some ulterior end. But an end ultimate in this sense need not be the complete good of the human person, as Thomas assumed when he tried to prove that one's will cannot be directed simultaneously to two or more ultimate ends (*Summa theologiae* I–II, q. 1 a. 5). Rather in loving various human goods for their own sake, human persons remain upright insofar as they remain open to integral human fulfillment. This fulfillment is naturally only an ideal, not a determinate goal to which all the acts of a

good life contribute. Thus, on the theory of human fulfillment proposed in chapters five and seven, the view that the human heart is naturally restless is based on a mistaken theory of human goal-directedness.[8]

Grisez says the "classical view" of Augustine and Aquinas that he wishes to revise held that the "Christian life in this world is only a means to be used to reach heaven." He thinks this has lead "to a sharp division within Christian life between religious and secular, supernatural and merely natural" and has "tended to depreciate human goods other than religion" and thus neglected the growth of the laity in holiness.[9] On the other hand he rejects the view "that human fulfillment will be found exclusively in this world" or that "heaven will inevitably follow this life, but that the positive meaning of this life is found entirely within it."[10]

To find a middle course between the otherworldliness of the classical view and the worldliness of secular humanism and liberal Christianity, Grisez proposes a doctrine of "fulfillment in the Lord Jesus."[11] As I understand him, he means that, as in Jesus divinity and humanity are united, so "fulfillment in Jesus" includes not only the beatific vision but also "the perfect human well-being which secular humanism falsely promises in this life."[12] Thus he believes that, in spite of the doctrine of the resurrection and of the inseparability of the love of God from the love of neighbor, the identification of human fulfillment with the good of contemplation has resulted in the neglect both of the value of bodily life and of the "communal aspect of heaven."[13]

This new revision of moral theory has many ramifications and hence has been criticized on many points,[14] but three of its theses stand out clearly and it is these alone that I want to discuss here:

---

[8] Grisez et al., *Christian Moral Principles,* 809–10.

[9] Ibid., 807–8.

[10] Ibid., 811–14.

[11] Ibid., 814–16.

[12] Ibid., 816.

[13] Ibid., 815.

[14] See Russell Hittinger, *A Critique of the New Natural Law Theory*; see also the reviews of Henry B. Veatch, *New Scholasticism* 62 (1988): 353–65; William H. Marshner, *Faith and Reason* 16 (2; Summer 1990): 177–99. Grisez answered in "A Critique of Russell Hittinger's Book, A Critique of the New Natural Law Theory," *The New Scholasticism* 62 (4; Autumn 1988), citing many "misreadings" by Hittinger. From a Wittgensteinian angle, see Garth Hallet, SJ, "Contraception and Prescriptive Infallibility," *Theological Studies* 43 (December 1982): 629–50; "Infallibility and Contraception: The Debate Continues," *Heythrop Journal* 49 (September 1988): 517–28; "The 'Incommensurability' of Values," *Heythrop Journal* 28 (1987): 373–87. More favorable to Grisez is James G. Hanink, "A Theory of Basic Goods: Structure and Hierarchy," *The Thomist* 52 (1988): 221–45.

1. Ethics is independent of a philosophical anthropology.

2. The human person, even if as Christians believe it now has a super-natural ultimate end, still also has a natural ultimate end.

3. The ultimate end of the human person is not a single good (and thus not just the good of contemplation, as Aristotle and Aquinas argued), but integral human fulfillment jointly constituted by several incom-mensurable basic goods.

This new theory is not alone in thus rejecting Aquinas's notion of a single ultimate end of moral decision. For example, John Rawls claims "human good is heterogeneous because the aims of the self are heterogeneous."[15] Although the new theory rejects classification as either deontological or teleological,[16] in view of the key role of the third thesis above I will refer to it as polyteleologism, "plural-goals-ism," although its proponents use no such label.[17]

II. Ethics and Anthropology

An Ethics Independent of Philosophical Anthropology

Polyteleologism (PT) implicitly assumes an Aristotelian logic according to which every true science is founded on indemonstrable first principles.[18] Sciences differ formally if they have different sets of first principles; or to put it in another way, if their conclusions reduce analytically to different types of knowledge. Generally PT uses the term "practical" for the knowledge that guides doing and the term "productive" for knowledge that guides making.[19] Yet PT also seems to identify with distinction the "ought" that pertains to making with the "is-to-be," although obviously also making a deal with the "is-to-be."

How then are we to know and formulate these first principles of the science of ethics? On the logical assumptions just made, these cannot be known by demonstration, that is, by reasoning. In a realist Aristotelian epistemology they are prior to reasoning and if knowable by humans can only be known by

---

[15] John Rawls, *A Theory of Justice*, 554. See his whole discussion of this question, 548–54.

[16] Grisez, Boyle, and Finnis, "Practical Principles," 101.

[17] Ibid., I class polyteleologism primarily as a teleology because it is based on the means-ends relation and not on the will of a legislator.

[18] Aristotle, *Posterior Analytics*, I, 75b37–76a 30.

[19] A usage derived from Aristotle, *Metaphysics* VI, c. 1, 1025b25 28; although in II, c. 1, 993b20 22 he seems to use *praktikos* generically. See Aquinas, *In libros Politicorum expositio*, Proemium, n. 6, where he divides *scientiae practicae* as a genus against *scientiae speculativae*, and then subdivides *scientiae practicae* into the *activae* (ethics, politics) and the *factivae* (arts in the broad sense). Cf. also *Summa theologiae* I, q. 18, a. 3 ad 1; I–II, q. 57, a. 4, c; a. 5, ad 1; q. 74, a. 1, c.

some form of intellectual intuition or insight *(intellectus)* ultimately based on sense knowledge.[20] Although Thomistic textbooks commonly say these axioms are "self-evident," for Aristotle it is not sufficient for the terms of a principle to be known nominally (from word usage). They must be known immediately or mediately from human experience to have real, existing instances.[21] Hence, in the case of ethics the first principles must be immediately evident from experience, and from a special kind of experience, namely moral experience.

Hence these first principles of ethics cannot be reduced to those of any other discipline, especially not to a theoretical discipline such as natural philosophy (which for Aristotle includes anthropology), nor even to metaphysics. Ethics is an autonomous science, formally distinct from the theoretical sciences.[22] Indeed, PT so emphasizes this autonomy, the irreducibility of the practical "is-to-be" to the theoretical "is," that it seems to cut ethics loose from any precise theory of human nature.

Yet PT grants that the moralist assumes many things about the human being, the world, and God (and of course logic), without demonstrating them.[23] By complaining that Augustine's "dualistic" anthropology injured ethics when it downgraded the bodily, worldly aspects of human existence,[24] PT recognizes that ethics needs a sound theoretical foundation. Moreover, Grisez in an early work[25] suggested a certain anthropology of his own based on the four orders of reasoning discussed by St. Thomas: the physical, intentional (logical), existential (ethical), and cultural (technological) orders. He explains,

The four orders are irreducibly distinct from one another. To reduce

---

[20] Aristotle, *Metaphysics,* 980a1–982a3; *Nicomachean Ethics,* 1139b 29; Aquinas, *Summa theologiae* I, q. 79, a.8; *De Veritate,* q. 15, a. 1. Grisez, Boyle, and Finnis, "Practical Principles," 106, 108, denies the first principles of ethics are known by "intuition," but defines intuition as "insights without data." For Aquinas *intellectus* is empirically grounded.

[21] *Posterior Analytics,* II, 93a14–21.

[22] Grisez argued this at length in "The First Principle of Practical Reason: A Commentary on the *Summa theologiae* I–I, Question 94, Article 2," *Natural Law Forum* 10 (1965): 168–201. His present position is found in Grisez, Boyle, and Finnis, "Practical Principles," 115–20.

[23] See Grisez. Boyle, and Finnis, "Practical Principles," 111, 113, 127.

[24] "The proposition that life is only instrumentally good implies that the human person or some parts of the human person are one thing and a person's living body is quite another thing. This implied position splits the person in two, and so it is called 'dualism.'" Grisez et al., *The Way of the Lord Jesus,* vol. 1 of *Christian Moral Principles,* 137–38. On this whole question of anthropological dualism, see my *Theologies of the Body: Humanist and Christian.*

[25] Grisez, *Beyond the New Theism: A Philosophy of Religion,* 232–43, 346–53. I am very grateful to Rev. William Virtue for calling my attention to these significant texts.

them to a single system, reason would have to relate them all to a single principle; reason would have to be related to the various entities in all of the orders in a uniform way. Thus, any attempt to unify the four orders into a single order amounts to relating every state of affairs included in all of them to a principle located in one of them, and to following the relationship by only one of the modes of causal reasoning. In other words, the orders are themselves related and unified, but not in only one way; each of them unifies by the special way in which it includes the states of affairs which are included in the others.[26]

These four orders characterize the human person or self.

A person is in all four of the orders, and he embraces all of them in himself. In the person the four orders are distinct, irreducible, yet normally inseparable. The unity of the person is unlike the unity of any entity that is enclosed within one of the four orders. The unity of the person is mysterious and must remain so. This unity is immediately given in human experience, and it cannot be explained discursively, since reason cannot synthesize the distinct orders in a higher positive intelligibility.[27]

Thus PT seems not to attribute, as does Aquinas, the unity of the human person as much to the specific difference that defines human beings as "rational animals" as to the mutual inclusion of these four irreducible and correlative orders. Is this perhaps the ultimate ground for PT's theory of the good life as a complex of incommensurable goods, unified only by their interrelations?[28] If so it bypasses Aquinas's insistence that since the intelligence is the specifying trait of human nature, contemplation is the final unifying teleology of that nature.

The Relation of Ethics and Anthropology

What then is the relation of ethics (and of the practical disciplines in general) to the other disciplines? For Aristotle and Aquinas metaphysics is first philosophy *in via judicii* but last *in via inventionis*. In the latter, epistemological order metaphysics is preceded by ethics, and ethics by natural philosophy. Ethics presupposes natural science because human practical activity

---

26 Ibid., 236ff. This fourfold distinction is based on Aquinas in *Nichomachean Ethics* I, lect. 1.

27 Ibid., 349.

28 For this distinction, see Jude Chua Soo Meng, "To Close a Generation Gap: Thomists and the New Natural Law Theory," *Quodlibet Online Journal of Christian Theology and Philosophy* 3 (2; spring 2001), www.quodlibet.net/meng-thomism.shtml, who supports this defense of Grisez with a reference to Robert P. George, "Recent Criticism of Natural Law Theory" in *University of Chicago Law Review* 55 (1988).

cannot be understood or even known to be possible before one has acquired sufficient knowledge of the human person to understand why we are capable of free activity and also to understand the teleologies of our human powers, which require such free activity to be satisfied. We also need to know in what ways the material world is subject to human practical action.

Therefore, while it is true that knowledge of the moral "is-to-be" cannot be formally reduced to the theoretical knowledge of the "is," nevertheless ethics epistemologically presupposes certain conclusions of a philosophical anthropology that is part of natural philosophy.[29] A merely commonsense grasp of what it is to be human will hardly do if serious errors in ethics are to be avoided, such as PT recognizes have been caused by dualistic anthropologies. Yet some defenders of Grisez's view have argued that the first principles of ethics, like the first principles of all the special sciences, pertain to metaphysics and are thus prior to and independent of the first principles of anthropology. This betrays the Neo-Scholastic tendency that I have discussed elsewhere[30] to read Aquinas in Scotistic fashion and place metaphysics epistemologically first among the sciences on the grounds that it deals with the first principles of all human reasoning. In any critical development of practical knowledge, however, one must first establish the nature and causal relations of the objects that one intends to act upon practically. How can one build a house without a theoretical knowledge of its materials, the tools to be used, and the purpose it is intended to serve? This type of knowledge is not practical, since its object is not what is to be done, but what really exists. Yet such knowledge need not be "metaphysical;" it can be theoretical knowledge at the level of natural science.[31]

Thus the formal autonomy of practical knowledge, and of ethics in particular, does not negate its need for material conditions that are supplied by natural science.[32] Therefore, it is unfortunate that PT so exaggerates the autonomy of ethics, that it remains content to make certain anthropological assumptions that require much more careful scrutiny.

At least the following conclusions of anthropology are required for

---

[29] On this point I agree with Hittinger, *Critique,* 193–94; but not with his discussion 194 and note 5, 223, nor the authors he refers to (Harry V. Jaffa, Frederick Coppleston) who find major differences between Aquinas's ethics and Aristotle's due to their supposedly diverse natural philosophies.

[30] See my article "Why First Philosophy is Last" in this collection.

[31] Aristotle, *Nicomachean Ethics* VI, c. 2, 1139b 14–35 shows that the order of learning *(via inventionis)* from data to principles is the reverse of the deductive order of wisdom *(via judicii)* from principles to explanation of the data. Also see *Metaphysics,* c. 29, V, 1025b–1026a 33, on the irreducible distinction of the sciences.

[32] Even if ethics depended on the anthropological conclusions of natural philosophy *formally,* it might still be autonomous, but *subalternate,* e.g., mathematical physics (a "mixed" science) is autonomous but subalternate to mathematics (see Aquinas, *Summa theologiae* I, q. 1, a. 2 c.).

ethics: (1) Humans are animals, living, sentient, having biological drives to eat, rest, defend themselves, mate and reproduce; (2) Species, specifically humans, are intelligent, free, and social in a way that requires language and the invention of culture and technology. (3) Human intelligence is dependent on the body to supply the instruments by which it is able to learn about the environment and the human person itself, but it is not identical with the activity of the body or of any bodily organ, not even the brain. Nor is it subject to the mortality of the body. Hence Aquinas lists health, reproduction, society, and truth as the four basic goods of human nature.[33]

PT, of course, rejects materialism and vigorously defends human freedom against determinism.[34] Nevertheless, it can be asked whether PT in its concern to avoid "dualism," sufficiently attends to the fact that, since the specific differentia of a thing makes it what it is, it is our intelligence that is the specifying and unifying factor that makes us human. The human body is human precisely because it is a body made for and used by intelligence. Why then should it be "dualism" to unify the human person by subordinating the goods of the body to the goods of the immaterial, free, and contemplative intelligence? Yet this subordination implies measurement of the subordinate by the superordinate, not the incommensurability of ends as posited by PT.

Moreover, free choice is possible only because humans have an intellectual understanding of means in relation to an end.[35] PT stresses that in practical activity the purpose (end) of a human action must be an intellectually anticipated "is," that is, an is-to-be. It argues in a way reminiscent of John Dewey,[36] that we seldom have in view a fully defined purpose, but generally only a rather vaguely conceived outcome, and it is precisely in the process and experience of working toward that intended result that the goal becomes more and more clearly defined. How true!

Nevertheless, it is also true that this "is-to-be" must somehow be specified, else our activity would become random. Nor can there be an infinite regress in final causes. Hence, all our free choices must ultimately be directed toward a specified end and this end cannot itself be freely chosen. It can of course be something to which we have previously committed ourselves by choice, but once again there can be no infinite regress in finality, so ulti-

---

[33] Human beings share with all things the inclination to self-preservation (in this case *life*) and with living things the inclination to *reproduction*, while the inclination to seek *truth* and live in *society* are specific to humanity; cf. *Summa theologiae* I–II, q. 94, a. 2 c.

[34] Joseph M. Boyle, Jr., Germain Grisez, and Olaf Tollefsen, *Free Choice: A Self-Referential Argument,* 100–2.

[35] *Summa theologiae* I–II, q. 1, a. 2 c.

[36] Grisez, *The Way of the Lord Jesus,* vol. 1 of *Christian Moral Princples,* 122.

[37] For Aristotle and Aquinas the final cause is the *causa causarum.* Hence the thesis that every system of per se causes depends on some unmoved mover applies principally to the final cause.

234 III. Moral Theology Issues

mately free choice depends on some final cause that is not free, but given.[37]

Thus although ethics has to do with the "is-to-be" of free human activity, it has to do with freely chosen means to ends that are ultimately given in the "is" of human nature. Errors in philosophical anthropology, therefore, are likely to generate errors in ethics from which the claim (justified when understood in a properly qualified sense) of the "self-evidence" of the principles of ethics will not absolve us.

PT in its present form seems to evade making a clear statement on the anthropology it presupposes. If in fact it is based on a four-dimensional anthropology in which the different aspects of human nature are united only by mutual inclusion, while the inner unity of the self remains inaccessible, rather than on a well-established anthropology in which this unity derives from human intellectuality, it is even more untenable than the dualism it rejects.

II. The Natural Fulfillment of the Human Person

The First Principle of Ethics

According to PT the first practical principle is "Do good and avoid evil," which it claims actually means "Don't do what is pointless," that is, what does not produce the practical effect intended. It is, therefore, a premoral principle, since the terms "good" and "evil" have a wider sense than moral good and evil. Moreover, just as the principle of contradiction is the first principle of all reasoning but does not enter any demonstration as a premise, so the function of this principle is not to serve as a premise of any ethical demonstration but only to exclude from consideration all actions that are "pointless," ineffectual.[38]

This contention seems to arise from the usage, already noted, of the term "practical" in a generic sense to cover both ethical and technical science. Certainly one can formulate a generic "principle of practicality" to cover both sciences and then distinguish two subordinate principles: (1) a first principle of technology: "If you are going to make X, do only what is technically effective to produce X, and do nothing that would be useless or harmful to its production"; and (2) a first principle of ethics: "Do only what is morally good, that is, helpful to human happiness, and avoid what is morally evil, that is, harmful to the same."

Note that the difference between the technical and the ethical is that the technical perfects the product, while the ethical perfects the human agent. Hence the technical issues only conditional imperatives, while the ethical issues unconditional imperatives. Thus every technical rule is subject to ethical qualification. When Aquinas said that the first principle of ethics is "do

---

[38] Grisez, Boyle, and Finnis, "Practical Principles," 119–22.

[39] *Summa theologiae* I–II, q. 94, a. 2 c.

good and avoid evil,"[39] and when we speak of the "is" and the "ought," the reference is not to the generic or premoral principle, but to the first moral principle. One cannot say technically that one "ought" to perform such and such an operation, but only that "If one is going to produce *X*, one should produce it by *Y* operations." To get an unconditional "ought" statement, one must then also add, "One has a moral obligation to produce *X* and of the possible ways of producing it *Y*, *Z*, and so on, are morally licit."

Thus the first moral principle on which ethics is based is, "Do the morally good, and avoid the morally evil" and means that "One has the unconditional obligation to do what leads to human happiness, and avoid what is harmful to it." The term "happiness," however, as Finnis has shown,[40] simply means "a fully satisfactory life" or, as the new theory commonly expresses it, "integral human fulfillment." As such it tells us only that the goal to be aimed at is the full actualization of the potentialities of the human person. This is based on the notion of teleology derived from natural philosophy according to which every substance tends to the realization of its nature.

Unlike voluntarism, PT does not make moral goodness depend simply on the will of a legislator, whether the legislator be external to the moral agent, or, as for Kant, the autonomous agent. Unlike consequentialism, PT does not make the moral value of an act lie exclusively in its extrinsic consequences, since it maintains that a moral act prior to its extrinsic consequences may have an intrinsic morality that renders the agent a better or worse human person. Thus PT is teleological in the fundamental sense that it judges actions to be performed or not according as they are foreseen to lead to or away from "integral human fulfillment."

Yet, as we have seen, one of the chief features of PT is that it rejects the notion that the goal of ethics is "conformity to human nature." Hence some critics have denied that it is a natural law theory at all.[41] Why does the new theory want to replace "conformity to human nature" with "integral human fulfillment"? It is because the first formula seems to reduce ethics to a theoretical science and thus to confuse the "ought" or "is-to-be" with the "is."

This charge originates in a too univocal reading of the term "nature" as used by Aristotelians. If nature is taken in a strictly physical sense as possessed by subhuman beings it excludes self-consciousness (and hence also freedom) because of the axiom "Nature is determined *ad unum*." The teleology of subhuman beings leads not only to one goal but also by one path to that goal. This saying, however, applies less and less strictly the higher one goes in the hierarchy of natural beings, since it is obvious that the higher animals can satisfy their instinctive drives by a variety of paths. For the human being at the end of the evolutionary line this axiom must be understood only in a very

---

[40] Finnis, "Human Good(s)," 23–36.
[41] See Hittinger, *Critique*, 198.

qualified way. Our intelligence makes us able to transcend the determination of nature and, within limits, freely choose the ways we attain our goals. Nevertheless, as PT itself has to admit, the most basic of these goals are determined by nature.[42] Our freedom is only to choose among a variety of ways to reach those goals, whether those ways be truly effective or only apparently so.

Thus to say, as did classical ethics, that morality is activity in conformity with human nature in no way reduces ethics to a theoretical science. But it does presuppose a natural philosophy, which, beginning with the generic study of human beings as natural objects, and then as animals, proceeds to show that these sorts of animals are intelligent, free persons who understand their own activities both theoretically and practically. The human nature (natural moral law) to which we must conform to be morally good human persons is a nature that requires us to make decisions about the unconditionally is-to-be.

Natural and Supernatural Fulfillment

Obviously, the next step after formulating the first principle of ethics in abstract form is to concretize it by saying just what constitutes "integral human fulfillment" or "life in conformity to human nature." For philosophers, like the authors of PT who are also concerned with Christian moral theology, this notion of "human fulfillment" needs to be untangled from the theological question of nature and supernature, since the finalities of each are of very different orders.

Aristotle's *Nicomachean Ethics* climaxes in an argument for the thesis that the best human life for the individual is not the life of sensual pleasure, but either a rational active life of moral virtue or the contemplative life of the philosopher for which the active life of virtue is a necessary preparation, and that of these alternatives the contemplative life is the happier one.[43] Furthermore, in his *Politics* Aristotle concludes that, since the good life is not possible except as the shared life of a community, the human community has as its purpose to foster the rational active life of moral virtue in order that the contemplative life can be attained by at least some of its citizens and the fruits of this contemplation shared as far as possible with the rest of the community.[44]

Realist that he was, Aristotle recognized that few states ever achieve that

---

[42] "The diversity of the basic goods is neither a mere contingent fact about human psychology nor an accident of history. . . . Rather, being aspects of the fulfillment of persons, these goods correspond to the inherent complexities of human nature, as is manifested both in individuals and in various forms of community." Grisez, Boyle, and Finnis, "Practical Principles," 107.

[43] *Nicomachean Ethics* X, c.6, 1177a12–1179a 33.

[44] "Since the end of the individual and of the state are the same, the end of the best man and of the best constitution must be the same." *Politics* VII, c. 15, 1334a 13 sq.

goal, and even the best come far short of sharing the wisdom and virtue of their philosophers with the others. Thus many human persons never attain the free life of citizenry but only a little security and pleasure in the status of slaves, that is, persons tolerated only for their useful services.[45] As a Christian, Aquinas believed that God has graciously begun to restore humanity from this fallen condition through his Son incarnated in sinless human nature. Moreover, God has begun to "divinize" that human nature. Hence the fulfillment of this restored and divinized or "super" nature can only be eternal life within the Trinity.

The entire argument of PT depends on the assumption that it is meaningful to speak of a "natural" as well as of a "supernatural" ultimate end in our actual human condition. It confirms this assumption by the Church's teaching that "human persons' calling to divine life is entirely gratuitous and supernatural" and refers to Pius XII's condemnation in *Humani Generis*[46] of "the theological opinion that God cannot create intellectual beings without ordering and calling them to the beatific vision." Grisez writes,

> My contention is that the human heart is not naturally oriented toward adoption as a child of God and the heavenly inheritance which goes with this status. It is naturally oriented toward human fulfillment, which is found in human goods in which one naturally can participate more and more. No single, complete good is naturally available to human persons as their determinate ultimate end.[47]

Hence the latest form of PT states flatly,

> And so the human will can have no natural disposition to fulfillment in divine goodness. In this sense the hearts of human persons, considered precisely according to their human nature, are not made for God; rather they are made for human fulfillment.[48]

And even more explicitly in his reply to Hittinger:

> I rule out Augustine's restless heart and Aquinas' argument that God is

---

[45] For a study of this much misunderstood topic in Aristotle's and Aquinas's political theory, see my dissertation, *The Theory of Natural Slavery.*

[46] Grisez, *The Theory of the Lord Jesus,* vol. 1 of *Christian Moral Principles,* 810, referring to *Enchiridion symbolorum, definitionum et declarationum de rebus fidei et morum,* edited by Henry Denzinger and Adolph Schönmetzer, 36th ed. rev., n. 931, nn. 3891/2318.

[47] Ibid., 809.

[48] Grisez, Boyle, and Finnis, "Practical Principles," 134.

man's final end by nature because these seem to me to imply what I believe to be impossible: proportionality between human nature and fulfillment in divine goodness, not in its participation, but in itself.[49]

Thus PT rejects the efforts of Blondel, de Lubac, and others to show that by the very fact of our humanity we tend toward intimate union with God, although that union can be achieved only by the help of grace. De Lubac argues for this on the grounds that although the Church Fathers did not clearly distinguish nature from supernature, they certainly believed that human nature is *capax dei*, capable of divinization.[50]

Finnis, however, seems to soften some of Grisez's statements on this topic by arguing for an analogy between the beatific vision and the naturally fulfilled life. He writes,

> Speculative questioning and understanding in contemplation discloses to us, already in this life, the existence of a God who is not Aristotle's purely contemplative *noesis noeseos* but rather the *dominus suorum actuum* and free creator and activator and governor of the universe. To attain the beatitude of a perfect human knowledge and love of God would be to attain the fullness of the image of God. So the imaging of God in this life (a life in which a very imperfect but real knowledge and love of God is possible) would be an imitation not of the Aristotelian divine contemplation, but of the fully practical (as well as contemplative) intelligence and will of the true God, creator of irreducibly many forms of good.[51]

While I am very sympathetic with efforts to free theology from Platonizing tendencies that neglect the value of the body, the doctrine of resurrection, and the communitarian character of eternal life, this suggestion of Finnis does not seem to me a happy one. Surely the blessed life of God consists in the mutual love and knowledge of the Divine Persons *ad intra*, to which God's works *ad extra* add nothing. Aquinas is only affirming common Catholic doctrine when he teaches that beatific vision alone constitutes perfect beatitude, so that the good of the resurrected body and the friendship of the blessed pertain to this beatitude only accidentally *(ad bene esse)* and not essentially *(ad esse)*.[52]

---

[49] "A Critique of Hittinger's Critique," 459–60.

[50] For the older controversies, see A. Gardeil, "Appetit," *Dictionnaire de théologie catholique* 1 (2): 1696–700, and A. Michel, "Surnaturel," ibid., 14 (2): 2854–59. For concise statements of the more recent controversy over *Surnaturel: etudes historiques* of Henri de Lubac, SJ, see his *A Brief Catechesis on Nature and Grace*, and on the other side J.-H. Nicolas, OP, *Les Profondeurs de la Grace*.

[51] Finnis, "Human Good(s)," 31–32.

[52] *Summa theologiae* I–II, q. 4, a. 7.

The principal way PT attempts to answer this problem of relating nature and supernature is to say that we are fulfilled by incorporation in Jesus in whom humanity and divinity are hypostatically united.[53] True enough the Church Fathers often say that "We became human, that we might become divine." Yet this answer only raises another question, "How can human nature, so infinitely inferior to the divine nature, be *capax Dei?*"

That Jesus as a man living earthly life was not only a *viator* as we are, but also a *comprehensor,* that is, he already possessed, even on the Cross, the beatific vision, is today widely questioned by theologians, but on the basis of official Church teaching Grisez defends it.[54] Thus the human nature of Jesus was united to his Father not only hypostatically but also by the beatific vision. Hence simply referring to the fact of the hypostatic union cannot solve the question of how human nature can be divinized by grace and the light of glory.

Some theologians think that even if sin had never entered the creation, yet the perfection of creation would have necessitated the Incarnation, opening the way to the beatific vision. Others abstract from this question and argue that de facto the human person has no natural ultimate end. To the accusation that both positions lead to Pelagianism, three types of answers are then given. One is that although our human nature demands the beatific vision as its perfection, we cannot achieve this perfection except by the grace of God. The weakness of this reply is that it accuses God of creating a being that lacks the capacity to achieve the end for which it was created.

A second answer is that since creation itself is a gratuitous act, even our nature is a grace. This reply, which eliminates the distinction between nature and supernature, seems to lead to the hyper-Calvinist notion of the total corruption of human nature after the fall from grace.

A third answer, the most cautious, is to admit that the distinction between the natural and the supernatural is valid in the abstract, but to maintain that in the concrete existential order the natural does not exist in its own right. Yet this theological position seems to deny to philosophy the possibility of developing a teleological ethics, since a knowledge of any ultimate end for the human person would be accessible only to faith. Yet why is there any philosophical difficulty in asserting that there are goods that are

---

[53] Grisez, *The Theory of the Lord Jesus,* vol. 1 of *Christian Moral Principles,* 814–16; cf. Grisez, Boyle, and Finnis, "Practical Principles," 146–47.

[54] *Summa theologiae* III, q. 10; Grisez, *The Theory of the Lord Jesus,* vol. 1 of *Christian Moral Principles,* 465, 475, n. 13, which he nuances on 529 and 547, nn. 5, 6; cf. *DS,* n. 3645/2183, 3812/2289. See also Karl Rahner, *Theological Investigations,* "Dogmatic Reflections on the Knowledge and Self-Consciousness of Christ," vol. 5, 193–218; William G. Most, *The Consciousness of Christ*; and my essay "Christology from Above" in this collection.

good in themselves, and therefore in a true sense "ultimate," yet which are not the Perfect Good and hence can also serve as means to that Perfect Good. Thus some goods are both ultimate in their own order, yet means to some greater good. They are intermediate ends in a hierarchy of ends.

The fundamental objection raised to this rather obvious solution of the problem by those theologians who deny a natural end to the human person is that it favors an "extrinsicism" that separates the life of faith from secular life, thus reducing religion to a very restricted area of the total life of the human person, a result PT emphatically wishes to avoid.[55]

Such objections seem based on a failure to see that if the natural ultimate end is subordinated to the supernatural end and the two ends are seen as pertaining to different and purely analogical orders, the natural end is not extrinsic to the supernatural end, but is subsumed to and included in it, so that the axiom "grace perfects nature" is realized. Grace perfects nature not by adding something extrinsic and accidental to it, but by profoundly transforming and elevating it to a higher, even an infinitely higher, order of being.

In the human person the generic animality we share with other animals is elevated to spiritual personality, yet it remains animality. In Christ human nature remains human nature yet by the hypostatic union becomes the instrument of divine acts. Human nature is *capax Dei* because it is personal, intellectual, and hence open to enter into a union with a personal, spiritual God if he graciously chooses to invite it to this union and empowers it by transforming grace.

In rejecting the position of de Lubac and others, PT also rejects Aquinas's notion of the "natural desire for the beatific vision," to which De Lubac appeals to bridge the gap between nature and supernature.[56] Different explanations have been given of St. Thomas's texts, and I will only state my understanding briefly without detailed exegesis.[57] The purpose of his argument is apologetic and is to show that the Christian doctrine that our unqualifiedly ultimate end is the beatific vision is not absurd and incredible. He does not try to prove that in fact the beatific vision of the Trinity is this

[55] Grisez, *The Theory of the Lord Jesus*, vol. 1 of *Christian Moral Principles*, chapters 21–35, argue for the specifically Christian character of moral life against the current tendency of moralists to identify all moral norms with natural law. Cf. Grisez, Boyle, and Finnis, "Practical Principles," 146–47.

[56] "Furthermore, there can be no *natural* desire for what is *not the natural* end of human persons, namely that [beatific vision]" (italics in the original), Grisez, Boyle, and Finnis, "Practical Principles," 134. On Aquinas's texts on the *desiderium naturale* and their history see the excellent article by Antoninus Finili, OP, "Natural Desire," *Dominican Studies* 1 (October 1948).

[57] I follow generally the classical interpretation of St. Thomas given by Sylvester Ferrariensis in his commentary on the *Summa contra Gentiles* III, c. 51, as ably explained by A. Finili, preceding note.

end, since that is a mystery of faith beyond rational proof. He speaks only of a knowledge of the essential nature of the First Cause whatever that may be. He does not even aim to prove strictly that this knowledge is possible (anymore than he tries to prove the Trinity or any other strictly supernatural mystery is possible), since for Aquinas possible existence can be proved only from known actual existence, not the other way around.[58] All he needs to show is that no argument for its impossibility has been established.

Therefore, Aquinas argues that the proper object of the human intelligence is *ens mobile* (sensible, changeable being) of which it can be proved that there is a first ultimate cause (the Unmoved Mover). Since every faculty naturally tends to ("has a natural desire for") its proper object (which cannot itself be understood except in the light of its ultimate cause, nor perfectly understood except in the light of a perfect understanding of that cause), it follows that the human intelligence, our highest human power, tends to seek to know the ultimate cause of all things as perfectly as possible. Since "Nature does nothing in vain,"[59] it follows that it would be absurd if a perfect knowledge of the First Cause were contradictory to human nature.

De Lubac's conclusion, however, that the fact of this natural desire to know God proves that at least in the present state the human person has no natural ultimate end, leads to what for an Aristotelian, at least, is an absurdity—a human nature that is not a nature. For Aristotle "nature" is defined dynamically as "an intrinsic principle of motion and rest" and "motion" implies a predetermined goal.[60] Thus a nature or essence that has no proper final cause is impossible, since an essence is a formal principle, and finality is simply the form considered as the goal attained, perfect and complete. Only chance entities lack an intrinsic final cause.

Hence, as *Humani Generis* taught, no impossibility appears why God could not have created human persons in a merely natural state, although in fact we were not so created. In such a world humans might be led by the "natural desire" of their intelligences to wonder if perhaps God would call them to perfect beatitude as sharers in his inner life. Nevertheless, when they found no signs that this was God's will, the virtuous would be humbly content with and grateful for the imperfect but marvelous beatitude proper to their own nature, an imperfect happiness specified by and culminating in

---

[58] The first "scientific question" *(An sit?)* concerns existence. Until it is answered affirmatively, the question of definition *(Quid sit?)* can only be answered nominally. Without a real answer to this second question no demonstration is possible. Aristotle, *Posterior Analytics,* II, c.1, 89b 23–35; Aquinas, *In Libros Posteriorum Analyticorum Expositio,* II, l. 2, nn. 407–17.

[59] Strictly speaking this principle does not mean nature absolutely never fails, but that the First Cause never fails, since it controls even chance events. Cf. Finili, 44–47.

[60] Aristotle, *Physics* I, c. 9, 192a 23; II, c. 7, 198b10–199b 32.

the contemplation of God's glory in creation.

Therefore I agree with PT that the human person even in our existential order has a natural finality that is ultimate in its own order, although God has graciously subordinated this finality to an infinitely higher supernatural one, so that while natural human fulfillment remains truly ultimate in its own natural order (i.e., as a relative or intermediate end), it is only relatively ultimate. Nevertheless, I am of the opinion that PT has obscured the harmony between grace and nature by rejecting the existence of the human person's natural desire to see God and especially by denying that the natural contemplation of God is our natural ultimate end.

Aquinas completed his theory of natural human fulfillment by considering in what sense death, apart from sin, is natural to the human person, and what might be the condition and happiness of the separated soul, apart from grace. Since such questions seem not to play an important role in PT I will not discuss them here.[61]

III: The Unity of Natural Fulfillment

The Complexity of Human Fulfillment

With these not unimportant qualifications PT's acceptance of a natural end for the human person seems sound. But what then is this end? PT admits: "Of course, in choosing, one seeks a good loved for itself. In this sense, one always acts for an ultimate end—that is, an end not pursued as a means to some ulterior end."[62] But PT also maintains that integral self-fulfillment is not simply one but a complex of at least seven ultimate goods, each sought for its own sake and not as a means to any other good, which are irreducible to any one concrete good and hence are incommensurable.[63]

Therefore, the first principle of morality should be understood to mean that the "integral human fulfillment" that is to be sought and its opposite avoided is a harmonious combination of all seven basic goods. The exact way in which they are combined and in what proportion thus becomes a matter of free choice, depending on the person's individual personality, circumstances, and freely chosen vocation. Hence, there is no best kind of

---

61 Grisez, *The Theory of the Lord Jesus,* vol. 1 of *Christian Moral Principles,* chapter 32, Appendix 2, "Penance, indulgences, purgatory, and temporal punishment," 785–86, is confined largely to an explanation of indulgences.

62 Ibid., 809.

63 According to Grisez, Boyle, and Finnis, "Practical Principles," 110, the "incommensurability" in question is not among different possible choices each with its unique, incomparable appeal, but consists in the fact that the basic goods are not "reducible to something prior," a common genus.

human life, but only what is best for the individual, namely the one he or she freely chooses and develops in the course of living it—provided, of course, that it does not violate the basic goods.[64]

In the *Summa theologiae* St. Thomas borrows from Aristotle's *Physics* the general theorem that "In every system of per se subordinate movers there is a first unmoved mover," which he then uses to prove the existence of God.[65] He applies the same principle to show that in human acts, every act must be for an ultimate end, and that this is true not only for a particular line of decisions but for the totality of human life.[66] Thus it follows that since God is the final cause of all things, he must be the final cause of every morally good human act, even a purely natural act.

Since God is Spirit, Self-Thinking Thought,[67] he can be attained as end only by persons (beings that can think and freely choose) and only by an act of the intellect, the beatific vision. As God is the plenitude of truth, absolutely one even in his Trinitarian life, so the beatific vision is a simple, completely unified act that constitutes our total beatitude without the necessity of any other good. At the same time this totality does not exclude other goods but rather becomes the superabundant source of them, so that the other faculties of the soul and the resurrected body share in the superabundant beatitude of the glorified intelligence.[68]

Nevertheless, for Aquinas the ultimate supernatural ordination of the human person to the beatific vision does not wipe out the natural end of the human person, ultimate in its own order. Consequently, it remains true that

---

[64] Ibid., 137–39, makes some important qualifications. "In sum, while the basic goods, considered as principles of practical knowledge, are not ordered among themselves, it does not follow that these basic principles are an unordered crowd. Prior to anyone's choice, unfettered practical reason, together with the conditions which human nature inevitably sets for moral life, establish certain natural priorities among a good person's basic interests. It follow that these priorities set necessary conditions for any morally good life."

[65] Aristotle, *Physics* VII, c. 1, 241b24–243a 2; Aquinas, *Summa theologiae* I, q. 2, a. 3, c.

[66] *Summa theologiae* II, q. 1, a. 6, c. In q. 5 Aquinas argues that we have only one ultimate end, because: (1) We all desire perfect fulfillment that leaves nothing else to be desired. (2) "Nature is determined to one goal," and by nature the will seeks fulfillment. (3) All moral goods are of the genus of things willed, of which some one species is the first principle. These reasons presuppose knowledge of the unity of human nature, but polyteleologism holds that: "The unity of the person is mysterious and must remain so." Grisez, *Beyond the New Theism,* 349.

[67] Aristotle, *Metaphysics* XII, c. 9, 1074b15–1075a 11; Aquinas, *In Met.* XII, l. 11, nn. 2600ff.; *Summa theologiae* I, q. 14, a. 2.

[68] Aquinas maintains, however, that the glory of the resurrected body will increase beatitude both extensively and intensively (but not essentially), *Summa theologiae, Suppl.* q. 83, a. 1; *Summa contra Gentiles* IV, c. 86.

III. Moral Theology Issues

the natural end of the human person is not a single good but an ordered complex of goods, of which the principal, specifying, and unifying good is the contemplated truth.

Nevertheless, while PT does not really differ from Aquinas as regards the complexity of integral human fulfillment in the imperfect beatitude practicable in this life, it does differ on two other points: (1) PT holds that perfect beatitude is also complex, while Aquinas holds it is simple; (2) PT holds that the unity of both perfect and imperfect beatitude ought not to be explained by the ordering of these complex goods to the one single good of contemplation, while Aquinas holds for such an ordering by which all other goods are to be regarded as instrumental to contemplation. Yet PT does admit that mature and virtuous persons ought to seek a unified life plan by the interrelations provided by the four "reflexive goods,"[69] and, at least for Christians, by the centrality of the virtue of religion.[70]

If this complex of ultimate and incommensurable goods that constitute integral human fulfillment are not subordinate to one principal good, what constitutes their unity and consistency? If they cannot somehow be reduced to harmony, it would seem that rational moral decision would be impossible. To answer this obvious difficulty, Finnis has recourse to the fact that when Aristotle establishes *eudaimonia* as the one ultimate end of human action, he has in mind a purely formal unity since *eudaimonia* "simply is the concept of the fully satisfactory life."[71]

Since for both Aristotle and Aquinas the "fully satisfactory life" is in fact not practicable in this vale of tears, Finnis argues it cannot be the principle of practical (ethical) reasoning, but can only serve as an "ideal" by which the "imperfect beatitude" that is practicable can be measured. Aquinas also says that this imperfect beatitude consists in "the operation of the virtues" and the virtues have a diversity of ends.[72] Therefore, Finnis concludes that the imperfect beatitude that is practicable in this life is complex but receives its unity from its approximation to the ideal of a fully satisfactory life.

I fail to see how this answers the difficulty, since the problem is not to find a merely formal unity such as is supplied by the terms *eudaimonia* or

---

[69] Grisez, *The Theory of the Lord Jesus*, vol. 1 of *Christian Moral Principles*, 124, and the latest formulation of these goods in Grisez, Boyle, and Finnis, "Practical Principles," 108, with their dialectical defense, 111–13. It does not follow that because goods are per se ends they are incommensurable.

[70] Grisez, Boyle, and Finnis, "Practical Principles," 141–43.

[71] Finnis, "Human Good(s)," 25, summarizing Troels Engberg-Pedersen, *Aristotle's Theory of Moral Insight*; cf. "Eudaimoneia and Praxis," 1–36.

[72] *Summa theologiae* q. 47, a. 6. Nevertheless, the plurality of the ends of the virtues is reduced to unity by their connection in charity, whose object is God, the ultimate end; see I–II, q. 65, a. 2.

"fully satisfactory life" or "integral human fulfillment" but to find some unity greater than a mere shopping list of items that are required for such a life to be "satisfactory" or "integral. It is true that Aquinas speaks not only of the ultimate end but also of the "ends" of moral decisions, of which he enumerated at least four basic goods of life, family, society, and truth.[73] Like Aristotle he held that the contemplation of truth is supreme among these goods, but that the individual without the aid of society cannot achieve it. Human society is not possible without the family and reproduction, and none of these are possible in this life without physical health, since Aristotle's epistemology, unlike Plato's, makes all human knowledge dependent on the senses.

Thus, for Aquinas, although contemplation is the highest good and therefore ultimate, to exist in this life it requires the complex of all four goods and thus can only constitute an imperfect beatitude. After the resurrection the condition of the body will follow the condition of the soul in contrast to this life in which the condition of the soul follows that of the body, the satisfaction of the body will result from the beatitude of the soul, not cause that beatitude.[74] These other goods, while characterized by Aquinas as instrumental,[75] are not for him "extrinsic" to integral human fulfillment. As we have already seen, a subordinate end can be ultimate in its own order, while at the same time serving as an instrumental means to a higher end. Each organ of the human body has its own proper function as an instrument of the total person but is not extrinsic to the person but necessary to its integrity.

PT, however, does not admit that the basic goods required for the good life may be at once good in themselves, and in that sense ultimate, and yet hierarchically ordered, so that it is possible to speak of a supreme good for which the others are means or necessary conditions and yet without which it cannot be attained. For PT, if these goods are per se good, they must be ultimate in that they are incommensurable and non-subordinate.

On the other hand I think that Garth Hallet is off the mark when he tries to answer the arguments of Grisez and Finnis for the incommensurability of these goods by the claim that the concept which unites them all and against which they can be measured is simply that they are values.[76] "Value" is an analogous term, and the fact these goods are all values only shows that they have some *secundum quid* similarity, not that they are essentially commensurable. Just as Finnis's suggestion that they are unified simply by the fact that they all

---

[73] Ibid., I–II, q. 94, a. 2, c.; cf. *Summa contra Gentiles* III, c. 129.

[74] Ibid., *Suppl.* q. 92, a. 2, ad 6; cf. 85, a. 1; *IV Sent.*, d. 48, q. 2, a. 1.

[75] "The body is for sake of the soul as matter is for the form; and as instruments are for the sake of their user *(motor)*, so the user can perform his actions through them." *Summa theologiae* I–II. q. 5.

[76] Hallet, "The 'Incommensurability' of Values."

contribute to a satisfactory life does not work, neither does Hallet's proposal.

Kevin Staley is more to the point when he shows[77] that Aristotle and Aquinas ordinarily do not speak philosophically about the end of earthly life so much in terms of a supreme good as in terms of the active and contemplative lives whose goodness requires not one but a complex of interrelated goods just as does the new theory.[78] As regards the imperfect beatitude of this life Aquinas and classical theology agreed with Aristotle that it consists in not one but several goods, while agreeing with the Platonists that the perfect beatitude of immortal life consists in one single Good.

The Goods that Constitute Integral Human Fulfillment

Because PT cannot accept Aquinas's hierarchical unification of the complex of goods that make up imperfect beatitude, it becomes important to find a way to at least interrelate them to each other in a kind of network. Thus Grisez has developed an elaborate theory of these goods, distinguishing between what he calls "existential" (or "moral" or "reflexive") goods because they are "both reasons for choosing and are in part defined in terms of choosing" and "substantive" (or "non-reflexive"), which "are not defined in terms of choosing" but "provide reasons for choosing which can stand by themselves."[79] The existential goods are (1) self-integration; (2) practical reasonableness or authenticity; (3) justice or friendship; and (4) religion or holiness. The substantive goods are (1) life (physical health, safety, reproduction); (2) knowledge of truth and appreciation of beauty or excellence; and (3) activities of skillful work and play.[80]

Interesting and insightful as it is, this classification is rather puzzling. Of the first of these existential goods, "self-integration," Grisez says, "Part of the meaning of self-integration is choice which brings aspects of one's self into harmony,"[81] hence it is "existential" because it "fulfills persons insofar as persons make free choices and are capable of moral good and evil," while the

---

[77] "Metaphysics and the Good Life," *American Catholic Philosophical Quarterly* 65 (1; Winter, 1991): 1–28.

[78] Aristotle, *Nicomachean Ethics* I, c. 7, 1098b9–1099a 7. Aquinas, after discussing the essence of beatitude in I, q. 3; goes on to discuss those things, e.g., rectitude of the will, health, exterior goods, and friends, which are also "required" *(exiguntur)* for beatitude.

[79] Grisez, *The Theory of the Lord Jesus,* vol. 1 of *Christian Moral Principles,* 124; cf. Grisez, Boyle, and Finnis, "Practical Principles," 106–8.

[80] In Grisez, Boyle, and Finnis, "Practical Principles," 108, these are listed and described somewhat differently: (1) harmony between individuals and groups of person; (2) interior harmony between desires; (3) harmony among feelings, judgments and choices-peace of conscience; (4) harmony "with God, or the gods, or some non-theistic but more-than-human source of meaning and value."

[81] Grisez, *The Theory of the Lord Jesus,* vol. 1 of *Christian Moral Principles,* 123.

substantive goods are those "in whose definitions choice is not included; they fulfill dimensions of the human person other than the existential one.[82] Yet, if choice is included in the definition of these existential goods, must they not be reckoned as means, not as ultimate ends? Free choice is possible only between practicable means; ends as such cannot be chosen, but only as means to some further end.[83] Yet surely we cannot reduce self-integration, reasonableness, friendship, and holiness to mere means. They are ends in themselves, and fall under choice only when regarded as subordinate ends that are means to some higher good.

On the other hand, the substantive goods of physical life and truth are clearly ends in themselves and not simply means. To say that "skill in work or play" is an end in itself is open to the objection that most people would regard work as a means, while play may very well be regarded as a form of contemplation or as a preparation for work or contemplation.[84] The real state of affairs is that all these goods (at least in some of their species) can be considered both as means subordinated to some higher end (and thus are existential, reflexive, and moral) or as ends in themselves, ultimate in their own order.

Furthermore, it is difficult to see how self-integration, authenticity, friendship, and holiness can be considered "basic," that is, elemental goods. Aristotle and Aquinas considered "friendship" not a virtue but the consequence of the virtues, that is, as the summation and integration of all the other goods of life—a synthesis of basic goods.[85] Similarly, for Aquinas, friendship as love of the common good (charity) sums up all other goods and is identical with "holiness."[86] Again self-integration and authenticity seem identical with the possession of all the virtues united in justice and charity. Thus it seems to me these "existential goods" are simply the whole virtuous life that must itself be defined by the possession of the more basic substantive goods in a duly adjusted order. This order results, according to Aquinas, precisely from the subordination of all other goods to union with

---

[82] Ibid., 124.

[83] Aristotle, "We will to be healthy, but we choose the acts which will make us healthy." *Nicomachean Ethics,* 111b26–29; Aquinas, *Summa theologiae* I, q. 82, a. 1, c. and ad 3.

[84] See Grisez, Boyle, and Finnis, "Practical Principles," 107. Aquinas, *Summa theologiae* I, q. 32, a.1, ad 3; II–II, q. 168, a. 2, argues that while activities that somewhat exceed our powers cause us pain and weariness (work); those proportionate to our powers please and rest us (play). Thus work (including the *effort* to contemplate) is for the sake of some end, not for its own sake; play is for recreation to ready us for more substantive virtuous activities, ultimately for contemplation.

[85] *Summa theologiae* II–II, q. 23, a. 3, ad 1; *De Virtutibus in Communi,* q. 2, a. 2, ad 8. Aristotle in Nicomachean Ethics VII and VIII argues the best kind of friendship is the sharing of a virtuous life culminating in contemplation. The contemplative life is solitary only *per accidens,* since perfect contemplation is communal; cf. Aquinas, *Summa theologiae* I–II, q. 4, a. 8, c.

[86] *Summa theologiae* II–II, q. 23, a. 1, 6, 7.

God, a union that is possible only through a loving contemplation imperfectly achievable in this life, perfectly achievable in the next.

Grisez develops beautifully the biblical notion of "peace"[87] as inner harmony. But what establishes this inner harmony if it is not the knowledge and love of God, that is, contemplation? For Aquinas the moral virtues are participations in reason, and reason is unified by wisdom, and the highest wisdom is the loving contemplation of God.[88] Thus the "existential" goods that PT enumerates are both the means to and, in their fullness, the fruits of contemplation.

PT's list of substantive goods is the same as Aquinas's four basic goods, except that it transfers the social good to the list of existential goods, combines the physical and the reproductive goods as one, and adds to the list the good of skill in work and play. But I prefer Aquinas's separation of the physical and the reproductive good, since the reproductive good pertains to the species and not just the individual, while the skills of work and play seem secondary, since they are not good in themselves but good as means (unless we rate play as a form of contemplation). Thus it seems that not much is gained by this classification over the simpler and still more basic one provided by Aquinas.

Truth as Unifying Life

For Aquinas the natural end of man is not the beatific vision, yet it is the contemplation of truth, because what makes us human is our intelligence.[89] The term "contemplation," therefore, refers to that act of the intelligence in which truth is enjoyed for its own sake, and not merely used instrumentally as a means to practical activity. Hence, to say that contemplation is the ultimate end of all human activity, is simply to say that all other goods satisfy us as human beings only when they culminate in what today we would somewhat awkwardly call a "meaningful experience."[90] Thus Aristotle says in a wonderful passage,

> Now for animals life is defined by the power of sensation, for man by the power of sensation and intelligence; and a power is defined primarily by its activity; therefore it seems that to live is to sense and to think . . . so

---

87 Grisez, *The Theory of the Lord Jesus,* vol. 1 of *Christian Moral Principles,* 127–28.

88 *Summa theologiae* II–II, q. 45, a. 1, c.

89 Ibid., I, q. 75, a. 4, ad 1; q. 76, a. 1 c.

90 The appropriation of raw experience is its "meaningfulness," its relevance to the self-conscious subject as in harmony with the subject's own projects. Not that this perceived purposefulness must be practical; ultimately its purpose (meaning) is its *beauty,* i.e., its truth as proportioned to the knowing subject, its *claritas.* Ibid., II–II, q. 145, a. 2; q. 180, a. 1, ad 3.

we sense that we sense, and we know that we know and hence know that in sensing and knowing we also exist, for to be is to sense or know intellectually. And it is pleasant to sense that one is alive.[91]

Even sensual pleasures are human only if they are meaningful. If sex is not expressive of love, or eating and drinking of conviviality, they are depersonalized. They must somehow express or reveal the truth of ourselves and our relations to others and to the cosmos, that is, they must be in some degree contemplative and reflective. It seems to me that in using the terms "existential" and "reflexive" Grisez is really pointing to this contemplative aspect of all truly human experience.[92]

Of course, Aristotle and Aquinas say that the natural end of human life is not just "contemplation" but supremely "contemplation of the Divine."[93] For them all truth leads to Truth Itself, to God. Thus contemplation is satisfying to the degree that it is able to discover God, the First Cause, in all his effects; but since all human experiences are in various ways effects of the First Cause that implies that all human experience finds its meaningfulness insofar as it enhances our contemplation of the Divine.

Does this mean, therefore, that for Aristotle only philosophers, or for Aquinas only monks, can attain happiness? Aristotle held that all free members of a community who have some share in virtue also have some share in contemplation, although only those whose lives are devoted primarily to the pursuit of truth, the philosophers, enjoy it fully. Those who are not free because they lack virtue are by that fact unable to share in the good of contemplation and can be accepted into the community only as slaves who thus attain a certain security and satisfaction of physical needs with their pleasures. They cannot become sharers in virtue because of the economic requirements of manual labor that hinder the education *(paideia)* needed to enable them to acquire the virtues. Without these moral virtues the discipline needed to develop the intellectual virtues is lacking, and without the intellectual virtues contemplation is not possible.

For Aquinas, the inescapable fact that so large a part of the human race seems excluded from the free and happy life by poverty and ignorance is due to original and actual sin;[94] while grace opens the door to supernatural beatitude even to the poor and ignorant. The virtue of faith makes a knowledge

---

[91] *Nicomachean Ethics* IX, c. 9,1170a 16–19.

[92] Grisez, *The Theory of the Lord Jesus,* vol. 1 of *Christian Moral Principles,* 135–36; Grisez, Boyle, and Finnis, "Practical Principles," 107–8, makes *choice* the *differentia* of these goods, yet describes them in terms of the "harmony" and "peace" that they produce. Is he not really describing contemplation, the rest we experience in knowing that everything is in order, i.e., that it is according to truth?

[93] *Nicomachean Ethics* X, c. 6, 1177a 12–1178a 7; *Summa theologiae* I–II, q. 3, a. 5, 6, 7.

[94] *Summa theologiae* I, q. 96, a. 4, c.

of God possible for all, and therefore a clue to the meaning of every experience, clearer and more profound than all philosophy can afford.[95]

Thus it seems that PT has not sufficiently taken into account the position of Aristotle and Aquinas on the natural end on the following points:

1. To say the natural end is contemplation does not deny the necessity for integral human fulfillment of other per se goods, ultimate in their own order provided they are subordinated to contemplation.

2. This subordination does not reduce these per se goods to mere means to contemplation, but instead renders them specifically human, by giving them existential meaning.

3. Such contemplation is not exclusively of the Divine, but includes all truth enjoyed for its own sake.

4. All human beings have the possibility of reaching this end to the degree that the society in which they live enables them to acquire the prerequisite moral and intellectual virtues and to share in the fund of truth acquired by the society as a whole.

If we grant that for humanity, truth is the ultimate good, then it becomes clear why the other three basic goods are also required. Understanding the world under God is possible only in the human community, because truth is a social enterprise,[96] and the human community cannot exist without reproduction and the family unit. Furthermore, the human mode of knowing requires the body and its senses, which cannot operate normally without a degree of health and the external possessions necessary to it. This does not mean, however, that community, reproduction, and health are mere means to truth since they are simply the actual existence of the human persons who share truth. To exist physically in health in a community of begotten persons is not a means but an end that is ultimately perfected by the sharing of truth.

Therefore has not PT, due to too narrow an understanding of the good of contemplation, labored needlessly to defend the complexity of earthly beatitude? If we all enjoyed good health, lived in a good family or at least were reared in one, found ourselves able to live friendly in a good society, and could make some sense out of our lives under God, would not that be a truly humane and integral self-fulfillment?

---

[95] Ibid., II–II, q. 2, a. 4 c.

[96] "In one way the search for truth is difficult, but in another way easy. Thus no person alone can attain much of truth, but all of us together can, for each makes some true statements about the nature of things. While singly we contribute little or nothing to the truth, by putting all our contributions together we accumulate quite a store." Aristotle, *Metaphysics*, 993b 1–4.

Inconsistency in Moral Life

PT, however, has touched on what does seem a grave weakness in Aquinas's analysis of human moral life: Namely, that it seems too unified to correspond to our actual experience of moral decision. Grisez writes:

> But, as a matter of fact, people can pursue diverse goods without ordering them to one another and without ordering all of them to anything ulterior. For example, a dissolute man can seek both sentient pleasure and status as a political leader. Similarly a Christian girl of fourteen can sincerely try to live her faith (and without serious sin) try to become a cheerleader for the sake of the activity itself and the status it will give her with her schoolmates. Hence, Thomas seems to have made a mistake in assuming that an ultimate end must promise integral fulfillment (see *ST* I–II, q. 1, a. 5). At least this premise needs to be proved. Thomas does not prove it; and his failure to do so renders question-begging his use of it to show that a person can have only one ultimate end.[97]

When we make moral decisions, we seldom seem to refer, as Aquinas claims,[98] to one ultimate end of our life to which everything else is leading. Rather we have in mind many different goods, all of which seem to us valuable in themselves without reference to anything else but which taken together form the fabric of a good life and thus constitute "integral self-fulfillment."[99]

PT accounts for these facts of experience by holding that moral goodness is simply the will to attain integral self-fulfillment by achieving some combination of the basic goods, and moral evil is the will to act against this fulfillment by violating any one of the basic goods. Thus, if by misfortune one lacks some of the basic goods, one can be morally good although not integrally fulfilled.[100] Sin, however, is not simply an evil but a "moral evil considered precisely insofar as it is contrary to the good of religion—contrary to the fulfillment of humankind's potential for harmony with God,"[101] which is only one of the "existential" basic goods, not the whole complex of such goods. It might seem, therefore, that PT is coming very close to the old error

---

[97] Grisez, *The Theory of the Lord Jesus*, vol. 1 of *Christian Moral Principles*, 393.

[98] *Summa theologiae* I–II, q, a. 6.

[99] John Rawls also writes "Although to subordinate all our aims to one end does not strictly speaking violate the principles of rational choice. . . . it still strikes us as irrational, or more likely as mad." *A Theory of Justice*, 554. But what is crazier than to strive after contradictory goals?

[100] Grisez, Boyle, and Finnis, "Practical Principles," 131–32.

[101] Grisez, *The Theory of the Lord Jesus*, vol. 1 of *Christian Moral Principles*, 314. Grisez here and in "Practical Principles" uses "religion" in a broader sense than Aquinas, for whom the virtue of religion is the readiness to worship God, and not a theological virtue that unites us to God (*Summa theologiae* II–II, q. 81, a. 8 c.) For Aquinas "charity," not "religion," is our "harmony" with God.

of the possibility of a merely "philosophic sin," that is, a moral evil that is not an "offense against God," but Grisez rejects that inference by maintaining that any act against our human fulfillment is always an act against God because it is against "God's plan."[102]

For Aquinas, on the other hand, although the happiness of this life is imperfect, if one faithfully adheres to the true end of life in its intrinsic unity one can still be said to be essentially happy, even if through misfortune some lesser per se goods, such as health, are deficient.[103] Unhappiness is the state of sin and sin is identical with moral evil[104] because it is any act inconsistent with the ultimate end, whether natural or supernatural. Since both the natural and supernatural ends are the possession of God (the former by natural knowledge, the latter through faith and the beatific vision) and this possession, although an act of the intellect, is attained through an act of the will, namely, the love of God, sin is primarily an act against the love of God.

In replacing St. Thomas's understanding of the ultimate end as a single supreme good, to which all other goods are subordinated, with the theory that it is unified only as the fulfillment of the human person whose unity remains mysterious, PT has also to face the current "mainstream" in moral theology that wishes to replace the concept of "ultimate end" with that of a "fundamental option."[105] PT holds that for Christians the fundamental option or commitment is not that of charity (as for Aquinas) but that of faith in the Lord Jesus,[106] so that mortal sin should be defined as "an act incompatible with faith's specific requirements" and venial sin as "an evil act not incompatible with the specific requirements of faith," but "incompatible with perfect [sic] charity."[107] Grisez also recalls the traditional problems about the relation of venial sin to the ultimate end, and adds some of his own.[108]

Do the inconsistencies in moral life require this "paradigm shift" from classical moral theory from monoteleology to polyteleology? It seems to me unnecessary if we concede that Aquinas presents a model of rational deci-

---

[102] Alexander VIII in 1690 condemned the theory of philosophical sin as rash and erroneous (*DS* 2291/1290 n. 2). For Grisez's arguments against the same theory, see *The Theory of the Lord Jesus*, vol. 1 of *Christian Moral Principles*, 316–18.

[103] In *Summa theologiae* I–II, q. 4, a. 5, 6, 7, Aquinas shows the various ways in which goods other than contemplation are required for human happiness.

[104] Aquinas simply says without distinction "a sin is nothing other than an evil human act" *(Peccatum nihil aliud est quam actus humanus malus)*. Yet he also says that a sin is proximately against human reason, but principally (formally) against Divine Reason. Philosophers consider the former aspect, theologians the latter. See *Summa theologiae* I–II, q. 71, a. 6.

[105] Grisez, *The Theory of the Lord Jesus*, vol. 1 of *Christian Moral Principles*, 382–90.

[106] Ibid., 395.

[107] Ibid. Is not a venial sin incompatible with charity, whether perfect or imperfect?

[108] Ibid., 391–93.

sion, rather than a description of the psychological complexities of moral decision. He is saying that whenever a new problem arises in our moral life that requires a new decision, highly prudent persons acting in full possession of themselves take into account what their decisions mean not just for today or tomorrow but, as far as can be foreseen, for the totality of their lives. Few of us are highly prudent, however, and even the highly prudent often act in situations of physical and emotional confusion. Young people and not a few adults seem to live for the moment or the day, as Grisez says, and it is difficult to discover any consistency of purpose in their behavior.

It is this inconsistency of human behavior that accounts for the possibility of "venial" sin. If we act without any freedom at all, there can be no sin, but when there is at least a modicum of free choice in our decisions, the failure to choose in a way that we perceive as consistent with our fundamental commitment to live according to the order decreed by God in creation is venial sin, more or less morally evil in proportion to the degree of freedom and the harm foreseen.

How then does Aquinas's principle that every human act is willed for the ultimate end apply to venial sins that are inconsistent with that end? First of all it is evident that they are at least negatively under the control of the commitment to the true ultimate end, since if the agent does not remain faithful to that end, he or she has no effective reason to stop at venial sin rather than to go on to mortal sin. Why not kill one's enemy rather than merely bruise him? But the ultimate end also positively finalizes the venially sinful act, since the agent is motivated to perform this sinful act as a step (although a misstep) in a life that as a whole remains directed to the true end. The fact that such an act cannot realistically serve this purpose since it is contrary to what reason tells us is an appropriate means to that end is precisely why it is sinful.

Thus to say that Aquinas's model of a unified moral life seems very abstract compared to the actual human condition of moral life is only to admit that our lives are at almost every point touched by venial sin. For the philosopher this predominance of human sinfulness is a mystery, but for the theologian it is explainable by the doctrine of original sin.

At certain points of our lives, however, we become aware that among the choices that lie ahead of us and seem attractive there are some that, if accepted, would require not only a certain inconsistency but a radical abandonment of our commitment to God because they are contradictory to that commitment. "You cannot give yourself to God and money" (Mt 6:24). For a good man to decide that after all nothing ultimately counts for him except making money is mortal sin and it makes him a radically bad man.

Our commitment to the natural ultimate end of life becomes fully conscious often only at those moments when we consider abandoning that commitment for another, that is, when the possibility of mortal sin presents itself. Since we are then considering the free choice of our commitment, it is no longer envisaged as ultimate end, but as a means to our happiness (integral self-fulfillment).

Thus in this sense PT is correct in holding that integral self-fulfillment, not contemplation of God or any other concrete good, is the ultimate end. Thomists traditionally recognized this by distinguishing between the ultimate end taken subjectively and abstractly (happiness), and objectively and concretely (God), and both these from the human act by which the objective end is actually possessed (contemplation, beatific vision).[109]

To say, however, that the objective and concrete natural end is a collection of incommensurable goods requires a distinction. In one sense, as PT maintains, physical life and truth are incommensurable because they have no common genus. Moreover, to say that truth is a human good superior to physical life runs into the difficulty that without physical life the pursuit of truth is impossible. The four basic goods are mutually dependent so that one cannot substitute for another and each is ultimate in its own order. In another sense, however, which PT without warrant rejects, goods that are ultimate in their own order are not incommensurable when they form a hierarchy of ends so that the lower goods are "measured" by the supreme good, which is ultimate for the whole hierarchical system.

In an Aristotelian metaphysics, only God contains the specific perfections of all lesser things, but among creatures the higher contain the lower only generically. Hence specifically considered every creature is unique and unsubordinated to any other being except God; but generically there is a linear hierarchy of creatures each containing the lower ones in a general manner.[110]

This is why the beatific vision of God himself requires no other goods, but the good of natural contemplation is superior to the other basic goods only generically, and cannot simply replace them. This means, however, that in moral choice the good of physical life can be sacrificed (in certain conditions to be mentioned later) for the sake of reproduction (the parent for the child), for the society (death in a just war), and for truth (the martyr). Also the good of reproduction can be sacrificed for the sake of society (the celibate statesman) and for truth (the celibate philosopher), and why the good of society can be sacrificed for the sake of truth (the hermit contemplative). This hierarchy, however, cannot be reversed; for example, one may not sacrifice the good of reproduction to one's physical health, as in the case of abortion.

---

109 Thus Aquinas, *Summa theologiae* I–II, q. 1, a. 1, speaks of beatitude abstractly, in a. 2 concretely, and objectively, in a. 3, of the act by which it is attained, and in a. 4 of goods necessary for its attainment or perfection but not of its essence.

110 *Summa theologiae* I, q. 45, a. 5.; q. 47, a. 1, 2. Cf. also Aristotle on the impossibility of classifying animals in a linear series of dichotomies, *De Partibus Animalium* I, c. 1, 642b 5–644b 20. See also the essay, "Hierarchy in Ecclesiology" in this collection.

The measurement of a lower by a higher good in the hierarchy of *per se* goods, however, does not result in a reduction of the lower to a mere means to the higher, as PT supposes. These four goods of life, reproduction, society, and truth remain ultimate in their own order, just as PT claims. Hence acts that directly contradict these goods are intrinsically evil and cannot serve as means to the ultimate end, although they are not equal but form a hierarchy.

For example, the good of (physical) life is the least in the hierarchy of basic goods and can be sacrificed to the higher goods, but only on the condition that the sacrificial act: (1) does not involve an injustice; and (2) is not intrinsically evil. For example, one may sacrifice one's life for truth by martyrdom as Jesus did, but not as Socrates did by suicide, because suicide is intrinsically wrong since it involves a direct intention against one's natural tendency to self-preservation.[111] One may sacrifice reproduction to the service of society by celibacy, but not by contraception, because contraception involves a direct intention to contradict the natural purposes of the human sexual act. One may sacrifice one's life for one's nation in a just war, but one may not intentionally kill the innocent for the good of society, because this violates justice. Thus the ultimate end measures the lesser ends in the hierarchy and unifies them without reducing them to mere means.

Although I agree with much that Grisez has written about the theory of the "fundamental option," he has not, to my knowledge, discussed its origin. As Richard McCormick has pointed out in its defense,[112] this theory does not maintain that the option is a mysterious unconscious choice, but depends on a distinction made by Max Scheler and Karl Rahner that was not between two kinds of act, but between two aspects of every human act.[113] Every free human act simultaneously has a transcendental and a categorial aspect. The categorial aspect is the choice of some particular concrete good, but the transcendental aspect is the fundamental attitude that this acts embodies, an attitude that must be either open to God or closed to him. Thus rightly understood, the "fundamental option" seems only to be Kantian-flavored language for the Thomistic "ultimate end."

Nevertheless, there is a real problem about the Scheler-Rahner theory. Scheler accepted the Kantian notion of the a priori, that is, an element of knowledge that is not derived from experience because it is the condition for possible experience. But since for Kant such knowledge is purely formal, Scheler wanted to go beyond Kant to an intuitive a priori that would not be merely formal but would be an apprehension of absolute values. This intuition

---

[111] *Summa theologiae* II–II, q. 64, a. 5.

[112] Richard A. McCormick, SJ, *The Critical Calling: Reflections on Moral Dilemmas Since Vatican II,* chapter 10, "Fundamental Freedom Revisited," 171–90.

[113] Scheler, *Formalism in Ethics and Non-Formal Ethics of Value.* Karl Rahner, *Theological Investigations,* "On the Question of a Formal Existential Ethics," vol. 2, 217–34.

was ascribed not to reason but to "feeling." The realization of these absolute values, however, pertains to the categorial realm of concrete experience and hence is always only approximative and relative.

This approximation to the absolute in complex, unique circumstances is, therefore, a creative act similar to that of the artist who knows that he can never realize his inspiration perfectly in actual stone or paint. This is the philosophical source of the present school of "proportionalism" in moral theology led by Fuchs, Knauer, Schüller, and McCormick that accepts absolute transcendental moral values but rejects the possibility of absolute categorial moral norms.[114]

If, therefore, we explain the fundamental option or commitment to God as transcendental and the choice of concrete means as categorial, we isolate this commitment to the ultimate end (whether natural or supernatural) from the realm of daily life and of public discourse. PT rightly criticizes this as a privatization of morals that would make moral guidance by the community and by the Church impossible.

As for the argument that the fundamental option of the Christian is not charity but faith, so that mortal sin should be defined as an act contrary to the moral prescriptions of faith, another distinction is necessary. The term "faith" in this assertion must refer to living faith, that is, faith informed by charity, since "dead" or unformed faith is compatible with mortal sin. Thus it is true that Christian commitment is the commitment of a living faith, that is, of a faith informed by charity. But when we compare "faith" and "charity" as distinct terms, "faith" in common Catholic theological terminology refers to an act of the intellect moved by the will to assent, and charity to an act of the will moved by the intellect when it contemplates God's goodness. Moral commitment, however, as the new theory itself maintains,[115] is not an intellectual act but an act of the will guided by the intellect's judgment of conscience. Hence it is charity that unites us to God in this life and not faith as distinct from charity.[116]

That PT in order to be self-consistent is forced into this novel position of seeming to define mortal sin as "an act incompatible with faith's specific requirements," rather than in the traditional way as "an act incompatible with the love of God and neighbor," reveals the danger of denying the unity

---

114 Sympathetic accounts in Bernard Hoose, *Proportionalism: The American Debate and Its European Roots,* and John A. Gallagher, *Time Past, Time Future: A Historical Study of Catholic Moral Theology,* 245–69. For my criticism, see Benedict M. Ashley, OP, and Kevin D. O'Rourke, OP, *Health Care Ethics: A Theological Analysis,* 2nd ed., 158–59, 165–69. The 4th edition (1998)-a 5th edition is now in preparation-omitted much of this discussion because the Encyclical of John Paul II, *Veritatis Splendor,* had definitely rejected proportionalism.

115 Grisez, Boyle, and Finnis, "Practical Principles," 140–43.

116 *Summa theologiae* II–II, q. 23, a. 6; q. 24, a. 1, 7.

of the ultimate end whether natural or supernatural or reducing it simply to a "will to integral self-fulfillment" by a complex of disparate goods. If logically pursued it could return us to a legalistic conception of morality as conformity to "God's plan," to a code, and only remotely as the true and effective love of God, self, and neighbor, the very opposite of what this impressive but flawed revision of moral theory seeks to achieve.

IV. The Scriptural Basis of PT

The Founding of Grisez Revision of Moral Theology

Surprisingly, in so vast a work as the still unfinished *The Way of the Lord Jesus* is proving to be, in which every question raised is treated in impressive detail, there is little attention given in the three published volumes to the question of how, even in principle, the biblical data as established by modern biblical scholarship is to be employed as the *norma normans* of Christian ethics. These volumes do, indeed, contain many citations of Scripture: The special index to volume 1 cites most of the biblical books and is over ten pages long and that to volume 2 is seven pages. Yet such citation is open to the common criticism that the author is merely "proof-texting," that is, quoting texts that seem to say verbally what he is saying but which in their proper context have quite a different sense or scope. Moreover, such a procedure, even when the citation is truly probative, does no more than confirm some thesis that the author has developed on the basis of natural reason. It does not root the assertion in the revealed Word of God.

There is one chapter in volume 1 of *The Way of the Lord Jesus*[117] where Grisez approaches this question, when he writes,

> Along with obvious differences, there are also similarities between the role of the Ten Commandments in the Old Testament and that of the Beatitudes in the New. As God gives the Ten Commandments to Moses, and then the rest of the law is unfolded from them, so Jesus gives the Beatitudes to his followers, and then the rest of the moral implications of the new covenant are unfolded. The Beatitudes provide a properly Christian moral framework. Although their relationship to the rest of the moral content of faith has never been clarified in detail, they have had an important place in moral instruction through Christian history. These are extrinsic, but not insignificant, reasons for taking the Beatitudes as organizing principles in analyzing Christian norms and virtues. . . . Although the New Testament provides no detailed moral code, one can expect to find in Jesus' teaching and example the basic guidance needed

---

[117] Grisez, *The Theory of the Lord Jesus,* vol. 1 of *Christian Moral Principles,* chapter 26, "Modes of Christian Response," 627–59.

for Christian life. . . . St. Matthew's Gospel is in a special way the New Testament book of moral teaching. The Sermon on the Mount is the primary synthesis of such teaching, and the Beatitudes are placed at the start of this synthesis. . . . Hence, it is reasonable to suppose that the Beatitudes express specifically Christian moral principles. . . . It is significant that in his expansion of the ancient creeds, the Credo of the People of God, Paul VI mentions the Beatitudes in his summary of Jesus' teaching . . . . Thus the Pope suggests that the Beatitudes be taken as the model summary of the specifically Christian content of Jesus' moral teaching.[118]

Thus, rightly I think, Grisez relates the moral teaching of the two Testaments by comparing the Ten Commandments to the *Sermon on the Mount* and then links this to the living catechetical tradition, the *kerygma*, of the Magisterium. He is able to quote such noted biblical scholars as John P. Meier, W. D. Davies, and Hans Dieter Betz to back up his claims, along with the moralist Servais Pinckaers, OP, who has examined the relevant interdisciplinary and historical questions in some depth.[119] Yet Grisez himself goes no further in exploring this topic than to attempt a correlation between the "eight modes of moral responsibility," which are a characteristic feature of his system and the eight Beatitudes.

My intention, therefore, is first to evaluate the success of this chief effort of Grisez to systematically ground moral theory in the Scriptures, and then to sketch what seems to me a more satisfactory program.

The Beatitudes as Incommensurable Goods

In Grisez's moral theory, the first moral principle (not norm) is "In voluntarily acting for human goods and avoiding what is opposed to them, one ought to choose and otherwise will those and only those possibilities whose willing is compatible with a will toward integral human fulfillment."[120] This fulfillment is possible only by the attainment of the eight "basic goods" that I have already discussed in Part III above. Further, Grisez argues that there must be specifications of that first moral principle, which he calls "modes of moral responsibility," each of which excludes "a particular way in which a person can limit himself or herself to a quite partial and inadequate fulfillment."[121] I have already mentioned these in Part III but will here repeat them in his more explicit formulation:[122]

---

[118] Ibid., pp 627–28.
[119] Ibid.. 657, nn. 1 & 2.
[120] Ibid., 184.
[121] Ibid., 191.
[122] Ibid., 225–26.

1. One should not be deterred by felt inertia from acting for intelligible goods.

2. One should not be pressed by enthusiasm or impatience to act individualistically for intelligible goods.

3. One should not choose to satisfy an emotional desire except as part of one's pursuit and/or attainment of an intelligible good other than the satisfaction of the desire itself.

4. One should not choose to act out of an emotional aversion except as part of one's avoidance of some intelligible evil other than the inner tension experienced in enduring that aversion.

5. One should not, in response to different feelings toward different persons, willingly proceed with a preference for anyone unless the preference is required by intelligible good themselves.

6. One should not choose on the basis of emotions that bear upon empirical aspects of intelligible goods (or bads) in a way that interferes with a more perfect sharing in the good or avoidance of the bad.

7. One should not be moved by hostility to freely accept or choose the destruction, damaging, or impeding of any intelligible human good.

8. One should not be moved by a stronger desire for one instance of an intelligible good to act for it by choosing to destroy, damage, or impede some other instance of an intelligible good.

Grisez points out that "Much that Scripture and Christian teaching say about morality is cast in the language of virtues."[123] For him "distinct virtues" are not separate entities but only aspects of a good person. They, and their corresponding vices, can therefore be distinguished in various ways. Hence he argues that it is best to treat the virtues simply as embodiments of the modes of responsibility.[124]

How then are these modes of responsibility specified as Christian? As we have seen Grisez's very original proposal is that the eight modes are embodied in the Eight Beatitudes. Thus the virtues embodying the eight modes of responsibility specify the first principle of moral theology and are intermediate between it and concrete moral norms, such as the Ten Commandments. In fact they are even enumerated in the *Gospel According to St. Matthew* in the same order as Grisez's systematic listing of the modes.

Thus to take only three examples: "Blessed are the poor in spirit" embodies the first mode of responsibility, that is, that one should "accept all good,

---

[123] Ibid., 192.
[124] Ibid., 193.

including the good fruits one's own work as God's gift." "Blessed are they who mourn" embodies the third mode, "One should not choose to satisfy an emotional desire except as part of one's pursuit and/or attainment of an intelligible good other than the satisfaction of the desire itself;" and "Blessed are the pure of heart," the second mode of responsibility, which requires that Christian "strive to conform one's whole self to living faith, and to recognize and purge anything which does not meet this standard." Furthermore, Grisez regards the traditional "Seven Gifts of the Holy Spirit" (Is 11: 1–2) as:

> virtues to the extent that they are dispositions to human acts, though of a specifically Christian sort, and as gifts insofar as their relationship to faith enlivened by charity makes them specifically Christian. Or, perhaps preferably, the gifts of the Holy Spirit might be identified with charity considered precisely insofar as it is the gift of the Holy Spirit which transforms the moral requirements articulated in the modes of responsibility into the characteristically Christian inclinations (or modes of response) proclaimed "blessed" in the Beatitudes.[125]

For the correspondence of each of the Beatitudes to a particular mode of responsibility, Grisez gives perceptive and plausible arguments, yet one is left with the feeling that this is an arbitrary and even fanciful accommodation to a system whose origin and justification is not biblical but philosophical. Is it really plausible that Jesus (or Matthew) promulgated the New Law by a series of Beatitudes corresponding to Grisez's modes of responsibility and in just that order? He may reply, of course, that his accommodation is no more farfetched than the diverse ways theologians, ever since Augustine, have matched the Aristotelian virtue list to the seven theological and moral virtues, the gifts of the Spirit, the beatitudes, the "spiritual fruits," the Ten Commandments, and the petitions of the Lord's Prayer. While some of these enumerations of "sevens" and accommodations to scriptural texts were merely catechetical and mnemonic, it is evident that for St. Thomas Aquinas this matching was a serious theological problem to which he devoted much attention not only in the *Summa* but also in many other works.[126]

It is helpful to compare Grisez's method of accommodation with that of Aquinas. At first sight it appears that Aquinas is a typical medieval who is determined to make everything fit into a neat set of niches. But further study shows he is trying to be true to the deepest principles of his theology as it is conceived to be *sacra doctrina*, a participation in the wisdom of God as he has revealed himself to us in Scripture and Tradition. In that wisdom there is first of all the revelation of what the Creator intended Adam and Eve

---

125 Ibid., 633.
126 For example, in his *III Sent., De virtutibus, De caritate,* and his Scripture commentaries.

and all those descended from them to be by nature and by grace, a divine intention finally realized in Jesus and Mary and ultimately in the communion of the saints. In other words, the basis of his moral doctrine is a Christian anthropology. Grisez emphatically concurs with Aquinas in making Jesus the model of Christian life.[127] Too much influenced, as I have already argued, by the dictum of modern analytical philosophy that the "ought" cannot be derived from the "is," he avoids establishing a Christian anthropology. Hence, he cannot make use, at least in the same systematic way that Aquinas does, of a taxonomy of the human powers, habits, virtues, acts, and objects as the basic principle for systematizing biblical doctrine.

Yet does not Aquinas also derive his listing of the virtues from Aristotle rather than from the Bible? I would not deny, of course, that this is the case *in via inventionis*. For Aquinas divine revelation has to be received into the human intelligence and made intelligible in human experience. Consequently, the Word of God in the Bible is expressed in human categories and a variety of literary forms. Theological wisdom has the task of ordering this revealed but humanly formulated data into a scientific order so as to show its unity and increase its intelligibility and credibility. Since theology, while eminently theoretical, is also truly practical, moral theology has the specific task of showing how human persons as free beings can, as it were, complete the work of creation and redemption in themselves and their community by freely chosen acts. Aquinas, therefore, uses Aristotle's psychology to help him read the Bible in a penetrating way but not to impose mere human philosophy upon it.

Does St. Thomas succeed in doing this as regards the moral data of the Scripture? Not perfectly, of course; medieval psychology and biblical exegesis both have serious defects upon which today we ought to be able to improve. Aquinas's theological anthropology is first of all based on Genesis 1–2, which teaches that like other living things we were created by God from the dust of the earth, yet also in his image as stewards of his material creation, and hence share in the Creator's spirituality and live with him in spiritual communion not only remotely by nature but intimately by the life of grace. This community in grace has been lost by sin, but is now restored in the God-Man, Jesus Christ. While Aquinas, uses the Aristotelian philosophy based on act and potency to formulate this biblical data, the total picture and its certitude transcend human reason.

With this understanding of the unity and complexity of the graced human person comes clarity about those human powers that constitute the human species as such. We could not be stewards of God's creation unless we were, like him, intelligent and free, which implies that we have the distinct powers of intellect and will. Yet because we are bodily beings, not pure angelic spirits, our

---

[127] Grisez, *The Theory of the Lord Jesus,* vol. 1 of *Christian Moral Principles*, chapter 19, "Fulfillment in Jesus and Human Fulfillment."

intellectual knowledge requires as its instruments sense organs, and our will requires bodily affections or passions. These physical cognitive and affective powers are instruments for and under the direction of the corresponding spiritual powers, since the intellect directs the senses, the will directs the passions.

Furthermore, the intellect and will are mutually interdependent. The complexity of human nature, and its need for a material body subject to chance, imply that the human person cannot direct itself toward God nor carry out the stewardship committed to it in a consistent and hence successful way without stability of character, acquired either by discipline or by the gifts of God, that is, by virtues acquired or infused. Moreover, success in attaining this goal of life is not possible by the individual alone, but only through the action of a graced community, a just civil community for temporal life, and a holy church looking toward eternal life.

While this picture of a virtuous Christian character in a just society and a holy Church is nowhere presented by the Scriptures in abstract terms, it is revealed in many concrete ways through images, precepts, exhortations, encomia, and examples. What Aquinas attempted to do, like Augustine and other Church Fathers before him, was to abstract the universal content from this biblical data and express it in appropriate terms taken from Greek philosophy, but modified to serve a scientific model. Central to this systematic reformulation of revealed data on the moral life in the New Testament is not a code of conduct like the Old Testament Ten Commandments, but the virtues that form Christian character and community as exemplified in Jesus.

Grisez, while admitting that an ethics that emphasizes individual acts at the expense of a consistent pattern of life is inadequate, argues against the centrality of virtue theory characteristic of St. Thomas's moral theology and ethics. He writes:

> Theories which emphasize character and the general trend of one's life nevertheless suffer from a major defect. They fail to realize that character itself—which is one's virtues or vices as a whole—is chiefly (although not solely) the enduring structure of one's choices.. . . . Character itself essentially is particular choices, and it manifests itself in further particular acts.[128]

Hence, Grisez devotes almost no time to the definition or classification of virtues and tends to reduce them all to modes of Christian response understood as aspects of the single virtue of charity. Of course, he is quite right in saying that character is formed by acts and is expressed in acts. It is entirely Thomistic to insist that virtues are for the sake of acts, not vice versa, and certainly it is entirely Christian to say that "a good tree bears good fruit." Never-

---

[128] Ibid., 193–94.

theless, theology as a science[129] is of the universal. Consequently moral theology does not attempt to explain individual prudential acts, but to develop general universal principles and more concrete norms to assist prudence in the ultimate judgment of conscience, but not to dictate it positively. The importance of the renewed emphasis on virtue theory today is that it frees us from the illusion, cultivated by the excessive development of casuistry in the moral manuals, that ethics can replace rather than serve prudence.

Again for Grisez the Thomistic account of the gifts of the Holy Spirit, and hence of the Beatitudes, which are their supreme, paradigmatic acts,[130] is mistaken because:

> the notion that human powers are actuated by the gifts of the Holy Spirit in a manner which reason enlightened by faith and human love enlivened by charity cannot account for. Thomas seems to admit an element of divine activity into the process of human action and to treat it as a principle on the same level with the principles of human action. (If it were not on the same level, it would not be an alternative to the movement of reason.) This appears to be a case of commingling."[131]

By "commingling" Grisez means a kind of monophysitism that confuses the order of grace and nature.[132] This reflects his constant concern in his revision of moral theology to eliminate what he regards as a certain "other-worldliness" in classical moral theology.

While Grisez's care for balance in this matter is certainly to be commended, it seems to me that his reduction of the Gifts and the Beatitudes to mere aspects of faith and charity is subversive of an extensive and deeply rooted tradition in the Church and in magisterial documents that deal with the theology of spirituality, but there is no room for me to demonstrate this here.[133]

---

[129] Ibid., 31–32. Grisez rejects Aquinas's arguments for theology being an Aristotelian *scientia per causas* that attains certitude and prefers to say that it is a "dialectic" "in Plato's sense of the word" (ibid., 7, 27–32). "By this method, one considers truths of faith by comparison *(analogia)* with truths of reason, with one another, and with the ultimate fulfillment to which God calls us in Christ Jesus" (ibid., 31). But, in my understanding, although for Aristotle "dialectic" means merely probable knowledge, for Plato "dialectic" attains certitude through at least the formal exemplary cause by an ascent to an innate knowledge of the Ideas. As far as I can see, nothing that Grisez says about theology shows that it is not a *scientia per causes* yielding certitude. Is Grisez, then, by preferring to call theology "dialectical" rejecting an Aristotelian epistemology for a Platonic one?

[130] *Summa theologiae* I–II, q. 69, a. 1 c.

[131] Grisez, *The Theory of the Lord Jesus,* vol. 1 of *Christian Moral Principles*, 632–33.

[132] Ibid., 589–90.

[133] See my *Thomas Aquinas: Selected Spiritual Writings,* co-authored with Matthew Rzeczkowski, OP.

What directly concerns my topic is the biblical data with regard to the guidance of the Christian by the Holy Spirit.

It is not monophysitic to emphasize that in his human nature Jesus the Christ was not only the Divine Son, but that he was also anointed by the Holy Spirit and guided by his inspiration, as narrated in the account of his baptism (Mk 1:10 and par.). Aquinas argues that our participation by adoption in the Divine Sonship is achieved by rebirth through sanctifying grace and the theological and infused moral virtues, yet these virtues, even charity, do not suffice, without the direct guidance of the Holy Spirit to attain to eternal life in the Trinity.

Hence, in order that the theological virtues should not only attain God as their object but should be exercised in the divine mode appropriate to our life in Christ, we must be rendered flexible to the Holy Spirit's guidance by his special gifts. The effect of this guidance is not spontaneity, as Grisez seems to describe it,[134] but connaturality with the Divine Mind and Will. No "commingling" of nature and grace are involved, but only a transformation by grace in which nature is at once integrally preserved yet elevated. Certainly the theological virtues work such a transformation in the human mind and will or they could not obtain God in himself as their proper object. The Gifts do not change this object but perfect the mode of union between the power and the object, as analogically an increase in light perfects the union of the eye with color.

Thus I find Grisez's principal attempt to give a biblical foundation to his moral theology by way of the Beatitudes unsatisfactory. What form, then, should this biblical rooting take in a revision of moral theology?

Seeking a More Secure Scriptural Foundation for Moral Theology

My proposal for working out a biblical foundation for a revised moral theology can be reduced to the following points:[135]

1. Such a revision should avoid "proof-texting" and fundamentalism and take into account the solid results of the various modern methodologies of biblical exegesis as explained in the Pontifical Biblical Commission's "The Interpretation of the Bible in the Church."[136] Of these methods, however, the most directly relevant to the work of a theolo-

---

[134] Grisez, *The Theory of the Lord Jesus,* vol. 1 of *Christian Moral Principles,* 634.

[135] I first proposed these ideas in "The Scriptural Basis of Moral Theology," *The Thomist,* 1987, also in *Persona et Morale,* Atti del I Congresso Internazionale di Teologia Morale, Rome, 1986. They are the basis of my book *Living the Truth in Love: A Biblical Introduction to Moral Theology;* cf. especially chapter 1.

[136] *Origins* 23 (January 6, 1994): 499–524, n. 29.

gian is "canonical criticism," because the guarantee of inspiration and doctrinal inerrancy applies to the canonical text only as this is interpreted in light of the canon as a whole and the tradition of the Church.

2. Consequently, even the finest of biblical studies of New Testament ethics, such as that of Rudolf Schnackenburg[137] or Wolfgang Schragge[138] based on the data supplied by individual biblical authors, or that of Ceslaus Spicq, OP,[139] based on biblical themes, although they supply excellent data, do not of themselves constitute a biblically based systematic moral theology.

3. A stance must be taken on the relation of Old Testament ethics to New Testament ethics and this presupposes a position on the canonical unity of each of the two Testaments, especially as regards their moral teachings. I would opt for the view that Old Testament moral teaching centers in the covenant of the Ten Commandments as "the way of life" chosen against the "way of death" (Dt 30:15). The rest of the Torah and the narratives and Wisdom literature render the practical meaning of the Commandments more concrete, while the prophets exhort an interiorization of the law. This interiorization of the law as the Law of the Holy Spirit is the work of Christ, who in the (Matthaean) Sermon of the Mount brings the Law to its perfect, universal, and permanent form. Thus the moral law of the Old and New Testaments is one and the same divine law, which includes but transcends the natural law. The ceremonial and judicial elements of this law continue to have instructive but not obligatory force, while the moral elements in the interpretation given them by Jesus and by apostolic authority in the Church will remain obligatory until the end of history.

4. Although the Law as interpreted by Jesus is permanent and final, not subject to change by any human authority, our understanding of it and its prudential application undergo development in the history of the Church, both positive and negative. At any given time, however, the understanding and prudential application of the law by the Magisterium of the church, even if defective, is obligatory on all members of the church. Theologians, therefore, although they have a duty to assist in the development of moral doctrine, may not do so by any

[137] Rudolf Schnackenburg, *The Moral Teaching of the New Testament.*
[138] Wolfgang Schrage, *The Ethics of the New Testament,* translated by David E. Green. See also David Clyde Jones, *Biblical Christian Ethics.*
[139] Ceslaus Spicq, OP, *Théologie Morale du Nouveau Testament,* 2 vols.; also his *Agape in the New Testament,* 3 vols.

form of "dissent" that might undermine the authority of the Magisterium as the guide of faith and conscience.[140]

5. The New Testament Torah shifts the emphasis on the legal norms of morality to the formation of the Christian in view of eternal life, and thus to the development of character through the virtues. Central to this virtue theory are the theological virtues of faith, hope, and love *(agape)* that directly unite the Christian to the Trinity. These, however, require support from the infused moral virtues and are perfected by the Gifts of the Holy Spirit through which alone the supreme acts of the Beatitudes become possible and through them connaturality with Christ in the divine Sonship.

6. The most difficult problem in systematizing the New Testament data on moral life is the relation of the many virtues named in the texts and illustrated in the lives of Jesus, Mary, and the saints. The four cardinal virtues of prudence, justice, fortitude, and temperance are recognized as such only in a single biblical text, Wisdom 8:7. Yet they are certainly portrayed as characteristic of the Christian in many other places in the New and Old Testaments as principal virtues and exemplified in Jesus' own practical wisdom (prudence), his zeal for justice, his patience in martyrdom (fortitude), and his virginity (temperance). In fact, they can be intimately related to the theological virtues in that faith is supported in practical matters by prudence, hope by the asceticism of temperance and fortitude, love by justice. Thus the traditional view that Christian character is formed by the seven virtues of faith, hope, charity, prudence, justice, fortitude, and temperance is a well-grounded systematization of the New Testament picture of the character of Jesus and his saints.

7. Traditional authors differed as to the relation of the seven Gifts of the Holy Spirit, the Beatitudes, the Fruits of the Spirit, and the Lord's Prayer to the foregoing seven virtues, as Grisez correctly notes.[141] Aquinas himself was not always consistent in his statements on this

---

[140] I do not deny, of course, the possibility that a Catholic in a rare instance could know with certitude that a particular ordinary teaching of the Magisterium is mistaken and may be bound in conscience in his or her personal life to follow the truth, taking responsibility for his or her acts. But even in such rare cases Catholics would not be justified in carrying on a campaign against magisterial teaching, nor in attempting to substitute their authority as theological experts over the superior doctrinal and pastoral authority of the Magisterium. See the Congregation for the Doctrine of the Faith, "Instruction on the Ecclesial Vocation of the Theologian," May 24, 1990, *Origins* 20 (July 5, 1990): 117–26, and my essay "The Truth Will Set You Free" in this collection.

[141] Grisez, *The Theory of the Lord Jesus,* vol. 1 of *Christian Moral Principles,* 632–33.

subject, and undoubtedly the fact that the names of virtues are not themselves very stable or easy to translate makes such attributions somewhat arbitrary. Nevertheless, Aquinas sought a sound basis for such attribution in his Christian anthropology in which the human powers involved in fully human, free, and morally responsible acts distinguish the virtues through their proper objects. These can also be systematically related to the basic human needs and to the principal problems that all human beings must meet in attaining integral human fulfillment. The Bible shows us that we cannot be intimately united to God except by faith, hope, and charity, and by infused virtues that enable us to think about what we are to do. We must also act with a prudence that is not carnal but spiritual, accept the Cross (fortitude), control our fleshly desires (temperance) in hope of eternal life, and love our neighbor as ourself in justice. In all this striving, we need the guidance of the Holy Spirit through the intellectual gifts of wisdom, knowledge, and understanding, which enlighten our faith to enter into the mind of Christ, the gift of counsel to use our prudence spiritually, the gift of fear of the Lord to remain chaste, and of piety to be just to others as our own brothers and sisters in Christ.

Only with these gifts that free us to follow Jesus in the Holy Spirit is it possible to obtain by fully Christ-like acts the blessings promised in the Beatitudes: that is, the poverty of spirit and the mourning for sin that free us to follow Christ in the fear of the Lord; the meekness that accepts the Cross; the mercy to the sinful, which is true counsel and prudence; the hunger for justice that is true piety; the knowledge that enables us to understand our sinful world and the Creator's original intentions; the purity of heart that enables us to believe truly; and the love of peace that establishes us in the love of God and neighbor.

8. Once the biblical virtues have been given an anthropological and Christological foundation, the norms of Christian behavior can be derived from the kind of acts that must be performed and avoided under temptation in order to conform the Christian to Christ in the community that is the Body of Christ. Among these norms are those of Christian prudence that submit the Christian to the guidance of the Holy Spirit in applying these norms to the circumstances of life in a sinful world. The supreme goal of such a life is the contemplation of God in a faith illumined by the intellectual gifts of the Holy Spirit and conformed to Christ in charity. All Christians even in this life share this life of contemplation, although the vowed life of the practice of the counsels and Beatitudes is (as St. Paul tells us) the most freed for its attainment.

9. A moral theology of this type is not only biblically rooted, it flows from the deepest dogmatic mysteries of the Trinity and Incarnation and is an ascetic and spiritual theology confirmed by the experience of the saints and the ordinary Christian. The *Catechism of the Catholic Church*, developed by a universal consultation of the Magisterium, also confirms it in #1830–31. The moral life of Christians is sustained by the gifts of the Holy Spirit. They are permanent dispositions that make man docile in following the promptings of the Holy Spirit. They belong in their fullness to Christ, the Son of David. They complete and perfect the virtues of those who receive them. They make the faithful docile in readily obeying divine inspirations.

As for the Beatitudes, which are discussed at some length in the *Catechism* (#1716–29), it is said (#1726): "The Beatitudes teach us the final end to which God calls us: the Kingdom, the vision of God, participation in the divine nature, eternal life, filiation, rest in God." Thus in the magisterial catechesis of the Church the solid tradition is maintained that the Beatitudes are not virtues as such but the perfect acts of Christian virtue by which the final reward of beatitude is attained. They are the ends, not merely the means, of a fully Christian life. The work of moral theology is to mark out the steps by which that goal is to be attained. Today the collaborative task of the revision and renewal of moral theology—to which Germain Grisez by his courageous, faithful, and philosophically rigorous work has made so powerful a contribution—will be finally achieved only when we can mark out the way of the Lord Jesus in the full light of biblical revelation.

Conclusion: Clerical and Lay Morality

I would agree with polyteleologism, therefore, that contrary to de Lubac and others, we must retain the notion of a natural ultimate end, but only if it is also understood that in God's actual dispensation this natural end is subsumed within the supernatural ultimate end, perfect beatitude in the Trinity. To reject the present existence of a natural end is to render absurd the very concept of human nature, hence of the hypostatic union and of the transformation of human nature by grace.

I would also agree that the natural ultimate end taken subjectively and abstractly is integral self-fulfillment (happiness in the sense of imperfect beatitude). While taken objectively and concretely this imperfect natural happiness is not one single good, but a complex of interdependent goods that are not mere means but ends in themselves and in this sense (but only in this sense) incommensurable. Perfect beatitude, however, can be found only in the all-sufficient beatific vision of God, although its superabundance includes the community of all the blessed and the glory of the transformed universe.

But I would follow Aquinas in holding that the per se goods that constitute natural happiness are sufficiently listed as physical life, reproduction, community, and truth, and in affirming that they are hierarchically unified and measured, with truth (the good of contemplation) as the supreme measure in the sense that it specifies the others as human. Hence, the fact that the beatific vision elevates contemplation to an order in which the other goods become secondary, is not contradictory to natural happiness but consummative of it.

I would also agree with PT in its criticism of current fundamental option theories as excessively subjective, but I would not accept the notion that mortal sin is to be defined as an act contradictory to our faith commitment rather than to the love of God and neighbor.

This leaves us with PT's basic concern that to insist on contemplation as the ultimate natural end of the human person reflects a clerical point of view and has stood in the way of making the Christian life intelligible to the laity who do not at all experience life in that way. I concede that much of our Catholic literature on the Christian life has been written from a clerical or even monastic point of view. This literature insufficiently reflects the actual life of the average Christian in that it tends to deal with only a legalistic and minimalistic casuistry. But this deficiency, it seems to me, has been caused by understanding the term "contemplation" in much too restricted a sense.

In fact, broadly understood "contemplation" simply means an awareness of God in all aspects of our world and our lives, even when that awareness remains rudimentary and nameless. The mystic attains this awareness intensely, but it is not beyond the simplest and earthiest human being even without the special elevation of grace to be aware that this is God's world and we are God's. This awareness is evidenced in all the great world religions, although sometimes confused or mixed with error. That for many in our modern culture this divine presence is so silenced is a comment on that culture, not a disproof of the unity of our ultimate end. Yet even in our culture studies have shown[142] that God remains a part of most people's experience not merely as a private but as a public fact.

Therefore, a revision of moral theory that does not retain the classical doctrine of the good of contemplation, natural and graced, as the ultimate good that gives meaning and unity to our lives and makes them truly human falls short of accounting for common moral experience. I hope that the school of thought that I have criticized, which has done so much to introduce a more objective philosophical approach to current moral theory, will give still more thought to the unity of moral life.

---

[142] See Andrew M. Greeley, *Unsecular Man and Religious Change in America*; Andrew M. Greeley and Gregory Baum, eds., *The Persistence of Religion*, Concilium; also George Gallup, Jr., and Jim Castelli, *The People's Religion: American Faith in the 90s.*

CHAPTER 16

Dominion or Stewardship?[*]

In the Old Testament

HUMAN PUZZLEMENT OVER THE ADVANTAGES AND risks of technology is by no means a new one, as the Bible shows. The ancient Jews lived between the two oldest urban centers of human civilization, the cities of Egypt and of Mesopotamia. The Jews, once a semi-nomadic cattle-herding people, eyed the great cities with both envy and with moral disgust.[1] Hence the Hebrew Scriptures had to face the technological question: "Is it better to live as close to nature as possible; or to transform nature by art so as to enrich human life and overcome its limitations?"

The Bible dramatizes this problem through a number of stories, some genuinely historical, others merely typical of historic experience. It was the sons of the first murderer Cain who invented urban technology (Gn 4:17–22).[2] The building of the Tower of Babel led to the division of the

---

[*] This was written for the International Study Group in Bioethics, International Federation of Catholic Universities, Brussels, March 29–31, 1990, and was published in Kevin M. Wildes, SJ, Franceso Abel, SJ, and John C. Harvey, eds., *Birth, Suffering and Death: Catholic Perspectives at the Edge of Life* (Dordrecht: Kluwer Academic Publishers, 1992), 85–106.

[1] See Roland de Vaux, OP, *Ancient Israel*, 13–15.

[2] I have consulted W. Gunther Plant, *The Torah: A Modern Commentary*; E. A. Speiser, Genesis in *Anchor Bible*; and especially Claus Westermann in his very extensive *Genesis 1–11: A Commentary*, whose exegesis I have generally followed in this paper (see also his short work *Creation and Beginning and End in the Bible*. Westerman (pp. 342–44) accepts the view of Jean Paul Audet, "Le Revanche de Prométhée ou Le drame de la religion et de la culture," *Revue Biblique* 73 (1966): 1–29, that the Bible is not making the point that the advance of technology took place among the wicked Cainites instead of the just Sethites, but is simply indicating that this advance brought with it opportunities for evil. "The Cain and Abel narrative says that when

human family (11:1–9). The establishment of the Davidic monarchy brought on corruption, idolatry, and tragic national division (1 Sm 8:1–22; 1 Kgs 12ff.).[3] On the other hand the Bible recognizes the inventiveness and skill of craftsmen as gifts of the Holy Spirit to be used in God's service.[4] Thus for the Bible the "progress of civilization" is the ambiguous result both of human pride seeking to rival God and of the Creator's empowerment of humanity to share in the divine dominion. Consequently, in the Old Testament God gives his people a detailed Instruction (Torah, Law) on the right use of the dominion we share with Him.

Thus the Mosaic Law of the Pentateuch contains many detailed regulations on the proper use of technology, such as those on sexual practices, hygiene, birth and death, agriculture, the preparation of food, clothing, and housing. Although the technology envisaged was still very primitive, these laws established principles which the Oral Law later recorded in the Talmud and in the countless rabbinic *responsa* of later Judaism have been applied to all the details of technology in its development down to our own day.[5]

Christians, following St. Paul, although accepting the God of Abraham, Isaac, and Jacob do not consider themselves bound by the Law of Moses.[6]

---

people created by God live side-by-side in brotherhood there is at the same time the possibility of killing. The song of Lamech indicates that the increased progress activated by the human potential increases the possibility of mutual destruction. With the growth of one's capacities there is a growth of self-assertion and *amour propre* that demands retribution without limit for even the smallest injury" (p. 337). "Civilization and its effects have a postive emphases in Israel; from the very beginning it is founded in God's will for his creatures" (p. 343).

[3] Cf. the commentary by P. Kyle McCarter, Jr., 1 Samuel in Anchor Bible, 153–62. On 1 Kgs 12ff.; cf. the commentary by Gwilym H. Jones, 1 and 2 Kings, *New Century*, vol. 1, 247–56.

[4] "See, I have chosen Bezalel . . . and I have filled him with a divine spirit of skill and understanding and knowledge of every craft. . . . I have also endowed all the experts with the necessary skill to make all the things I have ordered you to make" (Ex 31, 2–3, 6). Cf. also Sir 38 in praise of physicians, craftsmen, and scribes.

[5] See Jacob Neusner, *Invitation to the Talmud,* 2nd ed., 1–27, for discussion of the Jewish "Oral Law" as written down in the Mishnah and Talmud after 200 C.E.

[6] For a penetrating discussion of this much controverted question, see E. P. Sanders, "On the Question of Fulfilling the Law and Rabbinic Judaism" in *Donum Gentilicum: New Testament Studies in Honour of David Daube,* edited by E. Bammel, C. K. Barrett, and W. D. Davies, 103–26. Sanders shows that there are two themes in Paul: (1) the abolition of the Old Law by justification through faith; and (2) the extension of the call to faith to the Gentiles. On the first point the rabbis also admitted that the works of the Law render righteous only if they are the fruit of faith, but since for them only the Jews were elect, the practice of the Law was obligatory for all who believed. The second point is Paul's real message; hence the first is rhetorical and stated with some exaggeration, since he does really mean that the moral elements of the Old Law are abolished.

Nor have we received some new law like that of Islam's Qur'an. Instead Jesus called us back to the original order of Creation, to the natural law that has been elevated by grace to lead us to life in the Triune God. Thus when Christians open the Bible behind the details of the Mosaic Law they turn to the account of creation as God meant it to be in the first chapters of the Book of Genesis.

According to that account, among the varied array of beings that God created, the greatest in the visible world was humankind made in God's "image and likeness," destined to share in God's dominion over creation, God's wise, loving care by which he guides to their perfection and fulfillment whatever he has made.[7] Unlike the Mesopotamian and Greek notion that humans were made to be the slaves of the gods, jealous gods who feared the rivalry and rebellion of these slaves, Genesis portrays a generous God who invites us to be his co-workers.[8] Such cooperation implies that God has also endowed humanity with spiritual intelligence and will. Although like other earthly creatures we are made out of matter, we resemble God in our spiritual self-consciousness and freedom.

The somewhat abstract statements of the First Chapter of Genesis are fleshed out in the vivid narrative about Adam and Eve in Chapter 2. God created this pair and placed them in a perfect environment, the Garden of Eden, yet he also gave them a task to perform, "to work . . . and take care of" the Garden. Those two words are derived, of course, from one of the simplest forms of technological economy, the cultivation of garden crops. Adam and Eve are pictured not as hunters, but as vegetarians who use no

---

[7] Westerman, Genesis 1–11, 147–60 reviews all the complicated history of the exegesis of "image and likeness" and concludes that this phrase does not describe the nature of humanity but God's purpose in creating them, namely, to have a being with whom he could enter into a relationship of communication. Westerman's view, however, depends in part on his source theory. Taking the next verse as it stands it would seem that the following verse, "Let them have dominion," best explains in what sense humans are images of God: They have co-dominion with God over other creatures.

[8] Ibid., 221–22. According to the Mesopotamian myths, "Man was made to be the servant of the gods, to be a kind of breadwinner of his divine masters, to be the builder and caretaker of their sanctuaries. In the initial chapters of Genesis man was created to be the lord of the earth, the sea, and the air. The luminaries were created for the earth, and the earth was created for man. . . . A certain degree of human dominion over creation is understood in the Babylonian account . . .which charges man with the building of sanctuaries and the bringing of offerings. But in the first place, this is not explicitly stated. And in the second place, it is the dominion or authority of a *servant*, not of a lord. Each account stresses an entirely different aspect of man's place in nature." Alexander Heidel, *The Babylonian*, 2nd ed., 121. A similar contrast with the Greek account of human creation by Hesiod, *Theogony*, and *Works and Days* and Aeschylus, *Prometheus Bound* is made by Audet, "Le Revanche de Prométhée," with references.

violence and shed no blood. They were to "take care of" the Garden, that is, to protect the ideal environment given them by God, yet they were also to "cultivate" it. Moreover, since Adam could not cultivate the Garden without understanding God's purposes in creating the various creatures that compose it, the story tells us that Adam "named" the animals around him, thus exerting an intelligent control over subhuman nature.

Yet God also warned Adam and Eve that their co-dominion with God could not be absolute. They might eat of all the trees of the Garden, even the tree of immortality deep in the midst of the Garden, but with a single exception: They might not eat of the Tree of Knowledge of Good and Evil lest they die. The serpent explained this exception to Eve, "God has forbidden this because he knows that if you eat of it you will become as gods knowing good and evil."

The serpent's lie consisted in insinuating that God's command was motivated by his desire to protect his absolute dominion. This is a lie, as Jesus was to make clear in the Parable of the Two Sons (Lk 15:11–32) because God desires nothing of us more than that we should share his blessed life. The serpent suggested to Eve that to know "good and evil" is somehow better than to know God's good gifts only. Eve began to be ashamed of her humanity, ashamed of her creaturehood, jealous of God. No longer content to cooperate with God, she became ambitious to create her own world with its own laws of right and wrong. Seeking total autonomy, she persuaded Adam to join her in it, gaining over her partner a seductive domination.

This lying illusion was the deadly poison of the tree against which God had warned them, and, as Genesis goes on to narrate, from it flowed murder and death, slavery and corruption—all the miseries of our world, ever threatening, as in the Flood, the total destruction of humankind. These consequences follow not because God fears rebellion as Zeus feared Prometheus who had given fire to humans, but because the unassailable God permits Adam and Eve to go their own way, the way they have freely and foolishly chosen.

Thus the theological answer of Genesis to the technological problem can be summed up as follows: (1) In creating us intelligent and free, God has given us a share in his dominion over the world and our own lives; but (2) this co-dominion is a stewardship that is to be exercised in cooperation with God in the completion of his creation according to his wise plan for our own happiness; and (3) thus human technology is not an absolute but a relative dominion under the guidance of God's loving wisdom and care.

In the New Testament

In the New Testament Jesus reinforced and perfected this teaching of Genesis in five ways. First, by preaching the coming of the Kingdom or Reign of God, that is, by showing us that human happiness will be consummated not by our proud conquest of the world, but by service of the Christ, the Messiah, the only earthly king, the New Adam, who is himself a Servant who will hand over his kingdom to his Father.[9] Second, Jesus worked great miracles: healing, commanding the forces of nature, and feeding the poor. These miracles imply that we are empowered by God to regain the original rational dominion of Adam over nature, over disease, over poverty and want, provided we use this power as Jesus did, not for personal aggrandizement, but to serve others.[10] Third, in the Parable of the Talents Jesus taught us that we will be responsible to God for the use of the gifts he has given us, and that it is not enough merely to return these gifts, but we must use them creatively (Mt 25:14–30; Lk 19:11–27). Fourth, Jesus rebuked the Twelve because they contended with each other over who should be first in the Kingdom of God, saying to them:

> You know that the rulers of the Gentiles lord it over them, and their great men exercise authority over them. It shall not be so among you; but whoever would be great among you must be your servant, and whoever would be first among you must be your slave; even as the Son of man came not to be served but to serve, and to give his life as a ransom for many. (Mt 20:25–28)

Fifth, Jesus taught that in the Last Judgment the criterion between salvation and damnation would be whether the plaintiff had or had not treated all other human beings as if they were Jesus himself (Mt 25:31–46).

Thus for Jesus the moral norm for dealing with creatures was to respect them for what God made them to be—to use the subhuman creation in the service of humankind, and to serve humankind as the image of God. This image of God is fully manifest only in Jesus himself, the Son of God incarnate. (2 Cor 4:4; Col 1:15). In this way the order of things willed by the Creator in the beginning is restored and brought to completion by Jesus in his humanity joined to the community of his followers, the Church animated by the Holy Spirit that Jesus sends them from the Father. Of themselves, however, human beings are powerless to bring about this restoration, since their sin-tainted efforts serve only to further distort the order of creation and to return the cosmos to chaos.

---

9 "Then comes the end, when he [Christ] hands over the kingdom to his God and Father . . . so that God may be all in all." (1 Cor 15:24, 28b).

10 The miracles of Jesus should not be understood as making technology unnecessary, but as signs to us show us that with the help of God's grace we can use technology to overcome many human ills. For example, liberation theology interprets the miracles of the feeding of the multitudes (Mk 6:34–44; 8:1–9) as a summons to us to feed the poor by a proper distribution of the abundance with which modern technology has supplied us.

Nature, Art, and Grace

The development of theology in the Christian Church involved the translation of the concrete narrative, metaphorical, and legal biblical categories of thought and language into the more technical, abstract categories and language of Greek philosophy prevalent in the Hellenistic culture in which the Gospel was preached.[11] This entailed no difficulty for the concept of "dominion," but notions of "stewardship," of human cooperation with God were not so easy to translate because, as we have seen, the Greek and Roman gods were not wont to share their dominion.

Yet what was familiar to the Greeks was the idea that the visible world is a work of art produced by the wisdom of the gods. Thus natural objects as works of art reflect the purposes of the gods and therefore must be used by humans only for such purposes. Hence we humans are subject in our behavior to a "natural law" intrinsic to the very structure of natural things, including the human body and its soul.[12] Thus Greek ethics, in the main, is built on the principle that human behavior must be conformed to the intrinsic teleology or purposefulness of things.

Conformity to natural law for humans, however, was not for the Greeks merely blind instinct as for brute animals, but both an intelligent concord with nature and a transcendence of it. The concordance was expressed by the saying, "Art imitates nature;"[13] while the transcendence was expressed by "Art perfects nature."[14] Thus was meant that art (*techne,* in the broad sense

---

[11] See Jean Danielou, *Gospel Message and Hellenistic Culture,* vol. 2 of *A History of Early Christian Doctrine,* especially chapter 17, "Problems of Anthropology," 387–425.

[12] For a historical survey on natural law theories, see Michael Bertram Crowe, *The Changing Profile of the Natural Law;* A. P. D'Entreves, *Natural Law,* 11th rev. ed.; Leo Strauss, *Natural Right and History,* especially 81–164; Yves Simon, *The Tradition of Natural Law: A Philosopher's Reflections,* edited by Vukan Kuic; Josef Th. C. Arntz, "Die Entwicklung des naturrectlichen Denkens innerhalb des Thomismus," 87–120 in *Das Naturrecht im Disput: Drei vorträge beim kongresz der deutschsprachigen moraltheologen 1965,* in *Bensberg/Heraugegeben und zur diskussion gestellt von Franz Böckle,* edited by Franz Böckle; William A. Luijpen, *Phenomenology of Natural Law,* especially the criticism of the Thomistic neglect of subjectivity, 91–111; John Finnis, *Natural Law and Natural Rights;* Anthony Battaglia, *Toward a Reformulation of Natural Law;* and for an interesting attempt to salvage the Thomistic theory "without metaphysics," Martin Rhonheimer, *Natur als Grundlage der Moral: die personale Struktur des Naturgesetzes bei Thomas von Aquin: eine teleologischer Ethik.*

[13] Aristotle, *Physics* II, c. 2, 194a 22; St. Thomas Aquinas, *Summa contra Gentiles* II, c. 75. See article by W. Tatarkiewicz, "Mimesis" in *Dictionary of the History of Ideas,* edited by Philip P. Wiener, 3: 225–30.

[14] St. Thomas Aquinas combines the two principles neatly when he writes, *Ars imitatur naturam, et supplet defectum naturae in illis in quibus natura deficit* ("Art imitates nature and supplies the defect of nature in those things in which nature fails"), IV *Sent.,* d. 42, q. 2, a. 1 c.

of our "technology") derives its principles from nature, but it extends these principles to carry nature beyond itself through invention. These two maxims, "Art imitates nature" and "Art perfects nature" thus provided Christian theologians with a way to translate the biblical notions of "dominion" and "stewardship." The Christian is to use the work of the Creator and his own personal gifts, in accordance with nature, with the natural law, in imitation (mimesis) of the Creator, but at the same the Christian is called in freedom to perfect nature by technology.

A third dictum was added to these Greek sayings by the medieval theologians to give the first two a specifically Christian character: "Grace perfects nature" or "presupposes nature."[15] This meant that God through the Incarnation has begun to repair the Creation fallen into ruin through the sin of angels and human beings, and not only does he restore the world but he has chosen to elevate it by grace to a share in the divine life itself, to deify it.[16] Hence as nature ought not to be wiped-out by human art, so also nothing that is human, both from nature and from art, is obliterated but perfected by grace. For Christians, therefore, as Vatican II in *The Church in the Modern World* has declared,[17] technology becomes an instrument of grace in the redemption of the world when it is concordant with God's purposes, when, so to speak, it perfects nature by "imitating" God.

---

[15] For the history of this principle, see Bernhard Stoeckle, *Gratia supponit naturam.*

[16] The term "deification" *(theosis)* of the human person by grace, much favored by the theology of the Eastern Church, does not imply that Christians will be absorbed into God in a pantheistic manner, but that they will become "partakers in the divine nature" *(theias koinonoi physeos)* (2 Pt 1:4).

[17] "Individual and collective activity, that monumental effort of humanity through the centuries to improve the circumstances of the world, presents no problem to believers; considered in itself, it corresponds to the plan of God. Humanity was created in God's image and was commanded to conquer the earth with all it contains and to rule the world in justice and holiness: humanity was to acknowledge God as maker and to relate itself and the totality of creation to God, so that through the dominion of all things by humanity the name of God would be majestic in all the earth. (Ps 8:7 and 10). . . . Far from considering the conquests of human genius and courage as opposed to God's power as if humanity sets itself up as a rival to the creator, Christians ought to be convinced that the achievements of the human race are a sign of God's greatness and the fulfillment of his mysterious design. With an increase in human power comes a broadening of responsibility on the part of individuals and communities: there is no question then, of the Christian message inhibiting human beings from building up the world or making them disinterested in the good of their fellows: on the contrary it is an incentive to do these very things." Vatican Council II, *Gaudium et Spes,* "Pastoral Constitution on the Church in the Modern World," December 7, 1965, Chapter III, n. 34.

Science and Nature

Today, however, the biblical view of technology translated into these Greek terms by theologians is not so easy to translate into the language of a scientific and technological age. The principal area of conflict between theologians and scientists today is not, as many suppose, creationism, which is a problem only for fundamentalists.[18] Not creationism but the notion of nature is the real barrier between contemporary theology and science.

For Christian, and especially Catholic, theology it is a dogmatic truth that each of God's creatures has an intrinsic teleology on which is also based an extrinsic teleological relation to other human beings, to the cosmos as a whole, and to its Creator, and that this teleology or natural law provides the foundation for a Christian ethics or moral theology.[19] With equal dogmatism modern science rejects all teleological statements as unscientific.[20] Historians have demonstrated that the historical origins of this rejection of teleology by science were not from within science itself, but that this rejection of teleology was the result of the triumph of Nominalism in the theological faculties of

---

[18] On the recent "creation-science" controversy in the U.S.A., see Roland Mushat Frye, *Is God a Creationist? The Religious Case Against Creation-Science,* and Langdon Gilkey, *Creationism On Trial.* I am afraid these two books are not very sensitive to the genuine religious concerns of the fundamentalists. I agree with them, however, that scientific theories of cosmic evolution and of the evolution of life and the origin of humanity answer different questions than those which the author of Genesis aimed to answer. The Bible transcends the scientific account by seeking the ultimate spiritual cause of the very existence of the cosmos and of the spiritual element in the human being; while science only studies existing material processes and modestly admits that the ultimate question of "Why anything at all exists" is beyond its ken. Even if science asserts, as neo-Darwinianism does (Cf. Jacques Monod, *Chance and Necessity*) that evolution is ultimately a matter of chance rather than of law, this claim does not contradict the doctrine of creation, since God can not only use natural law, but also he can use both free actions and chance events to perfect his creation. For current discussion of this topic between scientists and Catholic philosophers see Ernan McMullin, ed., *Evolution and Creation.*

[19] Vatican I, interpreting Rm 1: 19–21, solemnly defined (sess. III, *Constitution on the Catholic Faith,* sect. 2, *On Revelation,* canon 1, *Enchiriidion symbolorum, definitionum et declarationum de rebus fidei et morum,* n. 3026, that the Creator can be known with certitude by the light of natural human reason from his creation. Catholics, therefore, cannot deny that created beings have an intrinsic teleology, since the various rational proofs of God's existence that have been historically formulated explicitly or implicitly refer to such teleology.

[20] See the standard treatise of Ernest Nagel, *The Structure of Science,* 401–46, in which he goes to great lengths to show how all teleological statements, even in biology, can be reduced to non-teleological statements. Cf. another discussion in Richard B. Braithwaite, *Scientific Explanation,* 322–41.

the late medieval universities.[21] It is necessary, therefore, to ask whether this rejection is really scientifically necessary or even possible.

To posit an "intrinsic teleology" in nature is not to resort, as scientists commonly suppose, to occult forces or to some theory of "vitalism" or "panpsychism" to explain natural phenomena. Rather it is to claim that it is empirically verifiable that all natural individuals are by their very structures and uniform activities purposeful, although only higher organisms act from conscious purpose.[22] If it seems an oxymoron to speak of an "unconscious purpose" in lower organisms and inanimate entities, one might speak rather of "unconscious directedness."[23] Thus an aimed arrow moves predeterminedly to the definite target to which it was directed at the outset of its flight. Note, however, that in this example the arrow is directed by an external agent, the archer, while intrinsic teleology is a directedness inherent in the very nature of a thing, as the eye is a structure for seeing, even when it is covered by the eyelid.

Since it is empirically verifiable that living organisms in their parts and as totalities develop themselves and perform characteristic activities such as feeding and reproduction to meet innate requirements of survival and thus are purposeful structures, biologists admit they exhibit "teleonomy," but deny they exhibit teleology.[24] Biologists argue that since this observable adaptation of living structures to the functions necessary for the organisms' survival can be explained as the result of the Neo-Darwinian natural selection of chance mutations through adaptation to the environment, any reference to teleological explanations would introduce an unnecessary and non-empirical factor outlawed by sound scientific method. Yet to admit into science the notion of "adaptation for survival," that is, of the relation of the structure to function and function to the very existence of the organism, is to admit the notion of the relation of "directedness," which is all that philosophers and theologians mean by the term "teleology." Thus "teleonomy" and "teleology" are not rival explanations but two correlative aspects of a single, empirically observable phenomena that of adaptive functions, considered on the one hand as to their origin in natural selection, and on the other precisely as adaptive.

---

21 For a discussion of the influence of late medieval theology on the development of modern science, see James A. Weisheipl, OP, *The Development of Physical Theory in the Middle Ages,* and my *Theologies of the Body: Humanist and Christian,* 2nd ed., with a new introductory chapter published in 1996.

22 See my articles in the *New Catholic Encyclopedia,* 1st ed., 1969, on "Finality," vol. 5. 915–19, and "Teleology," vol. 13, 979–81, and on "Change and Process" in *The Problem of Evolution,* edited by John N. Deely and R. J. Nogar, OP, 267–84.

23 The use of the term "directiveness" was proposed and strongly defended in biology by E. S. Russell, *The Directiveness of Organic Activities.*

24 "Teleonomy" (goal-lawfulness) is used by some evolutionary biologists to indicate functionality or adaptation without any implication of "purpose."

Some would grant the intrinsic teleology of organisms, but deny it of inanimate natural entities. Admittedly goal-directed activity is more evident in living than non-living things. Yet the sciences of physics and chemistry would not be possible without the distinction between natural, chance, and artificial processes. Natural processes arise from forces inherent in physical objects prior to human manipulation and thus differ from artificial processes that always presuppose them. Technology has to use natural processes; it does not create *ex nihilo*. Moreover, natural processes are also prior to chance events, which result always from some unique concurrence of natural processes. Thus we call a process natural, and therefore subject to scientific investigation, because it is not a unique event resulting from chance, but instead regularly reoccurs, can be repeatedly observed and then expressed by a natural law. Processes that regularly reoccur, however, can be identified only because they produce uniform results, and are thus predetermined to a goal, that is because they are teleological. Chance events are non-teleological; artificial processes are teleological, but not intrinsically such, since their directedness is imposed by man on nature.

Yet even if we grant a teleology intrinsic to organisms and even to inanimate natural units, can we speak of a teleology intrinsic to the environment? Our earthly environment, like the human organism, is also a system, the ecosystem, but unlike an organism it is not an *unum per se*, a substantial entity, but an inter-related collectivity of substantial entities.[25] It does not, therefore, have an intrinsic teleology in the same sense as do the parts of an organism or the organism as a whole. Yet it is one of the discoveries of ecology that the inter-relations of the various organisms and inorganic bodies that compose an ecosystem, although not substantial, are something more than merely accidental. These objects (or at least many of them) depend for their very existence and survival on the system as a whole. For example, the correlation between the anatomy of an insect and the structure of the flowers from which it gathers honey and which in the process it pollinates—this mutual adaptation—is clearly teleological. This mutual dependence of the various entities that make up our earthly environment is scientifically verifiable.

Some scientists today in proposing the so-called "Anthropic Principle" even want to extend this teleology vastly by showing that if the solar system, our galaxy, and the whole cosmos were even a little different than they actually are, human life here could never have evolved.[26] Without entering into

---

[25] Cf. D. J. Owens, *What is Ecology?* For various implications of the Ecological Movement, see the essays in *Cry of the Environment: Rebuilding the Christian Creation Tradition* by The Center for Ethics and Public Policy. For philosophical and theological discussion, see A. R. Peacocke, *Creation and the World of Science,* The Bampton Lectures, 255–318, and Jürgen Moltmann, *God in Creation,* especially "The Ecological Crisis," 20–52.

[26] See Barrow and Tipler, *The Anthropic Cosmological Principle* for detailed arguments favoring this view.

this broader question, we can at least conclude that in an important sense (although not in the same way as is an organism) the terrestrial ecosystem is intrinsically teleological. What is special to the relation of humanity to its environment, of course, is that by our intelligence we exercise a dominion over the other members of the system and even to a degree the system as a whole, a dominion that is increasingly effective.

This freedom proper to human nature along with our materiality, which subjects us to chance, are the reasons we are historical beings, but human historicity does not, as is often thought today, obliterate universal human nature, since, as we have seen, chance and freedom presuppose nature.[27]

Science and Ethics

If it is granted that science can contribute to the study of the intrinsic teleology of our environment in relation to the intrinsic teleology of the human person, we can now move to the ethical aspects of the technological application of science. Here two questions confront us: (1) Can we empirically discover in the human species a common nature, invariant through cultural variations, which is teleological, so that it will make sense to say that certain kinds of behavior are good because they contribute to making the human being fully what it was made to be, that is, what it "ought" to be?[28] (2) Can we empirically discover a teleological relation between the human environment on this earth and human nature such that it makes sense to say that certain manmade modifications of this environment are "good" for the human species and others are "bad"?[29]

---

[27] Many ethicists today so emphasize human historicity as to neglect human nature and thus tend to moral relativism. Some have been unduly influenced by the well-known essay of Bernard Lonergan, SJ, "The Transition from a Classicist World-View to Historical Mindedness" in *A Second Collection*, 1–9. On this topic, see my essay "Contemporary Understandings of Personhood" (1990) in the present volume.

[28] On the famous Humean problem of the "is" and the "ought," which has so plagued modern metaethics, see Finnis, *Natural Law and Natural Rights,* 36–48. That this problem may be a result of misreading Hume, see Alasdair MacIntyre, *Against the Self-Images of the Age,* 109–24.

[29] Recently there has been much discussion about the need for more emphasis on the theology of creation as the context of the theology of redemption, cf. G. S. Hendry, "The Eclipse of Creation," *Theology Today* (January 1972): 406; Leo Scheffczyk, *Creation and Providence,* who emphasizes that the Creator also cares for what he has made; John Macquarrie, "Creation and Environment," *Expository Times* (October 1971): 4–9, who while denying that God "needs" his creation, yet wants to make the relation between Him and the universe more mutual; John Reumann, *Creation and New Creation: The Past, Present, and Future of God's Creative Activity,* who in Lutheran fashion stresses the primacy of Redemption and mission over Creation and restricts the New Creation to the redeemed community; while Norman J. Young,

The second of these questions is subordinate to the first, since if we cannot determine what is good for human persons, it will be meaningless to ask how humans should use or modify the environment.[30] Is it not illogical to fight to conserve the ecological balance as if it were teleological, that is, intrinsically purposeful, while at the same time denying an intrinsic purposefulness to the human structure, and attributing ethical norms purely to cultural convention? Equally absurd is the extravagantly altruistic notion, put forward by some enthusiastic "Greens," that we should preserve the environment for the environment's sake, not for ours, or even to our disadvantage.[31]

Thus, if the ecological movement that maintains that the teleological structure of the environment can be scientifically studied and technologically perserved and enhanced in the service of humanity is a reasonable enterprise, then must it not also be acknowledged that an ethics based on the notion of "natural law," that is, of an intrinsic teleology of human nature, can be objectively developed and applied? In biblical terms this means that the human moral code can and should reflect not arbitrary

---

Creator, Creation, and Faith, is critical of Reumann, who analyzes the transcendentalist view of Karl Barth, the ontological view of Paul Tillich, the existential view of Rudolf Bultmann, and the eschatological view of Jürgen Moltmann, and argues that four attitudes to creation can be taken by Christians—*alienation* (withdrawal from world); *coalition* (identification with world); *innovation*; and *revolution*; and Bernhard W. Anderson, *Creation versus Chaos: The Reinterpretation of Mythical Symbolism in the Bible,* who emphasizes that the evil in the cosmos is not due to God but to the free choice of creature, and devotes much consideration to the ecological problem.

30 See Arend van Leeuwen, *Christianity in World History,* for a discussion of Christianity's role in developing a scientific technology. A controversy was stirred up by Lynn White, Jr., "The Historical Roots of Our Ecological Crisis," *Science* 155 (March 1967): 1203–7, which accused Christianity of causing the ecological crisis by fostering the notion of man's unlimited domination of nature based on Genesis 1–2, and which drew numerous replies, e.g., Karlfried Froelich, "The Ecology of Creation," *Theology Today* 27 (1970): 263–76; Eric G. Freudenstein, "Ecology and the Jewish Tradition," *Judaism* 19 (1970): 406–14; B. E. Santmire, *Brother Earth: Nature, God, and Ecology in a Time of Crisis,* who admits that the Church has indirectly encouraged anti-ecology; Gabriel Fackre, *Ecology Crisis: God's Creation and Man's Pollution*; Richard E. Sherrel, ed., *Ecology: Crisis and New Vision* (a symposium); Hans Jonas, "Technology and Responsibility" in James Robinson, ed., *Religion and the Humanizing of Man,* 1–19; Cyril Richardson, "A Christian Approach to Ecology," *Religion in Life* 41 (1972): 462–79; Lionel Basney, "Ecology and the Spiritual Concept of the Master," *Christians Scholars Review* 3 (1973): 49–50; and George S. Hendry, *Theology of Nature.*

31 Thus Peter Singer, *Animal Liberation: A New Ethics for our Treatment of Animals,* argues for rights of animals on a par with human rights. Some today even speak of "speciesism" as a sin similar to racism and sexism. On the other hand, the International Network for Religion and Animals, which publishes *Network News,* with more theological balance, promotes an ecumenical concern for animal welfare.

human willfulness but the order of the world established by its Creator. Questions of value, therefore, should not be relegated to the realm of human subjectivity, but rather should remain open to objective rational debate to which scientific discoveries are directly relevant. Science can sharpen our understanding of natural law, and natural law ethics can guide the technological application of science to human living.

But how could the empirical methods of science possibly contribute to the establishment of ethical norms? Is it not true that the classical ethical systems such as those of Aristotle or Kant have been developed independently of modern science? Must we admit that these traditional norms are open to falsification by modern scientific discoveries? Certainly it is fallacious to argue, as is so often done, that since Aristotle's natural science was completely overthrown by Galileo and that of Newton on whom Kant relied by Einstein, so must their ethics based on an obsolete science also be obsolete. Whatever modicum of truth there may be in Thomas Kuhn's famous theory of "scientific revolutions through paradigm shifts," the history of science shows a fundamental continuity from Aristotle to Einstein.[32] Einstein actually retrieved a more Aristotelian notion of space and time than Newton. Likewise ethics today continues to build on the foundations laid by Aristotle or Kant.

We can look to science therefore, not to create an ethics *ex nihilo*, but to assist in refining traditional ethics. The more science reveals to us about the structure and function of creatures, the more accurate will be our understanding of their teleology and hence of the natural law that furnishes the foundation of ethics. If art is to imitate nature and perfect it, the better we know nature the better will be our work of imitation and perfecting. The better also will be our stewardship of God's gifts.

The biblical and conciliar teaching that I have just expounded can in a more philosophical manner be formulated as a simple principle: Human beings are morally obliged to use and to modify the natural environment and their own bodies in accordance with their intrinsic teleology. If God's purposes are knowable, at least in part, through the intrinsic teleology of creatures and this teleology is manifested by scientific investigations, then an area of common interest for science and theology is opened up. Indeed, the Catholic tradition has always defended the existence of this common ground under the name of "natural moral law."

To illustrate and test this principle I will take two examples, the first from ecology, the second from bioethics, to exemplify the type of ethical argument that I believe is appropriate to each. In neither case will I attempt a detailed analysis, but only an illustrative outline.

---

[32] Thomas F. Kuhn, *The Structure of Scientific Revolutions,* with the criticism of William A. Wallace, OP, *Causality and Scientific Explanation,* vol. 2, 238ff.

Endangered Species

A prime concern of ecologists is the preservation of endangered species. According to the evolutionary reconstruction of the history of the earth, species arise from previous species and then disappear to make room for still newer species. Only a few species, usually in isolated niches of the environment, last for long. Why then is it a problem that the arrival of the human species is causing at an ever more rapid pace, increasing in our times to a panic, the destruction of other living species?[33]

The reason usually given for alarm is that this devastation of other life forms will so upset the ecological balance of the earth, that the human species also will be threatened with self-destruction. No doubt there is reason for alarm, if this alteration of the environment proceeds heedlessly and without planning. Is it not possible, however, that we can make plans so that as we displace other species we may create an artificial environment, a man-made ecological system even more suitable for human life than the so-called natural environment that has predominated until this century? Indeed as the human population increases and technology advances, is it not necessary for us to assume this control? Do we really need other animals than ourselves? Do we really need trees and flowers? Do we even need the sun and moon or the seasons, if we can more successively control and use nuclear fusion as the source of all the energy we need?

These questions reveal, I think, that there is a more basic reason for preserving the natural environment than the riskiness of radically altering it. Would we really want to live in a purely artificial environment, such as might be constructed on the moon—an environment without trees or flowers, birds or fish? Our need for a natural environment is not merely practical, it is also esthetic, or even more profoundly, contemplative. Biblical ethics, as well as that of Plato and Aristotle, hold that the ultimate fulfillment of human nature, its teleology, is the contemplation of God, and that the glory of God is revealed in the cosmos and especially in persons made in his image.[34] Hence, our need for the natural environment is not merely to supply us with energy, light, air, food, water, and a place to walk, but to provide us

---

[33] For summaries of the issues, see the special number of *Scientific American* 261 (September 1989), *Managing Planet Earth*, especially the articles "Managing Planet Earth" by William C. Clark, 46–57, and "Threats to Biodiversity" by Edward O. Wilson, 108–17.

[34] Aristotle, *Nicomachean Ethics*, Bk. X, c.7, 117a 12sq.; and St. Thomas Aquinas, *Summa theologiae* I–II, q. 3, a. 8. See also St. Augustine's *Confessions*, Bk IX, c.10, and the whole tradition of Platonic Christian Theology described in my book, *Theologies of the Body*, 103–47. Robert J. O'Connell in *St. Augustine's Confession: The Odyssey of the Soul* shows that Bks. XI-XIII of the *Confessions* that deal with time and the creation account in Genesis 1 are integral to the work because the soul returns to God through the contemplation of creation.

with the mirror in which we see God, both to delight our senses and to enrich our minds through scientific investigation. In short we have an ethical obligation to preserve our natural environment so that artists may paint it and scientists explore it for our delight, and to destroy a species is to lose an irreplaceable masterpiece.

You may object that the new technology of genetic reconstruction offers hope that some day we may get control of the very process of evolution and thus replace the present environment not just with parking lots, airports, and shopping malls, but with a new living ecosystem of far more wonderful lifeforms than we have today. I concede this is a real possibility, but a possibility that finally faces us with an oft-neglected truth that human "creativity" is not truly creation *ex nihilo* but imitation (the Aristotelian *mimesis*).[35] As stewards of God's creation, we are "co-creators" in that we can perfect nature, but only by imitating it, by realizing in more detail what is already present in outline in nature. Perhaps we can "control" evolution, but only by understanding and employing the forces and potentialities of nature and generating our "creative ideas" from contemplating the forms it already has. When we lose sight of this essentially mimetic character of human art, as modern art tends to do today, we end in an empty minimalism of ideas and feeling. Similarly in technology we end with an environment that is either too polluted or too sterile for human life.

Thus the ecological movement is profoundly right in declaring that we must treat our planet like a garden, to be perfected, yes—but to be reduced to a wasteland out of which we will create a new world for ourselves, no. Our human goal is to know God, the Divine Artist, in his works. Our art is like that of the performer who enters into the vision of the composer by interpreting his composition and thus shares that vision and delight, but who remains a performer and interpreter not a composer.

Euthanasia

Let us turn now from ecology to bioethics proper. A very controversial set of bioethical issues are those concerned with the obligation to treat dying or severely deteriorated persons and, more generally, issues of human control over life and death. Some, of course, deny that it is ever moral to destroy any living thing; others restrict this to sentient things. The Fifth Commandment is "Thou shalt not kill" (Ex 20:13) and Genesis seems to say that in the original design of God, men and even animals were vegetarians, and that the permission to eat meat was a concession to fallen humanity (Gn 1:30; 2:16;

---

[35] Cf. St. Thomas Aquinas, *Summa theologiae* I, q. 45, a. 5, against Neo-Platonizing Aristotelians who held that God can create (in the strict sense) lower creatures through the instrumentality of higher creatures.

9:2–5). Yet the Old Law sanctions capital punishment and just wars (e.g., Dt. 19:21–20:1). Jesus on the contrary seems to have taught non-violence, at least to other human beings (Mt 6:38–48), but Paul accepted law enforcement by the sword (Rm 13:4).

Catholic Tradition has harmonized these biblical teachings by holding that while humans may use plants and animals for any legitimate human purpose, they may not directly kill any innocent human being for any reason; yet the community may execute criminals to preserve the order of justice and the common good, and the community and individuals may defend themselves against aggression even if this results in homicide as an unintended although foreseen effect. Furthermore, it has usually been held by Catholic moralists that one may sometimes allow persons to die of injuries, disease, or old age, when the only means available to maintain their lives exacts too heavy a burden either on the victims or on those who have the responsibility of care.[36]

Why, in view of the various aforesaid qualifications of the commandment against killing, is it not permissible for intelligent and free human persons, knowing that death is inevitable at some time, to choose the most fitting time, and to kill themselves or permit others to do so? Are there not also situations in which it would be better for one human being to decide this for other sufferers who lack the competence or at least the courage to make this "death with dignity" decision for themselves?[37]

---

[36] See Cardinal Joseph Bernadin et al., *The Consistent Ethics of Life,* edited by Thomas G. Feuchtmann, for a general discussion; in which note especially the critical article of Frans Jozef van Beeck, SJ, "Weaknesses in the Consistent Ethics of Life: Some Systematic Theological Observations," 115–22. Also Germain G. Grisez and Joseph M. Boyle, Jr., *Life and Death with Liberty and Justice: A Contribution to the Euthanasia Debate.*

[37] The answer to these questions may depend on the more general issue of the methodology of moral judgement. Catholic moralists have generally held that there are some concrete negative moral norms founded on the fact that certain acts by their very nature are contradictory to the basic teleology of human nature. Hence in all circumstances and for whatever motive they are performed *objectively* morally evil *(intrinsice malum)* and thus are *exceptionless* ("absolute"). Thus Josef Fuchs, SJ, in his widely used treatise *Natural Law: A Theological Investigation* wrote, "For example, it can never happen that a prohibition of a direct destruction of unborn life-a principle of the natural law-could cease to be an absolute demand even in a difficult concrete situation, or out of charitable consideration for a mother and her family." The controversy over Paul VI's Encyclical *Humanae Vitae,* "On the Regulation of Birth," July 25, 1968, however, provoked an effort to revise this fundamental notion by a new methodology of moral judgement called by its critics (of whom I am one) "Proportionalism" because of its reliance on what is called the "principle of preference" or "of proportionate reason." Surprisingly, Fr. Fuchs himself led this revision by what still remains one of its clearest statements, "The Absoluteness of Moral Terms" (1970) reprinted in Charles E. Curran and R. A. McCormick, SJ, *Readings in Moral Theology, No. 1.*

In the Catholic tradition the basic problem on whose answer all these others depend has been from the beginning whether suicide is sometimes licit, as pagan moralists taught and as seemed to some to be the case in martyrdom. The veneration of the martyrs led to moralists making the distinction between indirect and direct killing, and later this distinction proved helpful in discussing the morality of war.[38] As for direct suicide the answer commonly accepted by theologians was that to kill oneself contradicts the fact that life has been given us by God only in stewardship, to use in God's service but not to destroy. As some recent writers have pointed out, this argument seems to presuppose what it is supposed to prove, namely, that God has in fact limited his gift of intelligent, self-determining life in this way.[39]

No doubt it was for this reason that other theologians, notably St. Thomas Aquinas,[40] bolstered this argument from God's dominion with two others. The first is that as social animals we share in the common good to

---

Moral Norms and Catholic Tradition. See also the important articles of Peter Knauer, SJ, and Louis Janssens in the same volume and Bruno Schuller, SJ, "The Double Effect in Catholic Thought: A Reevalution" in *Doing Evil to Achieve Good*, edited by Richard A. McCormick, SJ, and Paul Ramsey, 165–92. This position has been extensively criticized as both impracticable and self-contradictory; for the literature, see Germain Grisez, with the help of Joseph M. Boyle, Jr., et al., *The Way of the Lord Jesus*, vol. 1 of *Christian Moral Principles*, see references to "proportionalism" in the index, 943. The risks of this proportionalist method are evident from the fact that some, for example, Daniel Maguire, *Death by Choice*, think it justifies euthanasia in certain current circumstances, while others such as Schüller or McCormick reject suicide as forbidden by a *virtually* exceptionless concrete norm because they feel that only in very rare cases would its values outweigh its disvalues. Although proportionalism still influences some Catholic moralists, its denial that some moral acts concretely defined are "intrisically evil," that is, are evil in all circumstances and even with "good intentions" are evil, whether they concern serious or light matter, was definitely rejected by John Paul II, *Veritatis Splendor.*

[38] In an unpublished paper prepared for the National Conference of Catholic Bishops' official dialogue with Methodists, 1986–89, on "How the Roman Catholic Position on Euthanasia Developed," I traced this history. The most authoritative current statements of the Catholic Church relating to these pro-life issues are those of the Congregation for the Doctrine of the Faith, *Declaration on Procured Abortion,* 18 November 1974, *Declaration on Euthanasia,* May 5, 1980, and *Instruction on Respect for Human Life in its Origin and on the Dignity of Procreation,* February 22, 1987, and also the papal teachings of *Humanae Vitae* and *Veritatis Splendor* discussed above, the latter of which fully confirmed the instructions of the Congregation for the Doctrine of the Faith.

[39] See Bruno Schuller, SJ, "What Ethical Principles are Universally Valid," *Theology Digest* 19 (1971): 23–28.

[40] *Summa theologiae* II–II, q. 64, a. 5. The development of this by Francisco de Vitoria and Cardinal de Lugo are discussed in my paper "How the Roman Catholic Position on Euthanasia Developed" referred to in note 38.

which we therefore owe our services and our persons, but by killing ourselves we deprive society of these goods to which it has a right in return for the good shared with us. The objection to this argument from the common good is that it does not seem to exclude suicide by someone who is no longer of service to society, perhaps indeed has become a burden to it.

The third argument is that suicide is contradictory to the fundamental human need to live; that is, it is contradictory to the intrinsic teleology of human nature. It would seem that Aquinas in proposing this third argument from intrinsic teleology has made explicit a presupposition of the other two arguments without which they are inconclusive and even circular. It is because suicide contradicts the intrinsic good of human nature that it also contradicts the good of society, since society exists to aid the perfection of its members. Even when a member seems no longer useful to the community, and has even in some respects become a burden to it, he remains precious to that society precisely because it exists for the good of each and all of its members.

Again, we know that God has made us stewards of our life but has retained his own absolute dominion over its beginning and end, not simply by revelation, but by the natural law that is simply an expression of the intrinsic teleology that God has given to human nature. To take our own life is to deny who we are, persons made to live, to guard and cultivate ourselves as living beings. So understood, the traditional argument against suicide, and consequently against all forms of euthanasia, remains valid and free of tautology. We know that our dominion over ourselves is that of stewardship not of autonomy when we understand the intrinsic teleology of our own natures, physical and spiritual.

When we apply this general approach to the problems of bioethics and environmentalism, we get the following results. Every bioethical problem reduces to a question about the intrinsic teleology of the human person. This teleology must not be understood in a physicalist sense, but also it must not be understood dualistically.[41] To take a rather crass example, consider the discussion of homosexuality and the attitude to be taken toward it

---

41 Thus Charles E. Curran, *Tensions in Moral Theology*, writes, "[T]he primary problem with the official hierarchical teaching is its physicalism or biologism. The physical act must always be present, and no one can interfere with the physical or biological aspect for any reason whatsoever. The physical becomes absolutized. Most revisionist Catholic theologians today will argue that for the good of the person it is legitimate at times to interfere with the physical structure of the act. Note that it is precisely in questions of sexual morality that Catholic teaching has absolutized the physical and identified the physical with the truly human or moral aspect. For example, there has always existed an important distinction between killing and murder, since murder is the morally condemned act, whereas killing is the physical act which is not always wrong. However, artificial contraception understood as a physical act is said to be always and everywhere wrong" (76). This caricatures the "official hierarchical teaching."

by the physician and the psychiatrist. It would be physicalistic simply to say that male homosexuality is unnatural because the teleology of the genital organs shows that penis is adapted to the vagina and not other orifices; but it would be dualistic simply to deny that it is unnatural on the grounds that morality of physical acts depends wholly on the spiritual meaning they have for the actors, not on their mere physical details. The true reason homosexuality is wrong is that human sexuality as a dimension of the total human person has an intrinsic teleology that is not realized except in a male-female relationship of committed love consummated by using their bodies in accordance with their natural functions. Thus the teleology of the genitals is morally significant but not in isolation from the meaning of sexuality for the whole human person, and this spiritual meaning can be realized only by an appropriate use of the body.[42]

Another example can be found in the bioethical question about the obligation to use so-called "ordinary" or "extraordinary" means to maintain life in the severely deteriorated patient, such as one in the persistent vegetative state.[43] To argue, as some do, that intervenous nutrition and hydration are always ordinary and obligatory if they are necessary to maintain life on the grounds that to discontinue them is to kill the patient, or because life, even in this condition, is still an inestimable value outweighing most burdens of care, is to forget that the obligation to take means to preserve life diminishes as the value of this life, measured in terms of its intrinsic teleology, diminishes. Human bodily life by its intrinsic teleology has its value from its service to activities of the whole human person, and especially to those activities that are specifically human, the spiritual activities of knowledge and free choice. When these activities become permanently more and more difficult or impossible the corresponding obligation to preserve bodily life diminishes. That is why most moralists will admit that it is not obligatory to prolong life in the person who is actually dying if this becomes proportionately burdensome; and it seems to me that this holds also for such cases as the irreversibly unconscious vegetative state, even if one maintains that such a

---

[42] This is my understanding of the ethical basis of the "Letter to Bishops of the Catholic Church on the Pastoral Care of Homosexual Persons" of the Congregation for the Doctrine of the Faith, October 1, 1986, www.vatican.va/roman_curia/congregations/cfaith/documents/rc_con_cfaith_doc_19861001_homosexual-persons_en.html. For criticisms of that document, see *The Vatican and Homosexuality*, Jeannine Grammick and Pat Furey, eds., which includes my defense of the Church's position, "Compassion and Sexual Orientation," 105–11.

[43] For medical views, American Medical Association, Report of the Judicial Council, "Treatment of Patients in Irreversible Coma," March 15, 1986, American Academy of Neurology, 1986. "Care and Management of Persistent Vegetative State Patients," *Neurology* 39 (January 1989): 125–27.

stable patient is not dying is debatable.[44] In every instance the important thing is to establish intrinsic teleology as the ultimate measure of morality.

Conclusion

If modern science is understood in such a way that it does not exclude teleology, but recognizes teleological explanations as correlative to explanations through efficient agency in all natural (i.e., uniform) processes, then sufficient common ground is obtained between science and Christian theology to serve as the basis for profitable discussion on moral questions to which science can provide moral theology with necessary empirical understanding, and theology can provide scientists with ethical guidance.

From the side of theology this implies openness to the important contribution of science to the understanding of the structure and function of the human person in relation to the natural environment considered as a total ecosystem and the effects on this system of human behavior. The theologian will interpret this understanding gained from science as an enhanced insight into human nature as the work of the Creator, and hence as a way to understand God's plan and will for human life that can be confirmed by Revelation and integrated into the total Christian view of the cosmos and our role in it. The fundamental principle for this integration is the biblical teaching that God has created us in his image and given us a stewardship over his creation, a stewardship to be exercised creatively and harmoniously within the Creator's general purposes.

---

[44] In an address to an international medical meeting, John Paul II, "On Life-Sustaining Treatments and the Vegetative State" (March 20, 2004) accepted their medical judgment that it is not at present possible safely to distinguish a reversible state of minimal consciousness from a state of irreversible unconsciousness and so hydration and nutrition may not be withdrawn from patients unless they are actually dying, although he did not change the ethical principles in the documents cited in previous notes. The U.S. Bishops have requested a clarification from the Holy See. All sides of the debate admit that the decision must be based on conservative diagnosis and avoidance of seeming support for euthanasia. The case in favor of withdrawal of life support when it is morally certain that the patient will not regain consciousness is explained by Kevin D. O'Rourke, OP, "The Catholic Tradition on Foregoing Life Support," *The National Catholic Bioethics Quarterly*, Autumn 2005, 3, 537–53. For the opposite view, based on a polyteleological stance, see William E. May, et al. Feeding and Hydrating the Permanently Unconscious and Other Vulnerable Persons," *Issues in Law and Medicine* 3 (1987): 203–10. I favor O'Rourke's arguments but a final decision of the Magisterium should be obeyed.

CHAPTER 17

Spirituality and Counseling*

Physical, Psychological and Ethical Counseling

THE ULTIMATE AIM OF ALL "COUNSELING" IS TO ASSIST clients to make decisions that are realistic.[1] These decisions must also be ethical, because unethical decisions ignore the real requirements of human well-being. They will probably lead to consequences that are harmful to the one who decides as well as to others. Such help is needed for many types of decisions, only one of which is specifically and directly the client's *spiritual* welfare. What does "spiritual" welfare mean? Today that term and its related nouns "spirit" and "spirituality" are used so loosely as to be almost meaningless.[2] Therefore, I must begin this essay by trying to give a precise meaning to "spiritual counseling" in distinction from other forms of counseling.

Four types of counseling can be distinguished, so closely inter-related that they are often confused:

First, there is a range of kinds of counseling that we can group as *physical* because they deal directly with the counselee's bodily well-being. *Economic* counseling helps clients make realistic decisions about how to obtain the material goods necessary or at least useful for a good life. *Medical* counseling

---

* Published as "Spirituality and Counseling," in Robert J. Wicks, ed., *Handbook of Spirituality for Ministers,* Vol. 2, *Perspectives for the 21st Century* (New York: Paulist Press, 1995), 656–70.

[1] For a fuller discussion of the concept of counseling and its ethical norms, see B. M. Ashley, OP, and K. D. O'Rourke, OP, *Health Care Ethics: A Theological Analysis,* 4th ed., 89–106.

[2] For an introduction to this field, see Richard Woods, OP, *Christian Spirituality: God's Presence Through the Ages;* Cheslyn Jones, G. Wainwright, and E. Yarnold, SJ, eds., *The Study of Spirituality;* John Garvey, ed., *Modern Spirituality: An Anthology;* and my *Spiritual Direction in the Dominican Tradition.*

helps them make realistic decisions about health. *Security* counseling helps in making realistic decisions about how to protect oneself from injury by external physical forces.

Second, *psychological* counseling (including all types of psychotherapy except those that are purely medical) aims to free counselees from those emotional and cognitive factors that limit their ability to make decisions that are free and objective. Obviously the ranges of these first two kinds of counseling, the physical and the psychological, somewhat overlap, since mental problems can arise from economic, medical, and security conditions that must be corrected or ameliorated before successful psychotherapy is feasible. Conversely clients who lack the clarity of mind and freedom needed to make realistic decisions cannot deal successfully with physical problems.

Ethical counseling, too often confused with psychological counseling, deals with decisions that are fully conscious and fully free and that require us to choose among alternative ways of acting to reach the realistic goals of human living. Such ethical counseling extends both to the management of clients' own private behaviors and to their social relations with other persons. Sometimes the counselor and client agree on a worldview and value system—for example, when both are Catholics who accept the Church's faith and moral guidance. In that case the counselor helps the client form a prudent conscience based on the moral norms accepted by both and on a careful examination of the circumstances and possible consequences of alternative decisions. When, on the other hand, the counselor and client have different worldviews and value systems, moral counseling can only take the form of "value clarification."[3] In such cases the counselor can help clients clarify their personal values so as to recognize inconsistencies in their thinking or behaving, but only rarely are counselors in a position even to attempt to change the priorities of their clients. Hence a client's worldview and value system must be taken as a given, unless it is obviously unacceptable in the society in which the client has to live or becomes seriously dangerous to others. Hence ethical counselors, for example, a lawyer, cannot counsel a criminal to act consistently with his commitment to a life of crime. But they would exceed professional limits if they were to attempt to make a Protestant a Catholic, a Jew, or Muslim, or a Secular Humanist a Christian by changing their religious commitment from one set of moral values to another. Thus when moral counseling is limited to value-clarification it tends to overlap with psychological counseling since psychotherapists also generally make no attempt to alter the value systems of their clients unless they are obviously dangerous or socially unacceptable.

---

3 See Brian P. Hall et al., eds., *Value Clarification as a Learning Process: A Handbook for Religious Education,* and Hall's *The Personal Discernment Inventory: An Instrument for Spiritual Guides.*

When, however, the counselor and client have value systems that are the same or largely overlap, the ethical counselor ought not to confine his services simply to helping the client solve particular moral dilemmas. In moral matters it is not enough to make particular good decisions, it is also necessary to help clients develop moral integrity or good character. Character is formed by certain decisional skills or "virtues" that make it easier for a person to act in a consistently moral manner. In helping clients form such moral skills, counselors can profit from classical "virtue theory" that provides a psychologically based classification known as the *four cardinal virtues*.[4]

In this classification *temperance* (moderation) enables one to achieve a realistic control over one's drives for pleasure, *fortitude* (courage) over one's drives for aggression. These two sets of drives are essentially biological and the virtues that control them resemble such bodily skills as are developed by athletes and dancers. In contrast to these two cardinal virtues are two others that perfect the more spiritual aspect of the human person. In the spiritual will the virtue of *justice* prompts concern for the rights of others. In the spiritual intelligence *prudence* facilitates moral reasoning for making realistic decisions. Hence, the scope of temperance and fortitude largely overlaps with the field of the drives and emotions with which psychological counseling is concerned, but the field of justice and prudence is especially that of moral counseling.

In our culture various aspects of ethical counseling are performed by various kinds of experts. For example, decisions that affect human rights and hence have an ethical aspect often require the lawyer's advice. Most often, however, people make ethical decisions with the help of the informal counseling of friends or family and the clergy. Yet in my opinion although the clergy or others with a religious ministry are often called upon for ethical counseling this is not the type of counseling that more properly characterizes their role. The special role of the clergy is, I would argue, spiritual counseling, although I by no means intend to imply that it is exclusively theirs. Other non-ordained persons with adequate theological and pastoral training can perform this task successfully, often more successfully than clerics.

Aims and Objectives of Spiritual Counseling

For many people in today's culture "spirituality" is a term that connotes a certain distaste for "organized religion." Frederick M. Denny in an essay "To Serve Allah in a Foreign Land: Muslim Spirituality in the North American Diaspora,"[5] describes the situation well:

---

[4] See Josef Pieper, *The Four Cardinal Virtues,* and my *Living the Truth in Love: A Biblical Introduction to Moral Theology,* 34–40.

[5] *Listening* 33 (1998).

It might be that "spirituality" is not the best term for characterizing Muslims' religious lives in North America in general. The word has become a euphemism for religion in an age when many peopled do not choose to affiliate with traditional Christian or Jewish denominational religion, for example, but instead want to enrich their lives by means of a spiritual quest at a personal-individual rather than a tradition-institutional level. In other words, for many people, spirituality is "in" and "religion" is "out." There are various forms of contemporary spirituality, ranging from engagement with Asian religions, New Age movements and Neo-Paganism to non-denominational, usually strongly evangelical Christian churches including the growing "mega-churches" around North America.

Thus even the Religious Right tends to emphasize private religious experience at the expense of a visible church with the authority to guide the individual conscience. Yet if one considers the fact that we human persons are intensely social in nature it is difficult to see how an effective spirituality can be achieved except in a community of a common faith. Why would anyone need a spiritual counselor, or how can such a counselor be certified as trustworthy if individuals can find their own spiritual path without social support? The concept of "spirituality," therefore, cannot be separated from the concept of "religion" that implies some kind of human community that shares essentially the same convictions about life.

In my book *Theologies of the Body: Humanist and Christian*[6] I emphasized that it is a mistake to restrict, as is so often done, the term "religion" to faith in God or even some transcendent Absolute. Scholars of comparative religion point out that if we are to make meaningful comparisons between the great world religions we must abstract from the *content* of their beliefs and simply define them by their *function* as "worldviews and value systems." This becomes obvious when we note that though everyone considers Buddhism one of the great world religions, Buddhists do not believe in God or in the human person but in an ineffable Void.

If, therefore, we define "religion" as a worldview and value system shared by a community, I believe that we should also admit that the Secular Humanism so widespread in the world today is a genuine religion.[7] Though secular humanists reject the term "religion" as a name for their worldview and value system, it functions for them in much the same way that Christianity, Judaism, Islam, or Buddhism do for their own adherents. Although one of its chief values is "freedom of thought," Secular Humanism is a uni-

6 Ashley, *Theologies of the Body: Humanist and Christian.*
7 On the function definition of "religion," see Keith A. Roberts, *Religion in Sociological Perspective*, 3–26.

fied and coherent worldview in which the supreme value is the autonomy of the individual. Obviously there is a paradox in such an individualistic religion, but watching TV or reading most of our "self-help" books can easily demonstrate that Secular Humanism is the shared conviction and way of life of very many Americans. In Secular Humanism the autonomy of the individual is an article of faith, and dissent from that faith entails an excommunication or exclusion from an in-group not very different from the excommunications enforced in the more "organized" world religions. Thus the most workable definition of "spirituality" is a personal commitment to a worldview and value system shared with a committed community the members of which strive to live in an honest and consistent manner.[8]

Thus even if the worldview of and value system shared by secular humanists denies the existence of a spiritual realm transcending our sensible experience, it is not an oxymoron to speak of a Secular Humanist's spirituality. It is important to make this point because it means that there will be as many types of spiritual counseling as there are religions, including the spirituality of persons who think they have no "religion."

Since there are different kinds of worldviews and value systems[9] each with its own type of spirituality, unless we surrender all personal autonomy and simply conform to the community in which we find ourselves, we are each faced with the inescapable necessity of deciding which is the truest and best. Thus we must compare the range of what Paul Tillich called "ultimate concerns," that is, what a given person values most in life. Karl Rahner spoke of this decision and commitment as the "fundamental option" that involves the "fundamental freedom" of any person at the root of our "categorial freedom" to make particular concrete practical decisions.[10] In the classical moral theology of the Roman Catholic tradition this was called "the choice of one's ultimate end."

St. Thomas Aquinas argued that in every "human act," that is, every conscious and free choice no matter how trivial it might be, the prime motivator of every choice was the ultimate end to which the chooser was already committed. If this commitment was realistically in conformity with the needs of the human person, either those that are innate or those elevated by divine grace, then choices that further that commitment are respectively natural or

---

8 See William Herbrechtsmeier, "Buddhism and the Definition of Religion: One More Time," *Journal for the Scientific Study of Religion* 32 (1993): 1–18, who argues that "the belief and reverence for superhuman beings cannot be understood as the chief distinguishing characteristic of religious phenomena."

9 *Choosing a Worldview and Value System: An Ecumenical Apologetics* (Staten Island, NY: Alba House, 2000).

10 On this topic, see two other articles in this collection: "Can We Make a Fundamental Option?" and "Integral Human Fulfillment."

graced good acts. Choices contradictory to such a realistic commitment are sins, and if knowingly, freely, and deliberately made concerning serious matters are *mortal sins* that convert this commitment to some other ultimate value that is not true happiness. For example the deliberate choice to do serious harm to another person is a mortal sin that changes one's ultimate end from love of God and neighbor to a destructive self-interest.

Sins are said to be *venial* if they do not involve informed, free, and deliberate choices or do not concern serious matters. As such they do not change a person's commitment to true happiness but gradually weaken that commitment at the risk of eventual mortal sin. Thus spiritual counseling, since it concerns commitment to the authentic goal of human life, must help the client become free of mortal sin by conversion to this true goal and must support a consistent effort by the client also to eliminate venial sin. It is odd that so much writing about spirituality today says so much about love and so little about sin. Granted that the positive aim of spiritual counseling is to deepen the client's commitment to the true goal of life, namely, love of God and neighbor, helping clients free themselves from the bondage of sin, especially mortal sin, is a necessary objective. What physician would talk only about good diet and exercise, and never warn about the effects of bad eating habits and lack of exercise or fail to point out that surgery or chemotherapy for a cancer must not be refused? Spiritual growth is not possible without a struggle against its negation—sin.

Thus "spiritual counseling" in an analogical sense that abstracts from the differences between these religions can be defined as that form of counseling that aims to help clients discover their fundamental option (ultimate concern, ultimate end) or commitment to a worldview and value system. It also helps them consider whether they ought to change that worldview and values system and live consistently and honestly in conformity to that life goal. Clearly this presupposes that the client is making good physical, psychological, and ethical decisions in relation to this ultimate goal.

Yet too often, I believe, these other types of counseling founder on a failure of persons to recognize who they really are by reason of their fundamental option. Until one faces this issue realistically life can only be a succession of contradictions that gets one nowhere. Hence the specific counseling task the clergy and others in explicitly religious ministry is *spiritual* counseling, not simply ethical counseling, since it involves what a Christian would call "the salvation of one's soul."

The spiritual counselor, therefore, must help clients explicitly recognize the worldview and value system to which they are in fact committed and that is dominating their lives. They must then be helped to ask and answer for themselves whether they have committed themselves without proper reflection to the wrong goal and need to change it to a more realistic goal. In the process of spiritual counseling it may become clear to the client that his or her priorities are inconsistent, confused, or lacking in a dynamic motivation that will make the individual fully effective in practical life. Hence spiritual counselors or "directors" aim to help clients not only choose a worldview and value system for their lives, but also recognize the implications of this commitment and the need to make it more consistent, profound, and dynamic.

Spiritual Counseling and the Structure of the Human Person

In our present culture, however, the evaluation of these different types of human commitment often lacks any criteria or point of references. A principle source of this confusion is a faulty anthropology and psychology. Many psychologists today identify human thought and free choice with the activity of the brain. Certainly the marvelous human brain is a necessary instrument for the human activities of abstract thought and free choice. Nevertheless, these specifically human activities transcend the spatial-temporal capacities of a material brain and distinguish human life from animal life and constitute us *persons* whose souls are truly *spiritual*, that is, not of the material order and thus destined to immortality. This distinction from animal life by the capacity for abstract thought and freedom of choice is empirically evidenced by human creativity in language, diversity of culture, and technical control over nature that comes from our capacity to explore the laws of nature.

Secular humanists are generally materialists, yet by using the term "spirituality" they admit the possibility that we humans can somehow transcend purely material concerns. For example, they often speak of the "spiritual values" of the fine arts or of other forms of human creativity. Yet they also generally assume that science has established that these "spiritual" activities are purely emotional and subjective and can be accounted for by the identity of our minds with brain activities. Why then call them "spiritual"?[11] On the other hand, it is equally unconvincing to identify the human self with the human spirit alone, as does Platonism and many eastern religions. Such a claim that the true self is purely spiritual results in the doctrine that the spirit is reincarnated in successive bodies in contrast to the doctrine shared by Judaism, Christianity, and Islam that there will be a bodily resurrection of the total person in eternal life. Such a dualistic anthropology tends to support the notion that the human spirit is only a part of the Divine Spirit into which after many reincarnations it will be absorbed.

---

[11] Prominent scientists can be found, however, who question this notion of mind-body identity. See the Nobel Laureate Sir John Eccles, *The Human Mystery,* The Gifford Lectures, 1977–78; and Roger Penrose, *The Emperor's New Mind: Concerning Computers, Minds, and the Laws of Physics.*

Christian Spiritual Counseling

Christian anthropology shares with Judaism and Islam this conviction that the human person has been created with a material body and a immaterial soul so intrinsically related that God will restore their union after death in resurrection. Thus each one will exist in eternal life as the unique person the Creator created it to be; we will not be absorbed into some impersonal Absolute. These three monotheistic religions agree that the true destiny of every created person is an eternal life in God's presence. Christians further believe that this communion with a personal God has been made possible by free choice of the Son of God to became incarnate in order to free us from our sinful alienation from the Father by the power of the Holy Spirit.

If this Christian anthropology is accepted, then the counseling relation itself becomes a paradigm of the interpersonal relationships in which our relation to God is destined to culminate. The biblical God is our supremely wise and patient Counselor as well as our Creator who bestows on us our individual freedom and guides us on the way to our ultimate fulfillment in the community of all persons, divine and created, who freely choose each other in love. Thus Christian spiritual counseling is conceived as a participation in the activity of the Divine Counselor who is the Holy Spirit of the Son who has chosen to share our human condition and the Father who created us. This participation always has the character of a communion in meditative prayer in which the counselor and the client together seek to respond to the Holy Spirit.

Thus Christian spiritual counseling aims at cooperating with the Holy Spirit in forming human persons in the image of Jesus Christ by the gift of the three theological virtues of Christian *faith, hope,* and *love* bestowed in baptism. Faith transforms the human spiritual intellect; hope and love transform the spiritual will, and thus transform the human person into the likeness of Jesus, the God-Man. Eastern Christian spirituality even dares to speak of this as a 'deification" *(theosis)*.[12] While the cardinal moral virtues free the human person from undue attachment to temporal values, they also facilitate the work of the theological virtues by which the human person attains direct contact with the living God, Father, Son, and Holy Spirit.

For modern psychology under the influence of the anthropology of Sigmund Freud, our creative, specifically human activities that reach their highest realization in mysticism are attributed to the unconscious or subconscious psyche. It is supposed that a psychological function that Freud called the "Censor" commonly prevents these creative processes from entering into the Ego of self-conscious life. Carl G. Jung, though he had greater respect for

---

[12] See Thomas Spidlik, *The Spirituality of the Christian East,* 332–34. and references in the Topical Index, 446.

religious phenomena than did Freud, also attempted to explain these processes as the product of a primitive "collective unconscious." I have argued elsewhere,[13] however, that it is utterly paradoxical to assign the highest, most human, most personal, most creative and free activities of the human person to the *animal pole* of the psyche that is deterministically instinctive and unfree. The great mystics and theoreticians of mysticism, such as Meister Eckhart and Teresa of Avila, locate these activities at the *spiritual pole* of the psyche in a "Super-Consciousness," an *apex mentis* or *ratio superior.* (Note that this "Super-Consciousness" is not to be confused with the Freudian Super-Ego that pertains to subconscious life.)

Besides Freud's materialism, two valid clinical observations seem to have misled him. First, we are commonly most clearly aware of the contents of the Ego, because this is the area of the practical, verbalizable consciousness of everyday life. The superconscious level of the psyche, however, is the level of insights so profound that they are difficult or impossible to verbalize. Thus Jacques Maritain in his *Creative Imagination in Art and Poetry*[14] showed that an artist usually begins to produce a work with a formative idea that cannot be verbalized, but that is expressible only in the work of art itself. Again, true human love cannot be adequately verbalized yet it animates the very depths and center of the human spirit. This is why for many their commitment to matters of ultimate concern, their life goal, is very difficult to put into words and, with the help of the spiritual counselor, must gradually be formulated.

The second clinical observation that has led to confusing the spiritual superconscious pole of the psyche with its unconscious animal pole of instinctive drives and primary processes is that our creative moments often also involve a release of suppressed images and emotions. In psychoanalytic free association "a regression in the service of the Ego" takes place in the process of free association in the presence of a non-judgmental and supporting analyst.[15] Similarly in the process of "brainstorming" people find it easier to formulate creative ideas because the facilitator assures them that no one will criticize unconventional thinking. Nevertheless, there is a vast difference between the suppressed contents of the animal subconscious and the suppressed content of spiritual creativity. What they have in common is simply the lowering of the inhibitions (the Censor) necessary for us to carry on the routine of practical every day life. Perhaps when Jesus said, "Unless you become like little children you cannot enter the kingdom of heaven," he meant that the realm of the spirit can be closed by the practicalities of adult

---

[13] "A Psychological Model with a Spiritual Dimension," *Pastoral Psychology* (May 1972): 31–40.

[14] Maritain, *Creative Imagination in Art and Poetry,* and my *Theologies of the Body,* 312–19.

[15] On this see Silvano Arieti, *Creativity: The Magic Synthesis.*

life and must be again opened to spiritual realities by a childlike transparency.

Thus spiritual counseling resembles psychoanalysis in that in both processes the ego with its practical, routine concerns must be quieted in order that suppressed activities of the psyche can emerge and be recognized by the counselee. They differ in that what should be permitted to emerge in psychoanalysis are unconscious processes that are reducing the freedom of conscious life, while in spiritual counseling it is the creative superconscious processes that must be allowed to emerge.

St. Catherine of Siena, in her classic *Dialogue* with God the Father, received from him three rules of spiritual counseling.[16] These rules are characteristic of the whole Christian tradition of spiritual counseling from the time of the Desert Fathers.[17] The first rule is an application of Jesus' warning in the Sermon on the Mount: "Do not judge if you would not be judged." The counselor seeks to understand the working of the Holy Spirit in the client, knowing that the Holy Spirit alone can know the depths of any human person. Unless counselors take this attitude of humility before the client, they will be blinded by their own spiritual deficiencies and be tempted to dominate rather than help the client to spiritual freedom. This rule resembles the "unconditional acceptance" demanded of psychological counselors, yet it goes much further, since it is an awareness of the sacred character of the work of the Holy Spirit in the depths of the human person.

The second rule received by Catherine follows from the first. Since the activity of the Holy Spirit in the client (as well as in the counselor) is mysterious, neither must be fooled by superficial religious "experiences." This rule is especially important in our culture in which "experience" is so highly valued and often too much trusted. Too many seek out spiritual direction in the hope of novel experiences. While there is indeed an experiential aspect of spiritual life, spiritual progress is not to be evaluated by emotional, imaginative, or even intellectually insightful "experiences." St. John of the Cross urges us not to pay much attention even to genuine visions and revelations. He says that not only are most such experiences liable to illusion, but even when they are genuinely from God their purpose is accomplished for spiritual advancement by the very fact of God's gift. Hence they should be received simply with thanksgiving, not with attachment or with a demand

---

16 *St. Catherine of Siena: The Dialogue,* translation and introduction by Susanne Noffke, OP, preface by Giuliana Cavallini, with commentary by Noffke, *Catherine of Siena: Vision Through a Distant Eye.* For a modern manual that is up-to-date in its psychology, see Carolyn Graton, *Guidelines for Spiritual Direction,* vol. 3 of *Studies in Formative Spirituality,* ed. by Adrian van Kamm, CSSp., and Susan A. Muto.

17 See Ashley, "Catherine of Siena's Principles of Spiritual Direction," *Spirituality Today* 33 (March 1981): 43–52. Reprinted in Kevin G. Culligan, OCD, ed. *Spiritual Direction: Contemporary Readings,* 188–95.

for more.[18] Catherine and John and all the great Christian spiritual writers emphasize that growth in holiness is growth in love of God and neighbor, a love that is founded in faith in God's guidance and of God's love of the neighbor and fostered by hope of union with God and neighbor. Consequently the counselor should be concerned principally with whether the counselee is advancing in the theological virtues of faith, hope, and charity, since Christian holiness consists essentially in these virtues. All good counseling has moments of encouragement and of confrontation with reality. Good spiritual counseling, therefore, encourages every indication of growth in faith, hope, and love, and confronts the client with every indication of any other motivation or of any other reliance in the client's spiritual striving except on God in faith, hope, and love.

The third rule transmitted by Catherine is that the spiritual counselor should accept the uniqueness of every counselee. St. Thomas Aquinas says that God created each human person as a unique image of himself, reflecting something of his own perfection.[19] Every person reflects God in a unique way and thus makes an irreplaceable contribution to God's creation. Consequently the Holy Spirit, as the supreme Counselor, leads each person in a unique way to the Triune Community that is the One God.

Counseling Risks and Gains

In addition to these fundamental principles stated by St. Catherine, a number of other cautions and suggestions can be made based on certain actual cases. The first of these, common to all types of counseling, is the risk of co-dependence. Temporary dependence of the client on the counselor of course cannot be avoided since it is intrinsic to the relation. This dependence can also legitimately become permanent in cases where the client is a disciple of the counselor. Thus in the monastic tradition monks were often dependent on the guidance of the same abbot throughout a lifetime. It is noteworthy, however, that Jesus said to his disciples, "For if I do not go, the Paraclete will not come to you. But if I go I will send him to you" (Jn 18:7b). He was saying that the kind of dependence they had on him in his earthly life had to yield to a reliance on the interior guidance of the Holy Spirit if they were to fully mature in his image. A failure on the part of counselors to work to make their guidance *dispensable* by the client can lead to disaster. They are then no longer working primarily for the welfare of the client but to meet their own needs. I

---

[18] *The Ascent of Mount Carmel,* translated by E. Allison Peers, Bk. 11, ch. 11. For a discusson of such extraordinary phenomena, see Jordan Aumann, OP, *Theology of Christian Perfection,* 654–75.

[19] *Summa theologiae* I, q. 47, a. 2. Modern notions of "democracy" and "equality" fail in that they do not acknowledge the true uniqueness of the individual as especially gifted by God. On this see the essay in this collection on "Hierarchy and Ecclesiology."

know of a well-meaning and spiritual gifted priest who was of help to many as a spiritual director. One nun became increasingly dependent on him for guidance. To have an easier access to his direction than was possible in her cloistered situation, she finally left her community and religious life. The priest counselor in turn came to feel so responsible for her that he finally reluctantly left the priesthood and married her, thus deserting the other clients whom he had helped or might in the future have helped by his gifts as a spiritual director. Evidently, under the guise of a "responsibility" to one client, this priest had become dependent on his counselee to satisfy his own emotional needs.

On the other hand there are classic examples among the saints where counseling relationships developed into genuine friendships that were of mutual spiritual benefit. Typical examples are the spiritual friendships of the Dominicans Bl. Raymond of Saxony and Diana D'Andalo and of St. Catherine of Siena and Bl. Raymond of Capua. The Carmelites St. Teresa of Avila and St. John of the Cross worked together for the reform of their order and are honored as Doctors of the Church, while St. Francis de Sales and St. Jane de Chantal became founders of two religious congregations. The letters recording these friendships, however, show great sensitivity to the need to avoid co-dependency.

Again, spiritual counselors have a double task. On the one hand they must encourage the client and reinforce every indication of genuine spiritual progress. John of the Cross says that most Christians striving for holiness are like the Hebrews in the desert who came again and again to the edge of the Promised Land. Each time as they were about to enter they grew fearful and turned back to wander about in the wilderness for a long time before again approaching the border. "No pain, no gain," say physical trainers, and so in the spiritual life real progress is possible only by plunging into what St. John of the Cross called "the dark nights of the soul and of the spirit."[20] The first dark night is necessary to free the person from "consolations," the second and more profound to free the spirit from depending on anything but God possessed by faith, hope, and love. St. Catherine in her second rule speaks of these same periods of spiritual "dryness." It is at these times of darkness that the support of the spiritual counselor is especially necessary, just as is that of a psychological counselor in emotional crises, or the physician in depressions.

On the other hand, a spiritual director must not be afraid to confront clients with the hard facts of their defects to which they may be blind or to expose their illusions that arise from ambiguous experiences that can even have a demonic origin.

One of the very important contributions that St. Ignatius Loyola and the Jesuit tradition of spiritual direction is a special emphasis on the ancient

---

[20] *Dark Night of the Soul,* translated by E. Allison Peers, cf. II, c. 1, 91. for the distinction between the two spiritual "nights."

concept of "the discernment of spirits."[21] This meant attention to enabling the client to become more and more sensitive to the experiential difference between genuine spiritual insights given by the Holy Spirit and bogus insights arising from tainted sources interior or exterior to the person. As St. Catherine explains, the classic sign of the authentic guidance of the Holy Spirit is whether such experiences lead to an increase of effective love of God and neighbor. To this Ignatius added from his own experience that the genuine guidance of the Holy Spirit is known by the deep interior peace that it brings, while illusory "insights" produce, to the contrary, spiritual unrest and confusion. He also emphasized the importance of "thinking with the Church," of considering whether one's insights are really in conformity with orthodox faith. Yet beginners cannot consistently make this distinction by themselves and require a director's guidance to become sensitive to it.

The spiritual counselor must never forget that though the essence of spiritual growth is in the deepening of the theological virtues facilitated by the increasing operation of the Gifts of the Holy Spirit,[22] these cannot be authentically exercised unless supported by a corresponding growth of the cardinal moral virtues. Various types of currently popular "spirituality," often labeled "New Age," that claim to open the way to transcendence without strict moral discipline are false and dangerous. In the Sermon on the Mount, Jesus prefaced his call to his disciples by saying, "Be perfect as your heavenly Father is perfect" (Mt 5:48), with the emphatic statement that "Do not think that I have come to abolish the law or the prophets. I have come not to abolish, but to fulfill. . . . Whoever breaks one of the least of these commandments and teaches others to do so will be called least in the kingdom of heaven" (Mt 5:17, 19a). This warning follows from the supreme commandment of love of God and neighbor, since the theological virtue of love of neighbor requires that we respect the neighbor's rights that the moral law protects.

Thus, as Catherine says, the work of the spiritual director is not to impose his or her own spirituality on their counselees. Instead it is to strive to discern the guidance of the Holy Spirit in their lives that is leading them to an ever-deeper commitment to love God through loving their neighbor with a love rooted in faith and supported by hope. This journey cannot but also be a way of the Cross, since Jesus said, "Take up your cross and follow me."

---

[21] See Piet Penning de Vries, *Discernment of Spirits According to the Life and Teachings of St. Ignatius Loyola,* and Hugo Rahner, *The Spirituality of St. Ignatius Loyola: An Account of its Historical Development.*

[22] On these gifts see Ashley, *Spiritual Directions,* chapter 7, 133ff.; *Thomas Aquinas: Selected Spiritual Writings,* co-authored with Matthew Rzeczkowski, OP, and *Living the Truth in Love: A Biblical Introduction to Moral Theology,* 75–78, and Subject Index, 552.

CHAPTER 18

Jesus and Humor*

St. Basil the Great is reputed to have said that since the Gospels never record that Jesus laughed or even smiled, such behavior is not becoming a monk whose thoughts must always be fixed on divine truth. St. Benedict in his *Rule* also cautions against excessive laughter.[1] On the other hand, it is recounted of St. Dominic that when his friars complained to him of the laughter of some of the young novices, he replied, "Let them laugh! They are full of joy that by entering religion they have defeated the wiles of the devil!" St. Phillip Neri, founder of the Oratorians, a favorite of Cardinal Newman, was called the "laughing saint" for his humor.[2]

Did Jesus laugh?[3] He was, of course, "the man of sorrows." But since nothing good was alien to him, we must take St. Basil's remark as a bit of rhetoric aimed at empty-headed monks who failed in moderation in humor, rather than literally. In fact, while the Gospels, brief as they are, have more serious matters to relate than the recreation of Jesus and the Apostles, they

---

* This essay has not been published before.

[1] Adalbert de Vögue, *The Rule of St. Benedict: A Doctrinal and Spiritual Commentary*: "But as for buffoonery or silly words such as move to laughter, we utterly condemn them in every place: nor do we allow the disciple to open his mouth in such discourse," 96–97. "The tenth degree of humility is that he is not easily moved and prompted to laughter, because it is written, 'The fool lifeth up his voice to laughter,'" 114.

[2] Bibliography in *Dictionnaire de Spiritualité*, André Derville, "Humour," tom. 7, 1187–91.

[3] Some authors who have dealt with this questions are Jakob Jonsson, *Humour and Irony in the New Testament*; Elton Trueblood, *The Humor of Christ*; Henri Cormier, *The Humor of Jesus*; Cal Samra, *The Joyful Christ: The Healing Power of Humor*; M. Conrad Hyers, *And Created Laughter: The Bible as Divine Comedy*; Giorgio Conconi, *When Jesus Smiled*.

do tell us two things that indicate the Master's humor. The first is his blessing of the children (Mt 19:13–15). One cannot imagine anyone showing affection to a child without at least smiling and being a bit playful. Furthermore, it is evident from the Gospels that Jesus attracted people strongly, and in no culture do human beings find unremitting seriousness attractive.

More important is the second thing that the Gospels show us in many places, that Jesus exhibits a sense of humor as a rhetorical devise in his preaching to hold the attention of the audience and open them to persuasion. Exegetes too often neglect this use of humor by Jesus. Yet it is evident in the parables. Ought we not smile at the Parable of the Unjust Steward (Lk 16:1–8), who when caught in fraud says to himself, "I am not strong enough to dig and I am ashamed to beg," and who then craftily makes "friends of the Mammon of iniquity"? And the master [God] commended that dishonest steward for acting prudently. "For the children of this world," Jesus concludes, "are more prudent in dealing with their own generation than are the children of light." Who can miss the comedy of the Parable of the Persistent Widow (Lk 18:18), which portrays the comic situation of the widow knocking and knocking at the door of the "judge who neither feared God nor respected any human being," becoming afraid of this little, powerless woman. This is even more evident in Luke 11:5–8, a the parable also about prayer, where God is compared to a man wakened in the middle of the night and aroused out of his bed by an importunate caller.

Unless we read these parables as humorous they become blasphemous in comparing God to a hard master, an unjust judge, or a sleepyhead. Jesus' humor in these and many other places usually takes the form of a gentle but penetrating satire on people whose religion is not very honest, or of irony, as in the famous saying, "I have come not to bring peace, but the sword." Of course the Prince of Peace came to bring peace, but with an irony, that is both sad and touched with humor, he acknowledges that the Gospel will have divisive side effects. Spiritual directors cause their disciples to recognize their faults by exposing them in a witty or humorous manner. This humor becomes even more inevitable in community life in which the eccentricity, foibles, and little hypocrisies of everyone become very evident to all through daily contact.

To understand how the Christian should use humor, it is necessary to define it more exactly by placing it in an ethical context of the life of virtue. In Latin "humor" means "a liquid." According to ancient medical theory, human health depended on the proper balance of the physiological secretions of the body. To be in a "bad humor" therefore meant to be out of balance, while to be in a "good humor" was a state of health both physical and psychological. Because laughter is normally a sign of cheerfulness, the word came to mean certain activities that produce laughter. Laughter and smiling, however, are natural expressions of pleasure and joy.

There are, of course, many other reasons for pleasure and joy than the pleasure we take in what is "funny," "comic," "ludicrous," "jocose." The genus of such pleasurable activities is "play," defined as a human activity that exercises our faculties for the sake of recreative pleasure but without the risk of serious consequences such as failure or pain.

By "recreation" is meant pleasurable activities that refresh our faculties for activities of more serious importance. Thus humor pertains to recreation as a form of play. This is made more specific by the fact that humor involves, primarily at least, an exercise of the intelligence rather than of bodily faculties. It is true that "practical jokes" and certain kinds of performances, such as a clown's antics, are physical, but the humor lies not in the physicality itself but in the mental perceptions that arise from this. Thus humor is a kind of intellectual play or game. The emotions or passions associated with it, therefore, are not simply pleasurable as in, for example, the enjoyment of beautiful objects. Rather it is also related to more specifically aggressive appetites, as in the competition of games that end in the pleasure of victory or, at least, of having played well, but which involve playful combat.

Yet we would not call a chess game or the solving of puzzles humorous. What is specific to humor is that it involves a *discovery* (hence something surprising) that what has the appearance of truth and value is really false or valueless because it is contradictory, absurd, over-valued.[4] This discovery, however, must be such as to remain within the limits of play, that is, it must not involve serious consequences or pain. Thus we laugh at others who do something that is ridiculous or that is incongruous with what they are supposed to be, provided, however, that this exposure causes no serious injury, but will teach them or others to act more suitably in the future. We can laugh at ourselves for the same reason. In either case the pleasure of the game is that at least the one who laughs takes pleasure in the discovery of a truth.

The element of "suddenness" is important because it intensifies the insight and its pleasure, but it does not seem absolutely essential. "Wit" is often distinguished from "humor" in that in humorous events the emotional element is more evident, in "witty" events the purely intellectual element predominates. Thus humor can be defined as playful intellectual activity whose aim is recreative pleasure produced by the discovery of truth through the exposure of absurdity in thought or behavior in oneself or others. Humor so defined has a purely recreative purpose and as a skill pertains to the fine arts, yet, of course, it can also be employed by rhetoric and dialectic as a means of persuasion or teaching.

This fact manifests the recreative value of humor in ascetic life. St. Thomas Aquinas points out that no one can live a human life without some

---

[4] For theories of humor, see Henri Bergson, "Laughter," *Comedy: An Essay on Comedy*, edited by Wylie Sypher, and Bob W. Parrott, *Ontology of Humor*.

pleasure, yet the pleasures of life are much reduced in an ascetic life aimed at gaining control over the unruliness of our appetites for pleasure. Thus humor provides a kind of recreation that refreshes the monk or nun for the more painful struggle to gain holiness in contemplation by providing a kind of pleasure that because it is intellectual is more spiritual than physical. It is important of course that this humor be under the moderation of reason. St. Thomas Aquinas speaks of the virtue of *eutrapelia*[5] or skill in taking this kind of recreation without falling into the extremes of silliness, on the one hand, or undue seriousness, on the other. He characterizes it as a virtue auxiliary to that of the cardinal virtue of temperance in that it moderates a pleasure, but not the physical drives for pleasure that are more difficult to control and more dangerous.

It must be added, of course, that humor and wit, while they are properly intended to bring joy and pleasure, can be cruel and wounding when they exceed the limits of play and have serious consequences for those mocked, either in their loss of reputation or in their own proper self-respect.

In Christian history humor can be found not only in the New Testament, but in a moderate yet significant manner in the sermons of Fathers such as St. Jerome and St. Augustine. It is also present in more popular works such as the legends of the saints. In the Middle Ages it becomes much freer, and the various collections of stories for preachers such as that of the thirteenth-century Étienne de Bourbon, contain many funny and witty anecdotes for the preacher. In fact medieval preachers often overindulged in this sort of thing and we find that others rebuked them for being more entertaining than edifying.[6] With the rise of more secular literature in the Renaissance, humorous story-telling became a fine art, as Chaucer's *Canterbury Tales* is an outstanding witness, not to mention the wonderful comedies later of Shakespeare and Molière.

In this growth of secular humor, of course, humor of a pornographic sort appeared and has been often deplored by Christian moralists. The sexual aspect of human nature is likely to furnish material for humor and wit for several reasons. Above all there is something inherently comic in the way that the noblest aspirations of humanity for a self-giving love that is intensely spiritual is bound up with the sheer physicality of the sexual act itself so organically connected to the lowly needs of urination and menstruation! Moreover the possibilities of absurd rationalization and concealment of animal desires by all manner of pretenses of love and regard for the other are unlimited.

---

[5] *Summa theologiae* I–II, q. 60, a. 5; quoting Aristotle, Nicomachean Ethics IV, c. 8 1128a 17 sq; also II–II, q. 72, a. 2 ad 1; q. 160, a. 2 c; 172, a. 2, ad 1.

[6] Sophia Menache Horowitz, *L'humor en chaire: le rire dans l Église médiévale,* chapter 1, 19–54, is the best short treatment of negative attitudes. It gives many humorous exempla in sermons and illustrations in art, with a lengthy bibliography, 257–79.

There are several reasons that pornographic humor is not true humor and has serious moral risks. The first is that it can easily be, and probably usually is, an excuse for taking pleasure in deliberate lustful ideas that Jesus exposed as "already committing adultery in one's heart." Second, it is an occasion for lustful acts on the part of the hearer. Third, it tends to develop wrong attitudes about sexuality as a means for immoral sexual acts rather than its true God-given purposes in marriage. Since these are serious harmful consequences they render what is supposed to be humorous, and therefore without such harmful consequences, false humor. A fourth reason that pornographic humor is immoral is that its purpose is commonly commercial, which makes it akin to prostitution. It is true that a sophisticated person of tried virtue might accept only the humorous element in a "dirty joke" and not yield to its evil aspect, but this is possibly not easy for most people, and even for the sophisticate is "tempting God" or causes scandal to others. It is analogous to the use of the other fine arts in a pornographic manner.

The Christian today lives in a pluralistic society where absurdity is almost overwhelming and leads to nihilism. A strong sense of humor, therefore, is needed if one is not to be overwhelmed. At the same time the temptation to compromise with the confusions of this culture requires us to recognize our own inauthenticity even in smaller matters, lest we become blind to more important falsities. When Jesus said to the pious Pharisees, "You strain at a gnat, and swallow a camel" (Mt 23:24), he was using humor to expose that same loss of proportion and common sense that today besieges us on every side.

Bioethics
Issues

CHAPTER 19

A Christian Perspective on Scientific Health Care*

Four Ethical Limits on Medical Practice

THE MEDICAL PROFESSION ACKNOWLEDGES ITS ETHICAL obligations, but it tends to think that these obligations are determined exclusively by the recognized goal of the profession, namely to use the resources of science to improve the health of the patient. Any attempt to introduce other standards of conduct into medicine appears to many physicians to be an unwarranted intrusion by those who lack professional medical competence. Consequently, considerable resentment is felt when the Church, as in its recent document on human reproduction, seems to impose limits on medical research and practice.[1] What competence does the Church have in scientific medical matters?

The answer is of course, "None at all." Nevertheless, the Church no more intends to intrude on medical expertise as such than do the financial and political institutions that restrict the actual practice of medicine and medical research by far more powerful pressures than the Church can apply. The Church speaks up on medical questions only when she perceives that an issue involves the rights of the human persons who are the subject of medical practice and the correlative responsibilities of medical providers to these subjects. In all societies human rights are violated and it has always been the recognized duty of the Christian Church and indeed of all religious bodies

---

* Keynote address for *Giornate di studio e di riflessione in occasione del 120 Anniversario della fondazione dell' Ospedale Pediatrico Bambino Gesu,* Rome November 28–29, 1989 (not previously published).

[1] Sacred Congregation for the Doctrine of the Faith, *Donum Vitae, Instruction on Respect for Human Life in Its Origin and on the Dignity of Procreation,* translated in *Origins,* March 19, 1987. Popular reaction is evident from "Catholic Hospitals in Europe Defy Vatican on In Vitro Fertilization," *New York Times* (March 18, 1987).

to act as advocates for the victims of such violations, especially when they are powerless, the "preferential option for the poor" to which magisterial documents often refer.[2] This is not to imply that the medical profession is often guilty of conscious injustices to patients, but only that it—like other professions (and I by no means exempt the clergy from this same accusation),—sometimes, under the immense pressures of its services to humanity, becomes blinded to abuses incidental to its great services. Thus it is in terms of justice and respect for human rights[3] that I want to explain the few, but possibly very irritating, ethical restraints that the Church has urged on the medical profession. I say "urged" because the Church, unlike the worlds of finance and politics, has no power except that of persuasion to restrain the medical profession. She speaks only to the conscience of physicians, confident that by their commitment to so noble a profession, they are men and women of goodwill.

As I understand the teaching of the Church, it proposes only four major limits to medical research and practice that are in fact part of the tradition of the medical profession itself; thus when the Church proposes them it is only reminding physicians of their own commitment, classically expressed in the Hippocratic Oath. These principles are not inventions of the Roman Curia, as some have snidely claimed, but are derived very directly from the teaching and example of Jesus Christ. They simply formulate that respect for the human person, or human dignity, which is basic to all learned professions in the service of humanity.

The first of these principles is "respect for human life," which was formulated in the Ten Commandments as "Thou shalt not kill." The biblical context shows this should be understood as "Thou shalt not kill the innocent," thereby not applying to the unjust aggressor in an act of aggression or to capital punishment for a serious crime. Jesus' own advocacy of non-violence, even against enemies, is so well known that this point requires no elaboration here.[4] It is sufficient to point out that recent developments that have pressured physicians whose commitment is to save life into becoming executioners radically undercuts the tradition and meaning of the profession, as do those lawyers who use their knowledge of the law to break it.[5] The direct taking of human life by abortion or euthanasia cannot be excused

---

2 *Instruction on Christian Freedom and Liberation,* n. 68, translated in *Origins* 15 (April 16, 1986): 714–28, speaks of the poor as "the object of a love of preference," as regards not just poverty in the narrow sense, but every form of human rights violation.

3 *Theses de la comission theologique international: La dignité et les droits dela personne humaine, Documentation Catholique* 82 (1985): 383–91.

4 See Raymond Regamey, OP, *Non-Violence and the Christian Conscience* for the necessary distinctions.

5 See Leon Kass, MD, "Neither for Love nor Money: Why Doctors Must Not Kill" in *The Human Life Review* 15 (Fall 1989): 93–115.

on grounds that it is the pregnant patient who chooses to kill her child or the suffering patient who wants to die. In such cases the physician always and in all circumstances is morally obliged to refuse to cooperate in such direct attacks on human life.[6] Human life is not a human creation: It is a gift of God given in stewardship to be used well and not rejected.

A second principle is that the primary responsibility for one's own body is one's own, consequently no medical procedure may be applied to anyone without their free and informed consent, or if they are incompetent to make such a decision, that of their proper guardians acting for their benefit.[7] Jesus exemplified this principle in a wider sense when he respected the consciences of his followers, asking of them only their own voluntary commitment (Jn 6:60–69). This principle in fact liberates the physician from the obligation to make decisions for patients whose exact circumstances and dispositions are very difficult for their caretakers to know. The physician's obligation is to truthfully inform the patient or guardian of his diagnosis and recommendations for treatment, and its risks and benefits; it is not to decide for the patient whether in fact the recommendations are to be followed. Of course, as already mentioned, physicians ought not to cooperate in decisions made by their patients that the physicians themselves believe to be either medically or ethically unsound.

The third principle is really a corollary of the second: A physician ought not to insist on procedures that the patient (or, when patients are incompetent, the guardians) judges to be "extraordinary means," that is, which promise only a minimal benefit or at least one that does not compensate for the burdens of such treatment to the patient and to those who will have to provide aftercare.[8] It is sometimes seen that physicians, either from a laudable commitment to do all their art can provide, or from a reluctance to

---

[6] The tradition of the church on the sanctity of human life is clearly defined in Paul VI's Encyclical *Humanae Vitae*, "On the Regulation of Birth," July 25, 1968, and in many instructions of the S. Congregation for the Doctrine of the Faith, such as the "Declaration on Procured Abortion," 18 November 1974, "Declaration on Euthanasia," 5 May 1980, and *Donum Vitae*, "Instruction on Respect for Human Life in its Origins and on the Dignity of Procreation," February 22, 1987.

[7] On informed consent, see Benedict M. Ashley and Kevin D. O'Rourke, *Health Care Ethics: A Theological Analysis,* 4th ed., 47ff, and Edmund Pellegrino, MD, "The Moral Foundations for Valid Consent" in *Proceedings of the Third National Conference on Human Values and Cancer.*

[8] "It is also permissible to make do with the normal means that medicine can offer. Therefore one cannot impose on anyone the obligation to have recourse to a technique which is already in use but which carries a risk or is burdensome. Such a refusal is not the equivalent of suicide; on the contrary, it should be considered as an acceptance of the human condition or a wish to avoid the application of a medical procedure disproportionate to the results that can be expected or a desire not impose excessive expense on the family or the community." *Declaration on Euthanasia.*

admit its limitations, or from hesitation to make a difficult decision, or perhaps because of fears of litigation, have a tendency to propose procedures whose benefit is dubious or whose burden is excessive, even against the will of the patient or the guardians. The Christian attitude, expressed by Jesus in his own submission to death, is that bodily life is not the ultimate value but is relative to spiritual goals.[9]

The fourth principle concerns the most ethically controversial field of medicine—that of sexuality and reproduction. Before trying to formulate this principle, it is important to focus these controversial questions on the essential point.[10] The Church's concerns about sexuality are primarily not, as many suppose, that it fears the earthly pleasures that sex can provide as dangerous rivals to the heavenly joys that religion promises. No, the Church's primary concern regarding sexuality is a concern for justice, and above all justice to the child.

The wide adoption of contraception (against the solemn warnings of the Church as to its intrinsic moral deformity, despite the dissent of not a few moral theologians) has separated sexual activity from its relation to procreation. As a result, many Catholics no longer perceive the fact that the ultimate moral significance of sex cannot be understood unless we focus our attention on how each form of sexual activity affects children I would like to illustrate the way in which the Christian moral perspective affects medical practice from the field of pediatric medicine, at the same time noting that the same four basic principles apply to all medical fields.

Limits on Pediatric Medicine

Every child from the first moment of its existence is a human person with human rights. The Church's position on human rights from conception does not depend on the question of the time of ensoulment, since even if it were

---

9 "Normally [when prolonging life is in question] one is held to use only ordinary means-according to the circumstances of persons, places, times, and cultures-that is to say, means that do not involve any grave burdens for oneself or for another. A more strict obligation would be too burdensome for most people and would render the attainment of higher, more important good too difficult. Life, health, all temporal activities are in fact subordinated to spiritual ends." Pius XII, "Prolongation of Life," November 24, 1957, *The Pope Speaks*, vol. 4, 1958.

10 The most important magisterial documents are: Pope Paul VI, *Humanae Vitae: Encyclical Letter on the Regulation of Births*, 1968; SCDF, *Declaration on Certain Problems of Sexual Ethics*, December 29, 1975, translated in Flannery, *Vatican Council II: More Postconciliar Documents*, 486–99. To these must now be added, SCDF, *Donum vitae: Instruction on Respect for Human Life*, 1987 and John Paul II's encyclicals, *Veritatis Splendor: The Splendor of Truth*, 1993 and *Evangelium vitae: On the Value and Inviolability of Human Life*, 1995.

uncertain that the conceptus is already a human person, the benefit of the doubt must be in its favor. But, as a matter of fact, present scientific evidence removes reasonable doubt on this score.[11] Some argue that the conceptus is not an individuated organism until approximately the time of implantation in the uterus, because during this phase of development twinning or the fusion of twins can still take place. This view, however, does not sufficiently take into account the evidence that in mammals the genome controls the development of the embryo (or pre-embryo as some term it) from the first cell division. Yet in the morula and blastula phases the blastomeres remain totipotential and if separated can develop into complete new organisms by a kind of natural "cloning," as seems to happen with identical twins. From the first cell divisions however the human embryo already exhibits a tight compaction and interrelation as well as an organic polarity that indicates it is not simply a loose assemblage of cells but a true unified organism having human rights.

The first of these rights obviously is to be born, which is why abortion is a grave injustice to the child that cannot be excused by some lesser advantage to the mother. The child also has a right to be born within marriage, because only in such a stable environment can it have its full chance to develop physically and psychologically. It is unique to the human species that the male is bound to the female by the possibility of intercourse throughout the entire year. The deep psychological bond of complementarity and intimate personal communication that makes possible a union of true love perfects this biological bond. This bond of love between male and female spouses, rooted so deeply in their biology and psychology, is the best guarantee of the child's security. When it is broken, as we see so often today in divorce, the child suffers a very real deprivation. Such an unlucky child is truly handicapped, truly disabled in a way that is very difficult to remedy.

Not only does the child have a right to be born and to be born legitimate, it also has a right to be born to its biological parents. The adopted child is still a handicapped child, although its adoptive parents may do much to remedy the loss of its biological parents. Yet these adoptive parents, for all their loving care, cannot restore to the adopted child what children normally enjoy—the security and sense of identity that come from knowing they are bound to their parents not merely by the subjective ties of love, as wonderful as these are, but by the objective basis of love in flesh and blood.

Human experience throughout history and the accounts we frequently read in the newspapers of adopted children searching to find their biological parents are proof that this human longing is profoundly a part of our

---

[11] For documentation on this point, see the essay "When Does a Human Person Begin to Exist?" in this collection.

nature.[12] Hence, artificial reproduction by heterologous insemination from a donor other than the husband produces a child who lacks this biological link to its adoptive father.[13] When this insemination takes place in a surrogate mother, the bond to parents is still further weakened, since now the child is clearly the fruit of adultery.[14]

What then are we to think of artificial homologous insemination with the semen of the husband or of in vitro fertilization, where the child is no longer the result of intercourse at all but is the product of a technician who combines ova surgically removed from the mother with the father's semen— semen in both cases usually obtained by masturbation? The magisterial objection to artificial insemination by the husband (AIH) does not rest primarily, however, on the fact that the process usually involves self-stimulation to obtain the semen (although that too is illicit) but on the separation of reproduction from the marital act.

Undoubtedly the aim of such techniques is to produce a healthy child, one genetically linked to a couple who would otherwise have to adopt. Yet this child too is a handicapped child, because it lacks that ultimate objective link to the parents that the normal child has, namely, that it is fruit of the very act of love that binds the parents to each other. A child has the right not only to be born, to be born legitimate, to be raised by its natural parents, but also to be the co-creation with God through their unitive act of sexual love.

This point of the Church's teaching seems to many absurdly subtle. After all, they say, does it make that much difference to the child? Perhaps the child will never know that it was produced in a test-tube. Perhaps if it does know it will be willing to accept the fact that its parents wanted it so badly that they were willing to resort to high-tech procedures to beget it. No doubt such acceptance will in fact not prove especially difficult for many children, just as being adopted is usually accepted simply as a fact of one's

---

[12] See Jan De Hartog, *Adopted Children*; Erica Haimes and Noel Timms, *Adoption, Identity, and Social Policy: The Search for Distant Relatives*; Arthur D. Sorsky et al., *Adoption Triangle*; Jeanne Du Praw, *Adoption: The Facts, Feelings, and Issues of Double Heritage* for current information on this problem.

[13] "Recourse to the gametes of a third person, in order to have sperm or ovum available, constitutes a violation of the reciprocal commitment of the spouses. . . . Moreover, this form of generation violates the rights of the child; it deprives him of this filial relationship with his parental origins and can hinder the maturing of his personal identity." *Donum Vitae,* II, A, 2.

[14] "Surrogate motherhood represents an objective failure to meet the obligations of material love, of conjugal fidelity, and of responsible motherhood; it offends the dignity and the right of the child to be conceived, to be carried in the womb, to be brought into the world and to be brought up by his own parents; it sets up to the detriment of families a division between the physical, psychological, and moral elements which constitute those families." Ibid., II A, 3.

life. Certainly it is better to live and to live in a loving family as a wanted child than not to exist at all. Compared with this joy, the exact mode of one's coming into existence seems not of much importance. But to admit all this is not to admit that such children are not handicapped in a very fundamental way. They lack something to which they have a natural right.

This point becomes more telling when we stop to think of the social consequences of the gradual acceptance of artificial insemination and in vitro fertilization as a regular procedure. It is a psychological fact that even now many children fear that maybe they are really adopted children and not the biological children of their parents, with a consequent anxiety that they may ultimately be rejected by these "parents."[15] What will the situation be when all children begin to question whether perhaps their "real parent" was a nameless technician who concocted them in a laboratory? Today in developed countries where the environment has become highly artificial, the sense of the natural foundations of the family is already much weakened.[16]

In the United States the single-parent family is becoming a widespread phenomenon, and children are more and more raised in "day-care centers" with parents absent. Children deprived of the natural bonding that results from the intimate love expressed in intercourse that is the source of their very existence and identity are handicapped children, victims of a grave injustice.

But you may say, "But without these techniques this child would never have existed at all. How can there be an injustice to a child who does not yet exist?" I will answer that most physicians would agree that when a couple decides to beget a child with a serious genetic disease, they are responsible for its existence as a seriously defective child, and they probably should refrain from satisfying their own desire for a child, although unquestionably once such a child is conceived it has the right to be born and cared for. Similarly, an *in vitro* child once conceived has a right to be implanted in a mother, to be born, and to be cared for, but the parents who gave the ovum and sperm from which they were constructed by a technician bear a responsibility for bringing this child deprived of a normal origin into existence. The child is no longer viewed as a unique gift, but is reduced "to an object of scientific technology."[17] The Church's conception of human sexuality emphasizes "the language of the body." The *Instruction on Respect for Human Life* follows the Church's understanding of sexuality as a natural sacrament, a sign of a spiritual love.

---

[15] See the works of De Hartog, Haimes and Timms, Sorsky, and Du Praw previously noted.

[16] See excerpts from "The Family: Preserving America's Future," by the Working Group on the Family, a White House task force, *The Human Life Review* 13 (Winter 1986): 105–16.

[17] Sacred Congregation for the Doctrine of the Faith, *Donum Vitae,* II, B, 4, c.

Hence married couples express their unifying love not merely by spiritual but by bodily acts, because human beings are both body and soul and their mutual gift of self is bodily and spiritual. Their cooperation with God in the creation of a new human being, who is also both body and spirit, is therefore a truly sacred act of a higher order than that of human technology that may assist it but cannot substitute for it.

"Fertilization achieved outside" the body "remains by this very fact deprived of the meanings and the values which are expressed in the language of the body and in the union of human persons."[18] The concept of "the nuptial meaning of the body" as expressing the need of human persons to make a total gift of themselves to others, sexually or in other modes of self-giving, has been remarkably developed by John Paul II in his *Reflections on "Humanae Vitae"* and *The Original Unity of Man and Woman.*[19] Both the test-tube baby and the seriously defective child may well say, "I thank my 'parents' for having me produced, but it was an injustice to me to come into the world deprived of what other children enjoy." Moreover, when such deprivations are the result of merely natural or accidental causes beyond human control, we must accept them as part of our destiny, but when they are the result of human deliberation and choice we can rightly blame them on their perpetrators.

Further reflection shows that the other aspects of the Church's teaching on sexuality that seem over-restrictive to many today, stem first of all from this same concern for the rights of the child. Contraception does not guarantee that a couple engaging in extra-marital intercourse will absolutely avoid pregnancy. No form of contraception now known, except sterilization, is free from serious risk of pregnancy, as is evident from the very high rates of abortion, chiefly among the unmarried, in many countries where contraceptive methods are widely distributed and accepted.[20]

For unmarried couples to engage in even one act of intercourse involves a very real risk that a child may result, and this child will suffer the injustice of illegitimacy. If the relationship is adulterous there is the further injustice of grave injury to the marriage bond and to children already begotten in this bond. Thus the Church rejects extra-marital sex not only because it is an irre-

---

18 Ibid., V, 4, 6.

19 John Paul II, *Reflections on* Humanae Vitae (Boston: St. Paul Editions, 1984) and *The Original Unity of Man and Woman: Catechesis on the Book of Genesis* (Boston: St. Paul Editions, 1980).

20 See Stan E. Weed, "Curbing Births, Not Pregnancies," *Wall Street Journal* (October 14, 1986). According to the *World Almanac*, there were 1,300,760 legal abortions performed in the United States in 1981. This figure has remained stable to date. For the stand of the magisterium on contraceptive sterilization, see Doctrinal Congregational Statement on Sterilization, March 19, 1975, in *Commentary of National Conference of Catholic Bishops* (Washington, DC: United States Catholic Conference, 1975).

sponsible indulgence, but also because the more such relationships are countenanced in a society the more the security of children within stable families
is imperiled. The injustice done to children by divorce is even more serious.[21]
The same reasoning applies to homosexual activity, today so widely condoned, to other forms of sexual indulgence separated from any relationship to
procreation, and even to masturbation that habituates and even addicts those
who practice it to a depersonalized attitude toward sexual pleasure.[22] Such
activities, which seem to affect no one but those who freely engage in them,
in fact create in the culture an attitude to human sexuality that undermines
the security of the family and hence of the child. Persons enslaved to such
practices are incapable of forming the kind of stable marriage that children
need for their own growth, and the result is that they themselves may grow
up without clear heterosexual sexual identity and motivation.

The Church should and does defend the human rights of homosexuals
and other sexual deviants, but it cannot accept their claims that their condition is simply a normal variant nor that their indulgence of their abnormal
inclinations is morally justified. It is a false compassion to help disabled persons deny their disablements, and true and loving compassion to enable
them to acknowledge their defects realistically and to learn to live with dignity and virtue in spite of them. Thus the whole Christian view of sexual
ethics centers in the rights of the child.[23]

This is why, I believe, that while Jesus did not often preach about sexual
morality, and then only to correct the defects of the Mosaic Law with respect
to divorce, and to insist on purity of heart as well as of action, he often dwelt
on the dignity of the child, of the "little ones." When his disciples tried to
dismiss children lest they get in the way of the Master's preaching and healing, Jesus rebuked them and called the children to himself, blessed them,
and said "Of such is the kingdom of God." (Mt 19:13–15). He also warned
that anyone who corrupted the innocence of children deserved to have a
mill-stone hung around his neck and to be cast into the sea (Mt 18:5–7).[24]

---

21 See Zoe L. Frost, "Children in a Changing Society," *Childhood Education* (March/
April, 1988): 244ff.

22 Sacred Congregation for the Doctrine of the Faith, "Letter to the Bishops of the
Catholic Church on the Pastoral Care of Homosexual Persons," translated in *The
Vatican and Homosexuality: Reactions to the Letter*, Jeannine Grammick and Pat Furey,
eds., with my contribution, "Compassion and Sexual Orientation," 105–11. Most of
the other contributors (except Archbishop John R. Quinn, 20–27) are hostile to the
Letter. See also John Harvey, *The Homosexual Person: New Thinking in Pastoral Care.*

23 For concise explanations of the Christian understanding of human sexuality, see
Ronald Lawler, OFM, Cap., Joseph Boyle, Jr., and William E. May, *Catholic Sexual
Ethics,* and Paul M. Quay, SJ, *The Christian Meaning of Human Sexuality.*

24 The recent crisis over child abuse by priests has in considerable part been due, I
believe, to the influence of the "sexual revolution" on clergy who thought they were

Any service done to a child, Jesus said, was a service to Himself. Those who sincerely feel this Christ-like concern for children will come to see, I believe, the wisdom of what the Church has always taught and teaches today about sexual morality, however a "hard saying" it may be.

One of the saddest blots on the record of human history has been the neglect of children.[25] When we think that in the past in many countries half of all human beings died in infancy, and that this situation prevails in many places today, and we realize that most of this results from poverty, we cannot doubt that human greed is a major factor in their deaths. Again the history of abortion, infanticide, child abandonment, prostitution, neglect of education, polygamy, illegitimacy, and transmission of venereal disease and drug addiction to children is appalling. Even in wealthy, aristocratic, and royal families throughout history there is a shocking pattern of leaving children to the care of servants, sending them away to school to get rid of them, and neglecting their moral training. In today's climate of "dysfunctional families" the situation is little better.

Therefore, the role of the pediatrician in society is of immense importance. Modern medicine makes it possible to remedy many ills and defects that in former times had no answer. Anyone who has visited a modern hospital for children is deeply moved by the wonderful and truly loving care that suffering children receive there, and the profound understanding of the needs of the child that so enriches the Church's own experience as advocate of children's rights.

In the United States today there is tremendous concern for the abused child and stringent laws about reporting such abuse to public officials. Although Americans are sensitive to what they regard as public interference in the bedroom and jealous of the "right of privacy," which the Supreme Court has discovered as an implication of our Constitution and its Bill of Rights, few question the duty of the government to breach the privacy of the home to salvage the abused child or the battered wife. It is an anomaly therefore that the Supreme Court continues to declare that a woman's "right of privacy" permits her to destroy the child who, in a few months or even days, would be so rigorously protected from abuse. In the long run the facts of medicine will expose this contradiction for what it is. We must come to recognize that sexual activity by its very nature has a social dimension because of its relation to the welfare of children: It cannot ever be simply a private matter. Yet again some who are engaged in research may well say, "These

---

"catching up with the times." One bishop who resigned over the matter said in his own excuse, "At that time we were all experimenting."

25 See Philippe Aries, *Centuries of Childhood*. For a contrary view, see Thomas Fleming, "Affection and Responsibility in the Family in Classical Greece," *The Journal of Family and Culture* 1 (1985): 43–56.

restrictions that the Church puts on the development of new techniques stand in the way of the scientific research necessary to find ways to overcome genetic defects and in many other ways promote the health of children. Is not the Church therefore hypocritical in claiming to be the advocate of the rights of the child?"

The Church does not oppose, it strongly urges scientific research on genetic and developmental problems and the devising of better techniques to regulate procreation and overcome infertility, and to promote child health.[26] It prays for the success of such endeavors and encourages young people to enter into scientific and medical education for this motive. It originated the hospital and it has encouraged the commitment of religious sisters and brothers and priests to hospital ministry.

Nevertheless, the Church has to insist on the ethical principles that somewhat limit medical research and practice in order to be the advocate of the rights of children and of adults. This does not set the Church in opposition to the medical profession since both Church and medicine ultimately aim at the welfare of human beings. Rather it places the Church in a position of dialogue. The Church does not impose these principles, it simply brings them to the attention of the medical profession, confident that fair-minded discussion will permit the truth to prevail.

Difficulties arise chiefly in the case of Catholic health care facilities sponsored by the Church. When a hospital takes the name of "Catholic," and especially when it is controlled by a religious order, it publicly professes to those who seek its services that it shares the Church's advocacy of human rights. Consequently, if it were to cooperate in medical procedures that in the Church's judgment violate human rights, it would become a responsible party to making false claims to the public.

Today, Catholic hospitals are often staffed by physicians and nurses who are not professing Catholics, or who are Catholics alienated from the teaching authority of the Church. Moreover, many patients are not Catholics or are alienated Catholics. Finally, Catholic hospitals commonly are beneficiaries of public funds received from a secular, pluralistic state and would have great difficulty continuing their services without these funds. They seem, therefore, obligated to provide the public with all the medical procedures that are usual in non-Catholic institutions.

This situation raises both the ethical problems of cooperation in activities that have both good and bad effects and of respect for the consciences of those with whom one does not agree. Regarding conscience, it should be

---

[26] "Basic scientific research and applied research constitute a significant expression of this dominion of man over creation. Science and technology are valuable resources for man when placed at his service and when they promote his integral development for the benefit of all." *Donum Vitae*, "Introduction."

clear that a Catholic health care institution can never in any circumstances do or formally cooperate in doing anything that the Church has authoritatively declared to be immoral. While it is certainly true that the pastors of the Church, even the Supreme Pontiff, may on occasion err in their teaching, short of the solemn definitions of the universal episcopate or the pope that bear the mark of infallibility, their guidance because of its authoritative character is the only safe guide for an institution that by its name claims the support of the Church.

Individual Catholic professionals in their own personal decisions, apart from institutional policy, must of course ultimately act according to their own well-informed conscience, but it is difficult to see how in matters of ethics such a professional can honestly suppose that his own moral judgment is more reliable than that of the Church, even when he sees that the bishops are in fact mistaken with regard to some of the medical data. Of what service is a physician to a patient if the patient ignores the physician's advice and follows his own untrained understanding of medical matters? Of what service then is the Church to physicians if they ignore her teaching and follow their own, usually untrained, understanding of ethics in ethical matters?

On this score a great deal of confusion has arisen in recent years because a good many prominent theologians have dissented from the Church's teachings, especially on questions involving sex and reproduction.[27] Consequently some physicians have the impression that the existence of such dissent permits Catholics to select freely the theological opinion that seems most plausible or even most convenient and act on it, and for physicians to cooperate in the implementation of these preferences. Instead they should be aware that Vatican II sought to give great freedom (sometimes today seriously abused) to theologians to debate issues to promote the advancement of the discipline of theology.

Consequently, views are frequently put forth in a hypothetical manner for critical discussion among theologians, without any guarantee that these views will eventually prove sound. Indeed the odds are that most will prove unsound, just as most experimental drugs prove useless. Consequently, the views of theologians never have and never will be a sound basis for moral action until the pastors of the Church who alone have authority from their office to guide Christian consciences have approved them.

Physicians, therefore, should draw their ultimate practical guidance not from the writings of theologians, however distinguished, especially as often badly reported in the public media, but from the authentic declarations of the Church. I assure you from personal experience that today these declarations when they touch on medical issues are not made without care-

---

[27] See Archbishop Daniel Pilarcsyk, "Dissent in the Church," *Origins* 16 (July 31, 1986): 175–78.

ful consultation with the medical profession. The more difficult question is how to respect the consciences of those with whom we necessarily cooperate. How do Catholic physicians counsel patients whose moral convictions are different from their own? Can physicians accept the decision of such patients and act on them simply as agents of their clients? What if the patient insists and threatens to seek counsel from another physician? The answer to such questions must certainly be that although Catholic physicians must be respectful of the subjective conscience of their patients and not pressure them to act contrary to their consciences, for the same reason they must respect their own Catholic consciences and refuse to cooperate in what they believe to be objectively wrong. When a third party is involved, as in abortion or in the possible transmitting of a venereal disease, the physician should do what he can to protect the third party.

What if the Catholic health care institution or the individual Catholic physician or nurse is involved in a cooperative endeavor with non-Catholic institutions or professionals, or is receiving government funding, and thus becomes involved in actions that are forbidden by Catholic teaching? We have here the very delicate prudential question of what is technically called "formal and material cooperation." The Catholic Church has never taken the purist stand that it is wrong to cooperate in any activity with others if this cooperation involves even indirect support of some morally reprehensible actions. If we were to take that stand, we would have to withdraw from the world to which Jesus sent us to minister. He did not hesitate, in spite of the criticisms of the Pharisees, to dine with sinners even when his presence seemed to give some support to their sinful ways of life.

It is always wrong to cooperate "formally" with actions that are intrinsically evil either by actually sharing in their execution or by approving or advising them. The physician who will not perform an abortion but refers a patient to an abortionist cooperates formally and shares in the crime of abortion. A physician who works in a hospital where along with many legitimate services some abortions are performed, even though he does not perform them himself nor approve of them, cooperates only materially—that is, because through his own good work he helps to maintain the hospital and thus indirectly makes possible the abortions. To decide whether such indirect or material abortion is ethical, the physician must weigh the consequences of his continuing to work there or of withdrawing. If by withdrawing he can stop the abortions or bring about some other very good result, he should leave. But if his withdrawal will have little effect in preventing the evil, and will make it difficult for him to continue his own good services, it would be better for him to stay. Thus what needs to be considered is how "immediate" is his cooperation in the evil, the more immediate the greater the good accomplished or the evil prevented by his cooperation, to justify this cooperation.

In the case of a Catholic institution entering into some cooperative agreement with another, such questions must be thoroughly worked out and formalized in the written agreement before the cooperation is begun, as well as being subject to future revision based on experience. In the case of state funding and regulation, Catholic institutions in extreme cases must refuse such funding, even if this means closing the institution if the government fails to show proper respect for the rights of conscience. In such situations there may be a possibility of purely material cooperation, since it is possible that the evil of eliminating Catholic institutions and the witness they give to human rights in medicine may outweigh the evils involved in this cooperation. Yet it should be remembered even in such cases that material cooperation may sometimes have such an appearance of hypocrisy that the scandal given may weigh the scale against cooperation. The early martyrs refused even a pinch of incense to the idol of the Emperor.

A final doubt is raised by the fear of many in medical research that the Church's concern for human rights, as laudable as it may be, will become a serious obstacle to the advancement of the very knowledge that will enable medicine to better serve the child in the future and give it its rights. Why disapprove, for example, the use in research of fetuses obtained by abortion if this would not prevent their abortion, but would put the fetuses to a use that would help other children? Why completely forbid *in vitro* fertilization when this technique is so useful in learning how to remedy genetic diseases? Why forbid obtaining semen by masturbation, when this makes infertility testing and the discovery of remedies for it more effective?

Over all these questions hangs the shadow of historic incidents, such as the Church's opposition to the dissection of corpses or to Galileo's discoveries with the telescope![28] More accurate history demonstrates that such incidents have been relatively rare and can hardly count among the more serious impediments to scientific advance, such as the failure of governments to support basic research except for military purposes. Yet it should be granted in honesty that ethical considerations may close off some attractive research modes. Who does not grant that today we cannot simply use human beings as guinea pigs? Or that researchers must be content to experiment on animals before they try new drugs or new kinds of surgery on humans, even though direct experiments on humans would be more revealing? The ingenuity of scientists has always found ways to explore nature in spite of such necessary restrictions, and indeed it is likely that the very challenge of these restraints has spurred research. Who denies that research on living adults must be restricted by ethical considerations and that animals be used instead, although this makes research somewhat more difficult?

---

[28] See Bernard Vinaty et al., *Galileo Galilei: 350 ans d'histoire,* edited by Paul Poupard, with a declaration of John Paul II.

What the Church insists on is simply that the fetus ought to be treated as a human subject, not as subhuman. We would not use human persons marked by a Hitler for genocide for experimental purposes on the excuse they are going to die anyway. Nor, lest we seem to be partners in this crime, would we use their corpses. Why then should we experiment on fetuses created in the laboratory to be studied and then destroyed, or on ones obtained from an abortionist?

Therefore, the Catholic Church, as the community of which Jesus Christ, the healer, is head, speaking through its pastors who have received their commission of guidance from him, blesses research scientists, physicians, and nurses, in their self-sacrificing work for humanity, laying no burden or restriction on them except to remind them that all human beings, including children and the unborn, are created in God's image. They should come into the world in families that exemplify God's love and through the very act of love by which this mutual covenant of love is firmly established, and should leave this world consoled by the Church's sacraments, neither unwisely retained in life by some useless medical *tour de force*, nor rejecting the gift of life by so-called "mercy killing." The medical profession has won great esteem, in which it is still held, by this reverence for the dignity of the human person, even when obscured by the extremes of suffering; it will retain that honor only if it retains that reverence, today already somewhat tarnished by too many compromises with practices utterly contrary to human dignity.

History demonstrates that the rights of truth, including scientific truth itself, depend on our respect for human dignity.[29] Science is a human activity and achievement, one of the noblest of human activities and achievements, and it cannot flourish except in a society that appreciates and defends the great human values. When human life loses its sacredness, brute power rules the world and science becomes just another instrument of enslavement rather than a search for truth. Therefore, the health care profession, if it is to be loyal to its own dedication to science in the service of human health, must defend human rights, even at the inconvenience of certain reasonable restrictions on its own options. In fact such restraints do not inhibit scientific progress but rather guide it into more productive channels.

---

[29] See Robert Jay Lifton, *The Nazi Doctors: Medical Killing and the Psychology of Genocide.*

CHAPTER 20

When Does a Human Person Begin to Exist?*

Facing the Question

THE PRESENT CONTROVERSY OVER CLONING AND STEM cell research cannot be separated from that of abortion. *Roe* v. *Wade* argued that it is uncertain when life begins and hence it is not evident that abortion is the murder of an innocent human person. Therefore the certain rights of the woman to privacy and health trump the uncertain rights of the unborn fetus. If that argument is true, then it also seems that the need to do research in order to find new remedies for the diseases of those who are certainly human persons trumps any rights of a mere "embryo"[1] to life. Though cloning human persons involves additional questions it too presumes extensive prior research that also involves the killing of embryos. Thus the fundamental issue involved in abortion, cloning, stem cell research, and artificial reproduction is: "When does a human person having human rights come into existence?"

The moral importance of this question becomes evident when we recognize that if the beginning of human life is determined to be at the moment

---

* This unpublished lecture sums up material contained in several of my published articles: "A Critique of the Theory of Delayed Hominization," in D. G. McCarthy and A. S. Moraczewski, eds., *An Ethical Evaluation of Fetal Experimentation,* Appendix I, 113–33; and, co-authored with Albert S. Moraczewski, OP, "Is the Biological Subject of Human Rights Present From Conception?" in Peter J. Cataldo and Albert S. Moraczewski, OP, eds., *The Fetal Tissue Issue: Medical and Ethical Aspects*; and "Cloning, Aquinas, and the Embryonic Person," *The National Catholic Bioethics Quarterly* 1 (2; 2001): 189–202.

[1] The recent use of the term "pre-embryo" begs the question and was not used until it was found useful polemically in the ethical debates by those defending abortion or experimentation with embryos. As Lee M. Silver, *Remaking Eden,* 39, says: "I'll let you in on a secret. The term 'pre-embryo' has been embraced wholeheartedly by IVF practitioners, for reasons that are political, not scientific."

of the completion of the successful fertilization of the human ovum by a human sperm, then in the United States there have been four times as many innocent human beings legally killed as a result of *Roe* v. *Wade* as the number of Jews killed by Hitler and 10,000 times the number killed by terrorists in the Twin Towers. Already unknown thousands of embryos are being discarded in the process of artificial reproduction. Are many thousands more now to be killed in research because of the still highly speculative hopes for medical discoveries that we possibly may achieve in less violent ways? We must face this question in light of objective evidence and reasoned truth, striving to lay aside all prejudice and ideology. We must not, like the Germans who shut their ears to the rumors of the Nazi death-camps, blind ourselves to the bitter truth. But how can we hope to settle this question without appeal to the authority of the Catholic Church, which is not recognized by the majority of Americans?

In our culture the authority whose objectivity is the least questioned is that of science. Modern science, however, refuses to deal with anything more than probabilities and will not deal at all with questions of value. Yet our culture does maintain that human persons have human rights, including a right to life if they do not commit grave crimes. If this were not the case pro-choice arguments would be groundless since *Roe* v. *Wade* is based on the "human right to privacy." If the innocent human embryo has human rights, it is murder to kill it. How do we determine that something has human rights? Peter Singer at Princeton wants to say that animals have rights because they can feel pain;[2] but is pain the best criterion of what it is to be human? Surely there is some more significant mark of humanhood!

Can we settle such crucial questions about human rights simply by public opinion? The majority of Germans had little regard for the rights of Jews. The majority of white Americans formerly had little regard for the rights of other races. The enfranchised majority of men had little respect for the rights of disenfranchised women of the United States. Does that mean that Jews, other races, and women only got human rights when the times changed and a majority consensus developed that they were human? Or did they always have rights when these were denied them? We cannot, therefore, say that embryos do or do not have human rights because *Roe* v. *Wade* or some government-appointed scientific commission says so. Human rights must be grounded in objective facts by which human laws and cultural consensus are measured as just or unjust, not the other way round.

We must decide if our culture contradicts itself when it proudly claims to defend human rights while on the plea of the right of privacy, as interpreted by *Roe* v. *Wade*, it kills embryos. Such a contradiction, if it is such, threatens every human right, since it subordinates all rights to the whims of the court

---

2 Peter Singer, *Animal Liberation: A New Ethics for our Treatment of Animals.*

or the mob. There is no way to defend human rights unless we honestly face the question of whether killing an embryo is killing a human being, and we must first subject that question to the procedures by which modern science attempts to come to a critical judgment about facts. You may object that science itself does not claim to come to certainty but only probability. But in moral and legal matters we do not need absolute certainty, and we seldom can get it. What is sufficient, and usually all that is possible, is a high preponderance of probability. To take a course of action based on a lesser probability in the face of a greater one in matters of life and death is utterly irresponsible.

What is a "Human Person"?

The first difficulty in getting a scientifically probable way of distinguishing a human person with human rights from non-persons is to define a human person. This certainly cannot be done by race or gender or sexual orientation or education or social status. Any such definition goes directly against the notion of human equality on which our belief in human rights rests. One approach taken by those who seek to give an ethical justification to experimentation on human embryos (or "pre-embryos," as they prefer to term them) is to argue that the "potentiality" for human life begins even with the ovum and the sperm and develops continuously without any clear point at which human personhood, with human rights, emerges. C. Grobstein argued this view in 1988 in his *Science and the Unborn: Choosing Human Futures* and has been cited favorably by certain Catholic theologians.[3]

More recently this view has been defended even more forcefully by two biologists, Harold J. Morowitz and James S. Trefil, in *The Facts of Life: Science and the Abortion Controversy*. For them "humanness" seems to be only a legal concept relating to human rights; the question of "ensoulment" is purely religious and subjective, not scientific and objective. Moreover, since the human species is the product of evolution there is continuity between it and other animal species that makes any definition of "humanness" problematic. They grant, however, that "humanness" can at least be given objective biological distinction by the marked development of the cerebral cortex of the human brain that makes possible "new and unexpected functions."[4] For them this means, however, that the production of the one-celled zygote by the fertilization of the human ovum does not have the great significance given it by those who believe that this is when human life begins.

---

[3] Notably Richard A. McCormick, "The Embryo Debate 3: The First 14 Days," *The Tablet* (10 March 1990): 301–4; "Who or What is the Preembryo?," *Kennedy Institute of Ethics Journal* 1 (1991): 1–15; "The Embryo as Potential: A Reply to John A. Robertson," *Kennedy Institute of Ethics Journal* 1 (1991): 303–5.

[4] Harold J. Morowitz and James S. Trefil, *The Facts of Life: Science and the Abortion Controversy*, 100.

> There is no time in the sequence [from gametes to zygote] we've just
> described where life is created. In fact, from the point of view of the
> biologist, *at conception, two previously existing living things come together
> to form another living thing.*[5]

Moreover, they say, other systems than the zygote have "potential life."[6]
They further minimize the uniqueness of the zygote by saying that the fact
its nucleus contains a unique kind of DNA is not so remarkable, since this is
true of surgical tissues, such as cancers, that are gladly discarded.[7] The fact
that perhaps only one-third of fertilized eggs survive also seems to them to
indicate that the zygote is nothing special.[8] They argue, however, that what
is certain is that it is unreasonable to attribute "humanness" to the fetus
until its brain is sufficiently developed so that it can at least feel pain,[9] which
is possible at about 24 weeks of gestation. They support this argument by
emphasizing that any effort to help premature infants to survive "hits the
wall" at this time because before then both the brain and the respiratory system are too immature. Hence they draw the ethical conclusion that:

1. Until the burst of synapse formation in the cortex during the seventh
   month of pregnancy, the right of the woman to choose must take
   precedence. During this period, abortion should be a matter of choice.

2. In the third trimester, mechanisms for decisions should take account
   the concerns of the mother, the values of the community, and the
   realization that the fetus is acquiring a more and more fully functional cortex as times passes.[10]

Interestingly they also say that until synapses of the cerebral cortex develop,
"[w]e can't say that humanness *has* been acquired, but we can't say that it
hasn't either. This is a classical example of a gray area."[11] Although the
authors note that, previously in the book they had indicated unqualified
support for the "pro-choice" movement:

> The effect of sifting through the scientific literature, then, has been to
> move me both toward a less absolute position and to make me realize

---

[5] Ibid., 46ff.
[6] Ibid., 46–48.
[7] Ibid., 49–50.
[8] Ibid., 50–52.
[9] Ibid., 157–59.
[10] Ibid., 154.
[11] Ibid., 155.

that after the onset of humanness, the interests of the fetus must be taken into account along with those of the woman's reflections on the matter.[12]

The objective scientific certainty these authors' claim for denying "humanness" to the pre-embryo, embryo, and fetus up to 24 weeks is hardly convincing. Does it really make sense to speak, as they do, of the gametes or zygote as having "potential life"? The human gametes do not have the capability of becoming a mature human being, but the zygote does and it has this capability not "potentially" but *actually* since it immediately starts to self-construct into a mature human body through a series of phases determined by its genome. Although Morowitz and Trefil correctly say that the genetic information in the zygote is only "the blue-print not the building,"[13] they strangely neglect to note that the zygote itself as a living organism is both the builder and the building, since it is "self-organizing." Is it not also far-fetched to compare the zygote to a cancer or surgically excised tissue in order to show that zygote is disposable? Cancers and excised tissues cannot construct themselves into human persons.

What Morowitz and Trefil regard as the "strongest evidence" against human life beginning at conception, however, is the phenomenon of *parthenogenesis*,[14] demonstrated for amphibians, in which an unfertilized diploid ovum can be artificially stimulated to develop into a mature animal. This has not been observed in placental mammals probably because their ova have a gene necessary for the development of a placenta that is deactivated in the mature female gamete. Hence they need to receive this essential gene in an activated state from the male sperm that possesses it. Yet if we can discover a technique for activating this gene in the ovum, mammals also can be produced by parthenogenesis. Therefore they argue that if the zygote is a person, so must be every human ovum even before fertilization!

It is notable that Morowitz and Trefil only cite and refute arguments of "pro-life" authors who rely chiefly on denouncing the pain caused to the fetus by abortion or who are favorable to their position and hence do not really confront the stronger criticisms of that position. Because they regard the question of "ensoulment" as purely a religious issue, they entirely disregard pro-life arguments of a "philosophical" type that involve a non-religious critique of whether the definitions and principles they claim to be "scientific" are really such. Some court decisions seem based on the assumption of gradualism defended by these authors.

---

[12] Ibid., 165.

[13] Ibid., 48.

[14] Ibid., 52–57. If the "strongest" scientific argument for a case can only be based on something not yet empirically demonstrated, the case is rather weak.

Such distinctions between "human beings" and "human persons" must also be laid aside in our search for answers about the human rights of embryos: The right to life is more fundamental than any other human right since it is presupposed to them all. The embryo either has a right to life and consequently other rights, or it has no rights at all. How could one "gradually" have a right to life? One might, of course, argue that one human has a greater right to life than another; but then the notion of human rights as equal to all human beings has to be abandoned, which is contrary to the whole notion of human rights. In any case the talk of the pre-embryo, embryo, fetus, infant as "potentially" human is of no assistance in deciding when something is *actually* human.[15] The problem before us is: "When does an organism having human rights by nature—and not simply by majority opinion—come into existence?" To achieve an adequate answer we must systematically consider on the basis of current biological data all the major steps in the reproductive process that make it scientifically possible for an entity essentially identical with an adult member of the human species actually to exist.

1. As Grobstein claims and as Morowitz and Trefil argue by citing the evidence for parthenogenesis, this beginning of the human organism might even be prior to the completion of the fertilization of a human ovum by a human sperm. It could instead be some alteration in either the ovum or the sperm that occurs before "conception" in the sense usually given to that term.

2. Or it might be at "conception" in the sense of the completion of fertilization of the human ovum by a human sperm as pro-lifers generally maintain.

3. Or it might be when the zygote has begun to divide and form a small group of cells (the *morula*) and then the hollow *blastula* with the beginning of a differentiation of an inner cell mass from the rest of the cells that form the *trophoblast* or protective membranes and finally implants in the wall of the mother's uterus. Before the question of the ethics of such research was raised, embryologists used the term "embryo" for the phase of development extending from the first division of the zygote to implantation and the appearances of the rudimentary organs, when it was then called a "fetus." Recently, how-

---

[15] To have "potentiality" is to have an intrinsic capability of becoming what it is not actually here and now. A one-year-old child has the potential of becoming an adult human unless impeded by disease or accident—whereas a one-year-old chimp does not have such a potentiality, even if raised in a human environment, because it lacks the intrinsic potentiality of human maturation.

ever, some biologists have begun to call this developing entity a "pre-embryo" and hence speak of "conception" as taking place not at fertilization but at implantation. It is also important to note that up to implantation, identical twinning becomes possible.

4. Or, as Morowitz and Trefil suggest, hominization may take place only when the *primitive streak* that initiates the differentiation of the central nervous system and brain of the fetus appears. The fact that in the adult the great size and complexity of the brain specifies the organism as human seems to support this view.

5. Or does the fetus become human only when its brain is sufficiently developed for some degree of consciousness, even without any ability for abstract human thought, as in animals, as Peter Singer supposes?

6. Or, finally, might hominization be achieved only when the child "quickens," that is, moves in the womb and acquires human rights, as was formerly recognized by the common law? Or could it be, as the Jewish rabbinical tradition holds, or as "partial birth" abortionists claim is allowed by *Roe* v. *Wade*, that this is only when the head of the child emerges from the mother? Or is it, as at least one bioethicist has argued, a year or so after birth when it is evident the child has no serious genetic defects?[16] Or finally, could it only be when the child at about seven first gives clear indications of human moral responsibility?

I will next consider in order each of these possible stages in the reproductive process as a hypothesis to be biologically evaluated.

Which Hypothesis is Biologically the Most Probable?

There are arguments for each of these hypotheses and I grant some probability to most of them, but what has to be decided is which is the most probable since we can hardly ask more of biology. The fundamental concept of biology is that of a "living organism." Let us grant that from ovum to corpse we are talking about something that is living, but what do we mean by an "organism"? An organism is a material body and every material body has parts. To be a "living" organism, however, requires that (a) this body has parts; (b) that these parts be differentiated so as to be able to perform different functions for the survival of the whole body; and (c) that in order to do this the parts must be inter-related and ordered so as to form a unified whole. It is called an "organism" from the fact it has "organs," a term derived

---

[16] Tristram Englehardt, Jr., and others have actually argued in this vein, contending that personhood is a social construct; see his "Beginnings of Personhood: Philosophical Considerations," *Perkins Journal of Theology* (1973): 20–27.

from the Greek word for an "instrument." The many different parts under the control of some principle part perform different but related and coordinated functions to maintain and develop the whole living body.

It should be admitted that in the range of organisms from the most simple to the most complex there is also a range of clear differentiation of parts and their unification by a principal part. These degrees of organic structuring can be known only by observation and experimentation. In the human adult, however, this differentiation of parts is very evident—legs, arms, torso, head, and all their various tissues and special organs. The interrelating and ordering of these parts by a principal part is also very evident, since it is clear that the brain ultimately unifies the actions of the whole body and all its parts. Deprive the brain of oxygen for a very few minutes and the entire body ceases to function and dies. Yet this unification even in the human body is not such that the parts or systems of parts lack some real autonomy of function. After the brain dies, and with it the organism as a whole, some of the parts can—for a time and under special circumstances—continue to have life functions, although only those that are no longer specifically human functions. In some cases a brain-dead human body can continue to have metabolic functions if maintained on a life-support apparatus. What remains is not a human organism even if it seems for a while to be a human asleep. Gross appearances, therefore, are not very much help in answering our question. What we are looking for is exactly when a human organism as such, as a unified whole, first appears, and also when it ceases to be.

With this understanding of a living organism, Hypothesis 1 that places hominization before completion of the fertilization of the ovum by the sperm can be evaluated. According to this view either the ovum is already a human organism requiring only some external stimulus in order to begin developing to human maturity; or alternatively the sperm is already a human organism requiring only some nutrition from the ovum to develop to human maturity. The real difficulty with this hypothesis is that although, of course, a single cell can be a complete organism, neither the human ovum or the sperm cell is a complete organism. They first exist as parts of the two parents and only become detached from those bodies in the sexual process. They have a kind of life as instruments of the parents' bodies, but it is purely transitory life since they cannot live or reproduce on their own. Yet when they fuse to form the single-celled zygote (the term means "yoked," because the zygote is formed from the sperm and ovum) in a suitable environment, it can live on its own. The fact that the embryo is so tiny by no means indicates that it is not a complete organism. What enables a one-celled entity to live on its own, as so many bacteria do, is that it has a complete set of genes, while the human ovum and sperm each have only half the genes necessary for human organic life; they are *haploid*. Yet the moment they fuse in a single fertilized cell, normally in one of the Fallopian tubes of the mother who has supplied the ovum, a complete organism exists. Moreover, the genetic composition of this single cell is specifically human and already has that uniqueness that characterizes a human person as remarkably individualized. Thus it is certainly an organism that is a member of the human species.

What then of the argument from parthenogenesis, proposed by Morowitz and Trefil? If successful parthenogenesis could be artificially produced with a human diploid ovum, such an activated ovum would simply be the equivalent of a naturally fertilized ovum, that is, a zygote. Hence it does not follow that unfertilized ova that have not been thus artificially made into zygotes would already be persons.

Therefore Hypothesis 2, according to which hominization takes place at conception in the sense of the completion of fertilization and the initiation of the life of the one-cell zygote with a complete human genome in its nucleus, is far more probable than Hypothesis 1, which places hominization before fertilization. Indeed Hypothesis 1 is certainly false, because even though the ovum and sperm could be called organisms they are not one organism, nor is either a complete organism.

Yet is Hypothesis 2 more probable than Hypotheses 3 to 5 or any of the variations on Hypothesis 6? Proponents of Hypothesis 3, namely that the human being begins at implantation of the pre-embryo in the uterus, support their position by two main arguments. The first argument is that only a small minority of the cells that result from the progressive division of the zygote to constitute the blastula are ancestral to the body of the infant. The great majority go to form the trophoblast that becomes the protective membranes for the fetus during the rest of the pregnancy, as well as the placenta and the umbilical cord that connects the fetus to the mother. These organs are discarded in the afterbirth. This answer to our problem, however, has little if any probability, since the history of the trophoblast is that of a temporary organ of the fetus, which it needs only during its residence in the womb. Even in later life it is possible for an organ to atrophy when it no longer serves its natural function; for example, the thymus gland that is part of the human immune system begins to shrink at the age of fifteen, and the ovaries in women cease to function at menopause.

The second argument for saying that implantation initiates hominization is much more plausible because before implantation identical twins are sometimes produced. If it were true that as long as twinning remains possible the embryo must be simply a mass of independent totipotential cells *(blastomeres)*, then why are only two (or a very few) persons produced instead of as many as there are embryonic cells? Since each is totipotential and said to be independent of the others, each has as much potentiality to become human as any other. Why do they not all develop into a blastula with a neural streak?

How, on the basis of the delayed hominization theory, can we explain why *normally* the human zygote does not produce twins or multiples, but a single person? This theory would seem to demand that normally the cleavage of the zygote into what this theory claims is only a loose collection of totipotential cells would result in as many persons as there are such cells.

Norman Ford sees no difficulty in admitting that the zygote was a complete organism of the human species;[17] but he then goes on to say rather oddly,

> Whatever the cause of monozygotic twinning in the zygote at the two-cell stage, the fact that it cleaves into two individual blastomeres that may develop separately as identical twins does not mean the zygote itself is not a true ontological individual. We know it is a living ontological individual. But once it divides mitotically into two separate twin daughter blastomeres, it apparently ceases to exist and loses it ontological individuality to give rise to two new genetically identical, but distinct living ontological individuals within the zona pellucida.[18]

---

[17] "The zygote is not the same ontological individual as either one of the eventual twins that result from its development, notwithstanding its genetic identity continuing throughout all its subsequent cleavages." Norman Ford, *When Did I Begin? Conception of the Human Individual in History, Philosophy and Science,* 119. Cloning does not show, however, that the "ontological" individual *A* "ceases to exist" and in its place two "ontological" individuals come into existence, but that *A* existed before *B* and continues to exist when *B,* derived from *A,* comes into existence. This holds also for the zygote as the *A* clone; the facts in no way show that it ceases to exist but simply that once it has lost a cell, out of which *B* develops, it can by its regulative power supply this loss by again dividing. Of course, if twinning takes place at the two-cell stage, it may be arbitrary which of the two cells is called *A,* as the immediate successor of the zygote, and which *B,* since they come into existence simultaneously. If, however, further research demonstrates a polarity in the zygote, such as has been demonstrated in other mammalian species, as is probable, then that cell which contains the cytoplasm of the animal pole can properly be called *A,* that which contains the cytoplasm of the vegetal pole *B,* since the animal pole is more active and thus anticipates the head or primary organ than is the vegetal pole.

[18] The use of the term "ontological individuality" by Norman Ford (note 17 above) and Jason T. Eberl, "The Beginning of Personhood: A Thomistic Biological Analysis," *Bioethics: Journal of the International Association of Bioethics* 14 (2000): 134–57, misplaces the question into a different context than that in which Aquinas treats it and makes it difficult to relate it to the empirical data supplied by modern scientific embryology. Of course, if by "ontological" one simply means "real," there is, of course, no objection to saying that the individuality of the embryo is an empirical fact, but if the term "ontological" introduces metaphysical considerations, it is not relevant. Aquinas's so-called theory of "delayed hominization" originated not in Aristotle's *Metaphysics* but in his *De Generatione Animalium* and *De Anima,* works that form part of his *scientia naturalis* whose foundational principles are treated in his *Physics* and, hence, are not "metaphysical," but "physical," that is, empirical. Eberl in

This argument neglects a number of biological facts. Twinning in the human species is a reproductive abnormality since it is disadvantageous to both the mother and the offspring. Like the high rate of failure of pregnancies already mentioned, it is not surprising that, considering the extreme complexity of the reproductive process and the frailty of the embryo, such aberrations occur. About 65 percent of identical twinning takes place at the end of the first week when the blastocyst of some 50 or 60 cells (blastomeres) forms. The other 35 percent occurs during the first three days when cell cleavage, beginning about 30 hours after fertilization, is preceding rapidly until the time at about the 12-cells state when the cells undergo "compaction" into a globular cluster called the *morula*. Twinning at the first cleavage mentioned above by Ford is quite rare and its details have not as yet been much studied.

The argument in question is based on the notion that the cells into which the zygote divides are undifferentiated because their nuclei are *genetically* identical, but this is only one mode in which the parts of an embryo are differentiated. In fact cells that are genetically identical can be differentiated both by their *cytoplasmic content* and by their *position* within the embryo. Thus a cell or group of cells that can, when separated from the embryo, exercise their totipotentiality and produce a clone or twin, may not be able to do so when occupying a definite position in the embryo as one or several of its constituent cells. It has also been shown that early human embryos have remarkable "regulative" powers, that is, abilities to continue normal development even after its cells have been rearranged or some have been removed. This supports rather than negates the importance for future development of the actual position of a cell or cell group within the embryo, since it is that position that ultimately determines the outcome of genetic regulation on any cell.

Until implantation the embryo receives no additional material from the mother, except some fluids that enter at the blastocyst stage. Hence as the nucleus of the zygote is replicated to supply identical genetic material for each new cell produced by cleavage, the original cytoplasm of the zygote is portioned out among these cells. The new cells are for some time genetically totipotential, and hence in this respect undifferentiated, but from the beginning they are cytoplasmically differentiated. It is well known that generally in mammals, even in the unfertilized ovum, there is already an "animal" pole of the cell from which, if it becomes fertilized as a zygote, the central nervous system and senses will eventually originate, in contrast to a "vegetal"

---

a personal communication has assured me that he has now become convinced that the human person begins at conception. Ford himself, "The Human Embryo as Person in Catholic Teaching," *The National Catholic Bioethics Quarterly* 1 (2; Summer 2001): 155–60, also seems to have moderated his views, *When Did I Begin?* 84ff.

pole from which the digestive system will originate.[19] This axial polarity has not yet been demonstrated for human development, only a ventral-dorsal polarity in the embryo at the blastocyst stage.[20] Nevertheless, considering the basic similarity of embryo development among mammals, it would be strange if such a head-tail polarity of the embryo, even at the first cell division, were absent in the human species.

This differentiation by position, however, does not overcome the lack of genetic differentiation. Throughout the pre-embryo, pre-implantation phase, all or some of the newly divided cells do not have any of their genes turned off and hence are "totipotential," just as was the original zygote from which they have been formed. As long as such totipotential cells remain, as such cells normally do, in close contact with the other cells of the original organism, their differentiation by position prevents them from becoming new and distinct organisms in their own right.

Actually for some time as the organism divides its cells to form a morula and then a hollow blastula, all its cells are held together by a surrounding structure called the *zona pelucida* until they "compact" in such a way as to stick still more closely to each other. Thus it is false to claim, as at least some Catholic writers on this subject have asserted, that the pre-embryo is "a loose collection of cells"; it is always a unified organism in which cell division takes place in a specific order determined by the human genome present in the zygote and with interactions going on at all times between the cells. Of course this unity is less perfect at the beginning of cell division than it gradually becomes, and this is why identical twinning, although abnormal and quite rare, can occur. By implantation the pre-embryo has developed so complex and unified a structure that its cells are sufficiently differentiated by the turning off of genes that if some cells become detached they lack the potentiality that would permit them to live as distinct organisms. Thus what happens in identical twinning is as follows: The zygote is a complete though totipotential organism, but if during its first cell divisions some still genetically totipotential cells become separated, since they are no longer positionally differentiated, they can become new zygotes genetically identical to the first one. Thus the second twin organism is a few hours or a few days younger

---

19 "In this context [of the discussion of how the egg or ovum is asymmetrical] animal refers to typical animal organs such as eyes or the central nervous system, which often are formed in the vicinity of the egg's animal pole." The adjective "vegetal" refers to the future "vegetative organs that derive from the primordial gut and serve to 'lower' functions of life such as processing for food." Werner A. Müller, *Developmental Biology*, 1977, 12.

20 "Mammalian and human embryos appear to leave the site where the inner cell mass will segregate to chance. The position of the inner cell mass defines the future dorsal side. How the head-tail polarity is specified in unknown." Müller, *Developmental Biology*, 169.

than the first one, but—and this is the essential point—the first one has always existed as an organism and continues its development alongside its new twin. Thus while this explains the moment of origin of the second twin, it does not in any way contradict the reasons supporting Hypothesis 2, which remains much more probable than either Hypotheses 1 or 3.

Thus even from the first cleavage, one of the two cells, namely, the one from the animal pole, is related to the neural streak, or primordial central nervous system that Ford's argument considers the point at which ensoulment occurs. Moreover, through the early formation of the blastocyst the zona pellucida holds the cleaving cells together and "compaction" occurs. This zona must be considered part of the embryo, though a temporary one, not something extrinsic to the organism. There is never, therefore, a time in which after the zygote begins to divide within this zona that a loose collection of independent human cells exists. Even before compaction these blastomeres must be interacting physiologically or compaction and development of the blastocyst would not occur.

Most twinning takes place at the blastocyst stage in which there is already a differentiation of the inner cell mass or embryonic plate that is to become the permanent body of the fetus from the trophoblast that surrounds it. This trophoblast develops more rapidly than the inner cell mass because by it the embryo becomes able to implant in the mother's uterus so as to obtain nutrition and begin to grow quantitatively. Monozygotic twins are produced when the embryonic plate through some accident splits within the amnion and chorion that protect it and the detached portion of still totipotential cells begins independent development. But obviously this split occurs when the embryo is already considerably structured as a unified living entity that becomes cloned by the separation of part of its embryonic disc.

Thus there is no reason to think that the zygote, the morula, and the blastocyst are different organisms, nor that the embryo as it is transformed by successive cleavages has "lost its ontological individuality" at any point. If by a developmental accident twinning occurs at any point during these phases of growth of the human individual, the only reasonable explanation is that a clone of that individual has been formed by its loss of a part that by reason of its totipotentiality can begin an independent development. Thus organism A that was developing normally up to the point of accidental twinning continues its development alongside its somewhat younger clone, its monozygotic twin.

Furthermore, although the cells in the morula and blastocyst may not be as tightly bound together as they will later be in the fetus, they are already intimately connected and interacting with each other. Living cells are "sticky" and quickly form chemical bonds as is evident in the process of "compaction" that unites the blastomeres in the morula, a process that begins no later than the eight-cell stage. Protein synthesis has already begun in this early cleavage phase or development would cease. There is also clear evidence that cell cleavage is not a random process since it takes place according to a definite pattern and orientation that is regulated by the genome. Thus the notion that the jelly of the zona pellucida, once the zygote divides, holds only a loose collection of independent organisms is simply contrary to the evidence that a lively interchange of biochemicals is occurring between these cells as they continue to subdivide in an orderly manner and compact. Therefore the embryonic cells, even though when isolated from the embryo are genetically totipotential, as long as they remain in the embryo they are already the *differentiated* parts of a single self-developing organism predetermined by its guiding genome to form specific parts of its life structure.

Hypothesis 4 is that hominization begins with the appearance of the *primitive* streak in the embryo. Hypothesis 5 is that it begins much later when this streak has developed into a central system with a distinct brain. Hypothesis 6 is that it is only when this brain is so developed, at birth or even after birth, that some form of specifically genuine consciousness becomes possible. All three hypotheses rest on a single assumption, namely that it is the emergence of the human brain either at a primitive or developed stage that constitutes hominization.

This assumption goes back all the way to Aristotle, whose views will be examined at some length later, who argued that a unified organism requires a principle part that directed not only the functioning of the other organs but also their embryological differentiation and development. Since he thought mistakenly that in animals the heart is this primary organ, he concluded that animal life began only with the appearance, at least in rudimentary form, of the heart. Later biologists corrected his notion that the heart, not the brain, is the primary organ in adult animals, and hence concluded on the same principle that animal embryos, including the human embryo, were alive only at a vegetative level until their brains, at least in rudimentary form, had begun to differentiate. This was adopted in the common law that recognized the rights of a human person only when the fetus "quickened," that is, exhibited activities indicating a functioning brain.

Thus it is precisely this principle of organic order that is also presupposed by Hypotheses 4, 5, and 6. It is because we know that the brain is the primary organ of the specifically human body in its maturity that there is a probable argument for supposing that the human organism with human rights begins at the primitive streak, or some stage of brain development.

Nevertheless, modern embryology has shown that there is a flaw in the way in which these hypotheses apply the principle of order. While it is true that the brain emerges as the primary organ controlling human functions, the emergence of the brain itself is the work of the genome already present in the zygote. This is true not only in the sense that the gene contains the program for building the brain but also in the sense that since the genome first exists in the nucleus of the zygote as its primary organ that zygote has the intrinsic capacity to develop itself. What follows is the continuous growth of an already existing organism, not some new organism. The nucleus of the zygote is not only the program for building a human organism but it provides the zygote with the power to build itself into the mature differentiated structure that is the mature human being. Thus the nucleus, or primary organ of the zygote, contains not only the blueprint for a human being with rights, it is also its builder, its efficient cause. The so-called pre-embryo receives little or no nourishment from without itself, and even after implantation receives nourishment and protection only from its mother. Since this is the case, Hypotheses 4, 5, and 6 are less probable than Hypothesis 2, namely, that the human organism begins with conception in the sense of the completion of the fertilization of the ovum and the formation of the zygote as a true organism capable of developing itself into a mature human being. As a human organism it has equal rights with every other human organism, no matter what their stage of development. To deny this is to contradict the principle of human equality.

We can conclude, therefore, that on purely scientific, biological grounds the most probable conclusion—and its probability is high, approaching the type of certitude possible in such matters—is that the human organism originates at conception defined as complete fertilization of the ovum by the sperm. Moral decisions must be responsibly made on the basis of such objective fact and do not require absolute theoretical certitude.

Philosophical and Theological Considerations

The foregoing scientific conclusion, however, is at odds with a long tradition that deserves respectful and detailed attention. Nothing has yet been said about what philosophers and theologians, but few biologists, call the "soul" of the human being or its immateriality. Some philosophers, of course, deny that we can know whether the human soul as distinguished from the organization of other subhuman organisms is spiritual. Some of the greatest philosophers, however, have maintained this can be proved to be the case, and I am convinced by their best arguments. But this is not the place to take up that question. I will simply assume that most of us do believe that we are in some sense spiritual beings by reason of our intelligence and freedom. Indeed it is difficult to explain how we humans can be free and hence have human rights and moral obligations if we are merely material organisms whose behavior is wholly determined by natural laws and chance. The major religions of course maintain that we have a spiritual and immortal soul, and the Christian religion maintains both that this can be proved by reason and that it must be believed as infallibly revealed.

Moreover, as Pope Pius XII and the *Catholic Catechism* have declared, it is an infallibly revealed truth that the human soul is the vital form of the body generated by the parents but that it is itself not produced by them or by any biological process. It is instead created for the body by a direct divine act of creation *ex nihilo*.[21] The spiritual human soul, therefore, does not exist before the human body but God in the act of creating it brings to completion the biological process of human reproduction so that the beginning of human life is simultaneously the origin of both body and soul, that is, of the whole human person. This point is sometimes misunderstood because this marvelous event is often referred to as the "infusion of the human soul into the body," thus giving the false impression that the soul pre-exists the body. This much is theologically certain and is supported by good philosophical arguments.

Contrary to popular belief, even among some "pro-lifers," the opposition of the Catholic Church to abortion and direct killing of the pre-embryo, therefore, does not depend on the time of ensoulment. Even if the embryo is not yet ensouled, it has dignity from its role in the reproductive process as has been clearly stated by the Congregation for the Doctrine of the Faith, *Instruction on Respect for Human Life in it s Origin and on the Dignity of Procreation: Replies to Certain Questions of the Day,* 1987.

> The Magisterium has not expressly committed itself to an affirmation of a philosophical nature [as to the time of ensoulment], but it constantly affirms the moral condemnation of any kind of procured abortion. This teaching has not been changed and is unchangeable. The human being is to be respected and treated as a person from the moment of conception, and therefore from that same moment his or her rights as a person must be recognized, among which in the first place is the inviolable right of every innocent human being to life. (I, n. 1).

Actually, as stated earlier, from the time of Aristotle and later adopted by St. Thomas Aquinas and hence always respected by the Catholic Church, it was supposed that it was the appearance of the human heart, rather than of the brain, that marked hominization.[22] When medical advance showed that

---

[21] "In order that all may know the truth of the faith in its purity and all error may be excluded, we define that anyone who presumes henceforth to assert, defend, or hold stubbornly that the rational or intellectual soul is not the form of the human body of itself and essentially, is to be considered a heretic." Ecumenical Council of Vienne, 1312, Denzinger-Schönmetzer, n. 902; Pope Pius XII, *Humani Generis,* n. 36; *Catechism of the Catholic Church,* 2nd ed., n. 365.

[22] Aristotle's views are to be found in his *History of Animals, Parts of Animals,* and *Generation of Animals.* It has seemed to me unnecessary to document them here in detail.

the brain, not the heart, is the primary human organ that unifies the whole human organism, this position was modified but its essential reasoning was retained. The Church, however, although it accepted the cessation of cardiac function as certain evidence of human death, did not also conclude officially that the beginning of cardiac function was the sure sign of the presence of the human soul.[23] This is why some recent Catholic philosophers and theologians have revived the views of whether St. Thomas Aquinas and Bl. Duns Scotus who in different ways supported a theory of "delayed hominization" some weeks after conception. It was this view that led St. Thomas to hesitate

---

As for Aquinas, the chief texts relating directly to this question (in probable chronological sequence according to James A. Weisheipl, OP, *Friar Thomas D'Aquino*, 395ff, are as follows: *II Scriptum Sententiis* (1252–56): II dist. 8, q. l, a. 4 ad 2 (demons could generate only by using human seed); dist. 18, q. 1 a. 2 (notion of *rationes seminales*); dist. 78, q. 2 aa. 1 and 3 (mediate animation); dist. 20, q. 1, a. l and 3 (human persons are uniquely intended by God); a. 2 c. (reasons for sexual difference), ad 4, 5, 6 (semen is well-digested food); q. 2, a. 1, ad 1 and 2 (female is not unnatural); a. 2c and ad 5 (imaginative power is in forebrain); dist. 30, q. 2 a. 3 (human souls share inequality of human bodies); III. dist. 3 q. 2, a. l (male parent is agent of organization, female in preparing matter and nutrition); q. 5 a. 1 and 2 (Christ was animated at conception); IV d. 44, q. l, a. 2 sol. 3 and a. 5 ad 5 (embryo before animation will not be resurrected). *Summa contra Gentiles* (completed 1264): II, c. 58 (only intellective soul in man); cc. 68–69 (how soul is form of body); c. 72 (soul is whole in the whole, and whole in every part); c. 86–89 (mediate animation); IV cc. 48–49 (Christ was animated at conception); c. 8 (sex difference remains in resurrected body). *Compendium Theologiae* (possibly contemporary with *Summa contra Gentiles*): cc. 92–95 (mediate animation). *De potentia* (1265): q. 3 aa. 9–12 (mediate animation); q. 5 a. 9 (role of cosmic forces in generation). *De malo* (1266–67): q. 4 aa. 3, 6, 7 (original sin transmitted seminally). *De spiritualibus creaturis* (1267–68): a. 3 ad 13 (life in embryo); a. 4 and 5 (how the whole soul is in all the parts). *De anima* (1269): aa. 8–12, especially a. 1 ad 2 (mediate animation). (i) *Summa theologiae* I (1266–68): q. 76 (union of soul and body); q. 78 (powers of the soul); qq. 90–92 (creation of man); q. 99 (Adam's children); q. 118, aa. 1–3 (mediate animation); q.119 (propagation of human body); III (1272–73): q. 6 a. 4 (matter of Christ's body existed before Christ); qq. 27–28 (the Virginal Conception); q. 31 aa. 4–8 (conception of Christ); q. 33 (Christ was animated at conception). For information on the medieval discussions of Aristotelian embryology, see M. Anthony Hewson, *Giles of Rome and the Medieval Theory of Conception: A Study of the De formatione corporis humani in utero*.

[23] In the baptismal instruction of the *Didache*, dating from before a.d. 120, after the first commandment of love we read: "But the second commandment of the teaching is this, 'Thou shalt not procure abortion nor commit infanticide.'" *The Apostolic Fathers*, 311. For the history of the question, see John Connery, SJ, *Abortion: The Development of the Roman Catholic Perspective*; and on the history of this question, see John T. Noonan, Jr., "An Almost Absolute Value in History" in *The Morality of Abortion: Legal and Historical Perspectives*, which he edited, 1–59.

about the doctrine of the Immaculate Conception of the Blessed Virgin Mary, though Duns Scotus defended it. Perhaps it has been out of respect for these great Doctors of the Church that the Church has never infallibly declared when the creation of the human soul takes place.

The reason, however, that these theologians were hesitant was their lack of the biological information that I have given above. They reasoned that since the human soul and its body are made for each other and are correlative causes of each other as form and matter, the matter of the human body has to be in a condition of proximate preparation proportionate to the soul that God creates for it. Otherwise we would be "multiplying miracles," which good Catholic theologians are always reluctant to do. Human conception is a natural event belonging to the cosmic order set up by a wise Creator; it is not a miraculous intervention, although it is a creative act that exceeds all but divine power.

St. Thomas Aquinas, following Aristotle, argued that the human embryo is at first alive only with vegetative life, then with animal or sensitive life, and only after at least 40 days of development is it prepared to become a human person by receiving a human, intellective soul from the Creator. Consequently, induced abortion before 40 days is a serious "sin against nature," because it destroys an organism whose natural purpose is to be transformed into a human being, but such abortion is not, strictly speaking, homicide.

Strangely, this medieval theory is again the subject of discussion among Catholic theologians in spite of the fact that since Vatican II they are eager to free their thinking from a rigid "official" Thomism, and that they vigorously reject Aquinas's views, also derived from Aristotelian biology, about male superiority. Although ultimately the authoritative position of the Catholic Church does not rest on the acceptance or rejection of Aquinas's theory of "delayed hominization" (the term is not his but of recent origin), it requires careful examination, even at the cost of some scholastic subtleties, for two reasons.

First, it must be recalled that in the casuistic technique of traditional Catholic moral theology, weight is always given to traditional positions of notable authorities, even when these opinions appear to have only an extrinsic value, somewhat as in arguing from legal precedents. According to the principle of casuistic *probabilism*, it is safe in practice to follow such solidly probable opinions even when the opposite view is more probable. Consequently, a number of responsible moral theologians in recent publications have adduced the authority of Aquinas, of Alphonsus Ligouri, and numerous other "standard authors" to argue that there is solid probability that induced abortion in the earliest period of pregnancy is not homicide. Therefore in a conflict of right that involves grave risk to the life of the mother (or an equivalent risk), the rights of the mother, who is certainly human, may be preferred against those of the fetus who is probably not human in the earliest period of pregnancy.[24] Fr. Joseph Donceel, SJ, in several influential articles,[25] has not only strengthened this argument from authority by showing that the opposite view arose in the church in the seventeenth century, largely through the influence of Cartesian dualism, but has gone on to argue the validity of Aquinas's theory of "mediate animation" (or "delayed hominization," as Donceel more accurately names it) on its own intrinsic merits. He believes that when Aquinas's theory has been freed from medieval biology it remains valid as a philosophical theory, and when this theory is used to interpret the data of modern embryology, we can conclude with high probability, even certainty, that the embryo in its first three months of existence cannot be a human person. The only solid reason, therefore, for opposing abortion during this period is that this is a "sin against nature." Donceel is not alone in his views that were also supported by the Dominican theologian Fr. A. Plé, OP, and by two Catholic physicians, James J. Diamond, MD, and Bernard J. Bans, MD.[26]

Not only did Aquinas hold for delayed hominization, but the great Franciscan theologian Bl. Duns Scotus also accepted it and explained it by his famous "real but only formal" distinction between the "corporeity" of the body and the spiritual soul, a position that reflects the influences of Platonic dualism in which the soul inhabits a body alien to it. Recently this Scotistic view has been revived in the service of a theory of delayed hominization, but

---

[24] John Dedek, "Abortion," in *Contemporary Medical Ethics*, 109–85. Dedek takes the position that "[c]ontemporary theologians are only returning to an earlier theological position, saying that the prohibition of abortion is not an absolute one. Ordinarily the purposeful destruction of a fetus is morally wrong. But exceptions to this rule have to be made when a proportionate value, another life or its moral equivalent, is at stake" (p. 131); he quotes Karl Rahner, SJ, Robert Springer, SJ, Richard McCormick SJ, and Bernard Haring, CSSR in his support.

[25] Fr. Joseph Donceel, SJ, "Causality and Evolution," *New Scholasticism* 39 (1965): 295–315; "Abortion: Mediate and Immediate Animation," *Continuum* 5 (1967): 167–71; "Immediate Animation and Delayed Hominization," *Theological Studies* 31 (1970): 76–105; and, "Why is Abortion Wrong?" America (August 16, 1975): 65–67.

[26] A. Plé, OP, *"Alert au Traducianisme."* Plé does not say that mediate animation is more probable, but only that many current writers against abortion seem to use crypto-traducian arguments; that is, they forget that while the special creation of the human soul is *de fide*, there is no revelation concerning the moment of hominization. Plé continues the defense of St. Thomas's position maintained by several Dominican writers during the neo-Thomistic period, see e.g., H. M. Hering, OP, "De tempore animationis foetus humani," *Angelicum* 28 (1951): 18–19, and M. Hudeczek, "De tempore animationis foetus humani secundum embryologian hodiernam," *Angelicum* 29 (1952): 162–81, who makes a strong argument on the basis of twinning. James J. Diamond, "Abortion, Animation and Biological Hominization," *Theological Studies* 36 (1975): 305–24, and Bernard J. Ransil, MD, *Abortion*.

since it presupposed the same faulty embryological data as Aquinas's views, I will not discuss it here.[27]

On the contrary, I will argue that if the philosophical principles of Aquinas are correctly applied to the data of modern embryology, the theory of delayed hominization turns out to be quite implausible. Consequently, we must judge the traditional authority for this view in Catholic moral theology to be obsolete, since it would appear from the history of the question, as outlined by Donceel himself, that St. Thomas's defense of the theory was not only the most influential but also the strongest on its merits.

Fr. Donceel's argument is stated by him succinctly as follows:

> Philosophically speaking, we can be certain that an organism is a human person only from its activities. The most typically human activity is reflection, self-awareness, the power of saying, "I." Of course, if we had to wait until a child starts to say "I" or to use the word "true" (which implies some self-reflection), we would have to delay hominization until longer after birth. The Church has condemned this position (*DS* 2135) and rightly so. When we sleep or have fainted, we possess no self-awareness either, yet we remain human beings; we remain capable of such activities. A person in the ultimate stage of senility may give no more sign of self-awareness, yet he still possesses the organs required for such activity. The least we may ask before admitting the presence of a human soul is the availability of these organs: the senses, the nervous system, the brain and especially the cortex. Since these organs are not ready during early pregnancy, I feel certain that there is no human person until several weeks have elapsed.[28]

Donceel bases this argument on the Thomistic principle that since the human soul, although spiritual, is created by God as the substantial form of the human body, it can only inform matter sufficiently prepared for ensoulment, and this requires that this matter have: (a) a differentiation into organs, including (b) the proper organ of man's highest animal activities (the "internal senses"), which, according to modern understanding, must be the cerebral cortex.[29] He gives little attention to St. Thomas's concern with the question of the efficient cause of the preparation of the matter, although his-

---

[27] See Thomas Shannon and Alan Wolter, OFM, "Reflections on the Moral Status of the Pre-Embryo," *Theological Studies* (1990: 51): 603–26.

[28] Donceel, "Immediate Animation and Delayed Hominization," 101.

[29] According to W. J. Hamilton, J. D. Boyd, and H. W. Mossman, *Human Embryology: Prenatal Development of Form and Function*, "The primordium of the hippocampus is the first part of the human cortex to differentiate. It arises in embryos of about 12 mm" (p. 297). Such an embryo would be about 40 days old.

torically this is the principal question for Aquinas.[30] For Donceel the issue is simply that of the relation of the material to the efficient cause. We can formulate his essential argument thus:

> Hominization is possible only when there exists the organ (i.e., the actual capability) required for the specifically human operations of thought and will.

> This organ is the brain, and probably the cerebral cortex.

> Therefore, hominization is possible only when there exists the brain, or better, the cerebral cortex.

I concede the major premise of this argument, at least as a correct statement of Aquinas's hylomorphic philosophy of the unity of the human person, but I would distinguish the minor by substituting for "cerebral cortex" the expression "the epigenetic primordium *(anlage)* of the cerebral cortex." Clearly Donceel himself does not mean that the cerebral cortex in its full mature development must be present, since this would bring hominization to a postnatal period, but only that it must be present in some way that we can empirically verify its radical identity with the mature cortex. As he grants, it need not be actually operational.

Our problem, therefore, becomes to determine on the basis of current data at what point in human embryonic development this radical identity can be verified. Since preformationist theories of embryology are not scientifically acceptable today, and are certainly inconsistent with hylomorphism, what we are trying to determine is the epigenetic, and not the preformed, origin of the cortex. Following Aquinas's line of thought, then, what results do we arrive at in view of current data?

The Meaning and Implications of this Thomistic Theory

1. *What degree of preparation of the matter did Aquinas require for its union with the spiritual soul to be possible?*

To answer this query, we must understand the epigenetic theory of embryology, which Aquinas derived from Aristotle, but which is often overlooked by advocates of delayed hominization.[31] The basic axiom of Aristotle's philosophy of nature is

---

[30] For Aquinas, as for most patristic and medieval theologians, this question was discussed in the context of the problem of the transmission of original sin, in opposition to Tertullian's *traducianism,* i.e., the theory that the parents produced the spiritual soul of the child as well as its biological organism. For the history of this, see A. Chollet, *Animation,* and J. Bainvel, *"Ame"* in *Dictionnaire de theologie.*

[31] Aristotle's theory is developed in *De Generatione Animalium* II, c. 1, 733b 24 sq. Aquinas did not comment on this work, but he constantly refers to it. What Aristotle meant by *epigenesis* (the term today is sometimes vaguely taken simply to mean

that "whatever is moved is moved by another." At first sight the living organism seems to defy this law, because a living thing is precisely a substance that is self-moving, self-developing, self-reproductive. This self-activity is the empirical evidence that a thing is alive and ensouled, since by "soul" we simply mean the form of a material thing that is self-active. The different species of living things are specified and recognized precisely by different kinds of such self-activity. Man is man and is recognized to be such by the fact that he has characteristic human self-activities, such as speech, invention, free choice.

The soul of a living thing, however, is its principle as a formal cause, not as an efficient cause. It is only by mediation of its parts, each informed by a vital "power" (which is to the part as the soul is to the whole organism) that a living thing moves itself, one part moving another. Consequently, in every living being there must be parts, and these (unlike the parts of inanimate chemical substances) must be heterogeneous, at least to the extent that one part is active and the other passive, so that the organism can move itself with the active part used to move the passive part. This active part is the *primary* part; and the passive part is, at first, in the embryological development of the organism, undifferentiated. The organism develops *epigenetically* because of this original lack of differentiation. (In the theory of *preformism* the parts would exist in differentiation from the start, but in miniature.)

However, from the beginning this primary part must exist not only as actually differentiated but must also be actively efficient (i.e., it must be not only in "first act" but also in "second act") because it is the "prime mover" of the whole organic system, without which it could not be alive, nor develop to maturity. The organism is ensouled and alive at the instant when this primary part first appears and begins to act, and it dies when the primary part ceases to act and is destroyed.

Aristotle, however, did not mean by this that when the primary organ first appears, it is itself fully developed in its own structure, nor that it already has its highest and specifically characteristic functions. He had done embryological experiments with fertilized chicken eggs, and he knew that the heart (which he regarded as the primary organ of animal life that in maturity would be the energetic source of the specifying activity of the animal) was the first organ to appear in the chicken egg, where it becomes visible to the naked eye as a pulsating red spot. As this primary organ is the agent that causes the formation of all other parts of the organism, if in its adult form it is complex it must at first have some truly primary part or "primordium" that causes it to develop to this perfect state. Thus the primary

---

the opposite of "preformation") was that the organism when first constituted as an individual need have only *two* differentiated parts, one of which then acts as the agent to differentiate the other parts out of the matter of the other that at first is only *potentially* differentiated.

organ is first present in very simple form, and as it constructs the total organism it also constructs itself in mature form. Similarly, at maturity, this primary organ will be the source of the total activity of the organism, including its highest specifying functions. Thus Aristotle knew that some animals are born before they are able to exercise all characteristic functions proper to their species, especially of sensing and moving; and in all animals the power of reproduction is possible only when the animal approaches maturity.

Thus we can answer our initial question by saying that the human body is sufficiently prepared for the human soul when and only when its primary organ is actually present and beginning to perform its vital functions, but that (a) the other parts need not be differentiated; (b) the primary organ need be present only in primordial form; and (c) it need only be functioning to bring about the embryological development of itself and the whole, while its ultimate highest and specifying functions may still be in abeyance, awaiting the various auxiliary organs necessary for such functioning. Finally, we must note that the primary organ, even when it is acting at this more primitive level of functioning, is still acting specifically in a manner characteristic of the species of the organism. This is true because, according to the Aristotelian dictum, "an activity is specified by its term"; hence, since the primary organ is at work building a chicken, a dog, or a human being, its functioning is already the activity of a chicken, dog, or human.

2. *Why then, did Aristotle and Aquinas doubt that the primary organ of human life, and hence the human soul, was present even in primordial form earlier than 40 days of pregnancy?*

Aquinas's doubts, at least, were not based on any idea that the primary organ of human life had to be very large or evidently elaborated. This is clear from the fact that he believed that in the case of the conception of Jesus by the Holy Spirit, hominization took place simultaneously with conception. This was possible because the infinite power of the Holy Spirit was able to complete this necessary preparation of the matter in an instant. However, Aquinas concedes that, at this point, the quantity of Christ's body was very small, and it would be grotesque to suppose that Aquinas imagined this in some preformist, rather than epigenetic, manner.[32]

---

[32] "An individual has its minimum quality in the first instant of its formation and animation, which is so small that it barely exceeds the size of ant, as Aristotle says in IX *De Anima* (*Historia Animalium* VII, 3, 583b 17–18) that when a certain woman suffered an abortion on the fortieth day of pregnancy, the body of the fetus was found to have all its members differentiated, although it was only the size of an ant" (*II Sent.*, d. 3, q. 5, a. 2 ad 3m). Actually the fetus would be about 13 mm, i.e., one-half inch, in length.

Rather, the problem raised for Aquinas was that in non-miraculous conceptions, the efficient cause that must prepare the matter is a finite agent, i.e., the male parent.[33] Such a finite agent can bring about the formation of matter only through a sequence of changes that require some appreciable time. Now, according to the data available to Aristotle, the matter in question was the menstrual blood of the mother. The less organized this matter, the longer the time that would be required for the agent to carry out the series of steps necessary to prepare it for the human soul.

Aquinas explicitly discusses this question, and concludes that the menstrual blood is an inanimate chemical mixture of nutritional materials in the mother's body that has not been assimilated as an actual part of her living substance, but which has undergone digestive modifications until it is proximately prepared for such assimilation. Thus the efficient cause has the task of raising non-living material to the very high state of organization required to be suitable for the human body. In Aquinas's opinion, the flesh of the human body has to have the highest possible type of chemical balance or "temperament." The reason for this is that a sense organ can operate only if it is so tempered that it is neutral to all the contrary qualities found in sensible objects. If it were colored red, it could not be sensitive to green, or if it were hot, it could not be sensitive to cold, or if hard, to softness. This must be particularly true of the "internal senses" of imagination and the like, which are the necessary instruments of human thinking and willing, since they must be so delicately neutral as to be able to receive a limitless variety of images.[34]

Thus Aristotle and Aquinas could only conclude that the formative action of the male parent would have to take place over a considerable

---

[33] *Generation of Animals* I, c. 2, 716a 2 sq.; *Summa theologiae* I, q. 92, a. 1 c, and many other places in Aquinas's works. On the role of the female parent in ancient embryology as *actively* furnishing the matter of the fetus and fostering its growth and development, see Cletus Wessels, OP, *The Mother of God: Her Physical Maternity*, especially section 2, chapter 3, 124–51.

[34] "But nature never fails in necessary things: therefore, the intellectual soul has to be endowed not only with the power of understanding, but also with the power of feeling. Now the action of the senses is not performed without a corporeal instrument. Therefore it behooved the intellectual soul to be united to a body fitted to be a convenient organ of sense. Now all the other senses are based on the sense of touch. But the organ of touch required to be a medium between contraries, such as hot and cold, wet and dry, and the like, of which the sense of touch has the perception; thus it is potentiality with regard to contraries, and is able to perceive them. Therefore, the more the organ of touch is reduced to an equable complexion, the more sensitive will be the touch. But the intellectual soul has the power of sense in all its completeness. . . . Therefore, the body to which the individual soul is united should be a mixed body, above others reduced to an equable complexion. For this reason among animals, man has the best sense of touch. And among men those who have the best sense of touch have the best intelligence." *Summa theologiae* I, q. 76, a. 5 c.

period of time before it could temper the menstrual blood to the level of organization required for a human body that would be capable of the highest type of sensitive life

3. How was the manner in which the male parent carries on this formative action understood?

The answer to this question is crucial to the plausibility of the delayed hominization theory, yet its defenders have largely neglected it. For Aristotle and Aquinas, it is the major question. In fact this whole embryological question concerns Aquinas mainly because he wishes to refute the *traducianist* theory, which holds that the father transmits original sin to his children because the father begets the souls of his children, infecting them with his own sinfulness. Aquinas insists that because the human soul is spiritual it cannot be produced or infused by any material, biological process, but must be immediately created by God (a view which has become authoritative for the Catholic Church).[35] At the same time he is concerned to maintain that both male and female parents are true generators of their offspring, otherwise the doctrine of original sin would lose all meaning, and also the Incarnate Christ would not be truly a member of the human race.[36]

Consequently, Aquinas denies that the human father produces the human soul. Therefore, neither does the father bring about the *ultimate* formation of the matter of the human body, since this is effected by God alone in the very act of creating the soul as the substantial form of the body. What the father does is bring the menstrual matter to the stage of organization just prior to its hominization, that is, to a higher level of sensitive life. Because the father himself is infected by original sin his generative activity is in some measure defective, so that this work falls somewhat short of producing a completely "normal" body. Therefore, the soul created for such a body itself suffers infection with original sin from the body. Thus the transmission of human life in the defective condition we call "original sin" is due to the defective action of the male parent.[37]

The male parent, however, is not able directly to act on the menstrual matter because he is not in bodily contact with it, since it exists as unassimilated nutritional material within the mother's body. According to Aristotelian philosophy, no material efficient cause can act on another body except when the two bodies are in actual contact ("no action at a distance"), unless it acts through a "separated" instrument (i.e., another material body that acts as a medium of its efficient action). Aquinas, following Aristotle, believed this instrument of the male agent was the semen. Like menstrual

---

[35] See Elmar Klinger, "Soul," *Sacramentum Mundi,* vol. 6, 138–41.

[36] *De malo,* q. 4, a. 3, 6, 7; *Summa theologiae* III, qq. 31–35.

[37] Ibid., and III, qq. 118–19.

blood, semen was not itself alive, but only highly digested nutritional material ready to be assimilated but set aside in the body for another use. It consisted of two portions. One was merely an inactive fluid that, after intercourse, became mixed with the menstrual blood and constituted the male contribution (a minimal one compared with that of the mother's).[38] The other, active portion was a "vital spirit," which was the actual instrument of the male efficiency.[39]

The term "spirit" here does not mean that the active semen was a spiritual entity. Aristotelian biology (also reinforced after Aristotle's time by Stoic theories) thought that living bodies contain various "spirits" that were like hot, energetic gases (or even like our idea of electricity). This seminal spirit, of its own nature, had a high degree of the quality of "heat" and its proper efficient action was to act on the menstrual blood and refine it, just as it was thought that the heat of the body could digest nutritional material. As such, its action was purely chemical, and not strictly vital. However, as an instrument of the male parent, this spirit had been modified in the parent's body so as to have a much more specific efficiency by which it was capable of forming the menstrual blood to the specific neutral temperament required for the human body. This modification of the active semen constituted it a vital instrument, endowed with an intrinsic vital power *(virtus)*.[40]

---

38 "The likeness of the begetter to the begotten is on account not of the matter, but of the form of the agent that generates its like. Wherefore in order for a man to look like his grandfather, there is no need that the corporeal seminal matter should have been in the grandfather; but only that there be in the semen a virtue derived from the soul of the grandfather through the father." *Summa theologiae* I, q. 119, a. 2 ad 4. Yet Aquinas seems to admit that some part of the male seed mixes with the female seed, since he says (see next note) that the semen consists in two parts, only one of which is active. Consequently, the passive part must mix with the passive female seed.

39 Aristotle's theory of the semen and the vital *pneuma* that it contains is thoroughly discussed by A. L. Peck in Appendix B of his edition of *Generation of Animals*, 576–93, and is correctly reported by St. Thomas, *Summa theologiae* I, q. 118, a. 1, ad 4; *De potentia,* q. 3, a. 9 ad 15, and elsewhere in the texts given above. It is also commented on by Jean Poinsot (John of St. Thomas), *Cursus Philosophicus Thomisticus,* edited by P. Beato Reiser, II, q. viii, a. 111, 730 sq.

40 "The power *(virtus)* that is in the father's semen is an intrinsic and permanent power, not applied from without as is the moving power in a projectile. Therefore the power in the semen remains effectively, even when the father is removed to a distance. . . . Nevertheless, there is some similarity, since just as the finite power of the thrower moves the projectile only to a determinate distance of place by local motion; so the power of the parent moves [the fetus] only to a determinate form by the motion of generation." Since Newton we would have to modify this to read: "Just as the finite power of the thrower acting *against the resistance of the medium* moves the projectile only to a determinate distance of place, so the power of the parent moves the fetus only to a determinate form by the motion of generation *acting on the resistance of the matter from which it is formed.*"

Once the semen had been discharged in the maternal vagina, the passive portion was absorbed, but the active spirit remained as an independent agent acting on the menstrual blood. For Aquinas's theory this was necessary since "a thing cannot move itself," therefore the agent forming the menstrual blood had to remain separated from—but yet in contact with—it. Consequently Aquinas believed that the *semen remained as an active substance throughout the whole period* of preformation of the menstrual matter up to the point of hominization by the creative action of God. The proponents of delayed hominization have failed to notice that this is indispensable to the consistency of his theory.[41]

Is there any alternative that would be consistent with his philosophical principles? It would seem that one might be proposed. It is well known that in applying the notion of instrumental causality to the case of the falling

---

[41] "In perfect animals, generated by coition, the active force is in the semen of the male, as the Philosopher says (*Generation of Animals,* 11, 3); but the foetal matter is provided by the female. In this matter the vegetative soul exists from the very beginning, not as to the second act, but as to the first act, as the sensitive soul is in one who sleeps. But as soon as it begins to attract nourishment, then it already operates in act. This matter therefore is transmuted by the power which is in the semen of the male, until it is actually informed by the sensitive soul; not as though the force itself which was in the semen becomes the sensitive soul; for thus, indeed, the generator and generated would be identical; moreover, this would be more like nourishment and growth than generation, as the Philosopher says—And after the sensitive soul, by the power of the active principle in the semen, has been produced in one of the principal parts of the thing generated, then it is that the sensitive soul of the offspring begins to work towards the perfection of its own body, by nourishment and growth. As to the active power which was in the semen, it ceases to exist, when the semen is dissolved and the spirit thereof vanishes. Nor is there anything unreasonable in this, because this force is not the principal but the instrumental agent; and the movement of an instrument ceases when once the effect has been produced." *Summa theologiae,* q. 118, a. 1. ad 4. There is a difficulty of interpretation in this text because Aquinas here seems to say that the menstrual blood is alive vegetatively before the action of the male semen, which is contrary to his statement in q. 119, a. 2, where he shows that it is nutritive material that has never yet been assimilated to the actually animated state. Peck above interprets Aristotle as saying it is alive with vegetative life, so that the male only raises it to sensitive life; John of St. Thomas says also that it has an imperfect life. However, I believe that although Aquinas is not very clear on the point, it is more consistent to say that this nutritive material has never been actually alive, and that Aquinas when he says "the vegetative soul exists from the very beginning" means by "the very beginning" *(a principio)* from the very beginning of the action of the male semen, as he says in another passage: "Thus therefore through the formative virtue which is in the semen, after expelling the form of the [female] seed, another form is induced; and when this has been expelled, another is induced. And thus *first the vegetative soul is induced*; and then when this has been expelled, a soul which is both vegetative and sensible; and when this has been expelled there is induced not through the seminal power but by the Creator, a soul which is at the same time rational, sensitive, and vegetable" (*De potentia,* q. 3, a. 9, ad 8).

body, and also the projectile, later scholasticism invented the *impetus* theory.[42] Aristotle and Aquinas, in order to preserve the principles "No action at a distance" and "Nothing is moved without a mover distinct from itself," argued that although a projectile is set in motion by the projector, it can continue in motion only because it continues to be moved by the surrounding medium, which, unlike the projectile, still has contact with the projector and acts under its influence as its instrument. From the time of John Philoponus, (sixth century A.D.) and again with Robert Kilwardby (thirteenth century) and Jean Buridan (fourteenth century), the difficulties of this view were realized, and a new theory was proposed, which, in the form given it by the great Thomist Dominic Soto (sixteenth century), prepared the way for Newton's laws of motion. According to this new theory, the projectile continues to move not through any agency of the medium, but by a force *(vis)* given to it by the projector at the beginning of the motion when projector and projectile are in contact. This *vis* is an active quality that acts as the efficient cause of the motion, and which remains until destroyed by some resisting body encountered by the projectile.

Aquinas never accepted this impetus theory, although later Thomists, in their effort to answer the objections of Newtonian science, have adopted it.[43] For purposes of this discussion, however, I will concede that it is *not* inconsistent with Thomistic principles. Those who believe that it *is* would have to concede that in view of modern science and the Newtonian laws: (a) either the theory of the action of the medium has to be saved in some new way, or (b) the entire Thomistic argument, as well as his theory of delayed hominization, collapses.

Messenger and Dorlodot (on whom Donceel largely relies) revived the theory of delayed hominization, because it seemed to them to provide some Thomistic foundation for a theory of mediate creation of species by God through evolution.[44] In human embryology, there is a transformation of an

---

[42] A. J. Rozwadowski, "De motus localis causa proxima secundum principia S. Thomae," *Divus Thomas* (Piacenza) 42 (1939): 104–13, attempted to show that the theory of impetus is to be found in St. Thomas, depending largely on the text from *De Anima* quoted above. He was refuted by M. D. Chenu, OP, "Aus origines de la science moderne," *Bulletin Thomiste* 6 (1940–42): n. 351.

[43] See Antonio Moreno, "The Law of Inertia and the Principle *Quidquid movetur ab alio movetur*," *The Thomist* 38 (April 1974): 206–331. Moreno goes beyond the classical impetus theory by showing that in Einsteinian physics all motion involves a relation between the moving body and the *field* in which it moves, which may be the solution to the Thomistic difficulty.

[44] See E. C. Messenger, "The Embryology of St. Thomas Aquinas," and Canon Henri de Dorlodot, "A Vindication of the Mediate Animation Theory," in E. C. Messenger, ed., *Theology and Evolution*. Donceel, in his article "Causality and Evolution," seems to have first become interested in this whole problem by his effort to defend Teilhard de Chardin's evolutionary worldview in terms of Rahner's hominization theories.

embryo living by vegetative life into a second embryo living with animal life, and finally this into a truly human embryo by means of a certain power given to the vegetative embryo by the male parent. Therefore what objection could even strict Thomist metaphysicians, and these were in fact the most troublesome opponents of the theory of evolution, raise against a theistic theory of evolution in which the Creator gave to lower species an instrumental power to transform themselves into ever higher and higher species?

As I have argued elsewhere, such theories of a special "evolutionary force" are not necessary for a satisfactory theory of evolution compatible with Thomist views on causality.[45] But, if we take such an approach to the embryological problem, how could we work out a theory? We would have to suppose that the vegetative embryo is living only a vegetative life, which of itself would never result in the substantial change necessary to produce an animal embryo living with sensitive life. It would, however, in addition to its vegetative soul, be endowed with an intrinsic instrumental power *(virtus)* given to it by the male parent that would bring about these changes. It would seem that this *virtus* would have to reside, at least principally, in the primary organ first of the vegetative embryo and next of the sensitive embryo. If it did not modify the activity of this primary organ, which is the prime mover of all accidental changes within the organism, how could it guide these changes so as to prepare for the ultimate steps of substantial change?

Thus it would seem the two possible Thomistic theories would be:

1. Aquinas's own view that the male parent gives to the seminal spirit an instrumental power by which it is able (remaining a separate entity in contact with the maternal material) to act as the efficient cause to first form a vegetative embryo, then to transform this into a new animal embryo, and finally to perfect this embryo to the point that God, without a miracle, can directly effect the final transformation into a human person.

2. A modified Thomistic theory by which the male parent gives to the semen an instrumental power by which it first forms the vegetative embryo, along with the embryo's own primary organ. This it also endows with the instrumental power that is, until that time, possessed by the semen (the semen then becoming ineffective and incorporated into the embryonic matter), so that this vegetative embryo, by means of its primary organ, is able to transform itself into a new animal embryo, whose primary organ, in turn, receives

---

[45] See my article "Causality and Evolution," *The Thomist* 36 (1972): 199–230, in which I argue that theories like those of Karl Rahner, which posit a tendency of all creatures to transcend themselves, or Teilhard de Chardin's universal "law of evolution" are uneconomical in explaining the compatibility of scientific theories of evolution and the principle of causality.

the instrumental power by which this embryo raises itself to the point that God, without a miracle, can directly effect the final transformation into a human person.

An Evaluation of Delayed Hominization in Light of Current Embryological Data

After having made clear exactly what this Thomistic theory implies, we are now ready to evaluate it in terms of modern embryological data so as to see how it must be modified if its fundamental philosophical principles are to be retained.[46]

1. The first obvious modification, which is required, respects the maternal matter. Aquinas supposed that this was the menstrual blood, which was only inanimate refined nutritional material. In fact, the mother's contribution is the ovum, which, as long as it is a part of her own body, is ensouled by her own spiritual soul. At ovulation it is separated from the mother's body and becomes a distinct, living entity, very highly organized, with its own primary organ (the nucleus). There is every evidence that this ovum is very close to readiness for rapid embryological development: (a) because it contains within itself a considerable amount of cytoplasmic matter sufficient to fuel it until implantation and development of the placental system, since only then will any other source of nutrition be available; and (b) because, in the nucleus, it has the power to produce the messenger RNA, by which it will guide the early stages of embryonic development up to implantation.

In lower living things parthenogenesis is experimentally possible, and some believe that it occasionally takes place even in human reproduction, precisely because the ovum is haploid (has only one member of each paired set of chromosomes), but apparently this does not absolutely exclude development. Thus for Aquinas, the development *distance*, which the efficient cause of this initial embryological development must overcome, was very great and thus required a considerable time before the maternal matter was ready for the human soul. Modern biology, on the contrary, sees this developmental distance as much shorter, because the maternal matter—the ovum—is already very highly organized, and therefore proximately prepared. Amazingly enough the ovum was already present in the female before her birth and matured through many years. Thus logically, we should expect that

---

[46] The embryological data used here is from Keith L. Moore and T. V. N. Persaud, *The Developing Human: Clincally Oriented Embryology,* 6th ed.

hominization should occur much sooner than Aristotle and Aquinas would have imagined. Of course this still requires an empirical determination of what exactly is the duration of this period.

2. A modification of the Thomistic theory is necessary because we now know that the seminal fluid does not consist of a passive material (which is to be mingled with the maternal material) and active spirit, but material that is active by reason of the sperm, which, again, is already a living entity, originally part of the father's body, and living by his human life, which then becomes a separated entity living by its own very real, if brief and imperfect, life. This sperm does not remain separate from the embryo as an agent transforming it, but fuses at conception with the ovum. This process of fertilization is not instantaneous, but it is fairly complicated, though it ordinarily takes only a brief time. Its result is twofold: (a) the sperm, which, like the ovum, is haploid, contribute the second set of chromosomes to the nucleus of the new, fertilized zygote, which has a complete set of paired chromosomes, half from the ovum, half from the sperm, thus constituting a new and unique set of genes, different from those in the cells of either parent; (b) the sperm by its entrance into the ovum, *initiates* the process of fusing the two cells to form the new zygote, which at once begins to develop in the direction of a mature adult human being.

It seems plausible enough, therefore, that we retain the Thomist view that the semen (i.e., the sperm) is the *efficient cause* of the production of the new entity we call the zygote, and that it does this by virtue of an instrumental power received from the male parent. The empirical sign of its character as efficient cause is that the ovum remains in a resting state until the entry of the sperm initiates the fertilization process. That its power is instrumental seems consistent with the fact that the sperm is produced by the male parent as a functional instrument of self-reproduction, that it is an imperfect organism, haploid, and living only briefly, unable to nourish or reproduce itself. It also is evident that the sperm is able to perform its function in virtue of its own primary organ (its nucleus), which can thus be regarded as the seat of the instrumental power.

However, Aquinas's own unmodified theory is obviously disproved by the disappearance of seminal activity at the moment of conception. This would mean there is *no efficient cause for the rest of the embryological process*. Since "nothing can move itself," we thus have to resort to the second theory given above. By it the instrumental power resident in the nucleus of the sperm is transmitted to the nucleus of the zygote, which thus becomes the efficient cause of the embryological process. This nucleus, by its own inherent powers, is able to guide the vegetative life of the embryo only as regards vegetative functions, but, by its additional instrumental power, it will eventually be able to transform the vegetative embryo into an animal embryo, with some primary organ, which (in addition to its own proper power of directing sensitive life) will receive the instrumental power to pave the way for the creative action of God

3. Aquinas made no attempt to determine the primary organ of what he believed to be the vegetative embryo. According to Aristotelian botany, this was supposed to be located at the root end of a plant (analogous to the head-end of an animal).[47] According to modern data, it would clearly seem to be the nucleus of the zygote. But what is it once that cell division begins? It is now known that when the ovum divides, all the nuclei of the daughter cells are essentially equal, and all the cells up to the blastula stage (when implantation or nidation occurs) retain totipotentiality. Consequently, during this period, identical twins may be produced if the mass of cells divides, since each can develop into a complete organism; or separated cells may be rejoined and still form a normal organism. Hence, some have argued that at this stage, no determinate individual exists, but rather something like a colony of one-celled plants.

The biological data, as already explained, does not permit this conclusion. From the moment of fertilization there already exists in the zygote (and this was probably predetermined in the ovum) a metabolic *polarity* with the nucleus determining the upper pole of the metabolic gradient, and a *bilaterality* that will eventually be fundamental to the plan of the adult body. Consequently, as the first cell divisions take place, there is already some differentiation in the cytoplasm of the daughter cells. They may be totipotential when separated, but, as existing within the morula, they already constitute heterogeneous parts. At this stage it appears that the maternal RNA produced in the cytoplasm by the DNA of the nucleus of the original ovum plays a regulative role, and the nuclei, with their new unique DNA, are still relatively quiescent. Nevertheless, it was the nucleus of the zygote that initiated the whole process, and it will be the new nuclear DNA that finally takes over the regulation of the development from the blastula stage on. Thus, during this intermediate phase, it is still the nuclear DNA that has ultimate regulatory control, although it permits the maternal RNA to play its own role. We ought, therefore, to hold that during this time the primary organs are the daughter nuclei that originated from the nucleus of the zygote.

---

[47] *De Partibus Animalium* II, c. 10, 655b seq.

Since all are essentially similar, they can be said to act collectively, although it is probable that some of them, or even one, located at the superior pole of the organism, has the dominant effect, and can be identified as the primary organ of the whole.

At the blastocyst stage, when implantation occurs, a patch of cells called "the primary organizer" appears on the posterior lip of the blasto-pore. If this is removed, embryological development ceases, and if it is restored, it begins again. With its appearance, the totipotentiality of the cells ceases and from that time on differentiation of the parts of the organism is, for the most part, irreversible. Thus this "primary organizer" is clearly the primary organ of the blastocyst and is the epigenetic successor of the nucleus of the zygote, and of nuclei of the cells at the superior pole at the morula stage, as evidenced by the unbroken continuity of the polarity and bilaterality. By the end of the second week following fertilization, the blastocyst has become the gastrula, in which the three basic body layers—ectoderm, mesoderm, and endoderm—have differentiated. Out of the ectoderm, the nervous system, skin, and other sense organs will form. (It should be recalled that for Aquinas, it is the sense of touch that is the basic sense determining animal life, and it is the character of this sense that is specifically human.) Before this week is completed the *primitive streak* has appeared that is the primordium of the central nervous system; this already exhibits a polarity in the fetus that indicates at which end the brain will be formed. From this period on, the development of the central nervous system with the brain as its superior pole progresses in a clearly continuous manner.

Thus we can very reasonably interpret the biological data according to Thomistic terminology in the following manner: (a) The vegetative phase cannot last longer than two weeks in the human embryo; and, (b) even in this stage, an epigenetic continuity can be traced between the nucleus of the zygote as primary organ to the primitive streak as primary organ of the animal phase.

4. Since the embryological data establish this epigenetic continuity between the primary organ of the vegetative and of the animal stage, this can be interpreted in one of two ways: (a) by the modified Thomistic theory according to which these two organs are actually primary parts of two distinct substances, the first being transformed into the second by a substantial change whose efficient cause is an instrumental power derived from the sperm; or (b) by saying that the act of fertilization immediately produced not a vegetative embryo, but an animal embryo whose primary organ (the nucleus) is epigenetically and substantially identical with the primordial central nervous system manifested in the primitive streak.

The second interpretation seems far more plausible and economical. It is perfectly consistent with Thomistic principles, based on the following considerations: The sperm, as an instrument of the male parent who is genetically an animal, certainly has the power to produce a similar animal. Also, as was discussed above, the developmental distance to be spanned between the ovum and the zygote is very short and thus does not demand infinite power in the agent. In fact the first explanation may be eliminated as lacking any empirical confirmation and positing an unnecessary occult power in the first primary organ. It certainly lacks any authority from St. Thomas himself, since his explanation was quite different and, granted what we know about the disappearance of the sperm, untenable.

5. Having eliminated on empirical grounds any reason to believe that the human embryo is ever ensouled with a vegetative soul, we now have to ask whether it has a merely animal soul during some period prior to hominization. The reason for such a hypothesis, as given by Donceel, would be that this period is necessary for the development of the cerebral cortex, that is, for the elevation of the embryo from a lower form of animal life to the supreme level of nervous organization required for the functioning of the internal senses of imagination, the *vis aestimativa*, and so on.

Here it should again be recalled that St. Thomas himself believed that what is specific to the human sense organs is their high degree of neutrality, and that this is found primarily in the sense of touch. A man can be a man, can think and will, as long as he has the sense of touch, even if the other sense organs are lacking. Since, as we have already shown, Donceel cannot possibly be demanding the presence of the fully developed cortex for hominization, what is in question is the primordium of the specifically human capacity for the highest degree of sensitive life. Is there any reason to believe that this primordium is not initially present in the primitive streak of the blastocyst? We know that in the nucleus of the zygote there is already present all the *information* (order or formal cause) and the inherent developmental power (efficient cause) to construct the human nervous system, including the marvelously complicated neuronic pathways of the cerebral cortex. This does not mean that the nucleus contains a preformed, miniaturized cerebral cortex. The nucleus is the primary organ of a total organism that develops epigenetically, each part of the system reacting on the others at every point of development and maturity. What it does mean is that an existential and dynamic continuity can be traced from the nucleus of the zygote to the cortex of the human infant. There is at all times a central organ maintaining life and producing development and differentiation, and this constitutes an epigenetic identity

We must not merely understand the zygotic nucleus as a genetic "blueprint" and then argue, as some authors have done, that a "blueprint" is not identical with the building. The nucleus *does* contain a blueprint or exemplar of the adult in its genetic code. In addition, it has the active power to produce the finished building, and to produce it, not as something separate from itself, but as a transformation of the total organism of which the nucleus itself is a part. As we have seen, for a Thomist this can mean only one of two things: (1) either the zygote is already informed by the substantial form or soul of the adult into which it will develop; or (2) the transformation results from an instrumental power with which the central organ of the zygote has been endowed. We have shown that this latter explanation is uneconomical and empirically unverifiable.

Consequently, we must conclude that no substantial change takes place in the animal zygote at hominization, so that it must have been hominized from the moment that fertilization was complete.

A Brief Consideration of Three Common Objections to Immediate Hominization

I will now deal very briefly with three objections that are commonly posed against immediate hominization. They have already between touched on in the first part of this essay, but need to be directly related to Thomistic theology.

1. Many authors, including, as we have seen, Karl Rahner,[48] are disturbed by the fact that a very large number of fertilized ova, perhaps as many as 50 percent or even higher, do not develop. Does God create all these souls that are never able to live a human life?[49] Others even argue that this would logically lead to the absurd result that we should attempt to baptize countless minute zygotes or embryos.

---

[48] "For a few centuries Catholic moral theology has been convinced that individual hominization occurs at the moment of the fusion of the gametes. Will the moral theologian still have today the courage to maintain this presupposition of many of his moral theological statements, when he is suddenly told that from the start, 50% of the fecundated female ova never reach nidification in the uterus? Will he be able to admit that 50% of the 'human beings'—real human beings with an 'immortal' soul and an eternal destiny do not, from the very start, get beyond the first stage of human existence?" Karl Rahner, *Schriften zur Theologie,* 287, quoted by Donceel, "Immediate Animation," 99ff.

[49] "One cause [of spontaneous abortion of the conceptus] may be inadequate production of progesterone and estrogen by the corpeus luteum." See Moore and Persaud, *The Developing Human,* 36. The authors place the rate of failure at 45 percent.

The answer to these objections can be found in a distinction of the concept of "fertilized ovum." As indicated, fertilization is an elaborate process that often proves unsuccessful. There is good evidence that in most of those cases where the "fertilized" ovum fails to develop into a viable fetus, this process was never normally and perfectly completed.[50] Since I am arguing that hominization takes place at the completion of fertilization, it need not be concluded that God creates souls for all these hapless abnormal "zygotes." It might be noted also that this type of argument would lead to a denial of humanity to those countless infants who have died in the past when infant mortality was often as high as 50 percent. The difficulties about the duty to baptize arise from antiquated views concerning the salvation of unbaptized infants that few Catholic theologians would now support. As regards abortifacient contraceptives, the issue has to be decided not on general public attitudes, often based on misinformation, but on an objective evaluation of the issue as to when hominization begins.

2. The argument against immediate hominization based on the phenomena of twinning and recombination of cells at the pre-implantation stage has seemed very impressive to some theologians, including Paul Ramsey, and is supported by Diamond and Ransil with numerous subsidiary arguments (which I believe have been sufficiently refuted in the foregoing interpretation of the continuity of development), which purport to show that the individual identity of the embryo is only established at implantation.[51]

The basic facts, as have been demonstrated, are that even in the zygote prior to cleavage some differentiation already exists, and this

---

[50] Diamond, "Abortion, Animation and Biological Hominization," 311, says, "Emil Witschi, 'Congenital Malformations,' *Proceedings of Third International Conference* (Amsterdam) (*Excerpta Medica,* 1970), estimates that 58% of sperm-ovum conjugates never complete implantation: 16% terminate at conjunction, 15% never begin implantation, 27% are lost before the completion of implantation, and only 30% survive to birth. Many such failures would give a positive HCG test [a radioactive immune receptor assay test for pregnancy], despite the fact that differentiation and organismicization of somatic cells cannot occur due to defects intrinsic to the zygotes themselves. Hominizability, even *in potentia,* does not exist." This, of course, argues that not every pregnancy is certainly a true human conception, but it does not agree, as Diamond seems to think, that hominization is rarer than true conception, i.e., a normal and perfect fertilization.

[51] "The case of identical twins does, however, suggest a significant modification of any 'proof' from genotype. If there is a moment in the development of nascent life subsequent to impregnation and prior to birth (or graduation from Princeton) at which it would be reasonable to believe that an individual human life begins to be inviolate, that moment is arguable at the appearance of a 'primitive streak' across the hollow cluster of

continues in the cell mass that makes up the morula. During this period, the cells have totipotentiality only in the sense that if one cell, or a group of cells, are separated from the original organism they still retain the capability of developing into a second complete individual. Geneticists believe, on the basis of experiments with lower animals, that it is at least theoretically possible to "clone" new human beings from most of the body tissues of an adult human.[52] If this were to take place, when would hominization or ensoulment occur? Obviously, a Thomist must say that if at the moment there exists living cellular material sufficiently prepared for hominization, God, as the author of nature, will complete the natural process by the creation of a human soul. In such a case, the process is not that of true sexual generation (i.e., the clone would not be the "son" of the person from whom the tissue comes), but constitutes a sexual reproduction like that found in lower living things.

developing cells that signals the separation of the same genotype into identical twins." Paul Ramsey, "The Morality of Abortion," in Edward Shils et al., *Life or Death: Ethics and Options,* edited by Daniel H. Labby, 61–63. "I simply cannot find in the biological order any reason not to distinguish radically and categorically between the pre-implanted entity's vital capacity and that of the implanted entity. In short, the biologist holds that the numerous biological events converging in the general time area of the 14th to 22nd day weigh extremely heavily in any calculus of the beginning of the life of a homo." Diamond, "Abortion, Animation and Biological Hominization," 316. Certainly he is correct in saying that the gastrulation and implantation stage is a very important moment in embryological development, as is birth, but this does not indicate that it is the *initiation* of the life of the individual. Ransil presents a still weaker case because he depends largely on the following argument: "[T]he product of conception and its mother exist as a single system in a symbiotic relationship, in which a host organism (the mother) harbors and nurtures a dependent organism (the product of conception). Contrary to what seems to be a self-evident fact, two equivalent individuals (in the sense of two independent beings of equivalent morphology and function) are not involved. Present is a coupled system of a mother and a product of conception," *Abortion,* 82. But in this "coupled-system" are there not two *organisms*? Otherwise why call it "symbiosis?"

52 See James D. Watson, "Moving Toward the Clonal Man," *The Atlantic* 227 (1971): 50ff. For a Thomist there is a special difficulty in admitting that twinning involves asexual generation, since according to Aquinas original sin is transmitted by sexual generation. Would the twin then be "immaculately conceived?" But the same difficulty holds for the supposed possibility of a cloned human. However, contemporary theology understands original sin in a more inclusive way than did scholastic theologians, and would interpret the phrase used by the Council of Trent (Denzinger-Aldoph Schönmetzer, n.1513) when it declared that original sin is transmitted *per propagationem* in a broad sense. Consequently it would seem that if a human being comes into existence by the action of sinful human beings, whether naturally, or accidentally (as in twinning), or artificially (as in cloning), this human would still share in the sinfulness of the human family. Christ would remain an exception because his conception is the result of miraculous Divine action, not of human power.

Consequently, an adequate explanation of the facts, an explanation which is both economical and in line with the general theory I have elaborated, would be to say that the zygote is already a human being, whose central organ tends to retain its cells in a coherent and unified body as cleavage proceeds and gradually causes them to differentiate more and more perfectly. However, before this differentiation is complete the cells retain a certain totipotentiality, and, if separated by some accident from the original body, they become a new substance with its own form by a process analogous to asexual reproduction, budding, or cloning. Since these separated cells are still as prepared to live as was the zygote at the moment of fertilization, God supplies the twin with a human soul, just as he did the other twin. Both twins are truly children of the male parent, since it is the instrumental power of his sperm that has *initiated* the development of both, one directly, the other (as a result of an accidental occurrence) mediately, but by a mediation that is very simple and brief.

On the other hand, the view that individual identity is established only at the end of this period, when twinning becomes impossible, has to answer to very significant biological difficulties. (1) If, during this period, the morula or blastula is merely a mass of cells, lacking individuality as a distinct organism, what causes it to develop and differentiate according to definite laws, as we observe it does? (2) If, only after the twinning stage is passed, the single embryo, or the twin embryos, now each become self-identical organisms, what produces this new individual unity in each? *Ex hypothesi* this does not derive from an internal principle, since if it did, we would have to assume that one (or two) souls were already present *before* this stage. Clearly, also, it does not come from the mother, since there is no evidence that the mother is the agent of implantation. All the evidence indicates that the embryo implants itself. We are left with the possibility that it is God who individuates the cell mass by infusing the soul, but this is a recourse to divine intervention without attributing to biological processes their proper role. We can only conclude that the embryo at this stage already has its own individual vital unity, as all biological evidence indicates, but that in some cases by accident an asexual "cloning" event occurs that gives rise to a second, new individual organism.

It seems to me that this difficulty about twinning arises largely from a rather mechanistic idea of God's action in creating the soul. Rather we must suppose theologically that God, who controls not only natural but chance events, wills to create each human person, even when that person's body is produced by an embryological accident such as twinning,[53] and hence, it is inconsequential just how the properly prepared matter for hominization results.

A similar explanation can be given to recombination experiments.[54] The individuality of the embryo depends on its primary organ. If cells are separated from the morula and then rejoined to it, they become a part of the living substance when they fall under the directive influence of the primary organ, as does a transplant into an adult body. Also twins may partly fuse ('Siamese" twins), but if they have two brains remain two persons, or one may lose its primary organ and fuse with another which retains that organ and hence it alone remains a person that then is a "chimera" an individual having some alien tissues.

3. Some authors (notably Ransil) deny the individuality of the embryo because it is "symbiotic" with the mother.[55] They categorize it as analogical to a "parasite" or even a "tumor." To deal with such questions it is obviously necessary to distinguish between (a) parts of a single organism that are unified by a single "substantial form" manifested in a primary organ, and (b) distinct organisms interacting with each other, or a single organism reacting with its environment.

The biological data clearly indicate that no matter how intimate the reaction between the embryo (or fetus) and its mother or maternal environment, the embryo is still a distinct organism with the capacity to develop into another member of the same species as the mother. The fact that the embryo is a member of the same species as the mother makes it fundamentally different from a tumor or a parasite.

It is strange that Ransil and others continue to argue that the unborn embryo or fetus is not an individual because it is not independently viable. Obviously "independent viability" is a purely relative concept, not an absolute one like the notion of "human individual" or "person." No living thing has complete independent viability from other living things and the environment. The zygote, from the first moment after fertilization, has some independence in its life process,

---

[53] "MZ [monozygotic or identical] twinning usually begins in the blastocyst stage around the end of the first 8 weeks . . . and results from division of the inner cell mass or embryoblast into embryonic primordia." Moore and Persaud, *The Developing Human,* 134.

[54] Diamond, "Abortion, Animation and Biological Hominization," 312.

[55] "Perhaps the greatest difficulty for layman with the foregoing analogies and analysis will be his reluctance to view the fetus under the biological categories of parasite and tumor." Ransil, *Abortion,* 90. I would imagine most biologists, as well as laymen, might find this difficult! But then an analogy is between things which are "basically different, but in some respects the same."

although this is minimal compared with the adult that it will become, but then even the adult does not have complete independence.

Conclusion

We can only conclude that according to present biological knowledge, theories of delayed hominization lack any solid empirical evidence and that by far the most probable view is that hominization begins with completed, normal fertilization of the ovum by the sperm. Therefore, moral theologians should not use such theories as grounds for solving conflict situations in which the life of the conceptus and the mother are involved, and governments should do what is politically feasible to protect the right to life of every human person from the moment of conception.

CHAPTER 21

Humanae Vitae and Artificial Reproduction[*]

The Significance of the Contraception Controversy for Bioethics

GARY WILLS, LIKE MANY CATHOLICS TODAY, FINDS THE TEACHING of Paul VI's *Humanae Vitae* vigorously confirmed by John Paul II in many documents, including the *Catechism of the Catholic Church*, as outrageously absurd and dishonest.[1] Moreover it seems to be a fact that the majority of married Catholics simply ignore it. Yet much of the Church's teaching not only about contraception and sterilization but also about abortion and artificial reproduction and all questions of sexual ethics is intimately linked to this teaching. Hence it is important for Catholic bioethicists to have an accurate understanding of the controversy *Humanae Vitae* produced since the grounds for it both in natural law and in Christian revelation are often misunderstood and misrepresented. Although there are excellent published expositions of this question,[2] it seems worthwhile to present a brief but systematic summary of the results of the controversy and the implication of these results, since it has affected not only a broad area of bioethics but even the very foundations of ethics and Catholic moral theology.

---

[*] This essay has not been previously published.

[1] Gary Wills, *Papal Sins: Structures of Deceit,* 94–98. He attributes the teaching of the encyclical to Paul VI's psychology. "The Pope was a man obviously torn by doubts, tormented by scruples, haunted by thoughts of perfection, and above all dominated by an exaggerated concern—some called it an obsession—about the prestige of his office as Pope."

[2] See Germain Grisez, *Contraception and the Natural Law,* with a foreword by John Wright, and Janet E. Smith, *Humanae Vitae, a Generation Later and Why Humanae Vitae Was Right: A Reader,* edited by Janet E. Smith, foreword by John Cardinal O'Connor.

Humanae Vitae has been attacked as regards its concrete teaching on contraception but more fundamentally as regards the principle that it applies to this issue, namely, the *Principle of the Inseparability of the Unitive and Procreative Signification of the Marital Act*. It states this principle explicitly and formally for the first time in the teaching of the Church although it claims it pertains at least implicitly to the Church's traditional teaching. It also claims that this principle pertains to the natural moral law and John Paul II has further insisted that it is also confirmed by Christian revelation. The fact that *Humanae Vitae* did not attempt to show in more detail that it is also a truth pertaining directly to faith or at least closely connected to it is regrettable, but understandable in the circumstances because Paul VI was principally concerned to make a traditional teaching credible to the contemporary mind. It is necessary here, therefore, to separate the two questions and deal first with the principle in its purely rational, natural law character.

The Principle of Inseparability and the Natural Moral Law

By the "natural moral law" Catholic thought has generally understood that human happiness depends on a realistic choice of means to the fulfillment of certain needs that are essential to human nature according to their relative importance for such happiness. Today it is often questioned whether there is such a thing as "human nature" or, even if there is, whether it can be known in distinction from the need, real or apparent, created by the many cultures that have arisen in human history or that exist today. I will assume that it cannot be denied that the distinction between "nature and nurture" is a difficult one in some cases and will always require further research and refinement, but nevertheless this distinction is real and can be better known through the advances of the life sciences. Hence an agnostic cultural and moral relativism makes ethical dialogue meaningless.[3] Moreover in the life sciences the socio-biological debate makes evident that no understanding of human behavior is possible that does not attempt to distinguish and relate through their interaction genetic and cultural factors.[4]

---

3 Thus the Dutch Protestant theologian Pim Pronk, *Against Nature? Types of Moral Argumentation Regarding Homosexuality*, after dismissing biblical teaching as too culturally conditioned to be relevant as a moral guide today, eliminates human "nature" as mere biology that cannot be used in ethics without committing the "is-ought fallacy" (on this see the essay "Integral Human Fulfillment" in this collection). Pronk concludes that moral questions can only be decided by personal experience of what makes me happy. He also argues that since there is no moral obligation to reproduce, all arguments that homosexuality is "unnatural" fail because homosexual acts differ from heterosexual ones in no other morally significant way. Thus he considers that the physical manner in which sexual satisfaction is obtained is of no moral significance.

4 David S. Moore, *The Dependent Gene: The Fallacy of Nature vs. Nurture*.

Therefore, it must be granted that certain kinds of sexual behavior promote human happiness for the individual and the human community and are thus moral, and others are destructive of that happiness and are thus immoral. Moreover it must be granted that this is, at least in some respects, true not only for a given culture but can be proved to be the case for all human cultures because of the genetic unity of the human species. For example, it can reasonably be argued that "rape," defined as sexual penetration contrary to the consent of the victim, is destructive of human happiness in all cultures at all times, although in various forms it has been approved in some cultures.

Why is it that rape is always destructive of human happiness? The answer is found in observed fact that in the human species sexual intercourse is normally the result of a free consent of the partners and when it is the result of violence it has many harmful physical, psychological, and social consequences. To imagine a culture in which rape would be praiseworthy and judged to be moral is to imagine a culture that ignored the needs of human nature and was therefore eventually liable to extinction.

Thus questions of sexual morality involve an increasingly refined understanding of the sexual aspect of human nature. Furthermore in seeking this understanding it is important to seek objectively realistic judgments and not to be deceived by subjective desires whose pursuit may cloud objective judgment. No one trying to determine whether cigarette smoking or the use of addictive drugs promotes or destroys authentic human happiness would accept the judgment of a drug addict looking for a fix. It is an illusion to identify, as many people tend to do, physical pleasure with happiness, since in the case of addictions the pursuit of such pleasure results in great misery. Biology and psychology show that for all animals, including the human animal, the real significance of physical pleasure is that it can facilitate the behavior it accompanies and thus is of value not for its intensity and continuity but insofar as the reinforced activity is of value.

In human beings, therefore, endowed with a degree of freedom in their choice of means to happiness, physical pleasure ought to be sought only as it facilitates some behaviors essential to happiness. It should also be sought in moderation so that it does not become an end in itself and thus addictive, since addiction limits the human freedom essential to truly human happiness. It is true, of course, that one type of behavior facilitated by pleasure encompasses activities that *recreate* persons. This is so because the limitations of the human body makes other types of activities that are essential to happiness wearisome and even painful. Hence as bodily beings we at times need to be renewed in our energies by activities that in themselves may contribute little to essential happiness in themselves but do restore physical and hence psychological readiness for valuable action. For example, wine at a meal may contribute little to nutrition but is relaxing and promotes the social conviviality that strengthens human relationships if taken in moderation.

Thus in discussing the ethics of human sexuality realistic ethical judgment should be cautious in accepting popular views prejudiced by the immediate attractiveness of sexual pleasure. Any realistic ethics recognizes that this is an area of human behavior liable to tragic mistakes of judgment, grave exploitation and oppression, and depraved addictions favored by corrupt customs. A great part of world literature takes the miseries of sexual misadventures as its theme.

From a biological point of view it is obvious that evolution has produced many plants and all animals as sexual beings because this form of reproduction has survival value. Any consideration of the nature of human sexuality, therefore, must begin from the most evident and certain fact that its function is first of all reproductive (procreative).[5] Of course this is not sexuality's only place in human life, but it is its most evidently necessary one. It is not, however, essential to the survival of the species that all members reproduce. Thus, for example, among honey bees the worker bees whose work is needed for species survival are females whose eggs are never fertilized.

Hence among humans approximately the same number of males as females are produced, yet in certain circumstances it may be to the advantage of the species that some members remain celibate in order to devote their energies to perform other useful functions for the community. This also helps to regulate population growth in view of limited environmental resources. Since the happiness of celibates does not depend on reproductive activity, it is evident that such activity can be sacrificed to activities more essential to happiness.[6]

Human sexuality, however, differs in some essential ways from that of other animals due to the fact that our species alone is intelligent and free and thus capable of choosing among various means to happiness provided that basic human needs are satisfied and not violated. The most basic human need is physical existence, health, and security, since the survival of every individual and hence of the species depends on it. We come into physical existence through our biological parents, but our intelligence and freedom require a much more complex brain than other animals and hence a relatively long period of development in the womb and a protracted infancy and adolescence

---

[5] The term "procreation" has a wider meaning than "reproduction" because it includes not only the production of a child but its care, formation, and education to maturity.

[6] On these grounds it has been argued that homosexual activity is also justified, but as I argued in "The Theology of Hetero- and Homosexuality" in *Same-Sex Attraction: A Parent's Guide* (edited by John F. Harvey, OSFS, and Gerard V. Bradley), 75–88, homosexual acts are disordered and hence intrinsically wrong and ineffective means to true human happiness.

during which the child requires the care of its parents and learns from them the basic ways of behavior necessary for it to survive and achieve happiness.

In many animal species litters are produced at once and in some anthropoids the male role is simply impregnation of the female and the driving off of competitive males who might also injure his offspring. In the human species, however, normal reproduction is one child at a time and the female has a brief menstrual cycle that prepares her for reproduction throughout the year and thus makes her continuously attractive to the male. Hence the male is genuinely a "father" who not only impregnates the female but remains present to care for her during her long periods of pregnancy and child-care and to participate actively in that child care. Thus human happiness requires a two-parent sexually complementary family that stays together until the maturity of the child.

Thus through evolution male and female parents are adapted to genetically determined roles that are complementary in view of the happiness of each new individual of the species.[7] Yet the political atmosphere in the United States has led the largest group of anthropologist to issue the following statement:

> The results of more than a century of anthropological research on households, kinship relationships, and families, across cultures and through time, provide *no support whatsoever* for the view that either civilization or viable social orders depend upon marriage as an exclusively heterosexual institution. Rather, anthropological research supports the conclusion that a vast array of family types, including families built upon same-sex partnerships, can contribute to stable and humane societies. The Executive Board of the American Anthropological Association strongly opposes a constitutional amendment limiting marriage to heterosexual couples. [italics added]

While it is true that there are great cultural variations in the family, one wonders what is this alleged evidence that these cultural variations "contribute to stable and human societies." The example commonly cited at present is homosexuality: It exists in most societies, although its incidence is quite rare, and no one seems to have been able to show that it contributes to social

---

7 [Among primates] "[m]onogamous groups consist of an adult male and female with their children. When they are grown, the children leave to create their own nuclear families. While this group pattern is the most common one for humans, it is rare for non-human primates. It is found among the small Asian apes as well as some of the New World monkeys and prosimians. Specifically, monogamous family groups are the common pattern for gibbons, siamangs, titi monkeys, indris, tarsiers, and apparently some pottos." Dennis O'Neil *Behavior: a Survey of Non-Human Primate Behavior Patterns.*

stability. While it is true that comparative anthropology shows wide cultural variation in the form that human families have taken, the so-called "nuclear family" of one man and one woman and their children in a permanent relationship is by far the most common pattern globally and historically. No society that has survived long has failed to establish structures that involve the biological parents in child care. Polyandry is quite rare, and although polygyny is common it prevails mainly in ruling and richer classes in a society.[8] Because polygyny, the most common cultural variant, is unfair to women and deprives their children of full paternal care, it can hardly contribute to human happiness but only to the pleasure of the male and to addictive behavior on his part.[9] It is confined largely to rich males as a mark of prestige.

The union of the human male and female, in view of the welfare of their children, needs to be permanent because the child needs the same parents for fifteen or twenty years, at the end of which time it becomes more difficult, at least for the female parent, to find a new mate. The quarrelling or separation of parents during childhood and adolescence is a serious hindrance to the maturation, especially the emotional stability, of the child. The biological fact of the menopause or termination of female pregnancy supports this biological arrangement, since late pregnancy makes reproduction risky and menopausal sterility leaves her less attractive to males desirous of offspring. Thus the female very much needs the support and companionship by her male partner who fathered her children. The male also finds in his familiar wife and children a companionship and care he needs, especially as his own health declines.

Thus socio-biological facts favor monogamous families as necessary to human happiness and therefore a moral responsibility for individuals and society to support. Cultural or individual attitudes that deny these facts or are contrary to their implications must be judged as objectively harmful to human happiness and are thus to be condemned and if possible remedied by individual and social change in behavior. That such norms are not respected

---

[8] On this see Carol R. Ember and Melvin Ember, *Cultural Anthropology*, 175. They show that the commonly cited case of the Nayar who formerly existed in India is not valid; see also E. Kathleen Gough, "The Nayars and the Definition of Marriage," *Journal of the Royal Anthropological Institute of Great Britain and Ireland*, 1958, and Conrad P. Kottak, *The Exploration of Human Diversity* (pp. 399–401) also discuss this case, and show that another commonly cited case, of the Azande of Sudan, who first married a younger male and later married a woman and raised a family, is explained by the fact that they were a warrior tribe. "The Azande, flexible in their sexuality, had no trouble shifting from homosexual acts to heterosexual acts" in their second marriage (p. 401). Greek homosexuality seems to have been rather similar.

[9] On the relative incidences of marital forms, see Ember and Ember, chapter 10, 174–95. For a nuanced discussion of the findings of anthropology on the family institution and male and female roles, see Adam Kuper, *The Chosen Primate: Human Nature and Cultural Diversity*, 154–207.

in some cultures and are frequently violated in all cultures in no way invalidates them but rather accounts for much of the widespread suffering that is, like disease, poverty, and injustice, a *de facto* feature of the human condition. Different cultures have different food habits, but some are healthier than others, and in all cultures some persons have unhealthy diets; but this fact does not disprove that the basic nutritional requirements of the human species underlie all cultures and all preferences.[10]

Human happiness, therefore depends on the physical health, security, and successful maturation of its members, and hence on permanent, monogamous families to produce and form those members. Hence it is a primary responsibility of every culture to promote permanent marriage for the survival of the species and the happiness of its individual members. Thus any culture is to be judged morally good or bad first of all on its fulfillment of this responsibility. Sadly it must be admitted that U.S. culture today in many ways is more and more failing to meet this obligation.[11]

---

[10] On the history of the long controversy on the roles of nature and culture and a listing of common traits, see Donald E. Brown, *Human Universals.* Contrary to the statement of the American Anthropological Association, he shows that although in the culture of professional anthropologists there has always been a tendency to minimize the factor of "nature," recent development are counteracting this. In chapter 6, 130–41, he lists many such universals. As to the family he writes, "The core of normal UP (universal people) family is composed of a mother and children. The biological mother is usually expected to be the social mother and usually is. On a more or less permanent basis there is usually a man (or men) involved, too, and he (or they) serve minimally to give the children a status in the community and/or to be a consort to the mother. Marriage, in the sense of a 'person' having a publicly recognized right of sexual access to a woman deemed eligible for childbearing, is institutionalized among the UP. While the person is almost always a male, it need not necessarily be a single individual, nor even a male. The UP have a pattern of socialization: children aren't just left to grow upon their own" (p. 136).

[11] Although sociologists speak of "the myth of family decline," especially because the increasing age of the U.S. population skews the statistics and the rate of decline slowed or even slightly reversed in the 90s, we must face such facts from the U.S. Census Bureau as follows: 28 percent (20 million) of all children under 18 in the U.S. live with one parent; 84 percent of children who live with one parent live with their mother. The percentage of children who live with two parents has been declining among all racial and ethnic groups. Of all births in 1997, 32 percent were to unmarried women. Fifty-six percent of single-parent households had no other adult living in the house. The number of single mothers (9.8 million) has remained constant, while the number of single fathers grew 25 percent in three years, to 2.1 million in 1998. Men comprise one-sixth of the nation's single parents. Of children living with one parent 38 percent lived with a divorced parent; 35 percent with a never-married parent; 19 percent with a separated parent; 4 percent with a widowed parent; 4 percent with a parent whose spouse lived elsewhere because of business or some other reason.

Although good families are of primary importance for human happiness, they are not sufficient. The family unit alone does not provide sufficient resources either material or intellectual for a complete and rich human life; a larger society is needed of many individuals with different complementary gifts and skills. Human history shows that existence in small, isolated groups, or even in tribes, came to be recognized as inadequate to human fulfillment and larger, organized societies, with governmental structures had to be devised. Basic to such structures that exceed the satisfaction of biological drives and promote humanly invented cultures of considerable complexity is the human capacity not only to cooperate with others but also to find happiness in sharing with others one's aspirations, gifts, and personal accomplishments.

No adequate understanding of human moral responsibility can neglect the fact of this human generosity or self-giving and transcendence that leads to human friendships. While some friendships are based on mutual needs a higher type of friendship that we call "love" in the broadest sense of the term goes beyond the need to receive and produces also the need to give. While some philosophers, such as Thomas Hobbes, have tried to explain society as simply the result of human selfishness and competition, it is not sentimental but strictly realistic to recognize that without such genuine friendship based not on "altruism" (in the sense of more concern for others' happiness than one's own) but on the common sharing of the good things of life, human happiness is impossible. We cannot be happy unless we want others to be happy and to actively share our happiness with them. This fundamental fact of human nature is evidenced by the universal observation made by anthropologists that human beings as a species like to share their food rather than eat it alone. What is more human than to enjoy a feast celebrated together?[12]

In the light of this basic human need for social sharing, it becomes obvious why we need friends for more than strictly pragmatic reasons. Such true friendship is based on having something in common and growing in this commonness. Hence it is a universal feature of human nature that, apart from the family, people form friendships with persons of their own gender, men with men, and women with women. This phenomenon is especially evident in the unmarried adolescent who finds in his or her peers a commonality that supports personal development. It is more difficult, however, for male and female humans to become friends because of their physical and psychological differences that evolution has demanded in the interests of reproduction that make them so unlike that, as they find their own identity, they perceive how alien it is to that of the opposite gender.

Here the famous theory of androgyny, especially as propounded by Carl Gustav Jung, is of interest, although I mention with the caution that it is

---

12 For the controversy on the sociobiology of "altruism," see Kuper, *The Chosen Primate,* 137–41, and Donald E. Brown, *Human Universals,* 105–8.

more speculative than the other better-established data that I have relied on.[13] According to Jung the maturation of the human male and female was developed by evolution in function of the complementary role of the sexes in procreation and child care. Consequently the traits common to all members of the species are dichotomized so that males achieve their identity by suppressing some of their traits to the unconscious psychological level and females suppress the opposite traits. Since, however, the need for family permanence requires that it be based on a union of friendship in which each partner takes care of the other's interests, marriage leads to a progressive androgyny for both husband and wife. His *anima* or suppressed elements of human nature needed for the female role become gradually unsuppressed, while for the female her *animus* or suppressed elements needed for the male role become gradually unsuppressed. Neither male nor female lose their gender identity, since that is stabilized both by their genes and their formation in family and social life. Nevertheless they become more capable of empathizing and sharing with the other partner and hence also become role models that enable their children to mature in their respective sexual identities.

On the basis of our present scientific information[14] it is probable that persons who psychologically deviate in their sexual orientation from this

---

[13] See Carl Jung et al., *Man and His Symbols,* for the basic concepts.

[14] The report of the Catholic Medical Association, "Homosexuality and Hope," has an extensive bibliography of presently available research. From the side of the gay community, see John P. De Cecco, and David Allen Parker, editors of a survey on etiology of homosexuality, *Journal of Homosexuality* 28 (1995): Part I, 1/2, Part II, 3/4; *Sex Cells, and Same-Sex Desire: The Biology of Sexual Preference.* The *Journal of Homosexuality* publishes empirical studies clearly not biased in favor of the Catholic Church's position. James D. Haynes, in the same number of the journal, "A Critique of the Possibility of Genetic Inheritance of Homosexual Orientation," 91–114, gives four hypotheses to explain how homosexuality might be genetic. (1) If the trait is recessive but heterozygotes have survival fitness. (2) If homosexuals use the energy they did not use in having children to help their siblings have children, or parents do the same for their grandchildren. (3) If homosexuals by not having children reduce competition for resources, jobs, and mates so as to help their group to survive. (4) If homosexuality, at least in males, is a byproduct of the propensity for boys to masturbate. Since boys are denied intercourse with females until long after puberty, a boy may be become fixated on his own penis and come to prefer it to a vagina. Haynes concludes, "The available evidence forces one to consider that neither nature nor nurture provides the sole answer to the cause of sexual orientation, either heterosexual or homosexual" (p. 108). "[A]ll available scientific evidence points to the conclusion that sexual orientation, be it heterosexual, ambisexual, or homosexual, is a result of the interaction of genotype and environment. People are born with the innate ability to perform sexually, but the focus of that performance is no more immutable than language skills. Further, there is evidently great plasticity in orientation, as one moves from one point on the sexual continuum to another, for differing lengths of time, and at different periods of one's life. The constraints placed by the social order on

biological norm related to procreation are the victims either of genetic defect or much more probably of developmental accidents in which family dysfunction probably pays the major part. This seems to be the explanation not only of homosexual orientation but of transexuality, pedophilia, and other deviant tendencies that are obstacles to successful marriage and parenting.[15] Current efforts to mitigate such developmental barriers to human fulfillment by denying that such conditions are deviant from the human norm and hence oppose research to prevent or remedy them, or at least to support the victims of these defects from behavior destructive to themselves or to other individuals or the social order are deplorable and cruel.[16] Problems of abnormal tendencies in human beings are not to be denied but to be faced courageously and compassionately.[17]

To say that such deviance is just a "normal variation" in the human species flies in the face of the sociobiological data already cited. Individuals who remain incurable victims of these abnormalities cannot enter into successful marriages. What remains open to them, however, is celibacy of the type already described, in which an individual renounces marriage in order to seek happiness by other means.[18] Pseudo-marriage or promiscuity can only exacerbate such ailments of the individual and their social approval obscures the norms of sexual behavior that it is so vital for society to defend.

---

particular orientations have no basis in biology. Thus homosexuals should seek their liberation through political and social efforts rather than biological research" (p. 111). De Cecco and Parker, *Sex Cells, and Same-Sex Desire: The Biology of Sexual Preference*, say, "This dispute [over the American Psychiatric Association's denial that homosexuality is a defect] provides evidence for the claim that the decision regarding whether homosexuality is some sort of mental illness or not is basically a political one. This is largely due to the fact that what a mental illness is, is itself a normative question." (p. 17). They approvingly quote Quentin Crispo, "Health consists in having the same diseases as one's neighbors" (p. 19), and think that in the present stance of psychiatry, "We cannot see that any ethical argument *against* a choice to be homosexual can be explicated that is not religiously determined."

15 John P. De Cecco and David Allen Parker, "The Biology of Homosexuality: Sexual Orientation or Sexual Preference?" *Journal of Homosexuality* 28 (1995): 1–28.

16 See also Udo Schuklenk and Michael Ristow, "The Ethics of Research into the Cause(s) of Homosexuality," *Journal of Homosexuality* 31 (3; 1996): 5–30. They identify "normal" with "average" and thus argue that it is not always better to be "normal." They also claim that since "artificial" is not always better than "natural" it is irrelevant than homosexuality is not natural. For them the only ethical consideration is whether homosexual activity harms others, but they give no proof that it is not harmful.

17 See my article "Compassion and the Homosexual," *The Vatican and Homosexuality*, Jeanine Grammick and Pat Furey, eds., 105–11.

18 This is the purpose of the Catholic organization "Courage" established in many American dioceses.

Inseparability of the Procreative and
Unitive Meanings of the Marital Act

In the first half of the twentieth century a controversy arose as the result of the writings of Dr. Herbert Doms[19] who argued that the traditional formulation of theologians according to which the "primary end of marriage is procreation, the secondary end common life of the spouses" did not do justice to the sacredness of married love, since it seemed to subordinate that love as a mere means to procreation. Although the Holy See did not accept aspects of Doms's thesis, it is clear that Paul VI attempted to meet this objection by a new formulation of the moral nature of the marital act in terms of the "Two significations, unitive and procreative" and then declared the Principle of the Inseparability of these two "significations."[20] Unfortunately Paul VI did not explicitly show this new formulation was a legitimate development of the older doctrine founded in the Church Fathers and many of the great theologians, such as Thomas Aquinas, who certainly accented the procreative "purpose" of marriage.

How then are we to understand the term "signification" as "purpose" or "end" in the Encyclical? John Paul II, who was perhaps an influence in the writing of *Humanae Vitae*, in his extensive writings on this subject before and during his pontificate,[21] takes this to mean that the marital act as it signifies, symbolizes, or manifests the purpose and function of marital intercourse reveals the essential nature or truth of marriage and hence its conformity to its natural and God-given purpose. Thus the language is that of a phenomenological personalism in which the description of the experience of an interpersonal relationship is understood as revealing something essential to the human person.[22] Thus "signification" can also be translated "purpose" or "end," provided that "purpose" and "end" are not understood in a merely pragmatic sense but only as this purpose is seen as freely chosen in accordance with the understanding of its intrinsic teleology. To use Thomistic terminology, this distinguishes what is chosen as a mere means to an end and thus has no value in itself *(bonum utile)*, from those means that are also ends having intrinsic value but a value subordinate to some higher

---

[19] Herbert Doms, MD, *The Meaning of Marriage.*

[20] The original of the encyclical is not Latin but Italian and uses the term *il significato.* This was well translated by Fr. Marc Caligari, SJ, in a revised translation from the Italian published by Ignatius Press, see www.cin.org/docs/humanvit.htm as "signification" instead of the translation "meaning" that had become common in English translations.

[21] See his *Love and Responsibility*, www.catholicculture.com/jp2_on_l&r.html, and *Theology of the Body: Human Love in the Divine Plan.*

[22] On the sacramental, symbolic understanding of the natural order common in Christian faith, see my article "Catholicism as a Sign System" in this collection.

goal *(bonum honestum).*[23] If we seek to approach the issue more directly, it must be granted that the older insistence that procreation is the "primary goal" of marriage is true in the sense that sexual reproduction is *generic* to most living organisms and that if it were not, there would be no sexual differentiation in the human species and no males and females to seek each other in erotic love. Yet for the human species procreation is not the goal of life, but, as Aristotle says, "Perfect friendship is between those who are good and alike in virtue; for these wish well alike to each other because it is good, and they are themselves good,"[24] but this goodness is true happiness. Thus, true friendship requires the common sharing between friends of the truth about each other and about the world, that is of their common "worldview and "value system." According to Aquinas truth is the supreme human need and the true goal of life is contemplation whose supreme objects are persons, above all the Divine Persons in God.[25] From a purely rational point of view it can also be maintained that the "meaning" of life is found principally in human relationships and search for wisdom about the reality of human life and our world.

We have seen that the family is the institution that alone can put the young human person on the right road to this goal of human friendship and that it flourishes best when the relationship of the parents is precisely a genuine friendship, a sharing of life together for mutual fulfillment as human persons. Thus the relation between the procreative and unitive (or friendship) end of marriage was not adequately expressed by the formula of primary and secondary ends, which was appropriate to canon law but lacked theological profundity. Rather a good marriage is a friendship, yet it is a special kind of friendship, one that establishes a family and flourishes in it. Thus the teleology of human sexuality is best understood as the human specification of the procreative demands of biological life.

Human beings are best reproduced in a family of which friendship is the foundation. I use the term "friendship" because in current language "love" is a very ambiguous term and often is the selfish pursuit of individual satisfaction rather than of a mutual self-giving. Aquinas points out that true love implies both benefaction and communion, that is if we truly love someone we seek their welfare as our own and we hope to be united to them in that

---

[23] *Summa theologiae* I, q. 5, 6 c.

[24] *Nicomachean Ethics* VIII, c. 3, 1156b 7.

[25] *Summa theologiae* I–II, q. 3, a. 8, shows that perfect beatitude consists in the vision of the Divine Essence, which, in I, q. 27, a. 5, he shows is the most inclusive happiness, while in I, q. 30, a. 1, he shows that the essence of God is found in the Three Divine Persons, and in I, q. 29, a. 3, that this must be the case since to be a person is "what is most perfect in all of reality." It follows that it is in the true friendship of intellectual creatures that the Trinitarian nature of God and his perfect beatitude is most perfectly reflected.

good life. It is not enough to help another to be a friend; we can do that to a needy stranger and then walk away. To love is to give and to give oneself by living with as well as for another. Married love and the family it includes is such a friendship.

Thus it becomes clear why the unitive and procreative meanings of marriage cannot be separated from one another, anymore than a species can be separated from its genus. Sexual love is a specific kind of friendship based on the union of male and female designed by nature to procreate the species but in a manner specific to the nature of human persons. To seek to render marriage reproductively sterile, therefore, is to separate it from its generic biological purpose and thus to render its specific unitive purpose void. On the other hand to separate its procreative purpose from its character of human friendship between persons of opposite sex is to depersonalize it and render it more animal than human. While some might argue that such habits of easy sexual gratification differ from chemical dependency in that they cause less physical physiological damage, it cannot be reasonably denied that they have serious risks for either a successful celibate or married life.

Some Objections

Yet it can still be objected that although it is clear that the marital act has its perfection only when it is both unitive and open to procreation, yet it is still a fitting means to happiness when only one of these values is achieved. Would not an act resulting in pregnancy for a couple desiring a child be justified even if it were not sought for its pleasure or its unitive meaning? Conversely, why is an act that is deliberately sterile not justified if it gives a recreative pleasure or enhances the unity of relationship between the couple? Unquestionably this is the point that makes all rejection of contraceptive sex appear so unreasonable to many people.

To respond to this objection it is necessary to consider the morality of any act that deliberately produces orgasm in any manner other than by penile penetration of the vagina and the deposit of semen in the vagina. Contraception belongs to this class of acts since it fails to deposit semen in the vagina. The most obvious example of this class of acts is masturbation or self-abuse. Many argue today that this is physically and psychologically harmless and hence morally insignificant.[26] This neglects the fact that because such an act is easy to perform and has no obvious physical consequences yet yields

---

[26] The view that this is not always a grave sin was introduced into American Catholic discussion by Rev. Charles E. Curran, "Masturbation and Objectively Grave Matter" in *A New Look at Christian Morality*, 214. Fr. Curran first proposed this opinion at the Catholic Theological Society of America in 1966. On this question see Fr. John Harvey, OSFS, " Overcoming the Masturbation Habit," at www.couragerc.net/PIP-Masturbation.

intense physical pleasure it is highly addictive and thus tends to limit human freedom and lessen rational control over bodily urges. Moreover it tends to habituate the self-abuser to think of sex as immediate, individual satisfaction unrelated to the unitive and procreative meaning of sexuality. As such it becomes an inhibition against developing true sexual relationships and leads the person, probably males most particularly, to treat his marital partner in a depersonalized way as a "sex object." Because of its addictive character this perverse attitude toward sex, masturbation seriously distorts character and becomes a vice. This applies to even a single deliberate act of masturbation since the pleasure involved is as intense as that given by addictive drugs, and it is well-known that even one experiment with addictive drugs has a significant risk of leading to an addiction. This is even more obvious when animals or "sex toys" are used for what is essentially masturbation.

While mutual masturbation between male and female has the appearance of being interpersonal sex it remains depersonalizing since the bodies of the partners are no longer treated according to their natural function in the body, as is required by human dignity, but as if they were "sex toys." This is true even in the case of the use of unnatural orifices, in oral or anal sex and, of course, even more when orgasm is produced by masochistic and sadistic procedures. All such practices have as their purpose to obtain physical gratification without danger of pregnancy and hence addict the person. When to this is added sexual exploitation as in rape, sexual relations with children, adolescents, prostitutes, or even married partners imposing sex on one another without their true consent, it is evident that all such sexual behavior is rightly called "perverse" or—to avoid emotional connotations as much as possible—"disordered," in that it first injures the perpetrators by addicting them to behavior contrary to the true nature of their own sexuality and, where another person is involved, injures them similarly even when it is wholly or partly consensual. The current outcry about sexual abuse by Catholic priests puts the whole evil on the lack of full consent by the younger, pressured person, but even if there were free consent, the act would still be very gravely evil.

To become, or risk becoming, a sexual pervert, that is, someone habituated to the urge to seek self-gratification in a manner contrary to the inherent teleology of one's own sexuality, is an enslavement to a condition contrary to human dignity. The fact that in recent culture such perversity has been commercially exploited and widely condoned as a harmless exercise of personal freedom does not make it less dangerous to human happiness. History shows that societies that encourage widespread perversity become decadent and even fail to survive. Just as our society is deeply injured by alcoholism and other forms of chemical dependency, it is also being deeply affected by sexual perversity as the social sanctions against it decline. It can hardly be doubted that this is at least one important factor in the very marked decline of successful marriages in our society.

Many also argue that even if it is conceded that to be moral the sexual act must be between a husband and wife and be aimed at orgasm through penetration and vaginal deposit of semen, yet this does not forbid contraceptive acts within marriage by couples who already have the family for which their resources are adequate or that is reasonable in size in view of the population control necessary for social good. This position is supported by the apparent contradiction of the Catholic Church in forbidding contraception in such circumstances while promoting Natural Family Planning (NFP), which also seems to deliberately frustrate the procreative meaning of sexuality.

NFP can be used deliberately either to promote pregnancy or avoid it. Its purpose is the regulation of pregnancy in the interests of better family life and perhaps even of population control. Yet there is an essential ethical difference between NFP and contraception, namely, that NFP does not aim at *sterilizing* acts that may be fertile, but at making use only of acts that are probably infertile. Thus the precise moral evil of contraception is in the deliberate sterilization of the marital act. This evil is made even worse when that sterilization is deliberately rendered permanent by tubal ligation or vasectomy. Whether the sterilizing process is by condom, an intrauterine device, or chemical or surgical means does not change the essential character of the contraceptive act.

Thus it is entirely consistent to argue that NFP does not involve, as does contraception, a deliberate separation of the unitive signification of the marital act from its procreative signification. Instead it uses infertile acts to attain their unitive signification that they naturally possess. The procreative signification possessed by a fertile act is not, of course, explicitly expressed but it is implicit in the respect shown to the woman's reproductive cycle, as it is when a couple has intercourse throughout the cycle and when a couple is sterile. As has already been said, biologically evolution has provided in the case of the human species that the female is always ready for intercourse in order to keep the male with her continually, but since pregnancy is a complex and physically stressing process, the fertility cycle is not always at the point where pregnancy is possible, and furthermore after a pregnancy but during nursing of the child fertility is also suppressed. This does not imply, however, that the sexual act is deprived of its procreative teleology during these infertile periods since the very existence of such periods promotes the optimum reproduction of the species since it keeps the partners together, protects the health of the mother, and hence of the children conceived at a suitable time.

Thus the use of the sterile period does not separate the unitive and procreative meaning of the marital act when the knowledge of it is used to regulate pregnancy for the good of the family, although it would be unethical if its use were perverted simply by a selfish desire for gratification unrelated to the expression of union through personal self-giving. It could be objected, of course, that NFP is based on scientific findings unknown to the moralists of the past who long ago condemned contraception. Yet even when this was the case common experience showed that intercourse is not always fertile. This fact puzzled some ethicists who thought this implied that couples at least one of whom was known to be sterile could not legitimately have intercourse. The view quickly predominated, however, that since the right to marital intercourse does not depend on the certainty of procreation because this is naturally not predictable, it is not abrogated by circumstances beyond the deliberate causation by the partners. Hence partners known to be sterile can still ethically have intercourse and their acts retain the teleological orientation toward procreation just as does eating food tend to nutrition even when some digestive defect prevents this from actually occurring. Deliberately contraceptive acts, however, require that the agent freely choose not simply to perform what is known to be a sterile act but one that has been deliberately rendered sterile with the intent to destroy its natural teleology and signification.

Of course this argument seems to some too far-fetched and to close off to couples under financial or health pressures the possibility of the sexual union that is important to preserve their marriage. The fact that the practice of NFP is justified in such circumstances seems no solution because it is said not to be sufficiently safe, or to be too difficult for couples to practice, or to achieve the agreement of the other partner to practice.

To this it must be replied that neither are perverse actions that are intrinsically harmful to human virtue and happiness a solution to such hard cases. If it is granted that perverse acts are always wrong, so that single persons must remain celibate before marriage or when marriage for whatever reason is not possible or even advisable, and that often even for married couples long periods of abstinence and of separation are sometimes necessary, it no longer is unreasonable to suppose that married couples should be willing and able to abstain periodically for some fairly brief periods. Moreover, as for many other difficult situations in life, the real solution is more research to make the required sacrifices easier and more effective and the social support that will ease the circumstances.[27] When men go to war and leave their wives at home, the answer to sexual urges is neither military prostitution nor wifely promiscuity but sacrifice and work for peace and homecoming. Our present society does many things to make family life difficult but is very irresponsible in providing means to make family life easier. The advocates of

---

27 Even at present a correct use of NFP is as effective as any method of contraception except sterilization, and sterilization cannot always be reversed if a person later desires children. For a good explanation of the different methods of NFP, see Richard Fehring, Stella Kitchen, and Mary Shivanandan, *An Introduction to Natural Family Planning.*

NFP make a good case that the practice of periodic abstinence does not, in fact, usually weaken family life, but that it tends to strengthen it. It promotes the friendship of the spouses and their regard for the needs of the other, especially the husband's concern for his wife's needs and his acquiring unselfish habits against sexual self-indulgence that depersonalize his relationship to his wife. Statistics show that especially after the first years of marriage, which is the optimum time for having a family, the frequency of sex declines in most marriages and is not nearly as urgent as is often thought.

The issue of population control is not a new one to the human species. The spread of the human race from tropical Africa all over the globe, even to very inhospitable environments, must have been due in large part to the overcrowding of smaller areas of human hunting and cultivation. The histories of Greece, Rome, Phoenicia, and modern Ireland, to take notorious examples, show that these countries were forced by the overpopulation of the home territory to massive immigration and colonization. There are also historic counterexamples: The case of Rome again being notorious in that population decline was brought on in part deliberately by abortion and contraception and led to the extinction of a nation as more fertile peoples took over the territory. Today overpopulation is still only regional—and in many regions the population is declining—yet it must be admitted that it is a new feature of human history that medical science and great food production seem to be threatening us with eventual global overpopulation since it seems highly improbable that immigration to other planets will ever be feasible.

To solve this dilemma by abortion and forced contraception, as China is attempting, is obviously inhuman. To attempt to solve it by using these intrinsically unethical means is also to compound the problem by weakening the family institution that is required for true human happiness. It has been shown that in countries where the population lives above the poverty level and is educated, population increase comes rapidly under control. No doubt this is in considerable part, but by no means wholly, a result of the adoption of safe methods of abortion and contraception, since these have appeared to be easy and effective methods for society to support. The consequences of this type of solution, however, are already evident in advanced countries in the decline of family life and sexual decadence through perversity, as I have already argued.

Hence better solutions are needed and these can be provided by the social support of family regulation through the practice of NFP facilitated by more scientific research and proper family education in sexual behavior. This must be supported along with social disapproval of the commercial exploitation of so-called "sexual freedom" and also by social support of the single celibate life both before marriage and after the death of a spouse, as well as for those committed to organizations and professions engaging in social services that require freedom from domestic cares.

The advance of the movement for female rights has, unfortunately, often played into the hands of the same "sexual freedom movement" that formerly corrupted male behavior into being oppressive of women. But women's rights can also be promoted by the social support of celibacy, which will relieve the energies of more women from the domestic duties that inevitably fall mainly on them so that they can pursue careers on a par with men. In a society that demands more of men in family life and sanctions their extra-marital "freedom," men will also be more inclined to celibacy for the sake of their careers in service of the society. Men's excuse that they can neglect their family because of their public duties will be exposed as irresponsible. They must choose between marriage and fatherhood and a freer, but chaste, single life dedicated to their work.

To say that such proposals are utopian is to ignore the remarkable capacity of the human species to develop cultures that are viable in changing and difficult environments. Such a goal of a culture in which families are strong because of high sexual discipline on the part of its members will, of course, not be perfectly achieved, but it is not unthinkable as being relatively practical; perhaps the necessity of global limits will eventually make it unavoidable. The alternative is the self-extinction of the human species. This too is a real possibility that the increasing practice of abortion and contraception cannot ultimately prevent and certainly promotes.

Artificial Reproduction

At the same time that modern Secular Humanist culture promotes population control by contraception it paradoxically promotes artificial reproduction to correct sterility, some of which is caused by contraception. In various forms it is used widely today not to overcome infertility problems in marriage but also to supply same-sex couples or single persons with children, or even to help a parent have a child after the death of the spouse. Infertility in marriage is a condition due to the husband as often as to wife and has many causes, which in about 20 percent of the cases cannot be determined.[28] In order to determine a possible cause of male infertility the number and activity of mail sperm must be examined and hence physicians often ask men to masturbate, a practice that is ethically indefensible even for this legitimate purpose and an unnecessary one, since other ethical techniques of obtaining sperm for this purpose are also available. For women, ova, however, can be obtained for examination by a simple surgery that is ethically unobjectionable. The use of "fertility drugs" to mature several ova at once can result in

---

28 The Pope Paul VI Institute, Omaha, NE, under its founder and director, Thomas W. Hilgers, MD, has developed the Creighton Model and what is called NaPro Technology to perfect NFP, to make important advances in the treatment of infertility and other gynecological disorders.

multiple pregnancies that are disadvantageous to the development of the fetuses. To produce such multiple pregnancies and then resort to "selective pregnancy reduction" is abortion.

Current methods of artificial reproduction started with *artificial insemination* of the woman with the husband's sperm (AIH), which violates the Principle of Inseparability, or if the husband is infertile with a donor's sperm (AID), which is adulterous and renders the child illegitimate. More advanced technologies involve *in vitro* fertilization with embryo transfer (IVF-ET), in which fertilization is performed outside the woman by a technician and the embryo is then inserted into her reproductive organs through a variety of procedures. Commonly several embryos are produced *in vitro*, and some are preserved by freezing for use in case of a reproductive failure. In all these techniques the true efficient cause of reproduction is not the marital act of the couple, as required by the Principle of Inseparability, but a technician; thus the child is not bonded to the parents in this committed act of marital love. Some theologians have approved GIFT (gamete infrafallopian transfer), in which the ovum and sperm are collected in a tube with a separating air bubble and then inserted in the uterus of the woman where conception takes place. The Church has not passed judgment on this procedure, but I agree with those who say that this too violates the Principle because the conception is not directly the result of the marital act but of the act of a third party, the technician. What has become increasingly evident is that all these methods are relatively ineffective, very expensive, and have led to the death of many embryos that were eventually discarded.[29]

Many justify artificial reproduction pragmatically because the child it produces is indeed a precious being whose existence seems to justify almost any means to produce it.

On the contrary, however, the very dignity of a healthy child tells us that children have fundamental rights that cannot be ethically sacrificed to the desires of parents. A child is a gift of God, who alone is its Creator because only the Creator can produce the spiritual soul with its intelligence and free will.[30] The parents—God uses as his instruments to create the child's body for which he directly creates the spiritual soul that gives that body its human life with the capacity to think intelligently and to make free choices—do not own the child. They are only its caretakers.

We must, therefore, ask whether artificial reproduction is compatible with the rights of the child produced. It will not do to argue, "Well, the child has no rights until it exists." We might as well argue that future generations have no right to a good environment so we can violate its ecology. A

---

[29] See Benedict Ashley and Kevin O. Rourke, *Health Care Ethics: A Theological Analysis,* 4th rev. ed., 240–48, for a more detailed discussion.

[30] See my essay "When Does a Human Person Begin to Exist?" in this collection.

child does have rights to be born in a way that meets its essential needs.[31] That is why it is an injustice to bear a child outside wedlock, since it needs a stable family environment when growing up. Newspaper accounts of adopted children eagerly seeking their biological parents make this point very clear. It is true that adoptive parents may legitimately meet their own needs for a child by adoption and that it is a charitable act to provide the adopted child with a loving home. Yet adoption cannot wholly satisfy that fundamental need of the child to be biologically linked to its parents. It remains in one important respect deprived.

Yet does not artificial reproduction provide that biological link to the parents? Obviously it cannot do so completely if it is accomplished through a semen donor who is not the husband or by the husband's insemination of a surrogate mother. These cases are essentially no different than conception outside marriage. But what of artificial insemination or artificial conception outside the mother, in which a technician produces an embryo by combining gametes obtained from the parents? Since this procedure as usually practiced also involves the use of several ova to guarantee success in fertilization, and even cyrogenic preservation of several embryos to ensure success in implantation, it risks the danger of killing innocent human beings.

Yet even if only a single embryo is artificially produced and thus a certain biological link of the child to its parents is effected, this is not the full biological linkage to which the child has a right. The natural linkage is not only in the fact that the parents supply the matter for the body of the child and the genome, but that they cooperate with God in the act of creating a unique human person through their marital act of love. In philosophical terms, such as used by St. Thomas Aquinas, parents only provide the *material cause* of the child. They biologically prepare a body ready for the human soul but they cannot make it a living human person. The *formal cause* of the child is the spiritual human soul that gives life to the child as a person, including the information for the self-construction of its body contained in its unique genome formed in the nucleus of the zygote at the moment of conception. Therefore the *efficient cause* of the child is God using the parents in their marital act as the instrumental efficient causes of this act of conception. The *final cause* of the child is its growth to physical adult and the virtuous life by which it will attain perfect union with God in eternal life. This analysis can be restated without direct reference to God simply by reference to human nature as I have described it and as scientific and philosophical observation and analysis can determine it. Thus the child produced by artificial reproduction—even with the ovum and sperm derived from married

---

31 See my articles, "A Child's Right to His Own Parents: A Look at Two Value System," *Hospital Progress* (August 1980): 47–50, and "What is a Human Person?" *NaProEthics* 3 (July 5, 1998): 4–5.

parents and without killing other embryos—is still a child deprived of its rights to be born naturally linked to its parents, not only materially but efficiently. The instrumental efficient cause of its conception is not human parents but the laboratory technician. Even if a couple could perform the artificial procedures themselves, they would not be true parents of the child, which properly speaking simply has no parents.

Nor can it be argued that they are parents because they have chosen to obtain a child in this way, and therefore in employing a technician as their agent they are the remote efficient cause of its conception. There are some things that, if they are to be done, we must do ourselves and one of these is to be a parent. The natural linkage to the child is precisely due to the parents' *immediate* efficiency in the marital act of love. To reduce parenthood to hiring another to produce a baby is Cartesian dualistic thinking at its worst.

If this seems too subtle, consider what is actually happening in our society today. Few would deny that in recent years the family institution has been very seriously weakened. There are many causes for this, but a basic factor is the deteriorating public perception that the child should be intimately linked to a family. Contraception taught couples that the enjoyment of sex need not be linked to reproduction. This has been reinforced by gay and lesbian propaganda that sex need not be linked to heterosexual marriage and that adoption is as good for the child as procreation. Finally artificial reproduction spreads the view that reproduction need not be linked to the marital act within marriage. If this trend in thinking continues, the children of the next millenium will be deprived of the security to which they have a natural right, derived from their linkage to their parents as the true and proximate efficient causes of their existence. No doubt this alienation will be made even more dangerous by the fact that even naturally conceived children may not realize that in begetting them their parents were the instruments of God who alone is their Creator.

Bibliographies

Church Documents

PAPAL ENCYCLICALS AND MANY OTHER IMPORTANT PAPAL documents are available on the Internet: www.papalencyclicals.net. Vatican documents are available in translation on Internet Vatican: www.vatican.va. Other papal writings are listed under the author's name.

Enchiridion symbolorum, definitionum et declarationum de rebus fidei et morum. Edited by Henry Denzinger and Aldoph Schönmetzer. 36th ed. rev. Barcelona: Herder, 1976.
Code of Canon Law. 1983. www.intratext.com/X/ENG0017.HTM.
Catechism of the Catholic Church. 2nd ed. Vatican: Libreria Editrice Vaticana, 1997.

Leo XIII 1878–1903

Aeterni Patris, "Encyclical on the Restoration of Christian Philosophy." August 4, 1979. www.vatican.va/ holy_father/leo_xiii/encyclicals/documents/hf_l-xiii_enc_04081879_aeterni-patris_en.html.

Pius X 1903–1914

Doctoris Angelici, "Decree of Approval of Some Theses Contained in the Doctrine of St. Thomas Aquinas and Proposed to the Teachers of Philosophy." Translated by Jacques Maritain. *AAS* 6 (June 24, 1914): 336–41.
St. Thomas Aquinas. Translated by J. F. Scanlon. London: Sheed, 1951. Latin and English translated by Hugh McDonald, www.vaxxine.com/hyoomik/ aquinas/theses.eht.

Pius XII 1939–1958

Encyclicals Cited

Mystici Corporis Christi, "Encyclical on the Mystical Body of Christ, The Church." June 29, 1943. www.vatican.va/holy_father/pius_xii/encyclicals/documents/hf_p-xii_enc_29061943_mystici-corporis-christi_en.html.

Humani Generis, "Encyclical Concerning some False Opinions Threatening to Undermine the Foundations of Catholic Doctrine." August 12, 1950. www.vatican.va/holy_father/pius_xii/encyclicals/documents/hf_p-xii_enc_12081950_humani-generis_en.html.

Other Documents Cited

Apostolic Constitution. *Sacramentum Ordinis,* "On the Sacrament of Orders." November 30, 1947, *DS. AAS* 40 (1948). Partial translation available at www.fordham.edu/halsall/source/1438sacraments.html.

Animus Noster gaudio. AAS 45 (1953): 682–90. Translated in *Irish Ecclesiasical Record* (August 1965): 121–30, and *The Pope Speaks* 6 (1959–60): 325–28.

"Prolongation of Life." November 24, 1957. *The Pope Speaks* 4 (1958).

Singulari sane animi. September 16, 1960. Translated in *The Pope Speaks* 6 (1959–60): 325–28.

Paul VI: 1963–1978

Vatican Council II: The Conciliar and Postconciliar Documents. Edited by Austin Flannery. 2 vols. rev. ed. Northport, NY: Costello Publishing Company, 1988. The following cited in this book are available as noted on the Internet.

Sacrosanctum Concilium, "Constitution on the Sacred Litury." December 4, 1963. www.vatican.va/archive/hist_councils/ii_vatican_council/documents/vat-ii_const_19631204_sacrosanctum-concilium_en.html.

Lumen Gentium, "Dogmatic Constitution on the Church." November 21, 1964. www.vatican.va/archive/hist_councils/ii_vatican_council/documents/vat-ii_const_19641121_lumen-gentium_en.html.

Christus Dominus, "Decree on the Pastoral Office of Bishops in the Church." October 28, 1965. www.vatican.va/archive/hist_councils/ii_vatican_council/documents/vat-ii_decree_19651028_christus-dominus_en.html.

Optatum Totius, "Decree On Priestly Training." October 28, 1965. www.vatican.va/archive/hist_councils/ii_vatican_council/documents/vat-ii_decree_19651028_optatam-totius_en.html.

Gravissimum Educationus, "Declaration on Christian Education." October 28, 1965, #10. www.vatican.va/archive/hist_councils/ii_vatican_council/documents/vat-ii_decl_19651028_gravissimum-educationis_en.html.

Nostra Aetate, "Declaration on the Relationship of the Church to Non-Christian Religions." October 28, 1965. www.vatican.va/archive/hist_councils/ii_vatican_council/documents/vat-ii_decl_19651028_nostra-aetate_en.html.

Vatican II. *Dei Verbum,* "Dogmatic Constitution on Divine Revelation." November 18, 1965. www.vatican.va/archive/hist_councils/ii_vatican_council/documents/vat-ii_const_19651118_dei-verbum_en.html.

Apostolicam Actuositate, "Decree on the Apostolate of Lay People." November 18, 1965. www.vatican.va/archive/hist_councils/ii_vatican_council/documents/vat-ii_decree_19651118_apostolicam-actuositatem_en.html.

Dignitatis Humanae, "Declaration on Religious Freedom. December 7, 1965. www.vatican.va/archive/hist_councils/ii_vatican_council/documents/vat-ii_decl_19651207_dignitatis-humanae_en.html.

Presbyterorum Ordinis, "Decree on the Ministry and Life of Priests. December 7, 1965. www.vatican.va/archive/hist_councils/ii_vatican_council/documents/vat-ii_decree_19651207_presbyterorum-ordinis_en.html.

Gaudium et Spes, "Pastoral Constitution on the Church in the Modern World." December 7, 1965. www.vatican.va/archive/hist_councils/ii_vatican_council/documents/vat-ii_cons_19651207_gaudium-et-spes_en.html.

Humanae Vitae, "On the Regulation of Birth." July 25, 1968. www.vatican.va/holy_father/paul_vi/encyclicals/documents/hf_p-vi_enc_25071968_humanae-vitae_en.html .

Other Documents Cited

"Credo of the People of God." June 30, 1968. www.creeds.net/Misc/credo_paul6.htm.

"Declaration of the Commission of Cardinals on the 'New Catechism'" *(Die Nieuwe Katechismus).* October 15, 1968. www.ewtn.com/library/CURIA/CDFDCA/htm.

Homilies of September 27, 1970, and October 24, 1970. *The Pope Speaks* 15 (1970): 196–202, 218–22.

Apostolic Exhortation. *Marialis Cultus.* (February 2, 1974): 113–68. www.papalencyclicals.net/Paul06/p6marial.htm.

"Declaration on Procured Abortion." November 18, 1974. www.vatican.va/roman_curia/congregations/cfaith/documents/rc_con_cfaith_doc_19741118_declaration-abortion_en.html.

Apostolic Letter. *Lumen Ecclesiae,* "On St. Thomas Aquinas." *The Pope Speaks* 19 (4; 1975): 287–307.

Inter Insigniores. "Declaration on the Question of Admission of Women to Ministerial Priesthood." October 15, 1976. www.ewtn.com/library/CURIA/CDFINSIG.HTM.

John Paul II: 1978–2005

Written as Karol Wojtyla (Before Elected Pope)

The Acting Person. Translated by Andrezej Potocki; edited by Anna-Teresa Tymieniecka. *Anlecta Husserliana.* Vol. 10. Dordrecht, Boston: D. Reidel, 1979.

Love and Responsibility. www.catholicculture.com/jp2_on_l&r.html.

Encyclicals Cited

Redemptoris Mater, "Mother of the Redeemer." March 25, 1987. www.vatican.va/holy_father/john_paul_ii/encyclicals/documents/hf_jp-ii_enc_25031987_redemptoris-mater_en.html. *Mary: God's Yes to Man.* Introduction by Joseph Cardinal Ratzinger; commentary by Hans Urs von Balthasar. San Francisco: Ignatius Press, 1988.

Veritatis Splendor, "The Splendor of Truth." September 6, 1993. www.vatican.va/holy_father/john_paul_ii/encyclicals/documents/hf_jp-ii_enc_06081993_veritatis-splendor_en.html.

Evangelium vitae, "On the Value and Inviolability of Human Life." March 25, 1995. www.vatican.va/holy_father/john_paul_ii/encyclicals/documents/hf_jp-ii_enc_25031995_.

Fides et Ratio. September 14, 1998. www.vatican.va/holy_father/john_paul_ii/encyclicals/documents/hf_jp-ii_enc_15101998_fides-et-ratio_en.html.

Other Documents Cited

"Perennial Philosophy of St. Thomas for the Youth of Our Times." November 17, 1979. *L'Osservatore Romano* (English edition) (December 17, 1979): 6–8.

Lettera. *Sacerdotium ministeriale. Circa il ministro dell'eucaristia.* 1983. *Notificazione della Congregazione per la Dottrina della Fede.* September 15, 1986. *L'Osservatore Romano* (24 September 1986).

"Method and Doctrine of St. Thomas in Dialogue with Modern Culture." September 13, 1980. *L'Osservatore Romano* (October 20, 1980): 9–11.

"Declaration on Euthanasia." May 5, 1980. www.vatican.va/roman_curia/congregations/cfaith/documents/rc_con_cfaith_doc_19800505_euthanasia_en.html.

Ex Corde Ecclesiae, "Apostolic Constitution on Catholic Universities." August 15, 1990. www.vatican.va/holy_father/john_paul_ii/apost_constitutions/documents/hf_jp-ii_apc_15081990_ex-corde-ecclesiae_en.html.

Apostolic Letter Ordinatio Sacerdotalis, " On Priestly Ordination." May 22, 1994. www.vatican.va/holy_father/john_paul_ii/apost_letters/documents/hf_jp-ii_apl_22051994_ordinatio-sacerdotalis_en.html.

Original Unity of Man and Woman: Catechesis on the Book of Genesis; preface by Donald W. Wuerl. Boston, MA: St. Paul Editions, 1981.

Theology of the Body: Human Love in the Divine Plan. Boston, MA: Pauline Books, 1997.

"Instruction on Christian Freedom and Liberation." March 22, 1986. www.vatican.va/roman_curia/congregations/cfaith/documents/rc_con_cfaith_doc_19860322_freedom-liberation_en.html.

"Letter to Bishops of the Catholic Church on the Pastoral Care of Homosexual Persons" of the Congregation for the Doctrine of the Faith. 1 October, 1986. www.vatican.va/roman_curia/congregations/cfaith/documents/rc_con_cfaith_doc_19861001_homosexual.

"Instruction on Respect for Human Life." *(Donum Vitae), Origins,* 16 (40) (March 19, 1987): 697–709.

"Instruction on the Ecclesial Vocation of the Theologian." May 24, 1990. *Origins* 20 (July 5, 1990): 117–26. www.vatican.va/roman_curia/congregations/cfaith/documents/rc_con_cfaith_doc_19900524_theologian-vocation_en.html.

Sacred Congregation for the Sacraments and Divine Worship. *Pastoralis Actio,* "Instruction on Infant Baptism." October 20, 1980. www.ewtn.com/library/CURIA/CDFINFAN.htm.

Theses de la comission theologique international: La dignite et les droits dela personne humaine, Documentation Catholique 82 (1985): 383–91.

Pontifical Biblical Commission. "The Interpretation of the Bible in the Church." *Origins* 23 (29; January 6, 1994): 499–524.

United States National Conference of Catholic Bishops. "Doctrinal Congregational Statement on Sterilization." March 19, 1975. In *Commentary of National Conference of Catholic Bishops* (Washington, DC: United States Catholic Conference, 1975).

Committee for Pro-Life Activities. "Statement on Uniform Rights of the Terminally Ill Act." June 26, 1986. *Origins* 16 (12; September 4, 1986): 222–24, and Washington, DC: United States Catholic Conference, 1975.

The Ethical and Religious Directives for Catholic Care Services. Washington, DC: U.S. Conference of Catholic Bishops, 2001.

Works of Aristotle

The works of Aristotle cited in this book are available in standard translations classics.mit.edu/Browse/browse-Aristotle.html.

- *Categories*
- *Posterior Analytics*
- *Topics*
- *Physics*
- *De Caelo et Mundo*
- *De Partibus Animalium*
- *Historia Animalium*
- *De Generatione*
- *De Anima*
- *Nicomachean Ethics*
- *Politics*
- *Metaphysics*

Works of St. Thomas Aquinas

For full bibliographical information, see James A. Weisheipl, OP. *Friar Thomas d'Aquino: His Life, Thought,and Works.* Garden City, NY: Doubleday, 1974; Jean-Pierre Torrell, OP. "The Person and His Work." In Saint Thomas Aquinas. Vol. 1. Washington DC: Catholic University of America Press, 1996; and Thérèse Bonin's very full and up-to-date website, www.home.duq.edu/~bonin/thomasbibliography.html.

Commentary on the Sentences of Peter Lombard, Scriptum super Sententiis. Books I & II edited by P. Mandonnet. Paris: 1929. Books III & IV edited by M. F. Moos. Paris: 1933, 1947. There is no complete English translation; for translated excerpts, see bibliography at www.home.duq.edu/~bonin/thomasbibliography.html.

Summa theologica, Sancti Thomae de Aquino Opera Omnia. Vols. 13–15. Rome: Leonine edition, 1882. Translated by the Fathers of the English Dominican Province in the Benziger Bros. edition, 1947. www.ccel.org/a/aquinas/summa/home.html. Blackfriars bilingual edition, edited by Thomas Gilby, OP, and various translators. 60 vols. New York: McGraw-Hill, 1964–1973.

Summa contra Gentiles. Translated by Anton C. Pegis, James F. Anderson, Vernon J. Bourke, and Charles J. O'Neil. Vols. 22.1, 22.2, 22.3. Rome: Leonine edition.

On the Truth of the Catholic Faith (Summa contra Gentiles). 5 vols. New York: Doubleday, 1955–57. Reprinted as *Summa contra Gentiles.* Notre Dame, IN: University of Notre Dame Press, 1975.

Super Evangelium S. Ioannis Lectura, The Commentary on St. John. Edited by P. Raphaelis Cai, OP. Torino/Rome: Marietti, 1952. Only Part I, Chapters I-VII have been translated into English by James A. Weisheipl, OP, and Fabian R. Larcher, OP. Albany, NY: Magi Books.

Commentary on Boethius' "De Trinitate," Sancti Thomae de Aquino: Exposition super librum Boethii De Trinitate. Edited by E. Becker. 2nd ed. Leiden: 1955, reprinted 1959. Translated in part as *Thomas Aquinas: Division and Method of the Sciences* by Armand Mauer, with introduction and notes. 4th ed. Toronto: Pontifical Institute of Medieval Studies, 1986.

Quaestiones disputatae. Leonine vols. 23–25.2. Translated by Robert W. Mulligan, James V. McGlynn, and Robert W. Schmidt as *Disputed Questions.* Library of Living Catholic Thought. Chicago: Regnery, 1952–54; reprint, Indianapolis, IN: Hackett, 1994.

De Veritate. Leonine vol. 23. Translated by Robert W. Mulligan, James V. McGlynn, and Robert W. Schmidt as *Truth.* 3 vols. Library of Living Catholic Thought. Chicago: Regnery, 1952–54; reprint, Indianapolis, IN: Hackett, 1994.

De Malo. Leonine vol. 24, 1. Translated by Richard Regan as *On Evil*; edited with an introduction and notes by Brian Davies. Oxford: Oxford University Press, 2003.

De Potentia. Leonine vol. 24.2. Translated by Laurence Shapcote as *On the Power of God.* 3 vols. London: Burns, Oates & Washbourne, 1932–34; reprinted in 1 volume, Westminster, MD: Newman, 1952.

De Anima. Leonine vol. 25.1, 25.2.. Translated by James H. Robb as *Questions on the Soul.* Mediaeval Philosophical Texts in Translation, 27. Milwaukee: Marquette University Press, 1984.

De Unitate Intellectus Contra Averroistas. Leonine vol. 45, 1. Translated by Beatrice H. Zedler as. *On the Unity of the Intellect against the Averroists.* Mediaeval Philosophical Texts in Translation. Milwaukee: Marquette University Press, 1968.

Commentaries on Aristotle

Sententia super Posteriora Analytica. Translated by F. R. Larcher, OP. as *Commentary on the Posterior Analytics of Aristotle.* Albany: Magi Books, 1970.

Sententia super Physicam. Translated by Richard J. Blackwell, Richard J. Spath, and W. Edmund Thirlkel as *Commentary on Aristotle's Physics.* Rare Masterpieces of Philosophy and Science. New Haven, CT: Yale University Press, 1963; reprint, Aristotelian Commentary Series. Notre Dame, IN: Dumb Ox Books, 1999.

Sententia de caelo et mundo. Translated by Fabian Larcher, OP, and Pierre H. Conway as *Exposition of Aristotle's Treatise On the Heavens.* 2 vols. Columbus, OH: College of St. Mary of the Springs, 1964.

Sententia super De anima (distinct from the Disputed Question *De anima*). Translated by Robert C. Pasnau as *Commentary on Aristotle's De anima.* New Haven, CT: Yale University Press, 1999.

Sententia libri Ethicorum. Translated by C. I. Litzinger as *Commentary on the Nicomachean Ethics.* 2 vols. Library of Living Catholic Thought. Chicago: Regnery, 1964; reprinted in 1 volume with revisions as *Commentary on Aristotle's Nicomachean Ethics.* Aristotelian Commentary Series. Notre Dame, IN: Dumb Ox Books, 1993.

Sententia libri Politicorum (incomplete work). Translated by Ernest L. Fortin as *Commentary on Aristotle's Politics.* Thomas Aquinas in Translation. Washington, DC: The Catholic University of America Press, in preparation.

Sententia super Metaphysicam. Translated by John P. Rowan as *Commentary on the Metaphysics of Aristotle.* 2 vols. Chicago: Regnery, 1964; reprinted in 1 volume with revisions as *Commentary on Aristotle's Metaphysics.* Aristotelian Commentary Series, Notre Dame, IN: Dumb Ox Books, 1995.

Benedict M. Ashley, OP
Books, Articles, Reviews, Lectures

Note: This is a rough classification with considerable overlapping of categories.

Bioethics

Books

Health Care Ethics: A Theological Analysis. (Co-author with Kevin D. O'Rourke.) 1st ed. St. Louis: Catholic Health Association, 1977; 2nd ed. St. Louis: Catholic Health Association, 1982; 4th rev. ed. Washington, DC: Georgetown University Press, 1997; Italian translation, 1993. 5th ed. in preparation 2006.

Ethics of Health Care. Washington, DC: Georgetown University Press, 1986. A textbook version of *Health Care Ethics.*

Articles and Lectures

"Roman Catholic Medical Ethics." In Sylvester D. Thorn, *The Faith of Your Patients: A Handbook of Religious Attitudes Toward Medical Practices.* Houston: Privately published, 1972

"Ethics of Experimenting with Persons." In *Research and the Psychiatric Patient,* edited by J. Schoolar and C. Gaits. New York: Brunner/Mazel, 1975.

"The Religious Heritage of the Stewardship of Life: Perspective of a Moralist." In *Responsible Stewardship of Human Life*, edited by Donald G. McCarthy, 35–42. Inquiries into Medical Ethics II, The Institute of Religion and Human Development. Houston, St. Louis: The Catholic Hospital Association, 1976.

"A Critique of the Theory of Delayed Hominization." In D. G. McCarthy and A. S. Moraczewski, *An Ethical Evaluation of Fetal Experimentation,* Appendix I, 113–33. St. Louis: Pope John Center, 1976. (Note: The Pope John Center is now the National Catholic Bioethics Center, Philadelphia/Boston.)

"Problems in Medical Ethics." 5 video-taped cassette lectures commissioned by the Department of Health Affairs. Diocese of Lansing, Michigan, 1978.

"Ethical Assumptions in the Abortion Debate." In *Issues in Ethical Decision Making,* St. Louis: Pope John Center, n.d.

"Pro-Life Evangelization." *New Technologies of Birth and Death,* 80–97. First Bishops Workshop, Dallas, TX, 1980. St. Louis: Pope John Center, 1980.

"Principles for Moral Decisions about Prolonging Life." In D. G. McCarthy and A. S. Moraczewski, *Moral Responsibility in Prolonging Life Decisions,* 116–23. St. Louis: Pope John Center, 1981.

"Pro-Life Evangelization." In *The New Technologies of Birth and Death,* 80–97. St. Louis: Pope John Center, 1982.

"Genetic Engineering." Annual Thomist Colloquium. Washington, 1986. Unpublished.

"How the Roman Catholic Position on Euthanasia Developed." Official Methodist-Catholic Dialogue. 1987. Unpublished.

"Financial Burdens and the Obligation of Sustaining Life" & "Hydration and Nutrition: Ethical Obligations." In *Reproductive Technologies, Marriage, and the Church,* 113–18 & 159–65. Braintree, MA: Pope John Center, 1987.

"A Christian Perspective on Scientific Medicine." Keynote address for *Giornate di studio e di riflessione in occasione del 120 Anniversario della fondazione dell' Ospedale Pediatrico Bambino Gesu.* Rome, November 28–29, 1989. Unpublished.

"The Relevance of Ethics to Health Care." Annual National Conference of the Catholic Health Association of Canada. Victoria, British Columbia. May 16, 1990. Unpublished.

"Dialogue with William E. May on 'Normal Care.'" Discussion held at Providence Hospital, Washington, DC. 1992. Unpublished.

"Moral Inconsistency and Fruitful Public Debate." *Ethics and Medics* 17 (4; April, 1992).

"Dominion or Stewardship." A paper delivered at the International Study Group in Bioethics, International Federation of Catholic Universities. Brussels. March 29–31, 1990. In *Birth, Suffering and Death: Catholic Perspectives at the Edge of Life,* edited by Kevin M. Wildes, SJ, Franceso Abel, SJ, and John C. Harvey, 85–106. Philosophy and Medicine 41. Catholic Studies in Bioethics 1. Dordrecht/Boston/London: Kluwer Academic Publishers, 1992.

"Is the Biological Subject of Human Rights Present From Conception?" (With Albert S. Moraczewski, OP.) In *The Fetal Tissue Issue: Medical and Ethical Aspects*, edited by Peter J. Cataldo and Albert S. Moracczewski, OP. Braintree, MA: Pope John Center, 1994.

"Does 'The Splendor of Truth' Shine on Bioethics?" *Ethics and Medics* 19 (January 1994): 3–4.

"Health Care Ethics." In *Encylopedia of U.S. Biomedical Policy*, 119–21. Editors-in-chief, Robert H. Blank and Janna C. Merrick. Westport, CT: Greenwood Press, 1996.

"Anthropological and Ethical Aspects of Embryo Manipulation." Unpublished.

"Observations on the Document of the NCCB 'Moral Principles Concerning Anencephaly.'" *L'Osservatore Romano* (English Edition) 38 (23 September 1998): 8–10.

"Designer Babies or Gifts of God?" *NaProEthics.* (May 1, 2000).

"Cloning, Aquinas, and the Embryonic Person." (With Albert Moraczewski, OP) *The National Catholic Bioethics Quarterly* 1 (2; 2001): 189–202.

"Organ Donation and Implantation." Symposium sponsored by the John Cardinal Krol Chair of Moral Theology. Wynnewood, PA. April 19–21. In *Moral Issues in Catholic Health Care*, edited by Kevin T. McMahon, 1–18. Overbrook, MA: Saint Charles Borromeo Seminary, 2004.

Book Reviews

John Connery, *Abortion. New Review of Books and Religion* 2 (March 1978): 23

"Basis for Medical Ethics: A Triple Contract Theory." Robert M. Veatch, *A Theory of Medical Ethics. Hospital Progress* (January 1983): 58, 62.

Thomas A. Shannon and Lisa Sowle Cahill, "Religion and Artificial Reproduction: An Inquiry into the Vatican Instruction on Respect for Human Life in its Origin and on the Dignity of Human Reproduction." *The Thomist* 54 (1; January 1989): 153–55.

Psychology

Book

Healing for Freedom. Forthcoming.

Articles and Lectures

"A Psychological Model with a Spiritual Dimension." *Pastoral Psychology* (May 1972): 31–40.

"An Integrated View of the Christian Person." In *Technological Powers and the Person*, 313–33. St. Louis: Pope John Center, 1983.

"Theology and the Mind-Body Problem." In *Mind and Brain*, edited by Robert Brungs, SJ. St. Louis: Institute for the Encounter of Theology, Science, and Technology, 1985.

"Contemporary Understandings of Personhood." In *The Twenty-Fifth Anniversary of Vatican II: A Look Back and A Look Forward*, edited by Russell E. Smith, 35–48. Proceedings of the Ninth Bishops' Workshop, Dallas, Texas. Braintree, MA: The Pope John Center, 1990.

"John Paul II: Theology of the Body of the Acting Person." Paper given at the Catholic Theological Society of America, 1998. Unpublished.

"What is a Human Person?" *NaProEthics* 3 (4; July 1998): 4–5.

"Spirituality and Counseling." In *Handbook of Spirituality for Ministers*, edited by Robert Wicks, vol. 2, 656–70. *Perspectives for the 21st Century*. New York: Paulist Press, 2000.

"Study and Preaching" www.op.org/domcentral/study/ashley

"The Five Luminous Mysteries of the Rosary." 5 lectures, 2005. Unpublished.

Sexuality

Book

Justice in the Church: Gender and Participation. The McGivney Lectures, 1992. Washington, DC: The Catholic University of America Press, 1996.

Articles and Lectures

"From *Humanae Vitae* to *Human Sexuality*." *Hospital Progress* (July 1978): 78–81.

"A Child's Right to His Own Parents: A Look at Two Value System." *Hospital Progress* (August 1980): 47–50.

"Pastoral Problems in Sexual Morality." Paper for the National Conference of Catholic Bishops. St. John's University, Collegeville, MN. June 12–23, 1982. Unpublished.

"A Theological Overview on Recent Research on Sex and Gender." In Mark F. Schwartz, A. S. Moraczewski, and J. A. Monteleone, *Sex and Gender*, 1–47. St. Louis: Pope John Center, 1983.

"The Family in Church and Society." In *The Family Today and Tomorrow*, 101–12. Braintree, MA: Pope John Center, 1985.

"Compassion and the Homosexual." In *The Church and Homosexuality*, edited by Jeanine Grammick and Pat Furey, 105–11. New York: Crossroad, 1988.

"Gender and the Priesthood of Christ: A Theological Reflection." *The Thomist* 57 (3; July 1993): 343–79.

"Notes Toward a Theology of Gender." *National Catholic Register* 71 (53; December 31, 1995): 5.

"The Bible and Sexuality." 1997. Unpublished.

"Women's Participation in the Church." Lecture at Boston College. 1997. Unpublished.

"Sexism and Gender Imagery." in *Religion and the American Experience*, edited by Frank T. Birtel, Tulane Judeo-Christian Studies (Hyde Park, NY: New City Press, 2005), 81–93.

Interview. "Fr Ashley on Trotsky and Consecrated Virgins." *The Observer of Boston College* 14 (9; February 5, 1997): 12, 13.

"The Theology of Hetero- and Homosexuality." In *Same-Sex Attraction: A Parent's Guide*, 75–88. Edited by John F. Harvey, OSFS, and Gerard V. Bradley. South Bend, IN: St. Augustine's Press, 2003.

Theology

Books

Contemplation and Society. Lector in Theology dissertation. 1949. Unpublished.

Thy Kingdom Come! An Overview of Catholic Social Doctrine. Dubuque, IA: Archdiocese of Dubuque, Telegraph-Herald Press, 1976.

Thomas Aquinas: Selected Spiritual Writings. (Co-author with Matthew Rzechowski, OP.) Hyde Park, NY: New City Press, 1994.

Theologies of the Body: Humanist and Christian. St. Louis: Pope John Center, 1985. 2nd ed., with a new introductory chapter. Braintree, MA: Pope John Center, 1996.

Living the Truth in Love: A Biblical Introduction to Moral Theology. Staten Island, NY: Alba House, 1996.

Choosing a Worldview and Value System: An Ecumenical Apologetics. Staten Island, NY: Alba House, 2000.

Articles and Lectures

"The Beginner at Mental Prayer." *Cross and Crown* 12 (June 1960): 133–45. Reissued as a Cross and Crown reprint.

"Catholic Guilt for Anti-Semitism." From the Symposium on Christian-Jewish Relations. Rosary College, January 26, 1966. *At the Crossroad* 5 (Winter-Spring 1966): 6–8, 10–11.

"Theology in the Space Age." Interview. *Texas Catholic Herald* (1971).

"Religious Orders and Social Involvement." *Catholic Mind* (March 1971): 29–33.

"The Sacred in Art." Participation in a television program for Canadian national television. Published in *Artscanada* (April-May 1971): 17–25

"The Meaning of the Virgin Birth." *Texas Catholic Herald* (December 20, 1971).

"Aquinas and Process Theology." *University of Dayton Journal* (1975).

Columns on "Moral Directives." *The Christian Family Weekly* (September 4, 1978–August 1979).

"What Do We Pray in the Lord's Prayer?" *Spirituality Today* 31 (2; July 1979): 121–36.

"The Use of Moral Theology by the Church." In *Human Sexuality and Personhood*, 223–42. St. Louis: Pope John Center, 1981.

"Christian Moral Principles: a Review Discussion" of Germain Grisez's, *The Way of the Lord Jesus*, vol. 1, *Christian Moral Principles. The Thomist* 48 (3; July 1984): 450–60.

"The Development of Doctrine about Sin, Conversion, and the Following of Christ." In *Moral Theology Today: Certitude and Doubts*, 46–63. St. Louis: Pope John Center, 1984.

"Ethical Decisions: Why Exceptionless Norms?" *Hospital Progress* (April 1985): 50, 53, 66.

"The Coming Extraordinary Synod." *Catholicism in Crisis* (June 1985): 14–15.

"Liberation from What?" St. Catherine Symposium. Washington. 1985. Unpublished.

"Why is Breaking God's Law a Sin?" *Ethics and Medics* 11 (3; March 1986).

"A Response to John P. Boyle's, `The American Experience in Theology.'" *Proceedings of the 41st Annual Convention of the Catholic Theological Society of America* 41 (1986): 47–50.

"Science and Religion." 8 columns. *The National Catholic Register* (1987).

"Theological Method Today." Bishops' and Scientists' Dialogue of the NCCB, 1987. Unpublished.

"St. Thomas and the Theology of the Body." Annual Aquinas Address, University of St. Thomas, Houston, TX. In *Thomistic Studies II.* Houston: University of St. Thomas, 1987.

"The Scriptural Basis of Moral Theology." *The Thomist* (1987); also in *Persona et Morale, Atti del I Congresso Internazionale di Teologia Morale.* Rome 1986; Milano: Edizione Ares, 1987.

"Experience as a Theological Resource." Aquinas Lecture, University of Dallas, 1989. Unpublished.

"The Development of the Doctrine on Grace to the Reformation." A paper delivered at the Alliance of Catholic Theologians, Franciscan University of Steubenville, Ohio, October 1989. Unpublished.

"The Chill Factor in Moral Theology: An In-Depth Review of *The Critical Calling: Reflections on Moral Dilemmas Since Vatican II*" by Richard A. McCormick, SJ. *The Linacre Quarterly* (November 1990): 67–77. Awarded annual prize for best article in the journal.

"A Critique of Matthew Fox's *The Cosmic Christ* and the Notion of Creation-Centered Spirituality." Paper given at the Colloquium on New Age Sects. Franciscan University of Steubenville, June 1990.

"Creation-Centered and Redemption-Centered Spirituality." Paper given at "Defending the Faith II: A Conference on the New Age Sects." Franciscan University of Steubenville, June 1991. Published in cassette form by the University.

"Moral Theology and Mariology." *Anthropotes* 7 (2; December 1991): 137–53.

Review of Bernard Häring's *My Witness for the Church*. Introduction and translation by Leonard Swidler. New York: Paulist, 1992. *Catholic World Report* 2 (November 1991): 56–58.

"Elements of Catholic Conscience." *Catholic Conscience: Foundation and Formation,* 39–58. Tenth Bishops' Workshop of the Pope John Center, Dallas, Texas, February 4–9, 1991. Braintree, MA: Pope John Center, 1991.

"'The Truth Will Set You Free: A Commentary on the *Instruction on the Ecclesial Role of the Theologian* of the Congregation for the Doctrine of the Faith." Prepared for the NCCB Committee on Doctrine, 1991. Unpublished.

"Living in Christ." *Crisis* 11 (6; June 1993): 23–26.

"What is Moral Theology." *Medics and Ethics* Part I (July 1993); Part II (August, 1993); 3–4.

"Catholicism as a Sign System." *Journal of Semiotics* 10 (1–2; 1994): 67–84.

"What is the End of the Human Person: The Vision of God and Integral Human Fulfillment." In *Moral Truth and Moral Tradition: Essays in Honor of Peter Geach and Elizabeth Anscombe*, 68–96. Edited by Luke Gormally. Dublin and Portland, OR: Four Courts Press, 1994.

Encyclopedia of Catholicism. 25 short articles. Edited by Richard A. McBrien. San Francisco: Harper/Collins, 1995.

"The Loss of Theological Unity: Pluralism, Thomism, and Catholic Morality." In Mary Jo Weaver and R. Scott Appleby, *Being Right: Conservative Catholics in America,* 63–87. Bloomington/Indianapolis, IN: Indiana University Press, 1995.

"The Eucharist." *Catholic Dossier* 2 (September-October 1996): 12–18.

"The Documents of Catholic Identity." In *The Gospel of Life and the Vision of Health Care,* edited by Russell E. Smith, 10–16. Proceedings of the Fifteenth Workshop of Bishops, Dallas, TX. Braintree, MA: The Pope John Center, 1997.

"Fundamental Option And/Or Commitment to Ultimate End." A paper for a symposium of the Karl Rahner Society at the National Convention of the Catholic Theological Society of America, June 1996. *Philosophy and Theology* 10 (1; January 1997): 113–41.

"The Church's Message to Artists and Scientists." Keynote address for annual convention of the Fellowship of Catholic Scholars, San Francisco, August 25, 1987. Published in their bulletin, and in *The Battle for the Catholic Mind,* edited by William E. May and Kenneth D. Whitehead, 334–45. South Bend, IN: St. Augustine's Press, 2001.

"Modern Theology Needs a Renewed Modern Science." A paper for a conference of the Institute for Advanced Physics, headed by Dr. Anthony Rizzi, July 30-August 4, 2003, Notre Dame University. Unpublished.

Book Reviews

Ruth Mary Fox, *Dante Lights the Way. Cross and Crown* (1958).

Frank and Dorothy Getlein, *Christianity in Art and Christianity in Modern Art. The New World* (1965).

D. J. Silver, "Judaism and Ethics." *The Thomist* (January 1971): 199–202.

John Demaray, 'The Invention of Dante's Comedia." *The Review of Books on Religion* (mid-June 1974).

Northrop Frye, "Spiritus Mundi." *New Review of Books and Religion* (1 May 1977).

John McHugh, "The Mother of Jesus in the New Testament." *Cross and Crown* 29 (1977): 81–84.

Yves Congar, "Challenge to the Church: The Case of Archbishop Lefebre." *Cross and Crown* 29 (1977): 186–88.

David Little and S. B. Twiss, "Comparative Religious Ethics." *New Review of Books and Religion* (October 1979).

Anna-Maria Rizzuto, "The Birth of the Living God." *Spirituality Today* (December 1980): 375–76.

Stephen T. Katz, "Mysticism and Philosophical Analysis." *Spirituality Today* (December 1980): 366.

Hans Urs von Balthasar, "The Glory of the Lord: A Theological Aesthetics," vol.1, *Seeing the Form* (San Francisco: Ignatius Press and Crossroad, 1983). *Spirituality Today* (Summer 1984): 175–77.

Joseph Cardinal Ratzinger with Vitorio Messori, "The Ratzinger Report." *National Catholic Register* (October 4, 1987): 67.

Pseudo-Dionysius: the Complete Works, translated and edited by Colum Lubheid and Paul Rorem, et al. (New York: Paulist Press, 1987). *Spirituality Today* (Spring 1988): 87–88.

Philosophy

Books

The Theory of Natural Slavery. University of Notre Dame dissertation. 1951.

Science in Synthesis: Report of the Summer Session of the Albertus Magnus Lyceum, River Forest, Ill, 1952. (Co-author and editor.) River Forest, IL: Albertus Lyceum Publications, 1953.

Aristotle's Sluggish Earth. River Forest, IL: Albertus Magnus Lyceum, 1958. Previously published in *The New Scholasticism:* Part I: "Problematics of the De Caelo," 32 (1958): 1–31; Part II, "Media of Demonstration," 202–34; the treatment of Aristotle's biological works was not published.

St. Thomas and the Liberal Arts. (Co-author with Pierre Conway, OP.) Washington, DC: The Thomist Press, 1959.

The Way Toward Wisdom: An Interdisciplinary and Intercultural Introduction to Metaphysics. Houston, TX: University of Notre Dame Press, for the Center of Thomistic Studies, University of St. Thomas, 2006.

Articles and Lectures

"Research into the Intrinsic Final Causes of Physical Things." Published as "Problem: The Relation of Physical Activity to Essence and End," with comment by Robert J, McCall, SSJ. *American Catholic Philosophical Association Proceedings* (1952): 185–97.

"Social Pluralism in American Life Today." *Proceedings of the American Catholic Philosophical Association* (1959): 109–16.

"Are Thomists Selling Science Short?" In *The 1960 Lecture Series in the Philosophy of Science.* Cincinnati, OH: Mt. St. Mary's Seminary of the West, 1960.

"The Sociology of Knowledge and the Social Role of the Scientist." Reprint. River Forest, IL: Albertus Magnus Lyceum Publications, 1960.

"The Thomistic Synthesis." River Forest, IL: St. Albertus Magnus Lyceum Publications, 1961.

"Does Natural Science Attain Nature or only the Phenomena." In *The Philosophy of Physics*, edited by Vincent E. Smith, 63–82. Jamaica, NY: St. John's University, 1961.

"A Social Science Founded on a Unified Natural Science." In *The Dignity of Science: Studies in the Philosophy of Science, Festschrift presented to W. H. Kane, OP*, edited by James A. Weisheipl, 469–85. Washington, DC: The Thomist Press, 1961.

"Variations on the Scholastic Theme: Thomism." In *Teaching Thomism Today*, edited by George McLean, OMI. Washington, DC: Catholic University of America Press, 1962.

"A Phenomenological Approach to Christian Philosophy." In George F. McClean, *Christian Philosophy and the Integration of Contemporary Catholic Education*, 10–13. Washington, DC: Catholic University of American Press, 1964.

"A Priori and A Posteriori"; "Knowledge"; and "Logic." In *The Catholic Encyclopedia for School and Home*. New York: Grolier, 1965.

"Significance of Non-Objective Art." *Proceedings of the American Catholic Philosophical Association* (1965): 156–65.

Articles in New Catholic Encyclopedia. New York: McGraw-Hill, 1967. 1st ed.: "Christian Education, Papal Teaching on" (3: 637–8); "Education, II (Philosophy of) Historical Development, Ancient and Medieval" (5: 162–66); "Final Causality" (5: 162–66; 2nd ed., 5: 723–27).

"Causality and Evolution." *The Thomist* 36 (April 1972): 199–230.

"Change and Process." In John N. Deely and R. J. Nogar, *The Problem of Evolution*, 265–85. New York: Appleton-Century-Crofts, 1973.

"St. Albert the Great and the Classification of Sciences." In *St. Albert and the Sciences: Commemorative Essays,* edited by J. Weisheipl, 73–102. Toronto: Pontifical Institute of Medieval Studies, 1980.

"What is the Natural Law?" *Ethics and Medics* 16 (4; April 1987).

"The River Forest School of Natural Philosophy." Paper given at the International Congress of Medieval Studies, Kalamazoo, MI, May 1989. In *Philosophy and the God of Abraham, Essays in Memory of James A. Weisheipl*, edited by R. James Long, 1–16.. Toronto: Pontifical Institute of Medieval Philosophy, 1991.

"Thomism and the Transition from the Classical World-View to Historical-Mindedness." In *The Future of Thomism*, edited by Deal W. Hudson and Dennis Wm. Moran; preface by Gerald A. McCool, SJ, 109–22. Notre Dame, IN: American Maritain Association; distributed by the University of Notre Dame Press, 1992.

"Astronomy as a Liberal Art." *Semiotics* 1991, edited by John Deely and Terry Prewitt, 49–60. Lanham, MD: University Press of America, 1993.

"Truth and Technology." *American Catholic Philosophical Association Proceedings: The Importance of Truth* 68 (1993): 27–40.

"Cosmic Community in Plotinus, Aquinas, and Whitehead." In *Cultura y Vida (XX Semana Tomista, 1995)*, Appendix A, 1–27. Buenos Aires: Sociedad Tomista Argentina, 1995.

"Albertus Magnus on Aristotle's Metaphysics, Book I, Tract 1." In a special number of *American Catholic Philosophical Quarterly* edited by William A. Wallace, OP, and Michael W. Tkacz. (1996): 137–56.

"Albert the Great, Physics, Mathematics, and Metaphysics." Notre Dame University, Jacques Maritain Center, Thomist Summer Workshop, 1997. Unpublished.

"The End of Philosophy and the End of Physics: A Dead End." In *Postmodernism and Christian Philosophy*, edited by Roman T. Ciapalo, with an introduction by Jude P. Daugherty, 12–22. American Maritain Association. Washington, DC: The Catholic University of America Press, 1997.

"Foreword." Francis de Vitoria, OP. *On Homicide and Commentary on Thomas Aquinas, St. II–II, q. 64.* Translated by John P. Doyle. Medieval Philosophical Text in Translation. Milwaukee, WI: Marquette University Press, 1997.

"The Categories of Theology and Science." University of Notre Dame, Jacques Maritain Center, Thomist Summer Workshop, 1997. See www.nd.edu/Departments/Maritain/ti.htm.

"W. A. Wallace's The Modeling of Nature." (Co-author with Eric Reitan, OP) *The Thomist* 10 (1; January 1997): 113–41.

"Ethical Pluralism, Civil Society, and Political Culture." Ethikon Institute, San Francisco, 1998.

"The Demonstration of the Categories in Aristotle's Physics." University of Notre Dame, Jacques Maritain Center, Thomist Summer Workshop, 1998. Unpublished.

"The Validity of Metaphysics." In *Faith and Reason: The Notre Dame Symposium, 1999,* edited by Timothy L. Smith, 67–89. South Bend, IN: St. Augustine's Press, 2001.

"Cloning, Aquinas, and the Embryonic Person." (With Albert Moraczewski, OP.) *The National Catholic Bioethics Quarterly* 1 (2; 2001): 189–202.

"Science, Thomism, and the Future of Metaphysics." *Providence: Studies in Western Civilization* 7 (Spring/Summer 2002): 1–20.

Book Reviews

Jacques Maritain, *The Philosophy of Nature. Books on Trial* (December 1951).

Gabriel Marcel, *Problematic Man. American Ecclesiastical Review* (January 1967).

Marcia L. Colish, "The Mirror of Language: A Study in the Medieval Theory of Knowledge." *The Thomist* (April 1969): 377–24.

Bruce Wilshire, "William James and Phenomenology." *The Thomist* (January 1971): 199–202.

Jon R. Gunneman, "The Moral Meaning of Revolution." *The Thomist* 46 (January 1982): 164–66.

Lloyd P. Gerson, ed., *Graceful Reason: Essays in Ancient and Medieval Philosophy, Presented to Joseph Owens, CSSR. The Modern Schoolman* 64 (January 1987): 124–25.

Education

Books

The Liberal Education of the Christian Person. (Editor and co-author.) Chicago: St. Xavier University, 1954.

The Arts of Learning and Communication. Chicago: Priory Press, 1957. See also www.op.org/domcentral/study/ashley.

St. Thomas and the Liberal Arts. (Co-author with Pierre Conway, OP) Washington, DC: The Thomist Press, 1959.

The Challenge of Christ. (Co-author.) 3-vol. textbook series. Dubuque, IA: Priory Press.

Articles and Lectures

"The Thomistic Ideal of Education." St. Xavier College, Chicago, 1954, 43 pp.

"The Science of Mathematics." St. Xavier College, Chicago, 1954, 27-page outline.

"The Teaching of Poetics and of Fine Arts in their Relation to intellectual Development." St. Xavier College, Chicago, 1954, 64 pp.

"Integrated Education." *The Dominican* (Autumn 1954): 1–8.

"The Role of the Philosophy of Nature in Catholic Liberal Education." *Proceedings of the American Catholic Philosophical Association* (1956): 26 pp.

"Why a Liberal Arts Handbook." *Dominican Education Bulletin* (Spring 1959): 17–20.

The Story of the Kingdom of God. (Co-author with Sister Mary Dominic Merwick, RSM) 3 vols. A text for elementary schools, published in mimeo. Chicago: St. Xavier College, 1961.

"A New Curriculum of Christian Doctrine for Catholics Schools." *Religious Education* (July-August 1961): 1–7.

"Why Study Nature in the Elementary School." *The Catholic Educator* (November 1962): 223–26.

"On the Curriculum and Methods of the Philosophy Program." In *Philosophy and the Integration of Contemporary Catholic Education,* edited by George F. McClean, 320–23. Washington, DC: Catholic University of America Press, 1962.

"The Integration of Sacred Doctrine and Natural Science." *Proceedings of the Society of College Teachers of Sacred Doctrine* (1962): 24–28; discussion, 47–57.

"Philosophy in the Seminary." *Proceedings of the American Catholic Philosophical Association* (1965): 248–52.

"The Arts of Teaching and Studying (Syllabus)." River Forest, IL: Albertus Magnus Lyceum Publications, 1966.

"Making Philosophy Relevant: Methods of Teaching." Discussion with George Klubertanz, SJ. *Catholic University of America Affiliation Bulletin* 29 (January 1967).

Articles in *The New Catholic Encyclopedia* (New York: McGraw-Hill, 1967): "Christian Education, Papal Teaching on" (3: 637–38); "Education, II (Philosophy of) Historical Development, Ancient and Medieval" (5: 162–66); "Liberal Arts," (8: 646–99); "Finality" in 2nd ed. 5: 723–27; "Teleology," 13: 979–81.

"What Do You Mean 'You Will be Free'?" In John F. Choitz, *Christian Education in Transition, 26th Yearbook,* 32–34. River Forest, IL: Lutheran Education Association, 1969.

"The Discipline of Theology in Seminary and University." In Kendig Brubaker Cully, *Does the Church Know How to Teach,* 261–88. New York: Macmillan, 1970.

"Philosophy and Priesthood." *Omnis Terra* (March 1974): 211–88.

"Ethical Pluralism and Our Schools." *Iowa English Bulletin Yearbook,* 34–40. Ames: University of Iowa, 1975.

"Education in Chastity." Address to the Secondary Education Association of the Archdiocese of Boston, October 27, 1990. Unpublished.

"What the Church Lives: Faith and the Commandments" and "The Decalogue in Christian Moral Teaching." Portland Symposium on The Catechism of the Catholic Church, 1994. Unpublished.

"An Educator's Vision." In *The Quality of Mercy: A Festschrift in Honor of Sister Mary Josetta Butler, RSM, 1904–1995,* edited by Claudette Dwyer. Chicago: Sisters of Mercy of the America, Regional Community of Chicago, 1996.

"How the Liberal Arts Opened my American Mind." Lecture for Department of Humanities, University of Chicago, 1999. Unpublished.

"A Guide to Dominican Studies." Approved by General Chapter of Dominican Province 2003 to be submitted to and commended by the General Chapter of Dominican Order, 2004.

"The Anthropological Foundations of the Natural Law: A Thomistic Engagement with Modern Science." In *St. Thomas Aquinas and the Natural Law Tradition: Contemporary Perspectives,* edited by John Goyette, Mark S. Latkovic, and Richard S. Myers, 3–16. Washington, DC: Catholic University of America Press, 2004.

Dominicana

Books

Self-Study of St. Albert's Dominican Province. River Forest, IL: privately published, 1968.

The Dominicans. Collegeville, MN: The Liturgical Press/Michael Glazier: 1991. See also www.op.org/domcentral/study/ashley.

Spiritual Direction in the Dominican Tradition. New York: Paulist Press, 1995.

Friar's Folly: An Autobiography in Vatican II Times. Unpublished short version on www.op.org/domcentral/study/ashley.

Articles and Lectures

"A Self-Study as an Instrument of Religious Renewal." *Review for Religious* 26 (1967): 1034–46.

"The Essence of the Dominican Order and Religious Obedience." *Provincial Newsletter Forum* (1968): 12.

"Toward an American Theology of Contemplation." *Review for Religious* (March, 1971): 187–98. A longer version directed to Dominicans was published in the *Dominican Education Association Newsletter* (May 1970): 4–14.

"Whose Apostolate." *Exchange* 4 (March 1972): 1–3.

"Retirement or Vigil." *Review for Religious* (May 1972): 325–41.

"My Hopes and Concerns for St. Albert's Province." *Provincial Newsletter* 12 (July/August 1972): 3–5.

"O.P. Studies in Latin America." Report of Easter 1976 meeting of Permanent Commission on Studies with Regents of Latin America in Bogotá. *Dominican Newsletter Forum* (May 1976).

"Models for Dominican Relationships." *Exchange* (Fall, 1976): 5–9.

"Serving the Word: A Study Guide for Ministry in the Order of Preachers." Submitted to the Permanent Commission of Studies, OP, for General Chapter of 1977.

"A Guide to St. Catherine's Dialogue." *Cross and Crown* 29 (September 1977): 237–49.

"History of Dominican Spirituality." 19 cassette lectures. 1977.

"Three Strands in the Thought of Eckhart the Scholastic Theologian." *The Thomist* 42 (April 1978): 226–39.

"Catherine of Siena's Principles of Spiritual Direction." *Spirituality Today* 33 (March 1981): 43–52. Reprinted in *Spiritual Direction: Contemporary Readings*, edited by Kevin G. Culligan, OCD, 188–95. Locust Valley, NY: Living Flame Press, 1983.

"Common Life, 900–1200: Factors Which Shaped the Thinking of St. Dominic." (Co-author with David Wright, OP) In *Common Life in the Spirit of St. Dominic,* edited by Mary Nona McGreal and Margaret Ormond, 26–38. River Forest, IL: Parable, 1990.

Papers. (Some delivered at Dominican Studies Session, International Medieval Congress, Kalamazoo, MI, May 3–6, 2001): "Dominican Spirituality"; "The Ministry of the Word"; Blessed Osanna d'Andreasi and other Renaissance Italian Domincan Women Mystics"; "Dominic Cavalca and as Spirituality of the Word"; St. Antoninus of Florence and Christian Community"; and "St. Catherine and Contemporary Spirituality"; see www.op.org/domcentral/study/ashley.

Book Reviews

Catherine of Siena: Dialogue, translated by Suzanne Noffke, OP. Classics of Western Spirituality. *Spirituality Today* (March 1980): 69–70.

Richard A. McAllister, *Thomas McGlynn: Priest and Sculptor. Spirituality Today* (June 1982): 187–89.

Simon Tugwell, OP, *The Early Dominicans. Spirituality Today* (June 1982): 166–68.

Jordan of Saxony, On the Beginnings of the Order of Preachers, edited and translated by Simon Tugwell, OP. *Spirituality Today* (Summer 1983): 175–77.

Richard Woods, OP, *Eckhart's Way,* vol. 2, *The Way of the Mystics.* Wilmington, DE: Michael Glazier, 1986. *Spirituality Today* (Winter 1987): 371–73.

Art and the Word of God (Arte e la Parola di Dio): A Study of Angelico Rinaldo Zarlenga, OP, edited by Vincent I. Zarlenga, OP, text in English and Italian. River Forest, IL: Fra Angelico Art Foundation. *The Thomist* 58 (January 1994): 164–66.

General Bibliography

Albergio, Guiseppe, et al. *Une École de théologie le Saulchoir,* Paris: Cerf, 1985.

Alfaro, Juan, SJ. *Lo Natural y lo Sobrenatural: Historico desde Santo Tomas hasta Cayetano (1274–1534).* Madrid: Aldecoa, 1952.

Allen, William, J. C. D. "Abortion—Multiple Meaning." *Pastoral Life* (January 1976): 45–51.

Anderson, Bernhard W. *Creation versus Chaos: The Reinterpretation of Mythical Symbolism in the Bible.* Philadelphia: Fortress Press, 1987.

Anderson, Thomas C. *The Foundation and Structure of Sartrean Ethics.* Lawrence, KS: Regents Press of Kansas, 1979.

Aries, Philippe. *Centuries of Childhood.* New York: Random House, 1962.

Arieti, Silvano. *Creativity: The Magic Synthesis.* New York: Basic Books, 1976.

Arintero, Juan González, OP. *The Mystical Evolution in the Development and Vitality of the Church.* Translated by Jordan Aumann. St. Louis: B. Herder Book Company, 1949–51.

Armstrong, A. H. *The Architecture of the Intelligible Universe in the Philosophy of Plotinus.* Cambridge: The University Press, 1940.

Arntz, Josef Th. C. "Die Entwicklung des naturrectlichen Denkens innerhalb des Thomismus." In *Das Naturrecht im Disput: Drei vorträge beim kongresz der deutschsprachigen moraltheologen 1965* in *Bensberg/Herausgegeben und zur diskussion gestellt von Franz Böckle,* edited by Franz Böckle, 87–120. Düsseldorf: Patmos, 1966.

Audet, Jean Paul, OP. "Le Revanche de Prométhée ou Le drame de la religion et de la culture." *Revue Biblique* 73 (1966): 1–29.

Augustine of Hippo. *St. Augustine's Confessions.* Latin text with commentary by J. J. O'Donnell. www.stoa.org/hippo/frame_entry.html. Also, E. B. Pusey's English translation: www.ccat.sas.upenn.edu/jod/augustine/Englishconfessions.html.

Aumann, Jordan, OP, *Theology of Christian Perfection.* Dubuque: Priory Press, 1962.

———. *Christian Spirituality in the Catholic Tradition.* San Francisco: Ignatius Press, 1985. See Chapter 10, last section on "Systematic Spiritual Theology," and bibliography: www.op.org/domcentral/study/aumann/cs/cs10.htm#30.

Bainvel, J. "Ame." In *Dictionnaire de théologie catholique,* t. 1., cols. 967–1006.

Balthasar, Hans Urs von. *A Theological Anthropology.* New York: Sheed & Ward, 1967. Republished as *Man in History* by Sheed & Ward in 1982.

Bammel, E., C. K. Barrett, and W. D. Davies. *Gentilicum: New Testament Studies in Honour of David Daube.* Oxford: Clarendon Press, 1978.

Barrow, John D., and Frank J. Tipler. *The Anthropic Cosmological Principle.* New York: Oxford University Press, 1986.

Basney, Lionel. "Ecology and the Spiritual Concept of the Master." *Christian Scholars Review* 3 (1973): 49–50.

Battaglia, Anthony. *Toward a Reformulation of Natural Law.* New York: Seabury, 1981.

Beeck, Frans Jozef van, SJ. "Weaknesses in the Consistent Ethics of Life: Some Systematic Theological Observations." In Cardinal Joseph Bernadine et al., *The Consistent Ethics of Life,* edited by Thomas G. Feuchtmann, 115–22. Kansas City, MO: Sheed & Ward, 1988.

Belensky Mary F., et al. *Women's Ways of Knowing: The Development of Self, Voice, and Mind.* New York: Basic Books, 1988.

Bergson, Henri. *Creative Evolution.* Authorized translation by Arthur Mitchell, Ph.D. New York: H. Holt and Company, 1911. (French original 1907.)

———. "Laughter." In *Comedy: An Essay on Comedy.* Edited by Wylie Sypher. Baltimore: Johns Hopkins University Press, 1980.

Bernadine, Cardinal Joseph et al. *The Consistent Ethics of Life.* Edited by Thomas G. Feuchtmann. Kansas City, MO: Sheed & Ward, 1988.

Berstein, Richard J., ed. *Perspective on Peirce: Critical Essays.* Westport, CT: Greenwood Press, 1980, 1965.

Bertalanffy, R. Ludwig von. *General System Theory: Foundations, Development, Applications.* New York: G. Braziller, 1968.

Blackwell, Richard. "The Structure of Wolffian Philosophy." *The Modern Schoolman* 38 (1961): 203–318.

Bloch, Alfred and George T. Czucska, *Toward a Philosophy of Praxis.* New York: Crossroad, 1981.

Boerger, Egan, Erich Grädel, and Yuri Gurevich. *The Classical Decision Problem.* New York: Springer, 1997.

Bos, Abraham P. *Cosmic and Metacosmic Theology in Aristotle's Lost Dialogues.* New York: Brill, 1989.

Bouyer, Louis C. *The Word, Church, and Sacrament in Protestantism and Catholicism.* New York: Desclee, 1961; Crestwood, NY: St. Vladimir's Seminary Press, 1978.

———. "The Scriptural Themes of Mariology: The Divine Wisdom." In his *The Seat of Wisdom,* 20–28. Chicago: Regnery, 1965.

———. *Woman in the Church.* San Francisco: Ignatius Press, 1979.

Boyle, Joseph M., Jr., Germain Grisez, and Olaf Tollefsen. *Free Choice: A Self-Referential Argument.* Notre Dame, IN, and London: University of Notre Dame Press, 1976).

Braine, David. *The Reality of Time and the Existence of God.* New York: Oxford University Press, 1988.

Braithwaite, Richard B. *Scientific Explanation.* New York: Harper Torchbooks, 1960.

Brown, Donald E. *Human Universals.* Philadelphia: Temple University Press, 1991.

Brown, Raymond E., SS. *The Birth of the Messiah.* Garden City, NY: Doubleday, 1977.

————. "Gospel Infancy Research from 1976–1986." *Catholic Biblical Quarterly* 48 (3 & 4, 1986): 468–83, 660–80.

————. *The Death of the Messiah: from Gethsemane to the Grave: a Commentary on the Passion Narratives in the Four Gospels.* Anchor Bible Reference Library. 2 vols. New York: Doubleday, 1994.

————. *Introduction to the New Testament.* New York: Doubleday, 1997.

————, and John Meier. *Antioch and Rome: Cradles of Catholic Christianity.* New York: Paulist Press, 1983.

Bruce, F. F. *Tradition Old and New.* Grand Rapids, MI: Zondervan, 1970.

Brunning, Jacqueline and Paul Foster, eds. *The Rule of Reason: The Philosophy of Charles Sanders Peirce.* Toronto: Toronto University Press, 1997.

Burgess, Joseph A., and Brother Jeffrey Gros, FSC, eds. "Lutheran-Roman Catholic Dialogues: Justification by Faith." In *Building Unity: Ecumenical Documents, IV, Ecumenical Dialogues with Roman Catholic Participation in the United States,* 217–90. Preface by John F. Hotchkin. New York: Paulist Press, 1989.

Busa, Robert, SJ, ed. *Index Thomisticus.* Stuttgart-Bad Cannstatt: Frommann-Holzboog, 1974–1980, www.corpusthomisticum.org/it/index.age.

Buttiglione, Rocco. *Karol Wojtyla: The Thought of the Man Who Became Pope John Paul II.* Translated by Paolo Guietti and Francesca Murphy. Grand Rapids, MI: Eerdmans, 1997.

Calvin, John. *Institutes of the Christian Religion.* Edited by John T. McNeill; translated by Ford Lewis Battles. Wilmington, NC: Library of Christian Classics 1960.

Campbell, R. Alastair. *The Elders: Seniority Within Earliest Christianity.* Edinburgh: T&T Clark, 1994.

Cannon, Dale. *Six Ways of Being Religious: A Framework for Comparative Studies of Religion.* Belmont, CA: Wadsworth, 1996.

Capra, Fritjof. *The Tao of Physics: An Exploration of the Parallels between Modern Physics and Eastern Mysticism.* Boston: Shambhala, 1999.

Carr, Anne. *The Theological Method of Karl Rahner.* Dissertation Series, no. 19, directed by David Tracy. Missoula, MT: Scholars Press for The American Academy of Religion, 1977.

————. *Transforming Grace.* San Francisco: Harper and Row, 1988.

Cataldo, Peter J., and A. S. Moraczewski, eds. *The Fetal Tissue Issue: Medical and Ethical Aspects.* Braintree, MA: Pope John Center, 1994.

St. Catherine of Siena. *St. Catherine of Siena: The Dialogue.* Translation and introduction by Susanne Noffke, OP; preface by Giuliana Cavallini. The Classics of Western Spirituality. New York: Paulist Press, 1980.

"Catholic Hospitals in Europe Defy Vatican on In Vitro Fertilization." *New York Times* (March 18, 1987).

Catholic Medical Association. "Homosexuality and Hope." www.cathmed.org/publications/homosexualityarticle.html

The Center for Ethics and Public Policy (Berkeley, CA). *Cry of the Environment: Rebuilding the Christian Creation Tradition.* Santa Fe, NM: Bear and Co., 1984.

Cessario, Romanus, OP. *The Moral Virtues and Theological Ethics.* Notre Dame, IN: University of Notre Dame Press, 1991.

———. *A Short History of Thomism.* Washington, DC: Catholic University of America Press, 2005.

Chauvet, Louis Marie. *Symbol and Sacrament: A Sacramental Reinterpretation of Christian Experience.* Translated by Patrick Madigan & Madeleine E. Beaumont. Collegeville, MN: Liturgical Press, 1995.

Chenu, M. D., OP. Review of A. J. Rozwadowski. "De motus localis causa proxima secundum principia S. Thomae," *Divus Thomas* (Piacenza), 42 (1939): 104–13 in *Bulletin Thomiste* 6 (1940–42): n. 351.

———. "Aus origines de la science moderne." *Revue de Sciences Phiosophiques et Theologiques* 29 (1940): 206–17.

Chodorow, Nancy. "Feminism and Difference: Gender, Relation, and Difference in Psychoanalytic Perspective." In Mary Roth Walsh, *The Psychology of Women.* New Haven, CT: Yale University Press, 1987.

Cholij, R. *Clerical Celibacy in East and West.* Leominster, Herefordshire: Fowler-Wright Books, 1989.

Chollet, A. "Animation." In *Dictionnaire de théologie catholique,* t. I., cols. 1305–20.

Christian, William A. *An Interpretation of Whitehead's Metaphysics.* New Haven, CT: Yale University Press, 1967.

Ciapolo, Roman T., ed. *Postmodernism and Christian Philosophy* with an introduction by Jude Dougherty, American Maritain Association, Washington, DC: Catholic University Press, 1997.

Clark, William C. "Managing Planet Earth." *Scientific American* 261 (September 1989): 46–57.

Clarke, W. Norris, SJ. *The Philosophical Approach to God.* Winston-Salem, NC: Wake Forest University, 1979.

———. *The One and the Many.* Notre Dame, IN: University of Notre Dame Press, 2001.

Cochini, Christian, SJ. *Apostolic Origins of Priestly Celibacy.* Translated by Nelly Marans; preface by Alfons M. Stickler. Ft. Collins, CO: Ignatius Press, 1990.

Colson, Jean. *La Fonction diaconale aux origines de l'Eglise.* Paris: Desclée de Brouwer, 1960.

————. *Ministre de Jésus-Christ ou le Sacerdoce de l'Evangile: étude sur la condition sacerdotale des ministres chrétiens dans l'église primitive.* Paris: Beauchesne et ses fils, 1966.

Conconi, Giorgio. *When Jesus Smiled.* Staten Island, NY: Alba House, 1998.

Congar, Yves. *A History of Theology.* Translated and edited by Hunter Guthrie. Garden City, NY: Doubleday, 1968.

————. *I Believe in the Holy Spirit.* 3 vols. New York: Seabury, 1983.

————. *Esprit de 'l homme, Esprit de Dieu.* Paris: Éditions du Cerf, 1998.

Connery, John, SJ. *Abortion: The Development of the Roman Catholic Perspective.* Cambridge, MA: Harvard University Press, 1959–65.

Constitutions of the Order of Preachers: Fundamental Constitution. www.op.org/curia/ConstOP/const1_0.htm.

Conway, Pierre H., OP. *Principles of Education.* Washington, DC: The Thomist Press, 1960.

————, and Benedict M. Ashley, OP. *The Liberal Arts in St. Thomas Aquinas.* Washington, DC: The Thomist Press, 1959.

Copleston, Frederick, SJ. "The Nature of Metaphysics." In his *On the History of Philosophy and Other Essays,* 116–30. New York: Barnes and Noble/Harper and Row, 1979.

Cormier, Henri. *The Humor of Jesus.* Staten Island, NY: Alba House, 1977.

Crim, Keith, et al., eds. *The Perennial Dictionary of World Religions.* Reprint edition. San Francisco, CA: HarperSanFrancisco, 1990.

Crowe, Michael Bertram. *The Changing Profile of the Natural Law.* The Hague: Martinus Nijhoff, 1977.

Curran, Charles E. "Masturbation and Objectively Grave Matter." In *A New Look at Christian Morality.* Notre Dame, IN: Fides Press, 1968.

————. *Tensions in Moral Theology.* Notre Dame, IN: University of Notre Dame Press, 1988.

————, and R. A. McCormick, SJ, eds. *Readings in Moral Theology, No. 1. Moral Norms and Catholic Tradition.* New York: Paulist Press, 1979.

————, eds. *Readings in Moral Theology, No. 2. The Distinctiveness of Christian Ethics.* New York: Paulist Press, 1980.

D'Entreves, A. P. *Natural Law.* 11th rev. ed. Highlands, NJ: Humanities Press 1964.

Dalton, William J., SJ. *New Jerome Biblical Commentary.* London: Chapman, 1990.

Danielou, Cardinal Jean. *Gospel Message and Hellenistic Culture.* Vol. 2 of *A History of Early Christian Doctrine.* Philadelphia: The Westminister Press, 1973.

Dauphinais, Michael and Matthew Levering, eds. *Reading John with St. Thomas Aquinas: Theological Exegesis and Speculative Theology,* 241–52. Washington, DC: Catholic University of America Press, 2005.De Cecco, John P., and David Allen Parker. "The Biology of Homosexuality: Sexual Orientation or Sexual Preference?" *Journal of Homosexuality* 28 (1995): Part I, 1/2, Part II.

————, eds. *Sex, Cells, and Same-sex Desire: The Biology of Sexual Preference.* New York: Haworth Press, 1995.

De Hartog, Jan. *Adopted Children*. New York: Adama Books, 1987.

De Koninck, Charles. *Ego Sapientia . . . La sagesse qui est Marie*. Laval, Quebec: Editions de l'Université Laval, 1943.

———. "Introduction à l'étude de l'ame." *Laval Theologique et Philosophique* 3 (1947): 9–65.

———. "Sedeo, ergo sum." *Laval Theologique et Philosophique* 6 (1950): 343–48.

———. *The Hollow Universe*. London: Oxford University Press, 1960.

Dedek, John. "Abortion." In *Contemporary Medical Ethics*. New York: Sheed & Ward, 1975.

Deeken, Alfons. *Process and Permanence in Ethics: Max Scheler's Moral Philosophy*. New York: Paulist Press, 1974.

Deely, John N. *The Tradition via Heidegger: An Essay on the Meaning of Being in the Philosophy of Martin Heidegger*. The Hague: Martinus Nijhoff, 1971.

———. *Introducing Semiotic: Its History and Doctrine*. Bloomington, IN: Indiana University Press, 1982.

———. *Basic Semiotics*. Bloomington, IN: Indiana University Press, 1991.

———. *Four Ages of Understanding: The First Postmodern Survey of Philosophy from Ancient Times to the Turn of the Twenty-first Century*. Toronto: University of Toronto Press, 2001.

———, and R. J. Nogar, OP, eds. *The Problem of Evolution: A Study of the Philosophical Repercussions of Evolutionary Science*. New York: Appleton Crofts, 1973.

Delorme, Jean, Paul Bony, et al., eds. *Les ministère et les ministères selon le Nouveau Testament dossier exegétique et réflexion théologique*. Paris: Éditions du Seuil, 1974.

Denny, Frederick M. "To Serve Allah in a Foreign Land: Muslim Spirituality in the North American Diaspora." *Listening* 33 (3; Fall 1998).

Derville, André. "Humour." In *Dictionnaire de Spiritualité*, tom. 7, 1187–91.

Dewan, Larence, OP. "St. Thomas Aquinas against Metaphysical Materialism." Vol. 14, 412–34. *Studi Tomistici, Problema Metafisici*. Rome: Pontificia Accademia Romana di S. Tommaso d'Aquino, 1982.

Diamond, James J. "Abortion, Animation and Biological Hominization." *Theological Studies* 36 (1975): 305–24.

Dictionnaire de théologie catholique: contenant l'exposé des doctrines de la théologie catholique, leurs preuves et leur histoire. Paris: Letouzey et Ané, 1899–1950.

"Didache or Teaching of the Twelve Apostles." In *The Apostolic Fathers*. Translated by Kirsopp Lake. Cambridge, MA: Harvard University Press, 1959–65.

Doms, Herbert, MD. *The Meaning of Marriage*. Translated by George Sayer. New York: Sheed & Ward, 1939.

Donceel, Joseph, SJ. "Causality and Evolution." *New Scholasticism* 39 (1965): 295–315.

———. "Abortion: Mediate and Immediate Animation." *Continuum* 5 (1967): 167–71.

———. "Immediate Animation and Delayed Hominization." *Theological Studies* 31 (1970): 76–105.

———. ed. and trans. *A Maréchal Reader.* New York: Herder & Herder, 1970.

———. "Why is Abortion Wrong?" *America* (August 16, 1975): 65–67.

Donovan, Daniel. *What Are They Saying about the Ministerial Priesthood?* New York: Paulist Press, 1992.

Dorlodot, Canon Henri de. "A Vindication of the Mediate Animation Theory." In *Theology and Evolution,* edited by Ernest C. Messenger, 259–83. Westminister, MD: Newman, 1949.

Drees, Willem E. *Beyond the Big Bang: Quantum Cosmologies and God.* La Salle, IL: Open Court, 1990.

Drilling, Peter J. "The Priest, Prophet and King Trilogy' Elements of Its Meaning in *Lumen Gentium* and for Today." *Eglise et Theologie* 19 (1988): 179–206.

Du Praw, Jeanne. *Adoption: The Facts, Feelings, and Issues of Double Heritage.* New York: Messner, 1987.

Duffy, Eamon. *Saints and Sinners: A History of the Popes.* New Haven, CT: Yale University Press, 1997.

Duhem, Pierre. *Le système du monde: histoire des doctrines cosmologiques de Platon à Copernic.* 10 vols. Paris: Hermann, 1954–59.

Dunn, Patrick J. *Priesthood.* Staten Island, NY: Alba House, 1990.

Dussaut, Louis. *Synopse Structurelle de l'Epître aux Hebreux: Approche d'Analyse Structurelle.* Preface by Maurice Carrez. Paris: Éditions du Cerf, 1981.

Dyson, Freeman. *Infinite In All Directions.* The Gifford Lectures, 1985. Edited by the author. New York: Harper & Row, 1988.

Eberl, Jason T. "The Beginning of Personhood: A Thomistic Biological Analysis." *Bioethics: Journal of the International Association of Bioethics* 14 (2; 2000): 134–57.

Eccles, Sir John. *The Human Mystery.* The Gifford Lectures, University of Edinburgh, 1977–78. New York: Springer International, 1979.

Eco, Umberto. "The Role of The Reader." In *The Role of the Reader: Exploration in the Semiotics of Texts,* 3–43. Bloomington, IN: Indiana University Press, 1979.

Elders, Leo. "S. Thomas D'Aquin et Aristote." *Revue Thomiste* 88 (1988): 357–76.

———. *The Philosophy of Nature of St. Thomas Aquinas.* Frankfurt-am Main: Peter Lange, 1997.

Ellingworth, Paul. *The Epistle to the Hebrews: A Commentary on the Greek Text.* Grand Rapids, MI: W. B. Eerdman, 1993.

Ember, Carol R., and Melvin Ember. *Cultural Anthropology.* Englewood Cliffs, NJ: Prentice Hall, 1990.

Emmett, Dorothy M. *Whitehead's Philosophy of Organism.* 2nd ed. Westport, CT: Greenwood Press: 1981.

Engberg-Pedersen, Troels. "Eudaimoneia and Praxis." In *Aristotle's Theory of Moral Insight,* 1–36. Oxford: Oxford University Press, 1977.

Englehardt, Tristram, Jr. "Beginnings of Personhood: Philosophical Considerations." *Perkins Journal of Theology* (1973): 20–27.

Evans, Joseph W., edited by Jacques Maritain. *The Man and his Achievement.* New York: Sheed and Ward, 1963.

The Exegetical Dictionary of the New Testament. Edited by Horst Balz and Gerhard Schneider. Grand Rapids, MI: Eerdmans, 1990.

Fabro, Cornelio. *La nozione metafisica di partecipazione.* 2nd ed. Turin: Societa editrice internazionale, 1952.

Fackre, Gabriel. *Ecology Crisis: God's Creation and Man's Pollution.* St. Louis: Concordia Publishing House, 1971.

Faivre, Alexandre. *Naissance d'une hiérarchie: Les premières étapes du cursus clérical.* Paris: Ed. Beauchesne, 1977.

Falla, P. S. *Sources of Renewal: The Implementation of the Second Vatican Council by Cardinal Karol Wojtyla (Pope John Paul II).* San Francisco: Harper & Row, 1980.

Fatula, Mary Ann, OP. *The Triune God of Christian Faith.* Collegeville, MN: The Liturgical Press, 1990.

———. "*Contemplata Aliis Tradere*: Spirituality and Thomas Aquinas, The Preacher." *Spirituality Today* 43 (1; Spring 1991): 19–35. www.spiritualitytoday.org/spir2day/91431fatula.html.

Fehring, Richard, Stella Kitchen, and Mary Shivanandan. *An Introduction to Natural Family Planning.* Washington, DC: U.S. Catholic Bishops Conference, 1999.

Feuillet, André. *Jesus and His Mother.* Still River, MA: St. Bede's Publications, 1974.

———. "Le Femme vêtue de soleil (Ap 12) et la glorification de l'Epouse du Cantique des Cantiques (6, 10)." *Nova et Vetera* 59 (1984): 36–67, 103–28.

Finili, Antoninus, OP. "Natural Desire." *Dominican Studies* 1 (October 1948).

Finnis, John. *Natural Law and Natural Rights.* Oxford: Clarendon Press, 1980.

———. "Human Good(s) and Practical Reasoning." In *Proceedings of the American Catholic Philosophical Association, Practical Reasoning*, edited by Daniel O. Dahlstrom, vol. 40, 23–36. Charlottesville, VA: American Catholic Philosophical Association, 1984.

———. *Moral Absolutes.* Washington, DC: Catholic University of America Press, 1991.

Fitzmyer, Joseph A., SJ. *The Gospel According to Luke I–IX.* Garden City, NY: Doubleday, 1981.

Fleming, Thomas. "Affection and Responsibility in the Family in Classical Greece." *The Journal of Family and Culture* 1 (1985): 43–56.

Ford, Norman. *When Did I Begin? Conception of the Human Individual in History, Philosophy and Science.* Cambridge: Cambridge University Press, 1988.

———. "The Human Embryo as Person in Catholic Teaching." *The National Catholic Bioethics Quarterly* 1 (2; Summer 2001): 155–60.

Foster, Kenelm, ed. and trans. *Summa theologiae.* Bilingual ed. Vol. 9. New York: McGraw-Hill/Blackfriars 1968. "Appendix I."

Freudenstein, Eric G. "Ecology and the Jewish Tradition." *Judaism* 19 (1970): 406–14.

Froelich, Karlfried. "The Ecology of Creation." *Theology Today* 27 (1970): 263–76.

Frost, Zoe L."Children in a Changing Society." *Childhood Education* (March/April 1988): 244ff.

Frye, Northrop. *The Great Code: The Bible and Literature.* San Diego: Harcourt Brace Jovanovich, 1983.

Frye, Roland Mushat. *Is God a Creationist? The Religious Case Against Creation-Science.* New York: Charles Scribner's Sons, 1983.

Fuchs, Josef, SJ. *Natural Law: A Theological Investigation.* Translated by Helmut Reckter and John A. Dowling. Dublin: Gill and Son, 1965.

———. *Human Values and Christian Morality.* Dublin: Gill and Macmillan, 1970.

———. "The Absoluteness of Moral Terms" (1970). Reprinted in Charles E. Curran and R. A. McCormick, SJ. *Readings in Moral Theology, No. 1. Moral Norms and Catholic Tradition.* New York: Paulist Press, 1980.

Gadamer, Hans-Georg. *Truth and Method.* New York: Seabury/Continuum, 1975.

Gallagher, John A. *Time Past, Time Future: A Historical Study of Catholic Moral Theology.* New York: Paulist Press, 1990.

Gallup, George, Jr., and Jim Castelli. *The People's Religion: American Faith in the 90s.* New York: Macmillan, 1989.

Galot, Jean, SJ. *Theology of the Priesthood.* San Francisco: Ignatius Press, 1985.

Gardeil, A. "Appetit." In *Dictionnaire de théologie catholique*, tom. 1, 2, cols. 1696–1700

Garrigou-Lagrange, Reginald, OP. *Christian Perfection and Contemplation, according to St. Thomas Aquinas and St. John of the Cross.* Translated by Sister M. Timothea Doyle, OP. St. Louis, MO: B. Herder Book Company, 1937.

Garvey, John, ed. *Modern Spirituality: An Anthology.* Springfield, IL: Templegate, 1985.

Gaudemet, Jean. "The Choice of Bishops: A Tortuous History." In *Concilium*, vol. 3; and *From Life to Law*, edited by James Provost and Knut Walf (Maryknoll, NY: Orbis Books, 1996), 59–65.

Geertz, Clifford. "Religion as a Cultural System." In *Anthropological Approaches to the Study of Religion*, edited by Michael Banton, 1–46. New York: Frederick A. Praeger, 1966.

Gehring, R. B. "The Knowledge of Material Essences according to S. Thomas Aquinas." *The Modern Schoolman* 33 (1956): 153–81.

Geiger, L. B., OP. *La Participation dans la philosophie de S. Thomas d'Aquin.* Paris: Vrin, 1942.

Gelpi, Donald L., SJ. *The Divine Mother: A Trinitarian Theology of the Holy Spirit.* Lanham, MD: University Press of America, 1984.

Gensler, Harry J. *Gödels Theorem Simplified.* Landham, MD: University Press of America, 1984.

George, Robert P. "Recent Criticism of Natural Law Theory." In *University of Chicago Law Review* (55; 1988).

Gilkey, Langdon. *Creationism On Trial.* Minneapolis, MN: Winston Press, 1985.

Gilligan, Carol. "In a Different Voice: Women's Conceptions of Self and of Morality." Review by Ann Colby and William Damon in Mary Roth Walsh, *The Psychology of Women: Ongoing Debates.* New Haven, CT: Yale University Press, 1987, 274–322.

―――. *In a Different Voice: Psychological Theory and Women's Development.* Cambridge, MA: Harvard University Press, 1982.

Gilson, Étienne. *Being and Some Philosophers.* 2nd ed. Toronto: Pontifical Institute of Mediaeval Studies, 1952.

―――. *Painting and Reality.* New York: Meridian Press, 1959.

―――. *From Aristotle to Darwin and Back.* Notre Dame, IN: University of Notre Dame Press, 1984.

―――. *The Philosophy of St. Thomas Aquinas.* A translation of *Le Thomisme,* sixth and final edition by Laurence K. Shook and Armand Maurer. Toronto: Pontifical Institute of Mediaeval Studies, 2002.

Goergen, Donald J., OP, and Ann Garrido, eds. *The Theology of Priesthood.* Collegeville, MN: The Liturgical Press, 2001.

Gough, Kathleen. "The Nayars and the Definition of Marriage." *Journal of the Royal Anthropological Institute of Great Britain and Ireland* (1958). www.orion.oac.uci.edu/~dbell/html/body_gough.html.

Grammick, Jeannine, and Pat Furey, eds. *The Vatican and Homosexuality.* New York: Crossroad, 1988.

Graton, Carolyn. *Guidelines for Spiritual Direction.* Vol. 3 of *Studies in Formative Spirituality.* Edited by Adrian van Kamm, CSSP and Susan A. Muto. Danville, NJ: Dimension Books, 1980.

Gray, John. *Men Are from Mars, Women Are from Venus: A Practical Guide for Improving Communication and Getting What You Want in Your Relationships.* San Francisco: HarperCollins, 1992.

Greeley, Andrew M. *Unsecular Man and Religious Change in America.* Cambridge, MA: Harvard University Press, 1989.

―――, and Gregory Baum, eds. *The Persistence of Religion,* Concilium. New York: Herder and Herder, 1973.

Grelot, Pierre. *Église et ministères: pour un dialogue critique avec Edward Schillebeeckx.* Paris: Éditions du Cerf, 1983.

Griffith, David Ray, William A. Beardslee, and Joe Holland. *Varieties of Postmodern Theology.* Albany: State University of New York Press, 1989.

Grisez, Germain G. *Contraception and the Natural Law.* Foreword by John Wright. Milwaukee: Bruce, 1964.

―――. "The First Principle of Practical Reason: A Commentary on the *Summa theologiae* I–I, Question 94, Article 2." *Natural Law Forum* 10 (1965): 168–201.

————. *Beyond the New Theism: A Philosophy of Religion.* Notre Dame, IN: University of Notre Dame Press, 1975.

————. "A Critique of Russell Hittinger's Book, A Critique of the New Natural Law Theory." *The New Scholasticism* 62 (4; Autumn 1988).

————, and Joseph M. Boyle, Jr. *Life and Death with Liberty and Justice: A Contribution to the Euthanasia Debate.* Notre Dame, IN: University of Notre Dame Press, 1979.

————, with the help of Joseph M. Boyle, Jr., Basil Cole, OP, John M. Finnis, John A. Geinzer, Jeannette Grisez, Robert G. Kennedy, Patrick Lee, William E. May, and Russell Shaw. *The Way of the Lord Jesus.* Vol. 1 of *Christian Moral Principles.* Chicago: Franciscan Herald Press, 1983.

————, Joseph Boyle, and John Finnis. "Practical Principles, Moral Truth, and Ultimate Ends." *American Journal of Jurisprudence* 32 (1987): 99–151.

————, and Russell Shaw. *Fulfillment in Christ.* Notre Dame, IN: University of Notre Dame Press, 1991.

Grobstein, Clifford. *Science and the Unborn: Choosing Human Futures.* New York: Basic Books, 1988.

Haffner, Paul. *Creation and Scientific Creativity: A Study in the Thought of S. L. Jaki.* Front Royal, VA: Christendom Press, 1991.

Haimes, Erica, and Noel Timms. *Adoption, Identity, and Social Policy: The Search for Distant Relatives.* New York: Gower Publishing Co., 1985.

Haldane, John. "Thomism and the Future of Catholic Philosophy." Blackfriars Aquinas Lecture, 1988. www.holycross.edu/departments/philosophy/gcolvert/jjhbfl1998.htm

Hall, Brian P. *The Personal Discernment Inventory: An Instrument for Spiritual Guides.* New York: Paulist Press, 1980.

————, et al., eds. *Value Clarification as a Learning Process: A Handbook for Religious Education.* NewYork: Paulist Press, 1973.

Hallet, Garth, SJ. "Contraception and Prescriptive Infallibility." *Theological Studies* 43 (December 1982): 629–50.

————. "The 'Incommensurability' of Values." *Heythrop Journal* 28 (October 1987): 373–87

————. "Infallibility and Contraception: The Debate Continues." *Heythrop Journal* 49 (September 1988): 517–28.

Hamilton, W. J., J. D. Boyd, and H. W. Mossman. *Human Embryology: Prenatal Development of Form and Function.* 4th ed. London & New York: Macmillan Press, 1972, 1976, 1978 printing.

Hanink, James G. "A Theory of Basic Goods: Structure and Hierarchy." *The Thomist* 52 (April 1988): 221–45.

Harris, Errol E. *Cosmos and Anthropos: A Philosophical Interpretation of the Anthropic Cosmological Principles.* Atlantic Highlands, NJ: Humanities Press International, 1991.

Harvey, John, OSFS. *The Homosexual Person: New Thinking in Pastoral Care.* San Francisco: Ignatius Press, 1987.

————. "Overcoming the Masturbation Habit." www.couragerc.net/PIP Masturbation.html.

————, and Gerard V. Bradley, eds. *Same-Sex Attraction: A Parent's Guide.* South Bend, IN: St. Augustine's Press, 2003.

Hathaway, Ronald F. *Hierarchy and the Definition of Order in the Letters of the Pseudo-Dionysius.* The Hague: Martinus Nijhoff, 1969.

Hauke, Manfred. *Women in the Priesthood?* San Francisco: Ignatius Press, 1988.

Hawking, Stephen W. *A Brief History of Time* (Toronto: Bantam Books, 1988).

Hayes, John, and Frederick Prussner. *Old Testament Theology: Its History and Development.* Atlanta, GA: John Knox Press, 1985.

Haynes, James D. "Sex Cells, and Same-Sex Desire: The Biology of Sexual Preference." *Journal of Homosexuality* 28 (1995): Part I, 1/2, Part II, 91–114.

Heath, Sir Thomas. *Mathematics in Aristotle.* South Bend, IN: St. Augustine's Press, 1998, 1949.

Heid, Stefan. *Celibacy in the Early Church: The Beginnings of a Discipline of Obligatory Continence for Clerics in East and West.* Translated by Michael J. Miller. San Francisco: Ignatius Press, 2000.

Heidegger, Martin. *Being and Time.* Translated by John Macquarrie and Edward Robinson. New York: Harper and Row, 1962.

————. "Die Frage nach der Technik." In *Die Technik und die Kehre.* Prullingen: Günther Neske, 1962.

————. *The Question Concerning Technology and Other Essays.* Translated and with an introduction by William Lovitt. New York: Harper & Row, Colophon Books, 1970. See especially "The Turning," 38–39.

————. "On the Essence of Truth." In *Martin Heidegger: Basic Writings,* 130–35. Edited and translated by D. F. Krell. San Francisco: Harper and Row, 1977.

Heidel, Alexander. *The Babylonian.* 2nd ed. Chicago: University of Chicago Press, 1963.

Hendry, George S. "The Eclipse of Creation." *Theology Today* (January 1972): 406.

————. *Theology of Nature.* Philadelphia: The Westminister Press, 1980.

Henle, Robert J., SJ. "Transcendental Thomism: A Critical Assessment." In *One Hundred Years of Thomism: Aeterni Patris and Afterwards: A Symposium,* edited by Victor B. Brezik, CSB, 90–116. Houston, TX: Center for Thomistic Studies, University of St. Thomas, 1981.

Hennecke, Edgar, and Wilhelm Schneemelcher. *New Testament Apocrypha.* Translated by A. J. B. Higgins and others; edited by R. McL. Wilson. Philadelphia: Westminster Press, 1963–65.

Herbrechtsmeier, William. "Buddhism and the Definition of Religion: One More Time." *Journal for the Scientific Study of Religion* 8, 32 (1; 1982): 1–18.

Hering, H. M., OP. "De tempore animationis foetus humani." *Angelicum* 28 (1951): 18–19.

Herron, T. J. *The Most Probable Date of the First Epistle of Clement to the Corinthians.* Rome: Gregorian University, 1988.

Hewson, M. Anthony. *Giles of Rome and the Medieval Theory of Conception: A Study of the De formatione corporis humani in utero.* London: Athlone Press, 1975.

Hibbert, Giles, OP. "*Contemplata aliis tradere*: The Vocation of the Dominican Order. www.english.op.org/vocations/contemplata.html.

Hill, William, OP. *The Three-Personed God.* Washington, DC: The Catholic University of America Press, 1982.

Hittinger, Russell. *A Critique of the New Natural Law Theory.* Notre Dame, IN: University of Notre Dame Press, 1987.

Hollenbach, David, SJ. "Fundamental Theology and the Christian Moral Life." In *Faith Witness: Foundations of Theology for Today's Church*, edited by Leo J. O'Donovan and E. Howland Sanks, 167–84. New York: Crossroad, 1989.

Hoose, Bernard. *Proportionalism: The American Debate and its European Roots.* Washington, DC: Georgetown University Press, 1987.

Hopko, Thomas, ed. *Women and the Priesthood.* New York: St. Vladimir's Seminary, 1983.

Horowitz, Sophia Menache. *L'humor en chaire: le rire dans l Église médiévale.* Geneva: Labor et Fides, 1994.

Hudeczek, M. "De tempore animationis foetus humani secundum embryologian hodiernam." *Angelicum* 29 (1952): 162–81.

Hudson, Deal W. and Dennis Wm. Moran, eds. *The Future of Thomism*, Mishawaka, IN. American Maritain Association. Notre Dame, IN: Distributed by University of Notre Dame Press, 1992.

Hugon, Edouard, OP. *Les Vingt-Quatre Thèses: Principes de Philosophie.* 9th ed. Paris: P. Tequi, 1946.

Hyers, M. Conrad. *And Created Laughter: The Bible as Divine Comedy.* Atlanta, GA: John. Knox Press, 1987.

Ignatius Loyola, SJ, St. "Rules for Thinking, Judging, and Feeling with the Church to Have the Genuine Attitude which We Ought to Maintain in the Church Militant." In his *The Spiritual Exercises*, nn. 353–570, in *Ignatius Loyola: the Spiritual Exercises and Selected Works.* Edited by George E. Ganss, SJ, et al.; preface by J. W. Padberg, SJ. The Classics of Western Spirituality. New York: Paulist Press, 1991.

Iles, Susan, and Dennis Gath. "Psychiatric outcome of termination of pregnancy for fetal abnormality." *Psychological Medicine* 23 (1993): 407–13.

International Network for Religion and Animals. *Network News.* North Wales, PA and Silver Spring, MD. www.dd-b.net/~raphael/jain-list/msg02022.html.

Isaacs, Marie E. *Sacred Space: An Approach to the Theology of the Epistle to the Hebrews.* JSNT. Supplement Series 73.

Jaki, Stanley L., OSB. *The Road of Science and the Ways to God.* The Gifford Lectures 1975 and 1976. Chicago: University of Chicago Press; Edinburgh: Scottish Academic Press, 1978.

Jelly, Frederick M., OP. "The Relationship Between Symbolic and Literal Language in Naming God." In *Naming God*, edited by Robert P. Scharlemann, 52–64. New York: Paragon House, 1985.

John of the Cross, St. *Dark Night of the Soul.* Translated by E. Allison Peers. 3rd rev. ed. Garden City, NY: Doubleday/Image Books, 1959. www.thenazareneway.com/dark_night_of_the_soul.htm.

———. *The Ascent of Mount Carmel.* Translated by E. Allison Peers. www.thenazareneway.com/index_ascent_of_mount_carmel.htm.

John, Helen James. *The Thomist Spectrum.* New York: Fordham University Press, 1966.

Johnson, Mark F. "Did St. Thomas Attribute a Doctrine of Creation to Aristotle?" *The New Scholasticism* 63 (1989): 129–55.

———. "Aquinas' Changing Evaluation of Plato on Creation." *American Catholic Philosophical Quarterly* 66, 1 (Winter 1992): 81–88.

Jonas, Hans. "Technology and Responsibility." In *Religion and the Humanizing of Man,* edited by James Robinson, 1–19. New York: Council on the Study of Religion, 1972.

Jones, Cheslyn, G. Wainwright, and E. Yarnold, SJ, eds. *The Study of Spirituality.* New York: Oxford University Press, 1986.

Jones, David Albert, OP. "Was There a Bishop of Rome in the First Century?" *New Blackfriars* 60 (March 1999): 128–43.

Jones, David Clyde. *Biblical Christian Ethics.* Grand Rapids, MI: Baker Books, 1994.

Jones, Gwilym H. *1 and 2 Kings, New Century.* Grand Rapids, MI: Wm. B. Eerdmans, 1984.

Jonsson, G. A. *The Image of God: Genesis 1:26–28 in a Century of Old Testament Research.* Translated by Lorraine Svendsen; revised by Michael S. Cheney. Stockholm, Sweden: Almqvist & Wiksell, 1988.

Jonsson, Jakob. *Humour and Irony in the New Testament.* Reykjavick, Iceland: Bokautgafa Menningarsjods, 1965.

Jung, Carl Gustav. *Archetypes and the Collective Unconscious. The Collected Works of C. G. Jung.* Edited by Herbert Read, Michael Fordham, and Gerhard Adler; translated by William McGuire. New York: Pantheon, 1953–83.

——— et al. *Man and His Symbols.* New York, Dell, 1970.

Kane, William H., OP. Review of Jacques Maritain, *The Philosophy of Nature* (New York: Philosophical Library, 1951). In *The Thomist,* 16 (1953): 127–31.

Kasper, Walter. "Ministry in the Church: Taking Issue with Edward Schillebeeckx." *Communio* (Summer 1983): 185–95.

Kass, Leon, MD. "Neither for Love nor Money: Why Doctors Must Not Kill." *The Human Life Review* 15 (Fall 1989): 93–115.

Kauffman, Stuart A. *The Origins of Order: Self-Organization and Selection in Evolution.* New York: Oxford University Press, 1993.

———. *At Home in the Universe: The Search for Laws of Self-Organization and Complexity.* New York: Oxford University Press, 1995.

Keck, L. E., and J. L. Martyn, eds. *Studies in Luke-Acts: Essays Presented in Honor of Paul Schubert.* Nashville, TN: Abingdon, 1966.

Kerr, Fergus, OP. *Theology After Wittgenstein.* Oxford: Blackwell, 1986.

Keys, C. D. "Truth as Art: An Interpretation of Heidegger's *Sein Und Zeit and Der Ursprung des Kunstwerkes.*" In *Heidegger and the Path of Thinking*, edited by John Sallis, 65–84. Pittsburgh: Duquesne University Press, 1970.

Kirk, G. S. *Myth: Its Meaning and Function in Ancient and Other Cultures.* Cambridge: Cambridge University Press, 1970.

Klaaren, Eugene M. *Religious Origins of Modern Science: Belief in Creation in Seventeenth-Century Thought.* Grand Rapids, MI: Eerdmans, 1977.

Klinger, Elmar. "Soul." In *Sacramentum Mundi: An Encyclopedia of Theology*, edited by Karl Rahner et al., vol. 6, 138–41. New York: Herder and Herder, 1970.

Knasas, John F. X. "*Esse* as the Target of Judgment in Rahner and Aquinas." *Proceedings of the American Catholic Philosophical Association* 59 (1985): 114–31.

———. "Immateriality and Metaphysics." *Angelicum* 65 (1988): 44–76.

———, ed. *Jacques Maritain: The Man and His Metaphysics.* Bellaire, TX: American Maritain Association, 1988.

Knope, D. M. "Eucharist." In *The Perennial Dictionary of World Religions*, edited by Keith Crim et al., reprint edition, 637–40. San Francisco, CA: Harper San Francisco, 1990.

Kottak, Conrad P. *The Exploration of Human Diversity.* New York: McGraw-Hill, 2002.

Krapiec, Mieczyslaw. *I, Man: An Outline to Philosophical Anthropology.* New Britain, CT: Mariel, 1983.

Kuhn, Thomas S. *The Copernican Revolution: Planetary Astronomy in the Development of Western Thought.* New York: Random House, 1959.

———. *The Structure of Scientific Revolutions.* Chicago: University of Chicago Press, 1970.

Kümmel, W. G. "Luc en accusation dans la theologie contemporaine." In *L'Évangile de Luc: The Gospel of Luke*, edited by F. Neirynck, rev. ed, 3–19. Leuven: Leuven University Press, 1989.

Küng, Hans. *On Being a Christian.* Garden City, NY: Doubleday, 1976.

Kuper, Adam. *The Chosen Primate: Human Nature and Cultural Diversity.* Cambridge, MA: Harvard University Press, 1994.

Kwant, Remy C. *The Phenomenology of Social Existence.* Pittsburgh: Duquesne University Press, 1965.

La Nouvelle Eve, Bulletin de la Societe Francaise d' Etudes Mariales, 1954–57. Paris: Lethielleux, 1958.

LaCugna, Catherine Mowry. *The Theological Methodology of Hans Küng.* American Academy of Religion Academy Series, No. 39, 1982.

Lampe, G. W. H., and K. J. Woolcombe. *Essays on Typology, Studies in Biblical Theology.* Vol. 22. London: SCM Press, 1957.

Lango, John W. *Whitehead's Ontology.* Albany, NY: State University of New York Press, 1972.

Lasch, Christopher. *Haven in a Heartless World: The Family Beseiged.* New York: Basic Books, 1977.

Laurentin, René. *The Truth of Christmas: Beyond the Myths.* Preface by Joseph Cardinal Ratzinger. Petersham, ME: St. Bede's Publications, 1982.

Lawler, Michael G. *Symbolism and Sacrament.* New York: Paulist Press, 1987.

Lawler, Ronald, OFM, Cap., Joseph Boyle, Jr., and William E. May. *Catholic Sexual Ethics.* Rev. ed. Huntington, IN: Our Sunday Visitor, 1998.

Le Rohellec, Jospeh, CSSp. *Utrum juxta S. Thomae doctrinae essentiae rerum sensibilium statim in simplici apprehensione percipiantur,* Xena Thomistica, vol. 1, 285–303.

Leeuwen, Arend van. *Christianity in World History.* London: Edinburgh House, 1964.

Lemaire, André, *Les ministères aux origins de l'Église, naissance de la triple hiérarchie: évêques, presbyters, diacres.* Paris: Éditions du Cerf, 1971.

———. *Les ministères dans l'église.* Paris: Éditions du Cerf, 1971.

Lifton, Robert Jay. *The Nazi Doctors: Medical Killing and the Psychology of Genocide.* New York: Basic Books, 1986.

Lightman, Alan, and Roberta Brawer. *Origins: The Lives and Worlds of Modern Cosmologists.* Cambridge, MA: Harvard University Press, 1990.

Liska, James J. *A General Introduction to the Semiotic of Charles Sanders Peirce.* Bloomington, IN: Indiana University Press, 1996.

Little, Arthur, SJ. *The Platonic Heritage of Thomism.* Dublin: Golden Eagle Books, 1950.

Lonergan, Bernard J. F., SJ. *Insight: A Study of Human Understanding.* New York: Philosophical Library, 1957.

———. *Method in Theology.* New York: Herder and Herder, 1972.

———. "The Transition from a Classicist World-View to Historical Mindedness" & "Insight Revisited." In *A Second Collection,* edited by W. F. J. Ryan, SJ, and B. J. Tyrell, SJ. Philadelphia: The Westminister Press, 1974, 1–9.

———. *The Subject,* the Aquinas Lecture for 1968 delivered at Marquette University, March 3, 1968. Milwaukee: Marquette University Press, 1968.

Long, R. James, ed. *Philosophy and the God of Abraham: Essays in Memory of James A. Weisheipl, OP.* Toronto: Pontifical Institute of Medieval Studies, 1991.

Loscerbo, John. *Being and Technology: A Study in the Philosophy of Martin Heidegger.* The Hague: Martinus Nijhoff, 1981.

Lowe, Victor. *Understanding Whitehead.* Baltimore: Johns Hopkins Press, 1962.

Lubac, Henri de, SJ. *Surnaturel: Études historiques.* Paris: Aubier, 1946.

———. *The Mystery of the Supernatural.* Translated by Rosemary Sheed. New York: Sheed & Ward, 1967.

———. *The Sources of Revelation.* New York: Herder and Herder, 1968.

———. *A Brief Catechesis on Nature and Grace.* San Francisco: Ignatius Press, 1980.

Luijpen, Wiliam A. *Phenomenology of Natural Law.* Duquesne Philosophical Series 22. Pittsburgh: Duquesne University Press, 1967.

Lumbreras, Pedro, OP. *The XXIV Fundamental Theses of Official Catholic Philosophy.* Notre Dame, IN: University of Notre Dame Press, 1947.

MacIntyre, Alasdair. *Against the Self-Images of the Age.* Notre Dame, IN: Notre Dame University Press, 1978.

Macquarrie, John. "Creation and Environment." *Expository Times* (October 1971): 4–9.

Maguire, Daniel. *Death by Choice*. Rev. ed. Garden City, NY: Doubleday, 1984.

Maloney, George A., SJ. *Mary: The Womb of God—A Vivid and Powerful Study of the Greatest Woman Who Ever Lived*. Starrucca, PA: Dimension Books, 1981.

Manteau-Bonamy, H. M., OP. *The Immaculate Conception and the Holy Spirit: The Marian Teaching of Father Kolbe*. Libertyville, IL: Franciscan Marytown Press, 1977.

Maritain, Jacques. "The Philosophy of Nature." In his *Science and Wisdom*. New York: Scribner's Sons, 1940.

———. *The Philosophy of Nature*. New York: Philosophical Library, 1951. Reviewed by William H. Kane, OP, The Thomist 16 (1953): 127–31.

———. *Creative Imagination in Art and Poetry*. New York: Harper, 1954.

———. *Distinguish to Unite, or The Degrees of Knowledge*. 4th ed. Translated by G. B. Phelan. New York: Scribner's Sons, 1959. Reprint, Notre Dame: IN: University of Notre Dame Press, 1995.

Marshner, William H. Review of Germain Grisez, *The Way of the Lord Jesus*. *Faith and Reason* 16 (2; Summer 1990): 177–99.

Martinez, Raul Berzoa. *La Teologia del Sobrenatural en los Escritos de Henri de Lubac: Estudio Historico-Teologico*, 1931–80. Facultad de Teologia del Norte de España Sede de Burgos, n. 57. Burgos: Ediciones Aldecoa, 1991.

Maurer, Armand, ed. *The Division and Method of the Sciences: Q. V and VI of Aquinas' Commentary on the De Trinitate of Boethius*. 4th rev. ed. Toronto: Pontifical Institute of Medieval Studies, 1986.

May, William E. *An Introduction to Moral Theology*. Huntington, IN: Our Sunday Visitor Press, 1991.

———, et al., "Feeding and Hydrating the Permanently Unconscious and Other Vulnerable Persons." *Issues in Law and Medicine* 3 (1987): 203–10.

McCarter, P. Kyle, Jr. *I Samuel. In Anchor Bible*. Garden City, NY: Doubleday, 1980.

McCool, Gerald A., SJ. *Catholic Theology in the Nineteenth Century: The Quest for a Unitary Method*. New York: Seabury Press, 1977.

———. *From Unity to Pluralism: The Internal Evolution of Thomism*. New York: Fordham University Press, 1989.

———. *The Neo-Thomists*. Milwaukee: Marquette University Press, 1994.

McCormick, Richard A., SJ. "Fundamental Freedom Revisited." In *The Critical Calling: Reflections on Moral Dilemmas Since Vatican II*, 171–90. Washington, DC: Georgetown University Press, 1989.

———. "The Embryo Debate 3: The First 14 Days." *The Tablet* (10 March 1990): 301–4.

———." "Who or What is the Preembryo?" *Kennedy Institute of Ethics Journal* 1 (4; 1991): 1–15.

———. "The Embryo as Potential: A Reply to John A. Robertson." *Kennedy Institute of Ethics Journal* 1 (4; 1991): 303–5.

McCormick, Richard A., SJ, and Paul Ramsey, eds. *Doing Evil to Achieve Good.* Lanham, MD: University Press of America, 1985.

McInerny, Ralph. "The Prime Mover and the Order of Learning." In *Being and Predication: Thomistic Interpretations.* Washington, DC: Catholic University of America Press, 1986.

McMullin, Ernan, ed. *Evolution and Creation.* Notre Dame, IN: University Press, 1985.

Meng, Jude Chua Soo. "To Close a Generation Gap: Thomists and the New Natural Law Theory." *Quodlibet Online Journal of Christian Theology and Philosophy* 3 (2; 2001). www.quodlibet.net/meng-thomism.shtml.

Mercier, Cardinal Desiré-Joseph. *Cours de Philosophie* (1905), vol. 1, 26–30.

Merlan, Philip. *Monopsychism, Mysticism, Metaconsciousness: Problems of the Soul in Neo-Aristotelian and Neo-Platonic Tradition.* 2nd ed. The Hague: Martinus Nijhoff, 1969.

Messenger, Ernest C. *Evolution and Theology: the Problem of Man's Origins.* Preface by Cuthbert Lattey; introduction by Dr. Souvay. New York: Macmillan, 1932.

———. "The Embryology of St. Thomas Aquinas." In *Theology and Evolution,* 243–58. Edited by Ernest C. Messenger. Westminister, MD: Newman, 1949.

Mettinger, Tryggve N. D. *In Search of God: The Meaning and Message of the Everlasting Names.* Translated by F. H. Cryer. Minneapolis, MN: Augsburg Fortress Publishers, 1988.

Meyendorff, John. *Living Tradition.* Crestwood, NY: St. Vladimir's Seminary Press, 1978.

Michalski, Melvin. "The Relationship between the Universal Priesthood of the Baptized and the Ministerial Priesthood of the Ordained in Vatican II and in Subsequent Theology: Understanding 'essentia et non gradu tantum.'" *Lumen Gentium* no. 10. Lewiston, NY: Mellen University Press, 1996.

Michel, A. "Surnaturel." In *Dictionnaire de théologie catholique,* tom. 14, 2, cols. 2854–2859.

Miller, John, W. *Biblical Faith and Fathering.* New York: Paulist Press, 1989.

Minnerath, Roland. *De Jerusalem a Rome: Pierre et l'Unite de l'Eglise Apostolique.* Paris: Beauchesne, 1995.

Moltmann, Jurgen. "The Ecological Crisis." In *God in Creation,* 20–52. San Francisco: Harper and Row, 1985.

Monod, Jacques. *Chance and Necessity.* London: Collins, 1972.

Moore, David S. *The Dependent Gene: The Fallacy of Nature vs. Nurture.* New York. W. H. Freeman, 2002.

Moore, Keith L., and T. V. N. Persaud. *The Developing Human: Clinically Oriented Embryology.* 6th ed. Philadelphia: W. B. Saunders, 1998.

Mora, Jose Ferrata. "Suarez and Modern Philosophy." *Journal of the History of Ideas* 14 (1953): 528–47.

Moraczewski, Albert, OP. "Personhood Entry and Exist." In *The Twenty-Fifth Anniversary of Vatican II: A Look and a Look Ahead.* Edited by R. E. Smith. Braintree, MA: Pope John Center, 1990.

Moral Truth and Moral Tradition: Essays in Honor of Peter Geach and Elizabeth Anscombe. Edited by Luke Gormally. Dublin: Four Courts Press, 1994.

Moreno, Antonio, OP. "The Law of Inertia and the Principle *Quidquid movetur ab alio movetur.*" *The Thomist* 38 (April 1974): 206–331.

Morowitz, Harold J., and James S. Trefil. *The Facts of Life: Science and the Abortion Controversy.* New York: Oxford University Press, 1992.

Most, William G. *The Consciousness of Christ.* Front Royal, VA: Christendom College Press, 1980.

Muck, Otto, SJ. *The Transcendental Method.* Translated by William D. Seidensticker. New York: Herder and Herder, 1968.

Mullahy, Bernard, CSC. "Thomism and Mathematical Physics." 2 vol., typescript. Partially published as "Subalternation and Mathematical Physics," *Laval Theologique et Philosophique* 2 (1946): 89–107.

Müller, Werner A. *Developmental Biology.* New York: Springer, 1997.

Muniz, Franciscus, OP. *De Diversis Muneribus S. Theologiae Secundum Doctrinam D. Thomae.* Translated by John P. Reid as *The Work of Theology.* Washington, DC: The Thomist Press, 1953.

Murnion, Philip J., Msgr. *Catholic Common Ground Initiative: Foundational Documents.* New York: Crossroad, 1997. www.nplc.org/commonground/history.htm.

Nagel, Ernest. *The Structure of Science.* New York: Harcourt, Brace and World, 1961.

———, J. R. Newman and D. R. Hostadter, *Gödel's Proof,* rev. ed. (New York: New York University Press, 2002).

Nelson, Daniel Mark. *The Priority of Prudence: Virtue and Natural Law in Thomas Aquinas and the Implications for Modern Ethics.* University Park, PA: Pennsylvania State University, 1992.

Neusner, Jacob. *Invitation to the Talmud.* 2nd ed. San Francisco: Harper and Row, 1984.

New Jerome Biblical Commentary. Edited by Raymond E. Brown, Joseph A. Fitzmyer, and Roland E. Murphy; foreword by Carlo Maria Cardinal Martini. Englewood Cliffs, NJ: Prentice-Hall, 1989.

The New Jerusalem Bible. Garden City, NY: Doubleday, 1985.

Neyrey, Jerome H., SJ. "2 Peter" & "Jude." In *New Jerome Biblical Commentary,* edited by Raymond E. Brown, Joseph A. Fitzmyer, and Roland E. Murphy. Englewood Cliffs, NJ: Prentice-Hall, 1989.

Nichols, Aidan, OP. *The Art of God Incarnate: Theology and Symbol from Genesis to the Twentieth Century.* New York: Paulist Press, 1980.

———. *Holy Order: Apostolic Priesthood from the New Testament to the Second Vatican Council.* Oscott Series, No. 5. Dublin: Veritas Press, 1990.

Nicolas, J.-H., OP. *Les Profondeurs de la Grace.* Paris: Beauchesne, 1969.

Noffke, Suzanne, OP. *Catherine of Siena: Vision Through a Distant Eye.* Collegeville, MN: Michael Glazier/Liturgical Press, 1996.

Nolte, Ernst. "Heidegger and Nazism: An Exchange." *New York Review of Books* (April 8, 1993).

Noonan, John T. Jr., ed. *The Morality of Abortion: Legal and Historical Perspectives.* Cambridge, MA: Harvard University Press, 1970. See also his "An Almost Absolute Value in History," in this volume, 1–59.

O'Brien, Thomas C. *Metaphysics and the Existence of God.* Washington, DC: The Thomist Press, 1960.

———. "Names Proper to the Divine Persons." In St. Thomas Aquinas, *Summa theologiae.* Edited by Thomas Gilby, OP. Cambridge, UK: Blackfriars; New York: McGraw-Hill, 1964.

O'Collins, Gerald, SJ., and Daniel Kendall, SJ. "The Faith of Jesus." *Theological Studies* 53 (3; September 1992): 403–23.

O'Connell, Robert J. *St. Augustine's Confession: The Odyssey of the Soul.* Cambridge: Belknap Press of Harvard University, 1969.

O'Connor, James T. "Mary, Mother of God and Contemporary Challenges." *Marian Studies* 29 (1978): 26–43

O'Meara, Thomas F., OP. *Church and Culture: German Catholic Theology, 1860–1914.* Notre Dame, IN: University of Notre Dame Press, 1991.

O'Neil, Dennis. *Behavior: a Survey of Non-Human Primate Behavior Patterns.* www.palomar.edu/behavior/default.htm.

O'Rourke, Kevin D., OP. "Ethical Opinions in Regard to the Question of Early Delivery of Anencephalic Infants." *The Linacre Quarterly* 63 (August 1996): 55–59.

———. "The Catholic Tradition on Foregoing Life Support," *The National Catholic Bioethics Quarterly,* Autumn 2005, 3, 537–53.

Origen. *Origen on First Principles.* Translated by G. W. Butterworth; introduction by Henri de Lubac. New York: Harper Torchbooks, 1966.

"Origenism." www.newadvent.org/cathen/11306b.htm.

Osborne, Kenan B., OFM. *Priesthood: A History of the Ordained Ministry in the Roman Catholic Church.* New York: Paulist Press, 1988.

Overman, Dean L. *A Case Against Accident and Self-Organization.* Foreword by Wolfhart Pannenberg. Lanham, MD: Rowman & Littlefield, 1997.

Owens, D. J. *What is Ecology?* London: Oxford Press, 1974.

Owens, Joseph, CSsR. "St. Thomas and Modern Science." *Transactions of the Royal Society of Canada* 1 (June 1963): 283–93.

———. *An Elementary Christian Metaphysics.* Milwaukee, WI: Bruce, 1963.

Palmer, Richard E. *Hermeneutics: Interpretation Theory in Schliermacher, Dilthey, Heidegger, and Gadamer.* Evanston, IL: Northwestern University Press, 1969.

Pangallo, Mario. *L'essere come atto nel Tomismo essenziale di Cornelio Fabro. Studi Thomistici,* vol. 32. Rome: Officium Libri Catholici, 1987.

Parrott, Bob W. *Ontology of Humor.* New York: Philosophical Library, 1982.

Passmore, John. "Philosophy." In *Encyclopedia of Philosophy,* edited by Paul Edwards, vol. 6, 216–30. New York: MacMillan Publishing and Free Press, 1972.

Peacocke, Arthur R. *Creation and the World of Science.* The Bampton Lectures, 1978. Oxford: Clarendon Press, 1979.

Peck, A. L. *Generation of Animals.* Cambridge MA: Harvard University Press, 1979.

Peddichord, Richard, OP. *The Sacred Monster of Thomism: An Introduction to the Life and Legacy of Reginald Garrigou-Lagrange,* OP. South Bend, IN: St. Augustine's Press, 2004.

Peghaire, Julien, CSSp. *Intellectus et ratio selon S. Thomas d'Aquin.* Paris: Vrin; Ottowa: Institute d' Etudes Medievales, 1936.

Pegis, Anton. *The Problem of the Soul in the Thirteenth Century.* Toronto: St. Michael's College, 1934.

————. *A Gilson Reader.* Garden City, NY: Hanover House, 1957.

Pelikan, Jaroslav. *Imago Dei: The Byzantine Apologia for Icons.* The A. W. Mellon Lecture in the Fine Arts, 1987. The National Gallery of Art, Washington, DC. Bollingen Series xxxv, 36. Princeton, NJ: Princeton University Press, 1990.

Pelligrino, Edmund, MD. "The Moral Foundations for Valid Consent." *Proceedings of the Third National Conference on Human Values and Cancer.* Washington, DC: American Cancer Society, 1981.

Penning de Vries, Piet, SJ. *Discernment of Spirits According to the Life and Teachings of St. Ignatius Loyola.* New York: Exposition Press, 1973.

Penrose, Roger. *The Emperor's New Mind: Concerning Computers, Minds, and the Laws of Physics.* New York: Oxford University Press, 1989.

Pieper, Josef. *The Four Cardinal Virtues.* Notre Dame, IN: University of Notre Dame Press, 1966.

Pilarcsyk, Archbishop Daniel. "Dissent in the Church." *Origins* 16 (July 31, 1986): 175–78.

Pintard, Abbé. "Mater viventium." *La Nouvelle Eve* (1957): 61–86.

Plant, W. Gunther. *The Torah: A Modern Commentary.* New York: Union of American Hebrew Congregations, 1981.

Plé, A., OP. "Alert au Traducianisme." *La Vie Spirituelle* (Supplement) 24 (96–99; 1971): 59–71.

Plotinus. *The Enneads.* 3rd rev. ed. by B. S. Page. Translated by Stephen MacKenna; foreword by E. R. Dodds; and introduction by Paul Henry. New York: Pantheon Books, 1962.

Poddimattam, Felix M., OFM Cap. *Fundamental Option and Mortal Sin.* Bangalore: Asian Tradition Corporation, 1986.

Poinsot, Jean, OP. (John of St. Thomas). *Cursus Philosophicus Thomisticus.* Edited by P. Beato Reiser. Taurini: Marietti, 1930–37.

Powell, Ralph A., OP. "The Late Heidegger's Omission of the Ontic-Ontological Structure of Dasein." In *Heidegger and the Path of Thinking,* edited by John Sallis, 116–87. Pittsburgh: Duquesne University Press, 1970.

Power, David, OMI. *Ministers of Christ and His Church: The Theology of Priesthood.* London: G. Chapman, 1969.

Pronk, Pim. *Against Nature? Types of Moral Argumentation Regarding Homosexuality.* Grand Rapids, MI: Eerdmans, 1993.

Quay, Paul M., SJ. *The Christian Meaning of Human Sexuality.* Evanston, IL: A Credo House Book, 1985.

Quinn, John M., OSA, *The Thomism of Etienne Gilson: A Critical Study.* Villanova, PA: Villanova University Press, 1971.

Rahner, Hugo. *The Spirituality of St. Ignatius Loyola: An Account of Its Historical Development.* Westminister, MD: Newman, 1953.

Rahner, Karl, SJ. *Schriften zur Theologie.* EinsiedelnBenzige, 1954–98.

———. *Spirit in the World.* Translated by William Dych, SJ; introduction by Francis Fiorenza. New York: Herder and Herder, 1968.

———. *Hearers of the Word.* Translated by Michael Richards. New York: Herder and Herder, 1969.

———. "Angel." In *Sacramentum Mundi: An Encyclopedia of Theology,* edited by Karl Rahner et al., vol., 27–34. New York: Herder and Herder, 1970.

———. *Encyclopedia of Theology: The Concise Sacramentum Mundi.* New York: Crossroad/Herder, 1975.

———. "The Experiences of a Catholic Theologian." *Communio* 11 (4; 1984): 412.

———. *Theological Investigations.* 23 vols. Translated with an introduction by Cornelius Ernst, OP. London/Baltimore/New York: Dartman, Longman and Todd/Helicon Press/Herder and Herder/Seabury, 1961–92.

Ramirez, Santiago M., *De hominibus beatitudine in I–II Summa theologiae Din Thomae Commentaria,* 5 vols., Madrid, 1972.

Ramsey, Paul. "The Morality of Abortion." In Edward Shils et al. *Life or Death: Ethics and Options,* edited and introduction by Daniel H. Labby, 61–63. Portland, OR: Reed College, 1968

Ransil, Bernard J., MD. *Abortion.* Paramus, NJ: Paulist Press, 1969.

Ratzinger, Cardinal Joseph. *Principles of Catholic Theology: Building Stones for a Fundamental Theology.* San Francisco: Ignatius Press, 1987.

Rawls, John. *A Theory of Justice.* Cambridge, MA: Harvard University, Belknap Press, 1971.

Regamey, Raymond, OP. *Non-Violence and the Christian Conscience.* New York: Herder and Herder, 1966.

Reitan, Eric A. "Aquinas and Weisheipl: Aristotle's Physics and the Existence of God." In *Philosophy and the God of Abraham: Essays in Memory of James A. Weisheipl, OP,* edited by R. James Long, 179–90. Toronto: Pontifical Institute of Medieval Studies, 1991.

Renoirte, Fernand. *Cosmology: Elements of a Critique of the Sciences and Cosmology.* 4th ed. Louvain: Institut supérieur de philosophie, 1905. Translated by Thomas and Stanislaus Parker as *A Manuel of Modern Scholastic Philosophy.* 2nd ed. St. Louis, MO: B. Herder Book Company, 1919.

Reumann, John. *Creation and New Creation: The Past, Present, and Future of God's Creative Activity.* Minneapolis, MN: Augsburg, 1973.

Rhonheimer, Martin. *Natur als Grundlage der Moral: die personale Struktur des Naturgesetzes bei Thomas von Aquin: eine teleologischer Ethik.* Innsbruck: Tyrolia Verlag, 1987.

Richardson, Cyril. "A Christian Approach to Ecology." *Religion in Life* 41 (1972): 462–79.

Rist, J. M. *Plotinus: The Road to Reality.* Cambridge: Cambridge University Press, 1967.

Rizzi, Anthony. *The Science Before Science: A Guide to Thinking in the 21st Century.* Baton Rouge, LA: Institute for Advanced Physics Press, 2004.

Roberts, Keith, A. *Religion in Sociological Perspective.* 3rd ed. Belmont, CA: Wadsworth, 1994.

Roberts, Louis. *The Achievement of Karl Rahner.* New York: Herder and Herder, 1967.

———. *The Theological Aesthetics of Hans Urs von Balthasar.* Washington, DC: Catholic University of America, 1987.

Rodriguez, Alphonsus. *Practice of Perfection and Christian Virtues.* Translated by Joseph Rickaby. Chicago, IL: Loyola University Press, 1929.

Roof, Wade Clark, and William McKinney. *American Mainline Religion.* New Brunswick: Rutgers University Press, 1987.

Rosenthal-Schneider, Ilse. "Presuppositions and Anticipations of Einstein's Physics." In *Albert Einstein Philosopher-Scientist,* edited by Paul Arthur Schlipp. 3rd ed. La Salle, IL: Open Court, 1970.

Rozwadowski., A. J. "De motus localis causa proxima secundum principia S. Thomae." *Divus Thomas* (Piacenza) 42 (1939): 104–13.

Russell, E. S. *The Directiveness of Organic Activities.* Cambridge: Cambridge University Press, 1945.

Sallis, John, ed. *Heidegger and the Path of Thinking.* Pittsburgh: Duquesne University Press, 1970.

Samra, Cal. *The Joyful Christ: The Healing Power of Humor.* San Francisco: Harper and Row, 1986.

Sanders, E. P. "On the Question of Fulfilling the Law and Rabbinic Judaism." In *Donum Gentilicum: New Testament Studies in Honour of David Daube,* edited by E. Bammel, C. K. Barrett, and W. D. Davies, 103–26. Oxford: Clarendon Press, 1978.

———. *Jesus and Judaism.* Philadelphia: Fortress Press, 1986.

Santmire, B. E. *Brother Earth: Nature, God, and Ecology in a Time of Crisis.* New York: Nelson, 1970.

Schaff, Philip, and Henry Wace, eds. *Ante-Nicene Fathers.* Peabody, MA: Hendrickson Publishers, 1966. www.ccel.org/fathers2/.

Scheffczyk, Leo. *Creation and Providence.* New York: Herder and Herder, 1970.

Scheler, Max. *Formalism in Ethics and Non-Formal Ethics of Value: A New Attempt toward the Foundation of an Ethical Personalism.* Translated by M. S. Frings and R. L. Funk. Evanston, IL: Northwestern University Press, 1973.

Schelkle, Karl Hermann. *Theology of the New Testament.* Collegeville, MN: The Liturgical Press, 1978.

Schillebeeckx, Edward, OP. *Christ: The Experience of Jesus as Lord.* Translated by John Bowden. New York: Seabury-Crossroad, 1980.

———. *Ministry: Leadership in the Community of Jesus.* Translated by John Bowden. New York: Crossroad, 1981.

———. *The Church with a Human Face.* New York: Crossroad, 1985.

Schircel, Cyril L., OFM. *The University of the Concept of Being in the Philosophy of Duns Scotus.* Catholic University of America Press, 1942.

Schnackenburg, Rudolf. *The Moral Teaching of the New Testament.* New York: Seabury, 1973.

Schrage, Wolfgang. *The Ethics of the New Testament.* Translated by David E. Green. Philadelphia: Fortress Press, 1988.

Schreiter, Robert J., CPPS, and Mary Catherine Hilkert, OP, eds. *The Praxis of Christian Experience: An Introduction to the Theology of Edward Schillebeeckx.* San Francisco: Harper and Row, 1989.

Schuklenk, Udo, and Michael Ristow. "The Ethics of Research into the Cause(s) of Homosexuality." *Journal of Homosexuality* 31 (3; 1996): 5–30.

Schüller, Bruno, SJ. "What Ethical Principles are Universally Valid?" *Theology Digest* 19 (1971): 23–28.

———. "The Double Effect in Catholic Thought: A Reevalution." In *Doing Evil to Achieve Good,* edited by by Richard A. McCormick, SJ and Paul Ramsey, 165–92. Lanham, MD: University Press of America, 1985.

Schuurman, Egbert. *Technology and the Future: A Philosophical Challenge.* Toronto: Wedge Publishing Foundation, 1980.

Selling, Joseph A., and Jan Jans, eds. *The Splendor of Accuracy: An Examination of the Assertions Made by "Veritatis Splendor."* Grand Rapids, MI: Eerdmans, 1995.

Shannon, Thomas, and Alan Wolter, OFM. "Reflections on the Moral Status of the Pre-Embryo." *Theological Studies* (1990: 51): 603–26.

Sheehan, Thomas. "Heidegger and the Nazis." *The New York Review of Books* (June 16, 1988).

———. "A Normal Nazi." *The New York Review of Books* XL (1–2; January 14, 1993): 30–35. Review of Richard Wolin. *The Heidegger Controversy: A Critical Reader.* Cambridge: MIT Press, 1992.

Sherburne, Donald W. *A Key to Whitehead's Process and Reality.* Chicago: University of Chicago Press, 1981.

Sherrel, Richard E., ed. *Ecology: Crisis and New Vision.* Richard, VA: John Knox Press, 1971.

Shewmon, D. Alan, MD. "Recovery from 'Brain-Death': A Neurologist's Apologia." *The Lincacre Quarterly* 64 (February 1997): 30–96.

Sidgwick, Henry. *The Method of Ethics.* Originally published 1874. 7th ed. reissued. Chicago: University of Chicago Press, 1961.

Silk, Joseph. *The Big Bang.* Rev. ed. New York: W. H. Freedman, 1989.

Silver, Lee M. *Remaking Eden.* New York: Avon Books, 1997.

Silverman, Hugh J., ed., *Philosophy and Non-Philosophy Since Merleau-Ponty.* New York/London: Routledge, 1988.

Simard, Emile. "Le hypothese." *Laval Theologique et Philosophique* 3 (1947): 89–120.

Simon, Yves. *The Tradition of Natural Law: A Philosopher's Reflections*. Edited by Vukan Kuic. New York: Fordham University Press, 1965.

Singer, Peter. *Animal Liberation: A New Ethics for our Treatment of Animals*. New York: Avon, 1977.

Siraisi, Nancy G. *Arts and Sciences at Padua: The Studium of Padua before 1350*. Toronto: Pontifical Institute of Medieval Studies, 1973.

Smith, Janet E. *"Humanae Vitae," a Generation Later*. Washington, DC: Catholic University of America Press, 1991.

————, ed. *Why "Humanae Vitae" Was Right: A Reader*. San Francisco: Ignatius Press, 1993.

Smith, Vincent E. *The General Science of Nature*. Milwaukee: Bruce, 1958.

Snow, C. P. *The Two Cultures: A Second Look*. Cambridge: Cambridge University Press, 1964.

Sommerfeld, Arnold. "To Einstein's 70th Birthday." In *Albert Einstein Philosopher-Scientist*, edited by Paul Arthur Schlipp. 3rd ed. La Salle, IL: Open Court, 1970.

Sorsky, Arthur D., et al. *Adoption Triangle*. New York: Doubleday, 1984.

Speiser, E. A. *Genesis*. In *Anchor Bible*. Garden City, NY: Doubleday, 1964.

Spicq, Ceslaus, OP. *Agapè dans le Nouveau Testament; analyses des texts*. 3 vols. Paris: Editions Gabalda, 1958–59.

————. *Agapē in the New Testament*. 3 vols. St. Louis: B. Herder Book Company, 1963.

————. *Théologie Morale du Nouveau Testament*. 2 vols. Paris: Lecoffre, 1965.

Spidlik, Thomas. *The Spirituality of the Christian East*. Kalamazoo, MI: Cistercian Publications, 1986.

Spiegelberg, Herbert. *The Phenomenological Movement: A Historical Introduction*. 3rd rev. ed., with the collaboration of Karl Schuhmann. The Hague: Martinus Nijhoff, 1982.

Stoeckle, Bernhard. *Gratia supponit naturam*. Rome: Herder, 1962.

Strauss, Leo. *Natural Right and History*. Chicago: University of Chicago Press, 1953.

Suarez, Franciso, SJ. *Disputationes Metaphysicae, Opera Omnia*. Dist. I, Sect. iv, 13. *Disputationes Metaphysicae*. Hildesheim: G. Olms, 1965.

Swidler, Leonard, and Arlene Swidler, eds. *Women Priests: A Catholic Commentary on the Vatican Declaration*. New York: Paulist Press, 1977.

Szabo, P. Sadoc, OP, ed. *Xenia Thomistica*. Romae: Typis Polyglottis Vaticanis, 1925.

Tatarkiewicz, W. "Mimesis." In *Dictionary of the History of Ideas*, edited by Philip P. Wiener, vol. 3, 225–30. New York: Scribner 1973.

Teilhard de Chardin, Pierre. *The Phenomenon of Man*. Translated by Bernard Wall; introduction by Julian Huxley. New York: Harper, 1959.

Torrell, Jean-Pierre, OP. "The Person and His Work." In *Saint Thomas Aquinas*. Vol. 1. Washington DC: Catholic University of America Press, 1996.

Trueblood, Elton. *The Humor of Christ*. New York: Harper and Row, 1964.

Twetten, David B. "Why Motion Requires a Cause: The Foundation for a Prime Mover in Aristotle and Aquinas." In *Philosophy and the God of Abraham: Essays in Memory of James A. Weisheipl, OP,* edited by R. James Long, 234–54. Toronto: Pontifical Institute of Medieval Studies, 1991.

Vanhoye, Albert, SJ. *La Structure littéraire de l' "Épître aux Hébreux."* 2nd rev. ed. Paris: Desclée De Brouwer, 1976.

———. *Old Testament Priests and New Priests According to the New Testament.* Translated by Bernard Orchard. Petersham, MA: St. Bede's Publications, 1986.

———, and Henri Crouzel, SJ. "The Ministry in the Church: Reflections on a Recent Publication." *The Clergy Review* 5 (68; May 1983): 156–74.

Van Riet, Georges. *Thomistic Epistemology.* 2 vols. St. Louis: B. Herder, 1963.

Vass, George. *Understanding Karl Rahner.* Vol. 1: *A Theologian in Search of a Philosophy.* Vol. 2: *The Mystery of Man and the Foundations of a Theological System..* London: Sheed & Ward, 1985.

Vaux, Roland de, OP. *Ancient Israel.* New York: McGraw-Hill, 1961.

Veatch, Henry B. Review of Germain Grisez, *The Way of the Lord Jesus. New Scholasticism* 62 (Summer 1988): 353–65.

Vinaty, Bernard, et al. *Galileo Galilei: 350 ans d'histoire.* Edited by Paul Poupard, with a declaration of John Paul II. Tournai, Belgium: Desclee International, 1983.

Vögue, Adalbert de. *The Rule of St. Benedict: A Doctrinal and Spiritual Commentary.* Kalamazoo, MI: Cistercian Pubs., 1983.

Vollert, Cyril, SJ. *A Theology of Mary.* New York: Herder and Herder, 1965.

Vycinas, V. *Earth and Gods.* The Hague: Martinus Nijhoff, 1961.

Wagner, John V. *A Study of What Can and Cannot be Determined about "Separatio" as it is Discussed in the Works of St. Thomas Aquinas.* Ann Arbor, MI: University Microfilms, 1979.

Walgrave, John H., OP. *Person and Society: A Christian View.* Pittsburgh: Duquesne University Press, 1965.

Wallace, William A., OP. *The Role of Demonstration in Moral Theology: A Study of Methodology in St. Thomas Aquinas.* Washington, DC: The Thomist Press, 1962.

———. "The Existential Ethics of Karl Rahner: A Thomistic Appraisal." *The Thomist* 27 (1963): 493–515.

———. *Causality and Scientific Explanation.* 2 vols. Ann Arbor: University of Michigan Press, 1974.

———. "Demonstration in the Science of Nature. " In William A. Wallace, OP, *From a Realist Point of View,* 329–70. Washington, DC: University Press of America, 1979.

Walsh, Mary Roth. *The Psychology of Women: Ongoing Debates.* New Haven, CT: Yale University Press, 1987.

Watson, James D. "Moving Toward the Clonal Man." *The Atlantic* 227 (1971): 50ff.

Weed, Stan E. "Curbing Births, Not Pregnancies." *Wall Street Journal* (October 14, 1986).

Weisheipl, James A., OP. *The Development of Physical Theory in the Middle Ages.* New York: Sheed & Ward, 1959.

——, ed. *The Dignity of Science: Studies in The Philosophy of Science Presented to William Humbert Kane, OP.* Washington, DC: Thomist Press, 1961.

——. "Curriculum of the Faculty of Arts at Oxford in the Early Fourteenth Century." *Medieval Studies* 26 (1964): 143–85.

——. "Classification of the Science in Medieval Thought." *Medieval Studies* 28 (1965): 54–80.

——. *Friar Thomas d'Aquino: His Life, Thought, and Works.* Garden City, NY: Doubleday, 1974.

——. "Commentary on "Maritain's 'Epistemology of Modern Science' by Jean-Louis Allard." In *Conference Seminar on Jacques Maritain's "The Degrees of Knowledge,"* edited by R. J. Henle, SJ, et al., 174–84. St. Louis, MO: The American Maritain Association, 1981.

Wessels, Cletus, OP. *The Holy Web: Church and the New Universe Story.* Maryknoll, NY: Orbis Books, 2000.

——. *Jesus in the New Universe Story.* Maryknoll, NY: Orbis Books, 2003.

——. *The Mother of God: Her Physical Maternity.* River Forest, IL: Aquinas Library, 1964.

Westerman, Claus. *Creation and Beginning and End in the Bible.* Minneapolis, MN: Augsburg, 1972.

——. *Genesis 1–11: A Commentary.* Translated by John J. Scullion. Minneapolis, MN: Augsburg, 1984.

White, Lynn, Jr. "The Historical Roots of Our Ecological Crisis." *Science* 155 (March 1967): 1203–7.

Whitehead, Alfred North. *Process and Reality: An Essay in Cosmology.* Original edition, 1929; corrected edition by David Ray Griffin and Donald W. Sherburne. New York: Free Press, 1978.

Wills, Gary. *Papal Sins: Structures of Deceit.* New York: Doubleday, 2000.

Wilson, Edward O. "Threats to Biodiversity." *Scientific American* 261 (September 1989): 108–17.

Wippel, John F. *Metaphysical Themes in Thomas Aquinas.* Washington, DC: Catholic University of America Press, 1984.

Witt, Charlotte. "The Evolution of Developmental Interpretations of Aristotle." In *Aristotle's Philosophical Development: Problems and Prospects*, edited by William Wians. Lanham, MD: Rowman & Littlefield, 1996.

Wolff, Christian. *Discursus Praeliminaris de Philosophia in Genere.* 3. Verona: Haeredes Marci Moroni, 1779.

Woods, Richard, OP. *Christian Spirituality: God's Presence Through the Ages.* Allen, TX: Christian Classics, 1989.

Working Group on the Family. "The Family: Preserving America's Future." *The Human Life Review* 13 (Winter 1986): 105–16.

Young, Norman J. *Creator, Creation, and Faith.* Philadelphia: The Westminster Press, 1976.

Zimmerman, Michael E. *Heidegger's Confrontation with Modernity: Technology, Politics, Art.* Bloomington and Indianapolis IN: Indiana University Press, 1990.

Zukeran, Pat. "Buddhism." www.probe.org/docs/buddhism.html; www.onmark productions.com/html/schools-three-vehicles.html.

Index

Rahner, Karl, 40, 48, 255, 295, 363
  Aquinas and, 82–83
  ethics of, 209–11
  historical mindedness views of, 75
  theology of, 77, 203–8, 216, 221
  transcendentalism and, 120–21,
    196, 203–6
Ramsey, Paul, 364
Ransil, Bernard J., 364
rape, 371, 382
Ratio inferior, 214
Ratio superior, 214
Ratzinger, Cardinal Joseph, 196
Rawls, John, 229, 251*n*
Raymond of Capua, 302
Raymond of Saxony, 302
realism, 43
reason, harmony with faith, 4
reasoned inquiry, 125
Reconciliation, Sacrament of, 146
recreation, 307
Reflections on Humanae Vitae
  (John Paul II), 320
Reformation, 84, 90, 103, 168
reincarnation, 143
relationality of human person, 79–80
Religious Right, 294
Renaissance, 64
reproduction, 316
  artificial, 318, 329, 330, 369–89
  asexual, 366
Republic, The (Plato), 117
ressourcement, 17–18
resurrection, 143
Revelation, Book of, 134, 159
rhetoric, 34
Ricoeur on language, 80
right action, 125
RNA, 360
Rodriguez, Alonso, 144
Roe v. *Wade,* 329, 330, 335
romantic environmentalism, 72
Roof, Wade Clark, 79*n*
sacraments, 101. *See also* specific
  sacraments

sacred rites, 125
Sacred Scripture, 127
Sacred Tradition, 127
Sagan, Carl, 30
Saints and Sinners: A History of the Popes
  (Duffy), 127
Sales, Francis de, St., 302
Samson, 158
Samuel, 158
Sanders, E. P., 272*n*
Sarah, 158
satanism, 48
Scheler, Max, 195, 197–98, 206, 255
Scheler-Rahner theory, 255–56
Schillebeeckx, Edward, 75, 77, 82–83
Schmitz, Kenneth L., 193–94
Schnackenburg, Rudolf, 265
Scholasticism, 6, 7, 197
Schragge, Wolfgang, 265
Schüller, Bruno, 256
science. *See also* natural science
  division of, 34–35
  ethics and, 281–83
  hard, 32
  modern, 54–58
  moral, 222
  nature and, 278–81
  post-Galilean, 195–96
  sustained advance in, being held
    back, 64
scientific health care, Christian
  perspective on, 313–27
scientism, 5, 64, 72
  contemporary domination of, 27–32
  damage done to out culture by,
    28–34
  defined, 27
  polarization between, 64–65
  value-free, 29
Scotus, Duns, 31, 39, 42, 346
  delayed hominization and, 345–46
secular humanism, 28–29, 84, 228,
  294–95, 297
secular universities, 90

456 ■ | INDEX

suddenness, importance of, as element, 307
suicide, 288
Summa theologiae (Aquinas), 15, 39, 47–48, 109–10, 112, 115–16, 215, 243
Summum bonum, development of, in the ethical disciplines, 23
Super-Consciousness, 299
Super-Ego, 299
supernatural existential, fundamental freedom and, 207–8
supernatural fulfillment, 236–42
surrogate mother, 318
Synoptics, 128, 129
system, 171*n*
systematic theology, 86–88
    Catholicism as sign system, 95–108
    Jesus' human knowledge, 109–24
    moral theology and Mariology, 149–69
    priesthood of Christ, of baptized, and ordained, 125–47
    truth, 89–93

Taizé community (France), 147
Tao of Physics, The (Capra), 29
technological crisis, origins of our, 63
technology
    Heidegger on, 67–68
    in Old Testament, 271–74
    risks of, 271
    truth and, 61–73
teleological character of nature, 71
teleological ethics, 204*n*, 239–40
teleologism, 204*n*
teleology, 29, 70, 209, 215–16, 279
teleonomy, 279
temperance, 160, 266, 293
Ten Commandments, 144–45, 258, 260, 265, 314
Teresa of Avila, St., 107–8, 299, 302
theological virtues, 160

theology. *See also* moral theology; Systematic theology
    of Aquinas, 15, 83, 109–11, 215–16, 262
    building of, on anthropology, 48
    of consciousness, 199
    development of, in Christian Church, 276
    feminist, 81
    historical-critical approach to, 118, 213
    liberation, 81, 147
    political, 81
Theology of the Body, John Paul II on, 187–202
Theravada Buddhism, 143
thermodynamics, Second Law of, 55
Third Gospel, 153
Thomism, 6
    attempts to revitalize, 198
    canonization of, 4
    classical, 193–94
    contemporary value of, 6–7
    decline of, 13, 14, 38
    eight readings of, and their reconciliation, 39–44
    essential, 195, 199–200
    existential, 13, 38, 204–5, 205
    future of, 13, 25, 38
    Garrigou-Lagrange school of, 200
    papal support of, 7, 8
    revival of, in Neo-Scholastic form, 15
    transcendental, 15–16, 17, 40–41, 120–21, 194–95, 204–5
Thomistic God, 173–76
Thomistic metaphysics, 4–5, 24, 39–44
Thomist Revival, phases of, 39–44
Tillich, Paul, 295
Torah, 97
Tower of Babel, 81, 271–72
Tracy, David, process theology of, 196
tradition, Bible and, 96–97
transcendental anthropology, 206